Constantine Stephanidis (Ed.)

HCI International 2018 – Posters' Extended Abstracts

20th International Conference, HCI International 2018
Las Vegas, NV, USA, July 15–20, 2018
Proceedings, Part III

Editor
Constantine Stephanidis
University of Crete
  and Foundation for Research
  and Technology – Hellas (FORTH)
Heraklion, Crete
Greece

ISSN 1865-0929   ISSN 1865-0937 (electronic)
Communications in Computer and Information Science
ISBN 978-3-319-92284-3   ISBN 978-3-319-92285-0 (eBook)
https://doi.org/10.1007/978-3-319-92285-0

Library of Congress Control Number: 2018944385

Printed on acid-free paper

This Springer imprint is published by the registered company Springer International Publishing AG
part of Springer Nature
The registered company address is: Gewerbestrasse 11, 6330 Cham, Switzerland

Foreword

The 20th International Conference on Human-Computer Interaction, HCI International 2018, was held in Las Vegas, NV, USA, during July 15–20, 2018. The event incorporated the 14 conferences/thematic areas listed on the following page.

A total of 4,373 individuals from academia, research institutes, industry, and governmental agencies from 76 countries submitted contributions, and 1,170 papers and 195 posters have been included in the proceedings. These contributions address the latest research and development efforts and highlight the human aspects of design and use of computing systems. The contributions thoroughly cover the entire field of human-computer interaction, addressing major advances in knowledge and effective use of computers in a variety of application areas. The volumes constituting the full set of the conference proceedings are listed in the following pages.

I would like to thank the program board chairs and the members of the program boards of all thematic areas and affiliated conferences for their contribution to the highest scientific quality and the overall success of the HCI International 2018 conference.

This conference would not have been possible without the continuous and unwavering support and advice of the founder, Conference General Chair Emeritus and Conference Scientific Advisor Prof. Gavriel Salvendy. For his outstanding efforts, I would like to express my appreciation to the communications chair and editor of *HCI International News*, Dr. Abbas Moallem.

July 2018   Constantine Stephanidis

HCI International 2018 Thematic Areas and Affiliated Conferences

Thematic areas:

- Human-Computer Interaction (HCI 2018)
- Human Interface and the Management of Information (HIMI 2018)

Affiliated conferences:

- 15th International Conference on Engineering Psychology and Cognitive Ergonomics (EPCE 2018)
- 12th International Conference on Universal Access in Human-Computer Interaction (UAHCI 2018)
- 10th International Conference on Virtual, Augmented, and Mixed Reality (VAMR 2018)
- 10th International Conference on Cross-Cultural Design (CCD 2018)
- 10th International Conference on Social Computing and Social Media (SCSM 2018)
- 12th International Conference on Augmented Cognition (AC 2018)
- 9th International Conference on Digital Human Modeling and Applications in Health, Safety, Ergonomics, and Risk Management (DHM 2018)
- 7th International Conference on Design, User Experience, and Usability (DUXU 2018)
- 6th International Conference on Distributed, Ambient, and Pervasive Interactions (DAPI 2018)
- 5th International Conference on HCI in Business, Government, and Organizations (HCIBGO)
- 5th International Conference on Learning and Collaboration Technologies (LCT 2018)
- 4th International Conference on Human Aspects of IT for the Aged Population (ITAP 2018)

Conference Proceedings Volumes Full List

1. LNCS 10901, Human-Computer Interaction: Theories, Methods, and Human Issues (Part I), edited by Masaaki Kurosu
2. LNCS 10902, Human-Computer Interaction: Interaction in Context (Part II), edited by Masaaki Kurosu
3. LNCS 10903, Human-Computer Interaction: Interaction Technologies (Part III), edited by Masaaki Kurosu
4. LNCS 10904, Human Interface and the Management of Information: Interaction, Visualization, and Analytics (Part I), edited by Sakae Yamamoto and Hirohiko Mori
5. LNCS 10905, Human Interface and the Management of Information: Information in Applications and Services (Part II), edited by Sakae Yamamoto and Hirohiko Mori
6. LNAI 10906, Engineering Psychology and Cognitive Ergonomics, edited by Don Harris
7. LNCS 10907, Universal Access in Human-Computer Interaction: Methods, Technologies, and Users (Part I), edited by Margherita Antona and Constantine Stephanidis
8. LNCS 10908, Universal Access in Human-Computer Interaction: Virtual, Augmented, and Intelligent Environments (Part II), edited by Margherita Antona and Constantine Stephanidis
9. LNCS 10909, Virtual, Augmented and Mixed Reality: Interaction, Navigation, Visualization, Embodiment, and Simulation (Part I), edited by Jessie Y. C. Chen and Gino Fragomeni
10. LNCS 10910, Virtual, Augmented and Mixed Reality: Applications in Health, Cultural Heritage, and Industry (Part II), edited by Jessie Y. C. Chen and Gino Fragomeni
11. LNCS 10911, Cross-Cultural Design: Methods, Tools, and Users (Part I), edited by Pei-Luen Patrick Rau
12. LNCS 10912, Cross-Cultural Design: Applications in Cultural Heritage, Creativity, and Social Development (Part II), edited by Pei-Luen Patrick Rau
13. LNCS 10913, Social Computing and Social Media: User Experience and Behavior (Part I), edited by Gabriele Meiselwitz
14. LNCS 10914, Social Computing and Social Media: Technologies and Analytics (Part II), edited by Gabriele Meiselwitz
15. LNAI 10915, Augmented Cognition: Intelligent Technologies (Part I), edited by Dylan D. Schmorrow and Cali M. Fidopiastis
16. LNAI 10916, Augmented Cognition: Users and Contexts (Part II), edited by Dylan D. Schmorrow and Cali M. Fidopiastis
17. LNCS 10917, Digital Human Modeling and Applications in Health, Safety, Ergonomics, and Risk Management, edited by Vincent G. Duffy
18. LNCS 10918, Design, User Experience, and Usability: Theory and Practice (Part I), edited by Aaron Marcus and Wentao Wang

19. LNCS 10919, Design, User Experience, and Usability: Designing Interactions (Part II), edited by Aaron Marcus and Wentao Wang
20. LNCS 10920, Design, User Experience, and Usability: Users, Contexts, and Case Studies (Part III), edited by Aaron Marcus and Wentao Wang
21. LNCS 10921, Distributed, Ambient, and Pervasive Interactions: Understanding Humans (Part I), edited by Norbert Streitz and Shin'ichi Konomi
22. LNCS 10922, Distributed, Ambient, and Pervasive Interactions: Technologies and Contexts (Part II), edited by Norbert Streitz and Shin'ichi Konomi
23. LNCS 10923, HCI in Business, Government, and Organizations, edited by Fiona Fui-Hoon Nah and Bo Sophia Xiao
24. LNCS 10924, Learning and Collaboration Technologies: Design, Development and Technological Innovation (Part I), edited by Panayiotis Zaphiris and Andri Ioannou
25. LNCS 10925, Learning and Collaboration Technologies: Learning and Teaching (Part II), edited by Panayiotis Zaphiris and Andri Ioannou
26. LNCS 10926, Human Aspects of IT for the Aged Population: Acceptance, Communication, and Participation (Part I), edited by Jia Zhou and Gavriel Salvendy
27. LNCS 10927, Human Aspects of IT for the Aged Population: Applications in Health, Assistance, and Entertainment (Part II), edited by Jia Zhou and Gavriel Salvendy
28. CCIS 850, HCI International 2018 Posters Extended Abstracts (Part I), edited by Constantine Stephanidis
29. CCIS 851, HCI International 2018 Posters Extended Abstracts (Part II), edited by Constantine Stephanidis
30. CCIS 852, HCI International 2018 Posters Extended Abstracts (Part III), edited by Constantine Stephanidis

http://2018.hci.international/proceedings

HCI International 2018 Conference

The full list with the Program Board Chairs and the members of the Program Boards of all thematic areas and affiliated conferences is available online at:

http://www.hci.international/board-members-2018.php

HCI International 2019

The 21st International Conference on Human-Computer Interaction, HCI International 2019, will be held jointly with the affiliated conferences in Orlando, FL, USA, at Walt Disney World Swan and Dolphin Resort, July 26–31, 2019. It will cover a broad spectrum of themes related to Human-Computer Interaction, including theoretical issues, methods, tools, processes, and case studies in HCI design, as well as novel interaction techniques, interfaces, and applications. The proceedings will be published by Springer. More information will be available on the conference website: http://2019.hci.international/.

General Chair
Prof. Constantine Stephanidis
University of Crete and ICS-FORTH
Heraklion, Crete, Greece
E-mail: general_chair@hcii2019.org

http://2019.hci.international/

Contents – Part III

Interacting with Cultural Heritage

HCI in Commerce and Business

Interacting and Driving

Smart Cities and Smart Environments

Learning and Interaction

CLIP 4 Robotics: A Click-Based Programming Language

Ali Al-Bayaty[✉] and Christopher Martinez[✉]

University of New Haven, West Haven, CT 06516, USA
aalba3@unh.newhaven.edu, cmartinez@newhaven.edu

Abstract. CLIP 4 Robotics is an icon-based Visual Programming Language (VPL) that is designed for the novice programmer. The VPL program is written as a series of icons that represent program instruction syntax. The images allow for a wide age range to use the VPL from children to adults. Icons allow for users to feel less intimated with programming than with text-based languages. CLIP 4 Robotics has a user-defined syntax that helps the novice comprehend the language especially children. Icons allow children that have let master reading to program. Example programs are shown that demonstrate the CLIP 4 Robotics language in two different scenarios.

Keywords: Visual programming · Children programming · User interface
Novice programming environment

1 Introduction

With today's society relying heavy on technology in the near future there will be a need for the majority of people to have rudimental programming ability. One way to introduce a novice to programming is by using a Visual Programming Languages (VPL) rather than textual based languages. There have been a number of studies that have been done over the years that show VPLs are efficient at teaching the basic programming concepts [1, 2]. A VPL is less intimidating since graphical pictures are used to program instead of text. The graphics in VPL allow syntax to be express in simpler terms with tips for syntax shown through the user interface (UI) instead of relying on memorization of text rules.

We have developed a new VPL called 'CLIP 4 Robotics'. CLIP 4 Robotics is application specific to robotics and is based on the CLIP language. CLIP stands for a CLIck-based Programming language. The CLIP language is based on a UI approach of the programmer using the mouse to click on a command and then placing the command in an execution matrix. The CLIP language only requires clicks and no keyboard entry. We envision that the CLIP language can be extended beyond robotics in the future.

In this paper, we will present previous research on VPL languages, introduce the CLIP language, explain the user adjustable CLIP syntax, and the CLIP 4 Robotics implementation.

© Springer International Publishing AG, part of Springer Nature 2018
C. Stephanidis (Ed.): HCII Posters 2018, CCIS 852, pp. 3–10, 2018.
https://doi.org/10.1007/978-3-319-92285-0_1

2   Previous Research

VPLs have been a part of computer science since the early 1960s. As VPLs have developed the breakdown of VPLs fall into three different styles: iconic-based, diagram-based, and form-based. The iconic-based style has each command represented by a descriptive icon. The diagram-based style follows a flowchart layout to show the flow of a program visually. The form-based style uses templates that a user fills out to program a system.

Two of the most widely used VPLs are Alice [3] and Scratch [4]. Alice and Scratch are good examples of a form-based VPL. Alice and Scratch requires the programmer to select an operation and have selection that must be filled out. Figure 1 shows the options that must be filled out in a form analogy. The form-based VPL is good for beginners because the syntax is simple to understand since the form must be filled out. The VPL also gives clues to the syntax by using colors or drop boxes of correct attributes to use. ScratchJr is an example of an iconic-based VPL [5] (see Fig. 2). The programming of ScratchJr is done through selecting blocks with arrows showing the movement that would be programmed.

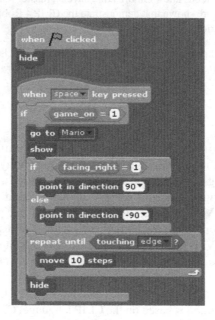

Fig. 1. Example of form-based VPLs.

By examining the previous research, we found that there are potential areas of improvement that could be made in VPLs. Alice and Scratch require the user be able to read to comprehend how to program. We feel that a simpler approach to programming could be accomplished by using iconic-based approach that young children can comprehend and provide more flexibility than ScratchJr. We also realize that syntax should adjust to the user based on their ability. We aim to develop an iconic-based VPL with a user adjustable syntax.

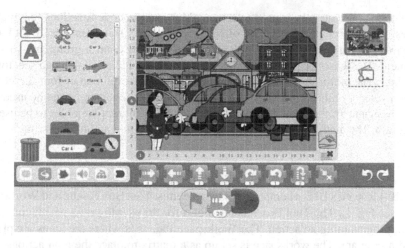

Fig. 2. Example of icon-based VPL ScratchJr [5].

3 CLIP Programming Language

When creating a programming teaching tool for a novice, a target application is selected to grab the attention of the new programmer. The popular target applications are storytelling and robotics. We developed the underlining principle for the CLIP language and aimed the first implementation towards robotics, hence CLIP 4 Robotics.

CLIP 4 Robotics is an iconic-based VPL; where each action is represented by an image. Using images allow for the CLIP 4 Robotics to be universal since it is not tied to the English language. The programming commands are broken down into the following categories: operations, flow control, sensors, motor movement, colors, numbers, variables, and math. Figure 3 shows the CLIP 4 Robotics icons commands. Depending on the age of the user all of the command categories could be used or a small subset.

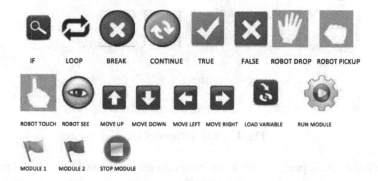

Fig. 3. CLIP 4 Robotics VPL Icons.

The operations category is used to set variables and run code functions that we call modules. The flow control categories offers support for IF statements and FOR loops; the number category is used to provide input into the flow control group and variable assignment. The sensors category provides the actions for the robot that can see, touch, and pickup. The motor movement category moves the robot in one of four directions. The color category allows predefine colors to be used by the sensor or can be used as a variable assignment; the variable group allows for four different variables to be used in the program. The math category allows for data manipulation and logic testing.

3.1 CLIP 4 Robotics Syntax

The CLIP 4 Robotics UI is a comprised of two palettes: Tool Box Palette and Workspace Palette (see Fig. 4). The Tool Box Palette allows for the user to select which command to use in programming an action. The Workspace Palette is where the icons are placed to build a program. The workspace is set up as a matrix to place the icon actions. The horizontal placement in the matrix is used to create one syntax correct line of programming instruction. The horizontal line forms one instruction and will have all the icons needed to check an IF statement, move the robot in the forward direction, or save a variable for example. The vertical direction of the matrix is used to set the sequential order of instructions to execute.

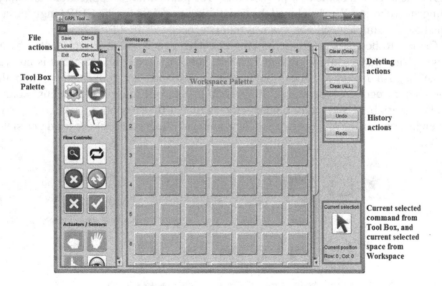

Fig. 4.   CLIP 4 Robotics UI.

To help the novice programmer form syntax correct command lines the UI provides tips when an icon is placed in the matrix. If the programmer places an icon from an incorrect category a popup message will show the programmer which category is expected next to complete the instruction. To form a correct instruction using icons, the programmer must follow a set of syntax rules.

3.2 Examples of User-Defined Language Syntax

The robot movement commands are examples where a user may modify the default syntax for a simplified version. The default syntax is defined as UP > > NUMBER:VARIABLE. The syntax is the UP ARROW icon followed by a NUMBER or VARIABLE icon. The command is expressed as a direction to move with an additional item of a number or variable telling how many units to move in the given direction. Figure 5(a) shows the graphical example. A young programmer may not be ready to learn about using variables. Leaving in the option to have variables would result in correct syntax but the execution would be incorrect if variables are not used properly. This may be a reason to modify the syntax to be UP > > NUMBER. With the modification only a number could be used to tell how many units to move. If the age of the programmer is so young that numbers are a difficult concept to grasp the syntax can be put into the most simplified version of only UP. In the simplified syntax the programmer is not able to provide any information about the number of units to move. The language would default to a single unit to move each time an UP command is given.

Another syntax example that may require modification is to work with assigning variables. To assign variables the default syntax is LOAD > > VARIABLE > > NUMBER:COLOR:TRUE:FALSE. The syntax tells that the LOAD icon must be followed by a VARIABLE icon and lastly followed by a NUMBER, COLOR, TRUE, or FALSE. The icon representation is shown in Fig. 5(b). A user may decide to alter the assignment of a variable to be LOAD > > VARIABLE ≫ = > > NUMBER:COLOR: TRUE:FALSE. The new syntax would require an equal sign be used to load a variable.

a) Move UP the amount   b) Load variable A with a number
in variable A

Fig. 5. Examples of CLIP 4 Robotics VPL syntax.

The following list is the default syntax that has been implemented in the CLIP 4 Robotic language.

```
LOOP >> NUMBER:VARIABLE
CHECK >> VARIABLE:TRUE:FALSE >> VARIABLE:SEE:TOUCH >>
       =:!=:>:>=:<:<= >> NUMBER:VARIABLE:COLOR
LOAD >> VARIABLE >> NUMBER:COLOR:TRUE:FALSE
VARIABLE >> = >> VARIABLE >> +:-:*:/ >> NUMBER:VARIABLE
CALL >> FUNCTION
FORWARD >> NUMBER:VARIABLE
BACKWARD >> NUMBER:VARIABLE
BREAK : CONTINUE : PICK : DROP : RIGHT : LEFT : STOP
FUNCTION
```

3.3   Example Programs

To show how programs are built using the CLIP 4 Robotics language the following example programs are shown. Example 1 is to sort colored boxes. A stationary robotic arm will be used to pick up boxes from a conveyor belt and put them in the corresponding containers based on the boxes' color. The robot will pick up the white colored box and put it in a container that is 90° to the left of the robot. The robot will pick the black colored box and put it in a container that is behind the robot. Finally, the robot will ignore any other colored boxes except the red color that indicates the robot should terminate the program. In this example inputs (sensors) include See to tell color and outputs (actuators) include Pickup and Drop. Figure 6 shows pseudo-code and the CLIP 4 Robotics graphical representation.

```
Forever loop
   If Sensor.See = Color.White Then
      Actuator.Pick
      Motors.TurnLeft(90°)
      Acutator.Drop
      Motors.TurnRight(90°)
   End
   If Sensor.See = Color.Black Then
      Actuator.Pick
      Motors.TurnLeft(180°)
      Acutator.Drop
      Motors.TurnRight(180°)
   End
   If Sensor.See = Color.Red Then
      Break
   End
End
```

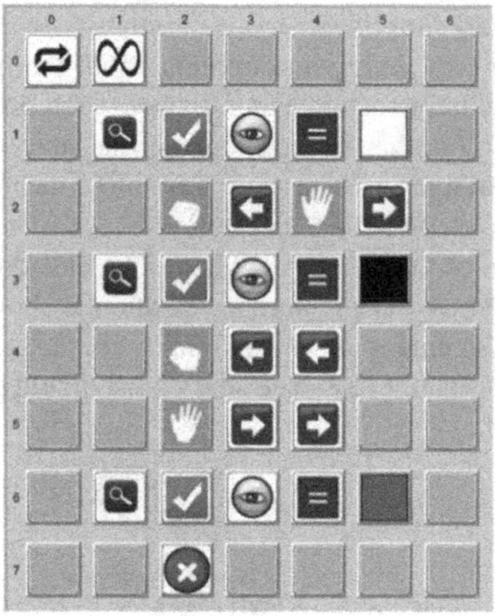

Fig. 6. Example 1: CLIP 4 Robotics example program for color sorting robot arm. (Color figure online)

Example 2 is a sweeper robot. A robot can be used sweep up obstacles along a straight path. The robot is programmed to sweep up to four obstacles on its path. The robot will stop at the last obstacle. The number of obstacle encountered is denoted as variable B. In this example inputs (sensors) include the Touch and outputs (actuators) include Pickup and Drop. Figure 7 shows the pseudo-code and the CLIP 4 Robotics graphical representation.

```
B = 0
Forever loop
  Motors.GoForward
  If Sensor.Touch = true Then
    Call Mod1
  End
  If B >= 4 Then
    Break
  End
End

Function Mod1
  B = B + 1
  Actuator.Pick
  Motors.TurnLeft(90°)
  Actuator.Drop
  Motors.TurnRight(90°)
End
```

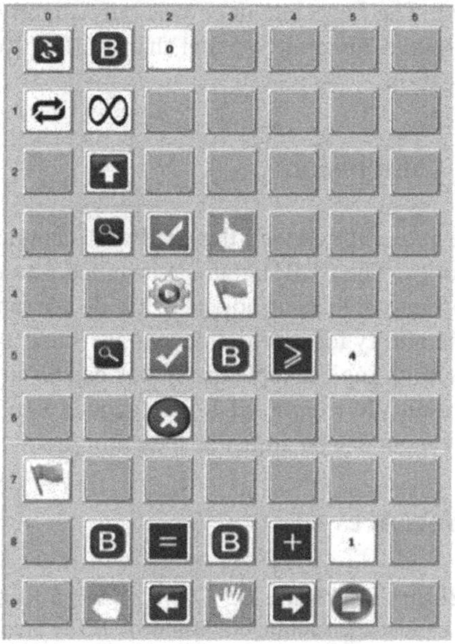

Fig. 7. Example 2: CLIP 4 Robotics example program for sweeper robot.

The two examples show that the CLIP VPL is able to introduce a novice programmer to a number of fundamental programming concepts. While the examples do require intermediate logic skills to create if statements and run a function preschool age children could still use the CLIP 4 Robotics language. Preschoolers would execute simple movement directions commands to get the robot to move from point A to point B.

To verify that the CLIP 4 Robotics language could be used and compile working code we create the CLIP 4 Robotics program to export code for a robot simulator. We pick RoboMind [6] as the robot simulator to test out the functionality of the language. We chose RoboMind since it does have support for interfacing with the Lego Mindstorm robots so that case studies could be done in the future.

4 Future Work

Currently the CLIP 4 Robotics language is able to work with the RoboMind simulator only. In the future, we hope to improve on the CLIP 4 Robotics application by develop our only robot simulator that can support instruction by instruction execution to aid in debugging. We also are working on making the CLIP 4 Robotics as a web application so that a wide audience can use it.

A formal case study would also be needed to verify the CLIP 4 Robotics effectiveness. We have run an informal study so far and compared CLIP 4 Robotics with Alice, Scratch and Lego NXT-G. Our study so far has shown the CLIP 4 Robotics was found to be easier than Alice and Scratch on a number of fundamental programming concepts. The focus group did find that Lego NXT-G was a better language to use to control a robot. The Lego language was only slightly better in ranking with our survey so with additional research we feel that CLIP 4 Robotics can have a place in programming education.

5   Conclusion

This paper introduced the CLIP VPL language in its current implementation focus on robotics. The CLIP language is an icon-based VPL that has been develop for a novice programmer that can appeal to a wide age range. A key component of the CLIP language is the ability for user-define syntax. Since a novice can easily become overwhelm with programming concepts the syntax can be adjusted to meet the current understanding of the user. We feel the CLIP language is a good language for young children to use since the syntax can be adjust as they progress.

References

1. Zhang, K., Zhang, D., Cao, J.: Design, construction, and application of a generic visual language generation environment. IEEE Trans. Softw. Eng. **27**(4), 289–307 (2001)
2. Good, J.: VPLs and novice program comprehension: how do different languages compare? In: Proceedings 1999 IEEE Symposium on Visual Languages, pp. 262 – 269 (1999)
3. Pasternak, E.: Visual programming pedagogies and integrating current visual programming language features. Master's degree thesis. Robotics Institute, Carnegie Mellon University (2009)
4. Resnick, M., Maloney, J., Monroy-Hernández, A., Rusk, N., Eastmond, E., Brennan, K., Millner, A., Rosenbaum, E., Silver, J., Silverman, B., Kafai, Y.: Scratch: programming for all. Commun. ACM **52**(11), 60–67 (2009)
5. Flannery, L.P., Silverman, B., Kazakoff, E.R., Bers, M.U., Bonta, P., Resnick, M.: Designing ScratchJr: support for early childhood learning through computer programming. In: Proceeding of the 12th International Conference on Interaction Design and Children (IDC 2013), pp. 1–10. ACM, New York (2013)
6. RoboMind. http://www.robomind.net

Complementary Learning Assist System: Guitar Performance Assist by Haptic Presentation

Kazushige Ashimori(✉) and Hiroshi Igarashi

Electrical and Electronic Engineering, Tokyo Denki University,
5, Senjyu-Asahi-Cho, Adachi-ku, Tokyo 1208551, Japan
{k.ashimori,h.igarashi}@crl.epi.dendai.ac.jp
http://www.crl.epi.dendai.ac.jp/

Abstract. Haptics is one of effective interface giving information as a position, force, and object texture. When people learn to motion like playing musical instruments, visual, hearing, and haptics feedback are valid. In this paper, we proposed haptic assist on musical instruments playing. As a method of haptic presentation, a haptic glove with bilateral control is developed. The glove has some small geared motors for each finger joint. As a result, the proposed method showed the usefulness of an intuitive learning teaching system by haptic feedback.

Keywords: Skill assist · Haptic glove · Bilateral · Guitar · Education

1 Introduction

Research on learning support is being conducted in various fields. The purpose of these research is considered not only for beginners but also for storage of craftsmanship technology and the use of rehabilitation. However, those studies mostly use visual information and auditory information, and there is no consideration of tactile information has not been developed [1–3]. Therefore, this research proposes to a method of learning support system by haptic presentation.

2 Proposed Method

Purpose of this research proposes a method of learning assist system. In general, education is only tell notice of the educator for the learner, and there is no feedback for the educator. Then, in this research, we propose complementary learning assist system (CLASS). This system aims to assist for the educator not only for the learner by giving haptic feedback to educators from the learner.

In this research, haptic glove is used as a method to present haptic information. The haptic glove proposed by this research is shown in Fig. 1. In the haptic glove proposed by this research, a small geared motor was attached to each finger joints. This haptic glove connects to only DIP joint of each finger to not disturb finger sense, and this glove can control thumb, index finger, and ring finger.

© Springer International Publishing AG, part of Springer Nature 2018
C. Stephanidis (Ed.): HCII Posters 2018, CCIS 852, pp. 11–16, 2018.
https://doi.org/10.1007/978-3-319-92285-0_2

Fig. 1. Overview of developed haptic glove.

3   Control Method of Proposed Haptic Glove

The control block diagram of the haptic glove proposed by this research is shown in Fig. 2. As a method to provide haptic information, we adopted force-sensorless bilateral control with DOB and RFOB [6,7]. This control method was developed by Iida et al., and haptic information interacted between master and slave each other [4,5]. In the Fig. 2, each term was defined as Table 1.

Control system has motor drivers: ESCON 24/4, and microcontrollers: Nucleo F746ZG for control of the geared motors. The control period is 1[kHz],

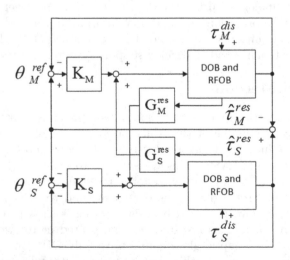

Fig. 2. Block diagram of haptic glove.

Table 1. Experimental parameters

Parameter	Value
θ_M^{ref}	Position of master
θ_S^{ref}	Position of slave
K_M	Position gain of master
K_S	Position gain of slave
τ_M^{dis}	Disturbance torque of master
τ_S^{dis}	Disturbance torque of slave
$\hat{\tau}_M^{res}$	Reaction force of master by RFOB
$\hat{\tau}_S^{res}$	Reaction force of slave by RFOB
G_M^{res}	Reaction force gain of master
G_S^{res}	Reaction force gain of slave

the resolution of the motor is 1200 [pulses/revolution], and the gear ratio is 50:1. The purpose of this research is to communicate haptic information of teacher to beginner via the glove, therefore, both operators have to wear the gloves.

4   Experimental Method

In this experiments, we divided the learner for three teams to confirm the effectiveness of haptic presentation and a method of CLASS.

- Group A: teacher gives only hearing and vision to beginner.
- Group B: Learner and teacher are wearing the globe, the learner is supported using auditory, visual and haptic.
- Group C: in addition to the environment of the Group B, the teacher is given haptic feedback from the learner.

For each team, the subjects of the learners were 12 men in twenties in men, and the educators were one male with 5 years guitar experience. Also, the task of the experiment was to play the F code of the guitar, and the procedure was as follows.

1. The teacher tells for the learner how to hold, and how to stroke the strings the guitar, minimum basic information in playing the guitar.
2. Show the tab notation of the F chord shown in Fig. 3 to the learner, the learner is instructed doing self-learning for one minute.
3. Guitar output of the learner is recorded. It is preparation sampling. (sampling: pre).
4. The teacher tells for the learner how to play F chord for 3 min. At this time, Group B and C wear gloves.
5. Guitar output of the learner is recorded as a first sampling. (sampling: first).

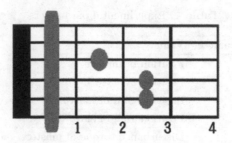

Fig. 3. F chord of the guitar

6. The teacher repeats to the teaching for 3 min and the guitar output is recorded again (sampling: second).
7. Similarly, repeats to the teaching, and the outputs is recorded again (sampling: third).
8. Learners take a small break and review themselves. Group B and C remove the glove.
9. Guitar output of the learner is recorded as a final sampling. (sampling: final).

5 Evaluation Method

In this research, we evaluate the output of the learner by three terms as follows.

5.1 Sustain

In the sustain, the output was evaluated on the length.

$$V_{sus} = 20 Log \frac{V_{in}}{V_{max}} >= -20[dB] \tag{1}$$

In the expression (1), Sustain of the output V_{sus} was calculated with input the maximum value V_{max} from the input value V_{in}.

5.2 Correlation Ratio

When guitar playing, supposing that tuning is constant, suppression at the correct position makes the similarity of frequency.

The frequency similarity was calculated by the correlation ratio r using Eq. (4). In the Eqs. (2) and (3); x is the number of data; y^T is the spectral intensity of the teacher; and y^L is the spectral intensity of the learner.

$$I_T = \sum_{i=1}^{x} (y_i^T + y_{i+1}^T + y_{i+2}^T - 3\bar{y}^T) \tag{2}$$

$$I_L = \sum_{i=1}^{x}(y_i^L + y_{i+1}^L + y_{i+2}^L - 3\bar{y}^L) \tag{3}$$

$$r = \frac{I_{TL}}{I_T I_L} \tag{4}$$

5.3   Output Signal/Noise Ratio

In this section, we compare to the S/N ratio between the teacher signal and the learner signals which fourier transformed. S/N ratio of the teacher I^E and S/N ratio of the learner I^L are calculated by Eqs. (5) and (6).

$$I^T = \frac{\bar{y}_o^E}{\bar{y}^E}, \tag{5}$$

$$I^L = \frac{\bar{y}_o^L}{\bar{y}^L}. \tag{6}$$

In the equation, $\bar{y}_E$ and $\bar{y}_L$ are average of the output for the educator and the learner, and y_o^E and y_o^L are average of peaks that beyond the each average value.

6   Experiment Result

Experimental results are shown in Fig. 4. The value of each result is the difference between "sampling: pre" and "sampling: final".

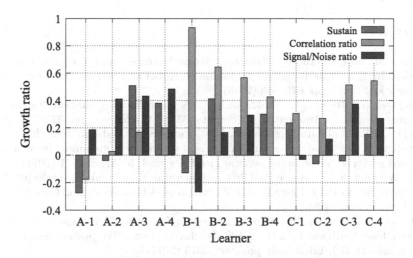

Fig. 4. Achievement result: total evaluation.

From the Fig. 4, high growth ratio was confirmed from the Team B and Team C on the term of correlation ratio. This result suggests the effectiveness of the proposed method.

In other hands, Team A shows high growth ratio on the term of S/N ratio, in spite of without correlation ratio growth. This result shows Team A learned about only "how to reduce the noise", and the learner could not learn about correct finger position.

From result of Team C, growth of both correlation ratio and S/N ratio teams were confirmed. This result shows the Team C learned correct finger position and reduction of noise. In the CLASS method suggested the learner could provide support suitable for the learner's finger movement since the teacher receives haptic feedback from the learner.

7   Conclusion

In this paper, we proposed learning support system using haptic gloves that were introduced bilateral control. Introducing bilateral control, the glove enabled human-to-human telecommunications. Purpose of this research is teaching the F chord of the guitar for a beginner; and evaluation was focused on three terms that guitar sustain, frequency similarity, and S/N ratio of output signals. As a result, in the evaluation of the correlation coefficient, mastery performance of the learner by the haptic glove was confirmed.

In the Team A (without haptic support team), high growth ratio of the S/N ratio was confirmed without growth of correlation ratio team. In the Team B (with haptic support team) and Team C (Complementary Learning Assist System: CLASS team) show high growth ratio on the term of correlation ratio. This result suggest effectiveness of haptic support.

References

1. Narita, M., Mastumaru, T.: Calligraphy-stroke learning support system using projection. In: IEEE International Symposium on Robot and Human Interactive Communication, vol. 7, pp. 640–645 (2015)
2. Takegawa, Y., Terada, T., Tsukamoto, M.: A piano learning support system considering rhythm. In: International Computer Music Conference, pp. 325–332 (2012)
3. Keebler, J.R., Wiltshire, T.J., Smith, D.C., Fiore, S.M., Bedwell, J.S.: Shifting the paradigm of music instruction: implications of embodiment stemming from an augmented reality guitar learning system. Front. Psychol. **5**, Article 471 (2014)
4. Iida, W., Ohnishi, K.: Reproducibility and operationality in bilateral teleoperation. In: 2004 The 8th IEEE International Workshop on Advanced Motion Control, AMC 2004, pp. 217–222 (2004)
5. Ashimori, K., Igarashi, H.: Skill assist system for musical instruments by skilled players force feedback. In: 2017 IEEE 26th International Symposium on Industrial Electronics (ISIE), Edinburgh, pp. 2008–2013 (2017)
6. Ohnishi, K., Shibata, M., Murakami, T.: Motion control for advanced mechatronics. IEEE/ASME Trans. Mechatron. **1**(1), 56–67 (1996)
7. Yamaoka, S., Nozaki, T., Yashiro, D., Ohnishi, K.: Acceleration control of stacked piezoelectric actuator utilizing disturbance observer and reaction force observer. In: 2012 12th IEEE International Workshop on Advanced Motion Control (AMC), Sarajevo, pp. 1–6 (2012)

Characterization of the Use of the Internet of Things in the Institutions of Higher Education of the City of Barranquilla and Its Metropolitan Area

Leonel Hernandez[1](✉), Genett Jimenez[2], Claudia Baloco[3], Angélica Jimenez[4], and Hugo Hernandez[4]

[1] Department of Telematic Engineering, Engineering Faculty, Institución Universitaria ITSA, Barranquilla, Colombia
lhernandezc@itsa.edu.co
[2] Department of Industrial Processes Engineering, Engineering Faculty, Institución Universitaria ITSA, Barranquilla, Colombia
gjimenez@itsa.edu.co
[3] Faculty of Education, Universidad del Atlántico, Barranquilla, Colombia
claudiabaloco@mail.uniatlantico.edu.co
[4] Department of Business Administration, Universidad del Atlántico, Barranquilla, Colombia
{angelicajimenez,
hugohernandezp}@mail.uniatlantico.edu.co

Abstract. The four pillars of IoT (People, Processes, Data and Things) have created the need to have an education system that empowers the new generations of digital citizens who understand the emerging technologies offered by IoT, the impact it has on the society the widespread adoption of the same and the correct application of the information that is captured. The purpose of this project is to diagnose the use of the Internet of Things (IoT) in the higher education institutions of Barranquilla and its metropolitan area and to develop a strategy that encourages the use of IoT in these institutions. There is great potential in the definition of new projects related to IoT, a series of opportunities that must be identified and developed within higher education institutions, which will improve the quality of life of the community in general. Currently, the IoT already offers added value and, over time, its potential will increase thanks to the work in innovation that is being carried out in various areas such as Sustainability and Energy Efficiency, Education, Health, Mining and Industrial Sector, Mobile vision and mitigation of proactive risks, among others. Education is not unconnected to this phenomenon and important developments have taken place in universities throughout the world, which will be described in the development of the work. This project aims, in addition to diagnosing the current state of IoT in our institutions of higher education and to define a strategy for its promotion, raise awareness about the role of IoT and the challenges it represents in formal education.

Keywords: Internet of Things · Institutions of higher education
Network design · Survey · Projects

© Springer International Publishing AG, part of Springer Nature 2018
C. Stephanidis (Ed.): HCII Posters 2018, CCIS 852, pp. 17–24, 2018.
https://doi.org/10.1007/978-3-319-92285-0_3

1 Introduction

Data and communications networks, in general, must meet the following basic conditions: security, scalability, high performance, redundancy, manageable and easy to maintain [1]. The key to complying with these conditions is to design a hierarchical network that allows the interconnectivity of the users to the various services of the network and the applications that it supports. The Internet has become a vital work tool for people's daily tasks. In this completely globalized world who are not connected to the great global network, and takes advantage of all its potential, it is simply designed to stay a step behind. It is estimated that by 2020, 50000 million devices will be connected to the Internet [2]. Today, approximately 99% of the objects in the physical world are not connected to the Internet. Internet of all things will tend because a large part of these objects connects to the global network. The Internet is becoming bigger, Internet of Things is expanding our interconnecting possibilities [3].

The objective of this project is to establish a characterization of the use of the Internet of Things (IoT) in the higher education institutions of Barranquilla and its metropolitan area. This detailed study will be done through descriptive and documentary research. The type of research design to be used is the qualitative/transactional - descriptive since it will analyze the current level or state of variables to be defined throughout the work and their relationship [4]. Lastly, a series of recommendations for the promotion of IoTs is established.

2 Literature Review About IoT and Conceptualization

Among all the essential elements for human existence, the need to interact is just after the need to sustain life. Communication is almost as important to us as air, water, food and a place to live. The immediate nature of Internet communications encourages the formation of diverse world communities. Being able to communicate reliably with everyone everywhere is vital for our personal and business life. To support the immediate sending of the millions of messages that are exchanged between people, and now between processes and even objects around the world, we rely on a web of interconnected networks [1, 5].

Reference [6] in its scientific Article entitled "Internet of Things" presented five articles that cover one of the most relevant areas in the field of IoT. Reference [7] carried out the research entitled "Intelligent Infrastructures on the Internet of the Future" in which they presented in a clear and understandable way the next technological leap, namely, the inclusion of the objects of daily life in the field of telecommunications, achieving a change in the communication paradigm. The research community has called this evolutionary step the Internet of Things. [8, 9] explain the most important concepts related to the Internet of Things and the applicability that the future of communications has in the future, the impact that this new trend has on society today.

Reference [10] in his research "Technological Evolution and the Internet of the Future" defined IoT as a global network of interconnected objects of unique addressing based on standard communication protocols. It managed to move forward regarding data exchange, processing and interoperability, considered the main challenges when using wireless sensor networks (WSN). These technologies are commonly used in automation, agriculture, home automation, logistics and security. Reference [11] in their thesis, "Evaluation of the reference model of Internet of Things (IoT), through the implementation of architectures based on commercial platforms, open hardware and ipv6 connectivity" made an evaluation of the IoT reference model through the design and implementation of network prototypes based on the Arduino, digi and IPv6 platforms. Reference [2] in his research refers to the impact of IoT in many sectors of the national economy, making a complete diagnosis of the transition from current connectivity to the total connectivity provided by the Internet of Things.

Internet of Things (IoT) can be defined as the meeting of people, processes, data and things to make network connections more relevant and valuable than ever, turning information into actions that create new capabilities, richer experiences and unprecedented economic opportunities for companies, individuals and the countries. Figure 1 shows the interactions between the elements that make up IoT [12]:

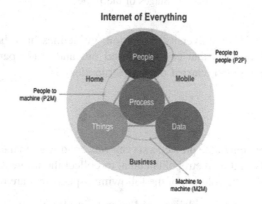

Fig. 1. Elements of IoT

3 Methodology

This detailed study will be developed using the documentary and descriptive research methodology as a research methodology, since for the elaboration of this project it is necessary to consult a series of documents and collect information through data collection techniques, to reinforce concepts and terms in the different stages in the optimal development of the object of study. The type of research design to be used is the qualitative/transactional - descriptive one since it is going to analyze the level or current state of variables that will be defined throughout the work and its relation.

A population has been chosen from a sample, following statistical criteria to be deepened in the project, to use data collection techniques such as direct observation and in-depth interview, to subsequently make a qualitative analysis of the data [13]. The wide number of Higher Education Institutions existing in the city and its metropolitan area are taken into consideration those that are accredited by the national education ministry and have ICT programs. Figure 2 shows the stages of the project.

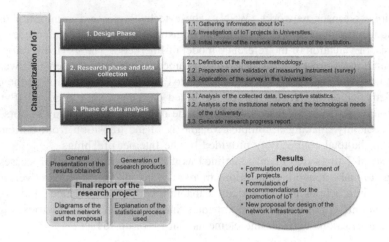

Fig. 2. Stages of the project

In the case of the ITSA university institution, guidelines have been given for the development of IoT projects that can be carried out and made part of the research seedbed, such as the research carried out by Hernandez [14].

4 Results

As part of the development of the project, a survey was conducted in the Higher Education Institutions of the city and its metropolitan area, to collect the impressions and draw the conclusions that lead to the solution of the following aspects that are required to know:

- Identify the existence of guidelines and/or policies for the use of the Internet of things of higher education institutions in the city and its metropolitan area.
- Evaluate the importance of the use of technological tools and latest generation trends, such as the Internet of Things, in the various processes (teaching/learning - administrative) of higher education institutions in the city and its metropolitan area.

The applied measurement instrument was called the IoT Survey. The chosen population is the set of Institutions of Higher Education, and the sample was those institutions with some program in Information and Communication Technologies and/or similar accredited by the Ministry of National Education. The statistical formula used to obtain the sample is shown in Fig. 3:

SIZE OF THE SAMPLE WHEN THE DEVIATION OF THE POPULATION IS NOT KNOWN	INFORMATION TO CALCULATE THE SIZE OF THE SAMPLE		SIZE OF THE SAMPLE
$n = \dfrac{k^{\wedge 2} * p * q * N}{(e^{\wedge 2} * (N-1)) + k^{\wedge 2} * p * q}$	Population Size (N)	15	14
	Probability of Success (p)	0,5	
	Probability of Non-Success (q)	0,5	
	Standard error €	0,05	
	Level of Confidence Chosen	1,96	
	DIAGNOSTIC INSTRUMENT SIG		

Fig. 3. Statistical formula for the sample

A reliability analysis of the measurement instrument was applied, calculating the Cronbach's alpha, obtaining a value of 0,761.

The Cronbach's Alpha coefficient is a model of internal consistency, based on the average of the correlations between the items. The closer you get to 1, the more reliable the measurement instrument and the greater the correlation between the variables. As can be seen, the alpha calculated for this work, using the SPSS tool, yields 0.761, which is quite good. The survey had 11 questions (variables). Table 1 shows the statistics by element, analyzed with SPSS software [15]:

Table 1. Element statistics

	Mean	Deviation	N
Familiarity with the concept of IoT	0,93	0,25	15
Development of research projects in IoT	0,20	0,41	15
Infrastructure network based on IoT at the University	0,20	0,41	15
Sufficient wireless network infrastructure	0,33	0,48	15
The possibility that Barranquilla becomes a smart city	0,86	0,35	15
Reliability of access to applications via web or smart device	0,80	0,41	15
Storage and access in the cloud of important applications	0,66	0,48	15
Process automation without human intervention	0,86	0,35	15
Technological leadership of the University thanks to IoT	0,93	0,25	15
Internet speed hired	2,53	0,74	15
Educational Level	1,80	0,94	15

It can see in Table 2 a summary of the statistics per element:

Table 2. Summary of Statistics per Element

	Means	Variance	N of Elements
Element means	0,921	0,484	11
Element variances	0,255	0,061	11
Correlations between elements	0,290	0,084	11

It can see in Table 3 some scale statistics:

Table 3. Scale Statistics

Mean	Variance	Standar Deviation	N of elements
10,1333	9,124	3,02056	11

The tabulated results and the histogram of a couple of the questions in the survey made are shown in Tables 4, 5, and Figs. 4, 5:

Table 4. Example 1 - Variable of the Interview

Answer	Percentage	Quantity
Yes	20,00%	3
No	80,00%	12

Table 5. Example 2 - Variable of the Interview

Answer	Percentage	Quantity
Yes	80,00%	12
No	20,00%	3

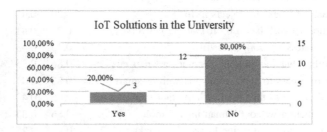

Fig. 4. Histogram Example 1 – variable of the interview

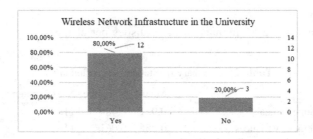

Fig. 5. Histogram Example 2 – variable of the interview

A. *Currently, are there solutions in the network infrastructure based on the Internet of Things in the University?*

B. *Does the University have a Wireless Network Infrastructure that allows the connectivity of the diverse users in any part of the campus?*

Given the results of the measurement instrument, it can be concluded that there is practically everything to do to promote the Internet of Things in the Higher Education Institutions of Barranquilla and its metropolitan area. That is why it is necessary to establish a series of recommendations (shown in Table 6) and formulate possible research and development projects (shown in Table 7) that can be carried out in the different institutions or companies [16].

Table 6. List of Recommendations for the Promotion of IoT

No.	Recommendation
1	Include within the curricular structures some type of training in the Internet of Things and in new technological trends
2	Train ICT teachers in this new technological trend to be multipliers of knowledge
3	The Institutions should promote in their seedbed of research the proposal and project proposals related to IoT
4	The institutions must strengthen their technological infrastructures, in such a way that prototypes, IoT solutions can be designed and implemented within it
5	Investment in technology

Table 7. List of Research and Development Projects in IoT

No.	Project
1	Design and implementation of an access control system managed by network sensors (WSN)
2	Design and implementation of a monitoring system of the health status of the academic community through sensors (WSN)
3	Design and implementation of a technological infrastructure that supports research and development in new technology trends such as the Internet of Things
4	Design and implementation of a control system on and off air conditioners and lights through network sensors
5	Design and implementation of a system for virtualization of the academic process

Among many others, since each sector has a wide range of possibilities, which may be well led by the University Institutions. The potential is enormous.

5 Conclusions and Future Works

The purpose of this project is to diagnose the use of the Internet of Things (IoT) in the higher education institutions of Barranquilla and its metropolitan area and to develop a strategy that encourages the use of IoT in these institutions, which has been developed to throughout the work. There is great potential in the definition of new projects related to IoT, a series of opportunities that must be identified and developed within higher education institutions, which will improve the quality of life of the community in general. Education is not unconnected to this phenomenon and important developments have taken place in universities throughout the world. This project aims, in addition to diagnosing the current state of IoT in our higher education institutions and to define a strategy for its promotion, raise awareness about the role of IoT and the challenges it represents in formal education.

The results of the application of the measuring instrument (survey and direct observation) give rise to two important conclusions: the first is that still in our educational environment, the potential of the IoT has not been understood; and secondly, educational institutions and those responsible for technological areas (both academic and administrative) are aware of the IoT potential and would consider, in one way or another, include it in their internal processes and encourage their use. Other future works may be to propose some hypotheses on which to perform statistical comparative tests and redesign the infrastructure of the ITSA network to support IoT.

References

1. Cisco Networking Academy: Cisco Networking Academy (2015). http://www.cisco.com/web/learning/netacad/index.html
2. García, L.: Estudio del impacto técnico y económico de la transición de internet al internet de las cosas (IoT) para el caso Colombiano. Univ. Nac. Colombia (2015)
3. Bujari, A., Palazzi, C.E.: Opportunistic communication for the Internet of Everything. In: Consumer Communications and Networking Conference, pp. 510–515 (2014)
4. Saravia Gallardo, M.A.: Metodología de investigación científica, Conacyt, pp. 1–18 (2006)
5. Hernandez, L.: Distributed Infrastructure for efficient management of network services. case: large company in mining sector in Colombia. In: 2016 2nd International Conference Science in Information Technology Proceedings, pp. 63–68. IEEE (2016)
6. Haya, P., Montoro, G., Schnelle-Walka, D.: Internet de las cosas: De los sistemas RFID a las aplicaciones inteligentes. Novatica **37**(209), 4 (2011)
7. Mansilla, D., Vega-Barbas, M., López, T.: Infraestructuras inteligentes en el Internet del Futuro. In: 1st Encuentro Investig. en Infraestructuras Intel., p. 5, March 2016
8. Saunders, A.: The Internet of Everything. Manag. Today **5**, 40–43 (2014)
9. Etzion, O., Fournier, F., Arcushin, S.: Tutorial on the Internet of Everything. In: Proceedings of the 8th ACM International Conference on Distributed Event-Based Systems - DEBS 2014, pp. 236–237 (2014)
10. Sosa, E.: Evolución Tecnológica e Internet del Futuro. In: XIV Workshop de Investigadores en Ciencias de la Computación (2012)
11. Abasolo, S., Carrera, M.: Evaluación del modelo de referencia de Internet of Things (IoT), mediante la implantación de arquitecturas basadas en plataformas comerciales, open hardware y conectividad ipv6. Universidad de las Fuerzas Armadas (2014)
12. Vazhnov, A.: La Red de Todo: Internet de las Cosas y el Futuro de la Economía Conectada, 1st edn. Andreidigital, Barcelona (2016)
13. Ronald, K.W., Myers, R., Myers, S., Ye, K.: Probabilidad y Estadística para Ingenierías y Ciencias, Novena Edi. Pearson, Mexico (2012)
14. Hernandez, L., Pranolo, A., Riyanto, I., Calderon, Y., Martinez, H.: Design of a system for detection of environmental variables applied in data centers. In: 2017 3rd International Conference on Science in Information Technology (ICSI Tech 2017), pp. 389–395 (2017)
15. IBM: IBM SPSS Statistics 21 Brief Guide. IBM SPSS (2012)
16. Lee, I., Lee, K.: The Internet of Things (IoT): applications, investments, and challenges for enterprises. Bus. Horiz. **58**(4), 431–440 (2015)

Development of Gesture Recognition Education Game for Elementary School Students Personality Education

Sunghee Hong[1,2(✉)] and Eunhye Kim[2]

[1] Major in Human Art & Technology, Morden Dance, Shinhan University,
Uijeongbu-si, Republic of Korea
hongsungh22@hanmail.net
[2] Major in Dance Sports, Department of Faculty of Liberal Arts, Shinhan University,
Uijeongbu-si, Republic of Korea
gracedance@hanmail.net

Abstract. The purpose of this study is to develop a game of education for children. By experiencing personality education game, participants respect their parents and learn to give consideration to their friends. Elementary school children feel joy when they can help a hard friend, and they are rewarding for themselves. But not all of the children who participated did it in a polite and polite way. A child who was proud of his polite behavior was very fond of writing it in his personality notebook. It is a difficult learning method to form good relationship with good behavior and friends while learning children's textbooks. Gesture recognition-based interface is a game that allows children to learn actively. It is an effective game tool that can be actively used to record daily action contents in a notebook. The game is divided into three types and it is done in 18 ways. The game is conducted in random form with a total of 100 points for 5 min with the narrator's explanation. Game music is used for children's songs. The game is the result obtained after the local governments of Korea. The behavior of the children depends on the animated picture problem. When they agree with the correct answer, as a means of complimenting audiovisual feedback, and they get a score for correct behavior. In cognitive learning that used this game, children were interested in the active behavior of their image on TV, and they were more interesting than teaching classes in traditional classrooms and actively engaged in learning classes. Children are interested, It's a good learning tool to raise awareness.

Keywords: Personality education · Seonbi-spirit practice manual
Gesture-based interface · Kinect

1 Introduction

Educational methods of personality education are meaningful for children to actively participate and practice. The personality education which is practiced by the Seonbi, known as virtuous scholar, spirit of Korean traditional culture is divided into 6 kinds. Personality education should be made so that children can act and decide by themselves

© Springer International Publishing AG, part of Springer Nature 2018
C. Stephanidis (Ed.): HCII Posters 2018, CCIS 852, pp. 25–30, 2018.
https://doi.org/10.1007/978-3-319-92285-0_4

in daily life habits, but it is not easy to do so. Therefore, this study was developed as an educational game to help children learn the personality education in their own using Kinect and motion image, It is the outcome of behaviors that children think in intellectual and moral aspects, such as personality education, and those outcome should be carried out by children in natural way. Educational games allow students to learn through the methods of beneficial games that they can learn through self-directed learning, so that they can carry out their habit of practicing themselves in daily life. Children need to have basic learning knowledge about personality education, so they can get higher score in game. The effort for learning becomes a factor of challenge and conflict. The more children immerse in the game, the higher the concentration and the higher the score. You can compare the score difference in scores and records in the game.

In the case of existing educational edutainment games, only the amusing part is emphasized, and necessary for learning is developed in accordance with commercial intention. It is difficult for adults in reality to have basic courtesy, consideration, humility and politeness in daily life, and finally to practice justice. The situation in this reality will be more difficult for children. Personality education game is a learning education for children to instinctively express and execute in reality. The purpose of this study is to help children actively learn gesture through physical body in relation with school, family and friends through the game of personality education game.

2   Educational Gesture Recognition Game Using KINECT

The KINECT used in this study uses the gestures of the hands and feet of the body without a separate controller such as a keyboard, mouse, or joystick. In the game, the child proceeds with the description of the game on the TV screen after the child selects the progress of the game. By using the motion image and the computer graphic screen with the camera, the correct answers are obtained by moving, typing, greeting, using hands or feet to the correct answer item in the presentation screen for each question. In the game, it proceeds by moving the body along the image of the computer graphic screen. Use Kinect's camera to let the participant's moving gesture appear on the game screen. This makes it easier to use the chromakey technique with Kinect. The purpose of this study is to practice the personality education behaviors learned through the content of study in children's daily life activities.

3   Game Program Scheme

The contents of education used in personality education were the 'Personality Education Practice Manual' which was enacted in Korea as 'Personality Education Promotion Act'. There are 18 ways to classify the game into three categories as "Anja Yookhun" of Oriental Humanistic Spirit of Ancient Teacher (1243), <Hyo, Choong> <Ye, Shin>, <Kyung, Seong>. The learned activities of the game in daily life are confirmed by the child to write in the 'self-examination notebook' (see Table 1). The game items (from 1 point to 5 points) checked in the notebook are recorded as scores.

Table 1. "Seonbi Spirit Manual" self examination handbook (Cover, Underprint)

Cover	One og the underprint	One of the underprint

For the active participation of children, it is necessary to generate interest. The participants, children, enjoyed the game with exciting Korean traditional music. The back screen shows the scene of the computer graphics screen drawn with the children differently as the game proceed.

The first screen is the screen of "Seonbi Spirit Manual" (see Table 2). The screen prompted the child to select the type of game. Whenever the correct answers are met, feedback is given to the "success" hearing. There are three categories of games and 18 methods are used (see Table 3). It gives 5 min to play once. After 5 min of progress, the result is given as a score. The result shows all the scores with the words "I did it very well" and I hear the exciting music with auditory feedback, and it shows on the screen how many as the total score. There is no difficulty depending on the level of the game.

Table 2. Screen shots of personality education game.

Start Screen	On-going	Result

Table 3. Content composition and total of 18 activity images

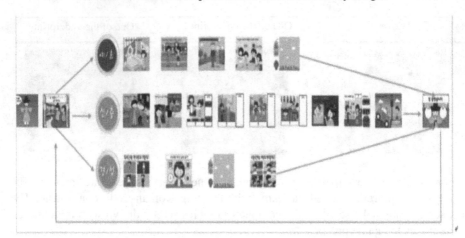

4   Children's Learning Courses in Personality Education Field

The personality education game designed in this study was conducted once a week for six months and it was subject to lower grades in 5 elementary schools of Yeongju city, Gyeongbuk province SOUTH KOREA. The chromakey technique, along with the graphic display using Kinect, is very useful for attracting children's interest

The rules of the game are to move the body to get the correct answer, or to move the hands and feet to move the correct answer and avoid the wrong answer. Not only does it challenge the intellectual challenges of learning, but it also involves physical challenges, and it also requires the agility of the gestures of the fast-moving players. Sometimes it is necessary to make a decision on the answer every moment. There is no game difficulty and level, but it requires shortening the time to get score. Along with the animation effect, the composition of the story of the game led to the success of the learning and made it possible to execute immediately in lifestyle habits. This is a learning scene where you move the body to avoid wrong answers (see Table 4).

Unlike the method of learning personality education by sitting in front of the existing classroom desk, personality education learning using game gesture in the field showed the following personality to children. The child enjoyed the appearance on the TV screen using the chroma key effect. Children began to engage harder to gain higher scores through the game, as well as to motivate learning, sensing hearing feedback and score increases in the way the body moves and gestures. The gesture appeared to be a game of using the body rather than using hands and feet.

Especially, the children were more interested in the motivation for correct personality learning in real life as well as the increase of the scores recorded in the personality education handbook. The children were not hesitant in their role to greet their parents, their superiors (bowing their heads), their brothers, the consideration of their friends,

Table 4. The place where the training is conducted by the participants

and their role in helping the hard work. It can be proved that games are possible alternatives to tools of traditional learning, and it is also consistent with the claim that it results in the same learning as traditional education.

Acknowledgement. The study was funded by the National Research Foundation of Korea (NRF) grant funded by the Ministry of Science and Technology (ICT & Future Planning). It is a private-led project and is being supported by local governments. It is a research and development (R & D) program for science and technology humanities research (1460-20170220).

References

1. Lee, E., Liu, X., Zhang, X.: Xdigit: an arithmetic Kinect game to enhance math learning experience. Retrieved 14 Feb 2013
2. Kim, N.: Designing Interactive storytelling game in location-based entertainment. J. Korean Soc. Comput. Game **23**, 227–236 (2012)
3. Freeman, S., Eddy, S.L., McDonough, M., Smith, M.K., Okoroafor, N., Jordt, H., Wenderoth, M.P.: Active learning increases student performance in science, engineering, and mathematics. Proc. Natl. Acad. Sci. **111**, 8410–8415 (2014)
4. Miles, H.C., Pop, S.R., Watt, S.J., Lawrence, G.P., John, N.W.: A review of virtual environments for training in ball sports. Comput. Graph. **36**, 714–726 (2012)

5. Taylor, P.: Transformative steam education for the 21st century. In: Proceedings of the Australian Conference on Science and Mathematics Education (formerly UniServe Science Conference) (2016)
6. Presnky, M.: The motivation of game play: the real twenty-first century earning revolution. On the Horizon 10.1, form (2014). http://www.marcprensky.com/writing/

Integration of Kahoot into EFL Classroom

Yen-ju Hou[✉]

Shu-Zen Junior College of Medicine and Management, Kaohsiung, Taiwan
yunju@ms.szmc.edu.tw

Abstract. Literacy reading was regarded complex and difficult for learners of English as a Foreign Language (EFL) and reduce their interest to read and reflect the materials. To increase students' motivation and reading comprehension, the study aimed to explore the effects of integrating questioning strategies with Interactive Response System (IRS), Kahoot, into English reading courses among junior college students in Taiwan. Together with motivation and attitude toward English learning, what students' feedback about the use of Kahoot in class was discussed as well. A total of 130 junior college students served as subjects of the study. They were all English majors enrolling in literacy reading courses for one semester and helped to complete a set of surveys regarding to English learning motivation and feedback toward the use of integrating Kahoot in class. Findings revealed that students had positive attitude toward using IRS, and their overall satisfaction of Kahoot, together with gender and English proficiency, was found to be relevant to their learning motivation in the end. Discussion and conclusion were provided.

Keywords: Interactive response system · Kahoot · English learning motivation
Literacy reading comprehension

1 Introduction

Nowadays, technology has been widely integrated into classroom, such as mobile devices, computers, media and software. Teachers could integrate various resources through online applications and platforms. Many researches explored the benefits of using interactive response system (IRS) via mobile devices, such as enriching environment, classroom participation, and motivation (Awedh et al. 2014; Chiang 2016; Huang 2016; Wash 2014). Therefore, many studies have been done to investigate the effect of technology on students' various aspect of learning outcome (Chen 2014; Huang 2016; Lin 2016; Wu 2017; Yang 2017). In Taiwan, studies have reported that IRS is proved to promote students' satisfaction and concentration (Lee 2017; Yang 2017; Wang 2016; Wang 2017) and academic performance (Chen 2014; Huang 2016; Kung 2016; Lin 2016; Tsai 2016; Wang 2017). However, some findings showed opposite results. For example, in Lin's (2016) study, the findings showed no significant difference among college students' situational attention and interest using Tablet IRS. Despite of the opposite findings, studies have showed the positive effects of integrating IRS into classroom to promote students' motivation and learning.

© Springer International Publishing AG, part of Springer Nature 2018
C. Stephanidis (Ed.): HCII Posters 2018, CCIS 852, pp. 31–37, 2018.
https://doi.org/10.1007/978-3-319-92285-0_5

In the research site, the huge class size of 50 to 60 students in an English classroom makes it difficult for the teacher to monitor all students' learning. Moreover, studies have showed significant effects of IRS on promoting learning motivation, and particular subjects (Chen 2014; Chiang 2016; Lin 2016; Tsai 2016; Wang 2016; Wang 2017). However, after researching current studies that are done in Taiwan, it is found that most studies on IRS have centered on elementary and junior high school students, especially in the area of science, social science and computer. How IRS affects language learning has not been discussed much in this decade.

To this point, the study aimed to investigate IRS into English courses which students were trained to use Kahoot to offer answers to different types of questions related to their literacy reading materials. By using Kahoot, both the teacher and students could see how well they comprehend the reading materials. Thus, it is hoped to inspire students to think actively and critically via questioning and then increase their motivation on English learning.

1.1   Research Resign

Quasi-experimental design of surveys was used in the study in order to investigate students' language learning motivation and feedback toward the use of Kahoot on English literacy reading courses.

1.2   Participants

Approximately three classes taught by the researcher participated in the study. Participants were all English-majors at a private junior college in Southern Taiwan. Class 1 consisted of 42 third to fifth grade students with English levels from low-intermediate to intermediate (M = 1.95, SD = .37), while Class 2 included 42 fourth grade students whose English levels mostly reached intermediate (M = 3.09, SD = .69), and Class 3 was composed of 61 third year students with low-intermediate English level (M = 2.30, SD = .72). Among the three classes, Class 2 had the highest English level than Class 1 (p < .05) and Class 3 (p < .05), while Class 3 had higher English level than Class 1 (p < .05). By removing the uncompleted surveys, valid samples were reduced to a total of 37, 38, and 55 students for the three classes, respectively. All participants were around 17 to 20 years old, and Chinese was their native language. Summary of the individual demographic background of the subjects were presented in Table 1.

Table 1. Summary for individual demographic background

Class	Total	Gender		CEFR level					M	SD	Sig
		Male	Female	A1	A2	B1	B2	C1			
1	37	6	31	4	31	2	0	0	1.95	.37	.000
2	38	6	32	0	6	23	8	1	3.09	.69	2 > 1*
3	55	12	43	3	42	12	3	1	2.30	.72	2 > 3*
All	130	24	106	7	79	37	11	2	2.43	.77	3 > 1*

Note: CEFR levels used here are based on ETS (2015). A1–A2 level ranks as basic user, while B1-B2 ranks as independent user, and C1–C2 for proficient user. *p < .05

1.3   Instruments

The research adopted 16 out of 21 questions developed from Wang (2017) to discover learners' perception toward teaching through IRS, Kahoot, with teaching interaction, engagement, self-efficacy and degree of learning satisfaction. Participants responded to each statement by using 5-point scale, from 1(not at all describes me) to 5 (best describes me). In addition, the survey of students' English learning motivation and attitude was adopted from Gardner (2004) with 7 point scale from 1 (not at all describes me) to 7 (best describes me), which was completed by the students twice, one was in the beginning of the semester (pre-test), and the other was in the end of the semester (post-test). The reliability of the research questionnaires were .932 for students' feedback about using Kahoot, as well as .838, and .872 for the pre-test and post-test of students' English learning motivation, respectively. As Gay and Airasian (2003) mentioned that "If a test were perfectly reliable, the reliability coefficient would be 1,00.... However, no test is perfect reliable" (p. 141), hence, with the reliability coefficient of between .838 and .932, the research instruments were quite reliable.

1.4   Mobile Assisted Learning Tasks (MAL Tasks)

MAL tasks were used mainly to access students' comprehension and to enhance their participation and attention on reading through Kahoot. Questions used in Kahoot were mainly multiple choice items, and used as review games for less than 10 min before the end of class. Students could submit their answers by individual or with peers based on their choice

1.5   Procedures

As the researcher obtained permission from school and participating students, the researcher explained the purpose of the study and MAL tasks, demonstrate how Kahoot were used. MAL tasks were used around 10–14 times in each class, and students completed tasks with pairs or individual depended on the classroom's learning atmosphere and the teacher's concerns. Participants were asked to complete the survey at the end of the semester. In addition, students helped to complete the survey of English learning motivation both in the beginning (pre-test) and in the end of the semester (post-test).

The survey was collected and coded for further analysis. The quantitative data was analyzed through SPSS, version 16. Descriptive statistics, t-test, one-way ANOVA, and Regression analysis were processed for means and standard deviation, class differences, and factors relevant to students' change of English learning motivation after the use of Kahoot.

2 Results

2.1 Students' English Learning Motivation Before and After the Use of Kahoot

Findings revealed that before the use of kahoot, students had favorable motivation on English learning with a mean of 4.99 out of 7 (SD = .71), and there was no significant differences among the three classes (F = 1.884, Sig = .172). But after the use of Kahoot, students' motivation to learn English was significantly increased with a mean of 5.12 out of 7 (SD = .78) (F = 7.016, Sig = .009). In particular, though among the three classes, Class 2 had the highest mean, followed by Class 3 and Class 1 both before and after the use of Kahoot, yet there was no significant difference among the three classes; however, after the use of Kahoot, Class 2 had significantly higher mean than Class 1(I-J = 1.6883, Sig = .011). In addition, females had stronger motivation than males (p < .05) after the use of Kahoot. The findings were shown in Table 2.

Table 2. Students' English learning motivation before and after the use of Kahoot

Motivation	Class 1		Class 2		Class 3		Total		Sig
	M	SD	M	SD	M	SD	M	SD	
Before Kahoot	4.79	.75	5.13	.63	5.06	.71	4.99	.71	.172 (F = 1.884)
Rank	(3)		(1)		(2)				
After Kahoot	4.86	.91	5.38	.70	5.13	.66	5.12	.78	.009 (F = 7.016)
Rank	(3)		(1)		(2)				Class 2 > Class 1*
									Females > Males*

Note. The answer to the items of motivation was from 1 to 7. *p < .05

2.2 Students' Feedback of the Use of Kahoot in Class

In light of students' feedback about the use of Kahoot in class, findings indicated that students had a high level of overall satisfaction of using Kahoot with a mean of 4.44 out of 5 (SD = .49). Additionally, among the groups, there was a significant difference on students' Satisfaction of Materials (p < .05) and Satisfaction of Performance (p < .05), particularly Class 2 students had significant higher mean than that of Class 1 (p < .05). In addition, except for Self Efficacy, females had significant higher means than their counterparts (p < .01–.05). The findings of students' feedback of the use of Kahoot were presented in Table 3.

Table 3. Students' feedback of the use of Kahoot in class

Categories	Class 1		Class 2		Class 3		Total		Sig
	M	SD	M	SD	M	SD	M	SD	
1. Interaction	4.25 (5)	.43	4.41 (5)	.46	4.36 (2)	.48	4.35	.46	.252 (F = 1.323)
2. Peer learning	4.26 (4)	.42	4.43 (4)	.45	4.43 (5)	.45	4.34	.44	.129 (F = 2.333)
3. Engagement	4.20 (6)	.49	4.3 (6)	.52	4.27 (6)	.54	4.27	.52	.333 (F = .944)
4. Self efficacy	4.29 (1)	.45	4.48 (3)	.46	4.31 (5)	.53	4.35	.49	.056 (F = 3.723)
5. Materials	4.27 (2)	.42	4.50 (2)	.47	4.36 (2)	.48	4.38	.47	.043 (F = 4.189)
6. Performance	4.27 (2)	.45	4.53 (1)	.50	4.40 (1)	.49	4.40	.49	.043 (F = 4.187)
7. Overall Satisfaction	4.27 (3)	.45	4.55 (1)	.50	4.47 (2)	.50	4.44	.49	.058 (F = 3.650) (I-J) = .282(*) Class 2 > Class 1*

Note. The answer to the items of feedback was from 1 to 5. $*p < .05$

2.3 Factors Predictive to Students' English Learning Motivation After the Use of Kahoot

By Regression analysis, among factors of class, gender and English proficiency, findings showed that the factors predictive to students' English learning motivation before the use of Kahoot were gender ($p < .01$) and English proficiency ($p < .01$). But after the use of Kahoot, together with gender and English proficiency, students' overall satisfaction of Kahoot was found to be predictive to their English learning motivation as well ($p < .01$). In other words, it could be predictive that in the study, students of Class 2, females, and those who had higher overall satisfaction of using Kahoot in class tended to have stronger motivation about English learning ($p < .01$). The findings were displayed in Table 4.

Table 4. Factors predictive to students' English learning motivation after Kahoot

Factors	Before using Kahoot		After using Kahoot	
	t	Sig	t	Sig
(Constant)	9.479	.000	2.341	.021
Class	.796	.428	.540	.590
Gender	4.802	.000	4.152	.000
English proficiency	4.624	.000	3.967	.000
Overall satisfaction of using Kahoot	–	–	3.221	.002

*Dependent variable: English learning motivation

3 Discussion and Conclusion

Literacy reading was complex and challenging for EFL learners and led to students became demotivated. To increase students' motivation and reading comprehension, the author adopted the IRS strategy to integrate Kahoot into classroom for 3 classes of literacy reading-related courses for one semester. Participants were 130 English majors in a junior college in Taiwan and the instruments included two main surveys dealing with students' English learning motivation and their feedback about the use of Kahoot. Findings revealed that students had favorable attitudes toward the integration of Kahoot into classroom (Lee 2017, Yang 2017, Wang 2016, and Wang 2017) and other benefits (Awedh et al. 2014; Chiang 2016; Huang 2016; and Wash 2014). Specially, comparing with their English learning motivation in the beginning of the semester, in the study, students' overall satisfaction about using Kahoot was found to be relevant to their motivation to learn English in the end, particularly, females. Moreover, in light of different classes with students having different English levels, it was found that it made a difference in students' English learning motivation before and after using Kahoot in class. Students with better English proficiency, especially females, had stronger motivation on English learning in the beginning and in the end of the semester. But after the use of Kahoot, together with gender and English proficiency, overall satisfaction was found to be relevant to students' English learning motivation. It has long been believed that motivation is the key to learning. Hence, when other things being equal, being satisfied with the strategy of integration of IRS into classroom seems to be potential to improve students' motivation and lead to more satisfactory learning outcome. However, not a strategy can fit everyone, hence, it's suggested that teachers be aware of students' individual differences when designing the curriculum, teaching activities, and evaluation prior to adopting the IRS as a teaching and learning strategy. Taking students' gender differences, previous knowledge, learning styles, and multiple intelligences into consideration can be a good tip for improving the effectiveness of teaching and learning.

References

Awedh, M., Mueen, A., Zafar, B., Mazoor, U.: Using Socrative and smartphones for the support of collaborative learning. Int. J. Integrating Technol. Educ. **3**(4), 17–24 (2014)

Chen, C.T.: Effects of Incorporating Interactive Response Systems in Flipped Classroom on Elementary Students' English Learning. (Unpublished master's thesis). Chung Hua University, HsinChu, Taiwan (2014)

Chiang, Y.F.: Effects of the Flipped Classroom Model of Elementary Students with Interactive Response System on Math Learning. Unpublished master's thesis, Chung Hua University, HsinChu, Taiwan (2016)

ETS: Mapping the TOEIC and TOEIC Bridge tests on the Common European Framework of Reference for Language (2015). https://www.ets.org/s/toeic/pdf/toeic_cef_mapping_flyer.pdf

Gardner, R.C.: Attitude/Motivation Test Battery: International AMTB Research Project. University of Western Ontario, Canada, pp. 1–12 (2004)

Gay, L.R., Airasian, P.W.: Educational Research: Competencies for Analysis and Applications, 7th edn. Merrill Prentice Hall, Upper Saddle River (2003)

Huang, C.P.: A Study of IRS Integrated Instruction Design-Implemented with Minnan Dialect Course in Elementary School. Unpublished master's thesis, Hsing Wu University, New Taipei City, Taiwan (2016)

Kung, M.F.: An Experimental Investigation of the Interactive Response System on Sixth Graders' Legal Education: The Example of Plickers Application. Unpublished masters' thesis, National Kaohsiung Normal University, Kaohsiung, Taiwan (2016)

Lee, C.C.: The Research on the Learning Effect by integrating an Online Instant Response System into Earth Science Teaching-A Case Study for the Middle School Students from the Rural Area. Unpublished master's thesis, National Taiwan Normal University, Taipei, Taiwan (2017)

Lin, T.Y.: The Effect of Integrating Feedback and Signaling Design with Tablet IRS on College Students' Situational Interest and Attention. Unpublished master's thesis, National Chiao Tung University, Hsinchu, Taiwan (2016)

Tsai, T.-H.: Relationships between Different Assessment and Learning Efficiency: Using Interactive Response System on Group Discussion as Examples. Unpublished master's thesis, National Ilan University, Ilan, Taiwan (2016)

Wang, C.W.: The Design and Implementation of Team-Game-Tournament with Instant Feedback System into a University Course. Unpublished master's thesis, Tamkang University, New Taipei City, Taiwan (2016)

Wang, C.C.: Correlations of Teaching through Interactive Response System with Teaching Interaction, Engagement, Self-Efficacy and Degree of Learning Satisfaction. Unpublished master's thesis, National Taipei University of Education, Taiwan (2017)

Wash, P.D.: Taking advantage of mobile devices: using socrative in the classroom. J. Teach. Learn. Technol. 3(1), 99–101 (2014)

Wu, T.H.: Exploring Pre-service Elementary Teachers' Intention toward Using Interactive Response System in Teaching: A Technology Acceptance Model Approach. Unpublished master's thesis, National Taipei University of Education, Taipei, Taiwan (2017)

Yang, T.H.: An Elementary Educational Study on Chinese Stroke Real-Time Response System. Unpublished master's thesis, National Taichung University of Education, Taichung, Taiwan (2017)

Utilizing HMD VR to Improve the Spatial Learning and Wayfinding Effects in the Virtual Maze

Tsuei-Ju (Tracy) Hsieh[✉], Yu-Hsuan Kuo, and Chun-Kai Niu

Chinese Culture University, 55, HwaKang, Taipei 11114, Taiwan R.O.C.
tracy.tjhsieh@gmail.com

Abstract. Human wayfinding strategy in an unfamiliar space has been an important research issue in the interface design of spatial navigation. This study aims at comparing the participants' spatial learning and wayfinding performance using two different visual displays - the regular PC screen and the head mounted display (HMD) virtual reality (VR) system. HMD VR (we used HTC vive) is the popularizing device which provides users the immersive visual experience and full body interaction with the virtual environment. We designed a target-finding experiment to examine three factors, the spatial complexity, the visual display, and the landmark type. The participants were divided into two groups and used PC screen with keyboard and VR with controller stick respectively to perform the task, namely finding a particular target in six virtual mazes in two different sizes. In each target finding trial, the participant received one of the three navigation aids, a given distant landmark, some local landmarks in every intersection, or local landmarks freely laid by the participant. We measured the complete time, the times of taking repeat routes, the times and duration of the pause, and the eye movements during target-finding in PC screen. Soon after the task, the participants were also asked to draw a maze map from memory. The preliminary results reveal the group of PC screen found target more quickly, but the VR group produced cognitive maps with higher spatial accuracy.

Keywords: Wayfinding · HMD VR · Navigation aids

1 Introduction

Human wayfinding behavior in unfamiliar virtual space had drawn researchers' attention in the interface design field of spatial navigation [1, 2]. This study aims at comparing the participants' spatial learning and wayfinding performance in two different visual displays, namely the regular PC screen and the head mounted display (HMD) virtual reality (VR) system. This study adopted a consumer VR product, HTC vive, as an experimental apparatus. HMD VR is a rapidly growing interface which provides users the immersive visual experience and full body interaction with the virtual environment [3]. HMD VR is a contemporary visual communication technology yet with room for improvements, such as imperfect user experience [4–6], high costs, and content shortage. Nevertheless, numerous VR applications for gaming, education, marketing and recreational purposes have been intensively explored in the past few years. VR technology was also used to investigate human wayfinding performance [7, 8], as manipulating the virtual space is much easier than manipulating a real space.

In this study, we designed a target-finding experiment which manipulates three factors, the spatial complexity, the visual display, and the landmark type. The fator of spatial complexity is varied in two sizes of Unity made virtual mazes with different numbers of intersections. The visual displays are a regular PC screen and HTC vive, while the three variations of landmark type include a given distant landmark, local landmarks in every intersection, or local landmarks laid by the participant. The influence of the three factors in spatial learning and wayfinding performance was evaluated through performance measures and the accuracy of the hand-draw cognitive map produced by the participant. Based on the theory of human navigation and motor skills [9], we hypothesize the users' spatial learning and wayfinding performance in the VR immersive environment could be better than that of in a flat display.

2 Method

2.1 Participants

The participants are undergraduates and graduate students enrolled in Chinese Culture University. There are 70 aged between 18–24 participants. The researcher recruited them in the classes and screened them with a short test of 3D sickness and illusionary motion sickness. Only the participants who are novice users of VR products and had no sickness reaction had participated in the experiment. There participants were divided into two groups: VR group and PC screen group. There are 35 participants in a group.

2.2 Stimuli

The Virtual Mazes
We created two sets of virtual mazes with different sizes and configurations, as shown in Fig. 1. It presents two bird view samples of the two different sized mazes. There are three different mazes in the small and larget set of mazes. From the start to the end of the wayfinding task, there are fixed four intersections in the small set of mazes and eight intersections in the large set of mazes.

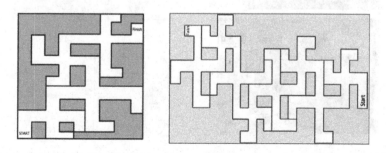

Fig. 1. Two sizes of virtual mazes represent two level of spatial complexity in the wayfinding experiment.

The Landmarks

Each participant was asked to complete the wayfinding task containing six trials, where each has to go through three small and three large mazes. In each trial, the participant would received a specific navigation aid, namely one of the three types of landmarks, a given distant landmark, local landmarks in every intersection, or local landmarks laid by the participant. Figure 2 shows these three types of landmarks from the participant's view. The distant landmark is a tree located constantly beside the maze. The local landmarks are different conspicuous objects such as a chair or a box placed in every intersection in the maze. The third type of landmarks is red disks that the participant can freely place on the floor in any route that he or she is taking.

Fig. 2. Three types of landmarks: distant, local, and local landmarks laid by the participant. (Color figure online)

2.3 Apparatus

Figure 3 shows the apparatus used to display the virtual mazes and control the participants' movement within them. The participants were divided into two groups and used either PC screen with keyboard HTC vive with controller stick respectively to perform the task.

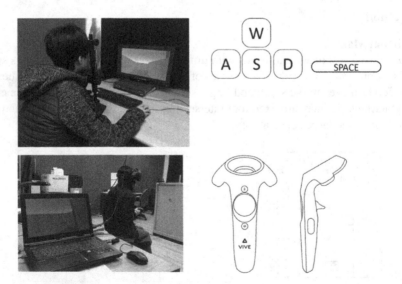

Fig. 3. Two types of interaction in the wayfinding experiment: PC screen with keyboard (upper) and HMD VR (HTC vive) with controller stick (lower)

2.4 Procedure

The participant accompanied by a research assistant have carried out the wayfinding experiment in the lab. The participant first takes a few minutes practicing the wayfinding task with either PC screen or VR interface. He or she has learned to control the movements in the mazes with the given interface, and also view three types of landmarks in the practice trial. The participants were informed that they would receive one of the navigation aids in every trial in the later experiment. During the practice, if the participant reports having difficulty with controlling the movement, then he or she will be given more time to practice.

There are two separated groups: VR group and PC screen group. There are 35 participants in a group. Each participant was asked to perform six times of wayfinding task (two sizes of mazes and three types of landmarks) using either PC screen or VR. The configuration of the mazes varies from trial to trial. The participant took around 40 to 60 min to complete all the six trials. They could have a short break if they ask. We measured the complete time, the times of taking repeat routes, the times of pause, and the eye movements during target-finding in PC screen. The participants were also asked to draw the maze map immediately after finishing the task from their fresh memory. The hand-draw cognitive maps (shown in Fig. 4) they produced would serve as a qualitative evaluation of the spatial learning. The researchers briefly interview the participant to access their experience interacting with the virtual environment.

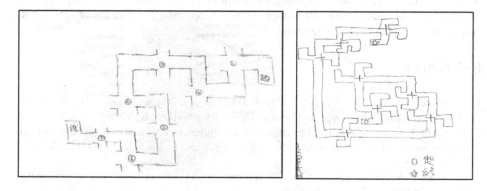

Fig. 4. Sample cognitive maps generated by two of the participants

3 Preliminary Results

Figure 5 shows the current results, where the two diagrams are mean complete time for PC and VR groups, with black, gray, and white bars to represent different conditions of navigation aids. The horizontal axis in the diagrams presents four sub-groups, male or female participants taking the large or small mazes.

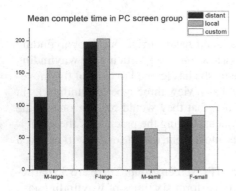 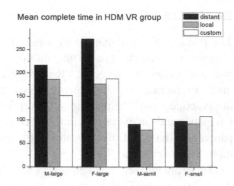

Fig. 5. Mean compele time of three types of landmarks in PC screen group and HD VR group

The primary results reveal that HMD VR group seems to require longer complete time (M = 146.47 s) than PC screen group (M = 114.30 s). However, if taking a closer look, the female participants in VR group result in shorter complete time in the condition of the small maze, and the females in VR group who were given local and custom landmarks also result in that of in screen group. Further more, based on our current collected hand-draw maps (see samples in Fig. 4), the participants of VR group are capable of generating the cognitive maps with better spatial representing of the mazes structure. Currently, we are increasing the number of the participants, analyzing the experiment datas and seeking for more evidence supporting the benefits of HMD VR system in the aspect of spatial learning.

References

1. Hedge, C., Weaver, R., Schnall, S.: Spatial learning and wayfinding in an immersive environment: the digital fulldome. Cyberpsychol. Behav. Soc. Netw. **20**(5), 327–333 (2017)
2. Zakzanis, K.K., et al.: Age and dementia related differences in spatial navigation within an immersive virtual environment. Med. Sci. Monit. Int. Med. J. Exp. Clin. Res. **15**(4), CR140–CR150 (2009)
3. Bowman, D.A.: Interaction techniques for common tasks in immersive virtual environments. Georgia Institute of Technology (1999)
4. Suznjevic, M., Mandurov, M., Matijasevic, M.: Performance and QoE assessment of HTC vive and Oculus Rift for pick-and-place tasks in VR. In: 2017 Ninth International Conference on Quality of Multimedia Experience (QoMEX). IEEE (2017)
5. Kelly, J.W., Cherep, L.A., Siegel, Z.D.: Perceived space in the HTC vive. ACM Trans. Appl. Percept. (TAP) **15**(1), 2 (2017)
6. Punkasem, T.-O., et al.: Vive Video Usability Report (2017)
7. Paris, R.A., et al.: A comparison of methods for navigation and wayfinding in large virtual environments using walking. In: 2017 IEEE Virtual Reality (VR). IEEE (2017)
8. Vilar, E., Rebelo, F., Noriega, P.: Indoor human wayfinding performance using vertical and horizontal signage in virtual reality. Hum. Factors Ergon. Manuf. Serv. Ind. **24**(6), 601–615 (2014)
9. Maguire, E.A., et al.: Knowing where and getting there: a human navigation network. Science **280**(5365), 921–924 (1998)

The Psychological Cost of College Math: Digital Learning Behaviors, Outcomes, and Genders Differences

Xing Huang[✉], Woonjon Hong, and Matthew Bernacki

University of Nevada, Las Vegas, NV 89154, USA
huangx2@unlv.nevada.edu

Abstract. Students' perception of the costs of engaging in learning has only recently been the focus of empirical study. Perceived costs include effort cost, opportunity cost, and psychological cost. This study focuses on the implications of psychological cost – the perceived negative psychological consequence of participating in a learning task –for learning behavior, performance, and the potentially greater prevalence of cost for women learning math. Research questions include: (1) Does perceived psychological cost of engaging in a calculus course predict undergraduates' behavior in the learning management system (LMS)? (2) Does psychological cost of engaging in a calculus course predict students' academic performance? (3) Which digital learning behaviors predict final exam score? (4) Do females perceive greater psychological cost than males? (5) Are there differences in course achievement by gender? And (6) Do male and females' digital learning behaviors differ? Contrasting theory and prior findings, psychological cost did not predict learning behavior or course performance. Students' use of policy documents and a tool to organize study sessions predicted final exam performance. Females perceived greater psychological costs than males when studying calculus, consistent with prior research. Female students also scored lower than males on the final exam. Results suggest that costs may differ by gender and may mediate gender differences in performance.

Keywords: Expectancy-value theory (EVT) · Psychological cost
Learning management system (LMS) · Math learning

1 Theoretical Framework and Background

1.1 Expectancy Value Theory

Motivation theories attempt to explain why individuals choose different tasks that they want to engage, how long they engage in those tasks, how intensive their engagement is, and what are their interpretations about task performance and goals (Eccles et al. 1998). Expectancy Value Theory (EVT) is one of the perspectives explaining motivation, arguing that individuals' expectations on the performance of tasks and their

© Springer International Publishing AG, part of Springer Nature 2018
C. Stephanidis (Ed.): HCII Posters 2018, CCIS 852, pp. 43–50, 2018.
https://doi.org/10.1007/978-3-319-92285-0_7

perceived value of tasks explain their choices and persistence on tasks as well as the vigor in carrying them out (Eccles et al. 1983). According to EVT model, expectancies and values are influenced by an array of psychological and social cultural determinants, such as beliefs of individuals' abilities, the perceived difficulty of different tasks, task goals, self-schema, and affective memories. Expectancy in the modern EVT is defined as the expectancies for success, which distinguishes from the beliefs about competence or ability (Wigfield et al. 2010). Task values in EVT consists of four major components: attainment value, intrinsic value, utility value, and cost. Attainment value can be understood as the personal importance of doing well on the task, intrinsic value is the enjoyment one gains from doing the task, utility value refers to how the current task benefits individuals' future plans, and cost refers to the negative aspects of engaging the task, such as performance anxiety or fear of failure. This study examines students' perceived cost, in particular, psychological cost in taking Calculus I, and how the psychological cost influence learning behaviors and the learning outcome.

1.2   The Role of Cost

Within EVT, cost is defined as "what an individual has to give up to do a task, as well as the anticipated effort one will need to put into task completion" (Eccles 2005). If a task is perceived as costing too much, individuals will be less likely to do it. EVT theorists hypothesized three types of cost: opportunity cost, effort cost, and psychological cost. Opportunity cost is how much alternatives one needs to give up in order to engage in the task, effort cost is how much effort will be needed to accomplish the task, and psychological cost refers to the negative psychological or emotional consequence of participating this task. Gaspard et al. (2015) found that females perceive more psychological and effort cost than males using a measure of cost found to be invariant between males and females.

Conceptualized as the mediator between individuals' affective reactions and performance, cost was introduced as one of the components of task values, along with attainment value, intrinsic value, and utility value (e.g. Barron and Hulleman 2015; Eccles et al. 1983; Eccles et al. 1998; Wigfield and Eccles 1992, 2000). Studies have shown that cost is empirically different from expectancies and values (Conley 2012; Kosovish et al. 2015; and Trautwein et al. 2012). Flake et al. (2015) extended these methodological confirmations and further elevated the treatment of cost and established costs as factors that influences outcomes alongside values, rather than as a subcomponent of values.

Prior empirical studies that examine cost as a component of value, primarily find that values were positively predict students' academic choices such as switching STEM majors (Perez et al. 2014) and enrollment intentions in math courses (Meece et al. 1990). In the studies that also measure perceived cost as an independent construct, perceived cost was found to negatively predict academic choice (Battle and Wigfield 2003). Barron and Hulleman (2015) also reported that students' value predicted their interest in the subject, but perception of cost can negative predict both their grades and interests in the subject. Debate continues: Barron and Hulleman (2015) proposed an expectancy-value-cost motivation model after a comprehensive review of the literature while Wigfield et al. (2017) maintain the argument that cost should not be elevated to a named component in Expectancy Value Theory. This study applies a contextual approach given prior evidence of the psychological variables previously shown to influence students engagement and achievement in undergraduate mathematics. We thus focus our examination on the implications of psychological cost across students, and focus further on its implications for the female students most apt to abandon their STEM career aspirations.

2   Methods

The primary purpose of this study is to examine the role of psychological cost in students' learning behaviors and outcomes in a face-to-face Calculus course in a Southwestern university. In addition, this study also seeks to answer whether or not there is discrepancy of psychological cost between female students and male students.

2.1   Research Questions

1. Does perceived psychological cost of engaging in a calculus course predict undergraduates' behavior in a learning management system (LMS)?
2. Does perceived psychological cost of engaging in a calculus course predict students' academic performance?
3. Which digital learning behaviors predict final exam scores?
4. Do females perceive greater psychological cost than males?
5. Are there differences in course achievement by gender?
6. Do male and females' digital learning behaviors differ?

2.2   Participants and Course

One hundred and twenty one undergraduate students (53% female; 33% Caucasian, 23% Asian, 20% Hispanic, and 24% others; 55% first generation college students) taking Calculus I in a Southwestern U.S. university participated in this study. Learning behaviors in the LMS were collected from server logs for two face-to-face Calculus course sections taught by instructors that hosted digital course content on their LMS course site.

2.3   Measures

Learning Behaviors. Eight kinds of students' learning behaviors are recorded. We traced and collected those learning behaviors explained by how frequently they clicked on the links (see Table 1).

Table 1. LMS learning behaviors observed via university server logs

Resource type	Behaviors (i.e., access of)
Content folder	Folders containing resources that an instructor shared with students
Content area	Link to an external website that provides a resource relevant to a course objectives
Monitoring process	Interactive worksheet designed to organize a study session
Lecture notes (partial)	Lecture notes to be completed in class
Lecture notes (complete)	Lecture notes to be used after class
Environmental Structure	LMS tools (e.g., settings, help)
Planning	Study guides and exam blueprints
Policy	Course schedules; course and university policies

Perceived Psychological Cost. Questionnaires assessing expectancies, attainment, intrinsic and utility value and effort, opportunity and psychological costs were adapted from Perez et al. (2014) and administered in weeks (4 items per value and cost; six-point Likert scale; Table 2).

Table 2. Items assessing psychological cost.

Please rate how much you agree or disagree with the following statement:	
1. I would be embarrassed if I found out that my work in my STEM courses was inferior to that of my peers	1.Strongly disagree
2. I'm concerned that I won't be able to handle the stress that goes along with my STEM courses	2.Disagree 3.Somewhat
3. It frightens me that my STEM courses are harder than courses required for other majors	disagree 4.Somewhat
4. It frightens me that my STEM courses are harder than courses required for other majors	agree 5.Agree 6.Strongly agree

Learning Outcome. A final exam provided a summative evaluation of students' learning in the course. This culminating exam assessed all course objectives and was composed of multiple choice and constructed response items. The majority of items were math problems to be solved. Some included prompts to provide written responses explaining concepts and procedures. These were scored using a standard rubric employed by multiple raters.

3   Results

Research Question 1: Does perceived psychological cost of engaging in a calculus course predict undergraduates' behavior in a learning management system (LMS)?

A series of multiple regression analysis regressing students' LMS behaviors on their level of perceived psychological cost revealed no significant predictive relationship, $Fs(3,115) < 2.69$, $ps > .05$.

Research Question 2: Does perceived psychological cost of engaging in a calculus course predict students' academic performance?

A multiple regression analysis regressing exam scores on values and costs produced a nonsignificant omnibus model, $F(6,113) = 1.141$, $p = .217$. In this model, psychological cost was not a significant predictor of exam scores, $\beta = -.166$, $p = .125$.

Research Question 3: Which digital learning behaviors predict final exam scores?

A model regressing final exam score on students' behaviors was statistically significant, $F(8, 110) = 2.491$, $p < .05$, $R^2 = .016$. Accesses to an interactive tool designed to organize study session (b = .013, SE = .007, $p < .05$, $\beta = .178$) and to policy documents (b = .012, SE = .004, $p < .01$, $\beta = .293$) predicted final exam grade.

Research Question 4: Do female perceive greater psychological cost than males?

In an independent samples t-test demonstrated variances were similar across groups (F = .531, $p = .468$) and that females students perceived significantly greater psychological cost when learning calculus than male students, $t(119) = 2.632$, $p = .010$, $d = .48$.

Research Question 5: Are there differences in course achievement by gender?

A second independent samples t-test demonstrated variances were similar across groups (F = .380, $p = .54$) and that males outperformed females on the final exam, $t(119) = -2.599$, $p = .011$, $d = .48$.

Research Question 6: Any gender differences on learning behaviors?

After a series of t-test, we did not observe significant gender differences on learning behaviors, $ts < .381$, $ps > .05$.

4   Discussion and Conclusion

This study builds on recent expectancy value theory research and examined the psychological cost induced when learning calculus, its relation to learning behaviors and achievement, as well as differences by gender. Results contrasted with theory and recent research and indicated psychological cost did not significantly predict behaviors or achievement.

Findings regarding the role of cost differ from EVT theory and previous studies of such relations. Prior research has revealed that high perceived cost results in lower frequency of learning activity (Chiang et al. 2011) and that perceptions of cost predict learning outcomes (Barron and Hulleman 2015). Because the courses observed were two face-to-face courses, where students had the opportunity to work both online and offline, the behaviors observed may comprise only a subset of learning activities. They do however provide a valid, granular record of learning events (Bernacki 2018). These findings should be understood to reflect only technology-based behaviors but to do so with precision. The modest relationship between psychological cost and achievement (i.e., β = .17) was not statistically significant, and was considerably smaller than the more general relationship between cost and achievement (i.e., r = .30; Flake, Flake et al. 2015). It may be that psychological cost is less associated with achievement than effort or opportunity costs, but contextual factors may also influence this relationship.

Digital learning (e.g. organizing study and policy document use) predicted achievement in calculus. Whereas relations between psychological cost and learning behaviors were not observed, two behaviors – monitoring study sessions with an interactive tool and use of policy documents – each predicted achievement. Monitoring one's study using this tool reflects a planful, metacognitive form of engagement in learning (Winne and Hadwin 1998). Attentiveness to policy documents reflect a kind of conscientiousness indicative of sensitivity to task affordances (Winne and Hadwin 1998; e.g. directives about learning objectives) and constraints (e.g., due dates) of the course during learning are more apt to understand and excel in the task. More nuanced analyses are warranted to better understand how events' impacts differ when they occur at different times in the semester, and in combinations or patterns (Bernacki 2018; Veenman 2013).

Females did perceive greater psychological cost than males when learning calculus, and they performed worse on a summative performance measure. Though we did not examine the casual relationship between female students' higher psychological cost and lower final exam scores, Fig. 1(a and b) document significant gender differences where females report greater psychological cost and achieve lower final exam scores. Additional analyses are ongoing to explore whether psychological costs may mediate these effects, and whether women might engage in different patterns of learning behaviors than

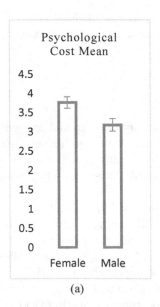

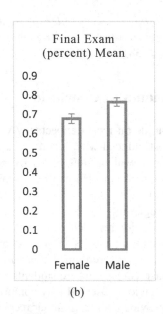

(a)   (b)

Fig. 1. (a) male and female students perceive different psychological cost, M_F = 3.746, M_M = 3.183, and (b) male and female students scored differently on the final exam, M_F = .677, M_M = .765.

men as a result of these perceived costs, and further, whether behaviors under such motivational state have differed predictive effects for achievement outcomes.

References

Barron, K.E., Hulleman, C.S.: Expectancy–value–cost model of motivation. In: Eccles, J.S., Salmelo-Aro, K. (eds.) International Encyclopedia of Social and Behavioral Sciences: Motivational Psychology, 2nd edn, pp. 503–509. Elsevier, New York (2015)

Battle, A., Wigfield, A.: College women's value orientations toward family, career, and graduate school. J. Vocat. Behav. **62**, 56–75 (2003)

Bernacki, M.L.: Examining the cyclical, loosely sequenced, and contingent features of self-regulated learning: trace data and their analysis. In: Schunk, D.H., Greene, J.A. (eds.) Handbook of Self-Regulated Learning and Performance, pp. 370–387. Routledge, New York (2018)

Chiang, E.S., Byrd, S.P., Molin, A.J.: Children's perceived cost for exercise: Application of an expectancy-value paradigm. Health Educ. Behav. **38**(2), 143–149 (2011). Official Publication of the Society for Public Health Education

Chow, A., Eccles, J.S., Salmela-Aro, K.: Task value profiles across subjects and aspirations to physical and IT-related sciences in the United States and Finland. Dev. Psychol. **48**(6), 1612–1628 (2012)

Conley, A.M.: Patterns of motivation beliefs: combining achievement goal and expectancy–value perspectives. J. Educ. Psychol. **104**(1), 32–47 (2012)

Eccles, J.S., Wigfield, A., Schiefele, U.: Motivation to succeed. In: Damon, W. (Series ed.), Eisenberg, N. (vol. ed.) Handbook of Child Psychology, 5th edn., vol. III, pp. 1017–1095. Wiley, New York (1998)

Eccles J.S., Adler, T.F., Futterman, R., Goff, S.B., Kaczala, C.M., Meece, J.L., Midgley, C.: Expectancies, values, and academic behaviors. In: Spence, J.T. (ed.) Achievement and Achievement Motivation, pp. 75–146. W. H. Freeman, San Francisco (1983)

Eccles, J.S.: Subjective task values and the Eccles et al. model of achievement related choices. In: Elliott, A.J., Dweck, C.S. (eds.) Handbook of Competence and Motivation, pp. 105–121. Guilford Press, New York (2005)

Ellis, J., Fosdick, B.K., Rasmussen, C.: Women 1.5 times more likely to leave STEM pipeline after calculus compared to men: lack of mathematical confidence a potential culprit. PLoS ONE **11**(7), e0157447 (2016)

Flake, B., Hulleman, M., Hulleman, C., McCoach, B.D., Welsh, M.E.: Measuring cost: the forgotten component of expectancy-value theory. Contemp. Educ. Psychol. **41**, 232–244 (2015)

Gaspard, H., Dicke, A., Flunger, B., Brisson, B., Hafner, I., Nagengast, B., et al.: Fostering adolescents' value beliefs for mathematics with a relevance intervention in the classroom. Dev. Psychol. **51**(9), 1226–1240 (2015)

Goetz, T., Bieg, M., Lüdtke, O., Pekrun, R., Hall, N.: Do girls really experience more anxiety in mathematics? Psychol. Sci. **24**(10), 2079–2087 (2013)

Kosovich, J.J., Hulleman, C.S., Barron, K.E., Getty, S.: A practical measure of student motivation: establishing validity evidence for the expectancy–value-cost scale in middle school. J. Early Adolesc. **35**(5–6), 790–816 (2015)

Meece, J.L., Wigfield, A., Eccles, J.S., Calfee, R.C., Schunk, D.H.: Predictors of math anxiety and its influence on young adolescents' course enrollment intentions and performance in mathematics. J. Educ. Psychol. **82**(1), 60–70 (1990)

Perez, T., Cromley, J.G., Kaplan, A.: The role of identity development, values, and costs in college STEM retention. J. Educ. Psychol. **106**(1), 315–329 (2014)

Trautwein, U., Nagengast, B., Nagy, G., Jonkmann, K., Marsh, H.W., Ludtke, O.: Probing for the multiplicative term in modem expectancy–value theory: a latent interaction modeling study. J. Educ. Psychol. **104**, 763–777 (2012)

Veenman, M.V.J.: Assessing metacognitive skills in computerized learning environments. In: Azevedo, R., Aleven, V. (eds.) International Handbook of Metacognition and Learning Technologies, pp. 157–168. Springer, New York/Berlin (2013). https://doi.org/10.1007/978-1-4419-5546-3_11

Wigfield, A., Eccles, J.: The development of achievement task values: a theoretical analysis. Dev. Rev. **12**, 265–310 (1992)

Wigfield, A., Eccles, J.S.: Expectancy–value theory of motivation. Contemp. Educ. Psychol. **25**, 68–81 (2000)

Wigfield, A., Cambria, J.: Expectancy-value theory: retrospective and prospective. In: Urdan, T.C., Karabenick, S.A. (eds.) Advances in Motivation and Achievement, vol. 16(A), pp. 35–70 (2010)

Wigfield, A., Rosenzweig, E.Q., Eccles, J.S.: Achievement values: interactions, interventions, and future directions. In: Elliot, A., Dweck, C.S., Yeager, D.S. (eds.) Handbook of Competence and Motivation: Theory and Application, 2nd edn., pp. 116–134. The Guildford Press, New York (2017)

Winne, P.H., Hadwin, A.F.: Studying as self-regulated learning. In: Hacker, D.J., Dunlosky, J., Graesser, A.C. (eds.) Metacognition in Educational Theory and Practice, pp. 277–304. LEA, Hillsdale (1998)

Effects of Video Games on HBCU Students

Erick K. Huston II[✉] and Joon Suk Lee

Virginia State University, Petersburg, VA 23806, USA
ehus5232@students.vsu.edu

Abstract. Our research focuses on how video games play a role in the lives of returning upperclassmen college students (sophomores to graduate level). In total, there were 34 participants, but due to unforeseen circumstances, only 32 of the college students (24 male, 8 female) could complete the distributed pre- and post-surveys. We then conducted weekly interviews with eight of the participants (6 male, 2 female) for 9 weeks. With the use of surveys, interviews and daily logs, our research concludes mixed results of both positive and negative effects of playing video games. Further research details life as a college student and the college experience.

Keywords: Video games · College students · Effects of gaming

1   Introduction

Video games are a type of electronic entertainment that has grown larger in businesses over the years, attracting diverse audiences of different ages, races, and genders. Video games are played on multiple devices such as consoles, computers, and smartphones. Each year, the video game industry increasingly sells more video games with over $24.5 billion dollars in sales for 2016 [19]. The Entertainment Software Association reports that 67% of homes across America are said to have video gaming consoles [3]. In addition, a study conducted by Pew Research states that 60% of people aged 18 to 29, and 53% of people aged 30 to 49 were said to play video games [6]. Since gaming is widely popular among all age groups all over the world, research has been done on video games to find the impact of video gaming on players [15]. Researchers conducted studies to understand who plays games [9] as well as interactions between those people and games [14]. Popular age groups for game-related research and studies are students of various age levels. While much previous research investigated negative impacts of gaming such as addiction [7, 10], aggression and violence [1, 2, 8], and poor school performance [4, 5, 17, 18], a growing number of research works have explored possibilities to use games to positively influence gamers [11–13, 16, 20].

While the answer to whether video games have negative or positive impact on college students' academic performance and their way of living is yet to be contested and confirmed, the fact that many current studies sometimes show contradictory and inconclusive results in turn hints to us that the more important question—instead of asking *whether* games have either positive or negative impacts—is to ask *how* these games affect college students. Moreover, in addition to video games that may or may not have

© Springer International Publishing AG, part of Springer Nature 2018
C. Stephanidis (Ed.): HCII Posters 2018, CCIS 852, pp. 51–58, 2018.
https://doi.org/10.1007/978-3-319-92285-0_8

an influence on students, we also need to consider if there are other factors that may influence students' daily lives and their academic performances. In our study, we explored the effects of video games in order to answer two questions, *"How do video games affect upperclassmen students?"* and *"What other factors impact college students?"*

2 Methodology

2.1 Overview

Our investigation took place at the Virginia State University campus in the Spring 2017 and Fall 2017 semesters. Our study sessions spanned two to three months' time and consisted of two surveys and weekly interviews. We advertised our study using mailing lists and flyers. The advertisement mentioned that (1) we are interested in studying the effect of video games in students' lives, (2) study participants would be asked to complete a pre-study survey at the beginning of the study and a post-study survey at the end, and (3) randomly selected participants would be asked to participate in weekly interviews and to keep logs of their video game activities.

2.2 Participants

Undergraduate students who completed 30 semester credit hours and graduate students were recruited for the study. This restriction was imposed to recruit students who at least had one year of college experiences. All participants were over 18 years old and received no monetary compensation. A total of 34 participants were initially enrolled in the study. However, two students dropped out in the middle of the study, leaving 32 participants (24 male, 8 female). Participants' age ranged from 19 to 34.

Among 32 participants, 28 were African American (87.5%) and 4 were Asians/Pacific Islander (12.5%). Twenty-six participants (81.25%) identified English as their first language, three Arabic (9.38%), one French (3.13%), one Fulani (3.13%) and one Twi (3.13%). Yet no one had problems conversing in English.

Twenty-three participants (71.88%) were Computer Science majors. The other 9 participants (28.13%) came from various other academic majors. Seniors made up the largest group with 11 students (34.38%). Both the juniors and graduate students were the second largest with 10 students (31.25%) in each group. Only 1 student (3.13%) was a sophomore at the time of participation.

2.3 Surveys

Pre-survey
After the consent process, the first survey was collected. During the consent process, students were informed that their personally identifiable information would be kept confidential. After the pre-survey data was collected, researchers categorized participants into four gamer types based on the information provided in the pre-study survey.

The four gamer types were Hardcore, Intermediate, Casual, and Non-Gamer. Researchers then used the gamer type information to randomly select students who would participate in the interview process.

Post-survey

The post-survey was given out to all the students who completed the first survey including those who were not involved in the interview process. The survey was distributed after the examination periods. The second survey served as a tool for the participants to reflect on the semester thus far, and judge the positive and negative effects that gaming may have had.

2.4 Interviews

To acquire the necessary information needed for the research, we chose 12 participants at random from each of the four categories between the Spring 2017 and Fall 2017 semesters (hardcore gamers, intermediate gamers, casual gamers, and non-gamers). Out of the 12 students who took part in interviews, 8 of the students (6 male, 2 female) successfully completed the full interview process.

Interviews for the selected participants were broken down into weekly interviews with scheduled one-hour sessions. All interviews were recorded with the use of an audio recording device. Questions asked were focused on the college experience which many times shifted to other themes such as other hobbies, time management, and school activities.

Interviewees classified as a hardcore gamer, intermediate gamer or casual gamer, were asked to maintain a digital gaming diary or a daily video game log. Researchers did not require participants to play games, nor did we specify which games to play; participants were asked to follow their usual daily routines and to write down the specifics of gameplay such as the date that each game was played, the title of the game and the duration that the logger played each game.

3 Findings

3.1 Pre-survey Data

The pre-survey included demographic questions as well as a series of Likert scale questions regarding participants' previous gaming experience. When answering the question *"How much do you enjoy playing video games?"*, almost half of the students (46.88%) gave a "7" as their enjoyment levels meaning *"Very Much."* A cluster of other responses came from the "5," "6" and "4" (in descending order) creating another total of nearly 46.88%. On the lower end of the scale, there were only a few students (6.25%) who said that they did not like playing games at all. Another question that was included in the survey was *"Why do you Play Games?"* The highest overall ranking was "Fun" followed by "Relaxation," then "Competition," "Personal Challenge" and "Other" reasons.

A few of the other gaming questions that we added were a little more specific in their intent in understanding how constant the time was that participants spent on video games. When asked *"How often do you play video games?"*, 18.75% played several times a day, 12.5% played at least once a day, 28.13% played several times a week, 12.5% played once a week, 9.38% played several times a month, 12.5% played once a month and 6.25% rarely played.

Furthermore, we wanted to grasp an idea of their social interactions while gaming by asking two questions. The first question was *"How often do you play video games with your friends?"* Only 6.25% of the participants played several times a day, 3.13% at least once a day, 34.38% several times a week, 12.5% once a week, 12.5% several times a month, 6.25% once a month and 25% rarely play with friends. In this question, participants' answers showed a shift with more of the students choosing several times a week and rarely. The second question *"How often do you play online multiplayer video games?"* was asked to consider not only friends but also the strangers that they may encounter while online. Responses for this question showed 9.38% of the participants playing several times a day, 12.5% at least once a day, 18.75% several times a week, 12.5% once a week, 12.5% several times a month and a higher increase to 34.38% who rarely play online multiplayer games.

3.2   Daily Logs

Students participating in the interviews were also asked to keep daily logs. Daily logs were then analyzed to extract individual students' video gaming patterns such as the total amount spent gaming, time spent gaming per week, time spent gaming in one sitting, time spent gaming during midterms, time spent gaming during fall break, and the number of games played. It is also important to note that one of the students who considered themselves an intermediate gamer, played a greater number of hours than one of the students who considered themselves a hardcore gamer. However, students are classified under their initial gamer types.

Total Amount Spent Gaming
After each of the interviewees' six-week period of gameplay, the total amount of hours was calculated for each gamer type by time spent during the week and during the weekend as well. "Hardcore Gamers" played for approximately 128 h and 26 min on the week and 102 h and 20 min during the weekend making a total of 230 h and 46 min. The "Intermediate Gamers" played for 93 h and 30 min during the weekday and 65 h during the weekend making a total of 158 h and 30 min. The "Casual Gamers" played for 24 h during the week and 16 h and 20 min on the weekend making a total of 40 h and 20 min. Overall, the trends of gameplay, as in "Hardcore Gamers" playing the most and "Casual Gamers" playing the least, was expected because of how much that they were inclined to play in their survey information. It is also interesting to note that most of the gameplay for all three groups did, in fact, occur during the week versus the weekends.

Time Spent Gaming During Midterms
Data was isolated for two periods of time. The first period was from September 25, 2017, through September 29, 2017. This was the week of midterms for Virginia State

University students. I wanted to know how much time would still be spent during this period. When comparing the midterms week numbers with the approximated school week numbers, the results for "Hardcore" and "Intermediate" gamers stayed relatively the same with a small increase of around three minutes. "Casual Gamers," however, showed a thirty-minute decrease in play.

Time Spent Gaming During Fall Break
The other period of isolated time was from September 30, 2017, through October 4, 2017, which lasted from the first Saturday until the following Wednesday. During this time, the campus was closed and there were no classes in session for students to attend. Compared to "Midterms," each of the gamer types had an increased amount of gameplay with "Hardcore Gamers" averaging almost 18 h, "Intermediate Gamers" averaging 13 h, and "Casual Gamers" more than doubling their play time with 3 h and 30 min.

3.3 Interviews

In each interview, the goal was to encourage participants to give their own perspectives on different subjects. Gaming remained one of the main subjects while conducting interviews, sometimes circling back from other topics.

Negative Effects
There were codes while reviewing the interviews that impacted these students in a negative way. An example can be found when P-14 talks about his experiences during his freshmen year. He says, *"My freshmen year, I was affected by playing games a lot. My grades weren't going down to Ds or low Cs, I would never let that happen, but I did notice that there would be sometimes where I would forget my homework or didn't even realize that I had homework because I would be playing Fallout 4 or I would be playing other games."* He was not prompted by a question he began to express this on his own. This code shows that gaming can be an obstacle in terms of schoolwork, but there are also limits or a certain set of standards to which some students hold themselves.

Another quote that expressed negative effects is that of P-01. P-01 on the topic of his organizational skills and getting work done states, *"...I plan stuff out. Then the plans go to shit. Then things happen and life goes down. Then I have a day, then I just fly it out and it works out. I don't know why it works out. I hate that it works out cause if it didn't work out, then it would force me to do it properly the next time..."* He mentions how life happens, which is an unexpected factor. Not to the extent of every assignment, but this is one of many examples where students said that they wait or are doing assignments last minute. In most cases, doing work last minute does not hurt them, but in hindsight, they do realize that they could do better.

Positive Effects
Positive effects were also found. Stress relief was a common consensus among participants. There were a few quotes mentioning learning real-world knowledge while playing. P-06 says, *"games help me learn plays. Most males...knock the ways females can think about sports, but honestly playing those video games really helped me know*

how to move the football." This is an example mixing stress relief with learning. She uses football as her stress relief. Games were said to be a substitute when football was not in season. She does not know all the plays, but she is able to use games to learn the real-world knowledge. In this way, she would not have to rely on her boyfriend for everything.

Something else mentioned among some gamers was social interaction, enjoying games with others. P-10 says that he likes to connect with people, socializing and building relationships. Video games are a way for him to do that. *"...you can meet new friends because you might find somebody that... like[s] the same game [as] you... Like, I've met a couple people that love Dragon Ball Z... and then from talking about Dragon Ball Z, we talk about something else so it's definitely a way to increase friendship using video games as a tool..."*

Motivation

A few of the questions asked were based on the motivation of students and their academics. When asked about this, P-15 says, *"I'd like to go into [gaming]... That's one of my main motivations for getting my education in computer science in general."* His response shows that gaming was the reason for his major choice. During the interview process, he would also show different codes and games that he made for his own personal gain.

Not all aspirations led towards games. P-14 found success in his major of hospitality management saying he takes school seriously. He elaborates, *"Over the summer when I got my internship, I brought my Xbox with me. When I went home, I left it there because I was like 'Hey, I need to focus on this and not focus on the game' ... I'm growing up pretty fast...realizing that I don't really have time anymore."* In other interviews, he shows this by explaining his leadership in being the president of his departmental organization and internships, which now leaves him busier than before. Interesting enough, he was not the only person who felt that way with multiple participants devoting free time to work, school and organizations.

Time Management

Students when asked about their time management, spoke on how much better they were with time than when they were a freshman. P-07 gives an example of his evolving time management skills saying, *"I learned I couldn't do my homework in my room...That was my freshmen year... It was always like 'Alright, I've been doing homework for 30 min. I'ma take an hour break now and play the game' ...It never goes like that... But I got better though. That was a freshmen year problem. When I get assignments [now], I normally go to the lobby."* Video games in his freshmen year were a distraction. Planning time never really worked out in his favor, further delaying time to get things done. He shows that he is proactive by finding more suitable workspaces.

4   Conclusion

The goal of our research was to investigate if video games caused problems in a college student's life while also taking other influences into consideration. Fun was found to be one of the main reasons why people were to play games. Our study helped us gauge participants' views on different aspects of gaming. Almost 1/3 of participants (28.13%) played video games several times a week. Throughout the interview process, participants shared with us their views of the video games, how playing the games impacted their day to day lives, and some positive/negative effects of video gaming. As upperclassmen, they still dealt with issues of being a college student. Gaming was not the sole activity they do in their daily lives. As students had many other obligations including work and school activities, most of them were quite busy with managing multiple tasks and were not spending as much time on games as in their previous years. Hobbies are used for fun and relaxation with video games being no exception. Though there are pros and cons to video games, like any other hobby that a person has, too much time spent on one activity can lead to negative effects.

References

1. Anderson, C.A., Dill, K.E.: Video games and aggressive thoughts, feelings, and behavior in the laboratory and in life. J. Pers. Soc. Psychol. **78**(4), 772 (2000)
2. Ashbarry, L., Geelan, B., de Salas, K., Lewis, I.: Blood and violence: exploring the impact of gore in violent video games. In: Proceedings of the 2016 Annual Symposium on Computer-Human Interaction in Play (CHI PLAY 2016), pp. 44–52. ACM, New York (2016)
3. Entertainment Software Association: Essential facts about the computer and video game industry, pp. 3–15 (2017). http://www.theesa.com/wp-content/uploads/2017/09/EF2017_Design_FinalDigital.pdf. Accessed 15 Mar 2018
4. Barlett, C.P., Anderson, C.A., Swing, E.L.: Video game effects—confirmed, suspected, and speculative: a review of the evidence. Simul. Gaming **40**(3), 377–403 (2009)
5. Block, J.J.: Lack of association between video game exposure and school performance. Pediatrics **119**(2), 413 (2007)
6. Brown, A.: Younger men play video games, but so do a diverse group of other Americans, September 2017. http://www.pewresearch.org/fact-tank/2017/09/11/younger-men-play-video-games-but-so-do-a-diverse-group-of-other-americans/. Accessed 15 Mar 2018
7. Brunborg, G.S., Hanss, D., Mentzoni, R.A., Pallesen, S.: Core and peripheral criteria of video game addiction in the game addiction scale for adolescents. Cyberpsychol. Behav. Soc. Netw. **18**(5), 280–285 (2015)
8. Bushman, B.: Effects of violent video games on aggressive behavior, helping behavior, aggressive thoughts, angry feelings, and physiological arousal. In: Rauterberg, M. (ed.) ICEC 2004. LNCS, vol. 3166, p. 22. Springer, Heidelberg (2004). https://doi.org/10.1007/978-3-540-28643-1_5
9. Greenberg, B.S., Sherry, J., Lachlan, K., Lucas, K., Holmstrom, A.: Orientations to video games among gender and age groups. Simul. Gaming **41**(2), 238–259 (2010)
10. Kim, D., Jeong, E.J.: Online Digital Game Addiction: How Does Social Relationship Impact Game Addiction (2016)
11. Liu, Y., Yan, N., Dili, H.: Chorlody: a music learning game. In: CHI 2014 Extended Abstracts on Human Factors in Computing Systems (CHI EA 2014), pp. 277–280. ACM, New York (2014)
12. Lyon, N., Valls, J., Guevara, C., Shao, N., Zhu, J., Zhu, J.: Little Newton: an educational physics game. In: Proceedings of the First ACM SIGCHI Annual Symposium on Computer-Human Interaction in Play (CHI PLAY 2014), pp. 351–354. ACM, New York (2014)

13. Papanastasiou, G., Drigas, A., Skianis, C.: Serious games in preschool and primary education: benefits and impacts on curriculum course syllabus. Int. J. Emerg. Technol. Learn. (iJET) **12**(01), 44–56 (2017)
14. Peever, N., Johnson, D., Gardner, J.: Personality & video game genre preferences. In: Proceedings of the 8th Australasian Conference on Interactive Entertainment: Playing the System (IE 2012), Article 20, 3 p. ACM, New York (2012)
15. Sanders, J.L., Williams, R.J., Damgaard, M.: Video game play and internet gaming disorder among Canadian adults: a national survey. Can. J. Addict. **8**(2), 6–12 (2017)
16. El-Nasr, M.S., Aghabeigi, B., Milam, D., Erfani, M., Lameman, B., Maygoli, H., Mah, S.: Understanding and evaluating cooperative games. In: Proceedings of the SIGCHI Conference on Human Factors in Computing Systems (CHI 2010), pp. 253–262. ACM, New York (2010)
17. Sharif, I., Sargent, J.D.: Association between television, movie, and video game exposure and school performance. Pediatrics **118**(4), e1061–e1070 (2006)
18. Sharif, I., Sargent, J.D.: Lack of association between video game exposure and school performance: in reply. Pediatrics **119**(2), 413–414 (2007)
19. Siwek, S.: Video Games in the 21st Century, pp. 2–36 (2017). http://www.theesa.com/wp-content/uploads/2017/02/ESA_EconomicImpactReport_Design_V3.pdf. Accessed 15 Mar 2018
20. Sweetser, P., Wyeth, P.: 2005. GameFlow: a model for evaluating player enjoyment in games. Comput. Entertain. **3**(3), 3 (2005)

Cognitive-Psychology-Based Study on Interactive Design of Preschool Children's Picture Books

Bin Jiang and Yuqiu Zhao[✉]

School of Design Arts and Media, Nanjing University of Science and Technology,
200, Xiaolingwei Street, Nanjing 210094, Jiangsu, China
617885531@qq.com, 18362903309@163.com

Abstract. The interactive picture book for children is the extension and development of the traditional picture book in the digital age. It is a multimedia picture book that children can read and interact with independently. Based on the research of the existing interactive picture books and the analysis of preschool children's cognitive psychology, this article presents the main points of interactive design for preschool children's picture books from the perspectives of usability and fun, and summarizes the design elements of interactive interface based on preschool children's cognition and the fun design methods.

Keywords: Children's cognitive psychology · Preschool children
Interactive picture book

1 Introduction

Picture books account for seventy percent of preschool children's books. Picture books dominated by pictures reading are suitable for the cognitive psychological characteristics of children, able to stimulate children's interest in reading, and benefiting the enhancement of logic thinking, artistic aesthetics, creativity and other aspects of children. Technology has changed lives, and it has also changed the way children are educated. Knowledge has shifted from traditional publications to electronic publications, and consumers' propensity to consume has shifted from single paper publications to interactive electronic publications. Children's interactive picture books are extension and development of traditional picture books in digital age, and the multimedia picture books that children can read independently and have interactive experiences, which are widely applied to the early education field.

After the investigation in the bookstore and on the Internet, I found that for the forms of preschool children's picture books, excluding the influence of electronic products on preschool children's eyesight, parents tend to choose low-cost alternative electronic picture books. Large-capacity, fast-renewal, easy to carry, environmental protection, and low cost are the main reasons for parents' favorite. At the same time, interactive e-books are more attractive to children. From the contents of the picture books, they also have the advantages of strong interactivity, full of interest, and the development of the children sensory system in all aspects.

Therefore, the author believes that electronic pictures of preschool children with interactive nature can meet parents' expectations and children's needs at the same time. This article takes the children's interactive picture book as the research object, takes the cognitive psychology of preschool children as the theoretical basis, and seeks an effective interaction design method from the perspectives of usability and fun.

Therefore, I believe, preschool picture books with interactive electronic properties will meet the needs and expectations of parents of children at the same time. This article takes the children's interactive picture book as the research object and the cognitive psychology of preschool children as the theoretical basis, and seeks an effective interaction design method from the perspectives of usability and fun.

2 Preschool Children's Cognitive Psychology

Users of this study are set to be preschool children, meaning the children that haven't reached school age yet. Such group of children is at the germination stage of imaginal thinking and intuitive thinking, they are able to use representational symbols to replace external things, and use representational system to reflect the objective world. This stage is the golden stage for the growth of linguistic, intelligent and thinking habits of children, so their picture books and digital publications are gaining more and more attentions, the operating characteristics of children in different age groups when using interactive modules and the attractiveness of children to different interactive methods are still the issues that need to be considered in current picture book design.

The cognitive development stage theory of the Swiss child psychologist, Piaget, divided the cognitive development characteristics of young children into four stages. Preschool children are in the "pre-computation stage". Their main features are as follows: Attention is not concentrated, and they cannot concentrate on the same thing for a long time; the abstract thinking is weak, and more intuitive, visual, and plot contents are needed to guide learning; the ability to express words is gradually strengthened, and simple communication and retelling can be performed; The purpose of the behavior is enhanced, but lack of thought before acting. Based on this, the author proposes that the interactive design of children's picture books should pay attention to the two key points: usability and fun.

3 Usability of Picture Books Interaction Design

3.1 Visual Design

The visual interface design including color, text, graphics and layout features and other important elements.

1. Add vivid color elements to attract children's attention. When using higher purity lightness and saturation, add mixed colors, pay attention to the color area ratio, and ensure the overall color harmony. The contrast between foreground color and background color is to cultivate spatial cognition of preschool children [1].

2. Minimize the boring sensation of the page brought by the text, use simple and straightforward, identifiable graphical and interesting words, and accompanied by appropriate voice prompts.
3. Pattern design should be more interesting. Make the abstract concept more concrete and the animals and plants anthropomorphic to meet children's cognitive characteristics.
4. The operation interface should be relatively simple and clear, adopt full-screen game scenes and peripheral function icons, and ensure the arrangement and size of each element.

As shown in Fig. 1, children's games hippo fishing, the overall picture is bright, with blue as the main color, and a high purity and saturation of the mixed colors, so that the screen is rich in color and no confusion to attract children's eyes. The interface graphic elements include various fishes and pieces, which are presented in an anthropomorphic and interesting form. The text elements are large and clear. The icon design is clear and the lines are rounded. The overall layout is reasonable, easy to operate and understand for children.

Fig. 1. Children's game hippo fishing interface design (Color figure online)

3.2 Rationalization of Animation and Sound Effects

Animation and sound effects are important ways to enrich children's perception through multi-channel interaction. The two factors complement each other. Through the feedback and prompts of voice and animation in the picture books, children's attention is drawn to help them understand the picture book frame and content. Adopt appropriate animation effects in the virtual reality world, and use a cheerful rhythm and beating notes to enhance the user experience.

3.3   Interactive Behavior

By analyzing children's tactile and physical characteristics and observing children's use of touch-screen devices, the author found that children mainly clicked contents, drew with their fingers on the screen or copy, dragged or slid the page. There are many gesture operations on the touch screen, such as clicking, swiping, long pressing, dragging, and double tapping. Clicking gently is the most natural interactive gesture used by children in the subconscious. If an element is fun, they will click repeatedly for a long time. Designing for children requires the user interface to reflect their input methods. The child's natural gesture is to press continuously after clicking, instead of releasing it after clicking. Avoid double-clicking at the same time. The timeliness of interaction must be taken into account when designing. Using double-clicking is an interactive gesture that requires learning, which can cause problems for children.

As shown in Fig. 2, the children's dinosaur puzzle interface, the interaction flow of the game is: click to enter the interface, click on the icon and continue to press, drag to the appropriate position and then let go, click to complete or return to leave the interface. These operations are tailored to the child's psychological expectations and minimize the cost of interactive learning, thereby maintaining children's interest in using the interface.

Fig. 2. Children's dinosaur puzzle interface design

4   Fun Interaction Design of Picture Books

4.1   Gamification of Book Contents

The famous linguist James Paul Gee observed that the game can give information embodied and contextualized presentation style, which is convenient for children's cognition and understanding [2]. And Raf. Coster proposed: "The game is to learn a certain skill in happiness." Nowadays, the concept of "light games" has also emerged. Light games are the intrinsic motivation of educational software plus mainstream games. Educational components are used as the main content, and they also possess certain characteristics of mainstream games, making full use of the intrinsic motivation of mainstream games, such as challenges, curiosities, goals, controls, etc. Pursue the intrinsic features of the game instead of the external form [3]. The game has four decisive characteristics: goals, rules, feedback systems and voluntary participation. In addition to voluntary participation, the other three features can be used to abstract the three basic modules of the gamification picture books design, namely to set key points, formulate key points in the series of rules, and timely feedback in multiple channels to build a picture book content framework.

Most of the picture books on the market are mainly popular science, art perception and story pictures. For any type of picture books, you can use the basic gamification module to build the content framework. Set The main knowledge points or storylines as key points, and conduct concatenation of key points according to the corresponding rules, such as completing tasks to promote plot development. By demonstrating progress and growth, people are motivated to learn new skills. Kindergarten uses small stars to reward children's good performance, although not in kind, the children are still keen, and it also shows that the sense of progress and accomplishment attracts preschoolers [4]. The difficulty of operation and understanding of task setting should meet the cognitive psychology of preschool children.

4.2 Multi-sensory Channel Feedback

The interactive types of children's picture books studied in this thesis mainly indicate multichannel interaction, meaning the interactive method of using two or more channels to communicate with computers in the input and output process. The multichannel perceptual system mainly involves the three sensory channels of vision, auditory sense and touch. The existing interactive picture books in the market can be roughly classified into the following three types according to the form of the interactive interface, namely electronic picture set, audition animation set and experience feedback set [5]. Among them, experience feedback sets can attract children's more interests by combining multichannel senses such as sight, hearing and touch. Research shows that the use of picture books in different materials will also have an impact on the understanding of preschool children's stories. The ingenious combination of images, texts, sounds, animations, etc. will transform the traditional static images into more dynamic and lively dynamic videos, providing children with multi-sensory experiences that can be seen, heard and felt [6].

Children can click anywhere on the interface. On the one hand, it must be designed to prevent misuse. On the other hand, this operating habit can be used to make the interface more interesting. The type and intensity of feedback is the most important difference between electronic and non-electronic [7]. Speaking of the reason why Tetris, is such a simple but charming game, reasonable feedback should be given first place. The three types of feedback that can be obtained when stacking Tetris: visual feedback – colorful cubes that are continuously generated and eliminated, quantitative feedback – rising scores, qualitative feedback – the challenge of continuing to rise.

The multi-channel and timely feedback is a supplement to the overall process after setting up the picture content and framework. Multi-channel feedback through key points and other important steps through graphics and sounds. This is Yu-kai's octagonal behavioral analysis framework hidden in the driving force - the feeling, brings a sense of pleasure, including touch, hearing, vision, etc. Visualization mainly consists of changes in the color, shape, and quantity of pattern elements in a single-page picture book and the display of picture book reading progress. Auditory can supplement timely audio feedback. Most of the tactile feedback is now based on vibration. It is divided into short vibration, long vibration and interval vibration. The supplement of feedback can better maintain children's interest, strengthen progress and sense of accomplishment in the process, thus forming a good circular reading framework.

5 Conclusion

Digital picture books would, no matter in the form of reflection or reading model, bring more interactive and entertaining experiences to children, with the development of intelligent terminal equipment and the wave of mobile internet, children's digital picture books are worthy of deeper discussions and researches.

Through the research of the current interactive picture book in the market and the analysis of preschool children's cognitive psychology, the key points of preschool children's picture book interactive design are proposed from the perspectives of usability and fun, hoping to provide the value of reference for interactive design of children's electronic picture books in the future.

References

1. Jing, H.: The study of game APP interface design based on preschool children's cognitive psychology. China University of Mining and Technology, Beijing (2015)
2. Gee, J.P.: An Introduction on Discourse Analysis: Theory and Method. Chongqing University Press, Chongqing (2011)
3. Junjie, S., Fangle, L., Haowen, L.: Light games – the hope and future of educational games. E-educ. Res. 1, 24–26 (2005)
4. McGonigal, J.: Reality Is Broken, p. 74. Huazhong University of Science and Technology Press, Wuhan (2017)
5. Jiayang, D., Daming, L.: An analysis of the manifestation of the interface of children's interactive picture book. Art Panorama 1, 124–125 (2017)
6. Yingmei, M.: The influence of different reading media on the understanding level of children. Mod. Prim. Secondary Educ. 32(1), 107–111 (2016)
7. Chou, Y.: Gamification and Behavioral Design. Zhejiang People's Publishing House, Hangzhou (2012). p. 24

Sketching as a Modality in Intelligent Tutoring Systems

Rodney Long[1(✉)], Ken Forbus[2], Tom Hinrichs[2], and Samuel Hill[2]

[1] Army Research Laboratory, Orlando, FL 32826, USA
Rodney.A.Long3.Civ@mail.mil
[2] Northwestern University, Chicago, IL 60208, USA
{Forbus,T-hinrichs}@northwestern.edu,
Samuelhill2022@u.northwestern.edu

Abstract. The Spatial Intelligence and Learning Center (SILC) pioneered the idea of *spatial learning*: improving learning about spatial concepts and using spatial concepts to facilitate learning about other domains. Spatial concepts are of significant importance in Science, Technology, Engineering and Mathematics (STEM) education including physics, chemistry, geoscience, and biology, as well as most branches of engineering. Spatial concepts are also important in the military. For example, sand tables are used to understand the terrain, since calculating Line of Sight (LOS) for cover and concealment on the battlefield can mean the difference between life or death. In addition, land navigation using topographic maps is a critical skill that all members of the military are required to obtain.

For this work in progress, the Army Research Laboratory (ARL) and Northwestern University, a member of SILC, are exploring sketching technologies to support spatial learning, as part of on-going research in adaptive training technologies. ARL's Generalized Intelligent Framework for Tutoring (GIFT) provides a software platform for developing intelligent tutoring systems. Adaptive learning, where the state of the learner is used to help select their path through activities, has been shown to improve learning. As part of our on-going research, we are in the process of integrating sketch worksheets into GIFT as a new type of instructional media. Sketch worksheets were designed to be general-purpose and use artificial intelligence to provide immediate feedback to students performing sketching assignments. To facilitate dissemination, an authoring environment was created for domain experts and instructors, to enable them to create new worksheets. This poster describes a work in progress to bring together the two lines of research to support the use of sketching in an adaptive learning environment.

Keywords: Sketching · Intelligent tutoring systems · Adaptive learning

1 Introduction

Spatial concepts are of central importance in STEM education (Montello et al. 2014) including physics, chemistry, geoscience, and biology, as well as most branches of engineering. STEM is also foundational for many areas of Army training (e.g. how equipment works, how to maintain and troubleshoot it, how to reason about terrain,

C. Stephanidis (Ed.): HCII Posters 2018, CCIS 852, pp. 65–72, 2018.
https://doi.org/10.1007/978-3-319-92285-0_10

etc.). The SILC pioneered the idea of *spatial learning*: improving learning about spatial concepts and using spatial concepts to facilitate learning about other domains. One of the tools for spatial learning that SILC has explored is sketching. Sketching is commonly used to convey ideas between people, and for people to work out ideas on their own. It has been argued that sketching is a powerful tool for STEM education (Ainsworth et al. 2011; Jee et al. 2014). The importance of sketching can be seen in a survey of geoscience instructors, 80% of whom believe that sketching is important for geoscience education (Garnier et al. in press).

While sketching is very powerful, it is underutilized in education because sketches are difficult and time-consuming to grade. That same survey indicated that, while instructors think sketching is important, fewer than 50% assigned graded sketching exercises more than three times a semester because of the difficulty of grading them. If intelligent tutoring systems could interact with people via sketching, it could have a revolutionary impact on education and training. This Work-in-Progress paper describes on-going research in using sketching technology in adaptive learning environments for the U.S. Army.

1.1 Related Work

There are two basic approaches to sketch understanding. The first involves recognition, i.e. a student draws something (e.g. a component of an electronic circuit) and the system automatically recognizes what it is intended to be, either labelling it or redrawing it more neatly. Several educational software systems have been fielded using this approach (e.g. De Silva et al. 2007; Valentine et al. 2012). However, this approach has fundamental limitations:

- It only works when a domain can be described in terms of highly conventional visual symbols, like analog or digital electronics. It fails when the mapping between visual information and conceptual information is many-to-many. For example, circles can indicate layers of the earth, planetary orbits, and latitude lines, even just within geoscience. When working with multiple STEM disciplines, the many to many problem becomes even worse, e.g. they can also indicate wall in a cellular or mechanical structure, among many other things.
- Most sketches involve elements that are spatialized, i.e. a road is sketched not as an abstract symbol, but as a spatial element whose relationships with other elements is important. Thus understanding sketches requires understanding the spatial relationships that people perceive (or learn to perceive during training) in sketches (Jee et al. 2014).
- Even for domains with conventional visual symbols, today's recognition technologies tend to be low-accuracy, providing fluid interaction when they work, and frustration when they don't. The domain-specificity of such systems means that, to date, a new system is needed for every category of sub-problem within a domain. Heuristics that work when dealing with professional users (i.e. interpreting a pause in drawing as the end of a visual element) fail when dealing with spatialized elements, because thinking through layout takes time, and with learners, because they stop to think about the domain.

1.2 Open-Domain Sketch Understanding

Over the last 15 years, Northwestern University has pioneered a different approach. It is based on an insight gleaned from observing human-to-human sketching. When people sketch together, they talk. They identify what something is intended to mean verbally, complemented by written annotations when needed. They use cultural conventions, but articulate them when needed (e.g. the length and shape of a road is intended to be to scale with the rest of the sketch, but the width is not, unless one is sketching some terrain in close detail). Our *open-domain sketch understanding* approach enables users to specify how they want their ink segmented into visual elements (called *glyphs*) and what those glyphs are intended to mean. Instead of using speech recognition plus natural language understanding – which is both beyond the state of the art for this task, and impractical in many classroom settings – we provide other interface modalities for communicating this information. The strength of the open-domain sketch under-standing approach is that it focuses on using human-like visual representations and processing to understand what someone has drawn.

2 Cogsketch

In developing CogSketch (Forbus et al. 2011) the goal was to both accurately model aspects of human visual and spatial reasoning and by doing so, provide a new platform for sketch-based educational software. We achieved this goal, to a large degree. In modeling, CogSketch has been used to model geometric analogies (Lovett et al. 2009), a cross-cultural visual oddity task (Lovett and Forbus 2011), and Ravens' Progressive Matrices (Lovett et al. 2010; Lovett and Forbus in press). In all three of these simu-lations, which use the same representations and processing, the system performs at human-level on the tasks and predicts aspects of human performance (e.g. reaction times and within-task problem difficulty).

2.1 Related Work

CogSketch has also been used to model learning of spatial prepositions (Lockwood et al. 2008a), solving conceptual physics ranking problems (Chang et al. 2014), rea-soning about depiction (Lockwood et al. 2008b) and learning by reading from texts and sketches (Lockwood and Forbus 2009; Chang and Forbus 2015). These capabilities enabled us to develop two new forms of sketch-based educational software:

- It only works when a domain can be described in terms of highly conventional visual symbols, like analog or digital electronics. It fails when the mapping between visual information and conceptual information is many-to-many. For example, circles can indicate layers of the earth, planetary orbits, and latitude lines, even just within geoscience. When working with multiple STEM disciplines, the many to many problem becomes even worse, e.g. they can also indicate wall in a cellular or mechanical structure, among many other things.
- Most sketches involve elements that are spatialized, i.e. a road is sketched not as an abstract symbol, but as a spatial element whose relationships with other elements is

important. Thus understanding sketches requires understanding the spatial relationships that people perceive (or learn to perceive during training) in sketches (Jee et al. 2014).

- Even for domains with conventional visual symbols, today's recognition technologies tend to be low-accuracy, providing fluid interaction when they work, and frustration when they don't. The domain-specificity of such systems means that, to date, a new system is needed for every category of sub-problem within a domain. Heuristics that work when dealing with professional users (i.e. interpreting a pause in drawing as the end of a visual element) fail when dealing with spatialized elements, because thinking through layout takes time, and with learners, because they stop to think about the domain.

The strength of the open-domain sketch understanding approach is that it focuses on using human-like visual representations and processing to understand what someone has drawn. In developing CogSketch (Forbus et al. 2011) the goal was to both accurately model aspects of human visual and spatial reasoning and by doing so, provide a new platform for sketch-based educational software. We achieved this goal, to a large degree. In modeling, CogSketch has been used to model geometric analogies (Lovett et al. 2009), a cross-cultural visual oddity task (Lovett and Forbus 2011), and Ravens' Progressive Matrices (Lovett et al. 2010; Lovett and Forbus in press). In all three of these simulations, which use the same representations and processing, the system performs at human-level on the tasks and predicts aspects of human performance (e.g. reaction times and within-task problem difficulty). CogSketch has also been used to model learning of spatial prepositions (Lockwood et al. 2008a), solving conceptual physics ranking problems (Chang et al. 2014), reasoning about depiction (Lockwood et al. 2008b) and learning by reading from texts and sketches (Lockwood and Forbus 2009; Chang and Forbus 2015). These capabilities enabled us to develop two new forms of sketch-based educational software:

1. *Design Coach* (Wetzel and Forbus 2010) helps students learn to explain their designs via sketching. Using sketching plus menus that help them craft a language-like explanation, they explain how their design is intended to work. Using qualitative mechanics (Wetzel and Forbus 2009), Design Coach looks to see if their design could actually work as intended. The use of qualitative mechanics is crucial because it provides more humanlike information, and numerical simulation is inappropriate for early stages of design, where most parameters are not yet known and shapes are roughly drawn. Design Coach was shown to significantly decrease student anxiety about communicating via sketching (Wetzel and Forbus 2015).

2. *Sketch Worksheets* (Yin et al. 2010; Forbus et al. in press) help students learn about concepts by creating sketches in response to a specific problem. For example, a geoscience student might be asked to identify the radiation flows in depicting the greenhouse effect, and a biology student might be asked to annotate a diagram of a human heart showing where the parts are and how blood flows through it. Sketch Worksheets are domain-independent: The same technology has been used in biology, geoscience, physics, and even knowledge representation. They work by the instructor using CogSketch to specify a problem and their desired solution(s), annotating facts that are important with feedback to give if they are not true, and grading rubrics. When

students download a Sketch Worksheet, they draw their own solution, asking for feedback whenever they like. Feedback is generated by comparing the instructor's sketch with the student sketch, using our model of analogy, presenting them with the instructor's feedback when there are problems.

Sketch Worksheets were designed to be broadly applicable, and have been used by over 500 students in classroom and laboratory experiments with students ranging from fifth grade (Miller et al. 2014) to college (Yin et al. 2010; Garnier et al. in press). Moreover, Northwestern's introductory geoscience course now routinely uses them for instruction, based on Sketch Worksheets authored by a geoscience graduate student at University of Wisconsin-Madison. Thus there is already evidence that this model can be effective and can scale. However, there is still work to be done. Sketch Worksheets are beneficial on their own, but could be even more powerful if integrated with other instructional media, such as provided in GIFT.

3 GIFT

To support adaptive training in the military, the Army Research Laboratory has developed the Generalized Intelligent Framework for Tutoring (GIFT). The framework allows users with no experience or expertise in computer programming to author intelligent tutors. The GIFT authoring tool provides a basic flowchart that walks the user through the process. As the author generates the ITS, various types of media can be used, e.g. PowerPoint, pictures, etc. The authoring tool also supports the Learning Tools Interoperability standard. As a result, GIFT can call other tutors and interface with various Learning Management Systems, e.g. edX. The next step in our research is to support learning content that includes sketching.

3.1 Integrating Sketch Worksheets into GIFT

Our first goal is to integrate CogSketch into GIFT, so that Sketch Worksheets can become a new type of instructional medium for GIFT. That is, an author for a new GIFT tutor can include Sketch Worksheets as one of the activities that students can do in that tutor. For example, a Simple Machines tutor could give a student a problem involving levers, implemented as a Sketch Worksheet. Based on their performance, it could either provide them with another Sketch Worksheet on the same topic, a different form of activity, or move on to the next topic. This adaptive sequencing goes beyond what CogSketch does.

To accomplish this, we will need to integrate CogSketch into GIFT. We plan to build a cloud-based version of CogSketch, based on Docker so that it is compatible with multiple cloud vendors. We have already implemented a prototype user interface for capturing digital ink and providing feedback in Sketch Worksheets being run remotely. We will integrate this user interface into the GIFT framework, as well as do the engineering necessary to make it compatible with the GIFT cloud. (We understand that the GIFT cloud is currently hosted on Amazon's service, which is supported by Docker.) We will also need to implement transducers that translate the kinds of tutoring data that Sketch Worksheets provide into GIFT domain knowledge files and metadata, so that student performance information gathered by CogSketch is available for other tutoring components.

To test this integration, we will develop a pool of Sketch Worksheets on a STEM domain that is important in K-12 education and for Army training, i.e. Simple Machines. Basic principles of mechanics typically start showing up in early education, communicating qualitative principles of forces, connectivity, and motion. They reappear in training technicians and in engineering education. We will develop a set of at least a dozen Sketch Worksheets covering principles of levers, pulleys, and gears, to provide a pool of Sketch Worksheets that can be used by a Simple Machines Adaptive Tutor. This tutor will be authored using standard GIFT tools, to ensure that the integration works smoothly and to explore how the data gathered by Sketch Worksheets can be used by such tutors.

We will gather evaluation data about this tutor by two means. First, we will make it available through the GIFT community distribution mechanisms. Second, we will set up an online *Sketch Academy* at Northwestern, where anyone can log in and try them out, and encourage undergraduates to use this as a learning resource. CogSketch already incorporates a "phone home" mechanism that does anonymization locally, so that no student identification data is ever transmitted to us. We will add a similar mechanism to the adaptive tutor, so that we can monitor and analyze student performance.

We note that once this integration is accomplished, anyone can author new Sketch Worksheets by downloading the Windows version of CogSketch and using its authoring environment. This should enable others to experiment with Sketch Worksheets for their own domains of interest.

3.2   Integrating Evaluate and Extend

We will continue to evaluate the data collected from our tutoring systems, improving and extending them as necessary to support better student learning. We also plan to explore some more advanced tutoring capabilities that the Companion cognitive architecture should support. For example, a hypothesis we plan to explore is that qualitative representations can help learners understand equations more deeply. Students often treat equations as disconnected from their daily life, as something to memorize for exams. Experts have additional tacit knowledge, things that equations tell them, which novices tend to not get. Qualitative representations make such tacit knowledge explicit. For example, $F = MA$ tells an expert that one can apply more force in a situation by using more mass, or make something go faster by pushing it harder. Qualitative representations provide a formal way to encode such tacit knowledge, making it available for tutoring systems to use in their domain models. Drawing graphs based on equations may be one way to help bridge from their spatial understanding of the world to their causal knowledge. Another example is giving students the opportunity to critique designs that have been proposed historically for perpetual motion machines. Determining why a design won't work could provide an engaging way to get students to think about friction and conservation laws. We plan to build a prototype perpetual motion machine tutor to explore this.

References

Ainsworth, S., Prain, V., Tytler, R.: Drawing to learn in science. Science **333**(6046), 1096–1097 (2011)

Chang, M.D., Forbus, K.D.: Towards interpretation strategies for multimodal instructional analogies. In: Proceedings of the 28th International Workshop on Qualitative Reasoning (QR2015), Minneapolis, MN (2015)

Chang, M.D., Wetzel, J.W., Forbus, K.D.: Spatial reasoning in comparative analyses of physics diagrams. In: Freksa, C., Nebel, B., Hegarty, M., Barkowsky, T. (eds.) Spatial Cognition 2014. LNCS (LNAI), vol. 8684, pp. 268–282. Springer, Cham (2014). https://doi.org/10.1007/978-3-319-11215-2_19

De Silva, R., Bischel, T.D., Lee, W., Peterson, E.J., Calfee, R.C., Stahovich, T.: Kirchhoff's pen: a pen-based circuit analysis tutor. In: Proceedings of the 4th Eurographics Workshop on Sketch-Based Interfaces and Modeling (2007)

Forbus, K., Usher, J., Lovett, A., Lockwood, K., Wetzel, J.: CogSketch: Sketch understanding for cognitive science research and for education. Top. Cogn. Sci. **3**(4), 648–666 (2011). https://doi.org/10.1111/cogs.12377. Scale Cognitive Modeling. Cognitive Science, 1–50

Forbus, K., Chang, M., McLure, M., Usher, M.: The cognitive science of sketch worksheets. Top. Cogn. Sci. (in press)

Garnier, B., Chang, M., Ormand, C., Matlen, B., Tikoff, B., Shipley, T.: Testing the efficacy of CogSketch geoscience worksheets as a spatial learning and sketching tool in introductory Geoscience courses. Top. Cogn. Sci. (in press)

Jee, B., Gentner, D., Uttal, D., Sageman, B., Forbus, K., Manduca, C., Ormand, C., Shipley, T., Tikoff, B.: Drawing on experience: how domain knowledge is reflected in sketches of scientific structures and processes. Res. Sci. Educ. **44**(6), 859–883 (2014)

Lockwood, K., Forbus, K.: Multimodal knowledge capture from text and diagrams. In: Proceedings of KCAP-2009 (2009)

Lockwood, K., Lovett, A., Forbus, K.: Automatic classification of containment and support spatial relations in English and Dutch. In: Freksa, C., Newcombe, N.S., Gärdenfors, P., Wölfl, S. (eds.) Spatial Cognition VI. Learning, Reasoning, and Talking about Space. Spatial Cognition 2008. LNCS, vol. 5248, pp. 283–294. Springer, Heidelberg (2008a). https://doi.org/10.1007/978-3-540-87601-4_21

Lockwood, K., Lovett, A., Forbus, K., Dehghani, M., Usher, J.: A theory of depiction for sketches of physical systems. In: Proceedings of QR 2008 (2008b)

Lovett, A., Forbus, K.: Cultural commonalities and differences in spatial problem solving: a computational analysis. Cognition **121**(2), 281–287 (2011)

Lovett, A., Forbus, K.: Modeling visual problem-solving as analogical reasoning. Psychol. Rev. (in press)

Lovett, A., Tomai, E., Forbus, K., Usher, J.: Solving geometric analogy problems through two-stage analogical mapping. Cogn. Sci. **33**(7), 1192–1231 (2009)

Lovett, A., Forbus, K., Usher, J.: A structure-mapping model of raven's progressive matrices. In: Proceedings of CogSci-10 (2010)

Miller, B., Cromley, J., Newcombe, N.: Using CogSketch to support student science learning through sketching with automatic Feedback. In: Proceedings of AERA (2014)

Montello, D., Grossner, K., Janelle, D.: Space in Mind: Concepts for Spatial Learning and Education. MIT Press, Cambridge (2014)

Valentine, S., Vides, F., Lucchese, G., Turner, D., Kim, H., Li, W., Linsey, J., Hammond, T.: Mechanix: a sketch-based tutoring system for statics courses. In: Proceedings of the Twenty-Fourth Innovative Applications of Artificial Intelligence Conference (IAAI) (2012)

Wetzel, J., Forbus, K.: Automated critique of sketched designs in engineering. In: Proceedings of the 23rd International Workshop on Qualitative Reasoning, Ljubljana, Slovenia (2009)

Wetzel, J., Forbus, K.: Design buddy: providing Feedback for sketched multi-modal causal explanations. In: Proceedings of the 24th International Workshop on Qualitative Reasoning, Portland, Oregon (2010)

Wetzel, J., Forbus, K.: Increasing student confidence in engineering sketching via a software coach. In: Hammond, T., Valentine, S., Adler, A., Payton, M. (eds.) The Impact of Pen and Touch Technology on Education. HIS, pp. 107–118. Springer, Cham (2015). https://doi.org/10.1007/978-3-319-15594-4_11

Yin, P., Forbus, K., Usher, J., Sageman, B., Jee, B.: Sketch worksheets: a sketchbased educational software system. In: Proceedings of the 22nd Annual Conference on Innovative Applications of Artificial Intelligence (2010)

Making Video Tutorials in the Classroom – Tacit Knowledge on Display

Gunver Majgaard[1(✉)] and Lykke Bertel[2]

[1] University of Southern Denmark, Campusvej 55, 5230 Odense M, Denmark
gum@mmmi.sdu.dk
[2] Aalborg University, Fredrik Bajers Vej 5, 9220 Aalborg Ø, Denmark
lykke@plan.aau.dk

Abstract. The paper presents the first experiences of teaching design of video tutorials in a ninth semester engineering cause titled "Learning and technology".

YouTube's popularity and easy to use programs for video production makes video tutorials a promising educational tool. Students tend to use video tutorial on their own initiative as supplement to curriculum literature or just for fun. The extensive use of simple video tutorials in both formal and informal settings makes it relevant to study in the classroom from a design angle.

The students developed simplistic and creative tutorials. They reflected on the design processes and how to compose efficient tutorials. Additionally, tacit knowledge were displayed visually due to interactions and system behavior. This tacit knowledge on display is one of the greatest potentials of video tutorials.

Keywords: Design processes · Tacit knowledge · Video tutorials

1 Introduction

What are the challenges and potentials of developing video tutorials in the classroom? The paper reports on the first experiences of teaching ninth semester engineering students design of video tutorials as part of a course in Learning and Technology. The students were from two educational programs: "Welfare technology" and "Learning and experience technology". The course covered learning theories and design of educational technology. As part of the course, the students analyzed and developed their own video tutorials in the field of health, learning and experience technology. Health technology covered applications for rehabilitation and of tracking health information. Learning technology covered e.g. tools to introduce programming and different digital devices. Experience technology were e.g. museums apps.

YouTube's rapid growth in popularity and easy to use programs for video production makes video tutorials a promising alternative to paper tutorials [10]. Students tend to use video tutorial on their own initiative as supplementary tutorials for new and hard topics [11]. They also see video tutorials just for leisure. The extensive use of video tutorials in both formal and informal settings makes it relevant to study in the classroom from a design angle [4].

© Springer International Publishing AG, part of Springer Nature 2018
C. Stephanidis (Ed.): HCII Posters 2018, CCIS 852, pp. 73–77, 2018.
https://doi.org/10.1007/978-3-319-92285-0_11

The learning approach was inspired by communities of practice and constructionist learning ideas [3, 4, 8]. In communities of practice students work actively together on common projects supported by experts [3]. The constructionistic approach comprises development and exploration of concrete systems in this case video tutorials while the students in parallel are developing internal cognitive learning processes [8]. The learning process is design based, experimental and experience oriented. The idea was for students to read about learning theory and in parallel develop tutorials in small groups.

2   Method

The students were required to develop short (maximum 5 min) instruction videos in the field of educational technology or health technology in pairs or groups of three. They were to develop storyboards as part of the preparation for the video production. The students developed tutorials using Flash Back Recorder, Camtasia Studio or similar to record screen, sound and webcam. The tools also had editing and sharing functions.

The students were to develop two versions of their tutorial and perform user testing in between in order to promote user centered design processes. Status meetings on the design process were conducted during classes. The student also received lectures on learning theory e.g. tacit knowledge [6], persuasive design [2] and evolutionary learning models [1, 9].

The research method was inspired by action research, supporting a reflective and iterative research process involving both researches and students in a community of practice. The process consisted of iterations of planning, action and fact-finding about the result of the action [5]. Empirical data were the students' tutorials and written assignments, curriculum, observations and a questionnaire.

3   Results

In the following, examples of students' tutorials are described. The students developed diverse tutorials in the field of educational technology and health technology, see Table 1. The tutorials were either screen recordings or web-cam recordings.

The tutorials in the first two rows in Table 1 shows traditional screen recorded video tutorials. The first row to the left shows a video recordings of a mobile app combined with power point bullets. The first row to the right shows a tutorial in Danish introducing two-dimensional arrays. The second row to the left shows a screenshot from a tutorial introducing the University of Southern Denmark's Learning Management System. The second row to the right shows a hand drawn animation.

The tutorials in the third row in Table 1 applied simple webcams. To the left a tutorial showing gestures for interacting with Hololenses and to the right a tutorial explaining how to program interactive building blocks developed as part of a master project.

Table 1.   Screen dumps from tutorials develop by the students.

 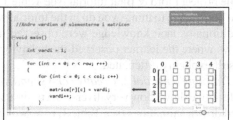 Applikation til Fjord&Bælt - Instruktionsvideo Tutorial explaining how to use an Argumented Reality Application for the Danish natural science museum "Fjord & Bælt" (AR-application was developed as part of master-thesis)	Tutorial in Danish explaining two-dimensional arrays in C#
 Tutorial explaining new students important elements of the University of Southern Denmark's Learning Management System	 Tutorial explaining how to use health-device to improve back health in sedentary work situations
 Tutorial explaining how to make gestures using Hololens before wearing the glasses	 Tutorial explaining how to use interactive building blocks to program robot car's behavior. (Robot system was developed a part of a master thesis)

4   Discussion

In the following, we discuss the learning potentials and challenges we discovered.

Learning potential 1: Tacit knowledge on display. Making their own tutorials facilitated deep learning for the students. For example, when they related learning theory to their designs or testing of observations. Often learning theory was a bit abstract for engineering students but the application of theory in the design processes made theory more concrete and relevant. Theory on tacit and explicit knowledge [6] gave them a language for articulated reflections on aspects of the learning processes. For example, in the project Fjord & Bælt tutorial (see Table 1, first row to the left), the students linked tacit knowledge to things you do in the tutorial while recording like clicking or touching. Additionally, tacit knowledge were observed in the programming of two-dimensional arrays where the learner observed the behavior of the programing environment, which wasn't explicitly articulated.

Learning potential 2: Creative and simplistic design of tutorials. The tutorials in the table above shows how very diverse the tutorials were. Some students developed creative hand drawn animations (see Table 1, row two to the right). Other students were creative in the way they manually zoomed in on the digital building blocks – simply by bringing blocks closer to the camera lens (see Table 1, third row to the right). This supports the idea of YouTube tutorial videos being simple, rudimentary and authentic [4].

Learning potential 3: From native tutorial consumer into reflective tutorial designers. It became clear that the students from time to time watched tutorials and during one of the lectures, they were to present their favorite tutorial for either entertainment or study. They also read about designing tutorials [4, 10, 11]. Finally, they developed and tested their own tutorials. Potentially, this gave the students a more reflected perspective on video tutorials. They became more aware of what was easy to visualize and what to expect from an effective video tutorial e.g. recap in the beginning, appropriate pace, length and clear language. They were also exploring the difficulty of making short tutorials no longer the five minutes and deciding what was the most important content. The students were able to reflect on the tutorials they were designing and improve the second version of their tutorial based on test results. Additionally, they were applying theory in the analysis of video tutorials in general.

Challenge 1: Video tutorials and future profession. The Learning and experience technology students could easily relate the design of video tutorial to their future profession and some of the students were making tutorials for their master thesis projects. Whereas, some welfare technology students didn't expect video tutorial to be a part of their future profession, even though they sometimes used them as part of their study. In the future, we as teachers must stress why design of tutorials can nuance evaluation of tutorials used in e.g. rehabilitation or requirement specification of tutorials.

Challenge 2: Diverse science cultures in the two educational programs. In the questionnaire, the students commented on the course project. Some students from the Welfare Technology program found it meaningless to make two iterative rounds of development. They also found it difficult to relate creation of video tutorials to their future profession. Whereas, the iterative design paradigm was a natural part of Learning and experience technology students' DNA. The Learning and experience technology students also found development of video tutorial relevant for their future profession. This might be due to the different research cultures and work practices. The Welfare technology students were used to a more positivistic approach of setting up highly structured experiments for testing hypotheses, gathering large samples of quantitative data for subsequently analysis [7]. The students from Learning and experience technology were more trained in qualitative design-based research methods and they were used to participatory iterative design methods [5]. As teachers, we were not aware of different cultures until very late in the semester, so next time we might propose two alternative semester assignments, which might fit better the diverse cultures. Additionally, we might also get the students to reflect on how they would be able to use video tutorials in their profession.

5   Conclusion

The paper reported on the first experiences of teaching ninth semester engineering students' design of video tutorials as part of a course titled "Learning and Technology". The challenges and potentials of developing video tutorials in the classroom are summarized below.

Regarding the potentials of teaching design of video tutorials in summary:

- Tacit knowledge on display.
- Creative and simplistic design of tutorials.
- From native tutorial consumer into reflective tutorial designers.

Regarding the challenges of teaching design of video tutorials, the most obvious was the diverse science cultures in the two educational programs. Which we plan to address in next year's teaching.

References

1. Bateson, G.: De logiske kategorier læring og kommunikation. Mentale systemers økologi: Skridt i en udvikling. Kbh: Akademisk forlag. Side, 282–308 (2005)
2. Fogg, B.J.: Persuasive computers: perspectives and research directions. In: CHI 1998. ACM (1998)
3. Lave, J., Wenger, E.: Situated Learning: Legitimate Peripheral Participation. Cambridge University Press, Cambridge (1991)
4. Majgaard, G.: Teaching mixed reality using video tutorials. In: Proceedings of the 11th European Conference on Game-Based Learning, ECGBL 2017, Graz, Austria, pp. 410–419 (2017)
5. Majgaard, G., Misfeldt, M., Nielsen, J.: How design-based research, action research and interaction design contributes to the development of designs for learning. Des. Learn. 4(2), 8–21 (2011)
6. Nonaka, I., Takeuchi, H.: The Knowledge-Creating Company: How Japanese Companies Create the Dynamics of Innovation. Oxford University Press, New York, Oxford (1995). Side 61
7. Olsen, P.B., Fuglsang, L.: Videnskabsteori i samfundsvidenskaberne - på tværs af fagkulturer og paradigmer. Roskilde univeristetsforlag. ISBN-13 9788778672780 (2004)
8. Papert, S.: Mindstorm – Children, Computers, and Powerful Ideas. Basic Books, New York (1980)
9. Qvortrup, L.: Knowledge, Education and Learning: E-learning in the Knowledge Society. Knowledge, Learning, Media and ICT. Forlag. Samfundslitteratur (2006)
10. van der Meij, H., van der Meij, J.: The effects of reviews in video tutorials. J. Comput. Assist. Learn. 32, 332–344 (2016)
11. Wells, J., Barry, R.M., Spence, A.: Using video tutorials as a carrot-and-stick approach to learning. IEEE Trans. Educ. 55(4), 453 (2012)

CyanoHABIT: A Novel Game to Identify Harmful Freshwater Algae

Elizabeth A. Matthews[1(✉)], Robin A. Matthews[2], Zaina Sheets[3], and Juan E. Gilbert[1]

[1] Computer and Information Science and Engineering Department, University of Florida, Gainesville, FL, USA
lizmatthews@ufl.edu
[2] Institute of Watershed Studies, Western Washington University, Bellingham, WA, USA
[3] College of Education, University of Florida, Gainesville, FL, USA

Abstract. CyanoHABIT (Cyanobacterial Harmful Algal Bloom Identifying Technology) is a proposed learning technology designed to give the general public the ability to self-teach identification of potentially harmful bloom-forming algae (HABs) in freshwater lakes. The primary users will be adults who are interested in helping government agencies distinguish potentially toxic algae blooms from other non-toxic blooms. Toxic algae in freshwater lakes present a serious threat to public safety, and while many algal blooms are not toxic, confirming toxicity can be time consuming and expensive. Many states have only one agency that is able to monitor, sample, and test water for HABs, and some states have no resources for this task [1]. Fortunately, relatively few freshwater algae are capable of forming toxins, and distinguishing between benign algae blooms and potentially toxic ones is a task that can be learned in a short time by most adults. With a better educated public, the time and resources of the professional public services can be concentrated on the cases where they are needed most. We developed a gamified trainer for use on smartphones and personal computers to teach this skill to the general public. Our focus was on education, enabling the user to learn the distinguishing features of toxic algae, and not provide a flip-book of pictures of algae. Preliminary testing indicates that the software is enjoyable to use, and that the users do acquire a valuable skill from its use.

Keywords: Cyanobacteria · Learning technology · Games
Algal blooms

1 Introduction

Freshwater algae can be found in almost any damp environment, including lakes and ponds, but also streams, wet soil, rocky areas in the spray zone of waterfalls, and standing water in birdbaths, fountains, livestock troughs, etc. Most

© Springer International Publishing AG, part of Springer Nature 2018
C. Stephanidis (Ed.): HCII Posters 2018, CCIS 852, pp. 78–84, 2018.
https://doi.org/10.1007/978-3-319-92285-0_12

freshwater algae are harmless, but one group, the cyanobacteria, have species that can release toxins that are harmful to humans, pets, and wildlife. Harmful cyanobacteria blooms (often called "CyanoHABS") are increasing in frequency and duration [2], partly in response to climate change [3,4]. The only definitive way to identify toxic cyanobacteria blooms is through chemical testing, but with training and access to an inexpensive microscope, most people can learn to separate the potentially toxic species from "all others."

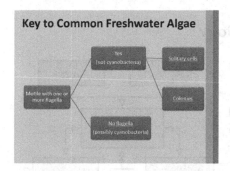
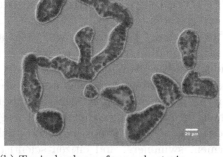

(a) Example of typical choices in algal identification.

(b) Typical colony of cyanobacteria (*Microcystis wesenbergii*).

Fig. 1. Examples of a typical keying approach to algal identification.

The CyanoHABIT (Cyanobacterial Harmful Algal Bloom Identifying Technology) game will provide a novel approach to learning how to recognize toxic cyanobacteria by incorporating the training into a game. Games have been considered ideal for visual scanning task training, given the game is selected to deliberately train the skills necessary for the task [5]. Identification of toxic cyanobacteria is typically presented in high-academic settings that present a steep learning curve for non-academics. Current work is in progress to increase the accessibility of this information, such as cyanoScope [6], but most of these efforts still rely on experts for the final identification. However, due to the limited number of features needed to identify toxic cyanobacteria, this process is ideal for gamification.

The CyanoHABIT game will use simple choices, with beginner, intermediate, and advanced settings, that allow the user to learn to identify potentially toxic species using clearly visible features described in nontechnical terms. Currently, the resources available for algal identification ask yes/no (dichotomous) choices for classification. For example, from "No flagella" (Fig. 1a), selecting "Colony" will bring up images of a typical colony of toxic cyanobacteria (Fig. 1b). As a learning technology, CyanoHABIT instead aims to train the user for a visual scanning task that will eventually be independent of the application. Users will be able to identify algae based on visual attributes and classification categories learned from the technology. The use of CyanoHABIT will provide the skills for citizen scientists to be able to identify a subset of "could be toxic," "definitely not toxic," and "too difficult to identify." In all cases, if there is concern about the health effects of an algal bloom, the identification should be confirmed by contacting a professional or the appropriate testing agency. But the ability to identify the first two categories may lessen the workload for state-based testing facilities, and can be used to contribute cyanoHAB citings to projects like cyanoScope, thus providing important information about the occurrence of algae blooms in the USA [6].

2   Proposed Learning Technology

The learning technology will use an instructional approach for the identification of toxic cyanobacteria. Our target user base will be people who are invested in the presence of toxic algal blooms in their freshwater lakes, ponds, and reservoirs, including, but not limited to, fishermen, swimmers, and citizen scientists. The design will focus on accessibility and limiting academic word barriers. Whenever possible, easy to understand descriptors will be used rather than technical terms. The app will be available on both mobile devices and desktop computers to increase accessibility.

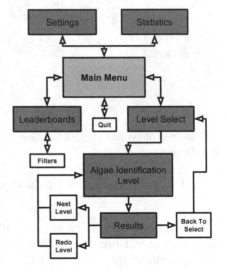

Fig. 2. The taskflow of the learning technology.

2.1   Design

Figure 2 shows the internal layout of the gaming system. The user starts on the Main Menu and can select from information about their progress, or continue learning about toxic cyanobacteria. The Level Select provides options between categories of identifiable process of elimination. For example, "Flagella and Cilia" are easily determined features of a microscopic organism; if present, they will disqualify the organism from being a toxic cyanobacteria. Figure 3 shows the workflow thought process involved in navigating CyanoHABIT.

Figure 4 shows a working example of the simple, clean design that will be used for the interface. When scientific wording must be used, such as "flagella" or "flagellum", simple definitions will be provided. Some examples of other screens as they may appear on the mobile version can be seen in Fig. 5 which displays wireframe mockups.

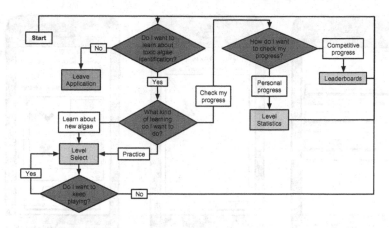

Fig. 3. The workflow of the learning technology.

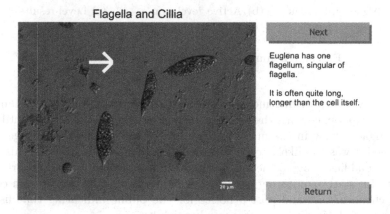

Fig. 4. A picture of the demo tutorial level on PC.

2.2 Personas

Primary Persona: Brandon Waters
Occupation: Fisherman; Technological Use: Expert

Brandon is a fisherman and spends 90% of his day either on or in the water. Brandon has recently taken a couple of different families out fishing on Lake Pine. He heard that some members of the family got sick after eating the fish they caught from the lake. Brandon was also informed one of the dogs got extremely sick after playing in the lake. He decided to take a trip to the lake where he noticed a macro-visible change in the water's appearance. He knew that the greenish color didn't necessarily mean a toxic algal bloom was occurring, but Brandon wanted to check whether there were cyanobacteria present in the lake.

Brandon had been using the CyanoHABIT game for some time now, so he collected a sample of the algae and took it to his local university's free-use

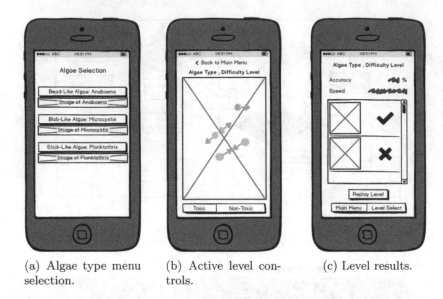

(a) Algae type menu selection.   (b) Active level controls.   (c) Level results.

Fig. 5. Wireframe mockups for the mobile version.

laboratory, which provided inexpensive microscopes for public use. Thanks to Brandon's experience with the learning technology, he was able to identify the type of algae he saw in the microscope as one of the common toxic algae, and determined it was the likely to have caused the illnesses. He informed his other fishermen buddies to avoid the lake until the bloom cleared up and reported the bloom to his state monitoring agency so that they could follow up with confirmatory chemical test and post a notice for the public indicating that fishing, swimming, or playing in the water was hazardous.

Secondary Persona: Rachel Keller
Occupation: Day Care Worker; Technological Use: Novice

Rachel works at Kiddie Cove, a daycare center promoted by the nearby elementary school. Kiddie Cove is located next to a popular lake where the kids love to wade and splash. Rachel grew up on a lake and loves taking the kids out to enjoy the lake. Often, the children's afternoon consisted of supervised, water-based activities.

Some of Rachel's coworkers mentioned that several children developed rashes while attending a weekend camping even at the lake. In addition to her concern for the daycare children, Rachel is a mother, and her son spends time at Kiddie Cove. One evening, at home, Rachel noticed a rash appearing on her son's leg. He had spent his afternoon playing in the lake, she began to wonder if it had something to do with the greenish water that she saw. Rachel spent some time online and learned that her son's rash might be caused by exposure to toxic algal. While looking into toxic algal blooms, Rachel came across a fun, algal identification game. This game could easily teach her how to conduct her own research on this issue. After playing a few rounds of the game she felt like this could be a great asset to have at the daycare.

2.3 Use-Case Scenarios

Task: Check Progress. Persona: Brandon

Brandon has been practicing most levels on CyanoHABIT and wants to check his learning progress. He opens the game and selects an option for "progress and statistics." The game shows Brandon a screen that lists his general progress and statistics for the entire game, such as accuracy and average time taken per image, as well as options to see statistics for individual levels.

Brandon clicks on the "*Anabaena* Statistics" option to see how well he can identify that particular type of algae. The algal-specific statistics page displays similarly to the general page, with accuracy and speed for the entire *Anabaena* category, along with the accuracy and speed listed for each of the various difficulty levels of easy, medium, and hard. He sees that, on average, for *Anabaena* he has a 95% accuracy rating.

After checking his personal statistics, Brandon wonders how his score compares to other people in his local area. Back on the main menu, Brandon remembers seeing a "Leaderboards" option, so he goes back and selects that option. The leaderboard, by default, lists all the scores available. Brandon wants to only see the local area, so he selects the local filter option. He had previously filled in his location for CyanoHABIT so the program knows where to list statistics from. Brandon's average accuracy lists him at 10th in his area, but his speed puts him in 2nd place. Satisfied with his progress, Brandon closes the game.

Task: Learn About Toxic *Anabaena* Persona: Rachel

Rachel is just beginning to learn the visual differences between the toxic algae types. In the evening, after dinner, and she has some free time to spare. Rachel wants to become sufficiently proficient with visually identifying cyanoHABs so that she can check the water samples herself, rather than sending out the samples for testing, which requires more money that her workplace, Kiddie Cove, can afford on a regular basis.

Rachel starts up CyanoHABIT and looks over her options. She wants to keep learning so she selects "Level Select." Rachel previously completed the "easy" level for algae that looked like beads on a string, but couldn't remember what the name for that type of algae. The menu for level select listed three different types of algae, using both the scientific names as well as a visual descriptors and images, with an option for "All types." Rachel selects the "Bead-Like Algae: *Anabaena*" section after recognizing the algae image. However, feeling confident from last time, she then selects the "medium" difficulty level.

The medium levels provide fewer hints to Rachel while she plays the game, selecting "toxic" or "non-toxic" on a series of algae images. After each selection,

CyanoHABIT provides the correct answer along with a list of the identifying features that Rachel should have used for identification.

After 10 randomly selected images, the level concludes with a results screen. The results show Rachel that while she was fairly accurate, her speed was slow. Rachel clicks on the one image she failed to identify correctly to review the identifying features again. Once she is satisfied with her ability to recognize that type of algae, Rachel closes the game.

3   Conclusion and Further Work

To test the efficacy of CyanoHABIT, several user studies will need to be completed. Expert opinions will be gathered from an algal identification workshop at Western Washington University to inform the design and scope of information covered in CyanoHABIT. The final development stages will use a traditional user study with between-subjects data collection measuring information retention.

Once CyanoHABIT is fully verified and developed, we want to work cooperatively with public outreach projects, such as cyanoScope, to increase awareness and access to our application. We are confident that CyanoHABIT will provide a means for citizens to contribute to improving watershed quality and public safety.

References

1. United States Environmental Protection Agency: States monitoring programs and information. https://www.epa.gov/nutrient-policy-data/states-monitoring-programs-and-information. Accessed 2 Oct 2017
2. Taranu, Z.E., Gregory-Eaves, I., Leavitt, P.R., Bunting, L., Buchaca, T., Catalan, J., Domaizon, I., Guilizzoni, P., Lami, A., McGowan, S., et al.: Acceleration of cyanobacterial dominance in north temperate-subarctic lakes during the anthropocene. Ecol. Lett. **18**(4), 375–384 (2015)
3. Paerl, H.W., Otten, T.G.: Harmful cyanobacterial blooms: causes, consequences, and controls. Microb. Ecol. **65**(4), 995–1010 (2013)
4. Chapra, S.C., Boehlert, B., Fant, C., Bierman Jr., V.J., Henderson, J., Mills, D., Mas, D.M., Rennels, L., Jantarasami, L., Martinich, J., et al.: Climate change impacts on harmful algal blooms in us freshwaters: a screening-level assessment. Environ. Sci. Technol. **51**(16), 8933–8943 (2017)
5. Achtman, R., Green, C., Bavelier, D.: Video games as a tool to train visual skills. Restorative Neurol. Neurosci. **26**(4, 5), 435–446 (2008)
6. iNaturalist: cyanoscope. https://www.inaturalist.org/guides/6092. Accessed 9 Mar 2018

iCE: An Intelligent Classroom Environment to Enhance Education in Higher Educational Institutions

Tarek H. Mokhtar[✉], Ahmed Oteafy, Abd-Elhamid Taha, Nidal Nasser, and Samer E. Mansour

The Intelligent Design and Art (iDNA) Research Group, Alfaisal University, Riyadh, Kingdom of Saudi Arabia
{tmokhtar,aoteafy,ataha,nnasser,smansour}@alfaisal.edu

Abstract. The intelligent Classroom Environment (**iCE**) promises to convey a rich and complex environment with the aim to achieve educational excellence and to provide world-class education in the university classroom environment. The classroom, the keystone for educational environments, is our first informational computer: a long-serving, complex, physical environment that embodies the education of human-minds; yet, classrooms are becoming an inadequate environment for tech-savvy generations. The **iCE** is a novel creative environment with the objective of enhancing education by embedding IT, Robotics, and Interactive Physical systems into the very fabric of the classroom's design. The **iCE** communicates a unique and flexible setting that allows for a better educational environment. The **iCE** will be developed to reconfigure and retune six basic scenarios of the different tasks needed in contemporary classroom environments, calling them: the Exploration, Collaboration, Meeting, Lecturing, Lounging, and Presentation configurations. In this paper, we will present **iCE**'s concept, design, and **iCE**'s kinetic wall explorations, as scaled prototypes.

Keywords: Design · Interactive systems · Cyber-physical platform
Classroom configurations, and education

1 Introduction

One of the greatest challenges facing education is the ever-growing need for the use of different learning tools, techniques and environments that enhance lifelong learning in academic institutions. Peter Lippman's research, an Associate AIA and architect, shows that there is a growing need to think of the connections between 21st century's learning tools and techniques in the ever-changing world and the "classroom," the physical environment. Additionally, a growing scholarship has emphasized the need to change our "classrooms and furniture to adapt to student's learning style[s]," [4, 3, 11]. Thus, the planning and construction of new classrooms should be undertaken with an awareness of the different teaching techniques and configurations [8–11].

On "Bridging Down the Wall," David Raths describes that, "the classroom setup does indeed have an effect on instructors' habits as well as student participation and

© Springer International Publishing AG, part of Springer Nature 2018
C. Stephanidis (Ed.): HCII Posters 2018, CCIS 852, pp. 85–93, 2018.
https://doi.org/10.1007/978-3-319-92285-0_13

collaboration" [2]. Moreover, in a 2011 comprehensive study conducted by Marko Kuuskorpi *et al.*, comparing a "traditional classroom environment" versus a "dynamic teaching environment," the researchers conclude by the need to have adaptable furniture to the different learning configurations with respect to the different working methods: formal teaching, informal learning, social, and individual learning [4]. "By using mobile tables and chairs, a learner can create the proper setting for the activity being performed," as stated by Hassel [3]. *Therefore, rethinking of the current traditional classroom-design comprised of the static petrified skins (i.e., walls and ceilings) and furniture, is becoming essential in developing teaching and learning experiences in our Higher Educational (HE) institutions.*

As our pedagogical approaches are getting more complex and dynamic; i.e., there is a *paradigm shift from passive learning to participatory learning*, using new technologies and new teaching methods and techniques, such as: game-storming, focus grouping, brainstorming, social and individual learning, multisensory stimulation, among others [1, 11]. Yet, if the classroom continues to communicate to and educate us, what is a classroom for the ever-changing Informational World? In today's Informational World, however, architects are largely under-prepared to design state-of-the-art electronic-based intelligent systems; and the classroom is likewise, today, an inadequate information technology environment.

Today, however, with our powerful electronic devices and gadgets, the use of architectural spaces as the physical interface to our educational interactions may seem quaint [5, 6]. iCE seeks to fill this gap by focusing on how a robotic environment on a room scale can respond and adapt to our different pedagogical needs.

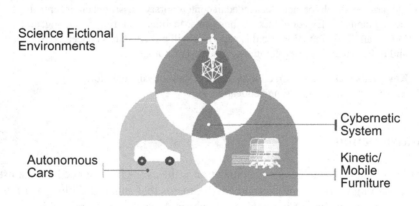

Science Fictional Environments

Cybernetic System

Autonomous Cars

Kinetic/ Mobile Furniture

Fig. 1. iCE's motivation and concept.

2   iCE's Motivation and Concept

iCE is an architectural-robotic environment that adapts to the continuously changing needs of its users. The design of iCE is motived by the technological advancements of the autonomous physical movements of mobile furniture and autonomous vehicles. The iCE's walls and ceilings are reconfigurable like a person who dreams that (s)he can change the surroundings based on his/her preferences, as in the bending city of the 2010 award-winning film "Inception" – Science Fictional Environment. We imagine that the chairs and tables autonomously move to set different configurations based on the different pedagogical and educational needs of its users, as described in **iCE**'s design. Literally, **iCE** is designed as a *cybernetic system that adapts to the continuous needs of its users* (Fig. 1).

3 Research Methodology

The design of **iCE**'s six different configurations is based on *iterative-design processes and prototyping techniques* (scaled and full-scale prototypes). A set of design guidelines for **iCE** informed by focus groups and brainstorming activities, informing the design of alternatives, and total virtual (i.e., computer generated models and videos) concepts for **iCE**. Finally, *a quasi-experimental research method* will be used to test and validate the effectiveness of such a system on real users, i.e., students and professors.

Our design of **iCE** is based on a human-centered design (HCD) approach, in which we use *personas and storytelling* as a research design approach to better understand the targeted users. For achieving this goal, we designed three different personas as described in the following section, Fig. 2.

Fig. 2. **iCE**'s three Personas employing the use of Storytelling technique

3.1 iCE's Personas

Personas and Storytelling techniques can help bringing to life the various users' needs and challenges. Accordingly, the research team had learned from creating these personas certain design drivers, which helped us in adopting the technologies that meet such needs. We had also taken a *design-driven technology* approach by getting immersed in the social life within the different classroom settings so as to create an evolutionary classroom environment. Not only from the understanding of the university's society and culture, but also from the ever changing needs and the evolution of the society, to *create new meanings* for all the classroom's stakeholders; *an autonomous classroom that can interact with us.*

Three different personas were developed for this research on the intelligent Classroom Environment, i.e., Andrew, Kate, and Prof. Adams.

1. *Andrew John* is an architectural student at Harvard University, he represents art students or what we called the *"creativity model,"* who is interested in design and art modeling, see Fig. 2.
2. *Kate Hogan* is a freshman electrical engineering student at Harvard, she is a tech savvy student representing a *"classical engineering student"*.
3. While Prof. *Annmarie Adams*, is in her 40s, researcher and professor of Mathematics at Yale University, prefers to use a mixed method in teaching. She uses the classical white board to show students *hands-on* the solution of complex math problems. She also prefers to use smart boards and tablets as new means in mixing the use of pen and paper method with the use of advanced software to solve such problems. Thus, representing a *"postmodernist model"*.

As presented in Fig. 2, our personas had been the characters of storytelling graphical formats that best describe the needs and the challenges for the three different models. Following the social immersion exercises and observing the targeted users, we came with the following design drivers to best fulfill the needs of the targeted users.

The Design Drivers for iCE, after creating the personas and storytelling, *should include:*

1- Minimal time for organizing space elements.
2- Physical and Digital tools.
3- New classroom arrangements for the ever-changing savvy tech users.
4- More than a place to sit and listen, it should embody social interactions.
5- Spatial and sensorial dimensions (sound, light, colors and texture), which are essential for the different user profiles, personas.
6- Open/reconfigurable environment.
7- User-friendly performance and system feedback.

3.2   iCE's Iterative Design Activities

Based on the above design drivers, the research team had identified three main challenges for the design of iCE, a. wall and ceiling robotic movements; b. table and chair design components; c. the centralized vs the distributed network of the system. The design team had employed the use of the iterative design approach in two studio-based design courses, semester-long projects for second and third year architectural students, to design physical kinetic walls and ceilings; and for interior design students to develop movable kinetic tables and chairs, Fig. 3. These iterative design activities led to the selected design of iCE.

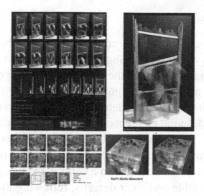

Fig. 3. iCE's interactive wall and roof panels while reconfiguring.

4   The Intelligent Classroom Environment (iCE)'s Design

4.1   iCE's Main Components

What we call "**iCE**" reflects the dynamic and inclusive character of our time. **iCE** is a robotic interactive physical-digital system for students and professors to connect with their classroom through the different components of the room; and, to reconfigure and retune it to the needed configuration, described below.

iCE is comprised of the following artifacts, a-self-organizing robotic desk; b-self-organizing robotic chairs; c-interactive wall panels; d- autonomous ceiling; e-auto-adjustable projector; and f-auto-adjustable sound and light systems, as in Fig. 4.

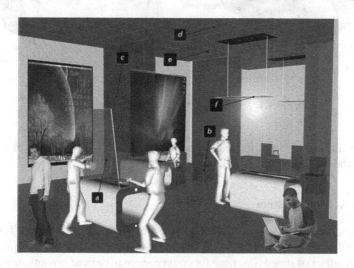

Fig. 4. iCE's different robotic and interactive components.

4.2   iCE's Architecture

iCE is a hybrid physical-digital system comprised of the above six elements, as in Fig. 4. The chairs, tables, walls, and ceiling are to be designed as architectural-robotic systems capable to reconfigure based on the six different configurations, more details in the following section. In achieving this goal, we incorporate the use of three robotic technologies: a. sensors that can help in detecting proximity to people and objects, and distances between iCE's different elements, i.e., ultrasonic sensors; b. Linear actuators, motorized wheels system, and servomotors to move the objects and components of the system; and, c. microcontrollers that work as the brains to process the inputs and the outputs, and to communicate wirelessly with a centralized computer/server.

As we envision iCE's table and chair designs, following the iterative design activities, the table is comprised of two movable on-track screens driven by linear actuators, LCD touch screen, ultrasonic sensors, three-wheel motorized systems, battery, and microcontroller, as in Fig. 5 (left). The chair is comprised of a movable back and two sides driven by linear actuators, ultrasonic sensors, two motorized wheel systems, battery, and microcontroller, see Fig. 5 (right).

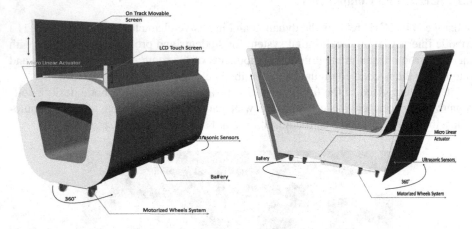

Fig. 5. iCE's Table (Left) and Chair Designs (Right).

For the walls and ceilings, the walls are comprised of foldable structures moving on motorized wheels, embedded in wall pockets when needed.

4.3   iCE's Network System

iCE involves the use of centralized and distributed network elements for module autonomy and independence. iCE incorporates the use of self-organization factors evaluated under metrics of speed (i.e., time for convergence to desired layout/configuration), energy, and safety [7].

The modular design approach also requires the development of reliable control schemes. Towards that end, a control algorithm will be created for each module with its own embedded system microcontroller, in addition to a centralized controller that coordinates the actions of the different modules. A hierarchical centralized control scheme must be developed for the different scenarios with reliability as one of its main design objectives, as in Fig. 6. In addition, an interfacing module is required and it will be programmed with a visual interface.

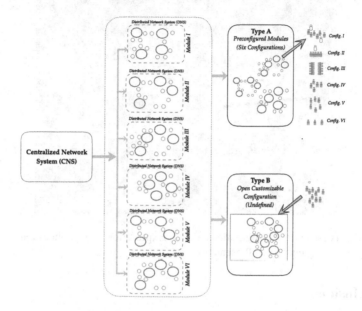

Fig. 6. iCE's centralized network system and distributed network systems

5 iCE's Configurations

As we envision the intelligent classroom of tomorrow, we conducted many design related exercises through the HCD methods and studio activities. This leads to understanding the different kinematics of the movable/mobile furniture and reconfigurable space elements. Based on the literature review on the different teaching methods, and on the brainstorming activities conducted by five professors from social and natural sciences, iCE's six basic configurations have been selected as, a. Exploration; b. Collaboration; c. Meeting; d. Lecturing; e. Lounging; and, f. Presentation configurations; in addition to the open customizable configuration that can be set by user's preferences, see Fig. 7.

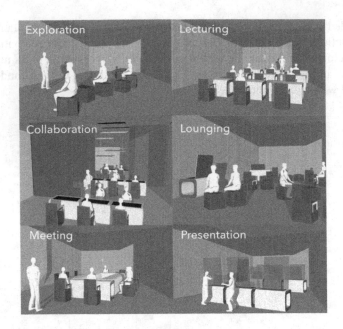

Fig. 7. iCE's Six Different Configurations, i.e., a. Exploration; b. Collaboration; c. Meeting; d. Lecturing; e. Lounging; and, f. Presentation.

6 Conclusions

While the use of the hybrid physical-digital platform in enhancing the classroom environment is not yet fully experimented, the vision of the hybrid reconfigurable environment is to open the possibilities for more explorations on the use of this system in universities and cultural centers to enhance human-space interactions. iCE's system suggests a novel research for designing social interactive systems for the classroom environment, and for enhancing both the human-hybrid interactions and our educational systems. The work has the potential for full-scale realization and evaluation on real users.

Acknowledgements. The authors acknowledge support from Alfaisal University under grant number SRG 220131502152.

References

1. Clarke, R.Y.: The next-generation classroom: smart, interactive and connected learning environments. A White Paper IDC Government Insights #AP779305 V (2012)
2. Collaborative Technologies Report: "Bringing Down the Wall," on Learning Environments in The Journal, (2013)
3. Hassell, K.: Flexible Classroom Furniture. American Sch. Univ. **84**(2), 18–21 (2011)
4. Kuuskorpi, M., Kaarina, F., González, N.C.: The future of the physical learning environment: school facilities that support the user. CELE Exchange (2011)

5. Meleshevich, A., Millin, J.: Building a technology classroom: lessons learned at a small liberal arts college. In: Proceedings of the 32nd Annual ACM SIGUCCS Fall Conference (SIGUCCS 2004). ACM, New York, pp. 13–17 (2004)
6. Mokhtar, T.H., Green, K.E., Walker, I.D.: Giving form to the voices of lay-citizens: monumental-it, an intelligent, robotic, civic monument. In: Stephanidis, C. (ed.) HCI 2013. CCIS, vol. 374, pp. 243–247. Springer, Heidelberg (2013). https://doi.org/10.1007/978-3-642-39476-8_50
7. Murata, S., Kurokawa, H.: Self-Organizing Robots, Springer Tracts in Advanced Robotics, vol. 77. Springer, Oita (2012)
8. Nilson, L.B.: Teaching at Its Best: A Research-Based Resource for College Instructors, 3rd edn. Jossey-Bass, San Franciso (2010)
9. Ogata, H., Saito, N.A., Paredes, J.R.G., San Martin, G.A., Yano, Y.: Supporting classroom activities with the BSUL system. Educ. Technol. Soc. 11(1), 1–16 (2008)
10. Sessoms, D.: Interactive instruction: creating interactive learning environments through tomorrow's teachers. Int. J. Technol. Teach. Learn. 4(2), 86–96 (2008)
11. Wurm, J.P.: Working in the Reggio Way: A Beginner's Guide for American Teachers, Red Leaf Press (2005)

CodeLab: Designing a Conversation-Based Educational Tool for Learning to Code

Enric Mor[1], Francesc Santanach[2(✉)], Susanna Tesconi[1], and Carlos Casado[1]

[1] Computer Science, Multimedia and Telecommunication Studies,
Universitat Oberta de Catalunya, Barcelona, Spain
{emor,stesconi,ccasadom}@uoc.edu
[2] eLearn Center, Universitat Oberta de Catalunya, Barcelona, Spain
fsantanach@uoc.edu

Abstract. This work presents the design and architecture of an educational tool for learning to code. The CodeLab tool is based on skill practice and assessment and is targeted for non-STEM students to develop computational thinking. The tool is designed to provide a lab experience and environment based on exercises to practice through a conversational interface.

Keywords: Conversation-based interaction · Dialogue-based interfaces
Interaction design · Virtual learning environments · Learning to code
Learning labs · Learning tools

1 Introduction

An educational lab is not only a repository of material and digital resources, but a multi-disciplinary space. In this space, knowledge is built through to social interaction, self-management, self-training, informal research and learning, as well as participation in expanded educational communities. In this sense, the laboratory is the space for experimentation for students, as well as the place where teaching practices are exchanged and peer training processes are activated. The laboratory is an ideal place to develop creativity, a flexible space for testing and experimentation that allows learning from mistakes and allows the acquisition of learning by practicing skills and learning by doing [1].

Learning to code can be considered as one of the most representative examples of learning by doing [2]. Accordingly, a laboratory-based learning environment seems to be the place where learning in programming take place more easily, especially for students from non-STEM (Science, Technology, Engineering and Mathematics) contexts. Learning to code in a laboratory-based environment allows students to build code-related knowledge through practice and social interaction with peers and experts. Also, a laboratory-based setting can help teachers create scaffolding strategies in order to support the acquisition of code-related concepts and practice [3]. The creation of those scaffolding strategies in online, virtual and asynchronous learning environments presents several problems, among them the difficulty in recreating the complexity of social and cognitive interactions taking place in a laboratory-based setting.

© Springer International Publishing AG, part of Springer Nature 2018
C. Stephanidis (Ed.): HCII Posters 2018, CCIS 852, pp. 94–101, 2018.
https://doi.org/10.1007/978-3-319-92285-0_14

Research in TELE (Technology-Enhanced Learning Environments) [4] in order to remove those barriers is moving forward from GUI (Graphical User Interfaces) interfaces and WIMP (Windows, Icons, Mouse and Pointer) environments toward the development of new interface formats and novel interaction paradigms such as wearable and tangible interaction as well as bots and conversational interfaces.

The use of artificial intelligence in education constitutes a research area with extensive background. For this research project, it is particularly interesting to note the advances in intelligent tutoring systems (ITS) and autonomous agents [5]. In recent years, conversational systems or agents, also called bots or chatbots (referring to the conversation-based bot), have experienced a large growth. We can find voice assistants in the main mobile and desktop operating systems. Conversation-based assistants can also be found in intelligent speakers and commerce-based web pages. In addition, we can also find bots in specific chat spaces such as Facebook Messenger (https://es-es.messenger.com/) or Slack (https://slack.com/). The current research in technology enhanced learning suggests that the impact of chatbots in the educational field will lead to a significant change in learning tools. Chatbots can provide, for example, teacher support, student guidance or perform formative assessment [6].

This work presents the design and architecture of the CodeLab learning tool. CodeLab is an ongoing project that aims to offer students a learning code laboratory tool that simulates the interaction that is carried out in a face-to-face programming laboratory. Thus, the system mimics a human tutor in a physical lab. Through the communication interface, a chatbot suggests a series of exercises and activities that the students have to solve or complete. Also, it is available to students to help them solve questions and monitor their progress; and if it identifies learners experiencing difficulties, it proactively addresses to them practice and solve the proposed activities.

2 Teaching and Learning to Code

This project takes place at UOC, Universitat Oberta de Catalunya (http://www.uoc.edu), a fully online university based in Barcelona, Spain. UOC offers a wide range of educational programs, and some of them are STEM oriented. Currently, the programming courses of the STEM area are based on three main elements: (1) learning materials; (2) teacher-student interaction and; (3) practice-based activities.

Learning materials with different formats and goals are used in order to introduce and help students to understand the basic programming concepts and ideas. Text-based resources are used as main material for understanding basic programming concepts. Video contents are used in order to foster a better understanding of advanced programming features and interactive videos are used to show students how code is executed and how variables are changing value along the process.

The teacher-student interaction is mainly based mail-based forums where teachers answer questions and solve problems in a way somehow similar to a traditional face-to-face course. In the case of theoretical questions, the teacher provides an answer based on the learning materials. But in the scenario with a more practical code-related questions is the teacher providing answers by examining and executing the code written by students, fixing it, if needed, and by delivering written feedback to students.

Hands-on activities are carried out autonomously by the student. Depending on the programming language, instructions are offered in order to download and install the IDE (Integrated Development Environment), if it's available, or the editor and the compiler or the editor and the interpreter. During the course several activities are proposed to students with the aim to foster their self confidence in programming and the acquisition of basic programming concepts.

Student assessment takes place through an exam and a practice-based test. The exam is theory oriented and students must show some understanding of the programming concepts included in the course learning itinerary. In the practice-based test students have to prove programming skills. Both assignments are reviewed and graded by the teacher. In the case of the practice-based test the teacher has to download, review and execute the code of every student in order to provide feedback and a mark.

This approach presents several issues for student's learning as well as for teacher's monitoring and assessment: (1) for novice students installing an IDE can be a difficult task; (2) collaborative coding tasks can be difficult because they require to interchange code by email or to install and learn version control tools; (3) in order to review the code the teacher has to download all the activities of every student and execute them, and; (4) for the teacher it is difficult to track the student's learning process, review all the activities or getting information about students practice. To address these issues and improve the experience of learners and teachers, a new approach is needed. With the CodeLab research project we aim to solve some of these issues and improve the experience of teaching and learning to code through a practice-oriented learning environment with a conversation-based interface.

3   The CodeLab Learning Tool

The CodeLab approach focuses on learning to code in a laboratory learning environment. The research is also focused on the definition and design of the most appropriate interface and interaction style for providing chatbot-based support. This is an ongoing interdisciplinary research project that combines ethnographic research, human-computer interaction research and technology enhanced learning, with the aim of designing and developing chatbots for educational environments.

Starting from the idea that learning to program is not easy [7, 8] and above all, it requires a lot of practice, we envision a learning environment that could foster the understanding of programming concepts as well as the acquisition of programming skills. The process we envision is quite simple: the student is provided with some basic concepts, then, he's invited to practice as much as possible in order to assimilate them correctly. Once the concepts are acquired, he can move on to more advanced ones. Whatever the teaching system and approach, this process is not easy to implement. It requires the teacher to stop and verify that students have acquired sufficient fluency with the concepts and lessons presented before progressing with new ones. In distance learning, the student is quite self-sufficient in determining both the number of hours he or she devotes to study and the times when he or she does so. This complicates the work of the teacher who cannot set a previously defined learning itinerary. Therefore, the teacher is only able to control the assimilation of concepts with the tests and assignments that are carried out throughout the course.

The main functionalities of the CodeLab learning tool are: (1) learner can write code and visualize its execution; (2) activities for practice and learn are presented in a consistent and logic order; (3) students can solve, visualize execution and save activities; (4) the tool can monitor the progress of learners as they practice and solve activities; (5) teachers can follow up on the student's activity and performance and, if necessary, step in and provide recommendations or feedback; (6) a dialogue-based interface allows learners and teachers to interact in order to answer questions and share comments; (7) in the conversational interface, a chatbot behaves as a participant in the laboratory, offering answers to questions or helping in specific aspects of algorithmic learning or programming language.

Currently, a number of programming tools to write and execute code can be found. There are both open source and paid tools that are being used in online educational settings where learners can write code, debug it and visualize its execution in real time. Nevertheless, most of these tools are coding tools but not learning tools. That is, they do not provide learning scaffolding for students. The aim of the CodeLab tool is to provide each student a collection of learning activities to be solved within the tool. Thus, the student can access to the theory and also to a set of activities designed to practice the key concepts of programming. The activities are presented in form of a sequence that is related to a previously defined learning itinerary. The development of activity-based learning itineraries are part of the teacher's educational work and it takes into account the skills to be developed on each learning stage. Learning itineraries can have different types of activities: predefined or template-based, that can automatically generate instances. The template-based activities allow CodeLab to provide different activities for each learner where the same learning concepts can be practiced.

CodeLab will track the programming practice carried out by each student as well as the activities that he or she solves, recording the time spent on the practice and the number of activities completed. This will allow both the system and the teacher to follow up on each student, see their progress and make relevant recommendations. Activity monitoring must also allow learners to deliver exercises directly from the CodeLab to perform a training evaluation. For example, a submission could take the form of solving a series of activities in a given time-period. Once the assessment period ends or the learner finishes, the teacher can review the work and, if necessary, provide a mark. This allows to advance towards a formative evaluation approach, especially indicated in areas as programming, that is based on practice and incremental learning.

Based on the monitoring and analysis of the activity carried out by learners (solving exercises, interaction with the environment, etc.), the CodeLab tool will provide feedback based on the learning itineraries and recommendations around activities and exercises to be solved. It will also recommend reading educational content if a learner needs to review basic concepts of programming. These recommendations will be similar to the ones provided by an intelligent tutoring system, but here will presented taking advantage of the dialogue-based interface mentioned above.

One of the design challenges of CodeLab is the design of a conversation-based interface that allow conversations to take place in the context where learners practice code. The goal is to facilitate conversations as they would happen in a face-to-face laboratory: when a student has a question, she asks the teacher or a colleague while she is able to point where the problem is, in a coding activity. Additionally, with the CodeLab project we are exploring the introduction of educational bots in the conversation-based interface of the laboratory. The interaction design of the chatbots is another design challenge that is being addressed. It takes into account ethnographic studies [9] of current programming labs and the state of the art from the HCI field [6]. We identified a set of functionalities that bots can support, from simply providing help with the programming language syntax to a more complex like providing feedback based on the monitoring and analysis of the activity carried out by learners (solving exercises, interaction with the environment, etc.). Chatbots can provide feedback based on the learning itineraries and recommendations around activities and exercises to be solved. They can also recommend learners to read educational content in the case they need to review basic concepts. Recommendations will be presented through the dialogue-based interface and chatbots will behave as any other participant in the learning laboratory.

Therefore, with the CodeLab project, we are facing several research and design challenges such as: (a) the conversational interaction within the tool; (b) chatbot design and training; (c) workspace for code practice and visualizing; (d) learning activities and itinerary and progress design; (e) formative assessment approach; and (f) dashboards and data for the instructors.

4   Architecture

CodeLab is a technology-based learning tool that can be used in both blended and online educational settings. In both cases, the learning tool needs to be integrated in a virtual learning environment where students can also interact with other courses and services. From the learner point of view, the dialogue-based interface of CodeLab needs to provide an integrated interaction experience with the different elements of the virtual learning environment. Therefore, the challenge here is to design and deploy the chatbot conversation-based interaction into the main application contexts of the virtual learning environment. In our case, a fully online higher education institution, we identified three main contexts: (a) learning materials or digital learning resources context; (b) virtual classroom context; and (c) communication interface.

In the digital learning resources context (a), the chatbot is deployed inside the learning materials, acting as a learner assistant, providing, depending on the topic or objective of each material section, the most appropriate exercises, activities and assessments. In the virtual classroom context (b), the chatbot is deployed inside the virtual classroom environment, it acts as an assistant, providing, through the chat interface, access to the resources and assessments available. In the communication interface context (c), the chatbot is deployed using Slack as communication environment. Slack is a communication tool that can act as an external space that unifies all learning and teaching communications in one place. In the case of CodeLab, there is a Slack that brings all code learners together in the same place, there are channels for each programming language and for promoting the community engagement. Here, the chatbot acts as an automatic lab assistant, solving the students' code questions, providing the appropriate lab resources for solving activities, providing assessments and transferring to the real lab instructor those questions that it doesn't understand or needs to be answered by a human teacher.

The chatbot is also an applications/systems aggregator and each of the application/ system in that ecosystem has also an interface with several design challenges that need to be faced. The number and distribution of that systems or applications could change depending on the products to integrate, but from the logical point of view, we can distinguish the following modules: (a) workspace for code practice; (b) assessment management system; (c) grading & feedback; (d) dashboards & analytics; and (e) the chatbot itself (Fig. 1).

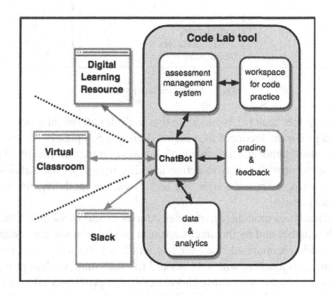

Fig. 1. CodeLab architecture.

The workspace for code practice (a) is essentially a cloud-base IDE for learning programming. In its first iteration, it provides P5.js as a programming language to learn. Since it is based on JavaScript, it does not require a server to compile and execute the code but can be directly interpreted and executed in any web browser.

The Assessment management system (b), is a system for managing the authoring and the deployment of the code exercises into the workspace for code. Through that module, is possible to connect with the authoring tools - like the workspace for code practice - and to set up specific learning activities for both, to be performed by students in specific time and to catalog for subsequent reuse (Fig. 2).

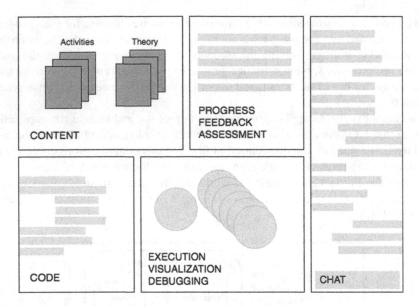

Fig. 2. CodeLab workspace

The grading & feedback (c), is a module that includes all the interfaces and services for grading and providing feedback to students. This is a complex issue, not only for the interaction with the chatbot and the other tools but also for the complexity of the grading process. It needs to provide a way to define learning itineraries and rubrics that could be very diverse such as the code style, the test cases, the legibility, the accuracy, the performance, and others.

The data & analytics module (d), includes interfaces and services related to the data gathered by the chatbot and by the other tools and modules in the ecosystem. It allows the chatbot provide recommendations for learners based on learning itineraries. This module also provides teachers with a dashboard to understand student progress.

The chatbot (e) is itself a module or application that provides dialogue-based inter-action for students and instructors. For instructors, the chatbot provides access to modules above for the authoring, delivering, grading and monitoring processes. For students, it provides assistance in context, recommending the most appropriate exercises to them. An important aspect here is the dialog-based interface language processing component. During the project we plan to evaluate different levels of chatbot commu-nication capacities, from a simple structured language to a natural language processing approach with the goal of measuring the importance of the human language proximity variable.

5   Discussion

With the CodeLab project, our goal is to provide a different approach to learn program-ming online, solve some common problems and provide a better learning experience through practice laboratories, learning by doing and conversation-based interactions. Therefore, we have two main goals: setting the architecture and design for the code learning tools and designing the chatbot that provides support to the tool. Introducing chatbots in online educational settings can be very challenging. In online learning the communication between teachers and students is a key element of its success and chatbots provide interesting opportunities to guide and support students. Also, chatbot deployment in virtual learning environments implies that different modules should be redesigned in order to introduce conversational interaction.

With our design and architecture, we are in the process of setting up a first version of the CodeLab learning tool. This tool will be evaluated with arts and design students in a P5.js course. Usually, non-STEM learners need more support and guidance when learning to code and we expect the CodeLab tool can provide it. From this pilot, we expect to get rich information to iterate the design of the learning environment and also the chatbot design in terms of guidance capabilities and its conversation design.

References

1. Romero, M., Lepage, A., Lille, B.: Computational thinking development through creative programming in higher education. Int. J. Educ. Technol. High. Educ. **14**(1), 42 (2017). https://doi.org/10.1186/s41239-017-0080-z
2. Hassinen, M., Mäyrä, II.: Learning programming by programming: a case study. In: Proceedings of the 6th Baltic Sea conference on Computing education research: Koli Calling 2006, pp. 117–119. ACM, February 2006. https://doi.org/10.1145/1315803.1315824
3. Van Merrienboer, J.J., Paas, F.G.: Automation and schema acquisition in learning elementary computer programming: implications for the design of practice. Comput. Hum. Behav. **6**(3), 273–289 (1990). https://doi.org/10.1016/0747-5632(90)90023-A
4. Veletsianos, G., Heller, R., Overmyer, S., Procter, M.: Conversational agents in virtual worlds: bridging disciplines. Br. J. Educ. Technol. **41**(1), 123–140 (2010). https://doi.org/10.1111/j.1467-8535.2009.01027.x
5. Roll, I., Wylie, R.: Evolution and revolution in artificial intelligence in education. Int. J. Artif. Intell. Educ. **26**(2), 582–599 (2016). https://doi.org/10.1007/s40593-016-0110-3
6. Song, D., Oh, E.Y., Rice, M.: Interacting with a conversational agent system for educational purposes in online courses. In: 2017 10th International Conference on Human System Interactions (HSI), pp. 78–82. IEEE (2017). https://doi.org/10.1109/HSI.2017.8005002
7. Gomes, A., Mendes, A.J.: Learning to program-difficulties and solutions. In: International Conference on Engineering Education–ICEE, vol. 2007 (2007)
8. Lahtinen, E., Ala-Mutka, K., Järvinen, H.M.: A study of the difficulties of novice programmers. ACM SIGCSE Bull. **37**(3), 14–18 (2005). https://doi.org/10.1145/1067445.1067453
9. Fink, R.D., Weyer, J.: Interaction of human actors and non-human agents. A sociological simulation model of hybrid systems. Sci. Technol. Innov. Stud. **10**(1), 47–64 (2014)

CognitOS: A Student-Centric Working Environment for an Attention-Aware Intelligent Classroom

Anastasia Ntagianta[1], Maria Korozi[1(✉)], Asterios Leonidis[1],
Margherita Antona[1], and Constantine Stephanidis[1,2]

[1] Institute of Computer Science (ICS),
Foundation for Research and Technology – Hellas (FORTH), Heraklion, Greece
{dagianta,korozi,leonidis,antona,cs}@ics.forth.gr
[2] Department of Computer Science, University of Crete, Heraklion, Greece

Abstract. The emergence of Intelligent Classrooms, and in particular classrooms equipped with facilities for identifying the students' attention levels, has raised the need for appropriate student-friendly tools that not only facilitate application hosting, but also acts as the means to re-engage inattentive students in the educational process. This work presents CognitOS, a web-based working environment that hosts several types of applications (i.e., exercises, multimedia viewer, digital book) that are utilized as channels to present interventions dictated by the intelligent decision-making mechanisms of the attention-aware classroom. This paper presents the functionality of CognitOS and the design process followed for its development.

Keywords: Intelligent classroom · Educational interventions
Educational working environment

1 Introduction

Paying attention to an educational activity is often considered as a fundamental prerequisite of learning [1, 2]; students need to be focused and motivated in order to benefit the most during their journey towards knowledge [3]. However, maintaining a constant focus of attention inside a classroom for a long period of time is difficult, since distractions either by internal stimuli (e.g., thoughts and attempts to retrieve information from memory) or external stimuli (e.g., sounds) are quite frequent [4–6].

Literature suggests several strategies to regain student attention and increase the level of engagement in learning activities; among them, Active Learning was acknowledged as the most effective instructional method in terms of resetting the students' concentration and decreasing attention lapses during lectures [7–9]. Currently, there is minimum technological support available to assist educators in maximizing student engagement, even in technologically advanced classrooms.

Envisioning an Intelligent Classroom capable of identifying inattentive behaviors and properly reacting to re-motivate students, the LECTOR framework [10] utilizes

© Springer International Publishing AG, part of Springer Nature 2018
C. Stephanidis (Ed.): HCII Posters 2018, CCIS 852, pp. 102–110, 2018.
https://doi.org/10.1007/978-3-319-92285-0_15

ambient facilities to observe the students' actions, identify the individuals who show signs of inattention and undertake the necessary actions to restore their engagement by applying appropriate interventions. This work presents CognitOS, a sophisticated web-based working environment that hosts educational applications utilized as channels to present LECTOR interventions. In this context, interventions are intended as system-guided actions that subtly interrupt a course's flow so as to re-engage distracted, unmotivated or tired students in the educational process.

2   Related Work

Desktop Graphical User Interfaces (GUIs) assist the user in easily accessing and editing files, while encapsulating the underlying complexity of the operating system. In [11] it is suggested that students prefer physical environments over desktop environments, especially if they create a unified working environment for performing educational activities. To that end, many approaches simplify the desktop environment of existing operating systems so as to and make it simpler and more child-friendly (e.g., 'Edubuntu' [12] and 'Puppy Linux' [13]), or create safe sandboxed environments that provides children with educational content and combine entertainment and learning [14–18].

Compared to passive working environments, attention-aware systems have much to contribute to educational research and practice. These systems can influence the delivery of instructional materials, the acquisition of such materials from presentations (as a function of focused attention), the evaluation of student performance, and the assessment of learning methodologies (e.g., traditional teaching, active learning techniques) [2]. However, existing approaches [19–23] concentrate mainly on computer-driven educational activities or self-paced learning environments [24] for monitoring and supporting student engagement in learning activities.

Subsequently, despite the fact that many approaches have tried to create child-oriented desktop environments that provide educational content in a fun and engaging manner, currently there is no infrastructure that transforms them into reactive attention-aware ecosystems that monitor student behaviors in a real classroom setting and intervene by suggesting improvements for the learning process.

3   The Intelligent Classroom Behind CognitOS

A traditional classroom consists of the students' desks and a board placed at the center of the room. Moving towards a technologically enriched intelligent classroom, new computer-equipped artifacts replace the class board and students' desks, enhancing educational activities with the use of pervasive and mobile computing, sensor networks, artificial intelligence, multimedia computing, middleware and software agents [25].

CognitOS is deployed permanently on the technologically augmented desks residing in the in-vitro simulation spaces of an Intelligent Classroom located at the FORTH-ICS AmI Facility Building. Each desk features a 27-in. multitouch-enabled All-in-One PC which integrates various sensors (e.g., eye-tracker, camera, microphone, etc.) and cooperates with other students' personal devices (e.g., smartphone, tablet, smartwatch).

The software architecture (Fig. 1) of the Intelligent Classroom consists of the AmI-Solertis middleware infrastructure [26], which is responsible for (i) the collection, analysis and storage of the metadata regarding the environment's artifacts, (ii) their deployment, execution and monitoring in the AmI-Solertis-enabled systems to formulate a ubiquitous ecosystem. Additionally, LECTOR [10] is an extensible framework offering a versatile mechanism for identifying behaviors that require system actions (e.g., unmotivated student) and an extensible intervention mechanism for intervening when the users need help or support. These mechanisms follow the trigger-action model [27, 28], which has been in the spotlight as a form of programming Ambient Intelligence (AmI) environments, using simple "if then" rules. LECTOR's sophisticated authoring tool, named LECTORstudio [29], supports both developers and educators in creating rules that dictate the behavior of the classroom.

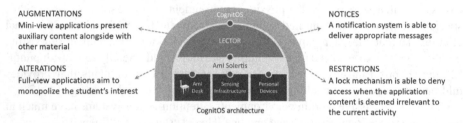

AUGMENTATIONS
Mini-view applications present auxiliary content alongside with other material

ALTERATIONS
Full-view applications aim to monopolize the student's interest

NOTICES
A notification system is able to deliver appropriate messages

RESTRICTIONS
A lock mechanism is able to deny access when the application content is deemed irrelevant to the current activity

CognitOS architecture

Fig. 1. CognitOS architecture and supported intervention types.

4 CognitOS as a Student Desktop

A desktop environment aims to offer an intuitive way for the user to interact with the computer using concepts similar to those used when interacting with the physical world, such as files and folders. In CognitOS, the Desktop constitutes the main working area – the base application – that covers the entire screen, manipulates the overall layout, prevents students from launching irrelevant applications and most importantly maintains and customizes the available educational applications and acts as the main control center that facilitates their execution (Fig. 2). The CognitOS desktop follows the metaphor of an actual desk containing virtual student items (e.g., books, pencils) that can be used to launch the respective applications. In more detail, the desktop contains: (i) a **pile of books** that offers a shortcut to the student's collection of books; the topmost book is related to the current course and through it the student can quickly launch the book application with the respective content, (ii) a **pile of notebook** pages that acts as a shortcut to student's collection of completed or pending assignments; the first page filters the assignments' list and displays only those related to the current course, (iii) the **personal card** that displays the student's name and provides access to the profile application with the detailed academic record of that student, and a **computer monitor** that can be used to launch the multimedia player.

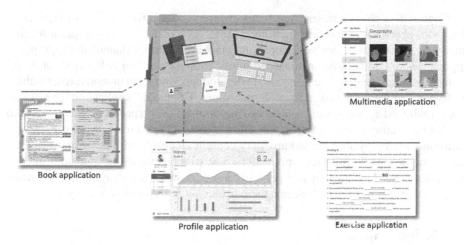

Fig. 2. Snapshots from the CognitOS applications.

A digital educational working environment should allow students to launch multiple applications simultaneously; therefore, it requires a mechanism that decides the placement of each newly launched application. To this end, a sophisticated algorithm was introduced ensuring that (i) if an application displays additional information related to another application, then they should always be launched next to each other, (ii) the application with which the user had interacted last will remain on top and (iii) secondary applications (e.g., calendar, calculator, etc.) will occupy less screen real-estate if more important ones are already or should be presented. Nevertheless, in addition to automatic layout, CognitOS permits the rearrangement of any launched applications so that each student can customize the environment according to his/her personal preference.

5   CognitOS as an Intervention Host

Apart from acting as a passive working environment that simply deals with application management, CognitOS has a more important role to fulfill. It is responsible for providing interventions to inattentive or unmotivated students so as to reengage them in the educational process. For example, a mini-quiz can be launched either explicitly by a student who selects a specific exercise on her book, or automatically when LECTOR intervenes to display a humorous quiz to keep her motivated in the reading assignment.

Literature review reports that several intervention techniques can prove to be beneficial in various situations occurring in an educational setting. Currently, two intervention techniques have been created in order to ensure active student participation in the main course (i.e., Active Learning). Particularly, the student desk is able to instantiate quizzes and multimedia presentations with appropriate content to keep students motivated. Furthermore, taking into consideration the fact that most students thrive in encouraging environments [30, 31] where they receive specific feedback, CognitOS is able to provide encouraging messages when deemed necessary.

CognitOS is able to present four types of interventions: (i) notices, (ii) augmentations, (iii) alterations and (iv) restrictions (Fig. 1). As soon as LECTOR plans a specific intervention, CognitOS receives a command via AmI-Solertis to launch the appropriate application(s). Particularly, an advanced notification mechanism is featured for delivering appropriate messages (e.g., notice) to the students who seem unmotivated, troubled or disengaged from the task at hand. Furthermore, CognitOS' applications (i.e., exercises, multimedia, book) can be launched on demand with specific content, so as to present motivating material. Each application is available in a mini- and a full-view; a mini-view is employed to present auxiliary content alongside with other material (i.e., augmentation), while full-view applications aim to monopolize the student's interest (i.e., alteration). Finally, they can get locked (i.e., restriction), denying access, when either the teacher or LECTOR deems them irrelevant to the current activity.

6   Design Process

Since CognitOS's philosophy evolves around the students' benefits, it was of foremost importance to concentrate on their needs, wants and limitations. In order to efficiently address this requirement the User-Centered Design (UCD) [32] approach was selected.

The users' characteristics and their tasks were analyzed through literature review and brainstorming sessions with a team of experts, which included members of various backgrounds, skills and perspectives (i.e., teachers, psychologists, designers, usability experts and developers). CognitOS focuses on students who have reached the formal operational stage [33]. At this stage, the children's thinking process is similar to that of adults, while their tastes and interests remain different. Consequently, students are able to apprehend – if not already familiar – abstract concepts (e.g., gestures, folders etc.) supported by computer systems. This is also a consequence of the fact that today's children are exposed from a very early age to a wide range of technologies, including multimedia systems, electronic toys and games, and communication devices.

According to [34], teenagers have much less research experience than adults, and therefore have more difficulty combing through and making sense of complex information. Furthermore, they tend to have less patience, thus they like getting answers quickly and dislike complicated interactions. Finally, as they are sensitive about their age, they prefer a clean and modest design, with visually meaningful icons and age-appropriate instructions easy to comprehend and remember [35], over a childish one.

Druin et al. [36] have found that children when using technology want to be in control, use technologies with others, and have at their disposal expressive tools. They pay attention to whether an application is "cool", easy to learn, appealing, and if multimedia is available. Regarding the latter, Said's studies [37] indicated that children (9–14 years old) become more engaged with multimedia when immediate feedback is provided, as well as when the environment allows them to be in control and set their own goals.

Socializing is another characteristic of children at this age; however, it is not limited to talking to classmates, but includes activities like sharing interesting resources with friends or collaborating to solve an exercise. Kaplan et al. [38] revealed that even though children (10–14 years old) may be co-present in the same space, they would like to be supported with tools to share their experiences with their friends and teachers.

Regarding student's goals and motives as drives for learning, several studies have taken place since the early 1960 [39–41]. Based on these studies, a list of tasks that the students should be able to perform was devised: (i) solve exercises of various types (e.g., multiple choice), (ii) get assistance on exercises, (iii) submit exercises that have been completed either during the lesson or at home, (iv) retrieve additional resources about something interesting or about an assignment dictated by the teacher, (v) have access to assistive applications (e.g., calculator, dictionary, etc.), (vi) have access to multimedia, (vii) maintain a personal area with access to history of homework, and (viii) collaborate with classmates to complete a task.

A scenario-based approach was adopted to further elaborate the characteristics of the aforementioned student tasks. Scenarios are really useful for providing realistic examples of how users carry out their tasks in a specified context. As soon as the developed scenarios were finalized, a series of interviews with children (5 children 11–15 years old) were conducted, in order to view them through the students' perspective. The children's opinions about the system during the interviews ranged from positive to enthusiastic. They were excited about the applications and the fact that they could share with the entire classroom interesting resources. Furthermore, the fact that they could work from their netbook appealed to them, as two of the children said: "studying would be much easier". Additionally, the interviews revealed that children enjoy playing educational and cooperative games both at school and at home, while they pointed out the importance of assistive applications, such as an organizer that displays homework or predefined exams, and a vocabulary that stores a list of words specified by the student for further studying.

In order to visualize plausible solutions, a set of prototypes were created and evaluated by children during a formative evaluation experiment. The goal of this experiment was to collect students' opinions about the functionality and applications supported by CognitOS. The results of this evaluation were taken into consideration during the development process in order to better meet the end users' needs. Once the development phase had advanced and interactive prototypes had been created, a heuristic evaluation was conducted, aiming to eliminate serious usability problems before proceeding to user testing. CognitOS was then improved according to the heuristic evaluation results. Finally, a full-scale user-based evaluation experiment is planned to be the next step of this work so as to acquire valuable feedback regarding the efficacy of CognitOS as an intervention mechanism and its acceptance by both students and educators.

7 Conclusions and Future Work

This work has presented CognitOS, a student-friendly web-based working environment for students that hosts a variety of educational applications. These applications also comprise the communication channel through which the attention-aware Intelligent Classroom presents interventions to students that need help or support. The formative and heuristic evaluation experiments revealed various usability issues which were incorporated in the current version of CognitOS. However, a full-scale user-based evaluation with students is being planned to fine-tune it before its final release.

Acknowledgements. This work is supported by the FORTH-ICS internal RTD Program "Ambient Intelligence and Smart Environments".

References

1. Szpunar, K.K., Moulton, S.T., Schacter, D.L.: Mind wandering and education: from the classroom to online learning. Front. Psychol. **4**, 495 (2013)
2. Rapp, D.N.: The value of attention aware systems in educational settings. Comput. Hum. Behav. **22**, 603–614 (2006)
3. Sousa, D.A.: How the Brain Learns. Corwin Press, Thousand Oaks (2016)
4. Johnstone, A.H., Percival, F.: Attention breaks in lectures. Educ. Chem. **13**, 49–50 (1976)
5. Bligh, D.A.: What's the Use of Lectures?. Intellect Books, Exeter (1998)
6. Bunce, D.M., Flens, E.A., Neiles, K.Y.: How long can students pay attention in class? A study of student attention decline using clickers. J. Chem. Educ. **87**, 1438–1443 (2010)
7. Prince, M.: Does active learning work? A review of the research. J. Eng. Educ. **93**, 223–231 (2004)
8. Burke, L.A., Ray, R.: Re-setting the concentration levels of students in higher education: an exploratory study. Teach. High. Educ. **13**, 571–582 (2008)
9. Bonwell, C.C., Eison, J.A.: Active learning: creating excitement in the classroom. 1991 ASHE-ERIC Higher Education Reports. ERIC (1991)
10. Korozi, M., Leonidis, A., Antona, M., Stephanidis, C.: LECTOR: towards reengaging students in the educational process inside smart classrooms. In: Horain, P., Achard, C., Mallem, M. (eds.) IHCI 2017. LNCS, vol. 10688, pp. 137–149. Springer, Cham (2017). https://doi.org/10.1007/978-3-319-72038-8_11
11. Fails, J.A., Druin, A., Guha, M.L., Chipman, G., Simms, S., Churaman, W.: Child's play: a comparison of desktop and physical interactive environments. In: Proceedings of the 2005 Conference on Interaction Design and Children, pp. 48–55. ACM (2005)
12. McKay, S., Rice, C.: Providing access to technology with Edubuntu Linux. In: Society for Information Technology & Teacher Education International Conference, pp. 2051–2052. Association for the Advancement of Computing in Education (AACE) (2007)
13. Puppy Linux Home. http://puppylinux.com/
14. What is Magic Desktop? http://www.magicdesktop.com/en-US/Landing
15. Sugar Labs. https://www.sugarlabs.org/
16. kidsmenu. https://www.glob.com.au/kidsmenu/
17. DoudouLinux - English. https://www.doudoulinux.org/web/english/index.html
18. Peanut Butter. http://www.peanutbuttersoftware.com/
19. Barrios, V.M.G., Gütl, C., Preis, A.M., Andrews, K., Pivec, M., Mödritscher, F., Trummer, C.: AdELE: a framework for adaptive e-learning through eye tracking. In: Proceedings of IKNOW, pp. 609–616 (2004)
20. Slykhuis, D.A., Wiebe, E.N., Annetta, L.A.: Eye-tracking students' attention to PowerPoint photographs in a science education setting. J. Sci. Educ. Technol. **14**, 509–520 (2005)
21. Wang, H., Chignell, M., Ishizuka, M.: Empathic tutoring software agents using real-time eye tracking. In: Proceedings of the 2006 Symposium on Eye Tracking Research & Applications, pp. 73–78. ACM (2006)

22. Merten, C., Conati, C.: Eye-tracking to model and adapt to user meta-cognition in intelligent learning environments. In: Proceedings of the 11th International Conference on Intelligent User Interfaces, pp. 39–46. ACM (2006)
23. Sibert, J.L., Gokturk, M., Lavine, R.A.: The reading assistant: eye gaze triggered auditory prompting for reading remediation. In: Proceedings of the 13th Annual ACM Symposium on User Interface Software and Technology, pp. 101–107. ACM (2000)
24. Chen, J., Zhu, B., Balter, O., Xu, J., Zou, W., Hedman, A., Chen, R., Sang, M.: FishBuddy: promoting student engagement in self-paced learning through wearable sensing. In: 2017 IEEE International Conference on Smart Computing (SMARTCOMP), pp. 1–9 (2017)
25. Leonidis, A., Korozi, M., Margetis, G., Ntoa, S., Papagiannakis, H., Antona, M., Stephanidis, C.: A glimpse into the ambient classroom. Bull. IEEE Tech. Comm. Learn. Technol. **14**, 3–6 (2012)
26. Leonidis, A., Arampatzis, D., Louloudakis, N., Stephanidis, C.: The AmI-Solertis system: creating user experiences in smart environments. In: Proceedings of the 13th IEEE International Conference on Wireless and Mobile Computing, Networking and Communications (2017)
27. Ur, B., McManus, E., Pak Yong Ho, M., Littman, M.L.: Practical trigger-action programming in the smart home. In: Proceedings of the SIGCHI Conference on Human Factors in Computing Systems, pp. 803–812. ACM, New York (2014)
28. Ur, B., Pak Yong Ho, M., Brawner, S., Lee, J., Mennicken, S., Picard, N., Schulze, D., Littman, M.L.: Trigger-action programming in the wild: an analysis of 200,000 IFTTT recipes. In: Proceedings of the 2016 CHI Conference on Human Factors in Computing Systems, pp. 3227–3231. ACM, New York (2016)
29. Korozi, M., Antona, M., Ntagianta, A., Leonidis, A., Stephanidis, C.: LECTORstudio: creating Inattention alarms and interventions to reengage the students in the educational process. In: Proceedings of the 10th Annual International Conference of Education, Research and Innovation (2017)
30. Abramowitz, A.J., O'Leary, S.G., Rosén, L.A.: Reducing off-task behavior in the classroom: a comparison of encouragement and reprimands. J. Abnorm. Child Psychol. **15**, 153–163 (1987)
31. Hitz, R., Driscoll, A.: Praise in the Classroom (1989)
32. ISO 9241-210:2010 - Ergonomics of Human-System Interaction – Part 210: Human-Centred Design for Interactive Systems. https://www.iso.org/standard/52075.html
33. Piaget, J.: Science of Education and the Psychology of the Child. Trans. D. Coltman, Oxford (1970)
34. Loranger, H., Nielsen, J.: Teenagers on the Web: Usability Guidelines for Creating Compelling Websites for Teens. Nielsen Norman Group, Fremont (2005)
35. Hanna, L., Risden, K., Czerwinski, M., Alexander, K.J.: The role of usability research in designing children's computer products. In: The Design of Children's Technology, pp. 3–26. Morgan Kaufmann Publishers Inc., San Francisco (1998)
36. Druin, A., Bederson, B., Boltman, A., Miura, A., Knotts-Callahan, D., Platt, M.: Children as Our Technology Design Partners+. Morgan Kaufmann Publishers Inc., San Francisco (1998)
37. Said, N.S.: An engaging multimedia design model. In: Proceedings of the 2004 Conference on Interaction Design and Children: Building a Community, pp. 169–172. ACM (2004)
38. Kaplan, N., Chisik, Y., Knudtzon, K., Kulkarni, R., Moulthrop, S., Summers, K., Weeks, H.: Supporting sociable literacy in the international children's digital library. In: Proceedings of the 2004 Conference on Interaction Design and Children: Building a Community. ACM (2004)

39. Covington, M.V.: Goal theory, motivation, and school achievement: an integrative review. Annu. Rev. Psychol. **51**, 171–200 (2000)
40. Midgley, C., Kaplan, A., Middleton, M., Maehr, M.L., Urdan, T., Anderman, L.H., Anderman, E., Roeser, R.: The development and validation of scales assessing students' achievement goal orientations. Contemp. Educ. Psychol. **23**, 113–131 (1998)
41. Urdan, T.C., Maehr, M.L.: Beyond a two-goal theory of motivation and achievement: a case for social goals. Rev. Educ. Res. **65**, 213–243 (1995)

Towards the Utilization of Diegetic UI
in Virtual Reality Educational Content

Gapyuel Seo and Byung-Chull Bae[(✉)]

Hongik University, Sejong 30016, South Korea
{gapseo,byuc}@hongik.ac.kr

Abstract. In this paper we introduce our ongoing VR learning program for fjord that can enhance the user's sense of immersion using the diegetic UI in virtual reality environment. Fjord is a typical example of glacier terrain, which is not very well known to our target users - junior high school students. As a method to naturally enhance the sense of immersion, we focus on the natural progression of the immersion senses by avoiding the use of non–diegetic UI (e.g., explicit head-up display menus) and employing the diegetic UI (such as the involvement of story characters who are helping the story progression, the use of props and inter-actable objects, and sound effects that can provide clues and aid in the process) in virtual reality environment.

We take three preliminary design issues into account – usability, utility, and satisfaction – when building diegetic UI in VR environments. First, usability addresses how easily and naturally learners (or users) can interact and use in the VR environment. Second, utility delineates how well learners achieve their goals in the VR environment. Third, satisfaction describes the learners' sense of satis-faction that they can obtain while experiencing the VR educational content.

Keywords: Virtual reality · User interface · UI · Diegetic UI

1 Introduction

Recently, the development of digital technology has been followed by active discussions on the use of virtual reality in various fields. Virtual reality (VR), in particular, provides users with active participation and realistic information. These advantages of virtual reality have attracted a great deal of attention as an educational medium by providing realistic information and enabling direct activity of learners. Thus ease of learning and immersion can be two essential factors for designing User Interface (UI) in educational VR contents.

Psychological immersion, which is also known as *flow* [1], refers to a psychological state in which the user can be completely immersed with the surrounding environment. The UI design in virtual environment can crucially affect the user's immersion and satisfaction [2]. The immersion process in VR can be achieved not just by an approach through sensory stimulation with multi-modalities [3], but also by the psychological immersion through the environment and the naturalness of the situation in flow [4].

© Springer International Publishing AG, part of Springer Nature 2018
C. Stephanidis (Ed.): HCII Posters 2018, CCIS 852, pp. 111–115, 2018.
https://doi.org/10.1007/978-3-319-92285-0_16

In the VR environment, interactivity is pivotal especially when we consider the user involvement process and conditions. The interaction between the virtual world and a user is generally performed through a user interface (UI). The game UI can be described as "the way players can interact with the game and receive feedback of their interaction" [5]. Thus it is necessary to maximize the user's feeling of immersion by natural interaction between the user and the contents in the VR environment. That is, a user needs a UI that can naturally interact with the user's behavior or movement without learning how to interact with the content. Regardless of the quality of its content, players would not be immersed with the virtual environment if they are not comfortable with interacting and receiving feedback on the content.

In this paper we introduce our ongoing VR learning program for fjord that can enhance the user's sense of immersion using the diegetic UI in virtual reality environment. A fjord is "formed when a glacier retreats, after carving its typical U-shaped valley, and the sea fills the resulting valley floor"[1]. Fjord is a typical example of glacier terrain, which is not very well known to our target users - junior high school students in South Korea.

2   Story

The narrative in our proposed VR project is an adventure genre. The player first accidently finds the amulets in the Viking-history relating books which were left by her grandfather. From the Viking history book, the player finds out a map of Norway. As soon as touching Norway on the globe in the room, the player finds herself that she just moved from her room to the inside of a boat in the sea of Norway, encompassed with fjords. Now the player's goal is to identify a place called Seven Sister Waterfall which was described in the book and move the boat safely to reach there using a given map. When the player almost comes to the Waterfall, she experiences a sudden change of weather with thunder and lightning. At this point the player recognizes an emergency bell that is being highlighted with an alarm sound. As soon as the player touches the emergency bell, the boat is struck by lightning and she falls into the floor. The player loses her consciousness and the scene fades out. In the next scene, the player wakes up in consciousness and finds out that she had time slips to the Viking era. Then, seeing a silhouette of a man at the outside of the boat, the player goes outside and meets a Viking. The player hears the story of fjords-related legend from the Viking, witnessing the creation process of the fjords.

3   Diegetic User Interface

The UI can be largely divided into Diegetic UI and non-diegetic UI in the opposite concept. Diegetic (or in-game) UI is "an interface that is included in the game world" [6], which is seamlessly included in the game world together with characters in the virtual world, background, props, and sounds. It can be seen or heard by the game

---

[1] http://norwaytoday.info/travel/what-is-a-fjord-and-how-is-it-formed/.

characters. Non-diegetic UI, on the other hand, refers to a typical UI that is "rendered outside the game world, only visible and audible to the players in the real world (e.g., heads-up display)" [6]. While it is arguable to say which type of UI is better for VR games, the choice seems to depend, more or less, on the user's preference in the first person shooting game genre at least [7].

As a method to naturally enhance the sense of immersion, we are currently focusing on the natural progression of the immersion senses by avoiding the use of the non–diegetic UI (e.g., explicit head-up display menus) and employing the diegetic UI (such as the involvement of story characters who are helping the story progression, the use of props and interactable objects, and sound effects that can provide clues and aid in the process) in VR environments. This section describes three elements in diegetic UI – character, props and interactable objects, and sounds.

3.1   Character – Informing the Progress of the Story

Virtual Reality (VR), compared to other media such as hypertext for interactive fiction or virtual environment for digital interactive narrative, could be an effective medium for building empathic relationship between the player and story characters [8]. In this project, we are creating UI design in connection with character design by presenting a diegetic UI through character. For instance, the player hears the fjord-related legend from the Vikings and experiences the creation process of the fjords as the story goes. Figure 1 shows the example of a diegetic character who plays the role of explaining about fjords.

Fig. 1. Screenshots of diegetic character

3.2   Props and Interactable Objects – Providing Clues and Aid in the Process

The props and interactable objects of VR need to be located precisely where they can naturally interact with each other according to the user's actions or movements. The props and interactable objects in our project are as follows:

- Props: Wooden chest, Viking history book, Amulet, Map, clock
- Interactable objects: Globe, Emergency bell

For example, the emergency bell is highlighted with an alarm sound when an emergency situation (e.g., storming in the sea) occurs. Then, the player can recognize that it is time to interact with it to progress the story. Figure 2 shows the example of props and interactable objects that we use in our project.

Fig. 2. Screenshots of props and interactable objects

3.3   Sound - Drawing the User's Attention

Interactable objects in the virtual world have their own characteristic (diegetic) sounds. Along with the sounds, the player can recognize when she needs to interact with some key objects in order to progress the story. For example, the wooden chest has specific sounds that can draw the player's attention so that the player can approach and open it. So has the emergency bell.

4   Conclusion and Future Work

In this paper we introduced our ongoing project focusing on the diegetic UI in which the player can explore some educational content on the fjords through three diegetic game elements – story characters, props and interactable objects, and sounds – without the explicit use of non-diegetic UIs (such as heads-up display) in VR environment. We are now implementing the project using Unreal game engine and HTC Vive.

As future work, we plan to conduct a user study after completion. We also plan to find out how usability factors such as ease of manipulation can affect the user's learning process.

Acknowledgements. This work C0564925 was supported by Business for Cooperative R&D between Industry, Academy, and Research Institute funded Korea Small and Medium Business Administration in 2018.

References

1. Csikszentmihalyi, M.: Flow: The Psychology of Optimal Experience. Harper Collins Publishers, New York (1990)
2. Llanos, S.C., Jørgensen, K.: Do players prefer integrated user interfaces? a qualitative study of game UI design issues. In: DiGRA 2011: Think Design Play (2011)
3. Chu, C.-C.P., Dani, T.H., Gadh, R.: Multi-sensory user interface for a virtual-reality-based computer-aided design system. J. Comput.-Aided Des. **29**(10), 709–725 (1997)
4. McMahan, A.: Immersion, engagement, and presence. In: Wolf, M.J.P., Perron, B. (eds.) The Video Game Theory Reader. Routledge, New York (2003)
5. The evolution of the UI in Games
6. https://medium.com/mobile-lifestyle/the-evolution-of-the-ui-in-games-2be067fcc4ef. Accessed 14 Mar 2018
7. Game UI Discoveries: What Players Want. https://www.gamasutra.com/view/feature/132674/game_ui_discoveries_what_players_.php. Accessed 14 Mar 2018
8. Peacocke, M., Teather, R.J., Carette, J., MacKenzie, I.S.: Evaluating the effectiveness of HUDs and diegetic ammo displays in first-person shooter games. In: IEEE Games Entertainment Media Conference (GEM) (2015)
9. Bae, B.-C., Kim, D.-G., Seo, G.-Y.: Study of VR interactive storytelling for empathy. J. Dig. Contents Soc. **18**(8), 1481–1487 (2017)

Teaching Introductory Programming Concepts Through a Gesture-Based Interface

Lora Streeter[✉] and John Gauch[✉]

University of Arkansas, Fayetteville, AR 72701, USA
{lstrothe, jgauch}@uark.edu

Abstract. The goal of our research is to create and evaluate a visual and gesture-driven interface to teach computer programming to non-traditional programmers, typically school-age children. By making the interface more enjoyable for young students, we hope to keep students engaged and increase their attention span while learning how to program.

Our system combines components from Google's Blockly, a visual block programming language with drag-and-drop puzzle pieces, and Microsoft's Xbox Kinect, which is used to perform skeletal tracking. We created pre-defined gestures to correspond to program functions and available actions, which were compiled from a survey conducted of over 100 grade-school students over three years who had very little to no programming experience before we met. After learning how to use Blockly and having a basic understanding of simple programming logic, the students were asked to create intuitive gestures for common programming constructs, while both standing up using full body movement, and sitting down at a desk, using only their hands. The specific programming constructs included in the survey were loops, conditionals, run program, and undo.

To detect the gestures, we have implemented and evaluated a number of gesture matching algorithms. One challenge is that the size, shape, and path of the gestures varied considerably, so the data has to be normalized for any comparisons.

Keywords: Blockly · Gesture matching · Kinect · Programming
Quantization · Visual programming

1 Introduction

Computer programming is an important field given the rapid advance of technology in recent years, but traditional programming classes are not necessarily directed to the masses. They are typically tailored to people who are either already interested in programming or are old enough (or have enough self-discipline) to sit in a class, take notes, and then go home and experiment with what they have learned in front of a screen. Could there be a better way to teach them? What if, instead of having them sit down and type, they could have a more interactive experience? These are two of the questions that motivate the current research.

© Springer International Publishing AG, part of Springer Nature 2018
C. Stephanidis (Ed.): HCII Posters 2018, CCIS 852, pp. 116–123, 2018.
https://doi.org/10.1007/978-3-319-92285-0_17

Programming is an integral part of the technologically driven society, so there is a need to provide a better way to teach programming to a broader audience. It is an essential career skill that teaches problem solving skills that are broadly useful. Hence, there is a need to grab the attention of non-traditional programmers, draw them into the world of computing, and hold their interest.

Programming with a language meant solely for text analysis or numerical computation can easily discourage people since learning syntax and rules is typically not as enjoyable as manipulating images and completing fun tasks. When people become immersed in learning and having fun, they are more likely to continue onto more challenging topics. It was discovered during some very controlled trials for first-time university level programmers that using a visual language like Alice increased retention by 41%, and the average grade in the class rose an entire letter grade [1].

The goal of our research is to create and evaluate a visual and gesture-driven interface to teach programming to non-traditional programmers, typically school-age children. We have discovered intuitive gestures for specific programming constructs for children, and are working toward recognizing pre-defined gestures. We are also working toward answering the question "Can we teach programming effectively without a mouse?" by using a gesture-driven interface utilizing the Kinect as an input device integrated with Google's Blockly. This paper discusses these intuitive gestures and our gesture matching algorithms.

2 Background and Related Work

2.1 Visual Programming Languages

Visual programming languages have a long history starting around the 1970's and have explored a number of programming paradigms and interfaces. They usually incorporate icons, have a drag-and-drop interface, or are mouse or graphics based – such as Google's Blockly, MIT's Scratch, Carnegie Mellon's Alice, and Berkley's Snap. Google's visual editor, Blockly, enables users to create programs by using a mouse to drag-and-drop connecting puzzle piece blocks together to accomplish a series of goals. After the user has completed a goal, Blockly shows them how many lines their program would have taken in JavaScript. Each task the user is given can be solved with the information they have been provided, and each puzzle builds on the previous in each game.

2.2 Gestural Programming Languages

A gestural programming language is one that takes input as a movement of the hands, face or other parts of the body instead of keyboard or mouse input [2]. Gesture-based languages can involve multi-touch gestures on a tablet device [3], using an image or video as input [4, 5], determining finger locations using a data glove [6], or manual selection of symbolic markers to control a robot [7]. Consumer devices, like mobile phones, tablets, and controller-free sensors such as the Kinect and LeapMotion, all of which are equipped with many sensors, cameras and multi-touch screens, have opened up new possibilities of promoting gestural programming to the broader public.

2.3 Kinect

The Kinect is a popular, inexpensive, three-dimensional camera that has revolutionized human-computer interaction by having depth and RGB cameras in the same easy-to-use unit. Although the Kinect was originally developed for video game input, it has been used as an input device for a wide range of applications, both because it provides a hands-free interface and because it provides physical engagement for users. The OpenNI framework provides an open source API for the Kinect that tracks and reports the positions of fifteen different skeletal joints, including hands.

3 Methodology

3.1 Student Population and Experimental Design

We have had the opportunity to teach and work with a number of young students who are interested in computer science and engineering, and to get feedback from them about gestures they thought were most natural for specific programming concepts. Using this information, we developed a prototype gesture-based visual programming interface that captures gestures using the Kinect and transfers this information to Blockly to create and run programs.

The students who participated in this segment of the study attended various engineering summer camps held at the University of Arkansas for rising 6th–12th graders. Some students arrived with absolutely no programming experience, while others had used a few languages already. Very few, if any, of the students had used Blockly before, although around half of the students had utilized Scratch in the past. For this experiment, we focused on Blockly.

The students got the opportunity to work with Blockly and then filled out a survey at the end of the session about the concepts they learned, and whether they would prefer to program while standing and using full body movements, or sitting and using only hand gestures. They were also asked to create their own gestures for the following programming concepts for both sitting and standing. The questions were left relatively open-ended to allow the students to either describe in words the gestures/movements they would make, or to draw the path of the gesture, or a combination of both. These programming concepts include:

- If statement
- If/else statement
- For loop
- While loop
- Run program
- Undo previous action

After filling out the survey, the students got the opportunity to record their gestures into the computer using the Kinect. Our capture gesture program is written in the language Processing that allows the user to draw a gesture with their hand and the Kinect. The program recorded the coordinates of all of the user's joints, even though all of our data was drawn one-handed, and made note of which joints comprised the gesture path (typically just the right or left hand). The gesture coordinates were saved into a text file, and a screenshot of the gesture path was saved into a jpg.

3.2   Comparing Gestures

Gesture Capturing

The gesture capture program code was designed to track the full skeleton, because when the research was started, we were not sure if standing and using full body movements or sitting and only using hand gestures would be more popular with students. In fact, 56% of all students surveyed would rather sit and use hand gestures, so we limited our subsequent research to that. However, when we asked the students to design their own gestures for both sitting and standing to see what kinds of results we got, and even when the student was standing and had the ability to use full body movements, the majority of students still chose a two dimensional, one handed gesture.

Common Gestures Among Students

While the students were given relatively open-ended prompts to generate gesture shape information, there were six distinct gestures that appeared consistently throughout the surveys. The most popular gesture was a circle or loop gesture, with 162 gestures being drawn or described under the "for loop" or "while loop" options, either while standing or sitting. 27 students chose a spiral gesture, with almost half of them choosing this gesture for one of the loop options while standing. An additional 22 students chose a "thumbs up" gesture, with 15 of them choosing it to run the program while they were seated at the computer. Finally 18 students chose a wave gesture, while 29 students chose either the figure eight or infinity sign. The rest of the gestures described or drawn were less common or unique.

Therefore, we decided to limit our gesture vocabulary to the circle/loop, infinity sign, figure eight, and wave. The spiral is very similar to a loop, so for the sake of simplicity and distinct gestures, we decided not to focus on it. The code we are currently using for skeletal tracking does not track individual fingers, so the thumbs up gesture was also discarded.

3.3   Gesture Matching Algorithms

An important part of controlling the computer with gestures is being able to recognize when a gesture has been drawn. By far, the most popular gesture created by students was a circle motion for a loop gesture. So to refine the gesture matching algorithms, it was decided to concentrate on matching the loop gesture first.

Template Matching for Loop Gesture

We started with a simple template matching algorithm, where a two-dimensional array was set up with a perfect circle plotted onto it. Instead of drawing the circle as a 1x1 pixel line, we used a 5x5 pixel mask to give the user's gesture some wiggle room so as to not require an exact 1-to-1 match. An advantage of using template matching is that it does not matter where the gesture starts or stops, if it is drawn clockwise or counter-clockwise, or how fast it is drawn. Plotting the user's gesture against the template and measuring hit and miss percentage should give us a good idea of whether or not the user's gesture matches the template.

The number of coordinates varied greatly between gestures and users, so we normalized all gestures to have the same dataset size of 50 uniformly sampled coordinates from the original saved gesture. We discovered there was no discernable loss of matching precision when comparing 50 pared coordinates instead of up to 195 for the longest recorded gesture.

Minimum/Maximum Scaling Algorithm

To use a template matching algorithm, we needed to normalize our data so that it fits onto the template. Our first attempt was to take the gesture, find the minimum x and y values, and the maximum x and y values, and linearly scale the gesture in both directions independently to fit the template.

As the coordinates for the drawn gesture are being plotted onto the loop gesture template, the number of hits and misses are counted, and then using these, the percentage match is calculated. If the percentage is above a certain threshold, the drawn gesture should be recognized as a match to the template gesture.

Standard Deviation Scaling Algorithm

While the minimum/maximum scaling algorithm works relatively well, one problem is that it is designed to match a saved gesture, not a real-time gesture. The files we are using for comparison were started when the user was ready to start and finished when they completed the gesture, so the minimums and maximums are relatively accurate to create a bounding box for the gesture. However, when trying to compare a gesture from a real-time feed, there is no predefined start and stop, so we still need to be able to detect it. For example, if the user reaches up and scratches their head before drawing a loop, how can we detect that and ignore it as irrelevant data?

Our first implementation was to try using standard deviation in the hope that it would help eliminate the irrelevant "straggler" coordinates before and after the intended gesture. The thought was that we should be able to take something like the number "9" and be able to detect where the loop section starts and ends without including the leg of the number. To this end, the x_{mean} and y_{mean} were calculated separately to come up with both x_{stddev} and y_{stddev}. Using this mean and standard deviation, we defined a bounding box that was k_x standard deviations units wide and k_y standard deviations tall, and we used those values to be the floor and ceiling of x and y coordinates of the gesture respectively.

Sector Quantization

Sector quantization is simply taking a large set of data and condensing it down to a smaller, more easily understandable set of data. We follow the path of the gesture and note which sectors it appears in and in what order. We have the paths of clockwise and counter-clockwise loops, figure eights, and infinity symbols predefined in the gesture matching code, and we compare each user provided gesture path to it, and then accept the largest matching percentage as the most likely candidate.

The current version of the code is written so that the predefined paths circle around twice. Instead of just 2, 3, 6, 9, 8, 7, 4, 1, 2 (see Fig. 1A) for a clockwise loop, the path is doubled to 2, 3, 6, 9, 8, 7, 4, 1, 2, 3, 6, 9, 8, 7, 4, 1, 2 so sub-lists of the arrays can be utilized without having to wrap the array index back to zero. Because the predefined paths are almost twice as long as the actual path we are trying to match, either the match percentage must be doubled, or the threshold of matching must be halved. We chose to go with the latter; therefore, the matching percentages look lower, but they are being compared to a predefined gesture that is almost twice as long as the expected gesture. An ideal loop gesture would visit eight or nine sectors, depending whether it starts and ends in the same one, or stops just short of completing the path. Our predefined loop gesture visits 17 sectors, visiting each one twice, and the initial sector three times. Thus, a valid loop gesture match should have at least a 47% match percentage (8 sectors/17 possible locations).

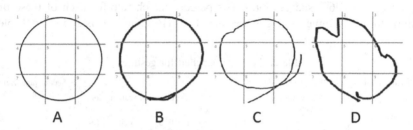

Fig. 1. Quantized gestures with sector grid; A. Ideal circle, and B–D. Three user gestures

4   Results and Analysis

4.1   Data General Analysis

Using the data collected in 435 gesture files, we have discovered that the average number of coordinates recorded for a gesture is around 94. This additional data was collected by giving young adults interested in programming or computer networking specific directions for what to draw ("draw a loop"), but not specifying where to start, which direction to go, or which hand to use. With the information in Table 1, we should be able to look at around 150 coordinates at a time to decide whether the person's movement contains a recognizable loop gesture. For the purposes of this paper, we will only be looking at the matching accuracy of the loop gesture.

Table 1. Data gathered

	Files	Total coordinates	Average coordinates	Minimum	Maximum
Figure eight	119	10973	92	42	195
Infinity	122	11953	97	39	185
Loop	129	10173	78	38	157
Spiral	40	5890	147	97	193
Wave	27	2138	79	53	131
All	437	41127	94	38	195

We tried a simple minimum/maximum scaling to linearly scale the gesture to a template. When the gesture was well-drawn and easily recognizable as a circle, this algorithm worked well (Fig. 1B). However, when the gesture had significant overlap (Fig. 1C), or was drawn shakily (Fig. 1D), the gestures did not match as well.

Next, to remove "straggler" points that were not part of the gesture itself, we tried a standard deviation scaling algorithm with many different values for sigma. Unfortunately, there was no one good value for sigma across all gestures, and the matching percentage rarely went above 50.

We are currently working with quantization, cutting down our gesture path to a three-by-three grid of nine total sectors. Requiring the gesture to match at least 47% of the path's sector order we expect to see for a loop gave us 124 matching files out of our test group of 129 (96% success rate). The percent match rate for each of these three algorithms for our sample three gestures (see Fig. 1B, C and D) is shown in Table 2.

Table 2. Percents matched for gestures

	Total coordinates	Template matching				Sector quantization
		Minimum/Maximum Scaling		Standard deviation scaling - all data		
		All data	Pared data	Sigma = 1.75	Sigma = 1.9	
B	68	91.18%	94.00%	12.50%	16.96%	58.82%
C	75	49.33%	48.00%	30.67%	6.67%	64.71%
D	112	33.04%	34.00%	11.48%	16.39%	52.94%

By requiring at least a 90% match for the template matching algorithms, and at least a 47% match on sector quantization to confirm that a drawn gesture matches what our program expects to see for a predefined gesture, template matching was not nearly as successful as sector quantization. When we break template matching into two sub-sections, none of the standard deviation scaling options give us a match, while only a very precise loop is matched using the minimum/maximum scaling. By using sector quantization, all three user drawn gestures are matched as a loop gesture.

While the minimum/maximum scaling algorithm gave better results on a consistent basis than the standard deviation scaling approach for template matching, we have discovered that sector quantization holds a lot of promise for future matching efforts.

5 Conclusion and Future Work

The goal of our research is to create and evaluate a visual and gesture-driven interface to teach programming to non-traditional programmers, typically school-age children. Based on surveys given to several groups of young students, we discovered that when given the option between sitting and using hand gestures, or standing and using full body movements, the majority of students choose a one-handed, two dimensional gesture, regardless of sitting or standing. This was counter-intuitive since we expected the students to use three-dimensional space and/or utilize more than their dominant hand.

Our current system has a limited gesture vocabulary that includes loops, figure eights, infinity signs, and waves. We would like to expand this in the future and allow students to create their own gestures for key programming constructs.

We have also implemented and evaluated several gesture matching algorithms. While template matching was not as successful as we were hoping, sector quantization holds a lot of promise and we are currently incorporating this into our application. When our gesture-based programming interface is completed, we would like to evaluate the effectiveness of this approach with additional groups of young prospective programmers.

References

1. Moskal, B., Lurie, D., Cooper, S.: Evaluating the effectiveness of a new instructional approach. SIGCSE Bull. 36(1), 75–79 (2004). https://doi.org/10.1145/1028174.971328
2. Hoste, L., Signer, B.: Criteria, challenges and opportunities for gesture programming languages. In: Proceedings of EGMI, pp. 22–29 (2014)
3. Lü, H., Li, Y.: Gesture coder: a tool for programming multi-touch gestures by demonstration. In: Proceedings of the SIGCHI Conference on Human Factors in Computing Systems (CHI 2012), pp. 2875–2884. ACM, New York (2012). http://dx.doi.org/10.1145/2207676.2208693
4. Kato, J.: Integrated visual representations for programming with real-world input and output. In: Proceedings of the Adjunct Publication of the 26th Annual ACM Symposium on User Interface Software and Technology (UIST 2013 Adjunct), pp. 57–60. ACM, New York (2013). https://doi.org/10.1145/2508468.2508476
5. Kato, J., Igarashi, T.: VisionSketch: integrated support for example-centric programming of image processing applications. In: Proceedings of Graphics Interface 2014 (GI 2014), Canadian Information Processing Society, Toronto, Ont., Canada, Canada, pp. 115–122 (2014)
6. Kavakli, M., Taylor, M., Trapeznikov, A.: Designing in virtual reality (DesIRe): a gesture-based interface. In: Proceedings of the 2nd International Conference on Digital Interactive Media in Entertainment and Arts (DIMEA 2007), pp. 131–136. ACM, New York (2007). http://dx.doi.org/10.1145/1306813.1306842
7. Dudek, G., Sattar, J., Xu, A.: A visual language for robot control and programming: a human-interface study. In: Proceedings of the International Conference on Robotics and Automation ICRA, Rome, Italy, April 2007

Design Research on Customized Online Education Platform Catering to Business Demands

Yajie Wang$^{(\boxtimes)}$, Xing Fang$^{(\boxtimes)}$, and Ying Luo$^{(\boxtimes)}$

Wuhan University of Technology, Wuhan, China
411349548@qq.com, 428037@qq.com, luoying1233@gmail.com

Abstract. Based on the search of the background information on the employment of Chinese college students, the analysis of the current status of online education and the investigation and studies of the different demands between schools education and companies, this paper analyzes the necessity of customized education and explores the unique strengths of customized online education catering to business demands. "Aoki Cloud" is chosen as the practice of design case to illustrate the design logic of customized online education platform catering to business demands. After that, the lo-fi main flowchart of the basic functions of "Aoki Cloud"(Student Version) is adopted to explain its design flow and the page turning procedures. The design strategy of "Aoki Cloud" as a customized online education platform catering to business demands is elaborated in the last part.

Keywords: Business demands · Customized education · Online education

1 Background

The Chinese College Graduates' Employment Annual Report (2017) (the annual blue book of employment) which is released by the third-party social investigation agency MyCOS in Beijing on June 12th shows that the number of college graduates has been continuously increasing in recent years. Comparing with the 7.7 million postgraduates in 2016, the number is expected to reach 7.95 million in 2017, with an increase of nearly 250,000 graduates. The employment rate of the 2016 college graduates six months postgraduate was 91.6%. Comparing with the percentage of 91.7% in 2015 and 92.1% in 2014, the proportion gradually decreased. In particular, the employment rate of undergraduates declines by 4% per year, while vocational graduates keep an employment rate at 91.5%, almost at the same level as in 2014. However, it is thought-provoking that according to the annual blue book of employment, the demand for professionals is 218 million people in the primary industry and 12.2 million people in the secondary industry, mainly in the areas of IT, microelectronics, automotive and environmental protection. The talent gap in the tertiary industry reaches 3.25 million people, so the total number of professional talents is still in short supply. In the face of the unbalanced situation of supply and demand of talents, graduates who have not been employed shortly after graduation can only re-employ their jobs through education and

© Springer International Publishing AG, part of Springer Nature 2018
C. Stephanidis (Ed.): HCII Posters 2018, CCIS 852, pp. 124–130, 2018.
https://doi.org/10.1007/978-3-319-92285-0_18

training. Therefore, many online and offline education and training institutions were created in the market. Although traditional offline education and training institutions are still the main focus of the education and training industry, the rapid development of online education has made itself an important part of the rising departments in the education industry (Fig. 1) .

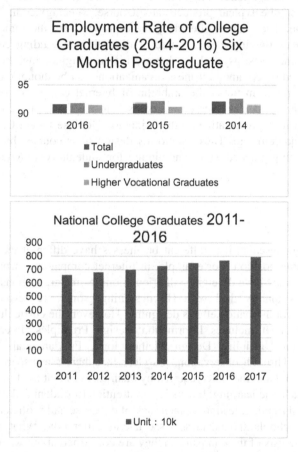

Fig. 1

2   Current Status

In recent years, online education has been developing rapidly and has attracted investment from various industries. The year 2013 was called as "the first year of online education in China" by education industry. According to statistics, there are more than 200 hot online education products designed for the purpose of student employment or improving students' professional abilities. The present paper will make a classification of online education products from the perspective of the industry nature of the products' developer.

Based on the industry nature of the products' developer, online education products can be divided into professional education institutions and common business institutions. MOOCs are the most representative ones of such products developed by professional educational institutions. In Chinese, "MOOCs" means Massive Open Online Courses, of which the typical products are iCourse, xuetangx.com, NetEase Open Course and so on. The courses offered by these products are the same as traditional university courses, covering a wide range of disciplines, including computers, economic management, tests, psychology, literary history, engineering, etc. This type of platform developed by common business organizations can be thought as an integrated online education platform under the umbrella of Internet companies of all sizes (including e-commerce). It can offer online courses in the form of recording and live broadcasting and its representative products include NetEase Cloud Class, Chuanke.com(Baidu), ke.qq.com, etc. These platforms design their courses by adopt leading platforms of learning practical skills and aiming for students' willingness to apply for jobs.

3 Research

It's found through research that different businesses have different technical requirements for the same position. For example, in Internet companies, visual designers of the same position may have different skill orientations. Some are responsible for banner designing, others mainly deal with H5 designing; some are responsible for UI designing, others for animation effects designing. However, the curriculum in school is different from that. It includes Information Design Principles, Interaction Design Principles, Design Discipline Design Methodology, Fundamentals of Interactive Technology, etc. Through observation, it's clear that there's a disparity between the curriculum in school and the skills required by businesses in that the former focus more on theory and academic learning. It pays lesser attention to students' skills teaching and intensive practical training, leading to their lack of expertise and proficiency in practice. This is because schools and businesses see talents differently. What matter to businesses are the interests of the company so they are concerned about whether the person is competent to the job responsibilities and acquires skills applicable to the company's business. While schools focus on "cultivation", that is to say, cultivating students' comprehensive abilities (both academic and practical abilities) and exploring students' potential to the best extent. Therefore, students need to improve their vocational skills in addition to learning school courses.

The education of vocational skills needs to be combined with the demands of the company. Vocational education combined with the needs of the company not only allows students to be more targeted and efficient in the learning process, but also can save the cost of pre-service training for employers and improve the economic efficiency. Therefore, customized education came into being. There are many kinds of customized education, including preschool education, basic education, exam-oriented education and so on. The purposes of these educations are to meet the different needs of different users. The present paper will discuss the customized online education platform catering to the business demands.

4 Practice of Design Research

"Aoki Cloud" is a customized online education platform catering to business demands and its service targets are companies who have specific requirements for the jobs they are providing. "Aoki Cloud" also customize courses for these companies. At present, 35 companies have settled in the platform. Through the platform, more than 80 kinds of professional customized services and courses are provided. These customized courses catering to business demands are learnt by students on the platform. These courses are in line with the company's operating strategies and there will be an assessment at the end of the courses. When students pass the tests of these courses, they will then have the skill qualifications to get the position of the company, as well as the opportunities to be employed. This kind of learning process and assessment mechanism will inspire students' learning motivation and speed up the employment process of those unemployed job-seekers. This clear teaching assessment model also solves the problems of recruiting talents faced by companies. At present, Huawei University and Alibaba Institute are both schools established by companies with certain strengths in China. The platform of "Aoki Cloud" will be able to establish a mechanism for training talents for small-sized and medium-sized companies with certain strengths, allowing more companies to develop their talents at relatively affordable costs and to save costs.

Figure 2 above shows the lo-fi main flowchart of the basic functions of "Aoki Cloud" (Student Version), in which the main function modules include "Course", "Company", "Message" and "Mine". There are two versions of "Aoki Cloud", namely Student Version and Enterprise Version. Students can view various customized education services developed by different companies on the homepage of "Course" module. These products of customized education service are all based on the company's own demands. If there are products of customized education service satisfying the student, then he can swipe right to add the product into his collection or he can apply for them directly. Only when the student's resume is examined by the company, can the student learn the products of the customized education service. This is also the protection of the company's own knowledge and achievements. Besides, this is also the guarantee of student's learning efficiency, ensuring that the student have the potential to get the position and guaranteeing fairness. Through the module of "Company", students can first select the company that they are interested in, and then look at some of the company's products of customized education service to continue learning. The module of "message" is mainly about the result of the resume delivery, that is, the feedback of qualification in course learning. The other part is the course list. The course list lists the courses that students have enrolled in. The courses are listed in time order. By clicking them, students can move forward to the live page of the course (as shown below) (Fig. 3).

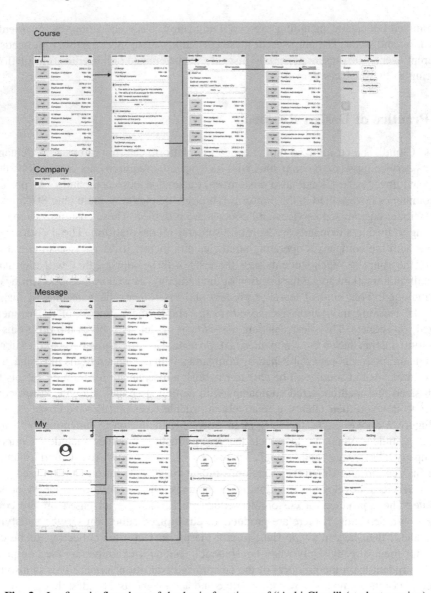

Fig. 2. Lo-fi main flowchart of the basic functions of "Aoki Cloud" (student version)

As shown in the Fig. 4, the design strategy of "Aoki Cloud" is that students can learn some featured courses catering to business demands on this platform. Enterprises can solve job recruitment issues on this platform while teachers can complete their teaching work through this education platform. Besides, schools can manage their own courses and assessment mechanisms in a better way through this platform while society can solve the problems of re-developing unemployed college graduates.

Fig. 3. Live page of "Aoki Cloud" online studying

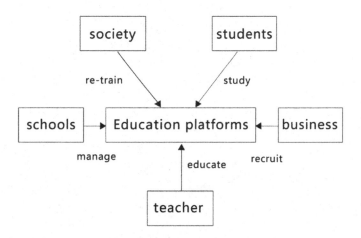

Fig. 4. Design strategies of "Aoki Cloud"

5 Conclusion

Unlike other vocational education online platforms, customized online education platforms catering to business demands permit direct participation of businesses. As proved by experiment, in the study of vocational courses, students can achieve higher efficiency while with specific targets than with subjective preference. Therefore, customized online education platforms realize the win-win situation between students and businesses while schools can be able to manage their curriculum and assessment mechanism with better effect and relieve the pressure of social employment.

References

1. Huangfu, Y.: Interaction design research of mobile internet vertical recruitment. Wuhan University of Technology (2017)
2. Zhang, G., Gao, Y.: Investigation and analysis of online information literacy education in agriculture and forestry universities based on users' demands. High. Agric. Educ. **2** (2014)
3. Liu, J.: Employment education strategies in the perspective of economic regional characteristics. Heilongjiang Res. High. Educ. **3** (2017)
4. Sheng, Y., Zhong, T.: Study on higher education training model based on mass customization. J. Zhejiang Gongshang Univ. **1**, 93–96 (2009)
5. Ulrich-Sundler: Industry 4.0. China Machine Press, Beijing (2014)
6. Kolko, Jon: Thoughts on Interaction Design. China Machine Press, Beijing (2012)
7. Dan, B.: Mass Customization - Building the Core Competence of the 21st Century. Science Press, Beijing (2004)

A Framework for Mobile Learning Technology Usability Testing

Ruth Wario[✉] and Bonface Ngari

University of the Free State, Bloemfontein, South Africa
wariord@ufs.ac.za

Abstract. Mobile devices have gained popularity among learners prompting educators to adopt mobile for teaching and learning. Despite high use of mobile devices amongst learners, there is no direct relationship between device ownership and its usability. Educators demand that a technological learning tool must be usable and effective in supporting the way learners learn, however, there are few tools to evaluate usability of mobile devices within the context of learning. Using focus groups and learners as participants, this study, developed a framework for usability testing. Suitable Human Interactive Elements (HIE's) were proposed by the focus group with their associated measurements to computer indexes. The framework was validated and used to evaluate iPad use in class at a tertiary institution. The results revealed that 88.1% of learners were satisfied learning with iPad with a correlation of .926 between learners' and lecturers usability testing.

Keywords: Mobile devices · Teaching and learning · Usability

1 Introduction

The ease of product or system use in the context of the user is determined by usability testing (Conyer 1995). The concept of usability testing is applied in human computer interaction (HCI) research, and has provided guidelines and principles of software designs especially user interfaces (Shneiderman 1992; Mayhew 1992; Nielsen and Lavy 1994). While good software user interface ensures high degree of acceptability, it is not a substitute for usability testing (Granic and Cukusic 2011). Usability is defined as the degree of ease as well as effectiveness of use (Shackel 1984) and usability testing is the evaluation of a product to determine whether it achieves the intended use satisfactorily in an effective and efficient manner (Rubin and Chisnell 2008).

According to Conyer (1995) there are two approaches of usability evaluation, namely user testing and usability testing. User testing involves the analysis of user behavior when using the product while usability testing is evaluation of the product to establish whether it meets the expected results satisfactorily when performing a task.

This study combines usability and user competence testing within the context mobile learning. The study is guided by the ability of user to perform a learning task by empirically measuring the human interaction elements of the product or prototype results (McLaughlin 2003) in relation to modified Bloom's taxonomical learning levels.

© Springer International Publishing AG, part of Springer Nature 2018
C. Stephanidis (Ed.): HCII Posters 2018, CCIS 852, pp. 131–136, 2018.
https://doi.org/10.1007/978-3-319-92285-0_19

It involves monitoring each interaction between device and user during a learning activity. Information is gathered through observation, user response, and measurement of user performance.

Mobile technology has been accepted and adopted quickly by learners, showing high ownership and preference. A longitudinal data survey indicates that despite high use of this device, the use in learning is not as widespread as the devices themselves (Dahlstrom and Bichsel 2014). Less than 50% of learners do classwork daily from mobile devices at home (Wright 2013), which is relatively small compared to percentage ownership. This indicates that device ownership is not a direct relationship to proficiency or usability especially in learning (Chen et al. 2015). Accordingly, usability testing methodology for e-learning or mobile learning systems do not exist (Granic and Cukusic 2011) and there is a need for research and empirical evaluation for mobile learning products. This study offers such an evaluation and contributed by combining Hans et al. (2008) usability evaluation model with educational evaluation (Nielsen 1993) by means of two sets of criteria, namely learning with software heuristics (Squires and Preece 1996) and pedagogical dimensions (Leslie 2016). It is expected that the contribution with its general findings will facilitate the understanding on how to evaluate and improve the usability testing of education technologies, especially mobile learning, before adoption.

2 Literature Review

This study reviewed literature on usability testing in general, and included ergonomics and pedagogical learning, as well as an assessment of previous research. After an extensive review, a conceptual model was built by combining elements of the Jigsaw model by Squires and Preece (1996); Kim and Han (2008) model, and a modified Bloom's taxonomy model through a logical decomposition framework of various elements. These models were found suitable for consideration in this study.

3 Aim of the Research

The aim of this study was to provide an innovative and systematic framework for mobile learning technologies usability testing.

4 Conceptual Framework of the Study

Previous models of usability evaluation were used to formulate the conceptual framework, which was used to develop the current usability-testing model. The conceptual model has three stages:

Stage 1: Classify usability dimensions
Informed by human interaction elements, the HIE was classified into design features of both hardware and software and user response features, which are impressive features that are purely subjective.

Stage 2: Develop usability measures of learning
Learner's specific learning tasks (Squires and Preece 1996) are identified and mapped onto the features of HIE then classified according to Bloom's taxonomy (cognitive, affective or psychomotor). The measures are leveled against learning outcomes based on the way operational tasks integrate to meet the learners' needs (Squires and Preece 1996).

Stage 3: Build usability model
The elements that show strong relationships between observation and perception of the learner are selected to construct the model.

5 Methodology

This study used a focus group method to identify, group and define the HIEs for the model. The researchers prepared the guidelines and schedule for the focus groups chosen from a tertiary institution. During the discussions, the researchers moderated the proceedings while each group appointed a rapporteur. The focus group was composed of 10 purposefully selected lecturers (5 from computer science and 5 from education) and 15 learners (10 from computer science and 5 from education). The sample size was the recommended number of participants in a focus group, which is between four to ten (MacIntosh 1993; Goss and Leinbach 1996; Kitzinger 1995), and the discussion sessions lasted between one to two hours (Powell and Single 1996).

6 Procedure

This study was granted ethical clearance and a go ahead by the University management where it was conducted. No participant was forced to participate in the study.

The researchers recruited the focus group participants and called for plenary sessions for briefing. Five groups were formed; each group had 2 lecturers and 5 learners. The group members were randomly selected. There were two sessions, the first was for brainstorming and the second was for defining HIE measures. Using the HIE's measures, a scorecard was developed to aid the usability evaluator to collect data.

The study begun by defining the usability dimensions through logical selection criteria, then usability measures for the model was developed. The model was tested in an iPad project, which was used for teaching in an extended program with 98 learners. The learners were each given an iPad, which they used for reading, referring and access to internet. Data were collected using a questionnaire that was given to the learners. Five computer science lecturers evaluated the usability of iPad using a score card. Learners were given a questionnaire to assess their experiences about iPad as a learning tool. The two results were computed and correlated.

7 Focus Group Activities

The first session required the group to identify suitable dimensions for usability testing. Researchers provided a list of dimensions from various models to choose from, but the groups were allowed to suggest new dimensions. The selection criteria were provided, as indicated in Fig. 1. After a break, a plenary session was called and each group's rapporteur presented their list of dimensions. The plenary agreed on the final list of dimensions to be used in the model.

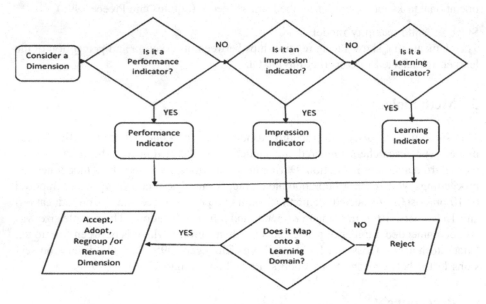

Fig. 1. A logical flow method for selecting usability dimensions

In the second session, each group was required to come up with HIEs for each dimension and also to suggest a measure for it. All reports were collected from the rapporteurs and a smaller group of lecturers who participated, evaluated and compiled the final elements of the model and measures for all HIE's.

The criteria for evaluating the dimensions is shown in Fig. 1. The dimensions were categorized as performance, impression or learning indicator and mapped onto the Bloom's taxonomical order. The mapping was an assessment to check if the dimension promoted any of the learning levels as classified by Bloom. If the dimension did not fit in any of the domains then it was rejected and if accepted, the dimension could be grouped together and renamed.

The final model of usability dimensions included Application Proactivity, Consistency, Memorability, Interactivity, Connectivity, Efficiency and Satisfaction.

8 Results and Interpretation

In this study, 64.8% of the participants were male and 35.2% were female. The average age was 20 years. The usability evaluations showed that most of the learners' (88.1%) were satisfied with iPad as a learning tool, with 59.5% strongly agreeing, 28.6% just agreeing, 2.4% neutral and 4.8% disagreeing. Table 1 shows the distribution of response to questions. From the results it is clear that the majority of learners were satisfied and had a good learning experience, however, there were a few who were not satisfied.

Table 1. Table a summary of learners' response to iPad usability

	Strongly agree (%)	Agree (%)	Neutral (%)	Disagree (%)	Strongly disagree (%)
Ease of use	45.2	38.1	11.9	4.8	0
Completeness of work	26.2	57.1	9.5	2.4	4.8
Comfortability	66.6	26.2	2.4	4.0	0
Ease to learn	47.6	40.5	7.1	4.8	0
Error recoverability	35.7	42.9	14.3	4.7	2.4
Impression	61.9	23.8	9.3	5.0	0
Connectivity	59.5	28.6	2.4	4.7	4.8
Interactivity	45.1	43.6	6.5	4.8	0

9 Conclusion

This study proposed a usability testing for mobile learning technologies comprising a collective set of human interactive elements' measures associated with mobile technology and learning. The results showed that there was a high correlation between evaluations of learners and experts (lecturers) and the overall mobile learning was perceived to satisfy learners.

References

Chen, B., Seilhamer, R., Bennett, L., Bauer, S.: Students' mobile practices in higher education: a multi-year study. EDUCAUSE Rev. (2015)

Conyer, M.: User and usability testing – how it should be undertaken? Aust. J. Educ. Technol. **11** (2), 38–51 (1995)

Dahlstrom, E., Bichsel, J.: ECAR Study of Undergraduate Students. EDUCAUSE Center for Analysis and Research (2014)

Goss, J., Leinbach, T.: Focus groups as alternative research practice **28**(2), 115–123 (1996)

Granić, A., Ćukušić, M.: Usability testing and expert inspections complemented by educational evaluation: a case study of an e-learning platform. Educ. Technol. Soc. **14**(2), 107–123 (2011)

Han, S., Yun, M., Kim, J., Kwahk, J.: Evaluation of product usability: development and validation of usability dimensions and design elements based on empirical models. Int. J. Ind. Ergon. **26**(4), 477–488 (2000)

Kim, J., Han, S.: A methodology for developing a usability index of consumer electronic products. Int. J. Ind. Ergon. **38**, 333–345 (2008)

Kitzinger, J. Introducing focus groups. Br. Med. J. **311**, 299–302 (1995)

Kreitzer, A., Madaus, G.: Empirical investigations of the hierarchical structure of the taxonomy. In: Anderson, L.W. (ed.) Bloom's Taxonomy: A Forty-Year Perspective. Ninety-Third Yearbook of the National Society for the Study of Education, p. 24. University of Chicago Press, Chicago (1994)

Leslie, O.: The second principle. Three domains of learning – Cognitive, affective, psychomotor (2016). http://www.thesecondprinciple.com/instructional-design/threedomainsoflearning/. Accessed 22 June 2017

MacIntosh, J.: Focus groups in distance nursing education. J. Adv. Nurs. **18**(12), 1981–1985 (1993)

Mayhew, D.: Principals and Guidelines in Software User Interface Design. Prentice-hall, Englewood Cliffs (1992)

McLaughlin, R.: Redesigning the crash cart: usability testing improves one facility's medication drawers. Am. J. Nurs. **103**(4), 64A–64F (2003)

Nielsen, J.: Usability Engineering. AP Professional, New York (1993)

Nielsen, J., Lavy, J.: Measuring usability: preference vs. performance. Commun. ACM **37**(4) (1994)

Powell, R., Single, H.: Focus groups. Int. J. Qual. Health Care **8**(5), 499–504 (1996)

Rubin, J., Chisnell, D.: Handbook of Usability Testing: How to Plan, Design and Conduct Effective Tests, 2nd edn. Wiley, Indianapolis (2008)

Shackel, B.: The concept of usability. In: Bennet, J.C. (ed.) Visual Display Terminals, pp. 45–87. Prentice-Hall, Englewood Cliffs (1984)

Shneiderman, B.: Designing the user interface: strategies for elective human computer interaction. AddisonWesley, Reading (1992)

Squires, D.: Preece, J. Usability and learning: evaluating the potential of educational software. Comput. Educ. **27**(1), 15–22 (1996)

Wright, E.: EDU Survey: How are University students, Faculty and administrators using technology? (2013). https://www.box.com/blog/edu-survey-how-are-university-students-faculty-and-administrators-using-technology/. Accessed 17 Apr 2017

Egocentric Distance Perception Control for Direct Manipulation Interaction on HMD Platform

Ungyeon Yang[1]([⊠]), Nam-Gyu Kim[2], and Ki-Hong Kim[1]

[1] VR & AR Technology Reserch Group,
Electronics and Telecommunications Research Institute (ETRI), Daejeon, Korea
uyyang@etri.re.kr
[2] Dong-Eui University, Busan, Korea

Abstract. At present, the simulation technique of sensory stimulation of virtual reality technology has limitations to reproduce imperfectly the sensory feedback learned while human grows. Therefore, the inconsistency of the sensory feedback is obstructing the popularization of the virtual reality service. This study deals with visual distance perception or sensory inconsistency experienced by users when using HMD. In addition, the feature of interaction that we study in this study is to restore objects in real space to virtual space and to manipulate the connected object in real time by hand. We carried out near-body-space interaction experiments to analyze the performance characteristics of subjects with various environments consisting of HMD-oriented hardware and a software focused on the 3D game engine, which is representing the VR market. We are investigating algorithms that can minimize the error of matching task in a virtual environment. We found the world scale parameter in terms of geometric field of view as a significant control factor. We report the results of applying the current research results to an indoor VR theme park application. The user can experience the visual feedback of the precisely associated virtual space while manipulating the physical object and receiving simultaneously the haptic feedback that interacts with other objects in the real space.

Keywords: Virtual reality · Head mounted display · Distance perception

1 Introduction

Virtual reality technology aims at delivering experience scenarios of contents to users' experiences naturally. In order to achieve the purpose, we study interface technologies that realize virtual space simulation and multisensory feedback at a high level of realism. The human sensory feedback process is naturally acquired as it grows. However, the sensory quality level of the HMD, which currently represents the VR interface technology, does not reproduce equally the feedback generated in the human visual sense organization. Thus, primarily, the visual satisfaction and the immersion feeling for the content are reduced. A secondary phenomenon is the induction of cognitive outcomes that differ from the actual situation, resulting in distortion and performance degradation of the work results and causing a negative after-effect during use (e.g. dizziness) or after use (e.g. a headache) have.

C. Stephanidis (Ed.): HCII Posters 2018, CCIS 852, pp. 137–142, 2018.
https://doi.org/10.1007/978-3-319-92285-0_20

This study has a goal to solve the real - virtual space discrepancy problem that occurs when HMD is used. Specifically, when the user directly manipulates the object in the near-body space, it can support the accurate interaction while recognizing the same distance perception as the real space. In order to achieve the goal, we quantitatively measure behavioral characteristics of various user groups according to VR system environmental conditions when we reproduce general interaction that can be experienced in real space in virtual space. Then, we develop an algorithm that corrects visualization related parameters of virtual reality contents to reduce the error so that the given task can be successfully performed in the experiment.

Generally, when working on objects located at over distance of more about 1–2 m from the user, there is no physical direct interaction phenomenon (e.g. contact and collision) due to user's actions. In this case, it is important to express the relative interaction results between virtual objects generated in the environment outside the user, rather than considering the user-oriented sensory perception such as proprioception by body motion. However, since our research targets the direct manipulation of near-body space, we developed a technology to control the virtual reality contents so that the user's sense of behavior and sensory stimuli formed in the real space are the same in virtual space.

2 Related Works

Human depth perception is determined by the interaction of multiple factors. One of the factors that recognize the depth of 3D space by the physiological structure of visual organs is disparity and convergence by binocular vision. In addition, factors that perceive depth from experience with a single eye are the focus, perspective, occlusion, lighting & shading, color intensity & contrast, and relative movement. Since the above factors are combined in the HMD experience environment, the interaction in the virtual space can be performed similarly to the real space only if the user is aware of the accurate depth/space.

We know that users get different experiences of distance from reality space in virtual space through past research cases [1–6] and many cases of HMD based virtual reality contents that are spread to the market. Renner et al. [7] suggested a solution to the problem that the subjectively perceived distance in the virtual environment becomes shorter than the real environment; they have reported that a rich virtual environment representation, including possible accurate disparity and high-quality graphic images, careful virtual camera setup, and floor textures to help sense distance, helps improve user sense of distance. Siegel [8] pointed out that the validity of the training or research performed in the virtual space can be questioned because of the tendency of the distance perception to be underestimated in the virtual reality space. To correct the underestimated distance, Siegel proposed a universal interaction task through interaction experiment. Altenhoff [9] also pointed out that the closer the distance is, the higher the degree of underestimation of distance is, and it is reported that it can be overcome by correction. Ziemer et al. [10] studied the relationship between the act of measuring distance perception in real and virtual environments and the effect of distance perception in other environments. Yang et al. [11] propose a technology that naturally connects the stereo 3D distance perception of reality and virtual space by controlling the hardware design parameters and propose a new EGD structure for direct interaction in near-body-space.

3   Egocentric Perception and Interaction in Near-Body Space

In this study, as a representative example in which a user interacts directly in a free space, we selected the situation where the key is inserted into the hole as shown in Fig. 1 among service scenarios of HMD based indoor experience type first-person-shooting (FPS) contents.

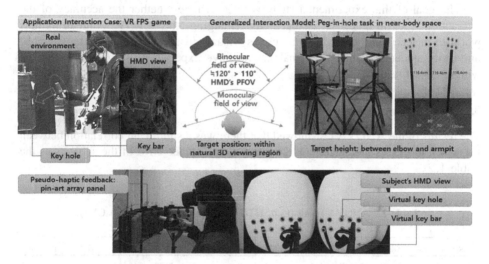

Fig. 1. Experiment design: Generalizing near-body space interaction in a real environment to peg-in-hole (target matching) task in a virtual environment with haptic feedback.

3.1   Experiment Design

To provide the same spatial feeling as the real space, the IPD (Inter-Pupil Distance) control part of the HMD hardware is changed to correspond to the measured IPD of the subject. First, the virtual camera of the real-time 3D rendering engine sets the default value of the hardware and generates the virtual space image reflecting the position of the IPD and the viewpoint of the subject. We also investigated the relationship between the GFOV (Geometric Field Of View), which is a software control element of HMD driving, and the distance perception in the near-body space interaction.

In order to compensate for the position discrepancy between the actual three-dimensional position space and the virtual space constituted by the tracking system, all the objects to be manipulated are placed in a constant tracking space by attaching tracking sensors to all mutual objects. As in the center part of Fig. 1, a number of keyholes, which are the target points, are placed within the field of view range of about 110° at a distance of 120 cm. The height of the keyhole was selected to be 116.4 cm, which is the height between the elbow and the armpit of an adult in the early 20 s, referring to the National Physical Size Database (Size Korea; sizekorea.kr) of the National Statistical Office. A pin art array device providing pseudo-haptic feedback was placed in order to provide a realistic feel to the subject's peg-in-hole task on the three-dimensional space that varies depending on various experimental conditions. Such as the bottom of Fig. 1, the subject is asked to perform a task of correctly pegging the bar-shaped key in a number of holes presented in an environment wearing an HMD. The Oculus Rift CV1 and three IR camera sensors were used to construct the experimental environment. And, the images of the experiment contents were changed to 98%, 100%, and 102% by controlling the world-to-meters parameters using the version 4.15 of UnrealEngine.

The goal of this experimental study is to determine whether the accuracy of the interaction (peg-in-hole) is changed by changing the GFOV (UnrealEngine's world-to-meters) and changing the user's visual distance. The subjects were 10 university students (7 male, 3 female), who have experience using HMD with the within-subject test.

3.2   Results and Discussions

The results of the ANOVA test showed that there was a significant correlation between the world-to-meters parameter and the interaction distance error of the subjects as the Table 1.

Table 1. ANOVA result (Left: HTC VIVE, Right: Oculus Rift CV1)

Source	DF	Adj SS	Adj MS	F-Value	P-Value	Source	DF	Adj SS	Adj MS	F-Value	P-Value
W2M	2	40.08	20.038	4.57	0.014	W2M	2	71.24	35.622	4.06	0.022
Error	69	302.64	4.386			Error	69	605.96	8.782		
Total	71	342.71				Total	71	677.20			

In order to apply the significance of the ANOVA analysis results to the improvement of interaction performance, regression analysis of distance error and world-to-meters parameter was performed and, although it is somewhat low fit(R^2), the regression line can be obtained as shown in the following Fig. 2.

When performing direct manipulation interactions within the near-body space range in the HMD environment, the value of world-to-meters was inversely calculated to make the distance error zero. The results are about 106.8 for HTC VIVE, and about 107.5 for Oculus Rift CV1. Therefore, it can be seen that it is helpful to the over-map world-to-meters parameter by about 7% for UnrealEngine. As shown in Fig. 3, the user interaction performance was improved by 83% in the short distance (40–60 cm) through 6 verification experiments by applying the corresponding correction values.

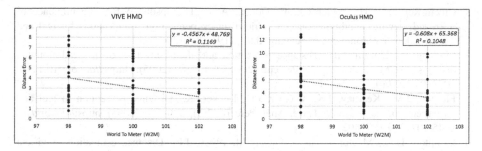

Fig. 2. Regression analysis between distance error and world-to-meters parameter

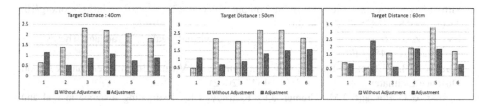

Fig. 3. Comparison of interaction distance error before and after calibration

4 Conclusions and Future Works

We propose a method to control the virtual camera parameters of the 3D engine so that it can help precise distance sense and perform accurate interaction when a user in a virtual space wearing an HMD manipulates a virtual object associated with real space. We propose a method of over mapping the world-to-meters parameter of the Unreal-lEngine, which is similar to the GFOV effect, to about 107% in order to compensate for the erroneous perception of near-body space. In addition, we observe that more than 80% of users increase the interaction accuracy. However, this study is a result of initial research on a limited scale group of subjects and hardware and software. Therefore, it needs to be expanded to research on various control elements for various HMD, tracking system and 3D visualization engine in the future.

Acknowledgement. This work was supported by Institute for Information & communications Technology Promotion(IITP) grant funded by the Korea government(MSIT) (R0118-16-1007, Immersive content experience enabling multi-user interaction based on high-speed and precise tracking in an indoor VR space).

References

1. Li, B.: Distance Perception in Virtual Environment through Head-mounted Displays. Open Access Dissertation, Michigan Technological University (2017)
2. Willemsen, P., Gooch, A.A., Thompson, W.B., Creem-Regehr, S.H.: Effects of stereo viewing conditions on distance perception in virtual environments. Presence Teleoperators Virtual Environ. **17**(1), 91–101 (2008)

3. Creem-Regehr, S.H., Willemsen, P., Gooch, A.A., Thompson, W.B.: The influence of restricted viewing conditions on egocentric distance perception: implications for real and virtual indoor environments. Perception **34**(2), 191–204 (2005)
4. Messing, R., Durgin, F.H.: Distance perception and the visual horizon in head-mounted displays. ACM Trans. Appl. Percept. **2**(3), 234–250 (2005). https://doi.org/10.1145/1077399.1077403
5. Plumert, J.M., Kearney, J.K., Cremer, J.F., Recker, K.: Distance perception in real and virtual environments. ACM Trans. Appl. Percept. **2**(3), 216–233 (2005). https://doi.org/10.1145/1077399.1077402
6. Lampton, D.R., McDonald, D.P., Singer, M., Bliss, J.P.: Distance estimation in virtual environments. In: Proceedings of the Human Factors and Ergonomics Society Annual Meeting, vol, 39, issue 20, pp. 1268–1272 (1995)
7. Renner, R.S., Velichkovsky, B.M., Helmert, J.R.: The perception of egocentric distances in virtual environments - a review. ACM Comput. Surv. **46**(2), 40 (2013). https://doi.org/10.1145/2543581.2543590. Article 23
8. Siegel, Z.D.: Improving distance perception in virtual reality. Graduate Theses and Dissertations. 14509 (2015)
9. Altenhoff, B.: "Effects of Interaction with an Immersive Virtual Environment on Near-field Distance Estimates". All Theses. Paper 1342 (2012)
10. Ziemer, C.J., Plumert, J.M., Cremer, J.F., Kearney, J.K.: Estimating distance in real and virtual environments: does order make a difference? Attention Percept. Psychophysics **71**(5), 1095–1106 (2009). https://doi.org/10.3758/APP.71.5.1096
11. Yang, U., Kim, N.-G., Kim, K.-H.: Augmented system for immersive 3D expansion and interaction. ETRI J. **38**, 149–158 (2016). https://doi.org/10.4218/etrij.16.0115.0750

Media and Cognition Course: How to Cultivate Technical Leaders in Artificial Intelligence

Yi Yang[✉] and Jiasong Sun

Tsinghua National Laboratory for Information Science and Technology,
Department of Electronic Engineering, Tsinghua University, Beijing, People's Republic of China
{yangyy,sunjiasong}@mail.tsinghua.edu.cn

Abstract. Artificial Intelligence technologies has been applied in each aspect of daily work and life and has dramatically changed the landscape of industry. The artificial intelligence and related fields have provided a large number of occupations. How to cultivate leaders and experts in artificial intelligence is one of the important issues in the high-education field. It is very significant for our EECS students to learn the developing histories and the state-of-the-art methods of artificial intelligence, such as Deep Neural Networks and Convolutional Neural Networks. In our Media and Cognition Course, students would be asked to propose and complete their own projects with machine learning and deep learning algorithms in the field of impressive artificial intelligence applications, such as speech recognition, image recognition and natural language processing. And they would have a new perspective that media signal processing/recognition solutions are all originated from the principles of human's perception/understanding. Both the advanced scientific knowledge and the practical technical expertise are involved in our class to improve students' performance by enriching their inside knowledge structures. At the end of course, the students showed their original and innovative outcomes, which expressed that they have the abilities to solve specific intelligent tasks in the given time/space structures. Our practice shows that the Media and Cognition Course can increase most of the students' interest in artificial intelligence. Some of students further researched on how to build smarter decision and prediction methods based on the spatio-temporal information and the cognition of human individuals/groups.

Keywords: Artificial intelligence · Cultivate leaders · High-education
Media and cognition course · Human's perception and understanding

1 Introduction

Artificial intelligence has created millions of jobs worldwide [1–5]. All the EECS students need some understanding of artificial intelligence and its applications. Our experience shows that students' intrinsic interest is one of the biggest drivers of learning. How to motivate students in lower grades with less professional background knowledge to focus on emerging cross-discipline directions (such as artificial intelligence, perceptual computing, and media cognition) is one of the important considerations in our media and cognition curriculum design. We build several experimental platforms involving multiple sensing and cognitive computing to provide more background knowledge and development environment for human cognition and media expression, which enable students to initially touch with the frontier of artificial intelligence technologies. The technical hotspots and challenges are emphasized in the class to push students achieve a variety of artificial intelligence technologies and solutions. The traditional verification platforms adopt goal-oriented or task-oriented setting, which lacks the cultivation faced to leaders and talents. In addition, there is a contradiction between the constantly expanding amount of knowledge in AI (Artificial Intelligence) field and the limited class hours.

There are several important teaching issues that need to be solved. One is how to utilize the advanced research achievements from the international Top-level Universities and our department to form our new education methods on intellect sense and machine learning. Another is how to establish an exploratory artificial intelligence technology teaching method, which includes interdisciplinary, multi-faceted and comprehensive learning and practice section. Meanwhile, it is able to improve the teaching effect and broaden the knowledge level while maintaining the same time of course and realizing the goal of training future leaders and talents.

This paper is organized as follows. In Sect. 2, the structure and content of the platforms are introduced in detail, following by the section introducing the research projects that students independently proposed and completed. This paper is concluded and the next step plan is given in Sect. 4.

2   Structure and Content of Platforms

In 2017, The media and cognition course include several primary parts: Realsense-based Human Computer Interaction platform, Multilingual text recognition platform and Face recognition platform.

2.1   RealSense-Based Human-Computer Interaction Platform

Intel RealSense platform [1] gives computing devices the same visual and audio capabilities as humans. RealSense can interact with users more naturally. RealSense is able to collaborate more intelligently with humans to create a symbiosis system of "machines plus people". Realsense has many specific application scenarios, such as 3D scanning, immersive collaboration, game entertainment, home improvement, smart robots and so on. The Realsense camera is a 3D camera that uses infrared imaging to provide depth information besides its another ordinary color camera.

To make it easier for developers to take advantage of highly integrated cameras, Realsense also offers a SDK that includes pre-developed computer vision algorithms to support the natural interaction of applications. The SDK supports multiple programming languages such as C++, C#, JavaScript, Java, Unity and more. Figure 1 shows the software architecture of the entire SDK.

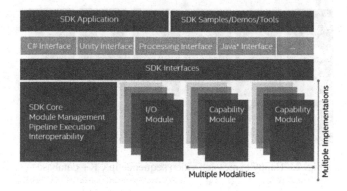

Fig. 1. The structure of Intel Realsense SDK.

2.2 Multilingual Text Recognition Platform

With the development of science and technology and the constant need of human society, extracting and recognizing Multilingual subtitles in video has become a real problem [2, 3]. Different from the regular character recognition of pure document images, the confusing background, indefinite text position, and various colors in the images have caused certain difficulties for text extraction and recognition. In order to correctly identify the text in the video image, the position of the text in the image must first be found, followed by the preprocessing of the size and color of the cut text line and finally the recognition of the text line.

2.3 Face Recognition Platform

Facial expression is an important feature to express human emotions. Research on face expression recognition is of great significance for computer understanding of human emotions. Face recognition has been a hot topic in the artificial intelligence and computer vision field. The specific tasks of our face recognition are as follows: face recognition is performed on one input face picture and the recognition result is one of the eight predefined expressions which include: Angry, Disgust, Fear, Sadness, Happy, Surprise, Contempt, Neutral.

We use some open academic datasets for facial expression recognition: CK+ datasets, JAFFE datasets, TFEID, and KDEF [4–7]. CK+ and TFEID contain eight kinds of facial expressions, and JAFFE and KDEF contain seven types of facial expressions (not including "flick" expressions). For example, the CK+ database shown in Fig. 2 includes 118 subjects, a total of 327 segments of expression video sequences, including 45 expressions of angry expression, 59 expressions of disgusting expression, 69 expressions of happy expression, 25 expressions of fear expression, 28 sadness, and 93 expressions of surprise expression. Emotion expression 18 segments.

Fig. 2. Happy expression video sequence in CK+ database

3   Proposed and Completed Projects by Students

3.1   Real-Time Three-Dimensional Reconstruction System Based on RGBD Camera

With the rapid development of computer hardware, three-dimensional reconstruction technology has attracted more and more attention. The basic principle of the 3D reconstruction process is to recover the 3D shape of the object or scene using the camera's picture in each pose. Based on the Realsense platform, the student research team independently developed and implemented two systems: The first system is to build a simple RGBD reconstruction system. It contains basic functions and real-time functions. However, it is limited to hardware problems and cannot be viewed in real-time, so this version is suitable for rebuilding by an offline data set. The scan program is started first to scan and save a series of RGB images and depth maps with an RGBD camera. The second system is to solve the problem of real-time, modify the best system ORB-SLAM2 in the current slam field [8], which proposes a robot positioning system based on sparse features for navigation and positioning. Besides this theory, students added the function of stitching the dense point cloud and reading the real-time equipment. Finally, it can achieve a robust reconstruction effect.

The whole system has two parts: the front end and the back end. The front end is also called the visual odometer. The role is to generate RGBD image point cloud and use the PNP algorithm to estimate the rigid body transformation matrix between two adjacent frames, to obtain the current This frame is relative to the pose of the previous frame. This frame is added to the keyframe when this pose transformation satisfies the implementation of the set parameters. The key frame is the bridge connecting the front end and the back end. In the real-time system version, the key frame will be regularly optimized, and the data set version will be optimized after all the key frames are obtained, and then the optimized camera bit will be taken out. At the end, all the point clouds are stitched together. The room shot based on this 3D reconstruction techniques are shown in Fig. 3.

Fig. 3. Room shot based on 3D reconstruction techniques proposed by students.

3.2   Printed-English Datasets Text Recognition in Video

Traditional segmented recognition methods can achieve better results for clear printed block text images (such as Chinese and Korean) based on higher image quality and correct character segmentation. If the image quality of the video and the shooting scene is not good enough, or deal with some languages with special writing rules (such as Arabic, the letters of each word in the sentence are closely linked, and the form is very different from the existence alone), it is extremely difficult to divide all the letters in the text line and the different forms of the single letter will greatly affect the recognition accuracy. We propose a no-segmentation method, which refers to the method of processing entire characters without dividing each individual character. Compared with the method of segmentation, this method is more adaptable on text recognition in video than segmented recognition. We established a Tensorflow-based RNN network for text line data set identification. There are 4 hidden layers in the network and the number of node units is 100, 100, 200, 200 respectively. The dataset was a printed English dataset we collected with higher image quality.

The first step is dataset preprocessing, which unifies the image width to 48, and then sends the image and truth information to the network for training. We used about 6,000 samples, 80% of which were train sets and the rest were test sets. The test accuracy was about 91.2%. All the 18,000 samples were used for the second time, of which 80% were used as test sets and the others were test sets. The test accuracy rate was about 96.1%. The results implied that the size of dataset has a positive correlation with the recognition accuracy.

3.3   Face Recognition Based on Color Recognition and Contour Detection

To the web databases and self-collected databases, the biggest problem is that the face occupies a small proportion of the whole face and the background is not uniform. Therefore, we need to design face detection algorithm for the feature extraction will have high interference. We deal with the black-and-white and color images separately. The color image is directly used for color recognition. A red component matrix is extracted and a pixel larger than a certain threshold is judged. The largest connected component is extracted to obtain a face. For black-and-white images, contour detection is performed because there is no significant difference in the gray-scale distribution between the background and the face. For the resulting profile, the noise is filtered first, then the non-dense contours (mainly the clothes and the background profile) are filtered out and the dense profile distribution is the facial features to finally obtain the faces.

It was found in the experiment that if the extracted features were directly classified by SVM, the effect was not very good. So, we performed non-linear processing after extracting features and mapped the features into higher-dimensional vector spaces, making it easy to classify using linear classifiers. We first divide the Gabor filter's output into small blocks, and each block takes the sum of squares of the gray value and re-opens the root number to obtain a compression of the feature. This kind of compression can retain much of the original information.

We reduce the amount of data and multiplied the compressed information with a random matrix to extend the data size of the feature by a factor of ten, where each element is a linear combination of the original features. The amplified features were combined with the original features to form a large feature that serves as the input to the final SVM classifier. Experiments show that this nonlinear processing greatly improves the SVM classification effect.

4   Conclusions and Future Works

Media and Cognition course covers various areas, such as human-computer interaction, media information processing, and virtual reality. The mission of artificial intelligence is to serve and integrate into human's society. To realize this goal, the direct thought is to make machine learn and interact by imitating humans.

We have explored and formed an artificial intelligence teaching method based on our cognitive interaction platform in our class to realize the design of composite multi-class cross-cutting technologies. It can achieve the purpose of improving teaching effectiveness and broadening the knowledge level of students within a limited teaching time, alleviate the contradiction between expansion of knowledge and limited time, and gradually realize the goal of training future leaders in the field of intelligent perception, and play an important role in talent cultivation. The student's on-site and after-class feedback shows that our teaching method has improved the students' willingness and ability to innovate to a certain extent and mobilized their intrinsic research interests.

Acknowledgements. Thanks to Tsinghua University Laboratory Innovation Funding.

References

1. Realsense overview. https://www.intel.com/content/www/us/en/architecture-and-technology/realsense-overview.html
2. Chung, J., Gulcehre, C., Cho, K.H., et al.: Empirical evaluation of gated recurrent neural networks on sequence modeling. arXiv preprint arXiv:1412.3555 (2014)
3. Gers, F.A., Schmidhuber, J., Cummins, F.: Learning to forget: continual prediction with LSTM. Neural Comput. **12**(10), 2451–2471 (2000)
4. CK+: The Extended Cohn-Kanade Dataset. http://www.consortium.ri.cmu.edu/ckagree/
5. JAFFE: The Japanese Female Facial Expression DataBase. http://www.kasrl.org/jaffe.html
6. TFEID: Taiwanese Facial Expression Image Database. http://bml.ym.edu.tw/tfeid/
7. KDEF: The Karolinska Directed Emotional Faces. http://www.emotionlab.se/resources/kdef
8. Dai, A., Nießner, M., Zollhöfer, M., et al.: Bundlefusion: real-time globally consistent 3D reconstruction using on the-fly surface reintegration. ACM Trans. Graph. (TOG) **36**(3), 24 (2017)

Interacting with Cultural Heritage

The Research of Applying Interactive Design for a New Experience into Taiwan Traditional Matsu Culture

Yi-Chieh Chen[1,2(✉)] and Chao-Ming Wang[3]

[1] Graduate School of Design, Doctoral Program,
National Yunlin University of Science and Technology, Yunlin, Taiwan
kikichen040271@gmail.com
[2] Chaoyang University of Technology, Wufeng, Taiwan
[3] Graduate School of Digital Media Design,
National Yunlin University of Science and Technology, Yunlin, Taiwan
wangcm@yuntech.edu.tw

Abstract. This research explores the use of electronic media in cultural related exhibition. It uses "Matsu Monopoly" interactive projection device as an example. Matsu Monopoly is an easy use device which allows people to understand the culture and the history of Matsu. Through the dynamics, images, and texts, visitors in the video, it will impressive the visitors for a strong visual feedback. We hope visitors will interact with the device, and profound experience a variety connotations of the Matsu culture in order to learn new knowledge from the game.

Keywords: Interactive device · Virtual experience · Interactive technology
Matsu culture

1 Introduction

The culture contains the relationship between peoples. In other words, it's the process of human evolution, many historical cultural products and ancient ceremonies are spread. The value of the culture will be changed by the interactive designing device. Human and environment should strengthen communication between each other. However, the essence of the design is not only the pursuit of beautiful shapes. Contributions should be made to the dissemination of the culture.

In a rapidly changing environment, people are used to be attracted to dynamic exhibitions. Computer networks and information technology continues to be developed and people began to have many activities in academic research and dynamic exhibitions. This new experience is to introduce Traditional Matsu culture into an interactive design. We hope to bring new creative idea and communication. It is also another new symbolic representation.

Y.-C. Chen—Chaoyang University of Technology, Wufeng, Taiwan (work unit)

Many people in Taiwan are slowly moving into the coastal areas. Therefore, many Matsu temples are built in the coastal areas. The Matsu Patrol and Pilgrimage in Taiwan was selected as Intangible Cultural Heritage in UNESCO (United Nations Educational, Scientific and Cultural Organization), and also was listed as the world's three major religious events in Discovery Channel.

We developed an interactive device by using a large map and large dice of a "Matsu Monopoly" as the basis. When dice is out of points, participants can go forward on the map. This research combines digital media technology with traditional Matsu culture, and use the technological interaction to spread cultural values. The purpose is to achieve educational and entertainment. Research through the design of a virtual interactive system, and it is similar to the traditional Monopoly game combination. Feel fun of realistic scenes in the virtual environment.

In this study a large-scale multiplayer parent-child interaction device as cultural communication. The objectives of this study were as follows:

- To design a multi-person and large-scale interactive device for parent-child, and to uses a concept of edutainment as cultural exchange. Device was proposed to provide customers with a device that enables them to enjoy the fun of an interactive experience. In addition, there is a different experience from the traditional practice of the past.
- Through the device can solve the busy people and they can also experience Matsu culture on weekends and this can solve the problem of time limit. The interactive device is an exhibition-style experience. It is different from the activities of the traditional Matsu Patrol and Pilgrimage, and there will be no bad weather or rain and work can't participate in activities of question.

2   Literature Review

There are many interactive technology design products are being developed in today's society. They are even used in large quantities in daily necessities. These interactive technology products are slowly changing people's visual habits. This research will be introduced through interesting interaction, and it makes people more relaxed and joyful learning culture and history.

2.1   Interactive Device Design

Ye in "The Principles of Interaction Design in the Post-digital Age" put forward "Triple E" indicators. It includes effective, easy and enjoyable [1]. Interactive design is to convert information into a simple and clear guidance. It creates an interesting process which motivates the people to learn.

The interactive system combines interactive design and culture feature. The interactive exhibition is to use projector to cast screen to the wall. They use for large-scale interaction in the field. In my opinion, interactive technology is to use computer technology, cultural and artistic performance all three combine together. It becomes an interesting form to present.

Although, it is a game, however, in the process of using interactive design, it spreads history and culture. Interactive design takes people's needs and cultural experience as the central consideration. It combines technology and art design as a link between people and people or people and devices. People will enjoy exploring cultural history during playing the game.

2.2 Virtual Experience

The virtual experience is to integrate and improve the existing technologies of sound, video, drawing, and text. It allows users to feel "live experience" without having to onsite visit. Ho (2005) once published that exhibition space is to create a situational experience space conducive to learning [2].

According to "Peripherals" and "Showing Methods", we can categorize Virtual Experience into "Desktop Emulator" and "Projection Virtual Reality" [3]. This research uses a large projection screen, with the projector and stereo sound output device. Projecting the entire scene, surround the user to create some kind of interactive experiential learning.

The rapid progress of science and technology and the concept of interactive technology are also emphasized. Many products in life through interactive technology and bring more convenience to people. Through the interactive technology to applying users receive information from one-way for Become a two-way communication with the operator. The core of interactive technology is human-oriented and humanity [4].

2.3 Interactive Technology of Case Studies

Interactive Technology is an innovative application technology and the combination of aesthetics, culture, technology and science. A good interactive device will attract users' attention and participation. Dix, Finlay, Abowd, and Beale (2004) also mentioned that the device wants good interaction and it is necessary to design the system with the user as the center. Let users quickly obtain information and with the add to user interaction of computers, projectors, sensors, etc. [5].

An interactive system consists of four parts: perception, display, control and feedback [6]. Humans understand computer status through computer display and self-perception and change the state of the computer through control and feedback [7]. For now under the general to uses of computers and computer science is closely related to the daily life of modern people and the importance of being deeply studied and explored of Human-Computer Interaction [8].

So, interactive technology is an important learning for humans and computers and people will get more different experiences through interactive design. Research is the following classification of several cases to discuss:

2.3.1 Hello, Miss Lin International Goddess Digit Dajia Matsu Pilgrimage (The General Association of Chinese Culture No. 1, 2017)

This exhibition uses projector with interactive technologies instead of using the traditional way to demonstrate the culture of Matsu. Figure 1a, we use a 12 m long projector wall to show and explain Dajia Matsu Pilgrimage. Interactive device through the touching system, you can have a dynamic interaction with the visitors. Figure 1b, there is an interactive experience area next to the palanquin. When visitor steps on the floor, it will produce the effect of smoke and firecrackers.

(a)   (b)

Fig. 1. Visitor interaction experience (Source: **The general association of Chinese culture, no. 1**)

2.3.2   Stamps of Landscape - NATIONAL PALACE MUSEUM 'Activities of the Twelve Lunar Months' (QIAN LONG GHAO 2015)

This device was made by using "Activities of the Twelve Lunar Months". The display we can see was composed from mountain, water, cloud, flower, tree, house, and people. It uses an "Augmented Reality" technology which allows visitors to manipulate the elements of mountain or water by themselves (For example, Fig. 2a and b).

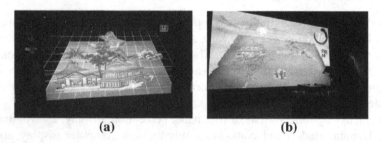

(a)   (b)

Fig. 2. An interactive wall that gives visitors a sense of time and space (Source: **Qianlong C.H.A.O. New Media Art Exhibition**)

2.3.3   National Palace Museum Digital Art Exhibition (Bright Ideas Design - Tang Dynasty Painting of Ladies, 2011)

The interactive device has a round button that can be used to measure people's weight. When people step on top of the button, the device will measure the weight and send the info to the computer. There are three buttons respectively stand for Taipei, New York and Paris. Use the button; it will represent the three different regions. There is an infrared sensor located on the right side of the exhibition. Figure 3a and b, adding some modern society elements into this picture (Table 1).

Fig. 3. Adding some modern society elements into this picture (Source: **Bright Ideas Design**)

Table 1. Interactive device design and organized

Works/Exhibition	Era	User interface	Display	Virtual content/ Feedback
Hello, Miss Lin/Hello, Miss Lin International Goddess Digit Dajia Matsu Pilgrimage	2017	Hand, Foot Touch Button	Projector	Floor interactive projection, Analog fireworks surround
Stamps of Landscape - National Palace Museum 'Activities of the Twelve Lunar Months'	2015	Augmented Reality, Gianlong Emperor Seal Button	Projector	Experience Gianlong emperor use the seal fun
National Place Museum Digital Art Exhibition	2011	Round Button	Infrared Sensor	Experience different times of fun in the area

The examples above are all used to the projection virtual reality. To uses a large projector screen, and projector to give the exhibition a new atmosphere of interactive experience.

2.4 Matsu Culture

The main culture for Coastal area is Min Nan culture. There are many ancient stories talking about how Matsu rescue people from the sea. People believe, when their life in dangerous in the ocean, Matsu will save them if they pray to her. This culture is slowly becoming people's faith. She is people's god; people believe in her and follow her.

People rely on Matsu, through the faith of believing Matsu will be able to educate people's mind. Therefore, it became a regional of the cultural phenomenon. Han (2006) had proposed a culture wants to continue to exist and develop and it needs continuous innovation and breakthrough [9]. This research is based on the interactive device of Matsu culture. Through the game, people will know more about the culture of Matsu.

3   Method and Prototype

3.1   System Design Concept

This interactive device experience allows visitors to operate on their own. The operation is easy to understand and it gives user a deeper impression through the images, words or videos of the visual communication. In this game, we experience the culture of Matsu. This game uses two of the 3E concept, "Effective" and "Enjoyable". The production process is to collect the information of the temple culture and make a video. The video contents are the cultural elements and it is used in the game.

3.2   Interactive Interface and Interaction Device

The first zone is the screen projection area. The main purpose for this area is let user to watch the virtual scene of the temple. The second zone is the interactive device of the map and dice. First of all, the game begins at the start point on the map. The visitor will hold a large dice and roll it on the round, how many numbers they get, then how many steps they move forward. After visitor move forward, if they stay on top of the temple spot on the map then they can step on GamePad button to trigger the system to send the information to the computer (Fig. 4). At the moment, the big screen on the wall will begin playing the temple's feature films. The person whom first arrives the final spot will be the winner of the game. Competing each other will let people have better interactive experience and fun.

Projection screen/ Taichung temple street scene

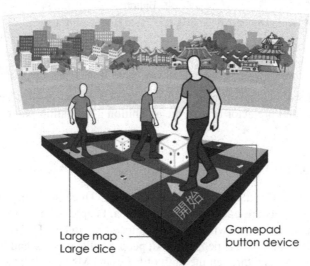

Large map ·
Large dice

Gamepad
button device

Fig. 4.   System diagram

3.3   Interactive Vision

3.3.1   Large Projection

The research exhibition is open space and takes the big screen as a focal point. Visitors can learn more about the culture of Matsu by watching the temple video.

3.3.2   Large Map, Dice, Poetry

Visitors get a chance or a fortune card by rolling the dice, as shown in Fig. 5. They learned about the activities or allusions of the temple from the question in the card. The first player who arrive the final destination is the winner and also learn the new knowledge from the cheerful interactive game.

Fig. 5. Opportunity card

3.4   Interactive System and Interactive Operation Process

The final winner will get a small gift (Fig. 6).

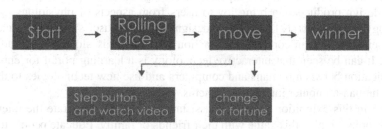

Fig. 6. Diagram of interactive process

4   Public Exhibition and System Evaluation

Kuan *et al.* (2007) put forward Scientific observations are based on researcher to finding phenomena of methods and systematically examine the course of events and people's reactions [10]. Li (2006) can also get results from observations and establish the theme of follow-up interviews [11].

When designers put the needs of users into their works properly and will increase the potential of the interactive system and it's easier for users to learn. Observing the operation of participants during the public display of this research and ass ess user interface operations and user behavior.

It is a combination of projection wall and interactive maps, dice, poetry. It is a multiplayer interactive device game. To begin the game, from the "starting point", rolling the dice to determine who goes first. The game has many stages that player has to go through each of them in order to complete the game (Fig. 7a and b).

(a)   (b)

Fig. 7. Exhibition site interactive device

This research exposes exhibitions and is through observation methods to observe user actions and responses. We need an assistant to help people understand how to operate the interactive device. Interviewee said that if there is a clearer way to use the operation process, it will be more convenient to use the device.

5   Conclusion and Suggestions

Based on the above discussion and experimental study. Green and Jorden (2002) pointed out that design products can bring joy to users from aspects of physiology, society, psychology and thought [12]. Interactive design is focus on user's experience and feedback. Therefore, human-computer interaction experience is slowly being added to pleasure. It can be seen that interactive technology is a learning portal for enhancing communication between humans and computers and use new technologies to develop multiple human-computer interaction systems.

People in this exhibition must have assistant to help them operate the interaction device. People can play this game with their friends or family. Educate people to know the culture and let people have fun is the main propose for the Matsu monopoly. It can reach the concept of entertaining, but also highly praised by participants.

1. The research results are as follows: This research uses Gamepad and other simple electronic media, combined with interactive multimedia design for a new experience into Taiwan traditional Matsu culture.
2. Experiencer learns a lot of the culture knowledge through the device.
3. The interactive device allows the experiencer to be experienced without the limitation of time and space.

References

1. Ye, J.-R.: The Principles of Interaction Design in the Post-digital Age, p. 29. Artist Publishing, Taipei City (2010)
2. Ho, L.-H.: Shorten the distance of people and things - talk about interactive exhibition of museums. Palace Mus. Mon. **270**, 100–105 (2005)
3. Chao-Yun, L., En-Dong, L.: The development and types of virtual reality. Audiov. Educ. Bimon. **40**(3), 18–26 (1998)
4. Jung-Tai, L.: The essence and research of cultural and creative industries. J. Des. **16**(4), 1–5 (2011)
5. Dix, A., Finlay, J., Abowd, G., Beale, R.: Human-Computer Interaction, 3rd edn., p. 225. Prentice Hall, Haddington (2004)
6. Kantowitz, B.H., Sorkin, R.D.: Human Factors: Understanding People-System Relationships, p. 332. Wiley, New York (1983)
7. MacKenzie, I.S.: Human-Computer Interaction: An Empirical Research Perspective. Newnes, Amsterdam (2012)
8. Blythe, M., Bardzell, J., Bardzell, S., Blackwell, A.: Critical issues in interaction design. In: Proceedings of the 22nd British HCI Group Annual Conference on People and Computers: Culture, Creativity, Interaction, British Computer Society, vol. 2, pp. 183–184 (2008)
9. Pao-Te, H.: Han Talks About Culture, p. 84. Collection Art Family, Taipei City (2006)
10. Hsing-Sheng, K., Lu-Yin, J., Ming-Tang, W., Lan-Ting, W., Pei-Ling, L., Hsin-Fa, K., Li-Shu, L., et al.: Design Research Methods, p. 206. Quanhua, Taipei (2007)
11. Li, C.-H.: Qualitative Research: Design and Project Writing, p. 168. Wunanbooks, Taipei (2006)
12. Green, W.S., Jordan, P.W.: Pleasure with Products: Beyond Usability, p. 390. CRC Press, New York (2002). ISBN 9780415237048, CAT TF1185

Research on Prototype Design Methods and Systems of Interactive Media Art in Public Space

Yuanyuan Chen[✉]

College of Design and Innovation, TONGJI University, Shanghai, China
chenyy@tongji.edu.cn

Abstract. The prototype design of interactive media art in public space is based on social place, and it is a kind of prototype design on systematic. The methods and systems of prototype design are not only design and construction in cultural, but also transformation and relational design of complex space. In this paper, I have taken Gaochun international cittaslow in Nanjing of China as an example, by using description framework, situation creation, visual mapping and other methods, described the prototype design methods and systems of interactive media art in public space.

Keywords: Public space · Interactive media art · Prototype design

1 Introduction: Prototype Design of Interactive Media Art in Public Space

The prototype design of interactive media art in public space, is based on social places, and it is built on the support of digital media and new social networking on the initial stage of design. It forms an active technology, art and social participation network. It designs and manages media space with interactive design ideas, methods and tools. This is a systematic prototype design. It involves the symbiotic relationship of interactive media art, people, community and urban space, and also relates to system of information physical and human computer interaction. The methods and systems of prototype design are not only design and construction in culture, but also transformation and relational design of complex space.

2 The Ways of Description on Methods and Systems

Compared with traditional design, prototype design methods and systems in public space, these new ways for describing, which are more tend to comprehensive arts, environmental science, architecture, communication, sociology, ecology, behavioral science, and experimental data in the process of solving problems. The prototype design methods and systems of interactive media art in public space, which involve such aspects as the regionalism of public space, the field character, community behavior design, city

© Springer International Publishing AG, part of Springer Nature 2018
C. Stephanidis (Ed.): HCII Posters 2018, CCIS 852, pp. 162–168, 2018.
https://doi.org/10.1007/978-3-319-92285-0_23

image, urban texture and so on, as well as interactive relationship between the phenomenal space, the personal space and the cultural space.

In prototype design of interactive media art in public space, I usually use the following methods:

The method of relational construction: Integration of interactive design methods, based on 4 steps and 8 themes[1], I introduce the design thinking and sources, conceptual metaphor and scenario description, modeling and task, design implementation and operation technology.

Framework description of design: Public space is established as an eco-circle model, in which, people, media and tools promote and symbiotic with each other.

Scenario: I transform complex social relations into humanistic narrative. With story scenarios, I explain the attention and promotion of continuity and effectiveness on design.

Mapping visual presentation: A method about design projecting into a region.[2] Combined with drawing geographic location (street information), it marks areas which integrate with media art and micro transformation design in space. And it provides design themes of possible space location, including media installation arts, media sculptures, media facades and so on.

Details of amplification design: This method designs for conceptual, including some possible operations, potential social behavior, and the action features of space interaction. For example, it is joined virtual character roles, it describes some complex and associated design tasks by using roles. For the media art design in public space, it will be confronted with validity of design and inclusive design.

3   Case Description

The prototype design methods and systems described in this paper, are from my practical experience. The prototype is drafted with using the above methods. Individual practice design of interactive media art in public space, is located in my hometown Nanjing, which is also the first Chinese cittaslow-GaochunYaxi. The project designs from the theme of "Slow City, Slow Life Space", which aimed to explore the combination and interaction of local culture and interactive media art, and to promote innovation of communication.

3.1   Thematic Elements of Interactive Media Space Design

The "slow" in Yaxi, is one of the main traditional features in this area. "Slow" is embodiment of the living and geographical environment about this region, not sluggish, but easy and leisurely, which means to enjoy the expression of life and time.

There is "Jinhua Festival" in Yaxi from March to May each year. Jinhua, namely rape flowers, are widely planted in Gaochun. Its roots are tough, flowers and leaves are dense,

---

[1] See [1].

[2] See [2].

and its flowering time is longer. It is easy to survive, bright and lively, and has the same simplicity and rugged as farmers who planted them. In traditional Chinese culture, the image of rape flowers symbolizes the simple ordinary life, which has the cultural characteristics of simplicity, cordial and easygoing. "Rape Flower" as a symbol of the mainly festival in Yaxi, it also represents the traditional thinking of "simple and pastoral traditional home feeling". It can be more aptly to reflect Yaxi regional features and geographical environment, besides, it is suitable for thematic elements of interactive media design in space (Fig. 1).

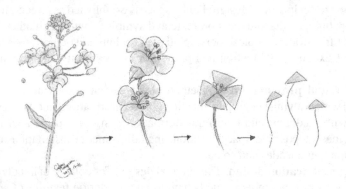

Fig. 1. Jinhua, namely rape flowers, is widely planted in Gaochun. "Rape Flower" is a symbol of the mainly festival in Yaxi. This figures shows the designing from the realistic to geometry of rape flower gradually. Finally, it is suitable for thematic elements of interactive media design in space.

3.2   The Spatial Level of Interactive Media Art in Public Space

In "Having an Experience" of John Dewey, his understanding of "art", was focused on the appreciation of entire creative process of consciousness, namely "an experience"; especially Dewey put forward three kinds of experience: Practical Experience, Aesthetic Experience, and Intellectual Experience.[3] The level of experience can be expanded to three levels of space (environment). Moreover, the spatial level of interactive media art in public space, that can also be understand from the progressive level.

The prototype design of interactive media art starts from the thematic elements and extends from the point to the physical space, the social space and the cultural space. I use the designing framework to describe the hierarchical of interactive media art design in public space (Fig. 2).

The Interactive Media Art Design in Traditional Physical Space
This is physical space. At this level, the prototype of interactive media art in public space embodies designing about "objects". It shows the cognition of tangible environment, physical environment and objects, which is the cognition of objectivity and scientific, and it is influenced by art and aesthetics. It is necessary to make an effective design and

---

[3] See [3].

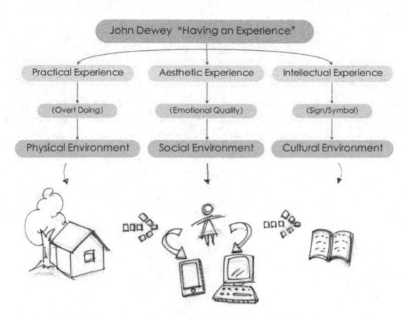

Fig. 2. The spatial level of interactive media art in public space

an inclusive construction of organization. In this case, I use the details of amplification method to put some possible designs, that can reflect the environment and culture into the public space of traditional streets, such as rape flower designing, the physical environment public space for rest and so on.

With the mapping visual presentation method, some modern urban culture and small gardening design are added to highlight the countryside pastoral flavor with rape flowers. More demands on the quality, much more needs about spirit of life and social, are enable interactive media art design to identify social values in public space. With the development of technology, the scope and depth of interactive media art design are expanding in public space, which are seeking the balance between the world and natural synergy by all creation (Fig. 3).

The Prototype Design of Interactive Media Art in Social Space
This is social space. At this level, design thinking is expressed as a factor of concern for "human". This kind of "human relationship" can be understood as the extensive design for interpersonal activities. It embodies multiple levels, such as the unity and harmony between man and environment, the relationship between human and products, and further to the design of relationship between human.

For the cultural and environmental features of Yaxi, interactive media art design needs to pay attention to social behavior and conceptual designing of cultural heritage in public space, through the simple media design or application. Meantime, APP application can be a greater range of promotion and information for social activity of Yaxi local culture. In the designing of APP applications and other information for virtual environment, I added some

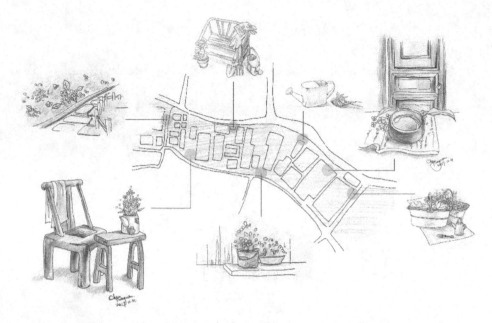

Fig. 3. The prototype of interactive media art in public space embodies designing about "objects", by using the methods of mapping visual presentation and details of amplification.

design elements about "Jinhua Festival". I designed APP application with bright color, I took watercolor painting of rape flowers as the main form (Fig. 4).

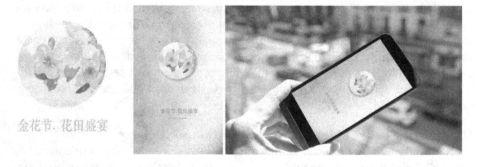

Fig. 4. APP application designing, with bright color and rape flowers as the main form

Design of Interactive Media Installation Art for Rape Flower Fields in Yaxi
This is for cultural public space. The interactive media installation art located at the main rape flower fields, which located in wooden pavilion (Fig. 5).

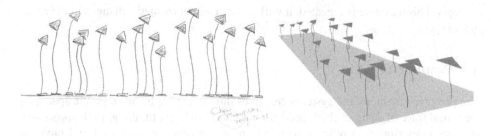

Fig. 5. The interactive media installation art located at the main rape flower fields, which located in wooden pavilion.

The theme of new media installation art is "Jinhua Festival. The Feast of Flower ", which focuses on the performance of rape flower as a symbol. It shows symbol and metaphor, 21 triangles with bright yellow, which means, rape flowers in the fields billowing in the wind. It helps transform rape flowers scene and local culture into tangible art in public space.

The device will be about three-square meters, it will metaphor and display the art scene narrative- rape flowers billowing in the wind, to audience, by using integration of mechanical and electrical, 21 metal triangles are propped up with the thin steel wires and animated with the help of mechanics, electronics and code (Fig. 6).

Fig. 6. The interactive media installation art

In terms of technology design, the work will use mechanical and electronic components, consisting of matrix metal erection devices. Each triangle will be sculptured by thin steel wires and independently controlled by motors. The construction and undulation of this media installation art, are performed in a choreographed sequence. Moving individually, it will gradually evolve from the beginning irregular movement to a definite form that appears later. The final shapes then emerge from this process, such as geometric and abstract rape flower petals. The continuous shapes will show fascinating changes. This narrative is repeated, it will look for visual thematic changes in the art of media space.

4 Summarize

The prototype methods and systems design of interactive media art in public space, on the initial stage of design, which need new methods and new thinking. In the processes of design description, it reflects symbiotic relations between media art and physical space, media art and community, media art and culture. It integrates information systems, human-computer interaction and art of performance. Not only to design for culture, but also to deal with complex transformation of city space and relational design. At the same time, the prototype methods and systems design of interactive media art in public space, can not only promote change of design behavior, but also perfect the social value and behavior orientation in public space.

Acknowledgement. This work was supported by the grants of MOE (Ministry of Education in China) Project of Humanities and Social Sciences (Project No. 15YJC760014), Humanities and Social Science Research Foundation of Nanjing University of Posts & Telecommunications (Project No. NYS214016).

References

1. Moggridge, B.: Designing Interactions, pp. 128–134. MIT Press, Cambridge (2006)
2. Manzini, E.: Design, When Everybody Designs: An Introduction to Design for Social Innovation, pp. 145–148. Publishing House of Electronics Industry, Beijing (2016)
3. Dewey, J.: Art as Experience: Having an Experience. Perigee Books, New York (1980). (Original work published 1934)

Flow: A Musical Composition Tool Using Gesture Interactions and Musical Metacreation

Jordan Aiko Deja[✉], Kevin Gray Chan, Migo Andres Dancel,
Allen Vincent Gonzales, and John Patrick Tobias

Center for Complexity and Emerging Technologies, De La Salle University,
Manila, Philippines
jordan.deja@dlsu.edu.ph

Abstract. Music composition is a delicate and disciplined art form that is tedious and repetitive. In this preliminary study, we explore the design of an interaction that aims to balance the work of composers with the help of a mobile application. The process of musical composition is not easy for composers. Certain tasks such as figuring out succeeding notes often requires trial-and-error, as well as knowledge of certain theories. Existing technology has employed musical metacreation to assist in this process. This endows machines with the artificial creative capacity to perform musical tasks. In review, the existing technology has not been generally-used in all stages of the musical composition process. By combining several interaction technologies, composers can benefit by being able to do their tasks with significantly less cognitive load and time.

Keywords: Interaction design · User interface design
Interaction techniques · Gestural input · Sound and music computing
Computational creativity

1 Introduction

In the process of musical composition, composers tend to follow a strict set of theories and guidelines to maintain the aesthetic quality of the music they create [5,7,9]. The process is usually not standardized and can be customized depending on the task of the composer. As such, one composer's approach might not work effectively for another [3,4]. To address this, we present a tool that will assist in the process rather than force composers to adapt to an unnatural approach. We intend to minimize cognitive load in every stage of the composition process. But generally, composers undergo a series of activities that allow them to draft their musical products, regardless of order or sequence [2,6]. These are (1) ideation, (2) sketching, and (3) revision. We developed a product that enables composers to undergo these stages, while ensuring a user-centric approach in the process.

© Springer International Publishing AG, part of Springer Nature 2018
C. Stephanidis (Ed.): HCII Posters 2018, CCIS 852, pp. 169–176, 2018.
https://doi.org/10.1007/978-3-319-92285-0_24

2   Framework and Methodology

We present the framework of this study as seen in Fig. 1.

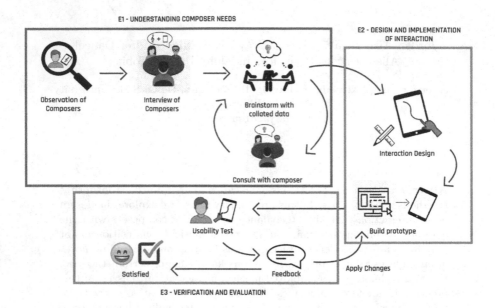

Fig. 1. Flow research framework

2.1   Participants

Five (5) subjects of both genders aged 18–40 were recruited through snowball sampling method to take part in the data collection and testing. Note that these subjects were categorized into two (2) user groups based on musical composition experience: amateur, and experienced. These groups were necessary to better understand the different processes that composers perform during composition.

2.2   Study Design

Our research approach was designed to be iterative, to allow for continuous development and improvement of the prototype. A single iteration involves building the prototype, testing it with composers, and using the resulting feedback and data to improve the next version of the prototype. In every iteration, we collected interaction data through the prototyping application: CogTool. This provided us with measurable data on KLM-GOMS, and Fitts Law [8] without having to measure them manually [1,10]. In each test, the subject was asked to participate in three (3) test setups. The first setup would make the subject use a bare music sheet for composition. The second setup would ask the subjects to use a different mobile musical composition application. The third will make use of our prototype, Flow. The purpose for these setups was to allow us to compare our prototype against existing musical composition approaches. Subjects were asked to perform certain tasks (i.e. adding a note, erasing/deleting a note, etc.) in all the test setups. This helped us see the differences of how the users interacted with the setup for a certain task. For the test setup of Flow, the tasks were also meant to test the features shown in Table 1. After finishing the tasks in all test setups, the subjects were asked to answer a questionnaire. The questions can be seen in Table 2. Note that each of the questions were repeated for each feature (Shown in Table 1). The questionnaire aims to get quantitative data on the subject's experience while using Flow. Answers are on a scale of 1–4, with 1 (Never or Strongly Disagree) being the lowest, and 4 (Frequently or Strongly Agree) being the highest.

Table 1. List of features

No.	Feature
F1	Add a note
F2	Edit a note
F3	Delete a note
F4	Move indicator/Cursor
F5	Move line/Space selector
F6	Selecting/Highlighting multiple notes
F7	Editing multiple notes
F8	Deleting multiple notes

Table 2. Feature related questions

No.	Question
Q1	How much did you use this feature to accomplish tasks?
Q2	Were you comfortable while using this feature?
Q3	Does this feature feel like how you naturally do the task when you're composing?
Q4	Is this feature new but easy to learn given enough time?
Q5	Does this feature make the task at hand way easier than how you do things?

2.3 Data Collection and Analysis

We performed the first round of testing with five (5) respondents. Two (2) of these were experienced while the rest were amateurs. Prior to testing, the subjects were asked to fill out a consent form outlining the tasks that will be performed. These tests were recorded through video, and audio, so that they could be reviewed later. Each test lasted for about 30–45 min. At the end of the first iteration's testing phase, we recorded the users' comments and the observed pain points. Through this, we were able to identify the more common problems in the design and used these to improve the prototype for the succeeding iteration.

3   Prototype

The prototype was built using Swift 4.0 for the iOS platform and is optimized for iPads. The interaction was designed to support a seamless method of musical composition using different types of gestures. The three main activities: *ideation*, *sketching* and *revision* were considered in the process of designing these interactions. The first method, *ideation*, is when a composer is in need of assistance in creative thinking. The system assists the composer in this task by providing audio feedback whenever they input a note. The audio feedback was found to be helpful because it let them figure out the flow of their music easier.

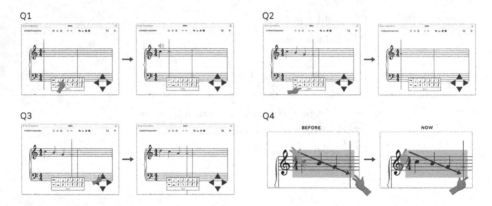

Fig. 2. Flow functions. Q1 demonstrates the add note function which plays a tune when a note is tapped into the digital sheet. Q2 shows the delete function. Shown in Q3 is the transposition function which increases or decreases the pitch of the selected notes using the up or down arrow keys respectively. Q4 illustrates the highlight interaction before and after changes were made due to the user testing.

The second method, *sketching*, is when the composer makes the draft of the initial melody of a composition. The application allows the composer to test out different rhythms while composing with just a tap. Users can simply tap a note from the menu which will then appear on the digital music sheet (see Fig. 2 Q1). The composer can then repeat this process to complete the composition. When the composer wants to revise a portion of his existing work then he can proceed to *Revising*.

Revising is supported by the system through different touch gestures as shown in Fig. 2 Q4 and Q2. In the initial prototype, to select a series of notes, the user performs the highlight by placing two fingers on the screen and dragging them in a diagonal direction until the rectangular highlight region covers the notes the they want to select. However, from the results of the testing and user feedback, we redesigned this interaction to require only one finger to highlight. We believe that this interaction not only uses less fingers, but is also less prone to failed attempts. After highlighting, the user can choose to either edit, delete, cut, copy, or paste certain notes by choosing the rights options from the top menu. Similarly, the user can tap on the up or down arrow keys to instantly transpose the selected notes to a higher or lower pitch respectively (see Fig. 2 Q3).

4   Results

4.1   Preliminary Results from CogTool

CogTool was used to collect preliminary cognitive interaction data for the prototype. Table 3 lists attributes that provide estimates on how efficient a person would be when using the application.

The attributes mentioned in Table 3 represent cognitive operations from the Keystroke-Level Model (KLM) [11] generated by CogTool. In the Motor Module, it is best to minimize the time it takes to perform tasks. Flow does this well according to its Minimum Fitts Time, which indicates the time it takes to move to an area based on the distance from the target and the width of the target [8]. This means that it takes approximately less than a second on average to locate buttons or targets in Flow's interface. Similarly, the Imaginal Delay notes the time it takes to respond to requests from the system like in confirmation buttons or pop ups. A value of 0.200 suggests that there's a very short processing time in between requests.

4.2   Testing Results

Table 4 lists an overview of the results from the questionnaire given after performing the test setups. As mentioned before, answers are on a scale of 1–4, 1 (Never or Strongly Disagree) being the lowest, and 4 (Frequently or Strongly Agree) being the highest. Each of the questions are repeated for each feature.

From the data gathered and analyzed, a clear difference in respondent sentiment was observed from features that needed multiple note selection (see F2 and F8) versus those that did not. This is most notable in the edit and delete features which had the lowest scores on average. Both of these features required the selection feature. Most of the respondents were not able to figure out and correctly execute the gesture for selection which was a two-finger drag. Although it is common for mobile applications to use one-finger drag to scroll, the results suggest otherwise. It was found that the gesture for highlighting (two-finger drag) would have felt more natural if it was switched with the scroll gesture (one-finger drag). Other than the note selection feature, respondents have expressed that most of the features worked well and felt comfortable to use. Although it was not

Table 3. CogTool results based on module

Attribute	Attribute description	Value
Motor module		
PECK fitts coefficient	b coefficient in Fitts's equation for PECK movements	0.075
Default target width	Effective width, in degrees visual angle, of targets with undefined widths	1.000
Minimum Fitts Time	Minimum movement time for an aimed [Fitts's] movement	0.100
Motor burst time	Minimum time for any movement	0.050
Motor initiation time	Time to initiate a motor movement	0.050
Motor feature prep time	Time to prepare a movement feature	0.001
Imaginal module		
Imaginal delay	Time in seconds to respond to an imaginal request	0.200
Temporal module		
Time noise	Temporal noise	0.015
Time master start increment	Temporal start interval	0.011
Time multiplier	Temporal multiplier	1.100

Table 4. Feature related questions

	Q1	Q2	Q3	Q4	Q5	AveF
F1	4.0	3.2	2.6	3.4	2.0	3.04
F2	2.2	1.8	2.0	3.0	1.8	**2.16**
F3	2.0	1.8	1.8	3.2	2.4	2.24
F4	4.0	4.0	3.4	3.6	3.4	**3.68**
F5	3.8	3.2	3.6	3.4	3.0	3.40
F6	2.4	2.0	1.8	3.2	2.8	2.44
F7	2.4	1.8	2.2	2.4	2.4	2.24
F8	2.2	1.8	2.2	2.4	2.2	**2.16**
AveQ	2.88	2.45	2.45	3.08	2.50	

like how they would regularly write music (i.e. pen and paper), Flow's method of composing was easy to learn and get used to. Majority liked the ease of using the cursor/indicator because they can simply tap on the location they want or use the arrow keys when they want to be accurate.

5   Conclusion and Future Work

This study provides a framework for designing mobile musical composition applications. To achieve this, we first had to perform user research which included performing interviews with composers and observing their creative processes. The results of the initial tests led to the design and development of a usable mobile musical composition tool that aided composers through musical metacreation. Given that only an initial prototype was used during the testing, some features were not yet implemented or fully working. The current prototype only included the functions necessary for a composer to create a complete composition. Similarly, the musical metacreation feature was not yet present in the prototype. However, the interviews and tests done during the early prototyping stage suggest that musical metacreation, or being given suggestions on possible notes to write next, would be a valuable tool for composers during their *ideation* activities. We have yet to incorporate the results from the second and third iteration and their corresponding feedback. We performed analysis using CogTool and these results are yet to be correlated with the results of the interaction testing. Future work would also include the integration of a machine learning inference engine that might possibly help composers in the events of a "creative block".

References

1. Bellamy, R., John, B., Kogan, S.: Deploying cogtool: integrating quantitative usability assessment into real-world software development. In: 2011 33rd International Conference on Software Engineering (ICSE), pp. 691–700, May 2011
2. Bennett, S.: The process of musical creation: interviews with eight composers. J. Res. Music Educ. **24**(1), 3–13 (1976)
3. Cheng, C.: On approaching a performance of paul hindemith's der schwanendreher (2016)
4. Collins, D.: The Act of Musical Composition: Studies in the Creative Process. Routledge, London (2016)
5. Collins, D.: A synthesis process model of creative thinking in music composition. Psychol. Music **33**(2), 193–216 (2005)
6. Graf, M.: From Beethoven To Shostakovich-The Psychology Of The Composing Process. Read Books Ltd. (2013)
7. Kikuchi, J., Yanagi, H., Mima, Y.: Music composition with recommendation. In: Proceedings of the 29th Annual Symposium on User Interface Software and Technology, pp. 137–138. ACM (2016)
8. MacKenzie, I.S.: Fitts' law as a research and design tool in human-computer interaction. Hum. Comput. Interact. **7**(1), 91–139 (1992)

9. Rothgeb, J.: Strict counterpoint and tonal theory. J. Music Theor. **19**(2), 260–284 (1975)
10. Sauro, J.: Estimating productivity: composite operators for keystroke level modeling. In: Jacko, J.A. (ed.) HCI 2009. LNCS, vol. 5610, pp. 352–361. Springer, Heidelberg (2009). https://doi.org/10.1007/978-3-642-02574-7_40
11. Sauro, J.: Measuring task times without users (2011). https://measuringu.com/predicted-times/

Interaction with Immersive Cultural Heritage Environments Using Virtual Reality Technologies

Giannis Drossis[1(✉)], Chryssi Birliraki[1], and Constantine Stephanidis[1,2]

[1] Institute of Computer Science, Foundation for Research and Technology Hellas,
N. Plastira 100, Vassilika Vouton, 70013 Heraklion, Crete, Greece
{drossis,birlirak,cs}@ics.forth.gr
[2] Computer Science Department, University of Crete, Heraklion, Crete, Greece

Abstract. The essential characteristic of Virtual Reality (VR) technologies is the enhancement of the user experience regarding perception and presence by immersing the users in a virtual world. The principles which are necessary in a VR experience are the system to be believable, that means feeling as if you are actually there, to be interactive, so when a user extends the arm the VR world must replicate those movements, to be explorable, so that each user is able to walk around an environment and finally to be immersive, which can be achieved by mixing exploration and believability in a way that the experience is enjoyable from any angle. This paper discusses ongoing work regarding immersive environments in which users can interact with cultural heritage 3d objects, navigate in a virtual reality environment and be informed using gestural interaction. The work can be adapted for diverse domains and has been created as a case study of a generic-purpose development framework for creating immersive and interactive virtual reality environments.

Keywords: Virtual reality · Cultural heritage · Gestural interaction
3D environments · Leap motion · Oculus rift

1 Introduction and Related Work

According to Greenbaum [9], "Virtual Reality is an alternate world filled with computer generated images that respond to human movements". Virtual Reality (VR) is an interdisciplinary field of research, including the domains of human-computer interaction (HCI), computer-generated imagery (CGI) and computer graphics. Virtual reality technologies (VR) offer unprecedented user experience when it comes to 3D visualization [18], constituting a domain that is employed in a variety of fields.

VR systems make users perceive that they are physically present in the rendered non-physical world. This feeling of immersion is accomplished through the combination primarily of vision and secondarily of sound. Other approaches involve additional human senses such as touch [12] and olfaction [5]. Virtual environments (VEs) are used to let users interact with places, characters or objects, where they should experience the feeling of "being there", also known as presence [2]. For various VR/MR/AR applications, such as virtual usability studies, it is fundamental that the participants have the

© Springer International Publishing AG, part of Springer Nature 2018
C. Stephanidis (Ed.): HCII Posters 2018, CCIS 852, pp. 177–183, 2018.
https://doi.org/10.1007/978-3-319-92285-0_25

feeling that they are really in the environment. Two important factors that influence presence are the level of immersion and the navigation method [14]. Jung's et al. [13] research showed that social presence in mixed (VR & AR) environments is a strong predictor of four realms of experience, i.e. education, esthetics, escapism and entertainment. Immersion in VR environments can be helpful for further engaging people into the virtual world, suspending the feeling of disbelief and stepping out of the real world into another dimension through which they can accomplish their own goals. These goals can be set by the creators of the virtual environments so that they are constructive and helpful across a variety of domains.

In the healthcare domain, the advantages of the application of Virtual Reality are twofold: it can be applied either for the training of doctors in a realistic environment without endangering a person's health (e.g. surgical skills training [8 and 19]) or for immersing patients in virtual environments and motivating them to perform rehabilitation exercises in a pleasant manner [4].

Tourism constitutes an additional area of VR application. Several implications of virtual reality are presented by Guttentag [11] in the domain of tourism, including planning and management, marketing, entertainment, education, accessibility and heritage preservation. Guerra et al. [10] claim that one of the promises of virtual reality is that when a user observes a monument, a building or a sculpture the perception of additional information will be straightforward and engaging.

VR is an extremely promising tool for the enhancement of learning, education, and training [16]. VR technologies are employed in collaborative virtual environments for the development of learning and communicating skills, such as E-Teatrix [15]. Furthermore, serious games are employed for telling stories and narrations for educational purposes [21], allowing users to experience a personalized view of mythology.

Cultural Heritage is an information-rich domain which is fruitful for visualization. Limitations in exploring institutions such as museums are obstacles often experienced by visitors [20]. Another issue when exploring public institutions is time constraints, which may force users to explore information at a higher speed than preferred [7]. In this direction, visualizations of virtual environments regarding cultural heritage can enrich and supplement, but not replace, in vivo visits to institutions. Sooai et al. [17] created virtual 3D environments presenting 3D models which users can experience by employing virtual reality views using mobile phones.

Furthermore, monuments can be inaccessible for a variety of reasons: the excavation process is not yet complete, renovations are taking place or even their state is fragile. Therefore, visualizations of such sites can provide access to people who would not be otherwise able to explore them. Additionally, items may be located in a protected area like a museum. In this case, the only way to perceive an environment containing the various elements found inside it is by augmenting existing environments with the items or by incorporating virtual environments containing the items.

Barsanti et al. [3] concluded that museums are among the first organizations to make use of advanced VR technologies to investigate their educational potential determining how they provide public education and amusement. The combination of information and images that can be interactively manipulated by the user and the immersive experience are two basic advantages of VR technologies: the user can both experience the sensation of being in an ancient world and can actively participate in the virtual environment. Finally, a 3D cave display enriched with haptic interaction modalities in order to recreate the process of an ancient monument construction is presented in [6], combining virtual reality with playful interaction.

This paper discusses ongoing work regarding immersive environments in which users can interact with cultural heritage 3D objects, navigate in a virtual reality environment and be informed using their bare hands. The proposed framework can be easily adapted to different domains, such as education or healthcare, keeping the information visualization components and interaction techniques the same, thus creating an immersive and interactive framework for VR environments.

2   Interacting with Cultural Heritage 3D Objects in VR

The visual representation of objects can be in the form of a three dimensional model, reconstructing digitally its physical shape in high detail. Digital 3D models can be utilized when the item itself is not available to exhibit, or when the item is too small or large scale, making it impractical to examine it in detail. In these cases, the exploration of an item can be performed through an interactive visualization of its reconstruction.

The system allows users to grasp three dimensional items and manipulate them, i.e., move, rotate or scale them in virtual space (Fig. 1). The application employs for each exhibit a mctallic item (manipulator) which the users can grasp with one hand to move and rotate. The manipulator only appears if the user's hand is near the item. Once holding an item from the manipulator, another metallic item appears below the item with a sphere on the other side, which the users can grab with their other hand in order to scale (maximize or minimize) the exhibit.

Fig. 1. Manipulation of a 3D cultural heritage object in a VR environment

The users' left hand is used as a menu which is shown when the palm is facing the users' eyes. This menu refers to the last item selected and can be pinned at any time using the pin button at the top right side. It contains an indicative title and image, along with a short textual description of the item. Furthermore, actions on the corresponding exhibit can be applied through the options at the bottom side of the menu. These currently include lighting, auto rotation and position reset. Upon lighting selection two draggable spotlights are enabled which users can place towards the exhibit in order to reveal more details of the item or to focus on a specific area. Users can disable the lighting whenever they want to. Auto rotating the exhibit is available so the users can position the object wherever they want, in their preferable scale and lighting and enable the auto rotation along Y axis in order to see a panoramic view of it. Finally, they can reset the exhibit to the initial position-scale and lighting.

The system can be employed in various domains, including:

- Education: it can be used for educating children on anatomy and biology, engineers by breaking down complex items into components, etc.
- Cultural Heritage: for items which are unavailable to citizens
- Healthcare: it can be used for rehabilitation (e.g. stroke) and fine motor skills improvement
- Professional environments: it can be used for employee training, like a simulation or a complex procedure
- Advertisement: preview and promotion of the advertised product

In general, it constitutes a case study of immersive visualizations using a VR headset and natural interaction through gestures, involving a one to one mapping to the physical world. The hardware used includes:

- Oculus Rift: A head-mounted display used for stereoscopic rendering, providing a virtual reality experience.
- LeapMotion controller camera, allowing the tracking of user's hands and providing tracking information about hand articulations, and therefore allowing the rendering of corresponding hands and the recognition of gestures.

2.1 Interaction

The interaction techniques for VR environment presented in this paper are based on the Leap Motion sensor placed in front of an Oculus Rift (Fig. 2), which displays a virtual world to the users. This setup allows free user movement in space, enabling them to turn their head towards any direction. Gesture recognition is accomplished with the camera placed in front of the user's head and therefore the user's hands are never occluded by the user's torso, which is a shortcoming for different setups where the depth sensor is placed in a static position. Egocentric manipulation techniques, such as the virtual hand, translate the user's hand movements to a simplified virtual representation of the hand, in which objects are typically glued to the virtual hand upon contact [1]. Virtual hand metaphors can be enhanced by providing an increased control of the virtual hand (e.g. finger motions) and providing additional visual feedback.

Fig. 2. User interacting with a virtual 3D statue

The developed system includes a fully animated virtual hand (including the forearm) which follows the user's arm, hand and finger movements. The 3D model was directly obtained from the Leap Motion SDK. Hand tracking was provided by the SDK, allowing to track the forearm, the hand and the fingers of the user's dominant hand. It was decided to use Leap Motion because it provides seamless finger tracking without the need to wear gloves or markers, thus providing unobtrusive tracking. The tracking quality ensures a correct animation for the realistic virtual hand for most situations, still, when the palm is in a vertical position finger tracking issues appear due to the palm inter-finger occlusions. The selection is achieved by a virtual "click in the air" with the pointer finger. The open left palm reveals the information menu accompanied with extra functionality which can be applied to the 3D object, such as lighting, position and rotation change. Finally, in order to select and move objects, a pinch with two fingers is sufficient, and upon release of the pinch the object is also released from grabbing.

3   Conclusion and Future Work

This paper has presented ongoing work regarding immersive and interactive environments in which users can interact with cultural heritage 3D objects using their hands and body movement, and therefore enhancing user experience in cultural heritage information visualization. The ultimate objective of this work is to explore the potential of creating a framework with which, regardless of the context of use, users will interact in virtual reality environments, manipulate 3D objects using only their hands/body without wearable devices and will perceive information through a common information visualization template. The system was temporarily installed in several public spaces where users had the opportunity to interact and provide feedback regarding their experience. The early users' comments on applying gestural interaction in combination with VR devices were very encouraging, as the approach proved to be natural, usable and entertaining. The next planned steps involve conducting an extensive evaluation, assessing the users' preferences both among the proposed alternate gestural approaches and in comparison to more traditional devices.

Acknowledgements. The work reported in this paper has been conducted in the context of the AmI Programme of the Institute of Computer Science of the Foundation for Research and Technology-Hellas (FORTH).

References

1. Argelaguet, F., Hoyet, L., Trico, M., Lécuyer, A.: The role of interaction in virtual embodiment: effects of the virtual hand representation. In: 2016 IEEE Virtual Reality (VR), pp. 3–10. IEEE, March 2010
2. Barfield, W., Zeltzer, D., Sheridan, T., Slater, M.: Presence and performance within virtual environments. In: Virtual Environments and Advanced Interface Design, pp. 473–513 (1995)
3. Barsanti, S.G., Caruso, G., Micoli, L.L., Rodriguez, M.C., Guidi, G.: 3D visualization of cultural heritage artefacts with virtual reality devices. In: The International Archives of Photogrammetry, Remote Sensing and Spatial Information Sciences, vol. 40, no. 5, p. 165 (2015)
4. Cameirão, M.S., Badia, S.B., Oller, E.D., Verschure, P.F.: Neurorehabilitation using the virtual reality based rehabilitation gaming system: methodology, design, psychometrics, usability and validation. J. Neuroengineering Rehabil. 7(1), 48 (2010)
5. Chen, Y.: Olfactory display: development and application in virtual reality therapy. In: 16th International Conference on Artificial Reality and Telexistence–Workshops, ICAT 2006, pp. 580–584. IEEE, November 2006
6. Christou, C., Angus, C., Loscos, C., Dettori, A., Roussou, M.: A versatile large-scale multimodal VR system for cultural heritage visualization. In: Proceedings of the ACM Symposium on Virtual Reality Software and Technology, pp. 133–140. ACM, November 2006
7. Gabellone, F., Ferrari, I., Giannotta, M.T., Dell'Aglio, A.: From museum to original site: a 3D environment for virtual visits to finds re-contextualized in their original setting. In: Digital Heritage International Congress (DigitalHeritage), vol. 2, pp. 215–222. IEEE, October 2013
8. Grantcharov, T.P., Kristiansen, V.B., Bendix, J., Bardram, L., Rosenberg, J., Funch-Jensen, P.: Randomized clinical trial of virtual reality simulation for laparoscopic skills training. Br. J. Surg. 91(2), 146–150 (2004)
9. Greenbaum, P.: The lawnmower man. Film Video 9(3), 58–62 (1992)
10. Guerra, J.P., Pinto, M.M., Beato, C.: Virtual reality-shows a new vision for tourism and heritage. Eur. Sci. J. (ESJ) 11(9), 49–54 (2015)
11. Guttentag, D.A.: Virtual reality: applications and implications for tourism. Tour. Manage. 31(5), 637–651 (2010)
12. Hoffman, H.G.: Physically touching virtual objects using tactile augmentation enhances the realism of virtual environments. In: IEEE 1998 Virtual Reality Annual International Symposium, Proceedings, pp. 59–63. IEEE, March 1998
13. Jung, T., tom Dieck, M.C., Lee, H., Chung, N.: Effects of virtual reality and augmented reality on visitor experiences in museum. In: Inversini, A., Schegg, R. (eds.) Information and Communication Technologies in Tourism 2016, pp. 621–635. Springer, Cham (2016). https://doi.org/10.1007/978-3-319-28231-2_45

14. Lorenz, M., Busch, M., Rentzos, L., Tscheligi, M., Klimant, P., Fröhlich, P.: I'm there! The influence of virtual reality and mixed reality environments combined with two different navigation methods on presence. In: 2015 IEEE Virtual Reality (VR), pp. 223–224. IEEE, March 2015
15. Pan, Z., Cheok, A.D., Yang, H., Zhu, J., Shi, J.: Virtual reality and mixed reality for virtual learning environments. Comput. Graph. **30**(1), 20–28 (2006)
16. Slater, M., Sanchez-Vives, M.V.: Enhancing our lives with immersive virtual reality. Front. Robot. AI **3**, 74 (2016)
17. Sooai, A.G., Sumpeno, S., Purnomo, M.H.: User perception on 3D stereoscopic cultural heritage ancient collection. In: Proceedings of the 2nd International Conference in HCI and UX on Indonesia 2016, pp. 112–119. ACM, April 2016
18. Tan, C.T., Leong, T.W., Shen, S., Dubravs, C., Si, C.: Exploring game play experiences on the oculus rift. In: Proceedings of the 2015 Annual Symposium on Computer-Human Interaction in Play, pp. 253–263. ACM, October 2015
19. Van der Meijden, O.A.J., Schijven, M.P.: The value of haptic feedback in conventional and robot-assisted minimal invasive surgery and virtual reality training: a current review. Surg. Endosc. **23**(6), 1180–1190 (2009)
20. Wang, N., Shen, X.: The research on interactive exhibition technology of digital museum resources. In: Green Computing and Communications (GreenCom), 2013 IEEE and Internet of Things (iThings/CPSCom), IEEE International Conference on and IEEE Cyber, Physical and Social Computing, pp. 2067–2070. IEEE, August 2013
21. Zikas, P., Bachlitzanakis, V., Papaefthymiou, M., Kateros, S., Georgiou, S., Lydatakis, N., Papagiannakis, G.: Mixed reality serious games and gamification for smart education. In: European Conference on Games Based Learning, p. 805. Academic Conferences International Limited, October 2016

Enhancing the Experience of Visiting Outdoor Heritage Sites Using Handheld AR

Mihai Duguleana$^{(\boxtimes)}$ and Gheorghe Daniel Voinea

Department of Automotive and Transport Engineering,
Transilvania University of Braşov, Braşov, Romania
mihai.duguleana@unitbv.ro

Abstract. Augmented Reality (AR) technologies are becoming mainstream, and with the support of big tech companies such as Alphabet and Apple, they are nowadays easily available. Narrowing down the niche, there is a vast research activity within the field of AR in outdoor museums and heritage sits. However, the influence of this technology over tourist behavior was not yet studied properly.

This study targets the process of building an AR application which can be used as a digital guide for outdoor museums, monuments or any other type of heritage sites. The quantitative results of this study are designed to help the development of AR applications for outdoor museums. This poster presents the result of 3 different experiment scenarios: visiting the remainings of an Etruscan tomb, walking through a central market square and inspecting an intangible monument (a catholic church destroyed decades ago). We compute several parameters based on a questionnaire which targets the manipulability and the comprehensibility. Following the experiments, we propose a list of guidelines for building mobile AR (MAR) applications with a focus on cultural heritage.

Keywords: Augmented reality · Cultural heritage · Mobile applications

1 Introduction

The research in MAR applications is effervescent. There is a vast interest in this field, particularly because of the recent technological evolution of smartphones. Many researchers try to steer their studies towards the adoption of AR technologies in contexts linked to cultural heritage. Some analyze the opportunities and the risks of using AR in tourism and history [1]. E.g., in [2], authors present an overview of the main challenges and prospects of using AR to enhance the tourism experience.

Others focus on specific test cases and implement custom AR solutions to solve particular problems [3]. Although still in the experimental phase, outdoor AR is targeted by studies such as [4]. In [5], authors make use of multimodal interfaces for offering a customizable experiences that can attract a broader spectrum of users in the case of indoor and outdoor cultural heritage sites. Considering the purpose of broadening the results and the contribution to science, some researchers present theoretical models of mobile augmented reality acceptance questionnaires, as it is in the case of the urban heritage tourism [6]. Their model evaluates AR applications through seven

© Springer International Publishing AG, part of Springer Nature 2018
C. Stephanidis (Ed.): HCII Posters 2018, CCIS 852, pp. 184–191, 2018.
https://doi.org/10.1007/978-3-319-92285-0_26

dimensions that should be, according to them, always considered in research: information quality, system quality, financial aspects, personal innovativeness, recommendations, risks and facilitating conditions. In [7], it is proposed a wearable augmented reality system for experiencing outdoor cultural heritage. The main issues with the system are the inconsistent tracking and the low brightness levels, especially when exposed to sunlight.

One interesting study which comes close to the subject of this manuscript is presented in [8], where authors investigate the use of a MAR application for cultural heritage, based on the Android platform. The proposed application superimposed virtual ancient elements on real scenes, thus creating the illusion of travelling in the past.

Sometimes, AR and VR technologies are mixed together to obtain a better user experience. Such is the case of the MAUS Museum [9]. Maintaining this idea, in [10], the authors studied the best approach to apply AR technologies to present the Egyptian cultural heritage. By choosing the best combination of techniques, users and sites, the appropriate AR display can be determined. The authors identified the ease of use and the technological and cultural accessibility as the main requirements of an AR application. A better user experience and an increased satisfaction are also the key elements pursued in [11]. Authors identified three factors that can maximize the tourist's satisfaction of using an AR application for heritage site: technology readiness, the visual and the situational factor.

In [12], researchers combine the concept of tourist binoculars with the AR technology, in order to enhance to interaction. However, tourists and their wellbeing were targeted from almost 20 years ago in [13], where authors implement and archeo-guide based on an incipient form of AR. Closer to the present, in [14] it is presented a mobile outdoor AR application for city visualization. What is close to the subject of this study, a set of guidelines was compiled and presented. This approach is beneficial for the scientific community, as guidelines can be adopted and used from the initial stages of the research. Continuing on this idea, a survey on AR technologies, applications and limitations is presented in [15].

Sometimes, the little details are the things impress people the most. This concept was behind the study presented in [16], where authors developed an AR application to help visitors explore hidden features of cultural heritage artifacts.

After extensively investigating the state of the art, we can conclude that AR technologies are today widely used and marketed. Most of the literature focuses on applications (museum guides, building virtual and augmented installations and exhibitions, and so on) instead of analyzing the influence of this technology over the behavior of travelers. In this paper, we present 3 test cases where we have used different types of MAR applications, the methodology behind the undergone experiments and the participants' characteristics. We apply the HARUS questionnaire presented in [17] to find out the details behind the manipulability and the comprehensibility of the applications. We compile based on these experiences several guidelines useful for anyone who wants to build an outdoor MAR application.

2   Materials and Methods

2.1   Procedure

We have constructed 3 different applications, for 3 different locations. The first scenario targeted the Etruscan tomb from Cecina, Italy. We have reconstructed in AR the entry, the ceiling and the central pillar of the tomb, and presented the application to the visitors of the museum. The second scenario was designed for the central square in front of the Colloseum from Rome, Italy. The year 2017 was the year which marked 2000 years from the death of Ovid, the famous roman poet. In order to celebrate this, we have built a MAR application which presented Ovid wandering around the Colloseum, reciting one of his famous poems. The third and last application was implemented in order to raise awareness about a lost monument from Brasov, Romania: the Reformed Church. The monument, a symbol of eclectic architecture which was built in 1893, was destroyed by the communist regime in order to make space for a state hotel (see Fig. 1).

Fig. 1. Pictures from all 3 applications, from Rome, Italy (top), Cecina, Italy (bottom-right) and Brasov, Romania (bottom-left)

Inspecting an intangible monument (a catholic church destroyed decades ago) was a good chance to measure the advantages and the limitations of the AR technology.

During all tests from all 3 scenarios, we investigate how much time tourists spend using the MAR system, as compared to exploring the museums/locations without a digital guide. We measure the "fatigue" resulted from using the interface (e.g. brought by holding the tablet, or playing with the UI) and analyze perceptual issues based on a questionnaire, such as the tracking stability, the content quality and the display-induced cognitive load.

2.2 Participants

8 participants tested the MAR application with the Etruscan tomb, 63 participants took part in the study outside the Colloseum and 21 participants inspected the lost Reformed Church from Brasov. The details about all participants and presented in Table 1.

Table 1. Individual characteristics of participant for each location

Variables	No.	Percent (%)	No.	Percent (%)	No.	Percent (%)
		Scenario 3		Scenario 2		Scenario 1
Gender						
Male	33	52.0	9	43.0	3	37.0
Female	30	48.0	12	57.0	5	63.0
Age						
18–25	1	33.33	9	42.85	1	9.09
26–35	11	30.16	3	14.28	4	36.36
36–49	11	26.99	6	28.57	3	27.27
50+	6	9.5	3	14.28	2	18.18
AR experience						
Yes	28	44.00	11	52.00	4	36.00
No	35	56.00	10	48.00	7	64.00

2.3 Questionnaire

We have used a slightly modified version of the HARUS questionnaire from [17] to assess the manipulability and the comprehensibility of the 3 MAR applications (Table 2):

Table 2. The questionnaire

Manipulability	Comprehensibility
I think that interacting with this application requires a lot of body muscle effort	I think that interacting with this application requires a lot of mental effort
I felt that using the application was comfortable for my arms and hands	I thought the amount of information displayed on screen was appropriate
I found the device difficult to hold while operating the application	I thought that the information displayed on screen was difficult to read
I found it easy to input information through the application	I felt that the information display was responding fast enough
I felt that my arm or hand became tired after using the application	I thought that the information displayed on screen was confusing
I think the application is easy to control	I thought the words and symbols on screen were easy to read
I felt that I was losing grip and dropping the device at some point	I felt that the display was flickering too much
I think the operation of this application is simple and uncomplicated	I thought that the information displayed on screen was consistent

3   Results

The questionnaire evaluates manipulability and comprehensibility. Each is characterized by a set of eight items and participants used a 7 point Likert-type scale (1 – Strongly disagree, 7 – Strongly agree) to rate them. The questionnaire contains both positive and negative worded items, as such we first inverted the results for the negative scale items for all the users. The new scores were then converted to a range of 0 to 6 and presented graphically in Fig. 2.

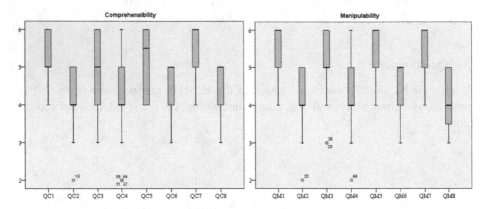

Fig. 2. Boxplot showing the results for manipulability and comprehensibility

We have computed separately the average time spent on using the AR handheld devices in selected locations (by tracking the time of each session inside the application, see Fig. 3) and the strong and the weak points of the application, by an open answer question.

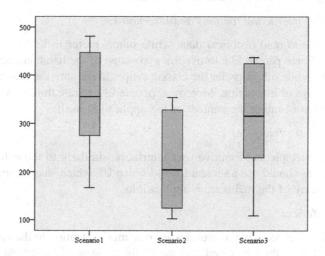

Fig. 3. Box plots showing the time spent (in sec) using the AR application for each scenario

4 Guidelines for Outdoor MAR Applications Designed for the Cultural Heritage Field

1. MAR applications need to be built for specific contexts.

Contexts are usually different. Each monument, each place, has its own particularities. Given the high variation in history, scenarios and objectives, it is hard to build an application flexible enough to cover the entire spectrum of use cases.

2. The historical data/context needs to be resumed well.

Because the presentation space in MAR applications is limited, special care should be put in retrieving and resuming the historical data.

3. Overcome limitations with good user interfaces and high quality models and textures.

The technology readiness level will never offer a full satisfaction. Even the best smartphones still encounter issues such as the glare effect, the limited brightness and the relatively small screen. Some of these problems can be augmented with a good implementation of the AR content, including well-rendered textures and intuitive interfaces.

4. Dynamic AR content and storytelling work better than simple 3D models display.

We've found that people are much more attracted by moving 3D objects, and retain much more information if it is served as a story instead of a billboard. MAR applications allow their creators to be as creative as possible. Implementing engaging AR scenarios will attract users with a multiplying effect.

5. Offer means of interaction, options and alternatives

Some people like to read historical data, while others prefer to listen it from a synthesized voice. Some people like to use the gyroscope of the handheld devices to see the AR content, while others prefer the classic swipe. Make sure the MAR application offers various ways of interaction. Moreover, people like to rate things. A good idea is to offer the option of rating the content or the application itself.

6. Build simple User Interfaces

Users appreciate simple and intuitive user interfaces, similarly to those found online. MAR applications should use a standard well-known UI, which share icons and button position with many of the mainstream applications.

7. Use quality devices

Many participants, especially those under 40, pay much attention to the capabilities of the handheld device they received for the trials. A state-of-the-art smartphone or phablet was always much more appreciated than an older model, even though the user interface remained unchanged.

5 Conclusions

This paper presents the results of a study undergone by a total 92 participants, almost equality spread among age levels, which tested 3 different MAR applications in 3 different locations. We used the diversity of the setup in order to find a common ground on which we've built a set of guidelines useful for anyone who is interesting in building an outdoor MAR application, with a particular focus in the cultural heritage field.

Acknowledgement. This paper is supported by European Union's Horizon 2020 research and innovation programme under grant agreement No. 692103, project eHERITAGE (Expanding the Research and Innovation Capacity in Cultural Heritage Virtual Reality Applications).

References

1. Kysela, J., Storkova, P.: Using augmented reality as a medium for teaching history and tourism. Procedia Soc. Behav. Sci. **174**, 926–931 (2015)
2. Kounavis, D.C., Kasimati, A.E., Zamani, E.D.: Enhancing the tourism experience through mobile augmented reality: challenges and prospects. Int. J. Eng. Bus. Manag. **4**, 10 (2012). Special Issue Digital and Mobile Economy

3. Cianciarulo, D.: From local traditions to "augmented reality". The MUVIG Museum of Viggiano (Italy). Procedia Soc. Behav. Sci. **188**, 138–143 (2015)
4. Han, J.G., Park, K.W., Ban, K.J., Kim, E.K.: Cultural heritage sites visualization system based on outdoor augmented reality. AASRI Procedia **4**, 64–71 (2013)
5. Liarokapis, F., Sylaiou, S., Moutain, D.: Personalizing virtual and augmented reality for cultural heritage indoor and outdoor experiences. In: The 9th International Symposium on Virtual Reality, Archaeology and Cultural Heritage, VAST (2008)
6. Claudia tom Dieck, M., Jung, T.: A theoretical model of mobile augmented reality acceptance in urban heritage tourism. Curr. Issues Tour. **21**(2), 154–174 (2015)
7. Caggianese, G., Neroni, P., Gallo, L.: Natural interaction and wearable augmented reality for the enjoyment of the cultural heritage in outdoor conditions. In: De Paolis, L.T., Mongelli, A. (eds.) AVR 2014. LNCS, vol. 8853, pp. 267–282. Springer, Cham (2014). https://doi.org/10.1007/978-3-319-13969-2_20
8. Fiore, A., Mainetti, L., Manco, L., Marra, P.: Augmented reality for allowing time navigation in cultural tourism experiences: a case study. In: De Paolis, L.T., Mongelli, A. (eds.) AVR 2014. LNCS, vol. 8853, pp. 296–301. Springer, Cham (2014). https://doi.org/10.1007/978-3-319-13969-2_22
9. Invitto, S., Spada, I., Turco, D., Belmonte, G.: Easy perception lab: evolution, brain and virtual and augmented reality in museum environment. In: De Paolis, L.T., Mongelli, A. (eds.) AVR 2014. LNCS, vol. 8853, pp. 302–310. Springer, Cham (2014). https://doi.org/10.1007/978-3-319-13969-2_23
10. Tahoon, D.M.A.: Simulating Egyptian cultural heritage by augmented reality technologies. In: BUE ACE1-Sustainable Vital Technologies in Engineering & Informatics (2016)
11. Chung, N., Han, H., Joun, Y.: Tourists' intention to visit a destination: the role of augmented reality (AR) application for a heritage site. Comput. Hum. Behav. **50**, 588–599 (2015)
12. Fritz, F., Susperregui, A., Linaza, M.T.: Enhancing cultural tourism experiences with augmented reality technologies. In: The 6th International Symposium on Virtual Reality, Archaeology and Cultural Heritage VAST (2005)
13. Gleue, T., Dähne, P.: Design and implementation of a mobile device for outdoor augmented reality in the archeo guide project. In: Proceedings of the 2001 Conference on Virtual Reality, Archeology, and Cultural Heritage (VAST 2001), pp. 161–168. ACM, New York (2001)
14. Lee, A.G., Dunser, A., Kim, S., Bilinghurst, M.: CityViewAR: a mobile outdoor AR application for city visualization. In: IEEE International Symposium on Mixed and Augmented Reality 2012 Arts, Media, and Humanities Proceedings (2012)
15. Van Krevelen, D.W.F., Poelman, R.: A survey of augmented reality technologies, applications and limitations. Int. J. Virtual Reality **9**(2), 1–20 (2010)
16. Ridel, B., Reuter, P., Laviole, J., Mellado, N., Couture, N.: The revealing flashlight: interactive spatial augmented reality for detail exploration of cultural heritage artifacts. J. Comput. Cult. Heritage (ACM), **7**(2), 1–18 (2014)
17. Santos, M.E.C., Polvi, J., Taketomi, T., Yamamoto, G., Sandor, C., Kato, H.: Toward standard usability questionnaires for handheld augmented reality. IEEE Comput. Graph. Appl. **35**(5), 66–75 (2015)

The Way to Preserve Korean Intangible Cultural Assets

Yang Kyu Lim[1]([✉]) and Jin Wan Park[2]

[1] Graduate School of Advanced Imaging Sciences, Multimedia and Film,
Chung-Ang University, Seoul, South Korea
lim0386@gmail.com
[2] School of Computer Science and Engineering, Chung-Ang University, Seoul, South Korea
jinpark@cau.ac.kr

Abstract. Korean traditional music and dance have a history of over 1,500 years. We intend to proceed with the process of preserving and digitizing these intangible cultural properties, especially in the traditional Korean music and dance. In this work, we connected gyroscopes and accelerometers to human joints. In order to save the characteristics of Korean dance, which is important for every single finger movement. We also installed a capture device that uses a small sensor on each finger. The stored data is applied to the 3D character in the computer so that it can be observed anytime and anywhere. Particularly, we implemented the experiment through the concert using the technique acquired in the research. In the future, we believe that the preservation of *Human Cultural Assets* in this way will be a good chance to store traditional cultural heritage of Korea if it is applied not only performances but also to other intangible cultural properties.

Keywords: Culture · Korea · Intangible Cultural Asset · Dance

1 Introduction

The percentage of music and dance performances in Korean cultural arts activities are 45.7% based on the data of the government in 2016. Among the 21,056 cultural performances, the number of Korean traditional performances is only 1,507, accounting for only 7.2% of the total [1]. In contrast, Western-style performances such as classical performance accounted for 9,907 cases, accounting for 47.1% [2].

Korean traditional music and dance have a history of over 1,500 years. However, domestic and international awareness is very low compared to its history. Particularly, efforts to preserve and develop it continue, but it is getting weaker. We are making a lot of efforts to save Korea's traditional cultural performances, which are becoming less popular (Table 1).

© Springer International Publishing AG, part of Springer Nature 2018
C. Stephanidis (Ed.): HCII Posters 2018, CCIS 852, pp. 192–195, 2018.
https://doi.org/10.1007/978-3-319-92285-0_27

Table 1. Number of performances by genre in performing arts in Korea [2]

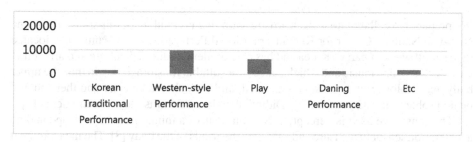

In Korea, there is a unique intangible cultural property protection system, *Human Cultural Asset*, to overcome this phenomenon. Cultural properties often refer to types of objects or buildings that have a long historical value. But within the category of culture, music and dance are included. In Korea, there is an effort to preserve this cultural heritage through *Human Cultural Asset* system. However, this method, which consists of only recording and human manipulation, causes many problems in terms of accuracy. The side effects are very serious. Many human cultural assets are selected by the relationship between man and man rather than skill and tradition. And by the passage of time, many variations of traditional dance and music have been created and many waves have been created due to the transformation. In terms of rediscovery of a new culture, it is a wonderful situation in the name of development. But it was a very difficult situation to preserve the original shape correctly.

We have tried motion capture that we have never tried in traditional dance. The goal of the research is to apply the ultra high density sensor to the traditional dancers. The data received from the movement is stored in the computer under the name Cultural Preservation.

2   Related Works

We have looked at a number of methods that have attempted to develop traditional performances in other studies. One of the typical examples of this was a performance performed with projection mapping. A Study on the Revitalization of Korean Traditional Dance Using Projection Mapping, which was studied for the purpose of education, plans the performances different from the existing traditional dance. However, we already use projection mapping in many performing arts fields. Performances such as performances in accordance with pre-produced videos are far from Korean traditional arts, which emphasize autonomy and improvisation [3].

Ensemble Sinawi is a leader in traditional culture that makes new attempts. It is popular not only for projection mapping, but also for realizing the sound interaction with music. It is famous for trying the latest trend with aggressive attitude such as selling CDs by using crowdfunding [4].

We have already been studying motion recognition pertaining to music several years ago and researching games that combine motion and sound. These studies can be used to digitize traditional Korean arts and further interact to create new content [5, 6].

3   Production Process

We prepared to collaborate with an artistic team that is credible for this study. We found Namwon National Center for Korean Traditional Performing Arts. Namwon is located in the southwestern part of Korea and has an excellent traditional culture and arts. First, we selected which music and which dances are suitable for storage. To do this, the upper body and the lower body must be separated, and they should be clear and there should be no problem in data generation. "Didim" is a dance that fits these requirements [7].

The sensor we used is Perception Neuron. It uses a miniaturized gyroscope and an acceleration sensor to measure and calculate the joints of the body [8]. The measurement sensor used the method of measuring the whole body by wearing rather than using the existing camera. A small module connected to the wifi transmits all the information of the sensor to the computer. Motion capture, reception, and storage were all created using Unity (Fig. 1).

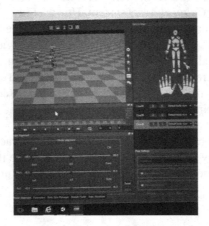

Fig. 1. Perception Neuron saves Korean traditional dance with Unity

We go through a process of filtering out unnecessary parts of the incoming information. One of the disadvantages of this sensor is the absence of position information. In this case, the characteristic of the dance is analyzed and the data is automatically moved to the expected path. As you can see in the picture, the action is saved by the music. Dance has a close relationship with music, and especially musicians and dancers perform improvisation through tuning during performance.

4   Evaluation and Conclusion

Storing dance as data is not a simple task. In particular, many attempts failed to save the same behavior each time. The reason is the improvisation that is characteristic of Korean traditional dance.

We used data that was stored successfully and loaded it into a 3D dummy object and played it back. The animation was provided to three professional dancers, including the dancer participating in the experiment. The boundary between fast and powerful motion and slow and smooth motion is ambiguous, and it is commonly evaluated that this system cannot be done yet. However, the evaluators advised that this system has another possibility for the popularization of Korean traditional dance. It is an interaction. Recent trends in the performing arts, there have been occasions when performances involving interactions have been most successful by the mysterious techniques (Fig. 2).

Fig. 2. Compares the dancing image with the computer generated animation.

It is still a long way to go as an early stage of research. However, we discovered new possibilities based on the technology that emerged during the process of researching on the theme of the preservation of *Human Cultural Asset* in Korea. In the future, we plan to save dance movements that require more complex operations through fine-tuning of sensors and diversification of measurement methods. We will also use the stored data to develop new genres of Korean traditional art performances.

References

1. Number of performances in Korea. http://www.index.go.kr. Accessed Dec 2017
2. Number of performances by genre in performing arts in Korea. http://www.index.go.kr. Accessed Dec 2017
3. Park, J.Y., Kim, U.M.: Promoting Korean traditional dance using projection mapping. Our Danc. Sci. **25**, 103–126 (2014)
4. Ensemble Sinawi and orchestra record maker. https://www.tumblbug.com/ensemblesinawi. Accessed Feb 2018
5. Lim, Y.K., Shim, B.K.: Shake it up: exercise intensity recognizing system. In: Stephanidis, C. (ed.) HCI 2014. CCIS, vol. 435, pp. 355–360. Springer, Cham (2014). https://doi.org/10.1007/978-3-319-07854-0_62
6. Lim, Y.K., Lee, E.J., Jung, H.C., Park, S.K., Park, J.W.: Motion detection and sound effect game for daily jogging. In: Stephanidis, C. (ed.) HCI 2016. CCIS, vol. 618, pp. 112–116. Springer, Cham (2016). https://doi.org/10.1007/978-3-319-40542-1_18
7. Kim, J.D.: Our Dance and Culture, Yeok Lak Korea (2017)
8. Perception Neuron. https://neuronmocap.com. Accessed Mar 2018

Digital Heritage Technology at the Archaeological Museum of Heraklion

Nikolaos Partarakis[1(✉)], Eirini Kontaki[1], Emmanouil Zidianakis[1], Giannis Drossis[1],
Chryssi Birliraki[1], George Metaxakis[1], Alexandra Barka[1], Vaggelis Poutouris[1],
George Mathioudakis[1], Ioanna Zidianaki[1], Antonis Chatziantoniou[1],
Panagiotis Koutlemanis[1], Xenophon Zabulis[1], George Margetis[1], Dimitris Grammenos[1],
Emmanouil Apostolakis[1], Emmanouil Stamatakis[1], Giorgos Paparoulis[1],
Margherita Antona[1], and Constantine Stephanidis[1,2]

[1] Foundation for Research and Technology – Hellas (FORTH), Institute of Computer Science,
N. Plastira 100, Vassilika Vouton, 700 13 Heraklion, Crete, Greece
{partarak,ekontaki,zidian,drossis,birlirak,gmetax,barka,
poutouris,gmathiou,izidian,hatjiant,koutle,zabulis,gmarget,
gramenos,apostolak,stamatakis,groulis,antona,cs}@ics.forth.gr
[2] Department of Computer Science, University of Crete, Heraklion, Greece

Abstract. This paper presents an Ambient Intelligence infrastructure that fuses
state-of-the-art technologies and related applications with digital cultural
resources to deliver interactive and immersive user encounters through on-site
Virtual Exhibitions (VEs) which respond to the demands of 'new museology'.
The practical exploitation of the concept is presented through the reformation of
the exhibition spaces of the Archaeological Museum of Heraklion which is one
of the most important Greek museums hosting representative artefacts from all
the periods of Cretan prehistory and ancient history, covering a chronological
span of over 5,500 years from the Neolithic period to Roman times.

Keywords: Information visualization · Interactive systems · Mixed reality
Augmented artefacts · Interaction with printed matter · Hand gestures
Skeletal interaction

1 Introduction

The term '**new museology**'[1] introduces a new philosophy around how museums function and a changed relationship between museums and their societies and communities,
shifting attention from museum collections towards visitors [1, 2]. It encourages
communication and new styles of expression, as well as **active participation**, in contrast
to more traditional, collection-centered museum models [3]. New museology demands

---

[1] 'New museology' is a discourse around the social and political roles of museums, encouraging
new communication and new styles of expression in contrast to classic, collections-centred
museum models (Mairesse and Desvallées 2010). It demands that the management of heritage
should be 'more open, inclusive, representative and creative' (Harrison 2013, 225).

© Springer International Publishing AG, part of Springer Nature 2018
C. Stephanidis (Ed.): HCII Posters 2018, CCIS 852, pp. 196–203, 2018.
https://doi.org/10.1007/978-3-319-92285-0_28

that the management of heritage should be more open, inclusive, representative and **creative** [4]. These developments can be argued to be part of a shift in focus from objects to ideas [5], with **language and education** now argued to have a **central position in museums** [6]. In this context, ICTs are and can further be used to enrich, transform and enhance the cultural experience.

The work reported in this paper delivers theme-specific interactive experiences aiming to communicate and shape CH in the context of CHIs. Virtual cultural assets and associated information and content (a) are combined, (b) organised appropriately to be transformed into interactive experiences, (c) displayed through suitable virtual environments and finally (d) delivered through digital platforms/devices on the basis of real-time interaction with visitors stimulating immersive experiences.

2 Background and Related Work

Virtual Museums have evolved from digital duplicates of "real" museums or simple online museums into complex communication systems, strongly connected with interaction and immersion in 3D reconstructed scenarios [7]. In such context, Virtual Museums mainly fall under one of the following categories:

Mobile Virtual Museums or Micro Museums, using Virtual Reality (VR)/ Augmented Reality (AR): Mobile applications using AR technology to explain history, architecture and or other artefacts visually, in an indoor or outdoor environment. Example applications include indoor virtual archaeology, embedded virtual reconstructions, and on-site data explorations.

On Site Interactive Installations: Multi-user environments, aimed at preserving the collective experience typical of the visit to a museum. A common characteristic is the use of 3D models reconstructing monuments, sites, landscapes, etc., which can be explored in most cases in real time, either directly or through a guide who acts as main driver of the application, usually mixed with other multimedia assets.

Web-Delivered Virtual Museums: Virtual Museums providing content through the Web. A wide variety of 3D viewers and players have been developed to provide 3D interactive applications "embedded" in browsers, activated by website exposing specific 3D content. Many of these tools are licensed as proprietary technology, charging for development tools/site license, while providing the closed player free of charge. Examples include Google Art, Inventing Europe[2], MUSEON[3], etc.

Multimedia Virtual Museums: Interactive experiences blending video, audio and interactive technologies (for examples 'DVD of Medieval Dublin: From Vikings to Tudors').

Digital Archives: Increasingly popular, as the amount of digital information increases, together with the wish of the public to gain access to information. It requires robust systems for storing information, but also intelligent tools to retrieve it. Examples

---

[2] http://www.inventingeurope.eu/.
[3] http://www.museon.nl/en.

of Digital Archives include **thesaurus** of terms describing a CH asset, digital reposito-
ries considering all possible different metadata schemes of its digital content, intelligent
searching/browsing systems, digital archives, etc.

Although much work has been done to date, museums still hesitate towards the
greater penetration of modern technology into the actual exhibition spaces to form novel
hybrid experiences that merge both actual artefacts and digital information displays. In
this paper an infrastructure for delivering such concepts to museums is presented,
focusing on a practical exploitation of the concept at the premises of the Archaeological
Museum of Heraklion.

3   System Architecture

One of the most challenging aspects of this research work is coping with the complexity
of the installation at the Archeological Museum of Heraklion. It was required to produce
a system architecture that could cope with the storage of knowledge, scenario building
upon knowledge sources, versioning and synchronization of scenarios, scheduling of
system functionality and tracking of system events for approximately 20 interactive
installations across the museum. The challenge was to create a system architecture that
could support these facilities in a way transparent to the museum personnel with automated handling of all systems (opening and closing systems based on schedules,
changing dynamically the scenarios presented by each system based on the time schedule
of each exhibit etc.).

To achieve this objective, a distributed architecture was designed and implemented
that addresses all the aforementioned requirements. In order to be able to administer the
large amount of digital information stored and facilitated by the interactive installations,
a centralized storage was set-up that has the required capacity to handle storage of digi-
tized 2D artefacts, 3D models, video content, presentations, interactive animations and
textual knowledge in structured ontology-based format. The centralized storage also
supports versioning and automated backup of these assets for further protection. Having
taken the decision to incorporate a centralized cloud based scheme for content storage,
it was required to create a mechanism for manipulating content and creating complex
content structures to be facilitated by interactive applications. This was delivered
through a content management system capable of producing, scheduling and versioning
scenarios, as well as dynamic installation management and control. On top of this architecture several interactive technologies are used to offer immersive experiences
including skeleton tracking, gesture/posture recognition, lateral touch detection and
localization. Based on this infrastructure, specific scenarios in the museum are implemented via specialized interactive applications such as:

Multimedia Viewer: Allows the reproduction of multimedia presentations with
structured content (scripts) and control of multimedia content, including images, videos,
descriptive texts, MS Power Point presentations, applications, mini games, etc.

Multimedia Content Enhancer: Capable of rendering content to extremely large
displays (video walls).

3D Objects Renderer: a control for rendering specified 3D models (scene graphs). The control can be simply embedded into internet browsers (e.g. IE) or .NET applications allowing users to interact using multi-touch devices.

Object Stream Visualizer: Comprises a collection of keywords, images and video thumbnails displayed on a very large touch screen.

Wall Game Presenter: presents a game scenario based on full body tracking using gamification technologies for keeping scores, calculating game levels etc.

Timeline Renderer: an application presenting an interactive timeline. Information is organized in the form of a tunnel in which users can navigate and explore different time periods and events.

Papyrus Renderer: a container that can present the content of a thematic category in the form of an interactive papyrus using an infinite multi-touch enabled canvas supporting dynamic embedding media elements through the CMS.

4 Universal Content Management for All Interactive Installation of the Archaeological Museum

The Content Management System coordinates a large amount of systems simultaneously, as the user is able to manage the content of each system remotely, as well as to define a variety of operating scenarios concerning which system will operate, when (i.e. which days of the year) and which content scenario will be presented. It is the most important component in the presented workflow, mainly because it controls everything that happens within the system from content management to scenario building and application delivery and scheduling (see Fig. 1). Using the CMS a number of low level facilities are offered in order to administer content, including versioning facilities and building interactive scenarios. Through the Installation Manager, it is possible to control what is happening in each installation and access its time schedule. Museum curators can control for each installation of the museum the interactive application that will be executed, for which time slot and days, what is the scenario that will be loaded for this application and what is the reusable interaction modality to be used for receiving input.

Fig. 1. Building a scenario using the CMS

5   Virtual Tour at the Archaeological Museum of Heraklion

The Heraklion Archaeological Museum is one of the largest and most important museums in Greece, and among the most important museums in Europe. It hosts representative artefacts from all the periods of Cretan prehistory and ancient history, covering a chronological span of over 5,500 years from the Neolithic period to Roman times. The Minoan collection contains unique examples of Minoan art, many of them true masterpieces. The installation of interactive exhibits at the premises of the Archaeological Museum of Heraklion covers the most important thematic categories of the museum. Interactive systems are scattered within the museum and occupy physical spaces where digital technology is used to "accompany" and "explain" physical exhibits and antiquities. A major challenge from a technological perspective was to automate all the functionality of the digital exhibits and integrate installations in an unobtrusive way within the museums architecture and rooms structure.

The Museum welcomes the visitors with a video wall consisting of 8 monitors accompanied by an artistic board depicting a simulation of the Minoan labyrinth and a design plan of the facilities. The video wall presents multimedia content related to the most important exhibits of the museum presented in chronological sequence, corresponding to the exhibition tour. Graphic designs smoothen the transitions between exhibits in order to give a pleasant overview of the exhibition (Fig. 2).

Fig. 2. Museum entrance, video presentation with the most important exhibits

The tour of the archaeological exhibits begins as visitors enter Hall no. II (Fig. 3a left). A screen embedded into the wall presents multimedia content related to the theme of the room, the Peak Sanctuaries. Physical environments of the sanctuaries, architectural conformation, dedicators, offerings and references of cult activity in modern times are illustrated. Proceeding to Hall no. VI (Fig. 3b), a presentation related to the theme "Music, dance, sports and spectacles" accompanies the room. In both halls, the **Multimedia Viewer** application is used together with the **Skeleton Tracking** and **Gesture/Posture recognition** interaction modality. Visitors may interact from distance and control the system with gestures.

Fig. 3. a. Left: Hall II "Peak Sanctuaries", b. Right: Hall VI "Music · Dance · Sports · Spectacles"

Hall No. V hosts two information kiosks (Fig. 4 left) displaying information about Minoan Diet, Minoan Architecture, Minoan Writing & Sealing and Minoan Technology (see Fig. 4 right). The info kiosks provide information categorized in the form of augmented digital book, enriched with additional features, through multiple touch screens. Each thematic contains texts, images, videos, 3D models or micro-games. Text may comprise hyperlinks which provide further information with related multi-media content through a pop-up window. The Papyrus renderer is used by the kiosks that integrate via the scenarios 3D objects Renderer, in order to offer interaction with 3D models. An edutainment micro-game is dedicated to provide information within two scenarios: the construction of a clay pot, and the construction of a bronze tool. Both scenarios unroll with the presence of a schematic human figure which users may manipulate through specific touch interactions.

Fig. 4. Left: Information kiosks located in hall V, Right: Minoan Diet, Minoan Architecture, Minoan Writing & Sealing, Minoan Technology

At the ground floor two other interactive systems are hosted. The system depicted in Fig. 5a presents multimedia content focused on the conservation of antiquities over time. The Multimedia Viewer application shell is used together with the Skeleton Tracking and Gesture/Posture recognition interaction modality. At the right side of the area (Fig. 5b) an interactive game provides visitors with an innovative experience of edutainment as they control the game using their "virtual" shadows projected on the display. The "virtual" shadow follows body movements as users stand in front of the screen. Minoan ancient objects have to be separated following specific criteria, such as material, usage, date, etc. The Wall game presenter application is used together with Skeleton Tracking and Gesture recognition interaction modalities.

Fig. 5. a. Left: Video presentation of the conservation of antiquities, b. Right: Entertainment game with interaction from distance

Proceeding to the first floor of the Museum, visitors get to learn about "Minoan thalassocracy" (Fig. 6a) and more specifically about the influence of prehistoric Crete in ancient times and the spread of Minoans around the Aegean Sea through descriptions of archaeological sites and objects, as well as reports of the Archaeological Secretariat concerning the tradition and the society of Cretans. In Hall XIV visitors are able to navigate through a multiple touch screen that provides information in the form of a constant flow of images and words. Accordingly, at the opposite aisle XXV, another touch screen presents information about "Daedalus & Icarus: The first flight and thereafter" (Fig. 6b). The Object stream visualizer is employed by both displays together with the embedded touch capabilities of the display.

Fig. 6. a. Left: Hall XIV "Minoan Thalassocracy", b. Right: Hall XXV "Daedalus & Icarus"

The conference room, in the first floor, hosts an interactive system that presents time-related information on a large scale display, while user interaction is achieved through remote gesturing. The system ensures a rich and immersive user experience, while providing information in a clear and unambiguous manner, and is suitable for the info-tainment domain, which combines information and entertainment. The information presented from the system is focused on the history of archaeological research and excavations in Crete through the establishment, operation and recent renovation of the Archaeological Museum of Heraklion, emphasizing key events. The Timeline renderer application shell is used in this installation together with the Skeleton Tracking and Gesture/Posture recognition interaction modalities. Content is synchronized in the form of scenarios by the CMS client.

6   Conclusion

This paper has presented the technological infrastructure deployed at the museum together with the specific interaction technologies and information systems used to blend digital information with the museum visiting experience. For this purpose technology is used to augment the information presented by museum exhibition to form novel experiences that blend physical artefacts with digital information rooted in new museology paradigm. The reformed exhibition is experienced, since 2015, by hundreds thousands visitors of the museum each year.

Acknowledgements. The installation at the Archaeological Museum of Heraklion was co-funded by the **European Regional Development Fund, National Strategic Reference Framework (NSRF 2007–2013), Operational Program "Competitiveness and Entrepreneurship"**. The development of the interactive systems presented by this research work was supported by the FORTH-ICS internal RTD Programme 'Ambient Intelligence and Smart Environments'[4].

References

1. McCall, V., Gray, C.: Museums and the 'new museology': theory, practice and organisational change. Museum Manag. Curatorship **29**(1), 19–35 (2014)
2. Falk, J.H., Dierking, L.D.: The Museum Experience Revisited. Left Coast, Walnut Creek (2012)
3. Mairesse, F., Desvallées, A.: Key Concepts of Museology, International Council of Museums. Armand Colin, Paris (2010)
4. Walker, K.: Structuring Visitor Participation, Digital Technologies and the Museum Experience, Handheld Guides and Other Media, pp. 109–124. Altamira Press, Lanham (2008)
5. Weil, S.: Rethinking the Museum and Other Meditations. Smithsonian Press, Washington (1990)
6. Hooper-Greenhill, E.: Museums and Education: Purpose, Pedagogy, Performance Abingdon. Routledge, London (2000)
7. Ferdani, D., Pagano, A., Farouk, M.: Terminology, Definitions and Types for Virtual Museums (2014).   http://www.v-must.net/sites/default/files/D2.1c%20V_Must_TERMINOLOGY_V2014_FINAL.pdf

---

[4] FORTH-ICS AmI Programme: http://www.ics.forth.gr/index_main.php?l=e&c=4.

Interactive City Information Point:
Your Guide to Heraklion City

Nikolaos Partarakis[1]([✉]), George Margetis[1], Emmanouil Zidianakis[1], Michalis Sifakis[1],
Giannis Drossis[1], Chryssi Birliraki[1], Antonis Chatziantoniou[1], Vassiliki Neroutsou[1],
Spiros Paparoulis[1], Thanasis Toutountzis[1], Panagiotis Koutlemanis[1],
Xenophon Zabulis[1], Stavroula Ntoa[1], Dimitris Grammenos[1], Emmanouil Apostolakis[1],
Emmanouil Stamatakis[1], Margherita Antona[1], and Constantine Stephanidis[1,2]

[1] Foundation for Research and Technology – Hellas (FORTH), Institute of Computer Science,
N. Plastira 100, Vassilika Vouton, 700 13 Heraklion, Crete, Greece
{partarak,gmarget,zidian,misi,drossis,birlirak,hatjiant,vaner,
spirosp,atout,koutle,zabulis,stant,gramenos,apostolak,
stamatakis,antona,cs}@ics.forth.gr
[2] Department of Computer Science, University of Crete, Heraklion, Greece

Abstract. The Tourism Office of the city of Heraklion is a truly original facility
that provides visitors with novel ways to access information through the use of
modern technologies and innovative interactive systems developed by ICS-
FORTH. This paper presents the innovative technologies employed at the tourist
information office in order to enhance the information provision capacity of this
type of facility in conjunction with traditional approaches, such as printed information material and human operated information provision. The info-point of
Heraklion deploys a mixture of systems that augment the visiting experience
while providing information through kinaesthetic interaction, Mixed Reality and
play.

Keywords: Information visualization · Interactive systems · Mixed reality
Augmented artefacts · Interaction with printed matter · Hand gestures
Skeletal interaction

1   Introduction

Public spaces have a social impact on people by involving necessary, optional and social
activities [1], and by hosting exhibits that provide public information. The latter include
for example advertising stands and bus-routes, as well as tourist information such as
weather forecast data, shop and sightseeing opening hours, shop offers, and city news
and events. To improve the quality of the information provided, researchers propose to
encourage user-interaction with the data in an aesthetic manner, instead of statically
displaying them on stands or screens. Modern information visualization techniques can
help towards conveying information without overwhelming users, and playful interaction can help towards arousing user interest and attracting the public. Especially in the

domain of tourist information, public information points have traditionally played an important role in delivering information to citizens regarding city attractions.

2 Background and Related Work

This work is rooted in the domain of interactive installations in public spaces and moves beyond into examining the process of applying such techniques into public information points. Interactive installations in public spaces have specific requirements in terms of interaction and setup. The installations need to adapt to fit to the space available, provide content which interests both experts and non-expert users, and also present thorough information on demand [2]. At the same time, the system design should provide information immediately and support straightforward interaction techniques. Multi-user interaction with public displays is an open issue and constitutes an active area of research. Once people approach the interactive display, they decide their actions with regard to the system. Especially in the context of MR applications, the initiation of interaction with a public display involves transitioning from implicit to explicit interaction [3] as the users become engaged to the pervasive display.

Tangible interaction is a form of interaction with mixed reality installations in which physical items act as mediators between the users and the environment. One aspect of tangible interaction refers to the augmentation of physical objects so as to become information displays. For instance, physical paper is employed as a portable display, augmenting maps or glass-protected models [4]. Interactive Maps [5] is a mixed reality application, where printed maps are augmented with additional multimedia information. Furthermore, tangible interaction can involve objects which have meaningful substance with a semantic meaning, such as smart objects (i.e. physical items equipped with sensors such as RFID tags) [6].

In this paper the concept of interactive installation for public information spaces is presented through a prototypical installation at the Heraklion Info Point. In this context a mixture of interaction techniques (augmented artefact, interaction with printed matter, hand gestures, body based interaction) are employed by different systems to communicate different types of information to visitors. All these different forms of interaction are combined together to offer an engaging, educational and fun experience.

3 The Heraklion Info Point

The Heraklion info-point promotes the island of Crete and provides visitors with novel ways to access information through the use of modern technologies and innovative interactive systems developed by ICS-FORTH. The seven (7) systems that have been deployed are:

- **Infocloud**, a colourful mosaic of photographs and other multimedia material showcasing the civilization and landmarks of Crete "flows" across a large touch screen.

- **Be There Now!** Photographs of many different locations and landmarks of Crete are projected one at a time on a wall. When visitors stand in front of an image they see themselves projected within it and they can e-mail themselves a souvenir photograph.
- **Paper View** presents a map of the entire island printed on a large table-top, which comes to life once the visitor places a piece of cardboard on the surface of the table.
- **Interactive Documents**: On a plain table surface visitors may place the printed map of the historical centre of Heraklion which is freely distributed by info-point. The system electronically augments the printed map with multimedia information in several languages and the user is able to interact through touch with the map in order to extract further information.
- **Media Gallery** presents an extensive collection of photographs and other multimedia materials about the flora and fauna of Crete that can be navigated by gesture.
- **Stater 360²** comprises a revolving disk which seems made of clay and on this surface the Phaistos Disk is projected in different states.
- **A Game Table** is a game kiosk that includes a multi-touch screen which can be used by one or more players and offers two educative and entertaining games that present images and information about Crete through playing.

There is one more system, which presents a synthesis of technology with art not only inside the info-point, but also at the window to the historic pedestrian way in front of the building. This is an interactive sculpture, where innovative technologies are combined with visual arts. Set in the main window, it draws inspiration from the myth of the Labyrinth, works of Nikos Kazantzakis and other elements of Crete's long cultural tradition to form a complex double-sided relief that welcomes visitors to explore it by touch. Visitors are invited to touch the mechanical devices embedded in the sculpture so as to reveal the scripture and set the ancient device back to life (see Fig. 1).

Fig. 1. Interactive sculpture inspired by the history of the city of Heraklion

3.1 Interaction with Information Flows

Infocloud comprises a collection of keywords, images and video thumbnails displayed on a very large touch screen. When a word is selected, an information window opens, which may contain an image or video accompanied by a short textual description. The keywords, images and video thumbnails constantly flow (e.g., from right to left), while (optionally) the background flows to the opposite direction. Items are positioned at multiple layers, each of which has different attributes (size, speed, dimness) (Fig. 2).

Fig. 2. Infocloud "Heraklion info-point"

3.2 Immersing Users to Landscapes to Create Digital Cartes Postales

Be There Now! is an interactive system that allows the exploration of different sceneries and immerses users in various landscapes, by depicting the visitors standing before it within the landscapes and the vistas projected, as if they were at that place (Fig. 3).

Fig. 3. Be there now! "Heraklion info-point

3.3 Alternative Forms of Interaction with Terrain-Based Information

PaperView is a **tabletop augmented reality** system that supports the exploration of **terrain-based information** (e.g., areas of interest on a 2D map, or a 3D scale model) using rectangular pieces of **plain cardboard**. The system allows users to view information and interactive multimedia using the cardboards as individual interactive screens; these cardboard screens can be lifted and held at various angles. Multiple users can concurrently use the table [7]. When a user places a cardboard piece over the table surface, an image is projected on it, adding details to the surface image. Furthermore, a pointer (i.e., a magnifying glass) is projected on the paper's centre, which assists the user in exploring the surface, guiding her/him to the information hotspots available. When a hotspot is selected, a multimedia slideshow starts. The slideshow comprises a series of pages, each of which may contain any combination of text, images, and videos. At the bottom area of the slideshow, a toolbar is projected containing an indication of the current page and the total number of pages available, as well as buttons for moving to the next/previous page (Fig. 4).

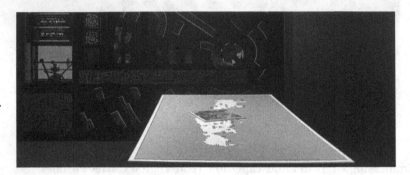

Fig. 4. Paper view at "Heraklion info-point"

3.4   Interacting with Printed Maps

The **interactive documents** system augments printed documents that are placed upon a surface (e.g., a plain table) with multimedia content and interactive applications. Such content is dynamically displayed in augmentation to the currently open page of the document, and is aligned in real-time with its 2D orientation upon the table surface. At the Heraklion Info Point visitors may interact with the printed map of the historical centre of Heraklion which is freely distributed. The system electronically augments the printed map with multimedia information in several languages and the user is able to interact through touch with the map in order to extract further information (Fig. 5).

Fig. 5. Interactive documents at the "Heraklion info-point"

3.5 Children Discover Crete Through Beautiful Pictures

Media Gallery is a system that allows browsing and exploring large collections of multimedia information using touchless remote interaction, by employing computer vision technologies. At the info point this system is targeted to attract the attention of visitors to a collage of landscapes, people, animals and plants of the island (Fig. 6).

Fig. 6. Media gallery at the "Heraklion info-point"

3.6 Physical and Multitouch Interaction with a Double Rotating Gimbal

Stater 360² comprises a revolving disk which seems made of clay and on this surface different views of the Phaistos Disk are projected. Visitors may turn the disk over in order to see both sides, while they can find out information about this legendary discovery of Minoan archaeology by touching the surface. The available information includes details of the Disk's discovery and a brief presentation of the latest findings of hieroglyphics, as well as attempts at understanding what the mysterious writing is about (Fig. 7).

Fig. 7. Stater 360² at "Heraklion info-point"

3.7 Game Table

The Game Table is a game kiosk that includes a multi-touch screen which can be used by one or more players and offers two educative and entertaining games that present images and information about Crete through playing:

1. Jigsaw Puzzle. Players are invited to complete a puzzle. They can select the difficulty level and image of their preference. As the puzzle is successfully completed, users can explore information related to that image,
2. Cryptolexon. Words are hidden within a grid of random letters, which users are called to detect. As the words are successfully selected, multimedia content with descriptive text is provided on the screen.

4   Evaluation

The info-point systems have been evaluated in-situ with actual visitors. In situ studies facilitate the exploration of the actual usage of a system in its real environment [8] and have the potential to reveal how the environment itself influences user experience [9], while they can result in revealing more usability problems than laboratory evaluations [10]. The evaluation employed observations, semi-structured interviews with users and employees, as well as questionnaires that were handed to the info-point visitors. In particular with regard to observations, since there was no audio or video recording, detailed observation notes were kept by the evaluation observers in custom observation sheets.

Upon entering the info-point, visitors were informed about the evaluation aims, objectives and procedures. Those who orally agreed to be observed during their inter-action with the systems were given an informed consent form to sign. Then, they were asked to continue their visit as they normally would, and only once they had completed their interaction with the info-point systems and/or with the staff for retrieving infor-mation, they were given the questionnaires to fill-in (one for each system they had inter-acted with) and finally they were interviewed.

Given that visitors were allowed to navigate in the info-point premises according to their own preferences and were not explicitly instructed to use all the systems, each of the systems was eventually evaluated by a different number and ensemble of users. A preliminary analysis of the results indicates that users found the systems fun to interact with and innovative, while they have suggested that in some cases additional useful information could be provided by the systems. Yet, it is interesting that despite the innovativeness of the employed interaction techniques, the majority of users easily identified how to interact and used the system without facing any significant obstacles or requiring assistance from the info-point employees.

The detailed analysis of the results from the evaluation of each one of the systems is an ongoing process and will be reported elsewhere, exploring three main hypotheses: (i) that the systems are easy to use with minimum guidance, (ii) that the interaction techniques employed by each system are natural to the users, and (iii) that each system yields a positive user experience [11].

5   Conclusion

This paper has presented the technologically enhanced City Information Point of Heraklion (Crete). In this context, eight interactive systems have been deployed that provide a complementary view of the tourism opportunities, history and culture of Heraklion and Crete through a mixture of novel information visualization techniques, Mixed Reality interaction with augmented artefacts and playful interaction. The info-point is up and running since August 2014 and has been visited so far by more than 40.000 tourists. The info-point has been evaluated in situ in terms of usability and user experience. Preliminary findings justify the initial hypothesis that novel forms of interaction can enhance information provision capacity and increase the interest of users by providing more immersive and memorable experiences.

Acknowledgements. The installation at the Tourism Office of the city of Heraklion was funded under the action L 313-1, priority 4, of the Programme «Rural Development of Greece 2007–2013» - (LEADER). The development of the interactive systems presented by this research work was supported by the FORTH-ICS internal RTD Programme 'Ambient Intelligence and Smart Environments'[1].

References

1. Brignull, H., Rogers, Y.: Enticing people to interact with large public displays in public spaces. In: INTERACT 2003, pp. 17–24 (2003)
2. Mortara, M., Catalano, C.E., Bellotti, F., Fiucci, G., Houry-Panchetti, M., Petridis, P.: Learning cultural heritage by serious games. J. Cult. Heritage **15**(3), 318–325 (2014)
3. Vogel, D., Balakrishnan, R.: Interactive public ambient displays: transitioning from implicit to explicit, public to personal, interaction with multiple users. In: Proceedings of the 17th Annual ACM Symposium on User Interface Software and Technology, pp. 137–146. ACM, October 2004
4. Grammenos, D., Michel, D., Zabulis, X., Argyros, A.A.: PaperView: augmenting physical surfaces with location-aware digital information. In: Proceedings of the Fifth International Conference on Tangible, Embedded, and Embodied Interaction, pp. 57–60. ACM, January 2011)
5. Margetis, G., Ntoa, S., Antona, M., Stephanidis, C.: Interacting with augmented paper maps: a user experience study. In: 12th Biannual Conference of the Italian SIGCHI Chapter (CHITALY 2017). 18th–20th September 2017, Cagliari, Italy (2017)
6. Petrelli, D., Dulake, N., Marshall, M. T., Pisetti, A., Not, E.: Voices from the war: design as a means of understanding the experience of visiting heritage. In: Proceedings of the 2016 CHI Conference on Human Factors in Computing Systems, pp. 1033–1044. ACM, May 2016
7. Grammenos, D., Michel, D., Zabulis, X., Argyros, A.: PaperView: augmenting physical surfaces with location-aware digital information. In: The Proceedings of the 5th International Conference on Tangible, Embedded, and Embodied Interaction (TEI 2011), Funchal, Portugal, 23–26 January 2011, pp. 57–60. ACM Press, New York (2011)
8. Fields, B., Amaldi, P., Wong, W., Gill, S.: In use, in situ: extending field research methods. Int. J. Hum. Comput. Interact. **22**, 1–6 (2007)
9. Rogers, Y., Connelly, K., Tedesco, L., Hazlewood, W., Kurtz, A., Hall, R.E., Hursey, J., Toscos, T.: Why it's worth the hassle: the value of in-situ studies when designing ubicomp. In: Krumm, J., Abowd, G.D., Seneviratne, A., Strang, T. (eds.) UbiComp 2007. LNCS, vol. 4717, pp. 336–353. Springer, Heidelberg (2007). https://doi.org/10.1007/978-3-540-74853-3_20

---

[1] FORTH-ICS AmI Programme: http://www.ics.forth.gr/index_main.php?l=e&c=4.

10. Nielsen, C.M., Overgaard, M., Pedersen, M.B., Stage, J., Stenild, S.: It's worth the hassle!: the added value of evaluating the usability of mobile systems in the field. In: Proceedings of the 4th Nordic Conference on Human-Computer Interaction: Changing Roles, pp. 272–280. ACM, October 2006
11. Margetis, G., Ntoa, S., Antona, M., Stephanidis, C.: Interacting with augmented paper maps: a user experience study. In: Proceedings of the 12th Biannual Conference on Italian SIGCHI Chapter, p. 18. ACM, September 2017

Toward Human-Magic Interaction: Interfacing Biological, Tangible, and Cultural Technology

Pat Pataranutaporn[1]([✉]) and Kimberly Lyle[2]([✉])

[1] Massachusetts Institute of Technology, Cambridge, MA 02139, USA
pat.pataranutaporn@gmail.com
[2] Arizona State University, Tempe, AZ 85281, USA
kelyle@asu.edu

Abstract. The ubiquitous and pervasive nature of computing fosters intimate relationships between humans and computers as the digital objects being entangled with "non" digital objects: biological, tangible, and cultural. We present the framework of the human-magical interaction, which defines the emerging interfaces as forms of "Magic" emphasizing the seamless interaction between humans and different technological mediums. To explore the framework of Human-Magic Interaction, we re-imagine the ecology of interactive systems and present three speculative technologies that demonstrate different aspects of the framework.

Keywords: Interface · Biological · Tangible · Cultural · Magic

1 Introduction

The current definition of Human-Computer Interaction focuses on the design, evaluation, and implementation of interactive computing systems for human use, specifically the interaction between human(s) and computational device(s) [1]. However, human computer interactions have undergone radical transformations in recent years. As the ubiquitous nature of computing fosters increasingly intimate relationships between humans and computers, this calls for a reimagining of the definition and framework for HCI. The growth of the digital era is not only defined by increased numbers of users and applications, but it also involves digital objects being entangled with 'non' digital objects. In a conventional context, 'non' digital objects are biological, tangible, and culturally rich. We propose a translation from the old framework of HCI to a new interface inclusive of these 'non' digital objects. This framework posits the existence of three new interfaces: natural, physical, and cultural. The Biological Interface encompasses systems that allow humans to interact with living and non-living things on a more intimate level, as design materials. The Tangible Interface incorporates physical objects as part of digital interactive systems. And the Cultural and Critical Interface considers both the global and personal effects that digital interfaces have on our values, beliefs, assumptions, and social relations as a society.

© Springer International Publishing AG, part of Springer Nature 2018
C. Stephanidis (Ed.): HCII Posters 2018, CCIS 852, pp. 213–221, 2018.
https://doi.org/10.1007/978-3-319-92285-0_30

2 Interfaces

2.1 Biological Interface

Researchers have developed interface systems that allow humans to interact with natural things (living and non-living) as design materials. For living things, researchers have developed a framework of Biological HCI to specify how biological materials can be computable through digital interfaces [2]. Projects that fall under Biological HCI include: the development of the Biology Cloud Lab architecture for online experiments involving living organisms [3], shape changing interfaces with the ability to produce morphable textiles [4] and biologically driven wearable technology [5] that responds to the human body [6], digital-biology hybrid games [7], and interactive biodesign installations [8]. These examples suggest how biological augmentation with digital objects provide a rich design space for arts, games, and experiments, which can lead to biotic processing units (BPUs) as future hardware architecture. Researchers also look at living organisms as the sensors for ubiquitous computing, which blur the boundary between computers and living organisms [9]. Beyond using organisms as interfaces, researchers have incorporated tattoos embedded into human skin that respond to changes in biochemical information within the body's fluids [10]. This demonstrates how humans have converted parts of the body into devices for displaying information.

2.2 Tangible Interface

Beyond conventional digital interfaces that are bound by the limitations of the display devices, researchers have also considered tangible interfaces, where the physical objects become part of an interactive system. An example of Tangible interfaces include shape changing devices and the use of everyday objects as interactive design materials. For instance, researchers have developed Shape Display [11], a new type of I/O device that can display physical 3D graphics, which leverages tangible interaction and collaboration through physical telepresence; Researchers have also looked into enabling technology for shape-changing materials using pneumatically-actuated soft composites, which integrate the capabilities of input sensing and active shape output [11]. Furthermore, researchers have developed everyday materials into interactive devices. For example, researchers have designed the Edible User Interface (EUI) [12], a multi-sensory design framework that utilizes food materials to create novel interactions such as TasteScreen, a display screen that allows people to taste different flavors by licking liquid residue released on the screen [13]. Researchers have also designed LOLLio, an edible interface made out of lollipops for playing games [14]. Beyond food, researchers also integrated multi-model sensor devices such as acoustic sensing, motion sensing, and accelerometers that allow non-digital objects to become an input device for computing [15, 16]. The integration and connectivity between everyday objects and the digital network "Internet of Things" broadens the scope of the computer interface. These examples demonstrate the programmability of everyday objects, allowing them to change shape or respond to the environment. This notion is captured in the vision "Radical Atoms", that propose how humans would interact with dynamic materials that manifest digital information [17].

2.3 Cultural and Critical Interface

The interface is the most important cultural form of our time [18]. The increasing prevalence of digital interface systems has reconfigured our cultural values, beliefs, assumptions, and social relationships. While culture is shaped by a wide range of factors, our framework for a Cultural and Critical HCI focuses on research divided into pre-digital human culture, digital interaction between humans, digital imitation of humans, and post-digital human culture. Shifts have been made from cultures that once revolved around oral storytelling and indigenous knowledges to digitally mediated cultures where humans interact through social media platforms that often spread more lies than truth [19], construct identity through online gaming communities [20], and communicate through forms of augmented reality [21]. The digital imitation of humans also continues to shape our social communities. For example, AI that recreates the dead through a chatbot version [22], robots that gain your trust by mimicking human nonverbal cues [23], moral decision making devices for self-driving cars [24], and real-time facial reenactment software that allows humans to digitally manipulate facial expressions of others [25]. The future of Cultural and Critical Interfaces, a post-digital culture, will oppose the hegemony of digital technology with tools that rebuild trust in social media by fostering civil discourse, allowing questions to be asked, and finding reasoned opposing views [26], location-based social networks [27] such as Action Path [28] which encourage community civic engagement, gaming environments that become a place for racial discourse [29], and continued research on anti-racial biased imaging software [30].

3 Toward Human-Magic Interaction

With the emerging interfaces spanning across domains of biological, tangible, and cultural systems, we observe a shifting trend in human-computer interaction. In the conventional model [1], there was a clear distinction between human and computer, and the bi-directional interactions that happen in between can be discerned as a linear line of interaction. To understand the holistic interactions between humans and computers, one must consider the ecology of human and machine enriched by the complicated network of interactivity and interaction between devices, and situated within a cultural context. We propose that this expansion of computing does not only change the scale and scope of HCI's study, but also creates a new paradigm shift in how we come to understand the computer.

By integrating the emerging interfaces, we present the framework of the human-magical interaction, which emphasizes the seamless interaction between humans and different forms of technological mediums. The convergence between biological matters, physical and tangible computing, and cultural technology allow humans to be fully immersed in an interactive environment, where bits and atoms are dynamically programmable [31]. This infrastructure of software, hardware, bio ware, physicalware, culturalware, and humanware are part of an interactive ecology that would allow humans to interface with technology in a "Magical" way. The "Magic" refers to the supernatural power that transcends beyond human's natural abilities. This definition of magic can be applied to the technology as they augment and expand human capabilities. Secondly, the idea of "Magic" embodies our unmet human desires as imagined in fairytales and stories where a human wish cannot be met without some form of magic.

Further, the idea of technology as magic also reflects how the technology has been used with minimal understanding as systems get more complicated as scholars have developed the term "Cathedral of Computation" [32]. The embeddedness of computing in our modern has been fabricated into our society. Therefore, the understanding between the interaction that happens between humans and technology can no longer be linearized, but rather viewed as symbiosis. This model reflects an ecology of human and technology driven by dynamic interactions, where each constantly effect and influence one another in unconscious and seamless ways.

To explore the future of Human-Computer Interaction, we look at the ecology of interactive systems through the lens of Human-Magic Interaction. These "Magical" Technologies place emphasis on the variability and ambiguity that happen in the progress of HCI expansion. We present three speculative technologies that demonstrate different aspects of the framework (Fig. 1).

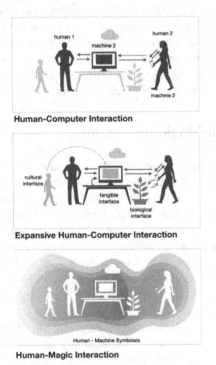

Human-Computer Interaction

Expansive Human-Computer Interaction

Human-Magic Interaction

Fig. 1. The Human-Magic Interaction model

3.1 Genie Machine

Genie machine is inspired by the character Genie from *Aladdin*. Genie is a powerful spirit residing in a magical lamp that can make the wish of his master come true. The character Genie resembles the form of an assistive intelligent agent that can complete tasks on behalf of a human. The notion of the intelligent assistant has been explored in various forms in areas of AI and robotics. Some of the examples include Apple's Siri, Amazon's Alexa, and IBM's Watson. The key component of the system is the language processing unit, which allows the system to listen to human commands and convert them into actions. By looking at Human-Magic Interaction, we speculate on the future of assistive intelligent agents that are embedded in wearable technology, which can work across biological, tangible, and cultural domains, extending the assistive capabilities beyond the digital realm. For example, the machine can be asked to check the status of plant growth by interfacing with a living system. Genie might also be asked to adjust the micro-climate around the plant by connecting with the internet of things devices, to change the environment. The ambiguity that arises here is the notion that the future computer is the machine of desire that mediates human experience from the micro to the macro level. By altering materials from bio to physical to achieve the task, the technology transforms digital abilities to magical power (Fig. 2).

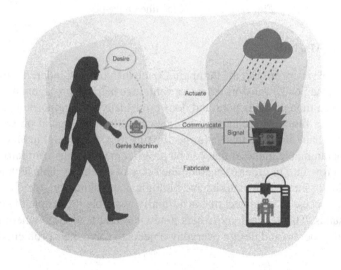

Fig. 2. Genie Machine interaction with various platforms

3.2 Pinocchio Machine

Pinocchio machine is inspired by the character Pinocchio, known for having a short nose that becomes longer when he is under stress, especially while lying. This feature of the character embodies the idea of body augmentation that responds to biological and cultural construction. We speculate a wearable technology that the user places on his/her nose to become self-aware of his/her actions. For example, the Pinocchio

Machine can be programmed to elongate when the user says something that has a low credibility score or violates social norms. This example serves as the kind of magical technology that allows humans to have part of their body become an interface for self-awareness, which is created through a feedback loop between biological and cultural status. This platform also visualizes the bio-political tensions between social constructs and individuality by demonstrating how the body can be altered if it doesn't conform with society (Fig. 3).

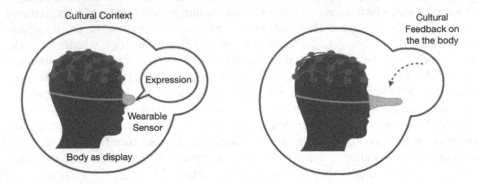

Fig. 3. Pinocchio Machine on the body

3.3 Pumpkin Machine

The final example is inspired by the Pumpkin Coach in the story Cinderella. In this story, the pumpkin is magically transformed into a vehicle to help the protagonist travel to her destination, even though she is poor and does not usually have opportunities to travel. We speculate the future of technology that can modify a biological object such as a pumpkin into a shape and form that has a specific function. The Pumpkin Machine would include a programmable material that can be programmed to transform into a mold for pumpkins to grow into in order to become the body of a vehicle. This technology is at the intersection of interactive material and biological augmentation, which can be used to decentralize access to the object that is normally available for people of certain socioeconomic status. This technology fosters a new cultural landscape where people are empowered to program and design everyday objects to solve their problems (Fig. 4).

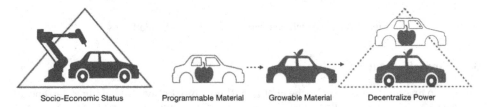

Fig. 4. Pumpkin Machine

4   Conclusion

The most recent HCI framework places emphasis on the interaction between human and machine as two separate entities that communicate back and forth with one another sequentially. Our proposed framework pushes this idea forward, citing how the context of the computer has radically expanded, becoming more inclusive of biological, tangible, and cultural interfaces. However, as the boundaries of human and machine continue to dissolve at an ever-increasing rate, these once clearly marked borders are beginning to blur further into one another. Full integration of human and machine then becomes an inevitable future, one where the machine is no longer a singular entity but encased seamlessly in our bodies, surrounding us in our environment, embedded in our cultural heritage, in our everyday objects, and even in the air we breathe.

As a result, we can no longer perceive technology as we have in the past. Technology becomes the new "Magic" that seeps into our culture, systems, and interpersonal interactions, while affecting us in ways that are mostly invisible. On the human level, as we slowly merge with our machines, our attention spans, mindfulness, and the full range of our human modalities will be mediated through technology as a human-machine symbiosis occurs. However, to fully understand the impact of this new framework, we must expand the picture further to consider the cultural context and ecology of things surrounding them. The term magic has negative connotations associated with it, which requires us to handle it with a high level of responsibility, criticality, and questioning.

This research article was created through a collaboration between an HCI research scientist and an artist, to imagine new possibilities, visualize the invisible tensions that are emerging, and ask questions about what this might mean for our society. We believe that the future of magical technology must be created through interactions between people across disciplines, as multiple perspectives will ensure a more well-rounded outcome. As the future of technology becomes seamlessly pervasive, what type of magic would you create?

References

1. ACM SIGCHI Curricula for Human-Computer Interaction: 2. Definition and Overview of Human-Computer Interaction. http://old.sigchi.org/cdg/cdg2.html
2. Pataranutaporn, P., Ingalls, T., Finn, E.: Biological HCI: towards integrative interfaces between people, computer, and biological materials. In: ACM Conference on Human Factors in Computing Systems Conference on Human Factors in Computing Systems (2018)
3. Hossain, Z., Blikstein, P., Riedel-Kruse, I.H., Jin, X., Bumbacher, E.W., Chung, A.M., Koo, S., Shapiro, J.D., Truong, C.Y., Choi, S., Orloff, N.D.: Interactive cloud experimentation for biology. In: Proceedings of the 33rd Annual ACM Conference on Human Factors in Computing Systems - CHI 2015, pp. 3681–3690. ACM Press, New York (2015)
4. Yao, L., Ou, J., Cheng, C.-Y., Steiner, H., Wang, W., Wang, G., Ishii, H.: bioLogic. In: Proceedings of the 33rd Annual ACM Conference on Human Factors in Computing Systems - CHI 2015, pp. 1–10. ACM Press, New York (2015)

5. Bader, C., Patrick, W.G., Kolb, D., Hays, S.G., Keating, S., Sharma, S., Dikovsky, D., Belocon, B., Weaver, J.C., Silver, P.A., Oxman, N.: Grown, printed, and biologically augmented: an additively manufactured microfluidic wearable, functionally templated for synthetic microbes. 3D Print. Addit. Manuf. **3**, 79–89 (2016)
6. Pataranutaporn, P., Ngamkajornwiwat, P., Unprasert, T., Umnajsasithorn, W., Luksanayeam, S., Loha-Unchit, S., La-O-Vorakia, C., Sakulkueakulsuk, B., Ngamarunchot, B., Assawaboonyalert, C., Pataranutaporn, P., Chatwiriyachai, S., Surareungchai, W., Jain, S.: Hormone couture: biopolitics, aesthetics, and technology. In: ACM Proceedings - International Symposium on Wearable Computers, ISWC (2017)
7. Gerber, L.C., Kim, H., Riedel-Kruse, I.H.: Interactive biotechnology: design rules for integrating biological matter into digital games. In: DiGRA/FDG 2016 - Proceedings of the First International Joint Conference of DiGRA and FDG (2016)
8. Lee, S.A., Bumbacher, E., Chung, A.M., Cira, N., Walker, B., Park, J.Y., Starr, B., Blikstein, P., Riedel-kruse, I.H.: Trap it!: a playful human-biology interaction for a museum installation, pp. 2593–2602 (2015)
9. Kuznetsov, S., Odom, W., Pierce, J., Paulos, E.: Nurturing natural sensors
10. Vega, K., Jiang, N., Liu, X., Kan, V., Barry, N., Maes, P., Yetisen, A., Paradiso, J.: The dermal abyss. In: Proceedings of the 2017 ACM International Symposium on Wearable Computers - ISWC 2017, pp. 138–145. ACM Press, New York (2017)
11. Rasmussen, M.K., Troiano, G.M., Petersen, M.G., Simonsen, J.G., Hornbæk, K.: Sketching shape-changing interfaces. In: Proceedings of the 2016 CHI Conference on Human Factors in Computing Systems - CHI 2016, pp. 2740–2751. ACM Press, New York (2016)
12. Gayler, T.: Towards edible interfaces: designing interactions with food. In: Proceedings of the 19th ACM International Conference on Multimodal Interaction - ICMI 2017, pp. 623–627. ACM Press, New York (2017)
13. Maynes-Aminzade, D.: Edible bits: seamless interfaces between people, data and food. In: CHI 2005 Extended Abstracts, pp. 2207–2210. ACM (2005)
14. Murer, M., Aslan, I., Tscheligi, M.: LOLLio. In: Proceedings of the 7th International Conference on Tangible, Embedded and Embodied Interaction - TEI 2013, p. 299. ACM Press, New York (2013)
15. Laput, G., Zhang, Y., Harrison, C.: Synthetic sensors: towards general-purpose sensing
16. Ono, M., Shizuki, B., Tanaka, J.: Touch & activate. In: Proceedings of the 26th Annual ACM Symposium on User Interface Software and Technology - UIST 2013, pp. 31–40. ACM Press, New York (2013)
17. Bonanni, L., Ishii, H.: Radical atoms
18. Johnson, S.: Interface Culture: How New Technology Transforms the Way We Create and Communicate. HarperEdge, San Francisco (1997)
19. Vosoughi, S., Roy, D., Aral, S.: The spread of true and false news online. Science **359**(6380), 1146–1151 (2018)
20. Costa Pinto, D., Reale, G., Segabinazzi, R., Vargas Rossi, C.A.: Online identity construction: how gamers redefine their identity in experiential communities. J. Consum. Behav. **14**, 399–409 (2015)
21. Pao, R.: Virtual reality: the new era of the future world. In: 2017 International Symposium on VLSI Technology, Systems and Application (VLSI-TSA), p. 1. IEEE (2017)
22. The AI that (almost) lets you speak to the dead | Ars Technica. https://arstechnica.com/information-technology/2016/07/luka-ai-chatbot-speaking-to-the-dead-mind-uploading/
23. Lee, J.J., Knox, W.B., Wormwood, J.B., Breazeal, C., Desteno, D.: Computationally modeling interpersonal trust. Front. Psychol. **4**, 893 (2013)

24. Awad, E.: Moral Machine: Perception of Moral Judgment Made by Machines—MIT Media Lab (2017)
25. Burgess, M.: Facial Recognition: Make Putin pout with this creepy face-tracking tech | WIRED UK. http://www.wired.co.uk/article/face2face-face-recognition-copy-putin-bush-trump
26. Fernbach, P.M., Rogers, T., Fox, C.R., Sloman, S.A.: political extremism is supported by an illusion of understanding. Psychol. Sci. 24, 939–946 (2013)
27. Zhang, A.X., Noulas, A., Scellato, S., Mascolo, C.: Hoodsquare: modeling and recommending neighborhoods in location-based social networks (2013)
28. Graeff, E.E.C.: Action path: a location-based tool for civic reflection and engagement (2014)
29. Nakamura, L.: Gender and Race Online
30. Wood, M., Hughes, S.: Why facial recognition software has trouble recognizing people of color. https://www.marketplace.org/2018/02/13/tech/why-algorithms-may-have-trouble-recognizing-your-face
31. Story, C., Ishii, H., Lakatos, D., Bonanni, L., Labrune, J.-B.: Radical atoms: beyond tangible bits, toward transformable materials. Interactions 19(1), 38–51 (2012)
32. Bogost, I.: The Cathedral of Computation

HCI in Commerce and Business

Using Multiple Research Methods to Inform Transformation of a Software Application into a Web Survey for Businesses

Amy Anderson Riemer(⌧)

U.S. Census Bureau, Washington D.C., USA
Amy.E.Anderson.Riemer@census.gov

Abstract. Every 5 years the U.S. Census Bureau collects detailed economic data from over 4 million business establishments for an economic census. Starting in 1997, a software application was offered as an alternative to paper forms. In 2018, businesses will be answering this complex survey using the Web as their only reporting option. In order to prepare for this change in platform, the Census Bureau undertook a multi-year/multi-method research program to identify key requirements and to test prototypes and early versions prior to launching the Web survey. In addition to ensuring that key functionality from the legacy software was transferred to the Web instrument, researchers also took the opportunity to identify potential enhancements to the design based on feedback obtained from respondents, internal Census Bureau staff, and user experience experts.

Various research methods were used to guide this transformation, using an iterative approach that took advantage of unique contributions offered by each technique. The process began with a detailed requirements gathering interviews with respondents and other key stakeholders and experts. A task analysis was conducted investigating processes and activities used by business respondents to complete surveys. Debriefing interviews were conducted with business respondents to evaluate features of the legacy software application, determining functionality critical for aiding respondents' work while also detecting tools that were under-utilized and identifying obstacles to their use. Usability testing was conducted using low-fidelity prototypes and early semi-functioning versions of the Web survey in order to test new and redesigned elements. Along the way, paradata from the legacy software and implementation of an early version of the Web survey were analyzed to further evaluate existing and revised features.

This poster will display how these various research methods complemented and augmented one another. It will also highlight challenges and lessons learned.

Keywords: Surveys · Usability testing · Prototypes · Paradata

C. Stephanidis (Ed.): HCII Posters 2018, CCIS 852, pp. 225–232, 2018.
https://doi.org/10.1007/978-3-319-92285-0_31

1   Introduction

Every 5 years the U.S. Census Bureau collects detailed economic data from over 4 million businesses of varying sizes and industry classifications for an economic census. Starting in 1997, a software application was offered as an alternative to paper forms. In 2018, businesses will be answering this complex survey using the Web as their reporting option. In order to prepare for this change in platform, a multi-year/multi-method research effort occurred that identified key requirements and tested prototypes and early versions prior to the economic census. In addition to ensuring that key functionality from the software are transferred to the Web instrument, researchers also took the opportunity to identify improvements.

This paper will discuss the research methods used to transition an electronic survey from a software platform to the Web, along with a discussion of challenges and lessons learned.

1.1   The Economic Census

The economic census is a mandatory survey that requests comprehensive accounting, payroll, and business activity information from all locations within a business. The data collected provides a measure of the U.S. economy and is used by a variety of stake-holders such as policy makers, trade and business associations, other federal agencies, and individual businesses.

Economic census forms vary by industry classification. During the 2012 Economic Census there were over 600 form types available. The software application included several features to assist in the management and collection of potentially thousands of pieces of data. In addition to moving the data collection entirely to the Web, the economic census will not be using paper forms as a response option for the first time during the 2017 collection. All respondents will be required to report using the Web instrument.

1.2   The Annual Survey of Manufactures and the Company Organization Survey

The Annual Survey of Manufactures (ASM) and the Company Organization Survey (COS) are annual surveys collected in the years between the economic census. These related surveys ask a subset of economic census questions from fewer businesses and use the same data collection platform. Because of the relationship between the surveys, changes to the economic census data collection instruments are often incorporated into the ASM or COS first. This strategy allows the Census Bureau to evaluate the impact of any changes and identify additional adjustments that may be necessary prior to a wider release during an economic census collection. Researchers were able to take advantage of this arrangement to develop and test early designs.

The collection software was phased out as a data collection tool in 2017 in time for the collection of the 2016 ASM/COS surveys. This gave researchers and survey managers a year to evaluate this change prior to the all Web collection of the 2017 Economic Census which will be collected in 2018.

2 Methodology

Moving all respondents to a Web only application that would support businesses of all sizes was going to be a massive undertaking that would require input from respondents and internal stakeholders from the beginning. The research effort began in 2014 with a focus on requirements gathering from all stakeholders. Once requirements were gathered, researchers worked with internal staff to create prototypes that were tested with respondents. After a final design was agreed upon, programmers developed early versions of the Web instrument for usability testing. Respondent debriefings were continually conducted to maintain communication with respondents about their actual use of the software application and later the newly designed Web instrument. During development, paradata analysis was used to evaluate the software application as well as the newly released Web instrument. The following Table 1 provides an overview of the research timeline for these multiple methods used across the past five years.

Table 1. 2017 economic census instrument redesign research timeline

2014	2015	2016	2017	2018
Requirements Gathering - Internal	High-Fidelity Prototype Testing (2 rounds)	Usability Testing (2016 ASM/COS)	Usability Testing (2017 Economic Census – 2 rounds)	Paradata Analysis (2016 ASM/COS)
Task Analysis & Respondent Debriefing	Respondent Debriefings (2014 ASM/COS)	Respondent Debriefings (2015 ASM/COS)	Respondent Debriefings (2016 ASM/COS)	Paradata Analysis (2017 Economic Census)
Paper Prototype Testing		Paradata Analysis (2015 ASM/COS)	Paradata Analysis (2016 ASM/COS)	Respondent Debriefings (2017 Economic Census)

The following sections will provide a brief description of the different methods that were used.

2.1 Requirements Analysis – Internal Stakeholders

The first step towards transitioning from a software based application to a web based application was to analyze and gather requirements for the new data collection platform. To achieve this, researchers met with internal stakeholders and respondents. The main goal for this initial step was to identify what features within the software application should be maintained, and which should be modified for the Web. Additionally, we solicited overall ideas for improvements to the data collection tool.

Researchers held several in-person meetings with internal stakeholders to gather this information. These included analysts and staff who worked closely with developing the software application and those that worked closely with the respondents during the past economic census.

2.2   Requirements Analysis – Respondent Task Analysis

In addition to meeting with internal stakeholders, researchers met with business respondents from various industries and company sizes in order to debrief about prior experiences with the data collection instrument and to conduct a task analysis. A task analysis is an early step in the user-centered design process that involves observing users in action to understand how they perform tasks in order to meet their goals [3]. In order to facilitate a task analysis, respondents were asked to provide a detailed description of the process they used when responding to the 2012 Economic Census.

Conducting real-time observation with businesses is very burdensome on the respondent and can be difficult for a survey like the economic census when it typically takes many hours across days or weeks to complete. In larger companies, the response process often involves multiple staff accessing multiple internal data sources to gather information [2]. In the absence of real-time observation, researchers often relied upon detailed exploratory questions that would reflect upon recent survey experience, where applicable.

The goal for the task analysis was to identify features from the software that respondents did and did not find useful and to solicit recommendations for improvements for the future system. Respondents were also asked to identify useful features from other electronic applications or websites that they felt could be pertinent for the economic census Web application.

2.3   Use of Prototypes

Feedback from respondents, internal staff, and user experience experts were translated into detailed requirements for the Web instrument and used to create various prototypes for testing. Prototyping [4] is the process of drafting versions of the final product in order to explore ideas and show the intent behind features or the overall design concept prior to programming the final instrument. Prototypes can range from paper drawings (low-fidelity) to semi-functioning instruments to a fully functioning site (high-fidelity).

A major benefit to prototyping is that early ideas can be quickly tested to see if they are successful before developers spend time on expensive programming. Prototypes are used early in the design process and are often tested iteratively as new features are identified or existing features are redesigned.

Testing for the economic census redesign involved the use of both low-fidelity and high-fidelity prototypes across several rounds of testing. Initial visits with respondents involved paper screen mock-ups that displayed new screen designs. After obtaining initial feedback with paper prototypes, a low-functioning prototype was programmed in HTML which allowed for navigation, branching, and the ability to input selected data. As data collection instrument requirements became more refined, programmers built two different high-fidelity prototypes for testing that showed a more realistic survey design.

2.4   Usability Testing

Usability testing is a method for evaluating a product, in this case a Web site, to identify issues. Web-site usability is about the ease at which a user can achieve their goals on a site. The goals in designing a usable web-site include making it learnable, efficient, and satisfying while preventing user errors. Usability testing can be conducted in a lab or in the field.

The usability testing for the economic census was conducted in the field. It is challenging to schedule meetings with business respondents that are outside of their place of business. Conducting testing with business respondents in the field was less burdensome and allowed researchers to observe the interaction with the instrument in the respondents setting [1]. In some cases, we were able to observe the use of records to fulfill their reporting requirements.

Once programmers, researchers, and stakeholders were comfortable with the design direction based off of prototype feedback, plans were made for launching the new design during the 2016 ASM/COS, the year prior to the collection of the 2017 Economic Census. In 2016, two rounds of usability testing were conducted prior to mail-out. The version tested during the first round had the overall look and feel of the final survey, but several features weren't fully functioning. A fully functioning version was available for the second round of usability testing several months later.

Although the economic census is similar to the ASM/COS, there are several necessary changes that need to be made to the layout and functionality of the web site for an economic census. The design was also updated to include improvements that weren't available for the 2016 ASM/COS. This resulted in significant changes and two rounds of usability testing were conducted in 2017.

2.5   Respondent Debriefings

Respondent debriefings are interviews that are conducted after respondents complete a survey to evaluate either survey content or the data collection tool. Respondent debriefings were conducted early in the process as a tool for requirements gathering. This method was subsequently used to continue evaluating the use of the software instrument until the web version was made available in 2017. At that time, researchers began debriefing respondents about their actual use of the newly released Web survey.

Findings from respondent debriefings were combined with feedback from prototype testing and usability testing to further refine prototypes or the final instrument. Research will not conclude with the mail-out of the 2017 Economic Census. Respondent debriefings are planned during 2018 to evaluate the instrument and provide feedback for continual improvement.

2.6   Paradata Analysis

Paradata from both the Web application and software application were analyzed throughout the research process and provided additional insight and direction for usability testing and respondent debriefings. The paradata also identified which features or functions were being most utilized in the Web application as well as indicating sources of burden in the instrument. Researchers reviewed software application paradata from the 2015 ASM to identify how often the various screens within the software application were visited and which features were used or under-utilized.

We are currently analyzing 2016 ASM/COS paradata and will be looking to dig deeper into how respondents are using key features within the Web application. We will be combining the paradata with response data in order to identify any potential characteristics (e.g., size of company, industry classification) associated with the degree to which Web application features were used or not used.

We are also preparing for analyzing paradata as responses are arriving from the 2017 Economic Census. The plan is to use paradata to help guide discussion topics during respondent debriefings. We also hope to use this information to help target which respondents to select for debriefings

3 Challenges

Given such a large research effort, it is no surprise that we faced several challenges along the way. One major challenge that we faced was dealing with the logistics of having multiple stakeholders. There are several hundred staff that work full or part time on the various survey lifecycle pieces on the economic census. Many of them have a stake in the data collection effort. During the research, several teams were created to help manage the development of the instrument and survey content. Where possible, researchers became a part of these teams in order to provide expert guidance and to keep members updated on research plans, progress, findings, and to solicit feedback. In addition, there were other stakeholders outside of the teams that needed to be updated on research plans and progress.

Managing the communication amongst all of these stakeholders was sometimes challenging. There were times when certain teams or stakeholders did not receive timely updates or have the opportunity to provide input. Because this project spanned many years, there was movement on and off teams. Teams were being formed and re-shaped, as survey managers tried to meet the needs of the work being accomplished.

Research plans were also continually in flux. We knew the overall goals and which methods we wanted to utilize and in which order, but schedules were constantly being adjusted because we were often dependent on results from previous rounds, adapting to the schedules and requests of our programmers, and adjusting for any delays along the way. During prototype development it was difficult to predict the amount of time that would be necessary or the amount of input that stakeholders would provide. There were rounds where prototype development would go quickly and the resulting design would have strong support. There were other rounds where the prototype discussion lagged and development was delayed. One common reason for delays were from stakeholders and respondents being reluctant to discard features that were present in the software.

Our respondents are not one size fits all. As mentioned earlier, we knew a priori that the response process amongst companies of different sizes can be different. There was a strong need to develop a 'one size fits all' design. Trying to develop a tool that met the needs of all types of respondents was a challenge, and in the end two paths were developed within the same instrument that allowed for select customization for small companies, but maintained many shared features for all.

Other challenges that we faced included finding resources, typically financial, in order to conduct the necessary research in person with businesses. Research schedules sometimes conflicted with the government budget schedule and we sometimes found ourselves dealing with limits on funding for travel. At times, we were able to find less costly local solutions.

Another challenge that we faced was fitting our work into the typical production schedule of the ASM and COS. These schedule often dictated, and sometimes conflicted, with the research schedule. The production schedule also meant that at times staff needed to focus on production related work and weren't able provide as much support for research efforts.

4   Lessons Learned

Overall, the research was successful. Results from the 2016 ASM/COS respondent debriefings were mostly positive. This was the first opportunity for researchers to evaluate the Web instrument that was released for collection.

Prototyping allowed programmers and researchers the ability to assess early design ideas before spending resources on full development. This was especially useful when programmers weren't available early in the design process or when they had conflicting schedules. Prototyping allowed for design discussion to continue without being reliant on costly programming resources.

Using prototypes also encouraged stakeholders, working closely with researchers, the ability to be creative. Researchers were able to discuss a variety of design ideas with respondents without much investment in resources. Researchers and stakeholders learned from the trial and error of evaluating a variety of designs while working towards the final design.

Knowing far in advance that the economic census was moving to an all Web collection allowed researchers and programmers time to discuss and test a variety of design options and incorporate thorough testing with respondents. Having additional time for development also allowed for the incorporation of a task analysis in the beginning. At times, development schedules are often so tight that there is a push to move right into testing of prototypes or early instruments. The task analysis allowed us the ability to truly learn about the economic response process and build requirements that would support these activities before prototype and instrument development began.

Using multiple methods over the last four years allowed us to incrementally identify what worked best for respondents and has resulted in a final design that respondents have found successful.

References

1. Nichols, B., Olmsted Hawala, E., Holland, T., Anderson Riemer, A.: Best practices of usability testing online questionnaires at the census bureau: how rigorous and repeatable testing can improve online questionnaire design. In: Proceedings of 2nd International Conference on Questionnaire Design, Development, Evaluation and Testing. Miami, Florida, 9–16 November 2016

2. Snijkers, G., Haraldsen, G., Jones, J., Willimack, D.: Designing and Conducting Business Surveys. Wiley, New York (2013)
3. Usability.Gov Task Analysis. https://www.usability.gov/how-to-and-tools/methods/task-analysis.html. Accessed 14 Mar 2018
4. Usability.Gov Prototyping. https://www.usability.gov/how-to-and-tools/methods/prototyping.html. Accessed 14 Mar 2018

Validating Self-reported Trends Using WiFi Tracking

Daniel Ebeling[✉], Zach Luker, Seth Pacheco, Angela Payne, and Nikki Rae

Information Technology, Brigham Young University, Provo, UT, USA
de6eling@byu.edu

Abstract. Observational data gathering is expensive as it traditionally relies on human intervention and intuition. However, with advances in Artificial Intelligence (AI) machines are gaining the capacity in making sense of the unstructured data observational methods yield [1]. With these advances in technology there is a new push to create innovative ways of gathering observational data to give context to self-reported user feedback.

Keywords: Wi-Fi tracking · Machine learning · Customer Experience
Location-based tracking · Time-based tracking · Probe requests
Observational tracking

1   Introduction

In commerce, Customer Experience (CX) is the relationship between a firm and its customers for the duration of their interaction [2]. Considering this definition, there exists significant overlap with Human Computer Interaction (HCI) in terms of goals: to create products and experiences that are usable, useful, and enjoyable [2]. However, there exists several discrepancies in methods between the two disciplines.

CX primarily focuses on gathering self-reported user feedback, most commonly gathered through surveys and questionnaires. The difference between firms often arise in the channel through which these surveys are administered; web applications, location-based triggered mobile phone notifications, text messages and experience kiosks to name a few [2]. However, HCI professionals understand that self-reported feedback alone carries a strong bias and is insufficient for informing design decisions that best support users. When self-reported data is coupled with observational data it provides a much more robust model for understanding user needs and desires.

Observational data gathering is expensive as it traditionally relies on human intervention and intuition. However, with advances in Artificial Intelligence (AI) machines are gaining the capacity in making sense of the unstructured data observational methods yield [3]. With these advances in technology there is a new push to create innovative ways of gathering observational data to give context to self-reported user feedback.

C. Stephanidis (Ed.): HCII Posters 2018, CCIS 852, pp. 233–237, 2018.
https://doi.org/10.1007/978-3-319-92285-0_32

2 Methodology

The participants in this study were anonymized students carrying a variety of devices who frequently visited a specific building on campus. No identifying information was collected. All tracking and load testing was performed using MAC addresses and the research team had no way of tying this hardware identifier with the individual owners. Methods of discovery around the specific problems to solve and the associated pain points for CX professionals included an academic literature review on tracking technologies, user observations by the team, and expert interviews with CX professionals. Based on this literature review, the team concluded that WiFi tracking is currently an underutilized method in the CX field for cross validating self report data and understanding user habits and choices.

2.1 Observational Tracking Methods

Currently, there are two leaders in gathering unstructured, observational data in the CX field. The first and most widely used method is bluetooth tracking. Bluetooth tracking requires customers to download an application to their mobile device and leave the bluetooth turned on while in the store. The systems observe user movements through the store through a series of strategically placed Bluetooth Beacons. While the bluetooth is fairly accurate in tracking device location it quickly drains the battery of mobile devices, and only updates the users location as long as the app is in the foreground [4].

Another more recent method relies on AI to recognize and tag customers actively through security camera footage. With this method firms are able to create accurate heat maps of customer activity in the store and gain valuable insights observing customer shopping habits. The drawback is that these systems are expensive. They are often required to be installed and calibrated by trained technical personnel and require some effort to maintain accuracy [5].

Finally, one of the newest observational data gathering methods leverages WiFi protocols to understand a users location. The benefits to using WiFi tracking are that it requires no additional software on user devices, however, it provides those conducting the tracking a universally unique identifier (the anonymized device's mac address) and it does not take any more than the devices normal battery usage [6]. For these innovative reasons, exploring WiFi protocols to observe user experiences is an exciting possibility for gathering observational data.

2.2 WiFi Probe Requests

As part of 802.11 WiFi protocol, WiFi enabled devices emit a signal called a probe request. Each probe request contains the devices MAC address, a universally unique identifier of the device, and the signal strength of the router with relation to the device. Probe requests are designed to find available networks the device is able to join. The router then returns a similar probe request to be received by all the proximal WiFi devices communicating their connection status [7].

2.3 Our Setup

In order to capture and analyze probe requests the team used three Raspberry Pi micro computers with 150 Mbps WiFi adapters (TP-LINK TL-WN722 N). Each Pi (or node) had a unique title and sent its logged probe requests to a central server where they were permanently stored and displayed with a web application. Each node sent its newly gathered probe request data to the server every ten seconds.

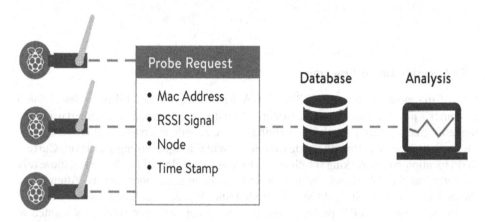

2.4 Time-Based Tracking

With the Raspberry Pi and server set up, gathering and analyzing time-based data was as easy as plugging the Pi into the wall and running a short Python script. There is significant value in gathering time-based data alone. Depending on the frequency of probe requests, CX researchers would gain contextual insight into when a user physically visited the store location and how long they spent there. Coupling this data with an unstructured survey administered to the user later yields valuable insights to the relationship of time spent in store and customer purchasing activity.

However, such insights rely on data being gathered accurately. To test the accuracy of time-based data tracking the team walked in and out of the WiFi range of the Raspberry Pi with two mobile devices. The first was actively recording a video with in order to log the time and location-based of the user. The second device was asleep in the testers pocket. The test yielded these findings.

Devices send 50% more probe requests when they are actively being used than when they are in standby mode. Further, android devices, specifically those manufactured by Samsung, consistently send 30% more probe requests than the next highest manufacturer. Devices manufactured by Apple send the least amount of probe requests from the devices measured. However, all devices correctly reflected the time spent in the target location with a deviation of only four minutes.

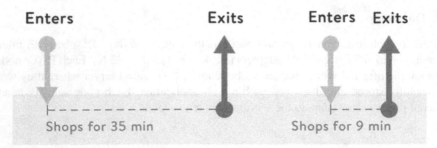

2.5 Location-Based Tracking

One of the most exciting possibilities of WiFi tracking is the ability to determine a customer's physical location within a store. A customer's location is identified using the logged signal strength from three receiving nodes. A node is a router that based on how far away the device is from the node (router) provides a signal strength or level. Current WiFi location-based tracking solutions use triangulation algorithms, however, these rely on a very predictable signal and tend to only work in more open spaces. Attenuation through walls or exhibits is difficult to predict and delivers unreliable results.

In interviews with CX professionals it became apparent that what they wanted to know was simply whether a user had visited a specific location or not. For example whether they had visited the checkout or a featured exhibit. The team chose to test a more simple method of tracking which would only log a users location in predetermined positions. With a simple machine learning algorithm and a learning interface on the web application store managers would train the algorithm by providing their own mac address and a specific location tag and then using their mobile device at that location. Once they have been there for 5 min the machine learning algorithm delivers a classifier which is used to measure the locations of all other devices.

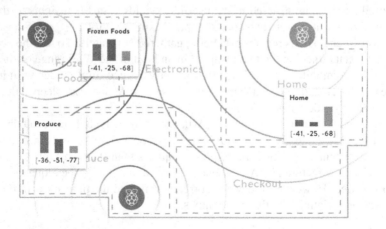

While the machine learning method cannot provide continuous location-based information, it does provides predetermined location-based information at roughly half of the computing cost. This method still requires a significant amount of modeling and reliability testing, however, early results are promising.

2.6 Privacy Concerns

The ethical considerations of implementing a technology solution with the capacity to track all WiFi enabled devices are significant. However, they are comparable to the use of security cameras in a business. To combat possible privacy concerns, business users will be made aware that they are being tracked by WiFi upon entering the store. Users will also be informed to disable the WiFi on their device if they wish not to participate. Awareness and transparency to the user are key to the ethical implementation of this technology.

3   Conclusion

Coupling self-reported user feedback with insights from unstructured tracking data may provide the necessary context for CX professionals to make impactful decisions for their products and brand experiences. Further, with the consent of the user there are valuable HCI research applications in understanding users habits and interactions in a variety of physical spaces at scale. While the concept has significant limitations as it is still in its infancy, it is ripe for further innovation, development and research.

References

1. Lohr, S.: Opinion—Big Data's Impact in the World," The New York Times, 11-Feb-2012. http://www.nytimes.com/2012/02/12/sunday-review/big-datas-impact-in-the-world.html
2. Customer Experience Defined. Forrester (2017). https://go.forrester.com/blogs/10-11-23-customer_experience_defined/. Accessed 16 Mar 2018
3. Sills, S., Song, C.: Innovations in Survey Research: An Application of Web-Based Surveys. Soc. Sci. Comput. Rev. **20**(1), 22–30 (2002)
4. Leddy, P.: 10 Things about bluetooth beacons you need to know. Learn Mobile Marketing. http://academy.pulsatehq.com/bluetooth-beacons
5. Vaniya, S.M., Bharathi, B.: Exploring object segmentation methods in visual surveillance for human activity recognition. In: Exploring Object Segmentation Methods in Visual Surveillance for Human Activity Recognition IEEE Conference Publication. http://ieeexplore.ieee.org/document/7955356/?reload=true&arnumber=7955356&SID=EBSCO%3Aedseee
6. Sapiezynski, P., Stopczynski, A., Gatej, R., Lehmann, S.: Tracking human mobility using WiFi signals. PLoS ONE (2015). http://journals.plos.org/plosone/article?id=10.1371%2Fjournal.pone.0130824
7. Freudiger, J.: Short: How Talkative is your Mobile Device? An Experimental Study of Wi-Fi Probe Requests. https://frdgr.ch/wp-content/uploads/2015/06/Freudiger15.pdf

Competitive Intelligence in the Service Sector:
A Data Visualization Approach

Oscar M. Granados[1]([✉]) and Oswaldo E. Velez-Langs[2]([✉])

[1] Department of Economics, Universidad Jorge Tadeo Lozano,
Bogotá, Colombia
oscarm.granadose@utadeo.edu.co
[2] Department of Computer Science, Universidad de Córdoba,
Monteria, Colombia
oswaldovelez@correo.unicordoba.edu.co

Abstract. This paper presents an alternative methodology for competitive intelligence through data visualization. The paper evaluates the possibilities offered by social media to collect data about the customer satisfaction with the service sector in order to develop a competitive strategy. Through data mining and algorithms, data visualization is incorporated to obtain a better understanding of the real-time situation of a brand, products, and services, creating knowledge that translates into tools for the definition of competitive intelligence. The analysis is done in two service sub-sectors that are antagonistic, banking and higher education, but that allows us to identify patterns and define strategies through data visualization and competitive intelligence.

Keywords: Competitive intelligence · Data visualization · Text mining
Strategy · Banking · Higher education

1 Introduction

The service sector stands out in the 21st century economy as an option that allows for the consolidation of production structures of countries that do not have a broad industrial base. Although these processes are not new, the service sector has entered an era where social media has become a benchmark for features, quality, and customer perception of them, as Twitter, Facebook, and social networks users express their opinions, desires, perceptions, feelings or, simply, post their experience with service companies. This document establishes a methodology for the service sector and evaluates two sub-sectors that are antagonistic but, with social media, these and other services, can come to define patterns in how to connect with their target market. The perception of service did not manifest only in the place of provision, now the dynamics of the market and the perception of the users can be understood in one place: the web. Not exclusively through a computer, but also from a mobile phone. Human mobility

© Springer International Publishing AG, part of Springer Nature 2018
C. Stephanidis (Ed.): HCII Posters 2018, CCIS 852, pp. 238–246, 2018.
https://doi.org/10.1007/978-3-319-92285-0_33

makes it easier for people in real-time to interact with the company that provides a service. The feeling is perceived immediately and without a filter.

Literature has several approaches to analyze feeling and opinion construction. The analysis of feelings and opinions based on the Web articulates different situations that users present when they interact in the social media [1–4]. Additionally, emotion analysis use algorithm techniques [5–8] and the processes where anxiety, emotions, and passions can direct and influence social media behaviors [9, 10]. However, they are not always articulated with specific industries and even less by companies that have directed their presence in social networks as a process of information and, occasionally, of marketing. In some countries, competitive intelligence processes have not been consolidated because the social media data mining, the feeling analysis, and the opinion construction are not very frequent. The competitive intelligence as part of knowledge management [11], not yet is an active part of the strategies of various companies and the social media data are not being fully exploited.

Consequently, it is necessary to provide appropriate data visualization tools for those companies that need to support their competitive intelligence tasks and improve the process of extracting knowledge from massive data in a reasonable time. The objective of this document is to identify non-explicit patterns, trends and interactions in data using data mining to extract non-trivial information contained in large volumes of data, machine learning techniques and data analytics that allow service companies to build competitive intelligence as part of their digital strategy and, also, make an intelligent exploitation of the data produced and disseminated in social media. The research is based on a heuristic, which establishes how the interaction of users in the service sector social media permits for several possible solutions to evaluate the guidelines and define a competitive intelligence strategy based on data from social media. To achieve this, the document is divided as follows: a first section where the methodology is presented, the data and the model, a second section that presents the results, and finally a discussion and final remarks section.

2 Method

2.1 Data and Competitive Intelligence

As a result of the Web democratization and the desire of people to participate more actively in social media, was the interest of customers to express an opinion and the emotion that comes out of a given situation. Users are motivated to participate based on their interests. Consequently, social networks became the agglomeration center of opinions and individual ideas about an issue and managed to bring them together regardless of the distance or geographical location where they were generated and consolidated the information that integrates a society [1] and created a digital community. Something that could not be developed previously due to geographical, spatial, cultural and linguistic limitations that made communication between communities more difficult.

Likewise, companies have developed strategies in social media as an initial part of a marketing process and participate in a new way of disclosing the relevant facts of their organizations, and sometimes of their products or services, but not at the same speed that is experienced in developed markets. In developing markets, the companies have not built a competitive intelligence structure that allows them to improve their position in the market or approach the users' interaction to obtain their feedback with the brand, service quality and their corrective schemes when presented with difficulties or develop strategies that allow them to offer new products.

However, the definition of competitive intelligence from data requires first of all the evaluation of the social media contents, where opinions and feelings that allow modeling are grouped based on what is considered text mining and the schemes of data mining in social networks [12, 13]. Subsequently, competitive intelligence is defined as a continuous cycle [14] where the processes of planning, collecting, processing, analyzing, disseminating, interacting and giving feedback are a factor that can optimize the competitive intelligence process [15, 16]. Finally, the integration of data visualization and competitive intelligence facilitates the determination of which tools and best practices can be applied to the selected sectors from the analysis of the Web [11, 17, 18].

2.2 Data

The data collection is defined from different aspects. First, the analysis uses monthly periods to do data mining in the official accounts of some service companies in Colombia. Second, the analysis focuses on the main banks and some of the most important universities. Third, it was identified that the social media activity of the universities intensifies in periods at the beginning of the academic term while in the banks there is a continuity during the whole year. This data collection allows to identify the interaction of selected companies in social media about brand analytics and the quality of services, in other words, an opinion mining. From a data collection, social media act in block and sometimes there may be a contagion as of a text that dissipates over time. This contagion can considerably affect the opinion about brand and quality of its products and services, while in other cases it can simply be an individual reaction. In some cases, this contagion can be framed in the formation of information clusters that also dissipate. Additionally, with the Twitter option to create hashtag to follow the trends that can be generated at a specific time [19], the selected companies and their data do not frequently use hashtag as part of their social media communication and the clients either, as result, breaking of the network of terms presented in Figs. 1c and 2c.

This is one of the definitions achieved by the collection of data that is reflected in the results of mining and subsequent visualization. This allows to advance in another element such as the information ecology in social media, this ecology identifies the parameters of user interaction on Twitter and Facebook and allows defining the populations formation and performance and their interactions [20], that is, a dynamic topology that establishes the necessity for a competitive intelligence in permanent transformation based on data. However, data mining identifies the shallowness of the information ecology in the selected companies and their way of developing their social media strategy.

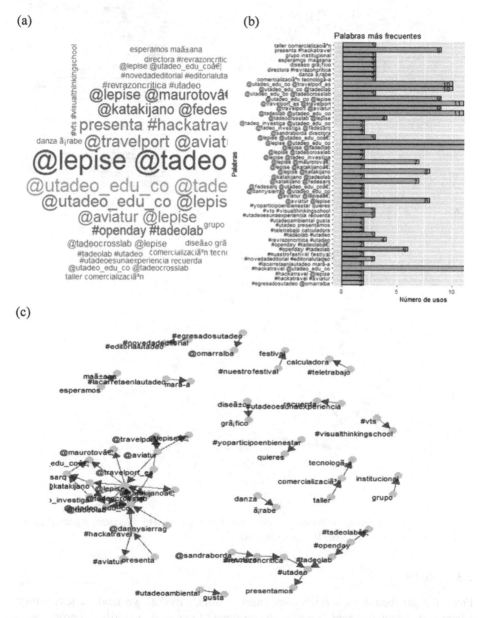

Fig. 1. Data visualization of education sector. (a) Word cloud. (b) Frequent words diagram. (c) Network of terms (Source: R Studio results)

(a)

(b)

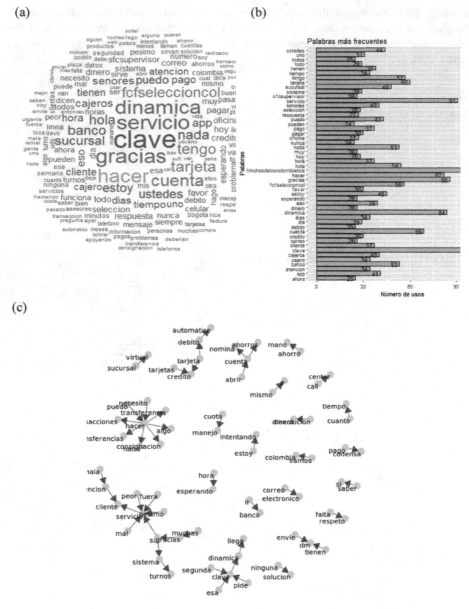

(c)

Fig. 2. Data visualization of banking sector. (a) Word cloud. (b) Frequent words diagram. (c) Network of terms. (Source: R Studio results)

2.3   Model

From the interaction of service companies in social media, we made a text mining where a representative set of words is incorporated to properly identify the processes of perception and additionally the likes and retweets. We use a N-Gram modify model that allows a better recognition of terms, defined comments, variables and parameters previously established in the data mining process. For the analysis has been developed some scripts in R language and Java application to advance the tasks associated with the project, such as download the information from social networks (Twitter and Facebook), pre-processing, initial statistical analysis, model generation and data mining visualization. After the pre-processed texts can be filtered according to different criteria, for example, we can select tweets from one specific user or group. We can also filter by a given date range or messages that contain certain terms. For the selection of the most relevant words, algorithms of attribute selection were used to determine the utility and the value of the attribute [21]. Likewise, the filter algorithms were used to evaluate attributes independently of learning algorithm and enveloping algorithms that use the learning algorithm performance to determine what is desired in a set of attributes [22]. These algorithms can define a way to classify the attributes that are derived from searches in data composed by text, that is, in text classifiers or text categorizations [23, 24]. Then:

$$H(C) = -\sum_{c \in C} p(c) log_2 p(c) \tag{1}$$

$$H(C|A) = -\sum_{a \in A} p(a) \sum_{c \in C} p(c|a) log_2 p(c|a) \tag{2}$$

If A is an attribute and C is the class, Eqs. (1) and (2) define the entropy class before and after observing the attribute. The amount by which the entropy decreases reflects the additional information about the class provided by the attribute and is called information gain, where each attribute Ai is assigned a score based on the gain obtained [22, 25].

3 Results

Data visualization is usually the best way to understand and analyze the results of data mining compared to other techniques because it facilitates in a simple way to understand and to analyze the knowledge [26, 27]. The visualization techniques of the neural methods to map the data are derived from the interaction of social media due to the large amount of data that is generated with the parameters and variables determined in the data mining process, allowing to classify the high amount of data and in turn to map the comparative opinions and feelings towards the selected organizations [28, 29]. The visualization of the data allows to understand the rapid changes in the market and the customer experience and, under these possibilities, a more agile strategy is articulated that takes advantage of the information in real time and identifies the events that can influence its performance. When confronting the results of two sub-sectors of antagonistic services such as banking services and higher education services, the following general results were found.

3.1   Higher Education

In the educational sector, we have the Educational Data Mining area (EDM) that emerges as a paradigm oriented to design models, tasks, methods, and algorithms for exploring data from educational settings. EDM pursues to find out patterns and make predictions that characterize learner's behaviors and achievements, domain knowledge content, assessments, educational functionalities, and applications. In this sector we studied the possibilities to use social media analysis to propose new (and relevant) programs in universities. In the last twenty years, the universities environment has experienced a new pressure because of competition among universities, new financing models, and the introduction of business methodologies in educational systems [30]. For these reasons, some universities need to adopt new tools to address the strategy, competitive advantage, and information systems that make it possible to understand the educational environment [31]. Additionally, in the selected universities, patterns were identified in different periods at the beginning of the academic term, where there is a greater connection of students with the university and academic activities and not exclusively with the claims (see Fig. 1a). Otherwise, they are closer to greater use of hashtags.

3.2   Banking

The most important banks were selected and through data mining in different periods, several patterns were found that can be seen in the Colombian largest bank. Figure 2a shows the word cloud generated by 1283 tweets during October 2017 and concentrates mainly on transactional issues and a customer service channel, rather than on a product strategy or an accurate identification of the different customer perceptions. There is a tendency towards negative comments because it is a channel of attention and not a digital strategy of services.

4   Discussion and Final Remarks

This work allows to identify brand and opinion elements about the services and products of some companies in the service sector in Colombia. Several alternatives of text analytics were proposed that better identify the sentiment towards selected companies. The results were not very encouraging because there is a strong inclination towards negative comments that allow us to identify that companies are not taking advantage of the social media space to incorporate improvements in their competitive strategy, but that it has become a client attention space. In our opinion, the use of social media is reactionary and in a very few events it is possible to identify elements that encourage competitive intelligence. The selected service companies show a similar pattern: Not exist a strategic use of social media except for some moments where universities achieve greater interactions with users (likes, retweets). We need to continue with some activities at the current stage of our project as: First, establish a process to know which the most frequently used hashtags are; second, sort the different tweet topics using clustering approaches; third, find the more frequent bigrams to generate a graph visualization; fourth, show how can associate the different terms in the analyzed texts. Finally, find a causal relation, in a graphical way, between the social media content and new proposal of university programs. Also, the future works will extend the periods and the selected companies, making it possible to specify the patterns identified here and verify the information ecology of the social media for the service companies and the networks that are generated from the proper use of a digital strategy.

References

1. Christakis, N., Fowler, J.: Connected: The Surprising Power of Our Social Networks and How They Shape Our Lives. Little Brown and Company, New York (2009)
2. Chau, M., Xu, J.: Mining communities and their relationships in blogs: a study of online hate groups. Int. J. Hum. Comput. Stud. **65**, 57–70 (2007). https://doi.org/10.1016/j.ijhcs.2006.08.009
3. Liu, B.: Web Data Mining: Exploring Hyperlinks, Contents, and Usage Data. Springer, Liepzig (2011). https://doi.org/10.1007/978-3-642-19460-3
4. Pang, B., Lee, L.: Opinion mining and sentiment analysis. Found. Trends Inf. Retriev. **2**, 1–135 (2008)
5. Allen, C., Machleit, K., Kleine, S.S., Notani, A.S.: A place for emotion in attitude models. J. Bus. Res. **58**(4), 494–499 (2005). https://doi.org/10.1016/S0148-2963(03)00139-5
6. Chmiel, A., Sienkiewicz, J., Thelwall, M., Paltoglou, G., Buckley, K., Kappas, A., Hołyst, J.: Collective emotions online and their influence on community life. PLoS ONE **6**, e22207 (2011). https://doi.org/10.1371/journal.pone.0022207
7. DeSteno, D., Petty, R., Rucker, D., Wegener, D., Braverman, J.: Discrete emotions and persuasion: the role of emotion-induced expectancies. J. Pers. Soc. Psychol. **86**, 43–56 (2004)
8. Prabowo, R., Thelwall, M.: Sentiment analysis: a combined approach. J. Inf. **3**, 143–157 (2009). https://doi.org/10.1016/j.joi.2009.01.003
9. Alkis, Y., Kadirhan, Z., Sat, M.: Development and validation of social anxiety scale for social media users. Comput. Hum. Behav. **72**, 296–303 (2017). https://doi.org/10.1016/j.chb.2017.03.011
10. Wakefield, R., Wakefield, K.: Social media network behavior: A study of user passion and affect. J. Strat. Inf. Syst. **25**, 140–156 (2016). https://doi.org/10.1016/j.jsis.2016.04.001
11. Chen, H., Chau, M., Zeng, D.: CI Spider: a tool for competitive intelligence on the web. Decis. Support Syst. **34**, 1–17 (2002)
12. He, W., Wu, H., Yan, G., Akula, V., Shen, J.: A novel social media competitive analytics framework with sentiment benchmarks. Inf. Manag. **52**, 801–812 (2015). https://doi.org/10.1016/j.im.2015.04.006
13. Barbier, G., Liu, H.: Data mining in social media. In: Aggarwal, C. (ed.) Social Network Data Analytics, pp. 327–352. Springer, New York (2011). https://doi.org/10.1007/978-1-4419-6287-4
14. Kahaner, L.: Competitive Intelligence. Simon and Schuster, New York (1996)
15. Miller, S.: Competitive intelligence: An Overview. John Wiley and Sons, Hoboken (2001)
16. Ashton, W., Stacey, G.: Technical intelligence in business: understanding technology threats and opportunities. Int. J. Technol. Manag. **10**(1), 79–104 (1995)
17. Bose, R.: Competitive intelligence process and tools for intelligence analysis. Ind. Manag. Data Syst. **108**, 510–528 (2008). https://doi.org/10.1108/02635570810868362

18. Xu, K., Shaoyi Liao, S., Li, J., Song, Y.: Mining comparative opinions from customer reviews for competitive intelligence. Decis. Support Syst. **50**, 743–754 (2011). https://doi.org/10.1016/j.dss.2010.08.021

19. Xintong, G., Hongzhi, W., Song, Y., Hong, G.: Brief survey of crowdsourcing for data mining. Expert Syst. Appl. **41**, 7987–7994 (2014). https://doi.org/10.1016/j.eswa.2014.06.044

20. Ulanowicz, R.: Information theory in ecology. Comput. Chem. **25**, 393–399 (2001). https://doi.org/10.1016/S0097-8485(01)00073-0

21. Kohavi, R., John, G.H.: Wrappers for feature subset selection. Artif. Intell. **97**, 273–324 (1997). https://doi.org/10.1016/S0004-3702(97)00043-X

22. Hall, M., Holmes, G.: Benchmarking attribute selection techniques for discrete class data mining. IEEE Trans. Knowl. Data Eng. **15**, 1437–1447 (2003). https://doi.org/10.1109/TKDE.2003.1245283

23. Pinheiro, R., Cavalcanti, G., Correa, R., Ren, T.I.: A global-ranking local feature selection method for text categorization. Expert Syst. Appl. **39**, 12851–12857 (2012). https://doi.org/10.1016/j.eswa.2012.05.008

24. Yang, Y., Pedersen, J.: Proceedings of 14th International Conference on Machine Learning, pp. 412–420 (1997)

25. Quinlan, J.R.: C4.5: Programs for Machine Learning. Morgan Kaufmann, San Mateo (1993)

26. Ganapathy, S., Ranganathan, C., Sankaranarayanan, B.: Commun. ACM **47**, 92–99 (2004)

27. Westphal, C., Blaxton, T.: Data Mining Solution. Wiley, New York (1998)

28. Edwards, D.: Introduction to Graphical Modelling. Springer, New York (2000). https://doi.org/10.1007/978-1-4612-0493-0

29. Ultsch, A.: Self-organizing neural networks for visualisation and classification. In: Opitz, O., Lausen, B., Klar, R. (eds.) Information and Classification, pp. 307–313. Springer, Heidelberg (1993). https://doi.org/10.1007/978-3-642-50974-2_31

30. Larsen, I.M., Maassen, P., Stensaker, B.: Four basic dilemmas in university governance reform. High. Educ. Manag. Pol. **21**(3), 41–58 (2009). https://doi.org/10.1787/hemp-21-5ksdxgpdnds1

31. Hammond, K.L., Harmon, H.A., Webster, R.L.: University performance and strategic marketing: an extended study. Mark. Intell. Plann. **25**(5), 436–459 (2007). https://doi.org/10.1108/02634500710774932

Chancho Assistant: Smart Shopping Guided by Consumer Habits

Fabián Gutiérrez Gómez[✉] and Rocío Abascal-Mena[✉]

Master in Design, Information and Communications (MADIC),
Universidad Autónoma Metropolitana, Cuajimalpa, Mexico
fabiangg@protonmail.ch, mabascal@correo.cua.uam.mx

Abstract. This paper presents a solution to consumer habits that, against of various economic and personal factors, affect the economy of the Mexican population. The solution is developed through a tool that offers different options of purchase in different places according to the cost of the product. Besides, the tool has an intelligent assistant which proposes other products according to the user consumption habits. In order to develop the tool an User-Centered Design process was conducted which allow to find user's needs. Also, iterative prototyping and evaluation was considered to give a pertinent solution by using a digital prototype.

Keywords: User-Centered Design · Iterative prototype · Intelligent assistant
Consumer habits

1 Introduction

This work has as a central element the design process of a proposal that helps to orient purchases through consumption habits and economic savings. For this, the starting point is to question and problematize what is a habit and the importance it has within the human-centered design methodology.

Later, in a second section, other proposals that have the same purpose are analyzed; that is, to help buy through the consumption of habits. In this point, the advantages and disadvantages of these proposals and the elements that characterise them will be explored.

A third section details the design process based on the User-Centered Design methodology, which was divided into 6 processes: observation, search scenarios and user's profile, delimitation and visualization of the proposal, and finally the development of a prototype. At each of these points the process was iterative, so the opinions and responses of the focus group were always taken into consideration.

The last section looks at the conclusions, which will be centered on the importance of habit in the development of interface design. The last section looks at the conclusions, which will be centered on the importance of habit in the development of interface design.

2 Habits

As will be detailed in the methodology section, the present work focuses on finding a proposal that will provide a solution to the needs of a certain group of the Mexican population, which considered young women between 25 and 30, who recently left university and are working and living independently.

It is then that the needs of this certain group are very specific, differing even for small periods of time. So a question arises: what is habit?

In the specific case of the design of tools that allow human-computer interaction, Pinder [1] comments that the habit has had little theoretical attention, since most of the questions have been addressed to a practical sense of habit generation. On the other hand, Frøkjær and Hornbæk [2] comment that discussions about the nature of habit have been on the psychology side. It is then that, on the one hand, the habit has been little questioned or taken as a tool to the psychological sciences.

For the present work, habit is considered from Peirce's semiotic studies and his work after 1907, which defines it as a state of fixed belief that occurs through the same kind of repeated conduct multiple times, and a tendency to similar behavior under similar circumstances [3].

Considering habit from Peirce's posture allows us to understand not only a relationship of the subject and his cognition, but also the relationship of the subject and the action he usually performs with the object; that is, a repeated action charged in principle by a mode of knowledge that later becomes something definitive. Moreover, the way in which the knowledge of something finally becomes habit allows us to understand also the moment in which this happens, thus assigning a temporality to the mode of action, of something seldom realized, to the formation of a habit.

3 State of the Art

In recent years, advances in artificial intelligence have allowed exiata a wide variety of applications and platforms that help and guide the user, in addition to those that come out more are those that work with a large database.

An example of this is the Mona app, developed by Atik in 2014 [4]; the Personal Shopping Assistant app, developed by Microsoft [5]; and Ps Dept [6]. All of these tools are characterized by a large database, stores that back them up, and a well-developed AI.

However, the problem observed is that it does not focus on the local market and does not take into account the context of users. This last part is of the utmost importance where there is a large wage gap, payments are not uniform and not everyone has access to online shops.

4 Methodology

The methodology used was based on User-Centered Design, which consists of bringing the end user to the centre of the product design and development process [7].

To do this, it was necessary to start from an empirical knowledge and to observe and ask about the needs of women between 25 and 30 years old. To achieve this objective, it was necessary to analyze a focus group of 4 women from different parts of Mexico, with the same degree of studies and a similar economic situation; that is, recently graduated from universities.

The reason why the sample was small is due to the generational generalities that exist in a certain sector of society, and whose needs are shared: i.e. lack of opportunities, unemployment, delinquency, etc.

An exploratory analysis was chosen first, but taking into account urban and semi-rural contexts.

4.1 First Step: Observation

In this step we observed the context in Mexico of middle-class youth and with the characteristics mentioned above. We considered the urban contexts of Mexico City and Guadalajara, and the semi-rural context of Sinaloa. It is important to emphasize at this point that culture and the signs to which young people are immersed are of vital importance in the process of acquiring habits.

4.2 Second Step: Interviews

The four persons interviewed share the same age range between 25 to 30. All are women and have a similar education (undergraduate degree). However, the place in which they live is different, since two live and work in the Mexico City and the other two work and live in the cities of Sinaloa and Guadalajara.

With the interviews performed, there was a disparity between the answers taking into account that there is a difference between their contexts and education. Users living at Mexico City with a constant relationship with technology in their daily activities (as at work) see the Internet and technology in general as necessary to the point of feeling bad when they don't have information. In contrast, people living in other states of the Mexican Republic (Sinaloa and Guadalajara) see the use of the Internet as indifferent to their activities.

The interviews were conducted with questions that went from the personal to general order, and trying to gain confidence and accelerate the answer, in order to obtained answers "without thinking". Therefore, there were no measures in the questions, and were opened while some observation was noted. It should be noted that the interviews were conducted through telephone calls.

In this way, the questions asked were:

- Say 5 habits that you have regardless of whether it's good or not;
- Say 5 harmful habits you'd like to change;
- Say 5 harmful habits that you observe in the Mexican people;
- What do you consider to be the country's three main problems?
- How much do you use technology?

- How much do you use Internet? What feelings do you have when you don't use Internet for a day?
- Say 3 apps you use the most;
- Say 3 possible solutions that may have the technology according your needs.

As can be seen, the series of questions was directed from the general to the particular, leaving a wide margin to different types of responses. And although it starts with the hypothesis that corruption is the main harmful habit in Mexico, it was never mentioned in the answers.

4.3   Third Step: Detection of Needs

There were three main problems that resulted from the interviews: (1) bad administration and economic inequality; (2) education; and (3) disinterest. It is then that within the opportunities that allow to improve the performance of innovation are those linked to the management and control not of these axes, but of its derivatives, such as, irresponsibility, procrastination, to mention a few.

Why not use what already exists to solve the different needs? One of the answers is because there is a total lack of knowledge about the offers that exist. Some users, at the interviews, referred to problems whose solution is already in progress (for example, to communicate with their dog). Another reference to consider is that they do not have adequate information about what technology can do (due to the time it took them to respond). So, it is necessary to improve the information that exists between the user and the technology.

Therefore, the 15 needs that were considered relevant, were:

- Need to have better control of expenses.
- Need to obtain accessible information.
- Need to change habits in the city.
- Good food handling.
- Need to change habits at work. Need to not leave everything to the last hour.
- Need to have better ways to know what to study.
- Better ways to do paperwork.
- Bad administration and ingrained habit.
- Habit of procrastination. Need to control it.
- Respect. Need for better respect among citizens.
- Administrative needs. How much and how do I dispose of my money?
- Finance knowledge. Need for non-specialized economic information.
- Improve the relationship between humans and animals.
- Change habits of time waste.
- Need to leave drinking alcohol.
- Need to have a better sleep.

4.4   Fourth Step: Scenarios and Profiles

At this point, it became necessary to delimit the outcome of the information given by the interviews and to offer alternatives to users and their needs. For this purpose, 4 scenarios were developed with 4 different types of users, considering the characteristic attributes of the focal group, such as the place where they live and their relationship with the technology.

For this development phase, two options were considered: a tool that brings together several people to exchange objects among themselves or an intelligent assistant to help with shopping. However, when the users were asked again, they replied that the second option seemed more interesting and useful.

4.5   Fifth Step: Inspiration Panel and Storyboard

At this point we proceeded to determine an aesthetic element and to determine the influence that would have with the users to whom it was directed. For the first point an inspiration panel was elaborated that had in principle the following guiding words: saving, simplicity, decisions, open, learning, alternatives, intelligent, intuitive, economic, and evolution.

In the aesthetic section, three options were considered. The first were the palette colors and icons taken from Royksopp video, Remind Me (2009) [8]. In addition, in the use of the interface was considered the Uber app [9] because it have a simple learning curve and intuitive interface. Finally, it was considered the limitation of not overloading aesthetics with banal functions, so it was considered, at this point, the Keiichi Matsuda video, Hyper-Reality [10] in which a society is observed with an information overload which impedes considering the reality and simplicity of it. In functional terms, Amazon Echo was considered for its design and its promising of the project. Finally, the computer Holly, from Red Dwarf series, was considered as an inspiration in the discursive section of what would be an assistant.

It was even in the storyboard where it was chosen at the end that the tool was going to be an intelligent assistant who helped in the purchases, both in offering cheap products, even in making the purchases completely. The scenarios and the chosen users were two: a young independent student, and a gentleman father of family. In both cases the help came in saving money, which allowed them to travel and be with their loved ones.

4.6   Six Step: Rapid Prototyping

In the process of making paper prototypes, a total of 26 windows were created resulting in a path with a task to be performed, and that was the purchase of a specific product. Taking into account the aesthetics of the tool, the functionality and the users to which it was focused, the work developed were the interface and navigation. As can be seen in the Fig. 1, the principal idea had been born, having then the idea of an assistant in a Mexican context, also with a geolocalization that would indicate a variety of purchase options.

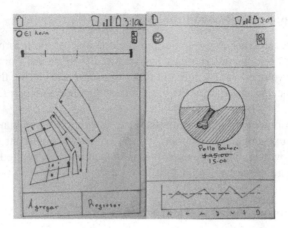

Fig. 1. Paper prototype with the some features, in this case the geolocalization and the product prices.

5   Usability Testing

The digital prototype was elaborated and evaluated with expert users; in other words, with the users to whom the tool was initially conceived. The platform that was used to create the digital prototype was JustinMind [11], which is characterized by the creation of wireframes through its own software and has the advantage of having more freedom than other tools for the same purpose. As can be seen in Fig. 2, the prototype, in its first phase, had aesthetic elements taken from the inspiration panel. In addition, during the process, a pet was created with the name of Chancho, that is a common name of the pig in America, a symbol that also means the act to save money.

Fig. 2. Home menu of Chancho Assistant which allows to insert the name and the password of the user and the first screen with products.

In the creation of the first digital prototype there were a total of 22 navigable windows which had as its main mission the purchase of a specific food.

The first tests of the tool were with users that have similar characteristics, which are postgraduate students of the career of communication sciences. These tests allowed to have some feedback and from this it was changed the interface and color palette. Within the same comments, it was also considered to change the iconography and homogenize all the icons. One of the most important contributions that were taken into account for a later development was about the cancellation of certain products and certain habits that the intelligent assistant may consider.

After the relevant changes, tests were continued with users of different context, whether experts or not. In addition, in this part, the users who previously participated emphasized,[1] like the others users, in changes over design and in the usability. In these evaluations, the tool, also rescues a similarity that had in the storyboard, and that was the initial test with a user between 45 and 50 years old who suggested a limit by brand.

Finally, in the opinions expressed by users, both the aesthetic changes and the idea of having an assistant guided by the local economy were discussed. One of the ideas discussed with users is that the idea of the habit will be exploited in order to change bad habits for good ones, especially in the area of nutrition.

6   Conclusions

Three elements in the Chancho Assistant process are considered, which are: the process itself, that has been reiterative and open considering the needs of a particular group; the medium itself, the Internet, which not only considers the user, but also the connectivity and the connection that makes it possible; and the elaboration of a general framework that guided the process from the hypothesis proposal, to the development of the prototype and the evaluation with different users.

Thus, the first section shows that the heuristics and the feedback generated by different tests with different users. This produced a series of changes that allowed an improvement in the aesthetics, in the interface, and the handling of the tool.

Secondly, is considered the iterative feedback of this tool in the medium where will be used: the Internet. Thus, feedback followed an emerging line of behavior, and these are individual reactions that are difficult to predict and depend on a global interaction of an exponential number of possibility, as mentioned by Demers and Vorn [12]. Therefore, the tool (Chancho Assistant) will not limited to browsing, but will allow an interaction with different users and various stores, both supermarkets and medium and small businesses.

In the third section, it emphasizes that the tool was not made without purpose, but always maintained a general framework that guided the process from the development of the hypothesis to development and testing through the prototype. It is then that this tool shows a solidity both theoretical and methodological.

Finally, we need to remember that this paper presents only the proposal and that ends with the prototype, and the tool itself is in the process of being developed. That

---

[1]   In this part, the test were made through the web, since no was possible by geographical limits.

said, we do not have the definitive results that give proof of both hypothesis, discourse, and development. However, given the solidity that underlies, there is no doubt that the elaboration is a minor problem.

References

1. Pinder, C.: Breaking and forming habits using technology: theoretical pointers from psychology. In: Proceedings of the 1st Habits in Human Computer Interaction Workshop, BCS HCI (2013)
2. Frøkjær, E., and Kasper, H.: Metaphors of human thinking in HCI: habit, stream of thought, awareness, utterance, and knowing. In: Proceedings of HF2002/OzCHI 2002, pp. 25–27 (2002)
3. Peirce, C.: Obras Filosoficas Reunidas. FCE (2012)
4. Mona (2017). http://www.monahq.com
5. PSA (2017). https://psa.microsoft.com/home/index.html
6. PS DEPT (2017). http://members.psdept.com/
7. Gracia Bandrés, M.A., Gracia Murugarren, J., Romero San Martín, D.: TecsMedia: Metodologías de diseño centradas en usuarios. Gobierno de Aragón (2015)
8. Royksopp (2009). https://www.youtube.com/watch?v=cy_h4Lc5QSE
9. Uber (2016). https://www.uber.com/es-MX/cities/mexico-city/
10. Matsuda, K.: Hyper-Reality (2016). https://vimeo.com/166807261
11. JustinMind (2016). https://www.justinmind.com/
12. Demers, L., Vorn, B.: Real artificial life as an immersive media (1995). https://users.hfg-karlsruhe.de/~ldemers/machines/alife/alife.pdf. Accedido el 5 de diciembre del 2016

Improve Onboarding Customer Experience and Reduce Airline Ground Staff Efforts Using Wearable

Abhishek Jain[1]([✉]), Shiva Subhedar[2], and Naveen Kumar Gupta[3]

[1] TATA Consultancy Services, Pune, India
abhishek.jain520@gmail.com
[2] Cognizant Technology Solutions, Pune, India
shivasubhedar05@gmail.com
[3] Mastercard, Pune, India
naveengupta1489@gmail.com

Abstract. Air transport has now turned out to be one of the prominent method of transport in India. Focused valuing, an ascent in per capita pay and so on are few of the drivers in charge of the development of flying industry in India. Due to in-wrinkle popular and promotion vantages of air travel, air terminal experts and airline companies are putting more endeavors in enhancing passenger experience to make their movement agreeable and critical. Passenger loyalty is key to repeat business. Dissatisfied passenger not only switch brands but also spread their dis-satisfaction. Passenger loyalty frequently relies on your item, administrations, activity and so on. Onboarding passenger in a flight is a successive procedure and every passenger needs to experience this procedure each time. Airline ground staff plays an important part in directing and dealing with every one of these stages. All things considered, onboarding flight is an intricate procedure for some passenger. Airline ground staff put their extraordinary endeavors to help a passenger who is in require, finding a passenger for a minute ago onboarding and so on. Very late scramble for discovering passenger expands their (Airline Ground Staff) function as well as leads burden to the kindred passenger, chance in flight timing delay and so forth. There are multiple factors which contribute to passenger onboarding experience like unable to travel within the airport, first-time traveler, un-familiar airport, language etc. In this paper, we are discussing how can we improve passenger experience in a repeatable way by improving indoor navigation within the airport using technology which might reduce efforts by airport ground staff in finding a last-minute passenger.

Keywords: Smart airport · IOT · Wearable · Customer experience
Process improvement

1 Introduction

Boarding plane is successive process and the passenger needs to experience it each time. Common process includes check in (scan travel documents, bag drop, SSR, seat

C. Stephanidis (Ed.): HCII Posters 2018, CCIS 852, pp. 255–260, 2018.
https://doi.org/10.1007/978-3-319-92285-0_35

selection, payment), security, immigration (if international), locate gate and lastly get onto the plane. For various procedures, passenger needs to experience distinctive zones inside an airport such as curb, lobby, mall and gate where they need to associate with stand, specialists, security work force, migration officer, and retailer and so forth to perform diverse exercises.

The time spent at the airport is a noteworthy bit of the whole travel so the experience that passenger has encountered noticeable all-around airport gigantically affects carriers and also on airport. Despite the fact that theirs is part of advances in airport frame-work in later past still passenger faces issues like administration interruption, bag lost, long lines, absence of data, expanded voyage times and so forth which affect their general travel experience. For airlines, a poor airport experience altogether impacts how its image is perceived, as passenger don't see the airport experience as partitioned to the administrations gave by the carrier specifically. For the airport itself, absence of passenger data and reconciliation with carriers can prompt lost incomes and decreased efficiency.

According to Karatepe and Choubtarash [1] passenger crowding as perceived by ground staff results in emotional dissonance that in turn heightens emotional exhaustion. Cheng Hua and Hsin Li [2] in their paper talks about Unruly Passenger Behaviors (UPBs) are a challenge for service provision enterprises, notably the airline industry and how airlines can improve UPB handling, including the establishment of appropriate service-staff authorizations, passenger education, complaint mechanisms, unruly passenger databases etc. Last minute rush for finding passengers not only increases their (Airport Ground Staff) work but also leads inconvenience to fellow passengers, risk in flight timing delay, loss to Airline industry [3] etc. To make passenger's inside flight experience to reduce stress using a new entertainment adaptive framework Liu et al. (2008) have illustrated their study [4]. In 2012, 25.8 million pieces of baggage were mishandled, of which 85% were delayed and 15% were damaged or lost, costing the aviation industry US $2.58 billion. mBELT (baggage management suite) was designed by Mercator [5], which will help airlines, ground handlers and airports to manage the entire life cycle of their passenger's bags. KLM Royal Dutch Airlines uses a robot to guide travelers through airport terminals [6].

In this paper we are talking about enhancing airport experience by making air terminals and indoor route experience smart and engaging. By this we are attempting to accomplish a. hassle free route inside air terminals by passenger, b. diminishment in endeavors of airplane terminal ground staff in discovering a minute ago traveler, c. upgrading the airplane terminal and aircraft passenger experience and opening better approaches for creating incomes.

2   Research

2.1   Method

A total of 40 subjects, volunteered to take part in this research (Age group from 24 to 51 years, M = 37.50; SD = 19.09). The paradigm utilized for choosing subject is (a) subjects have presentation to voyaging utilizing carrier and (b) Recent outside

(International) explorer (c) Frequent flyer local and worldwide. User Interviews have been con-ducted with subjects to comprehend their voyaging conduct, their past movement experiences and diverse inside airplane terminal encounters. In Secondary research, we have considered different looks into, contextual investigations identified with IOT impacting aircraft industry.

2.2 Findings

We have recognized some key subjective bits of knowledge from the study, which clarify the variables in charge of trouble in exploring inside the airport from passenger's perspective. Numerous subjects have thought that it was hard to explore in the airport in their first flight understanding. A few subjects revealed that they feel trouble in exploring inside a new airport. Size of the airport additionally influences inside air terminal route. The majority of the subjects announced that physical weariness influences their route when they head out through consecutive corresponding flights. Unfamiliar language is likewise influences ease in exploring inside an airport, some subjects found it difficult to understand signboards when they encountered an unfamiliar language.

3   Smart Airports – Reimagining Passenger Experience

Our proposed arrangement has 2 areas one is the way by which to upgrade the in-door course for the passenger and other is the way ground staff can track passenger and give them impromptu help when required. At the point when passenger is up for check in process they will get wrist band from carrier as a major aspect of administration. This wrist band will have vibrator, area sensor, little show and system network which will fill in as a virtual collaborator of passenger in airplane terminal for a given travel. Wrist band ought to be examined at key phases of the journey and in view of that band will give data about the following stages (security check, migration and so on). Passenger can whenever check the bearing which they have to check for getting onto the flight by along these lines they can undoubtedly explore inside the airplane terminal without any assistance. With the assistance of this band they would likewise be getting alarms in type of vibrations about flight, loading up entryway shutting and so forth. Passenger from various culture and dialect can likewise get profited from this band, it would give customized data in their own dialect. This band will be there with passenger inside airplane terminals and will be gathered back when they would get onto in flights, so same band will be reset and can be utilized for another traveler/flight (Fig. 1).

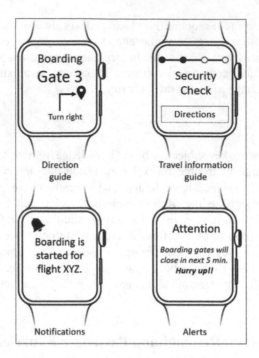

Fig. 1. Depiction of wrist band (wearable) views for passengers

For the ground staff group, they will have an application with the assistance of which they could bring passenger data like their present area, passenger's status, passengers who are in require or need support. This will incredibly lessen the ground staff issue in discovering last time passengers which is as of now one of their significant issue. Additionally, they can send alerts/notice to traveler who are lost or not landing at wanted area (loading up entryways) in given time. This alarm will be received by passenger in type of vibratory alert.

In Fig. 2, introduction of specialized elements is given. There are 4 key elements 'Wear-capable gadget (wrist band), IOT organize (in air terminal premises), Ground staff application and concentrated handling framework'. Every one of these elements are associated with airport wireless system for correspondence and information sharing. IOT system would incorporate arrangement of area sensor (for instance Wi-Fi positioning system [7] or Beacon Bluetooth Low energy [8]) in Indore positioning System structure. At whatever point Passenger's wearable gadget gets identified or comes quite close to IPS sensors, IOT framework will refresh area subtle elements with brought together handling framework.

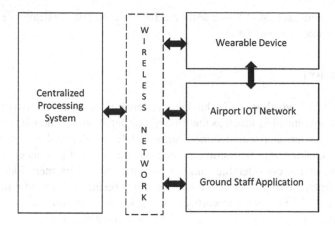

Fig. 2. Technical architecture of IOT based airport framework

4   Discussions

The new age passenger does not expect nonexclusive updates that has appropriated to all the passenger yet expect customized correspondence that address their worry. With our proposed arrangement we can give customized, area based and setting mindful constant data as route guides, alerts to the passenger. This will give more control to the traveler of their movement and make their development inside the air terminal engaged, improved and delightful.

From the carrier perspective if passenger travel is hassle free, error free then it brings about to general involvement, construct trust with carrier and enhances consumer loyalty. Carrier can use passenger information to pick up understanding into passenger needs and wants. For instance, understanding where the passenger is located and when they have to touch base at the door can manage the administrations offered to the passenger and the capacity to notify the carrier of genuine passenger delays. This arrangement will be helpful for the ground staff to find passenger any given time which will greatly diminish surge of discovering last time passenger which now and again result into flight delay. They can help passenger by activating alerts, guide when needed. This will enhance the correspondence amongst traveler and ground staff.

Passenger is the colossal wellspring of income for the airport however because of absence of passenger driven model and foundation airport loos revenue. Airport can utilize this course of action to pick up understanding about the passenger and based on that they can promote relevant services to the passenger. Promoted services should be customized based ion the passenger preference to encourage greater spend at airport terminal shops, eatery and so on.

For this course of action to work airport and airline should cooperate and share passenger data with each other to pick up understanding about the passenger which will enable them to serve better. Be that as it may, following and sharing data about the passenger could prompt protection issue for some traveler as they don't need anyone to track them or their exercises. There will be a lot of setup cost, endeavors and gadgets are required to make airport keen.

5   Conclusion

All of us that travel, whether it is for business or leisure, look forward to a day when we enjoy the journey almost as much as the time at our destination. There has been a piece of advances in air terminal establishment starting late to achieve this however there is still part of extension for progression is there and which won't be conceivable without the dedication of the considerable number of partners. All partners incorporate the aircraft, the airplane terminal and the passenger must be interconnected with electronic correspondence driving more noteworthy efficiencies and consumer loyalty. In spite of the fact that there is part of perspectives and procedures which influence general travel involvement in this investigation we have attempted to center around how passenger development in the air terminal can be made simple and how it can diminish the ground staff work. Our future degree is to search for different open doors that effect the movement experience of the passenger inside the airplane terminal and propose an answer for that.

References

1. Karatepe, O.M., Choubtarash, H.: The effects of perceived crowding, emotional dissonance, and emotional exhaustion on critical job outcomes: a study of ground staff in the airline industry. J. Air Transp. Manage. **40**, 182 (2014)
2. Cheng Hua, Y., Hsin Li, C.: Exploring the perceived competence of airport ground staff in dealing with unruly passenger behaviours. Tourism Manag. **33**(3), 611–621 (2012)
3. Cook, A., Tanner, G., Anderson, S.: Evaluating the true cost to airlines of one minute of airborne or ground delay. Performance Review Unit, University of Westminster (2004)
4. Liu, H., Hu, J., Rauterberg, M.: AIRSF: a new entertainment adaptive framework for stress free air travels. In: Proceedings of the 2008 International Conference on Advances in Computer Entertainment Technology (ACE 2008), pp. 183–186. ACM, New York (2008). https://doi.org/10.1145/1501750.1501793
5. Innovative Technology Paves the Way for Better Handled Baggage. https://w3.accelya.com/innovative-technology-paves-the-way-for-better-handled-baggage. Accessed 15 Mar 2018
6. Robot "Spencer" to guide KLM passengers at Amsterdam Airport Schiphol. https://news.klm.com/robot-spencer-to-guide-klm-passengers-at-amsterdam-airport-schiphol/. Accessed 15 Mar 2018
7. Wi-Fi positioning system. https://en.wikipedia.org/wiki/Wi-Fi_positioning_system. Accessed 15 Mar 2018
8. Bluetooth low energy beacon. https://en.wikipedia.org/wiki/Bluetooth_low_energy_beacon. Accessed 15 Mar 2018

Skip or Not to Skip: Impact of Empathy and Ad Length on Viewers' Ad-Skipping Behaviors on the Internet

Yongwoog Andrew Jeon[✉]

Stan Richards School of Advertising and Public Relations,
The University of Texas at Austin, Austin, TX 78712, USA
yongwoog@utexas.edu

Abstract. This exploratory research paper examines how viewers' empathy toward the spokesperson in a skippable, in-stream advertisement influence their skipping behaviors. Based on the emotional empathy theory (Batson et al. 1997), the current study predicted that the heightened empathy induced by the spokesperson in the ad may make it difficult for viewers to avoid (i.e., skip) the person to whom they empathize in the ad. Further, the longer the exposure to the spokesperson in the ad, the higher the level of empathy with the spokesperson, the better the ad-effectiveness (Escalas and Stern 2003). Results are three-fold. First, viewers' empathy with spokesperson in the ad mediated the effect of the ad length on skipping likelihood. The longer the ad the higher the empathy, resulting in less likelihood of skipping ad ($-.99 < CI < -.01$, b $= -.50$, z $= -1.98$, p $= .04$). Second, empathy with spokesperson in the ad did not significantly mediate the effect of the ad length on viewing duration and on the click-through rate. The results provide initial evidence that empathy may be effective in reducing likelihood of viewers' ad-skipping.

Keywords: Skippable ad · Ad skip · Empathy

1 Introduction

The growth of online advertising is overwhelming. With the spread of the Internet's wider bandwidth, in 2015, the market size of the Internet advertising was estimated about $51.64 billion, almost one third of the total advertising spending in the United States (Advertising Age 2015). Particularly remarkable is the growth of the in-stream commercial—which is video advertising that appears pre-, mid- or post-roll while watching the chosen content (YouTube 2016). Spending on in-stream commercials increased by 42% from 2014 ($5.24 billion) to 2015 ($7.46 billion) (eMarketer 2016). This growth may reflect the audience's changing viewing behavior. Compared to 2012 (35 min), Americans spent 27 more minutes (62 min) on digital video media per day (Advertising Age 2015). More and more video contents (whether user- or broadcaster-created) attract viewers to the video sharing platform. The uploaders of these videos can allow the in-stream commercials to appear before or in the middle of their videos for monetary incentives. Compared to television commercials, in-stream commercials have

© Springer International Publishing AG, part of Springer Nature 2018
C. Stephanidis (Ed.): HCII Posters 2018, CCIS 852, pp. 261–265, 2018.
https://doi.org/10.1007/978-3-319-92285-0_36

advantages such as the likelihood of matching consumers with relevant advertising based on their search behavior or choices of and preferences toward online video contents (Evans 2009). The cost of this advertising is about 0.09 dollars, which is relatively cheaper compared to traditional media channels (Carter 2016). One successful in-stream commercial brought about 450,000 impressions, 80,000 video views per month, and 3,500 website visits (Carter 2016). Consumers may understand that in-stream advertising is a tradeoff for watching a free content (AOL 2012); in other words, viewers are somehow willing to pay the cost of watching their chosen content in advance. Here the cost is likely to be "watching" the in-stream commercial. However, as research reported, viewers hate to wait and sit through the in-stream commercials (Burst Media 2008). While waiting for their chosen video content, viewers may want to know when the negative event—waiting for an ad to end—will end. Therefore, although viewers may watch the commercial, they are likely to be irritated by having to wait until the ad ends (Burst Media 2008). Perhaps this adverse impact of waiting experience is one of the reasons why in-stream commercials may have been unsuccessful so far.

To relive viewers' irritation, Ad Skip button is available for viewers. Those ads that can be skippable are often called "skippable ads." Google reported that skippable ads are more effective than conventional non-skippable ads (Pashkevich et al. 2012). However, the Industry reports and mangers' views on the skippable ads are not as rosy as Google predicted (Gesenhues 2014). Viewers are more likely to skip the ads than complete viewing (Gesenhues 2014; Kevin 2017). Also major media outlets such as NBC, FOX, and CBS may fear that the feature of skipping ad may jeopardize their financial foundations (Peralta 2012). With the rapid growth of the skippable ads, thus, it is indispensable for the media industry to find out the best message strategies to keep the viewers watch the whole ad instead of skipping or avoiding their advertisements.

For marketers and message designers, thus, it is indispensable to make in-stream commercials that delay or prevent viewers' skipping of ad, particularly given that the effectiveness of advertising is indexed by the amount of time that viewers spend on watching the ad (Teixeira et al. 2010). This raises a question: how can an ad delay or prevent viewers' skipping of ad? Despite its urgency of finding out the solutions, only few research has been done on how to reduce viewers' skipping behavior. The present study answers this question by showing that empathy may be another key component of a message that can reduce viewers' skipping behavior.

2   Literature Review

One previous study found that emotion can be used to reduce viewers' likelihood of ad skipping (Belanche et al. 2017). The study shows that the higher the arousal the ad content elicits in viewers the less viewers are likely to avoid (i.e., skip) the ad (Belanche et al. 2017; Heath et al. (2006). Along with arousal, the present study identifies and tests the other emotional concept that may be useful in reducing viewers' skipping behavior: empathy. Empathy refers to "another-oriented emotional response congruent with the perceived welfare of another person (Batson 1990, p.339)." Simply put, empathy is the experience of another person's emotion. Previous research shows that empathy can promote prosocial behavior (e.g., helping people in need) (Bagozzi and Moore 1994; Basil et al. 2008; Eisenberg and Fabes 1991; Leith and Baumeister 1998; Roberts et al. 2014; Shelton and Rogers (1981)). While these studies accumulated a large amount of evidence that empathy can change attitudes and behaviors, what is less known in the literature is the relationship between empathy and avoidance of message. Given that empathy can be seen as "an emotional engagement" (Busselle and Bilandzic (2009), the present study predicts that if viewers' empathy with the person appearing in advertisements is triggered and aroused, then viewers will pay attention to what the person says. Thus, the higher the empathy toward the spokesperson in the ad, the less likely viewers click the skip ad button; the longer viewers watch the ad. Also, the present study predicts that longer ad (e.g., 30 s ad) is typically more effective than short ad (e.g., 15 s) because empathy needs a certain amount of time to be aroused in viewers (Schacht and Sommer 2009).

3   Methods

A sample of 57 college students were randomly assigned to either short (15 s) or long ad condition (30 s). Across all conditions, participants were given a choice of 4 titles for 4 "different" animal-related videos, which actually lead to the same single animal video. Once they chose a title and starts viewing the video, an unexpected skippable ad appears. This skippable ad was shown from a video experiment platform that was developed for research purpose (see Fig. 1) The ad used for this study was a campaign by American Heart Association. In the ad, a NBA star Paul George appears as a spokesperson talking about his experience about his mother's heart attack and how to cope with such a sudden event. Participants can skip the ad after 5 s elapsed. Also, they can click the link for more information about the ad.

Fig. 1.   A screen shot of the skippable ad.

In terms of measurement, participants' skipping behaviors including whether or not participants click the "Skip Ad" button and how long they stayed on the commercial were recorded in the server. In addition, participants' clicking on the "more information on our website" appearing on the bottom of the screen was also recorded. To measure participants' empathy toward the spokesperson in the ad, Batson's 7-item scale of empathy was used. After viewing the videos, participants were asked to rate to what extent they feel "sympathetic," "compassionate," "softhearted," "warm," "tender," and "moved." (on a scale of 1[not at all] to 9[extremely]) Also, there were asked "while viewing the ad, to what extent did you concentrate on feelings of the spokesperson in the ad."

4   Results

The results showed first that the longer the ad the higher the empathy level ($\beta = 1.11$, $SE = .48$, $t = 2.28$, $p = .02$, $.14 < CI < 2.07$). Next, the empathy significantly mediated the effect of the length of the ad (15 vs. 30 s) on viewers skipping behavior (whether or not viewers clicked the skipping button, 0 = not clicked vs 1 = clicked), ($\beta = -.50$, $SE = .78$, $Z = -1.98$, $p = .04$, $-.9 < CI < .0061$). Yet, the mediation model was not significant with the other outcome variables, the duration of watching the ad ($-.39 < CI < 31$) and the clicking on the link ($-.22 < CI < 1.43$).

5   Discussion

The current study provides some evidence that empathy might be effective in reducing viewers' skipping behavior. The results showed that the longer the ad the stronger the empathy viewers experience. The aroused empathy then reduced the likelihood of viewers' skipping behavior. This is an initial evidence with a small sample size. Thus, the results await further examinations with more studies.

References

Advertising Age.: Marketing Fact Pack: Annual Guide to Marketers, Media, and Agencies. (2015) Accessed from http://adage.com/d/resources/resources/whitepaper/2016-edition-marketing-fact-pack

AOL.: ShortForm, Big Impact. (2012) Accessed from https://advertising.aol.com/sites/advertising.aol.com/files/insights/research-reports/downloads/onlinevideo-shortformforweb.pdf

Barthold, J.: AOL: short-form video content advertising most effective, in FierceCable (18 December 2012)

Basil, D.Z., Ridgway, N.M., Basil, M.D.: Guilt and giving: A process model of empathy and efficacy. Psychol. Mark. 25(1), 1–23 (2008)

Bagozzi, R.P., Moore, D.J.: Public service advertisements: Emotions and empathy guide prosocial behavior. J. Mark. 56–70 (1994)

Batson, C.D., Polycarpou, M.P., Harmon-Jones, E., Imhoff, H.J., Mitchener, E.C., Bednar, L.L., Highberger, L.: Empathy and attitudes: can feeling for a member of a stigmatized group improve feelings toward the group? J. Pers. Soc. Psychol. **72**(1), 105 (1997). https://doi.org/10.1037/0022-3514.72.1.105

Belanche, D., Carlos, Flavián and Alfredo Pérez-Rueda.: Understanding Interactive Online Advertising: congruence and product involvement in highly and lowly arousing, skippable video ads. J. Interact. Mark. **37**, 75–88 (2017)

Burst Media.: Consumers Shout "I Want My Online Video. (2008) Accesssed from http://www.burstmedia.com/pdf/2008_01_01.pdf

Busselle, R., Helena, B.: Measuring narrative engagement. Media Psychol. **12**(4), 321–347 (2009)

Carter, B.: Why YouTube Pre-Roll Ads Rock & How To Take Advantage of Them. (2016) Accessed from http://www.convinceandconvert.com/content-marketing/why-youtube-pre-roll-ads-rock-how-to-take-advantage-of-them/

eMarketer.: US Digital Display Ad Spending to Surpass Search Ad Spending in 2016 - eMarketer (2016)

Eisenberg, N., Richard, A.F.: Prosocial behavior and empathy: A multimethod developmental perspective (1991)

Escalas, J.E., Stern, B.B.: Sympathy and empathy: emotional responses to advertising dramas. J. Consum. Res. **29**(4), 566–578 (2003)

Evans, D.S.: The online advertising industry: Economics, evolution, and privacy. Journal of Econ. Perspect. **23**(3), 37–60 (2009)

Gesenhues, A.: Study: 56% of Viewers Skip Online Video Ads & 46% Say Any Ad Over 15-Seconds Is Too Long.http://marketingland.com/study-56-viewers-skip-online-video-ads-46-think-ad-15-seconds-long-88299. Accessed 20 June 2014

Kevin, G.: Millennials skip YouTube ads… and that's ok. Business Insider (2017)

Leith, Karen P and Roy F Baumeister.: Empathy, shame, guilt, and narratives of interpersonal conflicts: guilt-prone people are better at perspective taking. J. Pers. **66**(1), 1–37 (1998)

Pashkevich, M., Dorai-Raj, S., Kellar, M., Zigmond, D.: Empowering online advertisements by empowering viewers with the right to choose: the relative effectiveness of skippable video advertisements on YouTube. J. Advert. Res. **52**(4), 451–457 (2012)

Peralta, E.: No TV ads? Maybe not. NBC, FOX, CBS sue over ad-skip feature. NPR (2012)

Roberts, William, Janet Strayer and Susanne Denham.: Empathy, anger, guilt: Emotions and prosocial behaviour. Can. J. of Behav. Sci. **46**(4), 465–474 (2014)

Schacht, A., Sommer, W.: Time course and task dependence of emotion effects in word processing. Cognit. Affect. Behav. Neurosci. **9**(1), 28–43 (2009)

Shelton, M.L., Ronald, W.R.: Fear-Arousing and Empathy-Arousing Appeals to Help: The Pathos of Persuasion. J. Appl. Soc. Psychol. **11**(4), 366–378 (1981)

Teixeira, T.S., Wedel, M., Pieters, R.: Moment-to-moment optimal branding in TV commercials: preventing avoidance by pulsing. Mark. Sci. **29**(5), 783–804 (2010)

YouTube: Non-skippable in-stream ads. (2016) Accessed from https://support.google.com/youtube/answer/188038?hl=en

Research on Interactive Design of Interface Layout of Idle Resource Transactional Websites

Bin Jiang and Yitong Wang[✉]

School of Design Arts and Media, Nanjing University of Science and Technology,
200, Xiaolingwei Street, Nanjing 210094, Jiangsu, China
631603555@qq.com, yitongwang1011@163.com

Abstract. In recent years, with the continuous development of the Internet, the idle resource transactional websites has gradually sprung up and developed rapidly with the help of the Internet platform. And it has also gained more and more people's attention and favor. The layout design of the website is not only the first impression of the website, but also is an important factor for user experience. Either from the perspective of business profit or from the perspective of user needs, it is very important to research and explore the layout design of idle resource transactional websites. First of all, this paper analyzes and classifies the idle resources transactional website. Secondly, according to the classification of idle resources transactional websites, we propose the interface layout design evaluation index. We have evaluated three of the most visited idle resources transactional websites based on the proposed evaluation index. The result proves that interface layout design is a very important factor. Finally, we conclude some practical and useful design strategies which can be used as the reference for the interactive layout design of the website.

Keywords: Website interface design of idle resources · Interaction design

1 Interface Layout Design Interpretation of the Idle Resource Transactional Websites

1.1 The Definition of Idle Resource Transactional Websites

Idle resources transactional website is a commodity trading platform where users can not only sell or share their idle resources, but also can find cost-effective goods. And the benefit of idle resources can be maximized on the win-win platform.

1.2 The Classification of Idle Resource Transactional Websites

With the rapid development of the sharing economy, idle resource transactional websites have also started to go to the positive market. At present, there are two kinds of idle resource trading websites, free sharing and sale. Free sharing sites include Freecycle, YouRole, etc. These websites are very easy to use, where free information of idle resource transferring and help can be released. Sale sites include Xian Yu website,

© Springer International Publishing AG, part of Springer Nature 2018
C. Stephanidis (Ed.): HCII Posters 2018, CCIS 852, pp. 266–272, 2018.
https://doi.org/10.1007/978-3-319-92285-0_37

Mercari, Carousell, etc. Users can buy and sell idle resource in order to get paid through these websites.

2 Standard Extraction of Interface Layout Design

2.1 Grid Systems Theory

Grid systems design style is characterized by the use of digital proportions, the type page is divided into numerous uniform sizes through strict calculation. The page is divided into one column, two columns, three columns, or more columns. And the visual elements such as words and pictures are arranged into these columns. So that the layout has a certain rhythm change, formed the harmonious beautiful visual rhythm [1]. The grid system is developed from a planar grid system, and their design thoughts are intimately tied up, which guide and standardize the layout and distribution of information in the web page by using regular grid array [2]. For the interface design, the use of the grid system can not only make the web information more beautiful and easy to read, but also enhance the usability of the web page.

2.2 Symmetry and Equilibrium

The visual balance is to make each plate in the interface basically consistent, so as to achieve the balance. Visual balance is mainly divided into symmetrical balance and asymmetrical balance, also called equilibrium [3]. Although absolute balance does not have much use for websites interface design, left-right horizontal symmetry is often used in the layout of web pages. Equilibrium is one of the most common forms of composition and is often used in websites interface design. In two-column layout design of the websites page. We will find that the color of larger area with less content is usually light. While on the opposite, the color of small area, which we can use as navigation bar, is often dark. Such an asymmetrical layout will achieve a balanced effect, without causing a deviation of the center of gravity.

2.3 White Space

Chinese traditional aesthetics has this statement "white Shouhei" [4]. White space is a special way of showing no pictures in the version. Without very good white space, the page will be crowded. White space can lead the user's line of sight to the side of the page, making the design of the interface "breathable". In the design of the layout of the web, the beauty of white space is one of the factors that focus on the expressiveness of Art. The intention to leave white space is to leave enough room for the consumer to breathe, and it helps to highlight the contents that need to be emphasized, avoid accumulation of various elements without rhythm which makes visual fatigue and causes tension. It also strengthens space level, making layout compact and orderly.

2.4   Golden Section Method

To highlight the importance of attracting attention, people often habitually like to put important things in the center. However, according to the human visual habit, the center is actually a blind spot, which is often overlooked, so the information is placed in the center and does not cause the visual impact.

As is known to all, 0.618 is known as the golden ratio, which brings a harmonious and pleasant visual experience. Among them, the tripartite method is a method of using the golden rule. According to people's reading habits from left to right and from top to top, the visual impact of the four points as (shown in Fig. 1) is from strong to weak in order A (top left), B (top right), C (lower left), D (lower right). This reminds us that in order to enable users to obtain key information more accurately and efficiently, we should fully consider the overall picture and the reasonable arrangement of the visual center in the layout design of the interface.

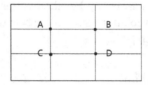

Fig. 1. Three-point page visual center

3   Case Analysis

We have selected three of the most visited idle resources transactional websites (Xianyu, Carousell and Mercari) based on the proposed evaluation index. The layout design of idle resource transaction website is analyzed according to the interface layout design standard.

3.1   Xianyu Website Layout Design Analysis

The Xianyu website has accumulated more than 100 million real-name authentication users and is the largest idle trading website in China. Users can log in using taobao or alipay accounts, without having to go through a complicated process of opening a store. Users can be used to upload and upload second-hand goods, and can be traded online and other functions.

Xianyu website layout structure is a comprehensive layout. This kind of layout structure is divided into three parts. Above the interface for Xianyu website is the Logo and navigation, in the middle is the main content of the website, at the bottom of the interface is the copyright information and contact information.

The reasonable arrangement and selection of interface layout structure is determined by the function of the website. There is a lot of information in the Xianyu website. So it is necessary to have a clear hierarchy of information in the layout structure, and the proportion of information content should be sufficient. In order to facilitate user browsing, the visual contrast relationship between the parts should be taken into consideration in the layout arrangement. The best way is to use the golden ratios the most reasonable way is to use the golden ratio to divide, so the main content in the middle is bigger space. The middle part of the proportion will be a little more. Usually account for about 60%, the top 10%, the bottom 30%. Below this way of dividing the closest to the golden ratio, visual center can be concentrated to the main information area. The overall layout and have some breathing space, bring more comfortable feeling to the user (Fig. 2). Xianyu homepage interface, the whole layout of segmentation is very close to the golden ratio. Commodity information is also on the layout along the center of gravity on the average distribution, to achieve the effect of visual balance. However, the content of the interface is too much. And there is no good white space, which leads to the accumulation of too much information. That can't effectively communicate the information, which can also cause the user's visual fatigue and cause the tension.

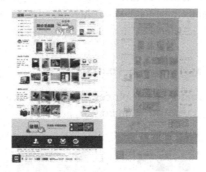

Fig. 2. Xianyu website interface

3.2 Carousell Website Layout Design Analysis

Carousell is a trading platform for idle resources in Singapore, which expanding to 13 major cities around the world, mainly in the asia-pacific region. In the mode, Carousell is similar to the Xianyu, simply edit the product information and upload the physical picture. And then users can free trade on the platform (Fig. 3).

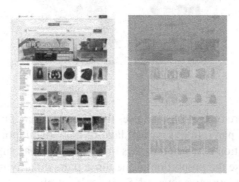

Fig. 3. Carousell website interface

The layout structure of Carousell website type is T layout structure, which is named for the similarity of capital letter T in English. At the top of the interface, the logo and Banner of the Carousell website are placed. The navigation bar menu is set on the left side. And the other part is the main information of the commodity. This kind of layout structure is characterized by simple and clear structure, clear interface information and strong visual impact. While bring us a simple and clear vision at the same time, the layout also has the disadvantages and problems of its own. First of all, information of the commodity content and navigation bar are not in accordance with the golden ratio, which will cause the feeling of imbalance because of the asymmetric layout, the deviation will lead to the center of gravity. In addition, the division of the upper and lower regions is too simple and rigid, and the lack of conciseness will give users a single empty visual sense.

So when idle resource trading website is used in the concise layout of T structure, we should pay attention to the way of arrangement of text, pictures and color elements. We also should enrich visual elements in smart layout, so as to avoid causing the overall interface imbalance.

3.3   Mercari Website Layout Design Analysis

Mercari is a trading platform for idle resources in Japan. Mercari raised more than $111 million, quietly becoming Japan's first unicorn.

Fig. 4. Mercari website interface

The layout structure type of Mercari uses the three-point method, which divides the whole page into three parts. In this type of layout, the most important thing is to grasp the reasonable proportion between the parts of division, and arrange the clear structure and hierarchy. Because the proportion of the three parts directly influence whether the information can be effectively conveyed. So it can't simply divide, attention should be paid to the relationship between the three. The overall layout proportion is unreasonable. The middle-upper part text information arrangement is too centralized. The Mercari website interface is based on the central axis, and the information content on the left and right sides is symmetrical. Such a form will make the consumer feel the visual balance, comfortable, the information is clear at a glance. The interface in the commodity display part and bottom of the part information has white space, and through the appropriate space. Make whole layout interface is breathable, users in the process of browsing more easily.

4 Research on Design Strategies of Idle Resource Transactional Websites

Based on the analysis and summary of the layout design of idle resource transactional website. It can provide practical suggestions and design strategies for the layout design of idle resource transactional website.

(1) Layout design based on user's visual habits and visual process

When designing the layout of idle resource transactional website. We should pay attention to the user's visual habit. Because only when we conform to the users' natural habits can we achieve the effective transmission of information. As you can see from the previous case analysis, the logo of the website is usually in the upper left corner. Because human visual habits generally begin from the upper left corner when browsing a website. And in the same interface, the content of the upper part of the region is more accessible to the user than the lower part of the content. And the left half of the area is more easily accessible than the right half. Psychological research also shows that in the same plane, the upper part of things can make people feel happy and comfortable, while the lower part of things will bring stability and depression. The reason is the same for left and right half. The contents on the left will be more favorable than the right side. Therefore, the layout of idle resource transaction website interface should be based on such a visual habit.

(2) Change and unity

Change and unity are the general principles of formal beauty and the application of the unity of opposites in the layout of the interface. The perfect combination of them is the most fundamental requirement of page composition. In idle resource transactional website layout design, the influence of shape, size, direction and so on is an important part of forming a sense of unity. For example, in the website interface design, the best way to make the page achieve a unified way is that the elements of the interface are less, and the form of the combination is richer. The use of some color blocks or color dots can make the whole page very unified.

The philosopher Heraclitus once said, "Nature is the original harmony of the object, not the union of the same kind, and the art is thus harmonious [5]. It can be seen that unification can bring about the harmony of the layout of the interface layout of the idle resource transaction. And the harmony also requires the opposition of the design change of the website interface. In the layout design of the interface, there are many ways to change the application. Such as the comparison of shapes, the comparison of size, the contrast of density and so on, that can bring harmony to the page from the comparison.

(3) Orderly and uniform

Regularity means ignoring differences and opposites, and pursuing consistent expansion and duplication of shapes, lines, colors, etc., so that all elements of idle resource trading website have strong regularity and uniform effect.

Mercari website interface (Fig. 4), we can see that the goods and copywriting are all the same size in the region and the location of the place also is the same in the rectangular area. And align each other up and down, the size the same modules are consistent. It is convenient for consumers to browse and find the rules to get the effective information of the goods quickly. Neat pages can make people visually relaxed and comfortable, and can feel the stability and calm of the page.

5   Conclusion

With the development of economic globalization, diversity has changed people's consumption and aesthetic perception. With the sustainable development trend and the idea of green consumption, more and more people begin to learn how to reduce the consumption on the basis of experience to gain a better life. The emergence of idle resource transactional websites provides a new way of thinking and perspective for realizing this idea.

However, there are some problems in the interface layout design of idle resource transactional websites. But the analysis of this situation is very limited. In this paper, idle resource transaction websites with high user volume are selected to analyze the current situation of their interface layout design. Furthermore, based on the advantages and disadvantages, we propose a practical value design strategy, and hope to provide reference value for the interactive design of the website interface of idle resource trans-action in the future.

References

1. Bosshard, H.R.: Layout Design Grid Structure. China Youth Publishing House, Beijing (2005)
2. Wang, S., Xu, S., Zhang, J.: Web Design and Page Matching, vol. 9, p. 131. Science Press, Beijing (2010)
3. Yi, X.: Research on the interface design of shopping in China. Central South University (2012)
4. Yang, F.: Research on shopping web page design in visual marketing. Tianjin Polytechnic University (2017)
5. School of philosophy of Peking University: Western aesthete on beauty and beauty. Commercial Press (1980)

Evaluation of Quality Management for Strategic Decision Making in Companies in the Plastic Sector of the Colombian Caribbean Region Using the TQM Diagnostic Report and Data Analysis

Genett Jimenez[1,2]([✉]), Leonel Hernandez[1,2], Hugo Hernandez[3], Luis Cabas[4,5], and Jenny Ferreira[4,5]

[1] Department of Industrial Processes Engineering, Engineering Faculty, Institución Universitaria ITSA, Barranquilla, Colombia
gjimenez@itsa.edu.co
[2] Department of Telematic Engineering, Engineering Faculty, Institución Universitaria ITSA, Barranquilla, Colombia
lhernandezc@itsa.edu.co
[3] Department of Business Administration, Universidad del Atlántico, Barranquilla, Colombia
hugoghernandezpalma@gmail.com
[4] Engineering Faculty, Systems Engineering Program, Corporación Universitaria Latinoamericana CUL, Barranquilla, Colombia
luiscabasvasquez@hotmail.com
[5] Economic Sciences Faculty, Financial Management Program, Corporación Universitaria Latinoamericana CUL, Barranquilla, Colombia
jennyosiferreira@gmail.com

Abstract. The plastic sector is considered one of the most dynamic industries with the highest competitive projection in the country. The incidence of this sector in the national and regional economy has led to the completion of various investigations, to learn about their behavior and detect opportunities for improvement. In this regard, previous studies carried out by entities in Colombia such as the Universidad del Norte [1], corroborated the growth potential of the sector; but one of its most relevant weaknesses was also identified in the quality factor and, at the same time, it was proposed as the main strategy for making decisions associated with productivity and competitiveness. Given this precedent, an analysis of the state of the art in this area was made, and it was found that there is not enough information on the current situation of quality management in the plastics processing and production industry in the Colombian Caribbean Region. Faced with this problem, a study was conducted to visualize the behavior of companies belonging to the plastics sector regarding quality management, identifying and analyzing the most significant needs for the approach of joint strategies to improve the sector.

Keywords: Quality management · Decision making · Plastic sector
Data analysis

© Springer International Publishing AG, part of Springer Nature 2018
C. Stephanidis (Ed.): HCII Posters 2018, CCIS 852, pp. 273–281, 2018.
https://doi.org/10.1007/978-3-319-92285-0_38

1 Introduction

The plastic industry is one of the productive chains of higher evolution, both in the growth in production, which reached 250 million tons in 2015 [2], with a growth rate in the consumption of plastic materials of the 4% up to 2030 [3]. In Colombia, this sector stands out as one of those that have best responded to the economic opening by establishing new markets, developing new products, improving its technological capacity and attracting foreign investment [4].

However, this growth will condition by latest trends in the manufacture and consumption of plastic, such as prices of raw materials, consumer demands, government and interest groups related to the impact of plastics on the environment and the possibility of Offer new products. Therefore, companies must implement standards and management tools to improve their products and processes continuously.

The Total Quality Management - TQM is a methodology that helps companies to be more productive and competitive in very dynamic markets but presents both endogenous and exogenous difficulties for implementation and certification [5]. Although there are some studies found in the literature, knowledge of quality management in the plastics sector is still limited, as well as the use of diagnostic methodologies.

This paper presents, in Sect. 2 a literature review on quality management. The methodology approach is explained in Sect. 3. Then, results and analyses are shown, in Sect. 4, with the description of the industrial and productive profile of the companies in the sector, and the diagnosis of enterprises taking into account the key variables of Total Quality Management, by city and company size. Finally, Sect. 5 presents the conclusions and future works.

2 Quality Management. A Literature Review

Quality Management is a management process based on quality, in which the activities, tools, and personnel involved interact in a coordinated manner towards the permanent search for satisfaction of the requirements, needs, and expectations of the clients, according to ISO 9001:2015 [6]. In this regard, we found different scientific articles that demonstrate the importance of knowledge management and quality management and their influence in companies [7]. In [8], shows the relationship between information systems quality and organizational impact. Other work shows the assessing information quality in manufacturing planning [9]. The quality management can be design using tools and methodologies. For example, in [10] shows the application of a methodology based on process management to increase the performance of processes and implementation of the Quality Management System in a Higher Education and in [11] shows the results of a similar study, but implementing an integrated approach based on the Balanced Scorecard and implementation of ISO 9001 in a service organization in Colombia.

Mainly, this research focuses on the application of quality management systems in the plastics industry. In this respect, very few studies were found in the scientific literature. In [12] explains a process for quality control of plastic injection using machine learning algorithms. Also, in other works, [13, 14], explain how to use the Taguchi Method and six sigma method for quality control of the plastic product and in [15] explains the implementation of a quality plan in a company in the plastics industry in Peru. In [16] describes a methodology for evaluation of Total Quality Management using Corporate Social Responsibility - CSR Company Reports.

In this regard, it can conclude that studies directly focused on improving the productivity and competitiveness in the plastic industry, with the use of the total quality management, are mostly limited. Therefore, this research contributes to the scientific literature and provides a diagnostic tool for companies in the sector based on the Total Quality Management.

3 Methodology

The investigative method [17, 18] used is described as follows. The project is framed within the analytical, descriptive and prospective study; because data and information of the present were collected and analyzed, with the purpose of proposing improvements towards the future. Given that a diagnosis of the current situation had to be made to propose solutions to the problems that arose during the investigative analysis, the study classified as transversal. It is also descriptive - explanatory, because the project, through a diagnosis of variables associated with total quality management, analyzed and classified the characteristics and behavior of Quality Management in the companies of plastic sector in the cities of Barranquilla and Cartagena, and the interrelation between the different variables that affect the management capacity of the companies in this aspect, to finally propose the action strategies.

Figure 1 shows the methodological design with the stages of the project, the procedure used to perform the entire investigative process, measurement techniques and data collection used.

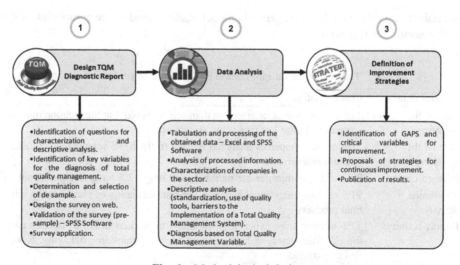

Fig. 1. Methodological design

For the data collection, a survey called TQM diagnostic report designed, which consists of three diagnostic components, as shown in Fig. 2. The TQM Diagnostic Report applied to a sample of 35 companies in the cities of Barranquilla and Cartagena using Eq. 1 for the calculation of the sample size (p = 0.5; q = 0.5; e = 0.05; k = 1.96; N = 39). The survey demonstrated a good level of reliability [19], with a Cronbach alpha of 0.96.

$$n = \frac{k^2 * p * q * N}{(e^2 * (N - 1)) + k^2 * p * q} \tag{1}$$

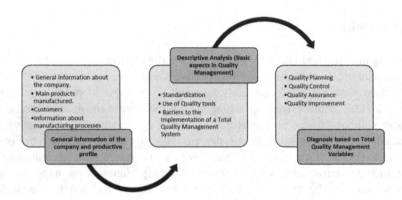

Fig. 2. Components of TQM diagnostic report

4   Results

4.1   General Information About the Companies of the Sector

In Table 1, are observed the main general characteristics found in the companies of the plastic sector are following:

Table 1. General information and productive profile

General data	Characteristics
Age of the company	34% of the companies are more than ten years old, but the creation of new companies in the last five years stands out
Size of the company	71% of the companies analyzed belong to the SME segment (Small and medium enterprises)
Foreign capital	88% of the companies are national, and only 12% have foreign capital
Economic activity	91% of companies are engaged in the transformation of plastic resins into final products
Export activity	57% of companies export their products to markets in Latin America and the US. The sectors of high demand for companies are packaging, food, and construction

4.2 Descriptive Analysis of Basic Aspects of Quality Management

In Fig. 3a–e, the primary results of the descriptive analysis are observed, taking into account essential characteristics in quality. The results show the potential that exists for companies to implement and certify their processes, use consulting services in quality management and certification and manage different tools to support quality. Likewise, the main barriers for companies in these processes are shown.

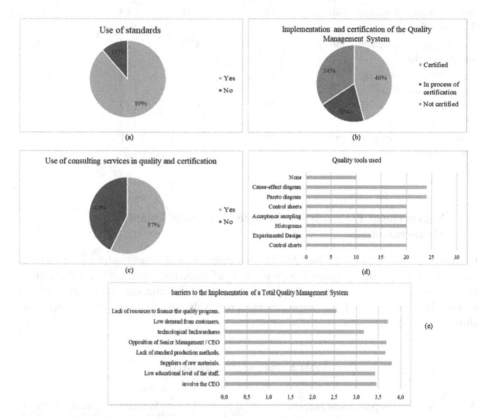

Fig. 3. Results obtained from the descriptive analysis: Use of standards (a), implementation of certification management system (b), use of consulting services in quality (c), quality tools (d) and barriers to implementation TQM system

4.3 Diagnosis Based on Total Quality Management Variables

In Table 2 shows a comparative table between the maximum scores of the TQM diagnosis for each of the critical variables (obtained from the multiplication of the number of questions by the Likert score scale) and the results obtained by the companies, according to the city and the size of the company. The results show a better performance of medium and large companies compared to small and micro companies. Likewise, companies in the city of Cartagena obtained better results than companies in the city of Barranquilla.

Table 2. Results of TQM diagnosis

	Variables				
	V1. Quality planning	V2. Quality control	V3. Quality assurance	V4. Quality improvement	Total score
Top score	65	45	140	30	280
Score obtained (average Cartagena)	60	41	123	27	250
Score obtained (average Barranquilla)	46	33	103	19	200
Score obtained (average big companies)	56	41	122	25	245
Score obtained (average medium companies)	61	40	123	27	251
Score obtained (average small companies)	46	30	99	17	192
Score obtained (average micro companies)	31	24	79	11	145

4.4 Improvement Proposals for Strengthening Total Quality Management

In an effort to underpin the Total Quality Management in the companies of the sector, a series of strategies are proposed with the aim of improving the quality management levels and, at the same time, increasing the productivity and competitiveness of this sector. The summary of the improvement proposals and the specific strategies are shown in Table 3.

Table 3. Improvement proposals

		Size of company			
Variables	Improvement proposals	Big	Medium	Small	Micro
Quality planning	Definition of the Mission, Vision and corporate values, to establish Quality Policies, objectives, and goals			✓	✓
	Incorporate strategic planning techniques (SWOT Analysis, Market Research)			✓	✓
	Development of the managerial capacity of the managers towards the Management of the Quality	✓	✓	✓	✓

(*continued*)

Table 3. (*continued*)

Variables	Improvement proposals	Big	Medium	Small	Micro
		Size of company			
Quality control	Implement statistical methods for the control of raw materials, processes, and products			✓	✓
	Encourage companies to use quality laboratories, research, and development		✓	✓	✓
Quality assurance	Sensitize Senior Management about the implementation of operational and administrative procedures		✓	✓	✓
	Encourage companies to use technical standards	✓	✓	✓	✓
Quality improvement	Development of an organizational culture suitable for quality and improvement	✓	✓	✓	✓
	Use of Management standards and indicators	✓	✓	✓	✓
	Use of statistical tools and techniques for the improvement of processes	✓	✓	✓	✓
	Training in soft management techniques	✓	✓	✓	✓

5   Conclusions and Future Works

This research constitutes a valuable contribution for the plastic sector of the Colombian Caribbean Region, by becoming a tool for analyzing the current situation of the same and for diagnosis in terms of Quality Management, achieving not only the description of the behavior of companies in the sector, but their classification taking into account their common characteristics, as well as the identification of key variables that affect their management capacity. The results of this research aim to raise the levels of productivity and competitiveness in companies in the sector, through the implementation of joint strategies with respect to Quality Management as a means for organizations to develop formal systems focused on customers, suppliers, the company and society in general, facilitating their growth and positioning in increasingly demanding markets.

As future work, the TQM diagnostic report will be applied to the selected companies to perform multivariate analysis, evaluate the levels of performance in quality management and establish correlational analyzes between variables and characteristics such as the size of the company, antiquity, and export orientation, among others.

References

1. Perez, H., Villamizar, V.: Análisis de competitividad del sector plástico de Barranquilla orientado a la identificación de macrocluster con alto potencial de desarrollo y formulación de estrategias para el mejoramiento continuo del sector. Universidad del Norte, Barranquilla, Colombia (2000)
2. Hacia un mundo que consume menos plástico: ¿Qué pasa con Colombia? http://www.dinero.com/economia/articulo/oportunidad-para-colombia-en-elmercado-mundial-de-plasticos-/217899. Accessed 08 Nov 2017
3. Arandes, J., Bilbao, J., Lopez, D.: Reciclado de residuos plásticos. Revista Iberoamericana de Polimeros **5**(1), 28–45 (2004)
4. Amar, P.: Un Estudio de la Innovación y la Gestión Tecnológica: Aplicación al Sector Plástico de la Región Caribe Colombiana. Universidad Politécnica de Valencia, España (2000)
5. Loesener, O., Wipplinger, G.: La certificación y la competitividad empresarial: temas clave para Latinoamérica. In: FOMIN/BIN-ONUDI, Washintong D.C (1999)
6. ISO, International Standard ISO 9001-2015: Quality Management System - Requirements. International Organization for Standardization, Switzerland (2015)
7. Tarí, J., Garcia, M.: Dimensiones de la gestión del conocimiento y de la gestion de la calidad: una revision de la literatura. Inv. Europeas de Dirección y Economía de la Empresa **15**(3), 135–148 (2009)
8. Gorla, N., Somers, T.M., Wong, B.: Organizational impact of system quality, information quality, and service quality. J. Strateg. Inf. Syst. **19**(3), 207–228 (2010)
9. Gustavsson, M., Wänström, C.: Assessing information quality in manufacturing planning and control processes. Int. J. Qual. Reliab. Manag. **26**(4), 325–340 (2009)
10. Jimenez, G.: Procedimientos para el mejoramiento de la calidad y la implantación de la Norma ISO 9001 aplicado al proceso de Asesoramiento del Centro de Investigaciones y Desarrollo Empresarial y Regional en una Institucion de Edicacion Superior basados en la gestion por procesos. In: Congreso de Gestion de la Calidad y Proteccion Ambiental GECPA 2014, pp. 1–22, Habana, Cuba (2014)
11. Jimenez, G., Zapata, E.: Metodología integrada para el control estratégico y la mejora continua, basada en el Balanced Scorecard y el Sistema de Gestión de Calidad: aplicación en una organización de servicios en Colombia. In: 51ª Asamblea Anual del Consejo Latinoamericano de Escuelas de Administracion CLADEA 2016, pp. 1–20, Medellin, Colombia (2016)
12. Tellaeche, A., Arana, R.: Machine learning algorithms for quality control in plastic molding industry. In: IEEE International Conference on Emerging Technologies and Factory Automation, ETFA (2013)
13. Mehat, N.M., Kamaruddin, S.: Quality control and design optimisation of plastic product using Taguchi method: a comprehensive review. Int. J. Plast. Technol. **16**(2), 194–209 (2012)
14. Safwat, T., Ezzat, A.: Applying six sigma techniques in plastic injection molding industry. In: International Conference on Industrial Engineering and Engineering Management, IEEM 2008 pp. 2041–2045. IEEE, Singapore (2008)
15. Moscoso, J., Yalan, A.: Mejora de la calidad en el proceso de fabricación de plasticos flexibles utilizando six sigma. Universidad de San Martin de Porres, Lima, Peru (2015)
16. Ochikubo, S., Saitoh, F., Ishizu, S.: Evaluation of total quality management using CSR company reports. In: Nah, F.F.-H., Tan, C.-H. (eds.) HCIBGO 2017. LNCS, vol. 10294, pp. 386–399. Springer, Cham (2017). https://doi.org/10.1007/978-3-319-58484-3_30

17. Saravia, M.A.: Metodología de investigación científica. In: CONACYT, pp. 1–18 (2006)
18. Hernandez, R., Fernandez, C., Baptista, M.: Metodología de la investigación, 5th edn. MacGraw-Hill, Mexico (2010)
19. George, D., Mallery, P.: SPSS for Windows Step by Step: A simple Guide and Reference, 4th edn. Allyn & Bacon, Boston (2003)

Diagnosis of Initial Conditions for the Implementation of the Integrated Management System in the Companies of the Land Cargo Transportation in the City of Barranquilla (Colombia)

Genett Jimenez[1]([✉]), Laxmi Novoa[1], Laura Ramos[1], Jairo Martinez[2,3], and Cesar Alvarino[2,3]

[1] Department of Industrial Processes Engineering, Engineering Faculty, Institución Universitaria ITSA, Barranquilla, Colombia
gjimenez@itsa.edu.co, laxmi.novoa_95@hotmail.es, lavarape@gmail.com

[2] Economic Sciences Faculty, Corporación Universitaria Latinoamericana CUL, Barranquilla, Colombia
jairoluis2007@gmail.com

[3] Engineering Faculty, Systems Engineering Program, Corporación Universitaria Latinoamericana CUL, Barranquilla, Colombia
cesaraugustoalvarinocruz@gmail.com

Abstract. The land cargo transportation represents one of the links in the logistics chain of great importance at the regional, national and global levels, due to its impact not only at an economic level but also at a social level. However, this sector shows operational deficiencies that affect not better productivity and competitiveness levels are obtained compared with other regions and countries. It is there where Integrated Management Systems become an alternative to support companies in achieving these objectives, especially in companies in this sector, where no diagnostic studies had found in the implementation of these management systems. This article presents a methodology for diagnosing the initial conditions for the application of Integrated Management Systems in companies belonging to the cargo logistics sector of the city of Barranquilla, taking into account the standards ISO 9001, ISO 14001, OHSAS 18001 and BASC. First, an instrument for measurement and diagnosis was constructed and statistically valid. Afterward, the general profile of the companies in the sector was described and categorized into four differentiated groups according to their level of performance, and the GAPS or percentage differences between the standard and the results obtained calculated. Finally, improvement plans proposed for the critical variables identified. The results show the importance in the application of diagnostic tools and the improvement of the conditions for the implementation of Integrated Management Systems, through a reliable data measurement and analysis instrument, with a Cronbach alpha of 0,96.

Keywords: Standardization · Integrated management systems
Land transportation · Cargo logistics · Continuous improvement
Productivity · Competitiveness · Data analysis

© Springer International Publishing AG, part of Springer Nature 2018
C. Stephanidis (Ed.): HCII Posters 2018, CCIS 852, pp. 282–289, 2018.
https://doi.org/10.1007/978-3-319-92285-0_39

1 Introduction

The land cargo transportation is a critical component of the logistics and supply chain of a country [1] since it seeks to minimize costs, time and assurance the delivery of products to customers in optimal conditions. Despite being an essential sector in the economy, it has problems that diminish not only the competitiveness of companies but also that of regions and countries, as in the case of Colombia. In this sense, the primary deficiencies related to the high logistic costs and the delay in the transport infrastructure [2, 3], the limited use of information and communication technologies and the non-application of business management methodologies [4].

Therefore, one of the keys to strengthening the land cargo logistics sector is through integrated management systems in its supply chain [5], through the design and implementation of strategies to improve its value chain, which allows them to guarantee the safety of human talent, the protection of the environment, control and security of commercial activities at national and international level, with a direct impact on productivity, quality and the relationship with interest groups.

In this sense, different researchers founded in the scientific literature related to the theory of Integrity Management Systems and their application in various industries. However, the evidence regarding the conditions and current behavior of companies in the land cargo transportation in the implementation of this methodology is limited and little explored.

The remainder of this paper is organized as follows: First, in Sect. 2, a brief literature review relating to theory and application of integrated management systems in different companies and sectors is presented. Then, in Sect. 3, illustrates the proposed methodology. Subsequently, in Sect. 4, describes and analyzes the results with the description of the companies in the cargo logistics sector, the diagnosis of initial conditions and the improvement proposals taking into account the key variables that affect the implementation of the Integrated Management System based on standards ISO 9001, ISO 14001, OHSAS 18001 and BASC. Finally, in Sect. 5 presents the conclusions and future work emanating from this study.

2 Integrated Management System: A Brief Literature Review

An Integrated Management System (IMS) is defined by [6] as a system that "integrates all of an organization's systems and processes into one complete framework, enabling an organization to work as a single unit with unified objectives." Authors like Garvin [7], Beckmerhagen et al. [8] and Llanes et al. [9] recognize the importance of integrated management as the degree of alignment of the organization in a single standard of administration, to achieve the efficiency, efficiency and flexibility planned.

In this sense, we reviewed the reported scientific literature where different academic articles showing the associated benefits for companies of the use of the Integrated Management System, such as the reduction of costs, the optimization of resources and the improvement of the corporate image [10, 11]. At the level of state of the art, the literature has reported scientific articles and academic works that analyze the factors, barriers, and integrated practices in management systems [12], as well as the development of diagnosis [13] and evaluation models of integrated management systems, considering the degree of maturity in the implementation in companies [14].

Also, we found studies that application of Integrated Management Systems - IMS in different companies, since biotechnological centers [15], thermoelectric companies [16]. Other applied works, explore some topics about the IMS like the most common elements and functions integrated in the certified Brazilian companies [17], the relationship between the level of integration and corporate benefits [18], the use of standardized methods for integration [19–21] and the impact of the level of integration of management systems on innovation capabilities of products and processes [22].

As a result of the review of the scientific literature, the academic literature on the integration of management systems applied to the cargo transportation sector is small and poorly developed [23]. Therefore, this research contributes to increasing the scientific literature and provides a methodology for diagnostic and improve the productivity, competitiveness, and sustainability of the industry.

3   Methodology

The methodology approach used in this work [24] is described as follows. The project is framed within the analytical and descriptive study; given the collected data were analyzed, with the purpose of diagnosing the behavior of the companies in this sector and finally, design improvement proposals. In this regard, a methodology comprised of three stages has been developed with the foresight to be applied in other industries. Figure 1 shows the methodological design with the phases of the project, the procedure used to perform the entire investigative process, and the techniques used.

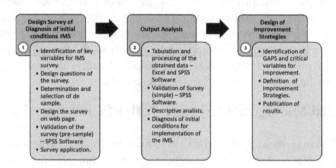

Fig. 1. Methodological framework for diagnosis of initial conditions for the implementation of the integrated management system

For the data collection, a survey for diagnosis of initial conditions for implementation of the IMS was designed based on international standards ISO 9001, ISO 14001, OHSAS 18001 and BASC. This instrument consists of two items, as shown in Fig. 2. In the first item, general aspects or profile of the companies were analyzed, such as antiquity, size, type of company, export orientation, certification, and the standard applied. Likewise, companies asked about the use of strategic planning tools, as support in the design and implementation of integrated management systems. In the second item, the objective is to diagnose the conditions of the companies concerning the application of Integrated Management Systems, to identify the critical variables in each company and the sector in general and design improvement proposals. This item consists of four components that evaluate the elements for the integration of management systems [24] and the cycle of continuous improvement for an integrated management system [25, 26] (refer to Fig. 2).

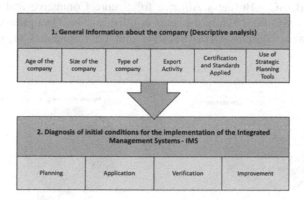

Fig. 2. Structure of the survey for diagnosis of the integrated management system

The survey was applied to a sample of 25 companies in the city of Barranquilla using Eq. 1 for the calculation of the sample size (p = 0,5; q = 0,5; e = 0,05; k = 1.96; N = 27). The results of reliability analysis demonstrated a good level of confidence of the survey [27], with a Cronbach alpha of 0,97.

$$n = \frac{k^2 * p * q * N}{(e^2 * (N-1)) + k^2 * p * q} \tag{1}$$

4   Results

4.1   Descriptive Analysis

In Table 1, are observed the main general characteristics found in the companies of the land cargo transportation:

Table 1. General information and productive profile

General data	Characteristics
Age of the company	Companies with more than ten years old predominate, 88% are between 10 and 20 years old
Size of the company	52% of the companies analyzed belong to the SME segment (Small and medium enterprises), and 48% are big companies
Export activity	32% of companies operate on a national and international scale

In Fig. 3a, b, and c, the results show that 56% of the companies analyzed use standards in management systems, but it is evident the potential that exists for companies to implement and certify their processes using the Integrated Management System. In the other hand, the implementation of integrated management systems is not still at a mature level in the sector since 64% of companies have management standards between 0–5 years and 36% of 6–10 years. The leading criteria implemented by the companies are BASC - Business Alliance for Secure Commerce and Quality Management System ISO 9001 while the least applied are the Occupational Health and Safety Management Systems OHSAS 18001 and Environmental Management System ISO 14001.

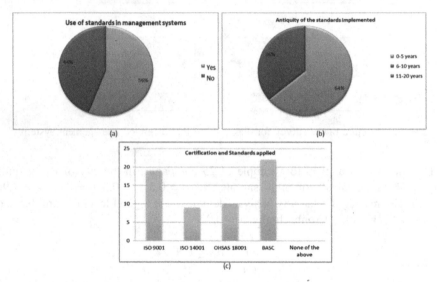

Fig. 3. Results obtained from the descriptive analysis: use of standards in management systems (a), the antiquity of the standards implemented (b), and certification and standards applied (c)

4.2 Diagnosis of Initial Conditions for the Implementation of the Integrated Management System - IMS

Table 2 shows a comparative analysis between the maximum scores of the diagnosis of initial conditions in IMS each of the variables (obtained from the multiplication of the number of questions by the Likert score scale) and the results obtained by the companies, according to the size of the company. The results show that big and medium-sized companies have better initial conditions for the implementation of the IMS, with an 86% and 75% respectively in comparison with small companies, with 43% of compliance.

In the other hand, the variables associated with planning and improvement, present a 70% of compliance while the variables of verification and application, with a 68% and 66% respectively. In this regard, there is necessary to establish priority improvement plans, considering the variables of the IMS diagnosis.

Table 2. Results of diagnosis of initial conditions in IMS

	Variables				
	Planning	Application	Verification	Improvement	Score
Top score	30	30	25	10	95
Score obtained (big companies)	26	26	22	8	82
Score obtained (medium companies)	23	22	18	8	70
Score obtained (small companies)	13	13	11	4	41
Total average	21	20	17	7	65
% of compliance	70%	66%	68%	70%	68%

4.3 Improvement Proposals for the Implementation of Integrated Management Systems

To support the implementation of Integrated Management Systems in the companies of the sector, we designed a series of strategies with the aim of underpinning the processes of continuous improvement and corporate sustainability. These strategies were proposed for each of the variables of the diagnosis, considering the type of company and its critical elements. However, improvement proposals can be generated for each of the companies. The summary of the strategies are shown in Table 3:

Table 3. Improvement proposals

Variables	Improvement proposals	Size of company		
		Big	Medium	Small
Planning	Define management responsibilities regarding Health and Safety at work, quality, BASC, and Environment		x	x
	Design and implement an integrated written policy about Health and Safety at work, Quality, BASC, and Environment		x	x
Application	Develop and implement training actions in the implementation of the integrated management system	x	x	x
	Design of procedures, processes or conditions in safety and health at work and environment		x	x
	Periodic reviews of the implementation status and progress of the integrated management system	x		x
Verification	Define mechanisms for data analysis of operations and processes, about the Integrated Management System	x	x	x
	Implement strategies for communication of results on the performance of the integrated management system, to collaborators and stakeholders	x	x	x
	Define and implement a program of integrated audits	x	x	x
Improvement	Implement programs to support continuous improvement and innovation in companies based on IMS	x	x	x
	Establish methods for evaluating the performance of the integrated management system, such as revisions by management, accountability, among others		x	x

5 Conclusions and Future Works

In this paper, a methodology was proposed for the diagnosis of initial conditions to improve the implementation of the IMS in the Companies of the Land Cargo Transportation based on criteria of quality, environmental management, safety and health at work, and security in logistics operations. The results demonstrated that the implementation of integrated management systems is not still at a mature level in the sector, being the big companies the leaders in the adoption this standard mainly BASC and ISO 9001. Besides, we identified the critical variables that affect the implementation of IMS (planning and evaluation), with compliance percentages lower than 70%. In this sense, we proposed a series of strategies to improve the levels of implementation for the companies in IMS.

This research enriches the scientific literature and contributes to the evidence base related to the use of methodologies for diagnosis and improvement of IMS. Nonetheless, it is necessary the commitment of the senior management and collaborators, define a plan of implementation with responsible, schedules and assign the resources. In this regard, as future work, the diagnostic of initial conditions in IMS will be applied to the selected companies in order to perform a multivariate analysis, evaluate the levels of performance and maturity of requirements for the implementation of the IMS and establish a correlational analyzes between variables and characteristics such as the size of the company, antiquity, and export activity, among others.

References

1. Chavarro, I., García, E.: Modelo logistico de transporte de carga con asignaciones mono-fuente a multi-destino empleando dinamica de sistemas - sector transportador de carga: Caso (Bogota-Buenaventura). Universidad Libre, Colombia (2013)
2. Ramirez, E.: Analisis de Comparativo de la Logistica de Transporte de Carga en Colombia - Bogota. Universidad Militar Nueva Granada, Colombia (2014)
3. Barbero, J.: La logística de cargas en America Latina y el Caribe: una agenda para mejorar su desempeño. Banco Interamericano de Desarrollo BID (2010)
4. Tipping, A., Kauschke, P.: Shifting patterns, the future of the logistics industry. PriceWaterhouseCoopers, Phoenix (2016)
5. Urbano, L., Muñoz, L., Osorio, J.: Selección multicriterio de aliado estratégico para la operacion de carga terrestre. Estud. Gerenciales 32(138), 35–43 (2016)
6. What is an Integrated Management System? http://integrated-standards.com/articles/what-is-integrated-management-system/. Accessed 21 Nov 2017
7. Garvin, D.: How the Baldridge Award really works. Harvard Bus. Rev. 69(6), 80–95 (1999)
8. Beckmerhagen, I., Berg, H., Karapetrovic, S., Willborn, W.: Integration of management systems: focus on safety in the nuclear industry. Int. J. Qual. Reliab. Manage. 20(2), 209–227 (2003)
9. Llanes, M., Isaac, C., Pino, M., García, G.: De la gestión por procesos a la gestión integrada por procesos. Ing. Ind. 35(3), 255–264 (2014)
10. Vidal, E., Soto, E.: Implantacion de los Sistemas Integrados de Gestion. Tourism Manage. Stud. 4, 1112–1121 (2013)

11. Fraguela, J.A., Carral, L., Iglesias, G., Castro, A., Rodriguez, M.J.: La integracion de los Sistemas de Gestion. Necesidad de una nueva cultura empresarial. DYNA **78**(167), 44–49 (2011)
12. Trierweiller, A., Bornia, A., Gisi, M., Spenassato, D., Severo-Peixe, B., Rotta, M.: An exploratory survey on the topic integrated management systems. Braz. J. Oper. Prod. Manage. **13**(2), 184–193 (2016)
13. Robaina, D., Hernández, M., Hechavarría, A., Sandoval, M.: Diagnostico para la gestion del proceso de cambio integrado. Ing. Ind. **29**(1), 3–7 (2008)
14. Domingues, P., Sampaio, P., Arezes, P.: Integrated management systems assessment: a maturity model proposal. J. Clean. Prod. **124**(15), 164–174 (2016)
15. Martínez, R., Agüero, B., Penabad, A., Montero, R.: Sistema Integrado de Gestión de Calidad, Seguridad y Ambiental en un centro biotecnológico. VacciMonitor **20**(2), 24–31 (2011)
16. Rodriguez, M., Zamora, R., Varela, N.: Propuesta de un procedimiento para lograr la integración de los sistemas de gestión implementados para la mejora del desempeño de la Empresa Termoeléctrica Cienfuegos. Universidad y Sociedad **7**(3), 133–139 (2015)
17. Nunhes, T., Ferreira, L.C., Oliveira, O.J.: Evolution of integrated management systems research on the Journal of Cleaner Production: Identification of contributions and gaps in the literature. J. Clean. Prod. **139**(15), 1234–1244 (2016)
18. Jesús Abad, J., Dalmau, I., Vilajosana, J.: Taxonomic proposal for integration levels of management systems based on empirical evidence and derived corporate benefits. J. Clean. Prod. **78**(1), 164–173 (2014)
19. Bernardo, M., Casadesus, M., Karapetrovic, S., Heras, I.: Do integration difficulties influence management system integration levels? J. Clean. Prod. **21**, 23–33 (2012)
20. Jimenez, G.: Procedimientos para el mejoramiento de la calidad y la implantación de la Norma ISO 9001 aplicado al proceso de asesoramiento del Centro de Investigaciones y Desarrollo Empresarial y Regional en una Institucion de Educacion Superior basados en la gestion por procesos. In: Congreso de Gestion de la Calidad y Proteccion Ambiental GECPA 2014, Habana, Cuba, pp. 1–22 (2014)
21. Jimenez, G., Zapata, E.: Metodologia integrada para el control estratégico y la mejora continua, basada en el Balanced Scorecard y el Sistema de Gestión de Calidad : aplicacion en una organizacion de servicios en Colombia. In: 51a Asamblea Anual del Consejo Latinoamericano de Escuelas de Administracion CLADEA 2016, Medellin, Colombia, pp. 1–20 (2016)
22. Hernandez, A., Bernardo, M., Cruz, C.: Relating open innovation, innovation and management systems integration. Ind. Manage. Data Syst. **116**(8), 1540–1556 (2016)
23. Rojas, J.: Elementos para la integración de sistemas de gestión y su importancia en la cadena productiva del transporte de carga terrestre en Colombia. Suma de Negocios **5**(12), 136–142 (2014)
24. Hernandez, R., Fernandez, C., Baptista, M.: Metodología de la investigación, 5ta edn. Mac Graw Hill, Mexico (2010)
25. Miguel, J.: PAS 99. Especificación de los requisitos comunes del sistema de gestión como marco para la integración. Revista Calidad, 8–12 (2013)
26. AENOR Norma No. 66177. Guía para la integración de sistemas de gestión (2005)
27. George, D., Mallery, P.: SPSS for Windows step by step: a simple guide and reference, (4.ª ed.). Allyn & Bacon, Boston (2003)

Developing Instructional Videos to Direct Business Respondents Through a Feature-Heavy Online Survey Instrument

Rebecca Keegan[(✉)]

U.S Census Bureau, Suitland, MD 20746, USA
rebecca.keegan@census.gov

Abstract. The economic census, conducted by the U.S. Census Bureau every five years, collects operational and performance data from roughly 4 million U.S. business establishments in non-farming industries. The level of detail requested, along with wide variation in the complexity of businesses, requires a highly sophisticated and flexible software design for online data collection. Thus, for the 2017 Economic Census, the Census Bureau redesigned and expanded its Web survey instrument, providing respondents with several new, more convenient features to help them complete the economic census.

Based on usability testing, debriefing phone calls, discussions with subject matter experts, and analysis of help calls received by the Census Bureau, we identified several features of the re-engineered website that were potentially problematic for users. Ten 'how-to' videos were created to assist respondents in navigating and utilizing these features to complete the Economic Census. Video topics included a general overview of the main screen, as well as specific action-items such as how to print, review data, and download spreadsheets.

Researchers conducted cognitive interviews with business respondents in order to evaluate and refine the how-to videos. The goal was to identify the best content for the videos that would address the most frequent user issues. During the interviews, participants completed several tasks designed to emulate the actions they would take when completing the actual survey. Participants then viewed the how-to videos, and provided feedback for each one.

Testing revealed strong support for the implementation of the videos. These videos helped orient respondents to the overall site and its key features. Ultimately, adding effective and readily accessible tutorial videos to the survey website may reduce help center workload and decrease the likelihood of respondent breakoff.

Keywords: Usability · Economic · Census · Instructional · Tutorial
How-to · Video

1 Introduction

The economic census is a survey produced by the Economic Directorate of the U.S Census Bureau that collects information on U.S. businesses. This survey collects data from more than 4 million U.S establishments in over 1000 industries. Respondents

C. Stephanidis (Ed.): HCII Posters 2018, CCIS 852, pp. 290–295, 2018.
https://doi.org/10.1007/978-3-319-92285-0_40

to this survey answer questions regarding their company's employment records, payroll, revenue and sales receipts among other information. The economic census is conducted every 5 years. Data gathered from this program contributes to key economic indicators such as the gross domestic product (GDP) and is an effective means of understanding the state of the American economy.

For the 2017 Economic Census, the Census Bureau updated its existing method of data collection. Up until the mid-2000's, data for the economic census was collected via a software program that respondents would upload onto their computer and enter their data into.

For the 2017 Economic Census survey, Census Bureau programmers developed an entirely new web-based electronic reporting system to host the survey. The web instrument titled 'Centurion' is a complex site that offers participants numerous ways to interact with their company's data and report for it. Respondents must navigate through several necessary steps built into the site in order to submit their data.

Due to the feature-heavy nature of the reporting platform, usability testing was conducted to ensure that the site was functional for novice users, and that all the necessary features were easily accessible and usable. This usability testing, as well as multiple debriefing phone calls and discussions with subject matter experts revealed several confusing features on the Centurion site that may be effectively addressed with short how-to videos.

Ten videos were designed to help orient respondents to the overall site and its' key features. Each video lasted no more than two minutes and detailed a feature on the site, while a narrator described the actions being taken on the screen. The short video topics included a walkthrough of the login process, a general overview of the site's main dashboard, as well as specific directions to complete different tasks that were problematic for respondents.

Areas of the site that were difficult for respondents to navigate were determined through usability testing, respondent debriefings and through analysis of the records of the calls received by Centurion customer service.

Preliminary testing was conducted to assess the effectiveness of these new tutorial videos, and to identify the optimal location within the website to place them. The study sessions were designed so that participant's feedback and actions would assist in identifying what improvements could be made to the videos once they are revised and finalized.

The goal of this study was to identify the best content for the videos that would address the most frequent user issues, as well as the best location for the videos. Effective and readily accessible tutorial videos may reduce call center burden, and decrease the likelihood of respondent breakoff.

2 Methods

Researchers conducted cognitive interviews with 12 respondents in order to evaluate and refine the new tutorial videos for the Centurion site. Testing was conducted during the winter months of 2017. Researchers traveled locally within the DC, Maryland and northern Virginia regions to interview respondents at their place of business. Participants were recruited via several Census Survey respondent files including the Economic Census and Annual Survey of Manufactures/Report of Organization (ASM/COS).

Attempts were made to recruit participants from businesses of varying sizes. In total, twelve businesses were recruited: four single-establishment businesses, six medium-sized (20–2499 employees) businesses and two small (1–19 employees) multi-establishment businesses.

Participants held a wide range of positions in their company, a plurality being associated with an accounting position. On average, participants were in their respective positions for 8.6 years. Participants for this study fell into a wide range of ages, with an average age of 38 years. Participants were well educated; all but one participant had earned a Bachelor's degree. See Table 1 for all participant characteristics.

Table 1. Participants' demographic characteristics (n = 12).

Age range (in years)	
18–25	2
26–35	3
36–45	2
46–50	3
51+	2
Educational level	
Less than high school	0
High school	0
Some college	0
Associates degree	1
Bachelors	9
Post bachelors	2

During the interviews, participants first filled out the consent form and several basic demographic questions. Every session was recorded with a screen-capturing program after getting consent. Following this, participants were brought to the Centurion website and asked to complete six tasks. These tasks were in line with the actions they would take while completing the actual economic census survey. All participants completed the same tasks.

The tasks outlined for participants were to (a) login to the site; (b) print the survey questions; (c) start the survey; (d) add a new location (e) download/upload Spreadsheet template; and finally to (f) find assistance on the site. These tasks were simplified versions of those that were used during usability testing of the Economic Census instrument in May and June of 2017.

After finishing these tasks, participants completed the second half of the study which involved viewing 5 how-to videos. Each video was less than two minutes long. There was a total of 10 how-to videos produced, but the number of videos the participants viewed was narrowed down to 5 due to time constraints. The topic of the videos that the participants viewed were predetermined to ensure that each video would be viewed approximately the same amount of times.

After viewing, participants were asked for feedback on the characteristics and content of the videos by answering on a Likert scale ranging from 1–7. The questions asked after each video included (a) how effective the video was in addressing the topic or target issue, (b) how appropriate the length of the video was, (c) how satisfied overall they were with it, (d) how likely they would be to recommend that someone who is having issues using the site watch the how-to videos, and finally participants were provided with a write-in box to describe any other thoughts or comments about the video.

After the viewing portion of the session was complete, respondents were asked several debriefing questions including what other ways the site can offer assistance, and how developers can best direct users to the how-to videos. They were also asked for their opinions regarding the ideal location for the videos on the website.

3   Results

Testing revealed several important aspects of the how-to videos that can be improved upon, as well as some potential improvements that can be made to the Centurion site to create a more user-friendly experience.

During the testing session, participants completed 6 tasks on the Centurion site that emulated the actions they would take when filling out the actual economic census. There was a 100% success rate for those that partook (technical difficulties prevented 1 participant from finishing the tasks). Although the tasks were relatively simple in nature, had there been substantial issues on the site, they likely would have been illuminated by participants attempting these tasks.

Participant feedback offered several findings and suggestions that can be generalized across all the videos. These included improving the sound quality, and improving full screen resolution. It was also recommended that the finalized videos include closed captioning. Overall ratings of the videos on a 7 point scale were very high. The average rating across all videos was 6.2. See Table 2 for the results of the video satisfaction questionnaire.

Table 2. Video satisfaction results (n = 12).

Video title	Run time	Number of views	Overall rating
Dashboard overview	1:20	7	6.0
Organizing dash	1:27	7	6.3
Print preview	1:47	6	6.7
Add/Delete	1:33	6	6.5
Messages feature	0:34	6	6.0
Download	1:25	5	6.4
Upload	0:50	5	6.4
Reviewing data	0:53	5	6.0
Submitting survey	1:10	5	6.5

After viewing the videos, participants completed a questionnaire designed to ascertain experience with internet and computer use. For this project, we amended the questions to include items regarding one's use of how-to videos in their daily life. The participants recruited for this study were all savvy internet/computer users. Their actions regarding use of how-to videos were more variable. This being said, all but one participant reported examples of how-to videos they've watched recently, and a majority, (n = 7) reported having viewed 1–2 how-to videos in the last month. Some examples of these video topics provided referred to handy do-it-yourself projects, and videos regarding complex software walk-throughs. See Tables 3 and 4 for several highlights of the how-to video use questionnaire.

Table 3. How-to video usage questionnaire (n = 12).

Question	Average (1–7)
How often do you seek out how-to videos when you need assistance with a task?	4.3
How likely would you be to access a how-to video if you're learning a new skill?	5.4

Table 4. How-to video usage questionnaire (n = 12).

If you have a need for assistance on a website, how are you most likely to get assistance?	
Prefer FAQ	3
Prefer to call	6
Prefer Video	3

Finally, at the end of the session participants answered several debriefing questions, some suggestions and responses resulting included bringing the link to the videos closer to the main reporting dashboard (as opposed to the uppermost banner of the site); offering a live chat as another means of assistance; and including a prompt in the overview of the site directing users to the videos.

4   Conclusion

The pretesting research offered valuable feedback on refining the content of the videos, and determining the best location for them within the website. The usability findings were overall positive with regard to both the functionality of the Centurion site, and the general effectiveness of the how-to videos. Hopefully, the implementation of how-to videos to the survey platform will be a valuable asset to respondents who are experiencing any difficulties during the reporting process.

Following the mail-out of the 2017 Economic Census, researchers will be able to examine the paradata generated by respondents, to analyze user behaviors such as how many times the how-to videos link has been clicked, and furthermore, how many views each videos has. Analysis of the paradata may also lead to informative debriefing calls with respondents who utilized them. Future paradata analysis will also reveal if there is a significant overall decrease in call-center inquiries and respondent breakoff.

This study revealed numerous lessons for any future videos that may be created. Some guidelines for video development include putting substantial effort into the creation of the video scripts that the narrator reads in each video. For this study, drafts were produced and then edited and reviewed by several subject-matter experts in various departments of the Census Bureau. Further work on the frontend of the project included putting extensive work into determining the best topic for each video. These decisions were informed by usability testing of the web-instrument, debriefing calls with past respondents, and discussions with help-center staff. Finally, if resources allow, having access to high-quality recording equipment and a quiet space to record the narration appears to go a long way in convincing respondents of the legitimacy and overall quality of the videos, as several participants noted that background noise was a distraction to them as they tested out the pilot videos created for this study.

Ultimately, no amount of guesswork can be a proxy for observing a novice user's interactions with an interface. Testing the survey platform and videos with participants was a critical component of understanding what improvements could be made. By employing multiple methods of analysis such as examining the accuracy of the tasks the participants completed, various Likert scales, and verbal feedback, researchers were able to use qualitative and quantitative means to assess the effectiveness of the videos and overall platform. Results of this study suggest future Census Bureau products may benefit from the implementation of how-to videos, particularly on websites and plat-forms that are newly developed and/or have numerous features built into the instrument.

Opinion Mining on Internet Primary Bank with Online News and Social Data

Dongmin Kim, Jihyung Hong, Yunjik Jeong, Jaehye Suk,
Kee Ok Kim(✉), and Hyesun Hwang

Sungkyunkwan University, Seoul, South Korea
kokim@skku.edu

Abstract. With the thriving smartphone industry, Fintech has spread worldwide due to the convergence of information technology and the finance industry. Among Fintech, internet primary banking is a fast-growing area of business that attracts consumers with convenience and cost-saving. An internet primary bank is a bank that has no branches at all. Thus, this bank has some obvious advantages such as no branch maintenance, fewer personnel costs, and no time and place limitations. This study explores the issue of and reaction to internet primary banking through online text from major newspapers and social data in Korea. Online text data for 2017 were collected with Trendup 3.0, a platform of a major data analysis company in Korea. This study analyzes positive and negative opinions about internet primary banks by opinion mining, making it possible to analyze internet primary banks from consumer and mass-media perspectives and seek the subsequent implications.

Keywords: Opinion mining · Internet primary bank · Big data analysis

1 Introduction

Internet primary banking was established after the development of information technology in the 1990s. One of the world's first internet primary banks was the Security First Network Bank (SFNB), which was launched in October 1995 [1]. Internet primary banking benefits consumers by offering services at a low cost; the banks can offer higher rates to depositors while charging lower rates from borrowers. Furthermore, internet primary banks can easily enter new markets and grow rapidly by using the internet [2].

Kakao Bank, a major internet primary bank in South Korea, gained wide consumer appeal after being launched on South Korea's highly accessible chat app Kakao talk, which has 42 million users among the country's 50 million population. Kakao Bank secured two million accounts in weeks. In addition, the deposit amount has reached 1 trillion won and loans amounting to 600 billion won have been awarded [3]. This study investigates the issues of internet primary banks, analyzes positive and negative opinions of them, and seeks to determine the subsequent policy implications.

© Springer International Publishing AG, part of Springer Nature 2018
C. Stephanidis (Ed.): HCII Posters 2018, CCIS 852, pp. 296–301, 2018.
https://doi.org/10.1007/978-3-319-92285-0_41

2   Method

This study analyzes positive and negative expressions through opinion mining of online texts from major newspapers and social media. Opinion mining analyzes people's opinions, appraisals, attitudes, and emotions regarding entities, individuals, issues, events, topics, and their attributes. This method analyzes sentence structure and separates facts and opinions by dividing them into positive or negative to measure their intensity [4]. Text data for 2017 were collected with Trendup 3.0, a platform of a major data analysis company in Korea. The numbers of texts in the data include 171,765 online newspaper articles and 152,445 social media posts. Opinion mining is analyzed with R 3.4.1.

3   Results

The results are summarized as follows:

First, social media buzz peaked in the period near the launch of the internet primary bank in July 2017, as shown in Fig. 1. Overall, more positive than negative words were used regarding Kakao Bank for one year (Fig. 2). However, the negative buzz in social media has rapidly increased since the bank opened.

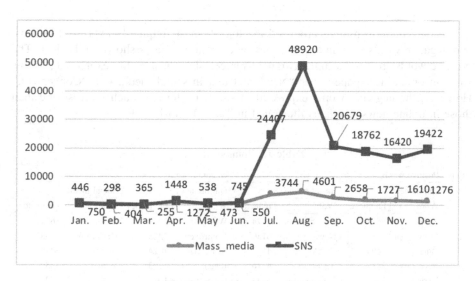

Fig. 1. Buzz for Kakao Bank

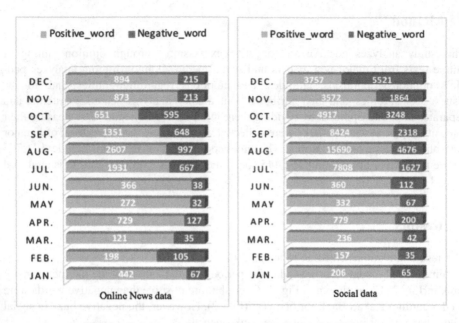

Fig. 2. Opinion mining of online news data and social data

Second, opinion mining produced the top 10 most frequently expressed positive and negative words in online newspapers and social media as shown in Table 1. The positive words are similar in the two data sources. The most highly expressed positive word in online newspapers was "New" and that in social media was "Convenient." However, the negative words expressed in social media are much more severe than those in online newspapers, as illustrated in Table 1 and Fig. 3.

Table 1. Opinion mining

Rank	Positive words				Negative words			
	Online news		Social media		Online news		Social media	
	Word	Frequency	Word	Frequency	Word	Frequency	Word	Frequency
1	New	6561	Convenient	13174	Worry	2912	Swindler	5624
2	Convenient	5518	New	6159	Controversy	2325	Discomfort	2968
3	Quick	3694	Quick	4503	Insufficient	1824	Illegal	3430
4	Necessary	2889	Necessary	4216	Illegal	1293	Worry	3359
5	Various	2867	Various	3432	Complicated	1065	Difficult	2723
6	Positive	2715	Familiar	2675	Out of order	790	Controversy	2491
7	Reliable	1002	Reliable	2630	Discomfort	668	Insufficient	2873
8	Cheap	998	Cheap	2496	Overdue	518	Out of order	2004
9	Familiar	958	Happy	2296	Lack	500	Lack	1810
10	Popular	262	Special benefit	623	Expensive	229	Overload	788

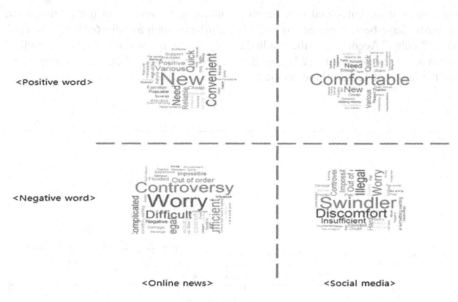

Fig. 3. Word cloud

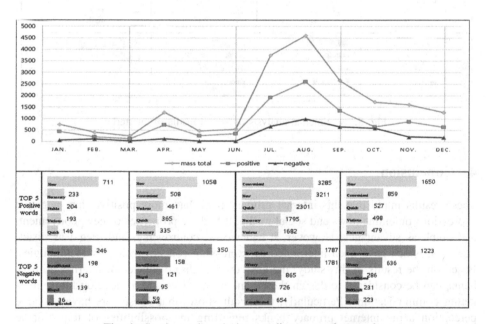

Fig. 4. Sentimental analysis on online news of quarterly

Third, the negative words in online newspapers are revealing the company's perspective, while those in social media are revealing the consumer's perspective, as illustrated in Figs. 4 and 5. Before the launch of the internet primary bank (first to second quarter), negative words related to concerns about the introduction of a new financial technology were seen. After the launch, the negative words are similar in online news data, but social data result is different. Compared to pre-third quarter, consumers have been experiencing negative attributes such as "discomfort," "worry," and "difficulty." According to the results from the fourth quarter of last year, "swindler" appeared. As the popularity of Kakao Bank grows, consumers' concerns are growing over the abuse of Kakao Bank accounts.

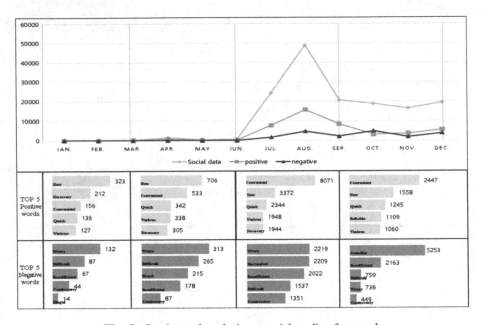

Fig. 5. Sentimental analysis on social media of quarterly

4 Conclusion

These results imply that this internet primary bank had more positive than negative expressions on online news and social media. It had the properties of new, convenient, and quick as advantages. However, it had worry, controversy, and illegal as disadvantages, which have been interpreted as expressing concern over new technologies. Based on the results of this study, the keywords of disadvantages of internet primary banks can be considered to design these banking services and to develop future marketing communications. Particularly, the result shows that consumers have negative perception about internet primary banks regarding the possibilities of unjustifiable transactions and confusing user experiences. In this regard, more reliable features of internet primary banking services need to be developed to lessen consumers' concerns about the services.

References

1. Christopher, B.: Thrift to offer services on the internet. FDIC Bank. Rev. **8**(3) (1996)
2. Yom, C.: Limited-purpose banks: their specialties, performance, and prospects. FDIC Bank. Rev. **17**(1), 19 (2005)
3. Lee, D.: Expectations and challenges of internet-primary bank. Korea Inst. Financ. Wkly. Fin. Brief **26**(18), 3–8 (2017)
4. Liu, B.: Web Data Mining: Exploring Hyperlinks, Contents, and Usage Data, 2nd edn. Springer Science & Business Media, Heidelberg (2011). https://doi.org/10.1007/978-3-642-19460-3

Modeling Conversational Flows for In-Store Mobile Decision Aids

Wi-Suk Kwon[1]([✉]), Veena Chattaraman[1], Kacee Ross[1], Kiana Alikhademi[2], and Juan E. Gilbert[2]

[1] Auburn University, Auburn, AL, USA
kwonwis@auburn.edu
[2] University of Florida, Gainesville, FL, USA

Abstract. Based on the Human-Elaboration-Object-Construal (HEOC) Contingency Model, we propose design principles for modeling conversational flows between consumers and an in-store mobile decision aid (MoDA) with artificial intelligence, functioning as a virtual sales associate. Through an on-going assessment of the quantity, type, and specificity of the decision preferences from the user's spoken input, MoDA is modeled to identify the user's levels of decision elaboration and construal, which leads to its recognition of the user's use of and shifts across four decision strategies commonly applied in consumer decision-making contexts. Upon identification of the user's decision-making strategy, MoDA is modeled to (1) identify strategy-relevant assistive tasks, (2) generate or access strategy- and task-relevant intelligence, and (3) utter strategy-, task-, and intelligence-relevant speech to naturally support the user's decision making strategy. The proposed design principles further map the types and examples of the agent tasks, intelligence, and speech required across the four consumer decision making strategies.

Keywords: Decision aid · Conversational flow · HEOC Contingency Model

1 Introduction

Consumer decision-making has changed with rapid technological advances including mobile technology. Physical retail stores have become merely one of many sources of product information for consumer decision making, along with a variety of online sources such as ecommerce sites, manufacturer sites, and online social media where user-generated product information (e.g., expert and customer reviews and ratings) is shared. With the abundance of information always available within a few clicks/taps, consumers no longer rush to make purchase decisions while they are in the store. The overload of product information makes it hard for consumers to acquire and process it fully within the store, motivating them to delay decisions until they have had the opportunity to review and compare choice alternatives online at a location and time of convenience to them. This trend naturally has led to the ever-increasing ecommerce

© Springer International Publishing AG, part of Springer Nature 2018
C. Stephanidis (Ed.): HCII Posters 2018, CCIS 852, pp. 302–308, 2018.
https://doi.org/10.1007/978-3-319-92285-0_42

sales [1]. In-store retailers are now compelled to offer consumers reasons to shop in the store instead of other channels, suggesting an acute need to reinvent their services to enhance customers' abilities to make decisions while in stores. In-store mobile decision aids (MoDA), which facilitate the acquisition and processing of product information and purchase decision making in the store while being able to physically examine the products, may address this need and provide in-store retailers with a competitive advantage over online retailers. In this paper, based on Chattaraman, Kwon, Eugene, and Gilbert's [2] Human-Elaboration-Object-Construal (HEOC) Contingency Model, we propose design principles for modeling conversational flows between a user and a language-based in-store MoDA which functions as a virtual sales associate and provides context-aware decision assistance in the way that caters to individual consumers' decision goals (e.g., product attributes or benefits sought) and constraints (e.g., time, product knowledge, cognitive resources).

2   Modeling In-Store MoDA Conversational Flows

The HEOC Contingency Model [3] postulates that an intelligent decision support system can predict a user's decision-making strategy based on the user's levels of decision elaboration (whether the user is likely to exert high or low effort in deliberating on the decision) and construal (whether the decision deliberation focuses on alternatives or attributes) identified from the user's decision preference input. Brand names and model names are examples of alternatives, whereas product features and functionality represent attributes. Specifically, the HEOC contingency model delineates the prediction of four common consumer decision-making strategies: lexicographic or LEX (low elaboration, attribute focus), satisficing or SAT (low elaboration, alternative focus), elimination by aspects or EBA (high elaboration, attribute focus), and weighted adding or WAD (high elaboration, alternative focus) [3]. Based on this model, we conceptualize a language-based in-store MoDA which

1. performs an on-going assessment and verification of the presence/absence, number, type, and specificity of the user's decision preference from his or her spoken input, with a goal of identifying the user's levels of decision elaboration (high vs. low) and construal (attribute vs. alternative focus),
2. predicts the user's adoption of and shifts across the four decision making strategies (i.e., LEX, SAT, EBA, WAD) based on the identified decision elaboration and construal levels,
3. identifies MoDA roles (e.g., decision preference prioritization aid, decision choice aid) and tasks that are relevant to the predicted decision-making strategy (see Table 1),
4. generates or accesses strategy- and task-relevant MoDA intelligence (see Table 1 for MoDA intelligence needed for each user strategy and task), and
5. utters strategy-, task-, and intelligence-relevant speech to naturally support the user's decision-making strategy (see Fig. 1 for the model and example of MoDA conversational flows for LEX decision makers).

Table 1. In-store mobile decision aids (MoDA) conversation flow design principles by user decision-making strategy: roles, tasks, and intelligence

MoDA role and tasks	MoDA intelligence	User decision-making strategy			
		LEX	SAT	EBA	WAD
Role 1: User Decision-Making Strategy Identifier (DMS_ID)					
1. Recognize alternatives voiced by user	• Ability to name alternatives (DMS_ID1)		✓		✓
2. Identify number of alternatives voiced by user	• DMS_ID1 • Ability to count alternatives (DMS_ID2)		✓		✓
3. Recognize attributes voiced by user	• Ability to name attributes (DMS_ID3)	✓	✓	✓	✓
4. Identify number of attributes voiced by user	• DMS_ID3 • Ability to count attributes (DMS_ID4)	✓	✓	✓	✓
5. Determine user's decision-making strategy	• DMS_ID2 • DMS_ID4 • Algorithm to determine user's decision elaboration level based on recognized alternatives and attributes voiced by user (DMS_ID5)	✓	✓	✓	✓
Role 2: Decision Preference Prioritization Aid (DPP_A)					
1. Inquire relative importance of attributes to user	• DMS_ID3 • Ability to process user language indicating level of importance (DPP_A1)			✓	
2. Recommend important attributes	• DMS_ID3 • Ability to prioritize attributes by widely-accepted degrees of importance (DPP_A2)	✓	✓		
3. Describe attributes to user	• DMS_ID3 • DPP_A2 • Knowledge of technical and practical meanings of each attribute and its levels (DPP_A3)	✓	✓	✓	✓
4. Inquire choice criteria per attribute	• DMS_ID3 • Knowledge of possible levels for each attribute (DPP_A4a) • Knowledge of attribute levels by alternative (DPP_A4b) • Ability to process user language that describes choice criteria (e.g., ranges, degrees, presence/absence) by attribute (DPP_A4c)		✓	✓	

(*continued*)

Table 1. *(continued)*

MoDA role and tasks	MoDA intelligence	User decision-making strategy			
		LEX	SAT	EBA	WAD
5. Recommend choice criteria per attribute	• Knowledge of widely-accepted criteria for each attribute (DPP_A5)		✓		
Role 3: Decision Choice Aid (DC_A)					
1. Show an alternative with highest value on the most important attribute	• DMS_ID1 • DMS_ID3 • DPP_A4b • Algorithm for rank-ordering alternatives by attribute (DC_A1)	✓			
2. Show an alternative that satisfies widely-accepted criteria on all attributes of importance to user	• DMS_ID1 • DMS_ID3 • DPP_A4a • DPP_A4b • DPP_A5		✓		
3. Help user with successive reduction of consideration set by applying attributes and their criteria in order of importance	• DMS_ID1 • DMS_ID3 • DPP_A1 • DPP_A4b			✓	
4. Show an alternative that meets user's choice criteria on all attributes voiced by user	• DMS_ID1 • DMS_ID3 • DPP_A4b • DPP_A4c		✓	✓	
5. Show a potential consideration set of alternatives and their attribute levels for user deliberation of trade-offs	• MS_ID3 • DPP_A4b • Algorithm for forming a consideration set (e.g., top alternatives on each attribute voiced by user, alternatives with top average ranks/ratings on all attributes voiced by user) (DC_A5a) • Ability to visualize the trade-offs (DC_A5b)				✓

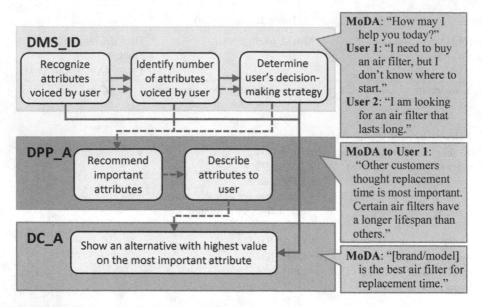

Fig. 1. Model and example of MoDA conversational flows for LEX decision makers. Note: dashed arrows are flows for User 1, and solid arrows are for User 2.

For example, through a conversation with a user, MoDA may find that the user is lacking product domain knowledge and unable to articulate decision preferences (see User 1 in Fig. 1), in which case MoDA initially predicts the user as a low elaborator who could be helped by learning about product attributes (i.e., a LEX decision maker). With this prediction, MoDA would now play a role as a decision preference prioritization aid (DPP_A) by recommending an important attribute (see Fig. 1 and DPP_A Task #2 in Table 1) and describing this attribute to the user (see Fig. 1 and DPP_A Task #3 in Table 1), and then shifting to a role as a decision choice aid (DC_A) by proposing an alternative that performs best on the recommended attribute (see Fig. 1 and DC_A Task #1 in Table 1). On the other hand, if the conversation with the user reveals that the user has a clearly preferred product attribute (see User 2 in Fig. 1), although MoDA may still classify this user as a LEX decision maker, it can skip the DPP_A role and directly engage in a DC_A role by proposing the best-performing alternative on the user-voiced attribute. In other scenarios (e.g., when user input reveals his or her preference for certain alternatives such as brands or models [i.e., SAT or WAD] and/or indicates the user's knowledge or motivation to process elaborately many types of attributes [i.e., EBA or WAD]), their respective roles, tasks, and types of intelligence implemented by MoDA will vary as outlined in Table 1.

3 Conclusion

Most intelligent agents in consumer environments such as ecommerce sites have served merely as navigational/procedural aids (e.g., Alaska Airlines' *Jen*). Previous literature on recommendation agents has assumed that users have well-defined decision preferences [4, 5], and hence has lacked in developing the aids for preference formation and prioritization. Previous work has also assumed that users are able and motivated to engage in an elaborative and rational decision-making strategy for an "accurate" decision [6–9]. However, consumer decision making tends to be constructive (i.e., consumers may form preferences as they learn about options) and is characterized by shifts across multiple decision-making strategies. Further, decision aid literature is scant on decision aids for the spoken language-based interface, which is the most natural mode of interaction between human agents and consumers in stores (cf., [10, 11]). The in-store MoDA conversational flow design principles proposed in this paper, based on the HEOC Contingency Model, articulate the specific roles, tasks, and types of intelligence (ability and knowledge) to be implemented in designing language-based intelligent agents that understand the consumer's use of and shifts across four common decision-making strategies during an in-store shopping process. The proposed approach contributes to advancing the intelligent agent literature by enlightening the *user intent* aspect of natural language understanding (NLU), which is a key area for current and future artificial intelligence research.

Acknowledgements. This material is based in part upon work supported by the National Science Foundation under Grant Numbers IIS-1527182 and IIS-1527302. Any opinions, findings, and conclusions or recommendations expressed in this material are those of the author(s) and do not necessarily reflect the views of the National Science Foundation.

References

1. Digital Commerce 360: Internet Retailer. U.S. e-commerce sales grow 16.0% in 2017, https://www.digitalcommerce360.com/article/us-ecommerce-sales/. Accessed 16 Mar 2018
2. Chattaraman, V., Kwon, W.-S., Eugene, W., Gilbert, J.: Developing and validating a naturalistic decision model for intelligent language-based decision aids. Hum. Fact. Ergon. Soc. Annu. Meet. **61**(1), 176–177 (2017)
3. Bettman, J.R., Luce, M.F., Payne, J.W.: Constructive consumer choice processes. J. Consum. Res. **25**(3), 187–217 (1998)
4. Chen, H., Lam, P.P., Chan, H.C., Dillon, T.S., Cao, J., Lee, R.S.: Business-to-consumer mobile agent-based internet commerce system (MAGICS). IEEE Trans. Syst. Man Cybern. Part C Appl. Rev. **37**(6), 1174–1189 (2007)
5. Xiao, B., Benbasat, I.: E-commerce product recommendation agents: use, characteristics, and impact. MIS Q. **31**(1), 137–209 (2007)
6. Lee, Y.E., Benbasat, I.: Interaction design for mobile product recommendation agents: supporting users' decisions in retail stores. ACM Trans. Comput. Hum. Interact. **17**(4), 17 (2010)
7. Swaminathan, V.: The impact of recommendation agents on consumer evaluation and choice: the moderating role of category risk, product complexity, and consumer knowledge. J. Consum. Psychol. **13**(1–2), 93–101 (2003)

8. Häubl, G., Trifts, V.: Consumer decision making in online shopping environments: the effects of interactive decision aids. Mark. Sci. **19**(1), 4–21 (2000)
9. Fleming, M., Cohen, R.: A decision procedure for autonomous agents to reason about interaction with humans. In: AAAI 2004 Spring Symposium on Interaction between Humans and Autonomous Systems over Extended Operation, pp. 81–86. (2004), http://www.aaai.org/Papers/Symposia/Spring/2004/SS-04-03/SS04-03-016.pdf. Accessed 16 Mar 2018
10. Maass, W., Kowatsch, T., Janzen, S., Varshney, U.: A natural language technology-enhanced mobile sales assistant for in-store shopping situations. In: Tuunainen, V., Nandhakumar, J., Rossi, M., Soliman, W. (eds.) 19th European Conference on Information Systems (ECIS), vol. 142. Helsinki, Finland (2011), https://www.alexandria.unisg.ch/72472/1/Maass%20et%20al%202011%20NLT-MSA.pdf. Accessed 16 Mar 2018
11. Kowatsch, T., Maass, W.: In-store consumer behavior: how mobile recommendation agents influence usage intentions, product purchases, and store preferences. Comput. Hum. Behav. **26**(4), 697–704 (2010)

Changed the Cup, Not the Saucer – NFC Payments in Supermarkets

Poornigha Santhana Kumar[1(✉)], Michael Bechinie[1], and Manfred Tscheligi[2]

[1] USECON, 1110 Vienna, Austria
{kumar,bechinie}@usecon.com
[2] University of Salzburg, 5020 Salzburg, Austria
manfred.tscheligi@sbg.ac.at

Abstract. Near field communication (NFC) payments are into play for many years now. Both card and mobile NFC's are widely accepted by almost all supermarkets in many countries. The usability of NFC payments not only depends on the NFC card/mobile used but also on the payment terminal used in the supermarkets. To evaluate the usability of NFC payments, observations and exit interviews were conducted in 6 different supermarkets in Vienna, Austria. We had a total 160 observations and 179 exit interviews. The above-mentioned data was analyzed and the results portrayed that NFC payments suffer several usability issues. The results show that users face lack of proper information, lack of feedback and consistency while paying with NFCs.

Keywords: NFC payments · Usability · User study

1 Introduction

NFC payments using card and mobile is replacing the traditional payment methods like cash and credit/debit card payments in many countries [1]. NFC payments outsmart the existing payment methods with its advantages [2, 3]. Since the user can pay (up till a particular limit) using NFC card/mobile by just holding them against the payment terminal, it is quicker than other payment methods and prevents attacks like shoulder surfing. The amount that can be paid using NFC card/mobile differs from various country and currency.

The acceptance of mobile payment has been studied in the literature. Some studies [4–6] also specifically study the acceptance of NFC payments. Most of these studies [4, 5] use TAM (Technology Acceptance Model) to evaluate the acceptance of mobile payment and NFC payment. Some studies also incorporate other psychological dimensions like trust [6, 7], social influence [5], perceived risk [5] and cost [5]. The acceptance of NFC payments has also been studied based on locations. [8] and [9] studies the state of NFC payments in Switzerland and Korea respectively. The above studies conclude by projecting the acceptance NFC's in those locations. Even though several studies have explored the acceptance of NFC's payments based on various dimensions, some aspect like usability and user experience of NFC remains as an unknown side in literature.

© Springer International Publishing AG, part of Springer Nature 2018
C. Stephanidis (Ed.): HCII Posters 2018, CCIS 852, pp. 309–313, 2018.
https://doi.org/10.1007/978-3-319-92285-0_43

An NFC payment consists of 2 components: the NFC card/mobile and the payment terminal at the supermarket. While considering the usability of NFC payments both the card/mobile and the payment terminal should be considered together. Both the component should work appropriately to be usable to the users. Only a few studies [10, 11] explore the usability of the NFC payment systems. The existing studies also state that the feedback, visibility and accessibility of the NFC system should be improved. This led us to explore further in this direction.

2   Methodology

Here, we present the methodology we used to understand the usability of NFC payments in supermarkets. We conducted a user study in supermarkets to understand the existing practice and the hassles faced by the customers while paying with NFC card/mobile. We conducted observations and exit interviews in 6 supermarkets in Vienna for 3 h in each supermarket. At the end of 6 days, we observed 160 customers who paid with NFC and we also received 179 exit interviews from the customers. During observation, the customers were observed on their attention to audio feedback, their attention to visual feedback and their familiarity with NFC payments. Despite the payment method used by the customers in the supermarket, they were asked for their interest in giving a short interview. Interested customers were questioned about the feedback given by the payment terminal, information provided in NFC card or mobile and were asked their reasons for using or not using NFC payments.

In exit interviews (N = 179), we had 78 (44%) male and 101 (56%) female customers with the mean age of 41.69 (SD = 15.61). The results from observation and exit interviews are summarised in Tables 1 and 2 respectively.

Table 1. Results from observations (N = 160)

Description	Number of customers
Perceives visual feedback	31 (19%)
Perceives audio feedback	49 (31%)
Perceives bill generation as feedback	66 (41%)

Table 2. Results from exit interviews (N = 179)

Description	Number of customers
Customers who found NFC payment and feedback incomprehensible	5 (3%)
Participants who perceived the visual feedback from the payment terminal	24 (13%)
Participants who perceived the audio feedback	43 (24%)

3   Results

3.1   Visual Feedback

Both the interview and observation data shows that customers were not able to perceive the visual feedback delivered by the payment terminal. When questioned about the visual feedback during exit interviews, most customers (155 customers) were not able to answer the visual feedback provided by the terminal. Some customers even wondered if the terminal will show something when they scan their card. This is clearly because customers scan their card on top of the payment terminal screen which hides screen thereby hiding the feedback provided the screen.

Since NFC payment is a new technology the terminals used in supermarkets were not designed for them exclusively. Credit/debit card was added with NFC functionality was printed with NFC symbol for users to understand that it is an NFC card. Whereas, the terminals previously used for credit/debit card payments has been just modified to support NFC payments. This difference led to unsuitable visual feedback for NFC payments.

3.2   Audio Feedback

Compared to visual feedback, the audio feedback delivered by the payment terminal was well perceived by the customers. 49 (31%) customers paid attention to audio feedback during observation and 43 (24%) customers recollected the audio feedback correctly during exit interview. As using NFC payment or credit/debit card does not affect the audio feedback, it was understood by customers easily. As supermarkets can be noisy, audio feedback cannot be unfailing all the times. Even though audio feedbacks are reliable than visual feedbacks in terms of NFC payments, it should be aided with appropriate visual feedback to improve the usability of the NFC payments.

3.3   Bill Generation as Feedback

During our observation, we noticed that customers paying with NFC also used feedback which is not from the payment terminal to know the end of the transaction. Customers while paying with NFC tend to hold their card against the payment terminal till the bill is generated. 66 (41%) customers were observed to treat bill generation as a feedback. Also in exit interviews, 2 customers mentioned that they identify the end of the transaction only using the generated bill. This is because the NFC system itself does not provide enough feedback to the customers. Using bill generation as feedback overpowers the main advantage of NFC payment. It makes customers hold their card against the terminal longer thereby increasing the total time of the process.

4 Discussion

The above results clearly state that there is a gap between the payment terminal used and NFC payments. This gap reduces the usability of NFC payments and also suppresses its advantages. NFC payments lack proper visual feedback, inconsistency in audio feedback and prolonged payment process because of mismatched payment terminal used in the supermarkets.

5 Limitations

The results above are based on the study conducted only in Vienna, Austria. We also observed only the terminals used in supermarkets in Vienna. This may have geographical limitations on the data and results presented in this paper. Also, different countries using NFC payments might have other types of payment terminals installed which may or may not overcome the above-stated shortcomings.

6 Conclusion and Next Steps

To conclude, we conducted a user study to evaluate the usability of NFC payments in supermarkets in Vienna. Our study results portrayed that NFC payment suffers several usability issues because of the payment terminals used in the supermarkets. The main reason for these usability issues is using the same payment terminal used for credit/debit card payments for NFC payments also. We propose to design or redesign the payment terminal to enhance the usability of NFC payments thus aiding the success of NFC payments. As a next step, we will be designing various experience prototypes of the NFC transaction based on the user study conducted. The prototypes will then be evaluated to find a usable NFC transaction design.

Acknowledgement. The project leading to these results has received funding from the European Union's Horizon 2020 research and innovation program under the Marie Sklodowska-Curie grant agreement No. 675730.

References

1. Leong, L.-Y., et al.: Predicting the determinants of the NFC-enabled mobile credit card acceptance: a neural networks approach. Expert Syst. Appl. **40**(14), 5604–5620 (2013)
2. Kerem, O., et al.: Current benefits and future directions of NFC services. In: 2010 International Conference on Education and Management Technology (ICEMT). IEEE (2010)
3. Massoth, M., Bingel, T.: Performance of different mobile payment service concepts compared with a NFC-based solution. In: Fourth International Conference on Internet and Web Applications and Services, ICIW 2009. IEEE (2009)
4. Paul Gerhardt, S., Schilke, O., Wirtz, B.W.: Understanding consumer acceptance of mobile payment services: an empirical analysis. Electron. Commer. Res. Appl. **9**(3), 209–216 (2010)

5. Tan, G.W.-H., et al.: NFC mobile credit card: the next frontier of mobile payment? Telematics Inform. **31**(2), 292–307 (2014)
6. Lu, Y., et al.: Dynamics between the trust transfer process and intention to use mobile payment services: a cross-environment perspective. Inf. Manag. **48**(8), 393–403 (2011)
7. Boes, K., Borde, L., Egger, R.: The acceptance of NFC smart posters in tourism. In: Tussyadiah, I., Inversini, A. (eds.) Information and Communication Technologies in Tourism 2015, pp. 435–447. Springer, Cham (2015). https://doi.org/10.1007/978-3-319-14343-9_32
8. Ondrus, J., Pigneur, Y.: An assessment of NFC for future mobile payment systems. In: International Conference on the Management of Mobile Business, ICMB 2007. IEEE (2007)
9. Shin, Seungjae, Lee, Won-jun: The effects of technology readiness and technology acceptance on NFC mobile payment services in Korea. J. Appl. Bus. Res. **30**(6), 1615 (2014)
10. Geven, A., et al.: Experiencing real-world interaction: results from a NFC user experience field trial. In: Proceedings of the 9th International Conference on Human Computer Interaction with Mobile Devices and Services. ACM (2007)
11. Tomitsch, M., Grechenig, T., Schlögl, R.: Real-world tagging in the wild: on the usability and accessibility of NFC-based interactions. In: Workshop on Future Mobile Experiences: Next Generation Mobile Interaction and Contextualization, Co-Located with the Nordic Conference on Human-Computer Interaction, NordiCHI 2008

Shadow-IT System and Insider Threat: An Assessment of an Opportunity Dimension for the Identity Theft

Asif Shaikh[✉]

Florida State University, Tallahassee, USA
asif.sarwarshk@gmail.com

Abstract. Shadow IT is taken as a key example of unauthorized use of IT resources/tools and is defined as collaborative systems for communication and sharing content among employees of an organization. Currently, organizations are struggling to understand the threats to their sensitive information assets and the necessary means to combat them. This research study seeks to understand such specific threats posed by insiders in an organizational context that facilitate such unauthorized use of Information technology. Using a survey design, this document systematically attempts to measure the fraud risk to Personally Identifiable Information (PII) as identity (ID) theft from insiders in varying security environments. By integrating the opportunity dimension, as explained in a fraud triangle, and the organizational context of insider threat to sensitive information, this research will present a theoretical model that may help explain the relationship between the various aspects of Shadow-IT system and the potential opportunity for the fraudulent behavior from respective shadow users.

Keywords: Shadow-IT system · Information security · Sensitive information

1 Introduction

Advancement in consumer technologies has given significant rise to *digital natives* (Zimmermann and Rentrop 2014) as employees who are blurring private and work-related spaces. Previous studies have largely conceptualized the phenomenon of Shadow-IT (SIT) as the voluntary use of any IT resource violating injunctive IT norms at the workplace as a reaction to perceived situational constraints (Haag and Eckhardt 2014). Some scholars (Györy et al. 2012) observe that user-driven innovations as a result of non-compliance are not necessarily the result of strict policies or limited user rights but may be caused by the inability of the IT department to fulfill business needs. This ability of end-users to bypass the central Information technology (IT) system at the workplace by using technologies that are often unsanctioned by the organizational network policy has challenged the authority to control IT use. The unauthorized use of information systems may expose organizations to various types of threats that can cause damage that might lead to significant financial losses. Information security damages can range from small losses to entire information system destruction. The effects of those threats vary considerably: some affect the confidentiality or integrity of data while others affect the availability of a system. This research will attempt to explore specifically the

© Springer International Publishing AG, part of Springer Nature 2018
C. Stephanidis (Ed.): HCII Posters 2018, CCIS 852, pp. 314–317, 2018.
https://doi.org/10.1007/978-3-319-92285-0_44

impact of the emerging phenomenon of Shadow-IT as a use of "unauthorized technologies at workplace" (Oliveira et al. 2016, p. 1) by creating opportunities for fraud that compromise data integrity. The focus of this research is specifically Identity (ID) theft (White et al. 2011) as a key fraud opportunity.

2 Theory and Method

This research conceptualizes two key concepts: First, **fraud theory** founded in the field of criminology by Cressey (1953) and Second, an organizational concept of **insider threat** to sensitive information (Cline 2016) in the information security literature. Cressey (1953) used a *Fraud Triangle* (see Fig. 1) to depict three psychological factors, pressure, opportunity, and rationalization that drive an individual's behavior to commit a fraudulent act. When insiders feel a perceived pressure to justify a fraudulent act will use an opportunity to violate organizational norms provides a rationalization to justify their actions. Cline (2016) is of the view that when insiders feel a perceived pressure to justify a fraudulent act will use an opportunity to violate organizational norms and create perceived pressure as a rationalization to justify their actions. Given such premises, this research assumes that an open, permissive IT environment with lesser control on the unauthorized use of IT system may eventually foster an environment that provides employees (insiders) with an increased opportunity to commit fraud. It assumes that use of a shadow-IT system may create a predisposition toward violating organizational norms and resultantly create an opportunity for a fraudulent behavior. The proposition that there is a positive relationship between use of shadow-IT systems and the susceptibility of organizations to fraudulent employee behavior is the basis of the theoretical and methodological decisions taken in this research.

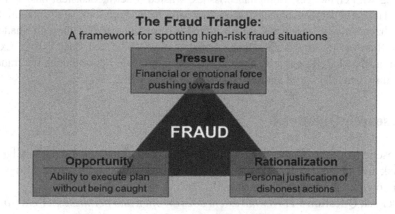

Fig. 1. Fraud Triangle (Cressey 1950)

Virtually all organizations deal with Personally Identifiable Information (PII) and are vulnerable to data breaches by insiderthreat. The current level of the research in identifying and evaluating Shadow-IT informs of three possible strategies for the collection of relevant information: (a) technical analyses (b) interpretation of help desk requests and (c) surveys of employees in the business departments (Rentrop and Zimmermann 2012). This research study will use survey of employees (IT managers) in order to address the research questions adequately.

Previous researchers used survey approach to find out which various aspects such as: IT tools employees use in their daily business (Rentrop and Zimmermann 2012) and how much employees use Shadow-IT (Silic 2015). This research study uses electronic survey method that seeks to understand whether and to what extent an open and permissive environment that facilitate Shadow-IT use can provide an opportunity for identity theft. For this survey research, IT professionals working in public sector organizations will be taken as sampling population.

3   Literature Review

Researchers (Dhillon and Backhouse 2000) are of the view that the widespread use of IT has given rise to "security blindness" on part of the users (p. 126) resulting in the improper use of information systems that could affect the privacy of critical assets of information. In several organizations, trend is evolving as a type of workaround from nontransparent and unapproved end-user computing (EUC), which challenges norms relative to IT controllability (Zimmermann and Rentrop 2014). Under this concept of Shadow-IT, the unauthorized use of IT resources is seen as violation of any IT resource injunctive or IT norms as a reaction to a perceived situational constraint with the intent to enhance work performance, but not to harm the organization (Haag and Eckhardt 2014).

Scholars (Köffer et al. 2015) support the view that consumer technologies have intensified the blurring between work and private spaces bringing more opportunities for innovation along with challenges. Compliance issues, wasted time, inconsistent business logic, increased risks for data loss or leaks, wasted investment, etc., are some of the potential risks that can have serious impacts on organizational information security through Shadow-IT users as 'Insiders' in any given organizational context (Silic and Back 2014). Existing research, acknowledges that a Shadow IT system can create opportunities for fraud and compromise data integrity of authorized systems (Allen et al., 2017).

4   Research Questions

Three research questions have been formulated in order to understand the link between fraud risk and unauthorized (or unsanctioned) use of IT systems in organizations while focusing on the opportunity dimension.

Research Question # 1: *To what extent does an open and permissive IT environment that allows the use of a shadow-IT system of an organization provide an opportunity for an identity theft?*

Research Question # 2: *What is the nature/pattern of opportunities for identity theft in using a Shadow-IT system?*

Research Question # 3: *What are the key technologies used within a Shadow-IT system that create more opportunities for insider threat in a given organization?*

5   Conclusion and Expected Outcomes

While no prior research addresses the distinct elements of fraud or malicious intent, several streams of research have acknowledged these security risks to organizational information systems likely to provide opportunities for fraud and/or the compromise of data integrity in authorized systems (Allen et al. 2017). In the current research literature, an opportunity to commit identity theft is seen as an ability to commit fraud created through weak internal controls, poor management oversight, use of one's position and authority, etc. However, unsanctioned use of IT systems can also create an opportunity to commit identity theft fraud and this is yet to be explored. The opportunity dimension of fraud is preventable as organizations can build processes, procedures, and controls that can inhibit or deter an employee's ability to commit fraud. The scant literature on shadow-IT usage and the opportunity dimension for shadow users towards fraudulent behavior in an organizational context reveals a strong need for future research that addresses such emerging challenges for organizational information systems.

References

Cline, H.G.: Understanding the insider threat (Doctoral dissertation) (2016). Accessed from ProQuest (10103896)

Cressey, D.R.: The criminal violation of financial trust. Am. Sociol. Rev. 15(6), 1–15, 738–743 (1950). Accessed from www.JSTOR.org

Cressey, D.R.: Other People's Money, pp. 1–300. Patterson Smith, Montclair (1953)

Dhillon, G., Backhouse, J.: Technical opinion: information system security management in the new millennium. Commun. ACM 43(7), 125–128 (2000)

Györy, A.A.B., Cleven, A., Uebernickel, F., Brenner, W.: Exploring the shadows: IT governance approaches to user-driven innovation (2012)

Haag, S., Eckhardt, A.: Normalizing the shadows–The role of symbolic models for individuals' shadow IT usage. In: Proceedings of the International Conference on Information Systems, Frankfurt, Germany (2014). Accessed from https://semanticscholar.org

Köffer, S., Ortbach, K., Junglas, I., Niehaves, B., Harris, J.: Innovation through BYOD? Bus. Inf. Syst. Eng. 57(6), 363–375 (2015)

Oliveira, M., Mallmann, G.L., Maçada, A.C.G.: Can shadow IT facilitate knowledge sharing in organizations? An exploratory study. In: Proceedings of the European Conference on Knowledge Management, Coleraine, UK (2016). https://academic-conferences.org

Rentrop, C., Zimmermann, S.: Shadow IT man-agement and control of unofficial IT. In: Proceedings of the Sixth International Conference on Digital Society, Valencia, Spain (2012). Accessed from https://researchgate.net

Silic, M., Back, A.: Shadow IT–A view from behind the curtain. Comput. Secur. 45, 274–283 (2014)

White, G.L., Mediavilla, F.A.M., Shah, J.R.: Information privacy: implementation and perception of laws and corporate policies by CEOs and managers. Int. J. Inf. Secur. Priv. 5(1), 50 (2011)

Zimmermann, S., Rentrop, C.: On the emergence of shadow IT-A transaction cost based approach. In: Proceedings of the European Conference on Information Systems 2014, Tel Aviv, Israel (2014). Accessed from https://researchgate.net

The Research on the Benefit of Telemedicine to Human Based on Evolutionary Game Theory

Qing Xue, Lingchen Zhou$^{(\boxtimes)}$, Jia Hao, and Minxia Liu

School of Mechanical Engineering, Beijing Institute of Technology,
Beijing 100081, People's Republic of China
{xueqing, haojia632, liuminxia}@bit.edu.cn,
1360829271@qq.com

Abstract. For situation that inadequate and overly expensive medical service as a result of medical and health resources are scarce and the distribution is not reasonable in our country, the paper uses evolutionary game theory to establish the evolutionary game model of the general hospital and patient based on telemedicine system, analyze the evolutionary process and the result of the two sides, and come to the conclusion that people can get the most benefit when choosing telemedicine. What's more, the paper use MATLAB to simulate the model, to further verify the benefits brought by telemedicine.

Keywords: Telemedicine · Evolutionary game theory · MATLAB

1 Introduction

The investigation found that the United States spends the annual cost of medical services is the largest in developed countries, while the per capita annual medical expenses in China is only 0.27% of that in the United States, indicating that the medical resources in China are extremely scarce. The medical and health resources in China are so serious shortage and are not evenly distributed, the city with a population of only 20% of the population has 80% of the country's medical and health resources, while the rural population is 80% of the total population but the medical and health resources account for only 20% of the country's total [1]. As a result, it is difficult for people to see a doctor, and telemedicine play an important role in improving the situation. As a new medical system, telemedicine connects the central hospital and the general hospital through the network, so that the patients can get the treatment from the central hospital in the general hospital, and it can improve health care resource utilization and patient flow issues better, to a large extent, the problem that people is difficult to see a doctor is greatly improved.

At present, telemedicine has been widely used both at home and abroad. The earliest application model of telemedicine is a two-way television system applied in radiology in the early 1950s [2]. From then on, more and more medical activities have begun to integrate with technology. In order to promote the development of telemedicine, developed countries in the West have successively developed some valuable projects. As a pioneer in developed countries, the United States has strong technological and economic strength and therefore has access to most areas of telemedicine, including pediatric far-reaching medical care and the UWGSP9 telemedicine project [3]. Since last century, China's economy has just started, the study of telemedicine far less than the developed countries in the West. At the end of the 20th century, telemedicine activities were carried out by General Hospital of PLA and Huashan Hospital, which enabled the start and breakthrough of telemedicine [4]. In addition, the Ministry of Health also created a telemedicine consultation system. Later, the People's Liberation Army General Hospital conducted a telemedicine consultation with a hospital in Jinan Military Region using E-mail, Videophone and ISDN, and established a "telemedicine center".

Telemedicine technology has broken borders and has a significant impact on the reform of the health care system. This article uses evolutionary game theory to analyze the benefits brought by telemedicine.

2 Model Establishment

2.1 Model Assumptions

Suppose general hospitals and patients is limited rationality during the game process; assuming that the patient must have a medical treatment, when the patient does not choose the general hospital treatment, he will choose the central hospital for treatment.

2.2 Model Factors

(1) Game sides

This paper studies the game of general hospital and patient under the telemedicine system, so the two sides of the game are general hospital and patient respectively.

(2) Strategy

General hospitals choose whether or not to carry out telemedicine cooperation with the central hospital. Therefore, the general hospital's strategy set is {cooperative, uncooperative}, and patients choose whether to go to a general hospital for treatment. Therefore, the patient's strategy set is {choose, no choose}.

(3) Income matrix

For hospitals, suppose that the ratio of general hospitals choose to cooperate with the central hospital with telemedicine is y ($0 < y < 1$) [5]. The benefits of general hospital choose to cooperate with central hospital are π_1, the benefits of general hospitals do not cooperate with the central hospital are π_2, As patients can get more trust from telemedicine, so $\pi_1 > \pi_2$; the cost to be paid that general hospital cooperates with central hospital (advocacy costs, operating costs and other fixed costs) is C_1, the cost to be paid when not cooperating with the central hospital (hospital fixed costs) is $C_2 (C_1 > C_2)$, in addition regardless of the general hospital how to choose, the cost in doctor when patients choose general hospital (bonus and salary of doctor) is C_3; the financial support provided by the government when the general hospital cooperate with the central hospital is W_1, and the financial support provided by the government which does not cooperate with the central hospital is W_2, now China is strongly supporting and promoting telemedicine, so $W_1 > W_2$. For patients, suppose the ratio that patients choose to visit a general hospital is $x(0 < x < 1)$ [6]. When the general hospital cooperate with the central hospital, the utility that patients choose the general hospital is V_1, when the general hospital cooperate with the central hospital for telemedicine, the utility obtained by the patients choosing general hospitals was V_1. When the general hospital do not carry out the telemedicine cooperation with the central hospital, the utility obtained by the patients choosing general hospitals was $V_2(V_1 > V_2)$; when the general hospital chooses to cooperate with the central hospital, the cost to be paid by the patient is P_1. When the general hospital does not choose to cooperate with the central hospital, the cost to be paid by the patient is P_2; the proportion of reimbursement of medical insurance in general hospital is σ, because the utility will reduce significantly when general hospitals do not cooperate with central hospitals, the patient will complain about the general hospital, and the cost is C_4, which result in the loss of the general hospital is L. Taking into account the patient must be medical treatment, this paper assumes that when the patient does not choose a general hospital for medical treatment, that is, choose the center of the hospital for medical treatment, the utility of the patient to the central hospital for treatment is V', the medical expense paid is P', and the reimbursement ratio of the central hospital is σ'. Additional costs paid such as transportation costs, time cost, and accommodation cost are E [7].

According to the above assumptions analysis: The actual expenses paid by patients when they choose to visit a general hospital are $P_1(1 - \sigma)$ and $P_2(1 - \sigma)$ respectively; when general hospital cooperate with central hospital, the patient's satisfaction with the general hospital increased, and the extra cost was saved, so the utility of the patient was $V_1 > (1 - \sigma)P_1$; when general hospitals do not cooperate with central hospitals, the patients are in doubt about the medical standards of general hospital doctors, so the patients may not be satisfied with the general hospital medical services, so the utility obtained by the patients is $V_2 < (1 - \sigma)P_2$ [8].

Based on the above assumptions and analysis, we can get the return matrix of both sides of the game, as shown in Table 1.

Table 1. The game income matrix of general hospitals and patients

		General hospital	
		合作 (y)	不合作 $(1 - y)$
患	选择 (x)	$V_1 - (1 - \sigma)P_1,$ $\pi_1 - C_1 - C_3 + W_1$	$V_2 - (1 - \sigma)P_2 - C_4,$ $\pi_2 - C_2 - C_3 + W_2 - L$
者	不选择 $(1 - x)$	$V' - (1 - \sigma')P' - E, -C_1 + W_1$	$V' - (1 - \sigma')P' - E, -C_2 + W_2$

Based on Table 1, the income matrix of patients is:

$$A = \begin{bmatrix} V_1 - (1 - \sigma)P_1 & V_2 - (1 - \sigma)P_2 - C_4 \\ V' - (1 - \sigma')P' - E & V' - (1 - \sigma')P' - E \end{bmatrix} \quad (1)$$

The income matrix of general hospital is:

$$B = \begin{bmatrix} \pi_1 - C_1 - C_3 + W_1 & \pi_2 - C_2 - C_3 + W_2 - L \\ -C_1 + W_1 & - C_2 + W_2 \end{bmatrix} \quad (2)$$

3 Model Analysis

Based on the above assumptions and analysis, the expected benefits of adopting two strategies of "selecting" and "not selecting" for a single patient are U_{11}, U_{12}, and the average income of patients are $\overline{U}_1$, respectively:

$$U_{11} = y[V_1 - (1 - \sigma)P_1] + (1 - y)[V_2 - (1 - \sigma)P_2 - C_4 \quad (3)$$

$$U_{12} = y(V' - (1 - \sigma')P' - E) + (1 - y)[V' - (1 - \sigma')P' - E] \quad (4)$$

$$\overline{U}_1 = xU_{11} + (1 - x)U_{12} \quad (5)$$

The dynamic equation for constructing the imitator is:

$$F(x) = \frac{dx}{dt} = x(U_{11} - \overline{U}_1) = x(1 - x)(U_{11} - U_{12})$$
$$= x(1 - x)\{y[V_1 - V_2 - (1 - \sigma)(P_1 - P_2) + C_4] - [V' - (1 - \sigma')P' - E]\}$$
$$(6)$$

Similarly, the imitation of general hospitals dynamic equation is:

$$F(y) = \frac{dy}{dt} = y(U_{21} - \overline{U}_2) = y(1 - y)[x(\pi_1 - \pi_2 + L) + W_1 - W_2 - (C_1 - C_2) \quad (7)$$

The evolvement behavior of the two sides in the process of game can be illustrated by the dynamic equation of imitators in both sides of the game. Let $F(x) = 0$, $F(y) = 0$, we can get five dynamic equilibrium point, respectively: $O(0, 0)$, $A(0, 1)$, $B(1, 1)$, $C(1, 0)$, $D(x^*, y^*)$, If and only if $0 < x^* < 1$ and $0 < y^* < 1$. Among them:

$$x^* = \frac{C_1 - C_2 - (W_1 - W_2)}{\pi_1 - \pi_2 + L}$$

$$y^* = \frac{V' - (1 - \sigma')P' = -E - [V_2 - (1 - \sigma)P_2 - C_4]}{V_1 - V_2 - (1 - \sigma)(P_1 - P_2) + C_4}$$

According to the above assumptions and the actual situation, the benefits of patients will much than the cost paid when they see a doctor, otherwise the patient will not choose to see a doctor, and when general hospitals cooperate with central hospitals and patients choose general hospitals, because of the additional cost was saved, so the benefits of patients obtain are much than that they choose central hospitals, so $0 < y^* < 1$.

According to Jacobian matrix analysis, constructing Jacobian matrix J [9]:

$$J = \begin{bmatrix} \frac{\partial F(x)}{\partial x} & \frac{\partial F(x)}{\partial y} \\ \frac{\partial F(y)}{\partial y} & \frac{\partial F(y)}{\partial y} \end{bmatrix}$$

Among them, the formula (6) and (7) derived partial derivation:

$$\frac{\partial F(x)}{\partial x} = (1 - 2x)\{y[V_1 - V_2 - (1 - \sigma)(P_1 - P_2) + C_4]$$
$$+ V_2 - (1 - \sigma)P_2 - C_4 - [V' - (1 - \sigma')P' - E]\}$$

$$\frac{\partial F(x)}{\partial y} = x(1 - x)[V_1 - V_2 - (1 - \sigma)(P_1 - P_2) + C_4]$$

$$\frac{\partial F(y)}{\partial x} = y(1 - y)(\pi_1 - \pi_2 + L)$$

$$\frac{\partial F(y)}{\partial y} = (1 - 2y)[x(\pi_1 - \pi_2 + L) + W_1 - W_2 - (C_1 - C_2)]$$

The determinant of Jacobian matrix J is:

$$det(J) = |J| = \frac{\partial F(x)}{\partial x} \cdot \frac{\partial F(y)}{\partial y} - \frac{\partial F(x)}{\partial y} \cdot \frac{\partial F(y)}{\partial x}$$

The trace of the Jacobian matrix is:

$$tr(J) = \frac{\partial F(x)}{\partial x} + \frac{\partial F(y)}{\partial y} \tag{8}$$

It should be pointed out that in the process of solving the model, we need to find out the evolutionary stability strategy of the game model to analyze the model. The evolutionary stability strategy has the corresponding criterion, when a certain equilibrium point of the game model makes the determinant of the Jacobian matrix positive and makes the trace of the Jacobian matrix to be negative, then this equilibrium point is the evolutionary stabilization strategy.

According to the patient's imitator dynamic equation analysis, When $y = y^*$, $F(x)$ always is 0, so all x are stable. When $y > y^*$, $x^* = 1$ is the ESS equilibrium point; when $y < y^*$, $x^* = 0$ is the ESS equilibrium point [10].

From the above three cases are available, the patient's imitator dynamic phase diagram is shown in Fig. 1(a–c).

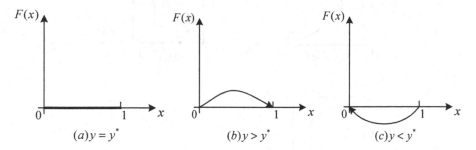

Fig. 1. The imitator dynamic phase diagram of patients

Similarly, we can obtain what through the dynamic equation analysis of imitators in general hospital strategy is: when $x = x^*$, $F(y)$ is always, that is, all y are stable; when $x > x^*$, $y^* = 1$ is the *ESS* equilibrium point; when $x < x^*$, $y^* = 0$ is the *ESS* equilibrium point [11].

From the above three cases are available, the general hospital's imitator dynamic phase diagram is shown in Fig. 2(a–c).

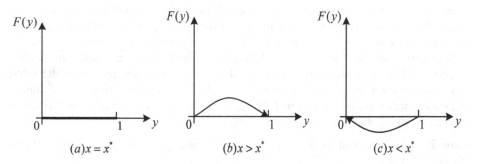

Fig. 2. The imitator dynamic phase diagram of general hospitals

According to the different values of x^*, there are three cases for analysis. According to the analysis, when the value of x^* is different, the general hospital and the patient's game strategy choice will be different. The dynamic phase diagram of the imitator is shown in the same coordinate system to obtain the dynamic evolution diagram of interaction between ordinary hospitals and patients under different x^* values, as shown in Fig. 3(a–c). It can be divided into three cases.

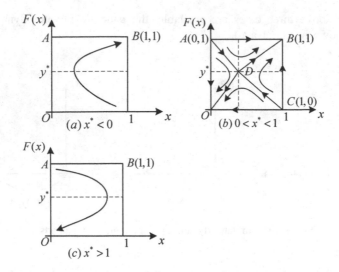

Fig. 3. Dynamic evolution of general hospital-patient interaction

Case 1. $x^* < 0$, that is $W_1 - W_2 > C_1 - C_2$

According to the above assumptions, in both cases whether general hospitals cooperate with central hospitals or not, the increase in the amount of money supported by the government to the general hospital can make up for the increase in the cost of the introduction of telemedicine in ordinary hospitals. That is to say, the general hospital benefit when cooperate with the central hospital. In this case, according to the Jacobian matrix determinant and trace symbol analysis corresponding to the equilibrium point of the dynamic system, $B(1, 1)$ is the *ESS* equilibrium point of the system. That is, the evolutionary result is that the general hospital chooses cooperate with the central hospital, and the patients choose the general hospital for treatment, and at the same time, the maximum benefit of both is achieved [12]. The Jacobian matrix determinant and trace symbol analysis shown in Table 2, the dynamic evolution of general hospital interaction with patients as shown in Fig. 3(a).

Case 2. $0 < x^* < 1$, that is $W_1 - W_2 < C_1 - C_2$ and $(\pi_1 - \pi_2 + L) + [(W_1 - W_2) - (C_1 - C_2)] > 0$

According to the above assumptions, in both cases whether general hospitals cooperate with central hospitals or not, the increase in the amount of money supported by the government to the general hospital can't make up for the increase in the cost of the introduction of telemedicine in ordinary hospitals. However, general hospitals have benefited in the long run by bringing increased benefits to general hospitals through telemedicine. In this case, according to the Jacobian matrix determinant and trace symbol analysis corresponding to the equilibrium point of the dynamic system, $O(0, 0)$ and $B(1, 1)$ is the *ESS* equilibrium point of the system. That is, the evolutionary result is that the general hospital does not choose cooperate with the central hospital, and the patients does not choose the general hospital for treatment, or the evolutionary result is that the general hospital chooses cooperate with the central hospital, and the patients

Table 2. Ranks and trace sign analysis of Jacobian matrix in case 1

Equilibrium	Determinant of J	Symbol	Trace of J	Symbol	Local stability
$O(0,0)$	$\{[V_2 - (1-\sigma)P_2 - C_4] - [V' - (1-\sigma)P' - E]\}\cdot$ $W_1 - W_2 - (C_1 - C_2)$	$-$	$\{[V_2 - (1-\sigma)P_2 - C_4] - [V' - (1-\sigma)P' - E]\}$ $+ W_1 - W_2 - (C_1 - C_2)$	$-$	Saddle point
$A(0,1)$	$[V_1 - (1-\sigma)P_1] - [V' - (1-\sigma')P' - E]\cdot$ $[C_1 - C_2 - (W_1 - W_2)]$	$-$	$[V_1 - (1-\sigma)P_1] - [V' - (1-\sigma')P' - E]$ $+ [C_1 - C_2 - (W_1 - W_2)]$	$+$	Saddle point
$B(1,1)$	$-\{[V_1 - (1-\sigma)P_1] - [V' - (1-\sigma')P' - E]\}\cdot$ $[(C_1 - C_2) - (W_1 - W_2) - (\pi_1 - \pi_2 + L)]$	$+$	$-\{[V_1 - (1-\sigma)P_1] - [V' - (1-\sigma')P' - E]\}$ $+ [(C_1 - C_2) - (W_1 - W_2) - (\pi_1 - \pi_2 + L)]$	$-$	ESS
$C(1,0)$	$-\{[V_2 - (1-\sigma)P_2 + C_4] - [V' - (1-\sigma')P' - E]\}\cdot$ $[\pi_1 - \pi_2 + L + W_1 - W_2 - (C_1 - C_2)]$	$+$	$-\{[V_2 - (1-\sigma)P_2 + C_4] - [V' - (1-\sigma')P' - E]\}$ $+ [\pi_1 - \pi_2 + L + W_1 - W_2 - (C_1 - C_2)]$	$+$	Instability point

Notes: *ESS is evolutionary Stable Strategy*

Table 3. Ranks and trace sign analysis of Jacobian matrix in case 2

Equilibrium	Determinant of J	Symbol	Trace of J	Symbol	Local stability
$O(0,0)$	$\{[V_2 - (1-\sigma)P_2 - C_4] - [V' - (1-\sigma)P' - E]\}\cdot$ $W_1 - W_2 - (C_1 - C_2)$	$+$	$\{[V_2 - (1-\sigma)P_2 - C_4] - [V' - (1-\sigma)P' - E]\}$ $+ W_1 - W_2 - (C_1 - C_2)$	$-$	ESS
$A(0,1)$	$[V_1 - (1-\sigma)P_1] - [V' - (1-\sigma')P' - E]\cdot$ $[C_1 - C_2 - (W_1 - W_2)]$	$+$	$[V_1 - (1-\sigma)P_1] - [V' - (1-\sigma')P' - E]$ $+ [C_1 - C_2 - (W_1 - W_2)]$	$+$	Instability point
$B(1,1)$	$-\{[V_1 - (1-\sigma)P_1] - [V' - (1-\sigma')P' - E]\}\cdot$ $[(C_1 - C_2) - (W_1 - W_2) - (\pi_1 - \pi_2 + L)]$	$+$	$-\{[V_1 - (1-\sigma)P_1] - [V' - (1-\sigma')P' - E]\}$ $+ [(C_1 - C_2) - (W_1 - W_2) - (\pi_1 - \pi_2 + L)]$	$-$	ESS
$C(1,0)$	$-\{[V_2 - (1-\sigma)P_2 + C_4] - [V' - (1-\sigma')P' - E]\}\cdot$ $[\pi_1 - \pi_2 + L + W_1 - W_2 - (C_1 - C_2)]$	$+$	$-\{[V_2 - (1-\sigma)P_2 + C_4] - [V' - (1-\sigma')P' - E]\}$ $+ [\pi_1 - \pi_2 + L + W_1 - W_2 - (C_1 - C_2)]$	$+$	Instability point
$D(x^*,y^*)$	$-u$	$-$	0	0	Saddle point

choose the general hospital for treatment [13]. The Jacobian matrix determinant and trace symbol analysis shown in Table 3, the dynamic evolution of general hospital interaction with patients as shown in Fig. 3(b).

In this case, the game model can evolve two evolutionary stability strategies, and the different initial states of each element in the model will cause the system to converge to different stable points, so as to obtain different evolutionary stabilization strategies. As can be seen from Fig. 3(b), when the initial state is in the area $AOCD$, the system will converge to $O(0,0)$, that is, general hospitals do not cooperate with central hospitals, patients do not choose general hospitals; when the initial state is in the area $ABCD$, the system will converge to point B $(1, 1)$, that is, the general hospital cooperate with the central hospital for telemedicine, patients choose the general hospital for treatment. And the larger the area of $ABCD$, the greater the probability that the system converges to the stable point $B(1,1)$, and the smaller the probability of converging to $O(0,0)$. Therefore, the factors influencing the evolutionary path of the analysis system can be transformed into the factors that affect the size of the $ABCD$. The area of $ABCD$ can be expressed as:

$$
\begin{aligned}
S_{ABCD} &= \frac{1}{2}(2 - x^* - y^*) \\
&= \frac{1}{2}\left[2 - \frac{C_1 - C_2 - (W_1 - W_2)}{\pi_1 - \pi_2 + L} - \frac{V' - (1 - \sigma')P' - E[V_2 - (1 - \sigma)P - C_4]}{V_1 - V_2 - (1 - \sigma)(P_1 - P_2) + C_4}\right]
\end{aligned}
\tag{9}
$$

Next, we discuss the effect of the change of parameters on the overall evolutionary result [14]:

(1) The cost increment of cooperative telemedicine in general hospital: $C_1 - C_2$.
To the formula (9), through the derivative with respect to $C_1 - C_2$, $\frac{\partial S_{ABCD}}{(C_1 - C_2)} < 0$, that is, S_{ABCD} is a decreasing function of $C_1 - C_2$, increases with decreasing $C_1 - C_2$ and decreases with increasing $C_1 - C_2$. So when the cost that general hospitals choose central hospitals for telemedicine increasing, S_{ABCD} will be reduced, the probability of the system to $O(0,0)$ points will be increased.

(2) The increase in government subsidies when general hospitals cooperate with central hospitals: $W_1 - W_2$.
To the formula (9), through the derivative with respect to $W_1 - W_2$, $\frac{\partial S_{ABCD}}{(C_1 - C_2)} > 0$, that is, S_{ABCD} is a increasing function of $C_1 - C_2$, increases with increasing $C_1 - C_2$ and decreases with decreasing $C_1 - C_2$. So The increase in government subsidies when general hospitals cooperate with central hospitals increasing, S_{ABCD} will increase, the probability of system evolution to $B(1, 1)$ points will increase.

Table 4. Ranks and trace sign analysis of Jacobian matrix in case 2

Equilibrium	Determinant of J	Symbol	Trace of J	Symbol	Local stability
$O(0,0)$	$\{[V_2 - (1-\sigma)P_2 - C_4] - [V' - (1-\sigma)P' - E]\} \cdot W_1 - W_2 - (C_1 - C_2)$	$+$	$\{[V_2 - (1-\sigma)P_2 - C_4] - [V' - (1-\sigma)P' - E]\} + W_1 - W_2 - (C_1 - C_2)$	$+$	ESS
$A(0,1)$	$[V_1 - (1-\sigma)P_1] - [V' - (1-\sigma')P' - E] \cdot [C_1 - C_2 - (W_1 - W_2)]$	$+$	$[V_1 - (1-\sigma)P_1] - [V' - (1-\sigma')P' - E] + [C_1 - C_2 - (W_1 - W_2)]$	$+$	Instability point
$B(1,1)$	$-\{[V_1 - (1-\sigma)P_1] - [V' - (1-\sigma')P' - E]\} \cdot [(C_1 - C_2) - (W_1 - W_2) - (\pi_1 - \pi_2 + L)]$	$-$	$-\{[V_1 - (1-\sigma)P_1] - [V' - (1-\sigma')P' - E]\} + [(C_1 - C_2) - (W_1 - W_2) - (\pi_1 - \pi_2 + L)]$	Unsure	Saddle point
$C(1,0)$	$-\{[V_2 - (1-\sigma)P_2 + C_4] - [V' - (1-\sigma')P' - E]\} \cdot [\pi_1 - \pi_2 + L + W_1 - W_2 - (C_1 - C_2)]$	$-$	$-\{[V_2 - (1-\sigma)P_2 + C_4] - [V' - (1-\sigma')P' - E]\} - [\pi_1 - \pi_2 + L + W_1 - W_2 - (C_1 - C_2)]$	Unsure	Saddle point

(3) The increase of return when general hospitals cooperate with central hospitals: $\pi_1 - \pi_2$.

To the formula (9), through the derivative with respect to $\pi_1 - \pi_2$, $\frac{\partial S_{ABCD}}{(C_1 - C_2)} > 0$, that is, S_{ABCD} is a increasing function of $\pi_1 - \pi_2$, increases with increasing $\pi_1 - \pi_2$ and decreases with decreasing $C_1 - C_2$. So The increase of return when general hospitals cooperate with central hospitals increasing, S_{ABCD} will increase,

Table 5. Model initial parameter assignment table

Factors	Assignment
W_1, W_2	600, 200 (million)
C_1, C_2	800, 300 (million)
π_1, π_2	400, 200 (million)
P_1, P_2	1.2, 1
σ, σ'	0.4, 0.6
V_1, V_2	1, 0.2
L, E	2, 0.2
C_4, P', V'	1, 2, 1.2

the probability of system evolution to $B(1, 1)$ points will increase.

(4) General hospital medical claims ratio: σ

To the formula (9), through the derivative with respect to σ, $\frac{\partial S_{ABCD}}{(C_1 - C_2)} > 0$, that is, S_{ABCD} is a increasing function of σ, increases with increasing σ and decreases with decreasing σ. So General hospital medical claims ratio increasing, S_{ABCD} will increase, the probability of system evolution to $B(1, 1)$ points will increase.

(5) Central hospital medical claims ratio: σ'

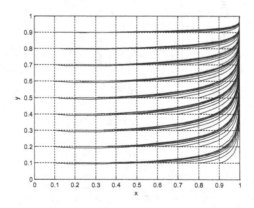

Fig. 4. Evolution trend simulation diagram of $x - y$ based on case 1.

To the formula (9), through the derivative with respect to σ', $\frac{\partial S_{ABCD}}{(C_1-C_2)} < 0$, that is, S_{ABCD} is a decreasing function of σ', increases with decreasing σ' and decreases with increasing σ'. So when the cost that general hospitals choose central hospitals

Table 6. Changed parameter assignment table

Factors	Assignment
W_1, W_2	700, 200 (million)
C_1, C_2	700, 300 (million)
π_1, π_2	400, 200 (million)
P_1, P_2	1.2, 1
σ, σ'	0.4, 0.6
V_1, V_2	1, 0.2
L, E	2, 0.2
C_4, P', V'	1, 2, 1.2

for telemedicine increasing, S_{ABCD} will be reduced, the probability of the system to $O(0,0)$ points will be increased.

Case 3. $x^* > 1$, that is $W_1 - W_2 < C_1 - C_2$, and $(\pi_1 - \pi_2 + L) + [(W_1 - W_2) - (C_1 - C_2)] < 0$.

According to the above assumptions, in both cases whether general hospitals cooperate with central hospitals or not, the increase in the amount of money supported by the government to the general hospital can't make up for the increase in the cost of the introduction of telemedicine in ordinary hospitals. And general hospitals don't have benefited in the long run by bringing increased benefits to general hospitals through

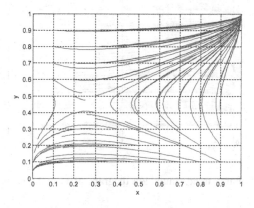

Fig. 5. Evolution trend simulation diagram of $x - y$ based on case 2.

telemedicine. In this case, according to the Jacobian matrix determinant and trace symbol analysis corresponding to the equilibrium point of the dynamic system, $O(0,0)$ is the *ESS* equilibrium point of the system. That is, when telemedicine can't make

Table 7. Changed parameter assignment table

Factors	Assignment
W_1, W_2	600, 200 (million)
C_1, C_2	1000, 300 (million)
π_1, π_2	400, 200 (million)
P_1, P_2	1.2, 1
σ, σ'	0.4, 0.6
V_1, V_2	1, 0.2
L, E	2, 0.2
C_4, P', V'	1, 2, 1.2

benefit for general hospitals, general hospitals will not cooperate with central hospitals and patients will not choose general hospitals for treatment. The Jacobian matrix determinant and trace symbol analysis shown in Table 4, the dynamic evolution of general hospital interaction with patients as shown in Fig. 3(c).

4 Simulation Analysis

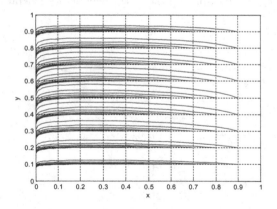

Fig. 6. Evolution trend simulation diagram of $x - y$ based on case 3.

From the above analysis we can see that when x^*, y^* have different values, the system will have different evolutionary path, resulting in different evolutionary results. In this paper, we use *MATLAB* to establish the model the about hospitals and patients. The paper simulate the model based on the three cases above, analyzing the impact of the initial state of the system on the game process of general hospitals and patients in different situations by graphics [15]. According to the evolution trend of the model in the graph, the factors that affecting the system evolution result will more clear.

Case 1. $x^* < 0$

In this case, the model initial parameter values are set to meet the situation 1, the specific assignment in Table 5.

Input the above model parameters into the *MATLAB* model, make the initial value of x, y is 0, In order to see the changing trend of the system clearly, make loop step is 0.05, running time is [0, 10] [16]. The $x - y$ chart of evolutionary game model of general hospital and patient running under the above conditions is shown in Fig. 4. The figure shows, when $x^* < 0$, all the points of x and y in the figure converge to (1, 1). That is, the final result of the evolution is that the general hospital chooses to cooperate with the central hospital and the patients choose to go to the general hospital for treatment. the system achieves a stable and balanced evolution at the (1, 1).

Case 2. $0 < x^* < 1$

In this case, the initial parameters of the model W_1, W_2, C_1, C_2 are changed so that the values of the model parameters meet the case 2 which is shown in Table 6.

Input the above model parameters into the *MATLAB* model, Same as case 1, make the initial value of x, y is 0, make loop step is 0.05, running time is [0, 10]. The $x - y$ chart of evolutionary game model of general hospital and patient running under the above conditions is shown in Fig. 5. The figure shows, when $0 < x^* < 1$, all the points of x and y in the figure converge to (0, 0) or (1, 1). That is, the final result of the evolution is that the general hospital chooses to cooperate with the central hospital and the patients choose to go to the general hospital for treatment or the general hospital does not choose to cooperate with the central hospital and patients do not choose to go to the general hospital [17]. the system achieves a stable and balanced evolution at the (0, 0) and (1, 1).

Case 3. $x^* > 1$

In this case, the initial parameters of the model W_1, W_2, C_1, C_2 are changed so that the values of the model parameters meet the case 3 which is shown in Table 7.

Input the above model parameters into the *MATLAB* model, Same as case 1 and case 2, make the initial value of x, y is 0, make loop step is 0.05, running time is [0, 10]. The $x - y$ chart of evolutionary game model of general hospital and patient running under the above conditions is shown in Fig. 6. The figure shows, when $x^* > 1$, all the points of x and y in the figure converge to (0, 0) [17]. That is, the final result of the evolution is that the general hospital does not choose to cooperate with the central hospital and patients do not choose to go to the general hospital. the system achieves a stable and balanced evolution at the (0, 0) [18].

From the simulation results, we can see that in the above three cases, when the general hospital chose to cooperate with the central hospital for telemedicine, both the patient and the general hospital can get the maximum return, that is, the model eventually evolves to (1, 1) point [19]. Therefore, it can be seen that the introduction of telemedicine technology can improve the current medical treatment in China.

5 Conclusion

Based on the serious shortage of medical and health resources and the extremely uneven distribution in China, this paper establishes an evolutionary game model of general hospitals and patients under the telemedicine system in order to improve people's problem of inadequate and overly expensive medical service [20]. According to the analysis of the game between the two sides, it can be concluded that when the general hospital chose to cooperate with the central hospital for telemedicine, patients can receive maximum benefit from their visit. This paper uses *MATLAB* to simulate the model, further illustrating that telemedicine technology can improve people's medical problems.

References

1. Zhu, H.C.: Analysis of the current situation and countermeasures of health resources allocation in China. Career Space **5**(5), 32–33 (2009)
2. Zhao, J., Cui, Z.: Analysis on the efficiency optimization of resource allocation based on telemedicine. Chin. Health Econ. **33**(10), 5–7 (2014)
3. Wang, X., Du, R., Ai, S., Zhang, Z.: The evolution analysis of the community hospital and patients' behavior selection under the background of telemedicine. Ind. Eng. Manag. **20**(2), 130–137 (2015)
4. Jie, Z., Cai, Y., Sun, D., Zhai, Y.: Discussing the status of development of telemedicine and its trend. Chin. Health Serv. Manag. **10**, 739–799 (2014)
5. Zanaboni, P., Wootton, R.: Adoption of telemedicine: from pilot stage to routine delivery. BMC Med. Inform. Decis. Mak. **12**(1), 1 (2012)
6. Rajan, B., Seidmann, A., Dorsey, E.R.: The competitive business impact of using telemedicine for the treatment of patients with chronic conditions. J. Manag. Inf. Syst. **30**(2), 127–158 (2013)
7. Armfield, N.R., Coulthard, M.G., Slater, A., et al.: The effectiveness of telemedicine for paediatric retrieval consultations: rationale and study design for a pragmatic multicentre randomised controlled trial. BMC Health Serv. Res. **14**(1), 546 (2014)
8. Wootton, R.: Twenty years of telemedicine in chronic disease management-an evidence synthesis. J. Telemed. Telecare **18**(4), 211–220 (2012)
9. Zhai, Y., Zhou, Y., Sun, D.: Studying on the policy restraints on the development of telemedicine in China and its counter measures. Chin. Health Serv. Manag. **31**(10), 728–731 (2014)
10. Cai, Y., Zhai, Y., Hou, H.: Cost-effectiveness analysis based on of telemedicine network roles. Chin. Health Econ. **33**(10), 8–10 (2014)
11. Rui, W.: Design and Implementation of Remote Consultation System Based on PACS, Shan Dong, Shan Dong University (2004)
12. Wei, W., Wang, D.: The status quo and systemic research of telemedicine consultation at home and abroad. Med. Inf. **12**(3), 31–33 (1999)
13. Chronaki, C.E., Katehakis, D.G.: WebO-nCOLL: medical collaboration in regional healthcare networks. IEEE Tans. Inf. Technol. Biomed. **1**(4), 257–269 (1997)
14. Li, J., Zhou, M., Geng, G.: The present and future of telemedicine at home and abroad. Foreign Med. Sci. **25**(5), 193–196 (2002)

15. Zhang, W.: Game Theory and Information Economics. Shanghai Joint Publishing, Shanghai People's Publishing House, Shanghai (1996)
16. Xie, Y.: Game analysis of hospital advertising strategies. Economist **9**, 26–27 (2005)
17. Ai, S., Fan, X.: Evolutionary game analysis of choice of medical app in hospital and patient. Chin. Manag. Sci. **S1**, 34–39 (2015)
18. Zhang, L.: Evolutionary game basic dynamic theory. China Econ. Rev. **3**(5), 58–64 (2003)
19. Zhang, L.: Evolutionary game: theory and method. J. Shunde Polytech. Coll. **5**(3), 39–42 (2007)
20. Zhang, L.: Evolutionarily stable equilibrium and Nash equilibrium - concurrent discussion on the evolution of evolutionary game theory. Econ. Sci. **3**, 103–111 (2001)

Training Demand Analysis for Airlines Safety Manager Based on Improved OTP Model

Yuan Zhang[✉], Yanqiu Chen, Yijie Sun, and Mingliang Chen

China Academy of Civil Aviation Science and Technology, Beijing, China
zhangyuan@mail.castc.org.cn

Abstract. The problems existing in the training demand analysis for airlines safety managers are analyzed. In view of the shortcomings of the OTP model, the OTP model is improved, which enriches the content and dimension of the OTP analysis. Based on the improved OTP model and the actual operation characteristics of airlines, the training demand analysis model for airlines safety managers is established, and the process, dimensions and methods of airlines safety manager training demand analysis are defined. Finally, taking an airlines as an example, the analysis of the training demand for safety manager was carried out, and the courses were determined. The case shows that the model is very practical.

Keywords: Training · Demand analysis · Safety manager · Airlines
OTP model

1 Introduction

Safety manager training is an important part of airlines safety management. It directly affects the knowledge, ability and performance of safety managers, and then affects the safety level of airlines [1].

At present, the courses of safety managers training in airlines are mainly based on experience, subjective desire, requirements of higher level units, or training plans of external training units. Basically, there is no systematic and comprehensive training demand analysis based on the actual situation of the airlines. Finally, the training content is not consistent with the actual work needs, and the training effect is not very well.

At the same time, there is lack of in-depth research on the theory and method of training demand analysis for airlines safety managers, and there are no detailed and operable methods and tools.

Therefore, it is necessary to establish an airlines safety manager training demand analysis model. It provides the basis for airlines to carry out the safety manager training and improve the safety management ability.

2 OTP Model and Its Improvement

2.1 OTP Model and Its Shortcomings

In academia and other industries, the organizational-task-personnel (OTP) analysis model proposed by Goldstein is often used to carry out the training demand analysis [2, 3].

1. Organizational Analysis. By analyzing the development strategy, development goals, resources and culture of the organizational, the problems and challenges faced by the development of the organization are identified. In order to improve the core competitiveness and achieve the established goal, what training needs to be carried out to all types of personnel at all levels are determined.
2. Task Analysis. In view of a particular task, the knowledge, skill and ability needed to complete the task are analyzed. The competency model [4, 5] is built, which defines what features the personnel should have.
3. Personnel Analysis. The gap between the actual situation of the existing personnel and the competency model is analyzed, and the content of the training are determined.

The OTP model analyzes the training demand of a job from the perspective of entire organization. The training demand of individual personnel is closely related to the organization development, the tasks and the current situation of individuals, instead of only being confined to specific tasks or personnel. The analysis of training demand is more comprehensive and the result of analysis is more scientific. However, there are some limitations and shortcomings in the OTP model, including:

1. In organizational analysis, the model ignores the influence of external environment and its changes on organizational strategy and objectives, and then the influence on training demand, such as natural environment, social environment, and industry development and so on.
2. In task analysis, the model ignores the predictable changes in the task, and the resulting requirements for the knowledge and ability of the personnel, which will impact the training demand, such as automated operation instead of manual operation, paperless office and big data analysis.
3. In personnel analysis, the model mainly focuses on the gap between the actual performance of personnel and the ideal performance. It focuses on what training is needed for personnel to achieve the ideal performance level, and ignores what training they want to get from the aspect of own development and career development.

2.2 Improve the OTP Model

In view of the limitations and shortcomings of the OTP model, the model is improved. The main idea of the improvement is to carry out OTP analysis in the perspective of developing and dynamic.

1. In organizational analysis, besides analyzing the internal factors of an organization, the external factors should also be analyzed, such as government management policy, industry development, natural environment, social environment, etc. Determine the impact of external factors on the development strategy and development goals of the organization, and then determine what training should be carried out to cope with these impacts.

2. In task analysis, in addition to analyzing the knowledge and ability required for the current task, the development trend of the task should also be analyzed and determined what knowledge and ability that personnel should have to complete the future task. And then what training needs to be carried out in advance are determined.
3. In personnel analysis, in addition to analyzing the difference between current performance and ideal performance, we should also consider the training from the perspective of their own development and career development. And then determine what training is needed for the personnel.

3   Establish the Training Demand Analysis Model for Airlines Safety Manager

Based on the improved OTP model and the actual operating characteristics of the airlines, the analysis model for training demand of airlines safety managers is established.

3.1   Organizational Analysis

See Table 1.

Table 1. Organizational analysis

Dimension	Analysis content	Information collection	Output
Internal factors	–Long-term development strategy –Core competitiveness –Long-term safety goals –Organize culture –Safety culture –Changes of operation scale –Change of operation contents; etc.	*–Airlines' development planning* *–Airlines' safety planning* *–Organizational culture construction program* *–Safety culture construction program; etc.*	By analyzing the organizational development strategy, resources and external environment, the problems, opportunities and challenges that exist in the development of organizations will be identified, and what training should be carried out to promote the realization of organizational goals will be determined
External factors	–State safety supervision policy –CAA safety supervision policy –Development of the industry –Changes of social environment –Change of natural environment; etc.	–The laws and regulations of the state and the CAA *–Development planning of civil aviation industry* *–Safety development plan of civil aviation industry* *–Development of civil aviation safety management* *–Analysis of the social environment of civil aviation operation* *–Analysis of the natural environment of the civil aviation operation; etc.*	

3.2   Task Analysis

See Table 2.

Table 2. Task analysis

Dimension	Analysis content	Information collection	Output
Current task analysis	–Law of state safety –Safety regulations of the CAA –Safety management system and procedure of airlines –Best practice of industry safety management –Practice of excellent employees –Contents of the airlines operation; etc.	–Law related to safety –Aviation safety management regulations of the CAA –Airlines' safety management manual –Airlines' safety management procedure –Experience in industry safety management –Operation manual of the airlines; etc.	The competency model is identified, and the characteristics of safety manager will be defined, which involves the following aspects: professional knowledge, safety management knowledge, safety management capability, safety management literacy and so on
Future task analysis	–Development of the means of safety supervision of CAA –Development of operation technology –Development of safety management theory –Development of safety management techniques and methods; etc.	–The development trend of the safety supervision policy of the CAA –The development trend of civil aviation operation technology –The trend of the safety management of civil aviation; etc.	
Competency factors	–Identify the characteristics that the excellent safety managers should have	–Analyze the typical events –Interview –Expert review; etc.	

3.3   Personnel Analysis

See Table 3.

Table 3. Personnel analysis

Dimension	Analysis content	Information collection	Output	
			Current status of personnel	Conclusion
Professional knowledge	The professional background of the current safety managers, as well as the knowledge of the operation	Information collection is carried out in the following ways: –Professional background survey –Work experience survey –Work inspection –Examination –Interviewing –Questionnaire; etc.	Through analysis, the current situation of safety manager in professional knowledge, safety management knowledge, safety management ability and safety management literacy is determined. The training expectation in the aspects of personal career development and quality improvement is determined	The current situation of safety managers is compared with the competency model, and the training needs of individuals are considered. And then what training needs to be carried out for current safety managers will be determined
Safety management knowledge	The safety management knowledge and experience of the current safety managers			
Safety management capability	The ability of the current safety managers to organize, communicate, coordinate, and so on			
Safety management literacy	The quality and working attitude of the current safety manager			
Personal training expectations	The training expectations of the current safety managers in the aspects of personal ability promotion, quality improvement, and career development			

3.4   Set up Training Program

Finally, the training content determined by the organizational analysis and the personnel analysis are integrated. In consideration of training resource, training time, training mode and so on, the training program of safety manager is finally determined.

4 Case Study

4.1 A Airlines Introduction

A airlines has been running for 3 years, and has 10 aircrafts. The main business is domestic passenger transport. Transportation routes mainly include coastal routes and plateau routes.

4.2 Training Demand Analysis for Safety Manager

4.2.1 Organizational Analysis

Through the collection and analysis of the internal and external information of the airlines, it is found that the organization has the following characteristics:

1. The airlines plans to increase the number of aircraft and the traffic volume gradually, and plans to open up international routes.
2. The company adheres to the corporate culture of efficient and quick, as well as the safety culture of positive and just.
3. The airlines regards safety as an important cornerstone of the development of the enterprise. It is one of the important tasks to ensure the safety of operation.
4. The state and the CAA have made clear requirements for the safe operation of the airlines and regard safety as the most important content of regulatory.
5. The public's demand for safety is getting higher and higher.
6. The plateau routes that the airlines operates has high operational risk.

Through the above analysis, the following training should be carried out to the safety managers in order to achieve the goal of the company (Table 4).

Table 4. Results of organizational analysis

Training content	Courses
Organizational culture	–Company development planning –Corporate culture and safety culture –Company operation content and key risk
Industry status	–Development trend of civil aviation industry –Operation characteristics and main risks of civil aviation industry –Development trend of safety management in civil aviation industry –The development trend of the safety supervision of the CAA

4.2.2 Task Analysis

Through the analysis of the current tasks and future tasks of safety manager, and the typical event analysis and personnel interviews, the competency model of the job is determined, including (Table 5):

Table 5. Results of task analysis

Dimension	Elements
Professional knowledge	At least one of the following items: –Flight Operations (FLT) –Operational Control and Flight Dispatch (DSP) –Aircraft Engineering and Maintenance (MNT) –Cabin Operations (CAB) –Ground Handling Operations (GRH) –Cargo Operations (CGO) –Safety Management (SEC)
Safety management knowledge	–Laws and regulations related to safety –Safety management system and procedure –Safety planning –Risk management –Safety information management –Safety check –Safety performance management –Event investigation –Emergency rescue –Safety training and education –Large data analysis –Safety management based on IT technology –Mathematical modeling of safety management
Safety management capability	–Organize and coordinate multiple departments to carry out work –Smooth horizontal and vertical communication –Team management and team collaboration –Planning management and time management –Good oral and written expression
Safety management literacy	–Self-confidence –Strict, meticulous, but not rigid –Keep learning and accepting new things –Service consciousness –Execution –Bear pressure –Dare to challenge –Calm and impatient

4.2.3 Person Analysis

The airlines has a safety management department with 8 safety managers. Through the investigation and analysis of the basic situation of these safety managers, the differences between these personnel and the competency model are determined.

1. Professional knowledge. At present, each of the 8 safety managers all has at least one operation professional knowledge.
2. Safety management knowledge and experience. At present, 8 safety managers have most of the knowledge of safety management, but lack of experience in risk management,

safety inspection and event investigation. There is little understanding of the trend of safety management and the safety management based on IT technology.

3. Safety management ability. At present, 8 safety managers have insufficient ability to communicate horizontally, and have poor oral expression ability.
4. Safety management literacy. At present, 8 safety managers lack of continuous learning consciousness for new theories and methods of safety management, and can not learn new things voluntarily. And the ability to work under pressure needs to be improved.

In addition, in terms of personal training expectations, some people want to be trained in leadership and fine management.

4.2.4   Set up Training Courses for Safety Managers

Integrate the training content determined by the organizational analysis and the personnel analysis. It is ultimately determined that the 8 safety managers need to be trained as follows:

- Company development planning;
- Corporate culture and safety culture;
- Company operation content and key risk;
- Development trend of civil aviation industry;
- Operation characteristics and main risks of civil aviation industry;
- Development trend of safety management in civil aviation industry;
- The development trend of the safety supervision of the CAA;
- Practice and experience sharing of risk management;
- Practice and experience sharing of safety inspection;
- Practice and experience sharing of event investigation;
- The concept, method and tools of safety management based on IT technology;
- Effective communication and oral expression;
- Continue to learn;
- Stress relief;
- Leadership;
- Fine management.

5   Conclusion

Some conclusions are given as follows

1. Safety manager training is an important part of airlines safety management. But there is no systematic and comprehensive training demand analysis in airlines.
2. Based on the improved OTP model and the actual operation characteristics of airlines, the training demand analysis model for airlines safety managers is established.
3. Through the model, the analysis of training demand for airlines safety manager can be carried out, and the courses can be determined.

References

1. International Civil Aviation Organization: Safety Management Manual, 3rd edn. International Civil Aviation Organization, Montreal (2012)
2. Zhao, D.C., Liang, Y.Z.: Training needs analysis: connotation, model and implementation. Teach. Educ. Res. **22**(6), 9–14 (2010)
3. Hu, J.P.: Study on the training of rural human resources based on Goldstein model. J. Anhui Agri. Sci. **39**(1), 554–555, 559 (2011)
4. Vickie, S.: Managing by competencies: a study on the managerial competencies of hotel managers in Hongkong. Hosp. Manag. **17**, 253–273 (1998)
5. Liu, M., Kunaiktikul, W., Senaratana, W., et al.: Development of competency inventory for registered nurses in the People's Republic of China: scale development. Int. J. Nurs. Stud. **44**(5), 805–813 (2007)

Research on Future-Oriented Manager Service Design Under the Background of New Retail

Shifeng Zhao[✉]

Hubei University of Technology, Hubei 430070, China
zhaoshifeng920@live.com

Abstract. At present, traditional management strategies in retail industry have gradually failed to meet the expectation of rapidly expanded consumers. Although some retail managers start to deploy new management strategies so as to establish better user connections with users, the management system is relatively isolated and not big enough to form big data. This paper begins with market research and user research, digs out the bilateral pain points of managers and consumers from the research, puts forward solutions and discusses the design and testing processes of establishing a manager service system taking consumers and managers as the main line under the background of new retail. The contributions of this paper to the research on new retail service design lie in a complete set of new retail service design process based on regional conditions and some discussions on how to serve bilateral audiences in service design.

Keywords: New retail · Service design · Smart retail

1 First Section

1.1 A Subsection Sample

Previously, retail and e-commerce were two relative concepts, and until August 2010 when Alex Rampell, founder of TrialPay, a US payment company, introduced the concept of O2O (Online to Offline) [1], the online and offline united communication drew a new blueprint for a business model. In the area of e-commerce, Liu Xiaohong indicated that Groupon in the US, the earliest ancestor of the group buying model, is the business paradigm of the Dian Ping and Meituan in China [2]. Similarly, Lu Yiqing and Li Chen also claimed in the study of the O2O business model that the group buying model is still the prevalent O2O business model in China around 2013 [3]. What's more, Sun Hua thought it has also profoundly affected the development of China's mortar retail industry [4]. In October 2016, Jack Ma aired his new viewpoints on the Alibaba Computing Conference, in which he introduced the concept of new retail. New retail utilizes AI computing and IoT technology and requires that online enterprises divert warehouses via inventory retailization to arrange offline channels overall, while offline enterprises highlight the efficiency advantages of traditional retail by using intra-city logistics and delivery to make offline business online [5, 6]. Further, from the perspective of retail format, Zhou Yong believed that the unmanned shops like Amazon GO will increasingly cater to the preferences of consumers and are the future development direction of retail industry, but the completely unmanned shop model is not suitable for the development of China [7]. Despite a few managers plus smart services are the main development direction of future retail shops, there is still a lack of relevant research on a few-people smart shops.

There are some problems with the current consumer management methods as well. First of all, Liping deemed that apart from carrying out execution and management, obtaining the consumer data serves as the most important part in the process of transforming the new retail business [8]. Previous retail enterprises relied on print media, marketing and other traditional advertising media for publicity, but Ni Ning and Jin Shao pointed out in the research on communication strategies in the big data age that under the background of the current huge information flow, the one-way output of traditional media is difficult for consumers to notice and capture among quick and complicated information [9]. Second, when propaganda and planning come into play and after consumers make the purchasing behavior, retail enterprises can merely count commodity data but cannot grasp peer-to-peer consumer data [10]. Then, even though purchase items, price ranges, consumption frequencies and consumption time data can be tracked by using membership cards, too small sample size and low data value still exist [11].

In order to address this problem, now many offline retail enterprises conduct data mining plans and their strategies are focused on: serving members in the form of own APP to achieve the conversion of entity membership cards. However, the fragmentation of current mobile device APPs is severe, and the number of the APPs actively used by a user per day is only about 9, making it rather hard for managers to collect large amounts of user data thereby. In addition, all enterprises and systems are relatively independent, and if they make research and development separately, the development are both costly and in a long cycle, and more importantly, data cannot be shared, resulting in "big data" not that "big" [12]. Consequently, the disjunction and separation of marketing, sales and evaluation systems are common and pervasive in the transformation process of traditional retail industry.

Through literature review, we found that a few-people smart shop service system is still a blank area. Although managers and consumers directly related to a few-people smart shops are in a service provider-receiver relationship, under the consumer-centered service design, the problems of efficient management and employee-friendly management systems are ignored. Vice versa, under the manager-centered service design, there is a service gap between systems, and user experiences would be inconsistent and non-fluent. In summary, relying on the a few-people smart shop service system, this paper will tease out the problem in the bilateral service design between consumers and managers.

2 Survey and Analysis of Strategies and Scopes

2.1 Survey Method Selection

Via the qualitative analysis with logical thinking, we have a fuzzy preliminary estimate of the products that have been made - the a few-people smart shop service system, then the correctness of the preliminary estimate needs to be tested through market research, and we need to find the typical target audiences of the developed product, dig out the audiences' pain points and potential needs through user research. Nevertheless, due to the particularity of the bilateral audiences in this study, except consumers, enterprises' managers are not the target users in the general sense, it is thus necessary to discuss and determine the research methods in view of this situation.

The most commonly used online questionnaire method at present is excluded by us. Although online questionnaires have various forms, are low in cost and large in sample size, because of the particularity of the surveyed respondents, there is no guarantee that online surveyed people are the managers and participants of retail enterprises. Therefore, we predicted that the received questionnaires would almost be unconvincing ineffective questionnaires, which fail to guide our judgments positively.

Hence, after evaluation, we determined two survey methods: field research and focus group. We carried out a single 30-minute short-time and high-frequency field research respectively on five typical retail shops through the three dimensions of time, places and marketing activities, conducted a focus group interview of 5 people based on the survey data and conclusions of the field research, delved deeper into the problems found during the interview and discovered new problems during discussion.

2.2   Survey Data Analysis

Field Research Analysis

As shown in Table 1, it's the problem observation and recording table during the field research on Lawson Convenience Store and preliminary analysis. As shown in Table 2, it's the product characteristics recording table of five stores. Because there were too many different variable elements in different shops, the data of the five stores were integrated in the summarizing process. The discovered problems were discussed in depth in the focus group.

Table 1. Problem observation and recording on Lawson Convenience Stores

Time	Activities	Potential problems
8–10	At the morning peak, when shift is completed, there are 2–3 employees in the store, 2 responsible for cashiering and 1 responsible for sorting goods and cleaning up the dining area	
11.30–13.30	Similar to the morning peak, the sales of ready-to-eat food and hot food grow, and microwave ovens are more frequently used	Due to being relatively busy, employees sometimes forget that the food in the microwave oven has been heated up
14–16	At leisure time, employees' main work includes cashiering, goods sorting, goods replenishment, and making an inventory of goods with a paper checklist and inputting it into the computer system	The use of paper checklists easily leads to missed inventory check, wrong inventory check; the secondary processing of manual inputting to the computer system is error-prone
21–23	11 o'clock everyday is the time for taking an inventory of goods and goods scrapping, which require employees to check the goods one by one	Manual inventory inspection is time-consuming and may result in missed inventory check. The scrapping of expired goods causes large losses
24–2	Every 15 min, the store with larger passenger volume has approximately 4 consumers, while the store with smaller passenger volume has approximately 2 consumers	The retention rate of night shift employees is low; training costs are high; and service efficiency is low

Table 2. Product characteristics of five Lawson Convenience Stores

Location	Crowd tendency	Product characteristics
University	College students, social people	Desserts, school supplies, snacks, drinks
Business district	Young people, 23–32, have slightly more women than men	Drinks, chewing gum, condoms, snacks
Community	Consumers are mixed	Daily necessities, alcoholic, tobacco, beverages, ready-to-eat food, bread
Office building	Staff mainly	Tobacco, alcohol, breakfast, ready-to-eat food, yogurt
Medical institutions	The tendency is not obvious. A little more middle-aged	Daily necessities, health care products, health gift boxes, eggs, milk
Transportation hub	Consumer attribute is not obvious	Comprehensive

Focus Group Analysis

Although the members in the focus group should be the testees with the same background and incomes, because the product requires a more macro management strategy and also the implementation details during the implementation process, the focus group consists of three direct salespeople, an assistant store manager and a store manager. For a clear expression, the needs and suggestions are summarized and listed in Table 3 in order of priority.

According thereto, we need to tap the immediate needs of audiences so as to find their real needs.

Table 3. Focus group summary

Requirements and recommendations	Demand priority (10–1)	Potential demand
What the goods that people around tend to buy	8	Increase sales
Estimate the quantity of fresh food stock to reduce scrap	7	Reduce loss
Timely reminder of near expired goods	6	Reduce loss
Shop address selection assistant service	6	Increase sales
Data of hot shelves and hot sales goods	5	Increase sales
Change offline promotions to achieve accurate marketing	4	Increase sales
A more convenient way to inventory replenishment goods	3	Reduce loss

2.3   Retail Management Needs Tapping

During the focus group discussion process, it was found that some of the problems we predicted did exist, such as the slight differences in the thinking perspectives between employees and managers. From the managers' point of view, the external target requires to increase the sales of high-margin products, and the internal target requires to reduce losses, cut down in-store expenses and reduce accidental goods damage and theft, thereby achieving the ultimate goal of maximizing profits. The thinking perspective of employees lies more in handling in-store issues more conveniently and efficiently and improving work efficiency, which directly and indirectly affect consumers' shopping experience and return rate.

According to qualitative analysis, firstly, increasing sales needs to enhance consumers' demand, so it is necessary to provide the goods more closely associated with consumers, which requires the sold goods match the consumers around the current store. Secondly, the reduction of losses needs to reduce expiry damage. As a consequence, not only the turnover rate of goods requires to be increased, but also products should be purchased in reasonable quantities. Both of these two issues need to be evaluated comprehensively based on the consumption needs, purchasing power, consumption desires and other relevant information of the consumers at specific locations so as to reduce the unsalable goods due to inaccurate judgment on surrounding consumers' needs and incorrect goods ordering.

Besides, the discussion among the focus group led us to new discoveries. Both managers were preparing new stores, and they all claimed that the scientific assessment of new store site selection is extremely difficult. Generally, without the market research data used for quantitative analysis, retail managers can only draw conclusions by means of repeated field visits and extensive qualitative analysis, which may result in the imbalance of passenger flow and rent, seriously affecting enterprise managers' return on investment. Therefore, the product we design should provide appropriate services ahead of audiences' shop setting-up to enrich the entire service process and form complete and smooth new retail solutions.

As a result, to sum up, we found that managers' most fundamental need is to have a tool that can help enterprises to understand consumers more accurately and locate potential consumption needs.

2.4   Retail Management Needs Subdivision

According to the problems collected during the process of designing survey and research as well as the potential needs, we tapped subdivision functions from the system service touchpoints, built a functional structure tree and wrote prioritizing needs documents, on which the iterative development orders in the future will be based as the priority thereof.

Table 4 describes that we divided the iterative development priorities according to users' needs into four categories - necessary, optional, user-expected and future-feasible.

Table 4. Functional requirements priority

Features	Demand level	Features	Demand level
Community product recommendation	Necessary	Directed music marketing	User-expected
Purchase information	Necessary	Check the community's basic attributes	Optional
Consumer location statistics	Necessary	User credit value match	Optional
Consumer purchasing statistics	Necessary	Consumer emotion recognition	Optional
Community Attribute Map	User-expected	Smart music service	Optional
Check community buying power	User-expected	Walking route thermogram	Optional
Check community interest	User-expected	Default product suggestions	Optional
Share store data	User-expected	A key to stop purchasing	Optional
Automatically identify consumers	User-expected	Share multiple types of retail data	Future-feasible
Match consumer information	User-expected	Consumer privacy protection	Future-feasible
Community promotion	User-expected	Spend voice service	Future-feasible
Unmarketable product promotion	User-expected	Smart price tag	Future-feasible
Recommended product display	User-expected	A key platform to promote access	Future-feasible
Stocking plan integration recommended	User-expected	Community tag redirects	Future-feasible
A key stocking	User-expected	Smart clearance	Future-feasible
Provisional reminder	User-expected	Promotion design guidance	Future-feasible

3   Analysis of the Service System Structure

At present, goods labels have been widely used in retail industry. As early as 1700, Europe printed the first batch of labels used on medicines and cloths for goods identification. From "Identification Label" to "Value Recommendation Label", labels have been refined and personalized. Goods exist because of consumers and consumers have different attributes due to purchasing, and the two influence each other [13]. The labels of goods enable consumers to find the goods they want more quickly; whereas managers can efficiently recommend potentially demanding goods based on consumer labels. Therefore, in combination with the previous design research, the project will focus on consumer labels as the core to make a bilateral friendly service management application between managers and consumers – so that enterprise managers are provided with scientific management programs, and consumers can get high-quality service by using this system. Furthermore, data labeling not only can make data more intuitive, but build privacy protection policies to minimize the risks caused by the leaks of consumers' privacy.

3.1 Service System Architecture Combing

According to the detailed user needs documents, the system architecture takes "searching for stores" - "operating stores" - "promotions" as user paths for information architecture combing.

According to the conclusions of the design research, this system takes the consumer label as the core to implement highly efficient and precise management service, so the above three journey phases are corresponding to three service tools: Consumers Community Analysis Tool, Consumers in-Store Service Tool and Community Marketing Decision Tool. The 3C tools include a number of sub-tools, and the main function hierarchy structural diagrams thereof are shown in Fig. 1.

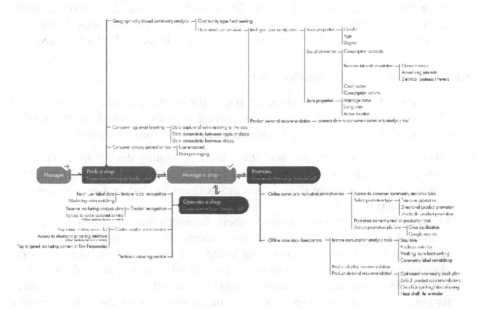

Fig. 1. Main function hierarchy structural diagrams.

3.2 Consumers Community Analysis Tool

As a service tool in the store searching stage, the consumers community analysis tool includes three sub-modules: respectively, (a) location-based community analysis, (b) consumer label smart learning and (c) consumer privacy protection tool:

(a) This system has already been prepared for providing service for retail managers before their store setting-up. First, the insight into location-based consumers will predict the passenger flow of the site selected by managers and make scientific stocking recommendations based on community personality label attributes. Compared to the previous ways that managers relied on the observation at selected spots and in-person visits, etc., this system can help retail managers make site selections more easily and scientifically. Second, this system can effectively reduce unnecessary store losses brought about by inaccurate stocking during the trial run by analyzing the attributes of passenger flow around the store. Since the system needs to be based on a large amount of social label data, it should consider accessing the Tencent MIND with the most abundant community resource data in order to achieve the goal of precisely targeting communities.

(b) Each purchase by a user is a piece of valuable data, so the purchase behaviors under this system will be transformed into label data to be fully prepared for the all-way marketing activities. The system needs to connect retailer's own APP data to retain users' habits; and multiple stores jointly manage and data are connected to one another... The data information of users gained through each channel is multi-dimensionally integrated to shape complete consumer labels.

(c) Since the system involves multiple user privacy, privacy protection policies must be designed at the system hierarchy. Thus, in this system, the system unifiedly generates user identification codes for all users, and all user data exist in the form of labels. In this way, all user information will not be manually backtracked.

3.3   Consumers in-Store Service Tool

As a service tool in the store operating stage, the consumers in-store service tool includes four sub-modules: respectively (a) entering-store face recognition, (b) emotion recognition, (c) centrally controlled voice service and (d) electronic price tag service:

(a) When a consumer enters the store, the cloud computing device inside the store starts to match and lock in the user, and retrieve the business interests under the user's label library to see if there is a promotional product in line with the consumer's interest label.

(b) When a user views the products on the shelf, the user's micro-expressions (positive emotion, hesitation or negative emotion) are identified at a certain frequency. When decision-making hesitation occurs, the voice assistant service is accessed at the electronic price tag to aid decision-making. Somber expression data would be recorded to reserve marketing analysis data (which will be used as the data source for goods personality analysis). To reduce development costs, the Azure cognitive service API is accessed in the storefront system.

(c) Replacing traditional centrally controlled broadcasting, the voice assistant can play music based on in-store consumers' music interests most of the time; and also broadcast targeted marketing contents to in-store consumers at a very low frequency. Broadcasted voice cannot be heard for being personal to someone, but the broadcasted marketing contents match the users' interests.

(d) Dynamic electronic price tags can conveniently adjust the displayed price and names of products in real time, and meanwhile can change interface display in some particular occasions, such as accessing the voice assistant image for users; the dynamic highlighting and flashing of promotional products and so on.

3.4   Community Marketing Decision Tool

As a service tool in the promotion stage, there are two sub-modules under the community marketing decision tool: respectively (a) online community marketing and promotion tool, (b) offline store stocking predicting tool. They are used to guide managers' marketing activities and complete complex tasks via one click.

(a) The online promotion module helps managers to reduce the barriers to Internet marketing technology, use the data of the consumers community analysis tool, provide the one-click production tool for promotion contents and directly access the landing pages on promotional platforms.

(b) The offline decision tool can provide managers with optimized stocking suggestions. A comprehensive analysis is carried out according to store sites, community labels, in-store consumption situations, consumption decision-making hesitation data, expired goods destruction and other data, and the longer the system is used, the more complete and the cleverer the self-learning of the system is. In addition, the tool is also directly connected with the stocking warehouse, so that it can be adjusted according to the stocking suggestions and generate a stocking plan via one click. For long-term backlogged goods, it will suggest stopping/reducing stocking, provide promotional advice so as to reduce losses.

4   Service System Interaction and Visual Design

Interaction and visual design processes are designed in accordance with the high-level, multi-channel, interactive-card design strategies. During the prototype design phase, according to the testing results of the alpha version, we need to visualize a large amount of data, simplify the bottom button and summarize the functional structure tree as three sections of "Dynamic Billboard", "Cloud Service" and "Me". Moreover, the "one-click completion" button is upgraded to the card to reduce click paths and improve operational efficiency. The high-fidelity prototype of the second version of shopkeep APP is shown in Fig. 2, and its visual design is shown in Fig. 3.

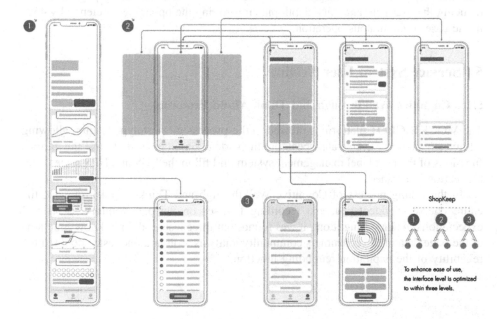

Fig. 2. Shopkeep APP high-fidelity prototype.

Fig. 3. Shopkeep APP visual design.

The interface color of the design can be changed according to stores and personal preferences, and the use of linear design allows users to better focus on the changes in data to meet the users' "exhilarating points". Also, most of the three-level and four-level operations are integrated into the one-level and two-level pages, greatly reducing the user path and click depth plus improving the operating efficiency by 45% in the case of continuous operation.

5   Service System User Testing

5.1   Cognitive Walkthrough and Think-Aloud Protocols

The MOCKINGBOT platform is utilized in the process for prototype testing, allowing 12 investigators to traverse and speak out their ideas simultaneously to test the various functions of the user label management system and fill in the SUS and NPS scales after the testing is finished.

In the testing process of Cognitive Walkthrough and Think-Aloud Protocols, the entire course is videotaped, and recording focuses on the part contrary to testees' expectations. After sorting it out, it was found that three testees did not know functions of the page data of the consumers community analysis tool; and one testee doubted the reliability of the expiration-reminding function.

5.2   SUS Testing

After traversing the system, the testees filled in the System Usability Scale, and the obtained SUS score was 82.5. The specific scale data are shown in Table 5.

Table 5. SUS scale results

Features	Original	Converted	SUS score
I think that I would like to use this system frequently	4.7	3.7	82.5 (A)
I found the system unnecessarily complex	2.1	2.9	
I thought the system was easy to use	4.3	3.3	
I think that I would need the support of a technical person to be able to use this system	1.2	3.8	
I found the three modules in this system were well integrated	4.1	3.1	
I thought there was too much inconsistency in this system	0.9	4.1	
I would imagine that most people would learn to use this system very quickly	4.1	3.1	
I found the system very cumbersome to use	1.8	3.2	
I felt very confident using the system	3.9	2.9	
I needed to learn a lot of things before I could get going with this system	2.1	2.9	

What's more, the score of learnability scale calculated based on the data was 83.75; and the score of usability scale was 82.19, which has increased by 10.6% compared with the testing results of the alpha version. The increase in SUS score shows that the service system provides a clearer interaction structure design after the second iteration, effectively lowering testees' cognitive difficulty and learning threshold.

5.3   NPS Testing

After the SUS testing, we collected testees' Net Promoter Score - 8.6, which has increased by 22.1% compared with that of the alpha version - 6.7. We interviewed three testees who participated in the testing twice. They held the application interfaces of the second version are more comfortable and modern, clearer in the differentiation of functions in the visual senses and easier to learn and use. Besides, we asked the testees who scored relatively high and low in terms of NPS about their scoring reasons, among which the testee scoring 6.7 said the application functions are not prominent enough to easily find the function he needs; and the testees scoring 9 to 10 said similar tools for guiding management are extremely scanty in the market, and the subdivided functions will be a tremendous help to them.

6   Conclusion and Prospect

After accomplishing the prototype design, multiple design testing is required to make the whole system more reasonable and easy to use. During the testing, it was found that the older testees with poorer learning ability have lower acceptance of the system, so the subsequent iterative design needs to focus on strengthening learnability.

This paper mainly discusses a manager service system and the entire service design process of its subsequent mobile application, starts with the social insight and demand survey to grasp the function needs of the system, establishes the system concepts and digs out the subdivided demand points in order to sort out the structure tree of the entire system, and finally in accordance with interaction strategies, conducts rolling design - testing - feedback – design on the system prototype to continuously improve services and application. Although the consumption characteristics and managers' business vary from region to region, the overall research framework and design process are of sustainable use and reference.

Furthermore, the limitation of this study lies in this system is a future-oriented manager service system in retail industry. Therefore, some modules and functions of offline stores currently require a relatively large amount of investment to be executable, but it's still feasible. The costs of the system will decline as technology costs in the future drop, enabling the business systems in smart cities to run more efficiently and provide better services by making good use of the big data at the retail level.

References

1. Say Goodbye to The Long Tail of Product Resellers. At Least on the Internet. https://techcrunch.com/2011/02/13/bye-bye-long-tail/. Accessed 13 Feb 2011
2. Xiaohong, L.: China O2O business model research. Jilin University (2015)
3. Yiqing, L., Chen, L.: O2O business model and development prospects. Bus. Econ. **11**, 98–101 (2013)
4. Hua, S.: Research on smart retail in big data environment. J. Xi'an Univ. Finance Econ. **02**, 41–46 (2016)
5. Ma: Pure electricity business will die! New retail era has come. http://www.sohu.com/a/116073016_188668/. Accessed 13 Oct 2016
6. Hongchi, S., ZhengJie, L.: Application research of B2C network marketing based on big data - a case study of retailing enterprises in China. J. Nat. Bus. **12**, 3–6 (2016)
7. Yong, Z.: Future Unmanned Convenience Store. Chin. Bus. **08**, 48–49 (2017)
8. Liping, X.: "New retail" Storm Struck. Shanghai Informatization **12**, 64–67 (2016)
9. Ning, N., Shao, J.: Precise advertising in the big data era and its propagation strategy - based on the perspective of field theory. Modem Spread (J. Commun. Univ. China) **36**(02), 99–104 (2014)
10. Junyang, L.: New Retail Concept Cannot Represent Future Dir. Retail Dev. Shanghai Bus. **02**, 18–19 (2017)

11. Gerrikagoitia, J.K., Castander, I., Rebon, F., et al.: New trends of intelligent e-marketing based on web mining for e-shops. Procedia – Soc. Behav. Sci. **175**, 75–83 (2015)
12. Changjie, L., Haydock, M.P.: IBM account analyst: big data prevents "hall phenomena" in retail stores. World Sci. **7**, 34, 28 (2014)
13. Qian, W.A.: "New Retail": from "Things to Gather Together" to "People in Groups" **12**, 48–49 (2016). Author, F.: Article title. Journal 2(5), 99–110 (2016)

Interacting and Driving

Human-Automation Interaction in Automated Vehicles: An Innovative HMI Design Approach. The Case of Elderly and Cyclists

Federico Fraboni, Marco De Angelis, David Plesnik, Andrea Altini, Marco Depolo,
Bruna Zani, Gabriele Prati, and Luca Pietrantoni[✉]

Department of Psychology, Alma Mater Studiorum, University of Bologna,
Via Berti Pichat 5, 40126 Bologna, Italy
luca.pietrantoni@unibo.it

Abstract. In recent years, significant progresses have been achieved in automated driving technologies and highly Automated Vehicles (AVs) are expected to become available to end-users within a decade. At the same time, many countries around the world are facing a demographic shift toward an aging society. Level 3 to 4 AVs will allow users to be released from the driving task for extended periods; however, they will be requested to take back control of the vehicle in specific situations. In the specific case of older road users, take over request stations could lead to significant complications in safety as well as mobility. Furthermore, communication needs to grant safe interactions between AVs and vulnerable road users, such as cyclists, should be deeply investigated and solutions should be proposed. This highlights the importance of designing AVs interfaces that are user friendly, safe, adaptable, and accessible for elderly drivers and for vulnerable road users.

The present study aims at developing and testing an innovative framework for designing inclusive and adaptive HMIs, both addressing AVs users' (elderlies) and other traffic participants (cyclists) basing on the Efficient Driver-Vehicle Cooperation Model proposed by Kraus et al. [1], integrating driver behavior models and user state assessment technologies. The model foresees that successful human-automation cooperation can be understood as the result of a relationship building process comparable to human relationships. Antecedents of safe and enjoyable interactions with highly AVs have been assessed and used as a basis for developing the framework, focusing on the psychological processes during the initial encounters with a system, in which system features interact with personality factors in building up beliefs and attitudes about a system affecting the further usage of the system. The proposed framework is integrating driver state assessment technologies and knowledge on human behavior to establish situation appropriate task function allocation between the driver and the vehicle. Our study is providing insights specific on vulnerable road users (e.g. elderly) characteristics and needs in designing interfaces.

Keywords: Automated vehicles · HMI adaptation · Elderly users · Cyclists

C. Stephanidis (Ed.): HCII Posters 2018, CCIS 852, pp. 359–366, 2018.
https://doi.org/10.1007/978-3-319-92285-0_48

1   Introduction

Automated vehicles (AVs) are seen as one of the key technologies and major techno-logical advancements with the potential to influence and shape our future mobility and quality of life [2]. In recent years, significant progresses have been achieved in auto-mated driving technologies and level 3 to 4 AVs are expected to become available to end-user market within a decade [3]. The advent of autonomous vehicles and automated driving have the potential to bring considerable benefits to modern societies, specifically: increasing road safety through reducing accidents caused by human errors; increasing transport system efficiency, reducing road congestion, energy consumption and emission of vehicles; increase users' comfort and freedom, enabling users to engage in other activities when on board of AVs; ensure mobility for impaired users and elderly.

This last point is particularly relevant considering that many countries around the world are facing a demographic shift toward an aging society. Because of higher life expectancy and consistently low birth rates there is a shift of the age distribution in global population. According to predictions of UN [4], the number of people aged 60 and above will double from 962 million in 2017 to 2.1 billion in 2050, while the number of people aged 80 and over will triple from 137 million in 2017 to 425 million in 2050. Level 3 to 4 AVs will allow users to be released from the driving task for extended periods, however they will be requested to take back control of the vehicle in specific situations. The increase in the elderly population will result in a growing demand of transport systems in many countries and an increase of older road users, which could lead to significant complications in safety as well as mobility and sustainability. This highlights the importance of designing user friendly, safe, adaptable and accessible for elderly drivers AVs interfaces.

Furthermore, [5], through an aggregation of the material found on Scopus, indicate that social science references linked to AVs represent less than 6% of the total. This suggests that most AV related research, primarily academic, has focused on technical and technological aspects of AVs and not on the associated social and behavioral issues. With that said, one of the major research needs in the field of AVs is the integration of human factors in the design of HMI for AVs, considering human needs, behaviors and users' characteristics, aiming at developing ways to foster efficient human-automation interaction and collaboration.

Vulnerable Road Users (VRU) are defined in the ITS Directive as "road users, such as pedestrians and cyclists as well as motor-cyclists and persons with disabilities or reduced mobility and orientation". According to this definition, traffic participants can be included in the VRUs category according the mode of transport used (e.g. bicycle, mopeds, etc.) and by user characteristics (e.g. elderly with different for of disabilities).

1.1   Gender and Age Differences in Automated Vehicles Studies

To design HMIs and effective strategies to foster efficient and safe human-automation collaboration it is crucial to consider users' personal characteristics. Recent studies focused mostly on gender and age differences in acceptance, considering attitudes, trust and intention to use as its components. Trust and Intention to use are classic constructs of technology acceptance models [6–8] and represent the degree of users' trust in automation and their intention to actually use the system, respectively. König and Neumayr [9] studied differences in attitudes dependent on personal characteristics, and they found that females, older people and people living in urban areas (as opposed to rural ones) tended also to bear less positive attitudes towards AVs. Many studies have tried to assess the difference between male and female about technology-related anxiety. There is a tendency to find greater anxiety among females than males about technology use [10]. Similarly, some research reported more driving anxiety among women than men [11]. Hohenberger et al. [12] explored anxiety and pleasure related to AVs' usage and found that men were more likely to feel pleasure than women whereas women were more likely to feel anxiety than men. A recent meta-analysis of the effect of gender on attitudes towards technology use show that men have more positive attitude towards the use of new technologies than women [13]. The authors investigated the components of attitudes and observed that the gender difference in affect and self-efficacy is decreasing, while the difference regarding beliefs about the use and societal function of new technologies remain constant. Our research considers these gender-related specificities when proposing a theoretical framework for HMI in AVs. It is of utmost importance to consider those results when designing HMI for AVs in order to reduce barriers to acceptance.

As level 3 to 4 AVs require the driver to take over in specific situations (i.e. take-over request scenarios), driving behavior continues to be a relevant subject of study when considering AV usage of elder population. The effects of age on driving behavior were studied extensively in psychological literature. While the most examined set of variables mediating this relationship are cognitive abilities, researchers in more recent works [14] call for greater attention for integrating affects in research of elders' driving behavior. A meta-analysis of the association between driving anger and driving outcomes [15] shows that this link is weaker in younger adults than in elders, suggesting that older drivers have a lower risk of driving disruptively because of anger. It is important to note that the negative stereotypes about elderly drivers are the major cause of lower cognitive abilities [16].

1.2 User Interface for Elderly

An efficient and useful human-computer interface must consider the abilities of the users who will operate it and anticipate the eventual difficulties that different users (e.g. elderly) must adapt and deal with [17]. A study by Phiriyapokanon [18] (2011), highlighted that layering different modes of information in interface design can reduce older users' cognitive workload. Another relevant concept to be taken into account when designing user interfaces are interactive interfaces [19, 20]. Furthermore, Hasan and Ahmed [21] found that the interactive interface concept has direct influence on users' perceived ease of use and perceived usefulness.

1.3   External Interfaces Addressing Cyclists

Nowadays, the interaction between motorized vehicles and vulnerable road users, such as cyclists is particularly critical in terms of traffic safety [22–24]. To maximize the potential benefits of introducing AVs in urban roads it is crucial to address the interactions and communication between AVs and vulnerable road users (i.e. cyclists and pedestrians). This topic has received limited attention in literature so far, but the number studies addressing vulnerable road users' interactions with AVs is increasing [25]. These interactions rely on the interpretation of two clusters of signals: (a) vehicle dynamics and other vehicle-centric cues using signs, lights and sound; and (b) through gestures, postures, and eye contact between drivers and cyclists [26]. Establishing eye contact serves as a confirmation that a driver and a cyclist have noticed each other [27]. In AVs, with the transfer of control from the driver to the vehicle, there is a risk that pedestrians will not be able to rely on these driver-centric cues anymore. Observational studies have shown that cyclists, when crossing red-light controlled intersections, heavily rely on visual search strategies to find a gap in the oncoming traffic flow [28].

Recent findings indicate that the communicative needs may change due to use of vehicle automation [26]. To sustain a high level of cyclists' perceived safety in the interaction with AVs, it could be beneficial to provide the cyclist with the corresponding information in some other way (e.g., by means of an external vehicle interface). Those interfaces could also be integrated with wireless detection technology of cyclists, increasing the communication potential and thus the perceived safety [29]. Furthermore, it is important to take into consideration that negative attitudes towards cyclists can influence the acceptance of safety system technologies addressing cyclists [30].

1.4   Human-Machine Cooperation in Automated Driving

In the studies focused on automated driving (AD) systems of SAE Level 3, the focus is mainly on transitions of control between manual driving (MD) and AD [31]. Specifically, the requests for switching from AD to MD from the side of the system in takeover scenarios ("take-over request", TOR) receive a great degree of attention [32, 33], since this situation can raise significant safety concerns, especially if the driver fails to take over vehicle control. However, there is an evidence gap for scenarios in which an operating AD system shares the control authority with the human driver and our research aims to expand the knowledge base of this issue.

In our view, design of AV HMIs with the capacity of mutual communication with the driver should consider that the driver has to be aware of the system limits in advance, especially in take-over situations [34].

Furthermore, the users tend to attribute intentionality and rationality automated systems, which, in some cases, are considered to be "team members" [35]. This shows that humans are inherently interested in understanding the functioning of automated systems in the attempt to understand and predict behavior of such systems.

The means used by the system to communicate with the driver are another topic covered by our study. As the driver is likely to be engaged in secondary tasks, it is necessary to direct her or his attention to the relevant information about the traffic situation and provide this information in clear and understandable way. Given that elder drivers might have difficulties perceiving certain types of alerts, we hypothesize that the use of multi-modal alerts (i.e. of those that use a combination of visual, haptic, and auditory stimuli) will elicit quicker driver responses than single-mode alerts. This effect was reported by Ho et al. [36], who showed the benefits in term of response time when using a multi-modality warning signals. In multi-modality conditions, the information processing was performing better as well as the spatial experience.

Shared control framework for vehicle control is a frame of reference for research focused on human-machine cooperation within the automotive domain [37].

According to Guo et al. [38], HMI design is one of key factors which enable efficient cooperation between the system and the driver. These authors state that the following HMI principles should be applied when designing AV HMIs:

- Showing the driving context. This principle follows the concept of common frame of reference as proposed by Hoc [39]. The system should be able to provide information about the driving context so that it shares the perception of the driving situation with the driver.
- The system communicates its intentions to the driver and provides available alternatives.
- The system provides a way for the driver to choose an alternative.

Sethumadhavan [40] provides several suggestions about designing safer Human-Automation Interaction:

- Automation user interfaces should increase the situational awareness of the driver and enable her or him to understand the traffic situations;
- As the behavior of the system changes because of learning, it should communicate these changes to the user to enable her or him to update the mental model of the system's functioning;
- The system should be able to cooperate with the driver, coordinate their intentions and behavior, and collaborate to reach the destination safely.

1.5 Challenges in Human-Automation Interaction and Cooperation

According to the aforementioned notions, in order to foster efficient human-automation collaboration and pleasant interactions between the vehicle and its user, AVs interfaces should be strictly interconnect with the vehicle artificial intelligence. Such artificial intelligence and it's HMIs should be capable of:

- Dynamically recognize partially unknown behavior patterns that were not originally implemented in the system;
- Interacting with humans through fine, low-latency yet socially acceptable control strategies;
- Use natural and multi-modal communication strategies which mandates common-sense knowledge and the representation of possibly divergent mental models;
- Assess user states and identify the user's individual and collaborative cognitive skills;
- Planning and distributing tasks for the driver and the vehicle based on the situation;

The present study focuses focus on a specific class of interactions: human–robot collaborative task achievement supported by multi-modal and situated communication.

The study will contribute in defining and test an innovative framework for AVs' HMI design, capable of achieving efficient human-automation collaboration by taking into account, at every stage, the intentions, skills and behavior of its human partner. According to the proposed concept, AVs must be able to recognize, understand and participate in communication actions. As for the driving task, the vehicle should be able to take part in joint actions, both pro-actively (by planning and proposing resulting plans to the human) and reactively, similarly to what has been tested for automated robots by Lemaignan et al. [41].

Acknowledgments. This work was supported by the European Commission under the Horizon 2020 Framework Program of the European Union (2014–2020). Project XCYCLE contract number: 635975.

References

1. Kraus, J.M., Sturn, J., Reiser, J.E., Baumann, M.: Anthropomorphic agents, transparent automation and driver personality: towards an integrative multi-level model of determinants for effective driver-vehicle cooperation in highly automated vehicles. In: Adjunct Proceedings of the 7th International Conference on Automotive User Interfaces and Interactive Vehicular Applications, pp. 8–13. ACM (2015). https://doi.org/10.1145/2809730.2809738
2. Fleetwood, J.: Public health, ethics, and autonomous vehicles. Am. J. Publ. Health **107**(4), 532–537 (2017). https://doi.org/10.2105/AJPH.2016.303628
3. ERTRAC Automated Driving Roadmap (2017). http://www.ertrac.org/uploads/documentsearch/id48/ERTRAC_Automated_Driving_2017.pdf
4. United Nations (2017). https://www.un.org/development/desa/publications/world-population-prospects-the-2017-revision.html
5. Cavoli, C., Phillips, B., Cohen, T., Jones, P.: Social and behavioural questions associated with automated vehicles: a literature review. Department for Transport, London (2017)
6. Davis, F.D.: Perceived usefulness, perceived ease of use, and user acceptance of information technology. MIS Q. **13**(3), 319–340 (1989). https://doi.org/10.2307/249008
7. Ghazizadeh, M., Lee, J.D., Boyle, L.N.: Extending the technology acceptance model to assess automation. Cogn. Technol. Work **14**(1), 39–49 (2012). https://doi.org/10.1007/s10111-011-0194-3
8. Venkatesh, V., Morris, M.G., Davis, G.B., Davis, F.D.: User acceptance of information technology: toward a unified view. MIS Q. **27**(3), 425–478 (2003). https://doi.org/10.2307/30036540
9. König, M., Neumayr, L.: Users' resistance towards radical innovations: the case of the self-driving car. Transp. Res. Part F Traffic Psychol. Behav. **44**, 42–52 (2017). https://doi.org/10.1016/j.trf.2016.10.013
10. Schottenbauer, M.A., Rodriguez, B.F., Glass, C.R., Arnkoff, D.B.: Computers, anxiety, and gender: an analysis of reactions to the Y2K computer problem. Comput. Hum. Behav. **20**(1), 67–83 (2004)
11. Gwyther, H., Holland, C.: The effect of age, gender and attitudes on self-regulation in driving. Accid. Anal. Prev. **45**, 19–28 (2012). https://doi.org/10.1016/j.aap.2011.11.022

12. Hohenberger, C., Spörrle, M., Welpe, I.M.: How and why do men and women differ in their willingness to use automated cars? The influence of emotions across different age groups. Transp. Res. Part A Policy Pract. **94**, 374–385 (2016). https://doi.org/10.1016/j.tra.2016.09.022

13. Cai, Z., Fan, X., Du, J.: Gender and attitudes toward technology use: a meta-analysis. Comput. Educ. **105**, 1–13 (2017). https://doi.org/10.1016/j.compedu.2016.11.003

14. Jeon, M.: Towards affect-integrated driving behaviour research. Theor. Issues Ergon. Sci. **16**(6), 553–585 (2015). https://doi.org/10.1080/1463922X.2015.1067934

15. Zhang, T., Chan, A.H.: The association between driving anger and driving outcomes: a meta-analysis of evidence from the past twenty years. Accid. Anal. Prev. **90**, 50–62 (2016)

16. Lamont, R.A., Swift, H.J., Abrams, D.: A review and meta-analysis of age-based stereotype threat: negative stereotypes, not facts, do the damage. Psychol. Aging **30**(1), 180 (2015)

17. Hsiao, S.W., Lee, C.H., Yang, M.H., Chen, R.Q.: User interface based on natural interaction design for seniors. Comput. Hum. Behav. **75**, 147–159 (2017). https://doi.org/10.1016/j.chb.2017.05.011

18. Phiriyapokanon, T.: Is a big button interface enough for elderly users? Toward user interface guidelines for elderly users. Masters thesis, Computer Engineer, Malardalen University, Vasteras, Sweden (2011)

19. Chen, C.L., Xie, S.: Freehand drawing system using a fuzzy logic concept. Comput. Aided Des. **28**(2), 77–89 (1996). https://doi.org/10.1016/0010-4485(95)00026-7

20. Han, J.Y.: Multi-touch interaction wall. In: Proceedings of the ACM SIGGRAPH 2006 Emerging Technologies (2006)

21. Hasan, B., Ahmed, M.U.: Effects of interface style on user perceptions and behavioral intention to use computer systems. Comput. Hum. Behav. **23**(6), 3025–3037 (2007). https://doi.org/10.1016/j.chb.2006.08.016

22. Marín Puchades, V., Prati, G., Rondinella, G., De Angelis, M., Fassina, F., Fraboni, F., Pietrantoni, L.: Cyclists' anger as determinant of near misses involving different road users. Front. Psychol. **8**, 2203 (2017). https://doi.org/10.3389/fpsyg.2017.02203

23. Prati, G., Marín Puchades, V., De Angelis, M., Fraboni, F., Pietrantoni, L.: Factors contributing to bicycle–motorised vehicle collisions: a systematic literature review. Transp. Rev. **38**, 184–208 (2018). https://doi.org/10.1080/01441647.2017.1314391

24. Prati, G., Fraboni, F., Pietrantoni, L.: Using data mining techniques to predict the severity of bicycle crashes. Accid. Anal. Prev. **101**, 44–54 (2017). https://doi.org/10.1016/j.aap.2017.01.008

25. Schieben, A., Wilbrink, M., Kettwich, C., Madigan, R., Louw, T., Merat, N.: Designing the interaction of automated vehicles with other traffic participants: a design framework based on human needs and expectations. Cognition, Technology and Work (2018)

26. Lundgren, V.M, Habibovic, A., Andersson, J., Lagström, T., Nilsson, M., Sirkka, A., Saluäär, D.: Will there be new communication needs when introducing automated vehicles to the urban context? In: Advances in Human Aspects of Transportation, pp. 485–497. Springer, Cham (2017). https://doi.org/10.1007/978-3-319-41682-3_41

27. Šucha, M.: Road users' strategies and communication: driver-pedestrian interaction. In: 2014 Proceedings of Transport Research Arena (TRA) (2014)

28. Fraboni, F., Marin Puchades, V., De Angelis, M., Prati, G., Pietrantoni, L.: Social influence and different types of red-light behaviors among cyclists. Front. Psychol. **7**, 1834 (2016). https://doi.org/10.3389/fpsyg.2016.01834

29. Dardari, D., Decarli, N., Guerra, A., Al-Rimawi, A., Marín Puchades, V., Prati, G., Pietrantoni, L.: High-accuracy tracking using ultrawideband signals for enhanced safety of cyclists. Mob. Inf. Syst. **2017**, 1–13 (2017). https://doi.org/10.1155/2017/8149348

30. De Angelis, M., Marín Puchades, V., Fraboni, F., Pietrantoni, L., Prati, G.: Negative attitudes towards cyclists influence the acceptance of an in-vehicle cyclist detection system. Transp. Res. Part F Traffic Psychol. Behav. **49**, 244–256 (2017). https://doi.org/10.1016/j.trf. 2017.06.021

31. Marinik, A., Bishop, R., Fitchett, V.L., Morgan, J.F., Trimble, T.E., Blanco, M.: Human factors evaluation of level 2 and level 3 automated driving concepts: concepts of operation (2014)

32. Lorenz, L., Kerschbaum, P., Schumann, J.: Designing take over scenarios for automated driving: how does augmented reality support the driver to get back into the loop? In: Proceedings of the Human Factors and Ergonomics Society Annual Meeting, vol. 58, no. 1, pp. 1681–1685. SAGE Publications, Los Angeles (2014)

33. Walch, M., Lange, K., Baumann, M., Weber, M.: Autonomous driving: investigating the feasibility of car-driver handover assistance. In: Proceedings of the 7th International Conference on Automotive User Interfaces and Interactive Vehicular Applications, pp. 11–18. ACM (2015)

34. Wiedemann, K., Schömig, N., Mai, C., Naujoks, F., Neukum, A.: Drivers' monitoring behaviour and interaction with non-driving related tasks during driving with different automation levels. In: Proceedings of 6th International Conference on Applied Human Factors and Ergonomics, Las Vegas, USA (2015)

35. Naujoks, F., Forster, Y., Wiedemann, K., Neukum, A.: A human-machine interface for co-operative highly automated driving. In: Advances in Human Aspects of Transportation, pp. 585–595 (2017). https://doi.org/10.1007/978-3-319-41682-3_49

36. Ho, C., Reed, N., Spence, C.: Multisensory in-car warning signals for collision avoidance. Hum. Factors **49**(6), 1107–1114 (2007)

37. Sentouh, C., Popieul, J.-C., Debernard, S., Boverie, S.: Human-machine interaction in automated vehicle: the ABV project. IFAC Proc. **47**(3), 6344–6349 (2014)

38. Guo, C., Sentouh, C., Popieul, J.C., Haué, J.B., Langlois, S., Loeillet, J.J., That, T.N.: Cooperation between driver and automated driving system: implementation and evaluation. Transp. Res. Part F Traffic Psychol. Behav. (2017, in press)

39. Hoc, J.M.: Towards a cognitive approach to human–machine cooperation in dynamic situations. Int. J. Hum. Comput. Stud. **54**(4), 509–540 (2001)

40. Sethumadhavan, A.: Self-driving cars: enabling safer human–automation interaction. Ergonom. Des. **25**(2), 25–25 (2017). https://doi.org/10.1177/1064804617697283

41. Lemaignan, S., Warnier, M., Sisbot, E.A., Clodic, A., Alami, R.: Artificial cognition for social human–robot interaction: an implementation. Artif. Intell. **247**, 45–69(2017)

Driver Drowsiness Detection Using EEG Features

Se-Hyeon Hwang[1], Myoungouk Park[1], Jonghwa Kim[2],
Yongwon Yun[2], and Joonwoo Son[1(✉)]

[1] DGIST (Daegu Gyeongbuk Institute Science and Technology),
Daegu 42988, Republic of Korea
json@dgist.ac.kr
[2] KATRI (Korea Automobile Testing & Research Institute),
Hwaseong-si 18247, Republic of Korea

Abstract. The objective of this paper is to discover the EEG (Electroencephalogram) features that expressed meaningful changes during drowsy driving state compared to the normal driving. For this purpose, 8 healthy male and female participants were recruited to conduct drowsy driving experiment in a fixed-base driving simulator, which reproduced the inside of the actual vehicle. The experimental scenario was driving a 37 km straight highway without any obstacles. The data obtained through this experiment were analyzed using brain wave analysis software. As a result, we found that the alpha RMS (Root mean square) and differentiated alpha RMS waves showed meaningful changes during drowsiness state compared to normal state. In addition, we suggested new brain activity index, which was composed of four brain waves that are alpha, beta, theta and delta, to amplify meaningful change in transition from normal state to drowsiness.

The statistical significances of the selected EEG features were tested using One-way ANOVA (Analysis of variance). The result indicated that all three EEG features showed statistical significance ($p < 0.005$). In conclusion, this paper suggested EEG features which have high accuracy for drowsiness detection. Currently, EEG measurement equipment such as dry type and non-contact type is actively developed. Therefore, it is expected that the drowsiness prevention system using the EEG features will be available in the near future.

Keywords: Drowsy driving · EEG (Electroencephalogram)
Brain activity index · Drowsiness detection

1 Introduction

1.1 A Subsection Sample

The SHRP 2 NDS (Second Strategic Highway Research Program Naturalistic Driving Study) survey to determine the prevalence of driver drowsiness before the crash showed that drowsiness driving is far more dangerous than our perception [7]. Currently, drowsiness driving detection is performed using various factors such as EEG,

© Springer International Publishing AG, part of Springer Nature 2018
C. Stephanidis (Ed.): HCII Posters 2018, CCIS 852, pp. 367–374, 2018.
https://doi.org/10.1007/978-3-319-92285-0_49

EOG (Electrooculography), PERCLOS (Percentage closure of eyes) and so on. The EEG-based studies uses the ratios of EEG slow and high frequency bands, VSWs (Vertex Sharp Waves), and the changes of alpha wave to detect drowsiness [8, 15]. However, EEG has a disadvantage that is difficult to accurately detect drowsiness because there is a large difference between individuals.

This study suggests EEG features that can be used to detect drowsiness for any drivers using Z-score values of EEG features. Furthermore, these factors have the possibility that can be made into a real-time model because the state of driver can be calculated in 100 ms interval. In addition, the ANOVA result shows significant difference for the three EEG features.

2   Method

2.1   Apparatus

Figure 1 showed the fixed-base driving simulator used in the research. The device consisted of a DLP (Data loss prevention) projector, a screen, a control PC, and a simulator vehicle that reproduced the interior of Hyundai Genesis's interior. The driving simulation software was STISIM Drive of Systems Technology, Inc. of USA.

Fig. 1. Fixed-based driving simulator

2.2   Data Collection

B-ALERT X10 [1] was used as a device to measure the EEG data of participants. The EEG data was collected by attaching electrodes to 9 positions, i.e. POz, Fz, Cz, C3, C4, F3, F4, P3, P4 according to 10–20 system. We used decontaminated signals window that eliminates five disturbance factors caused by EMG, eye blinks, excursions, saturations, and spikes. To analyze the measured EEG data, BIOPAC AcqKnowledge 5.0 Software was used [5]. The EEG frequency bands were set to 0.5–4 Hz for delta wave, 4–8 Hz for theta wave, 8–13 Hz for alpha wave, 13–30 Hz for beta wave, and 36–44 Hz for gamma wave.

2.3   Experiment Procedure

The experiment procedure was designed so that the participants visited twice. On the first day, the participants were checked about the eligibility and wrote consent of the experiment. On the second day, we checked the compliance and conducted the drowsy driving experiment twice. During the experiment, the face of participant was logged as shown in Fig. 2. Then, the time when the participant's drowsiness was marked based on the predefined drowsiness state (Table 1) through manual video inspection. Table 1 shows the criteria for judging the status of participants. The criteria were developed based on the Karolinska sleepiness scale (KSS) [2].

Fig. 2. Face image of participant

Table 1. Table captions should be placed above the tables.

State	Drowsiness pattern
Awakening state (0)	Eye blinking was relatively constant and stable driving
Initial drowsiness state (1)	Eye blinking was slower than arousal and the eyelids were closed and did not open for more than 2 s
Drowsiness state (2)	If the driver lost the center of gravity of the head, If the accident was occurred, If the eyelids were closed and did not open for more than 3 s

2.4   Data Collection

Based on the previous study [6], the values of alpha, delta, alpha RMS(or A RMS, it is windowed root mean square value of the signal using a window width of 0.25 s) wave were obtained by averaging waves measured from POz, Fz, and Cz. Theta wave was obtained by averaging waves measured from POz and Fz. Beta wave was measured from POz.

2.5   Data Reduction

We extracted 240 s length of each EEG data. Each data was extracted between 10 s before the beginning of drowsiness period and 10 s after the end of drowsiness period and included all drowsiness periods. All data were normalized by converting the data into Z-score values and reduced by averaging the data values at every interval of 100 ms for ANOVA test.

3   Results

3.1   Simulated Driving Experiment

Fourteen experimental data were obtained from 8 participants. One participant's data was seriously contaminated by movement artifact, e.g., he had heavy arm movements during the experiment and moved his head very severely at the drowsiness state. Therefore, the data was removed from the analysis. Finally, we used 13 data from 7 participants in the study.

3.2   EEG Feature Selection

In this study, we suggested three EEG features for drowsiness driving detection. The first EEG feature was A RMS. Based on the previous studies [4, 12] that showed the relationship between RMS and human state, we used A RMS as a drowsiness detection factor. Figure 3(a) shows that the value of A RMS increased dramatically at the drowsy state.

The second EEG feature was the value of differentiated A RMS that is called dA RMS. It was devised in view of the sudden increase in the value of A RMS at the drowsy state. Figure 3(b) showed that the average value of dA RMS at the drowsiness state was generally lower than the average value at the normal state even if there were several sudden sharp rises at the drowsy state.

The third EEG feature was the most emphasized function expression in the paper. It is called the BAI (Brain activity index). Equation (1) represented the expression of BAI.

$$\mathrm{BAI} = \left| \left(\frac{dAlpha\,value}{dt} + \frac{dTheta\,value}{dt} \right) * \frac{dDelta\,value}{dt} - \frac{dBeta\,value}{dt} \right| \quad (1)$$

Based on the previous study [3], BAI used the differential values of the four bands of alpha, theta, delta and beta of the EEG. In addition, based on the other studies [6, 9, 14], we summed the differential values of alpha and theta waves and then multiplied by differential value of delta wave, and subtracted the differential value of beta wave. The BAI had large values at the drowsiness state as shown in Fig. 3(c).

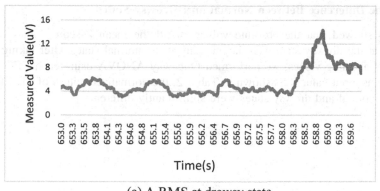

(a) A RMS at drowsy state

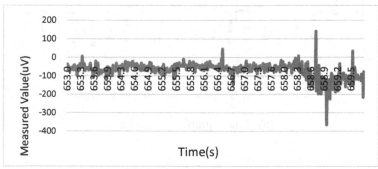

(b) dA RMS at drowsy state

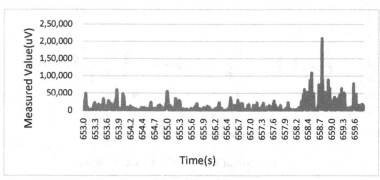

(c) BAI at drowsy state

Fig. 3. EEG features at the drowsy state of the same participant (In these graphs, it entered the drowsiness state at around 658 s)

3.3 The Difference Between Normal and Drowsy States

Figure 4 showed that the absolute values of all the mean Z-score values of EEG features at the drowsy state were larger than at the normal state. After taking all the values as absolute values, we performed One-way ANOVA using each EEG feature and state as input values. As shown in Table 2, the normalized values of EEG features between normal and drowsy states were significantly different.

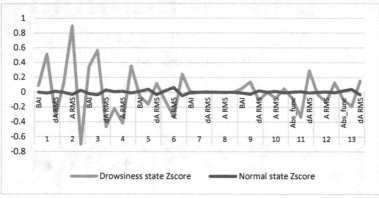

(a) Linear graph of EEG Features

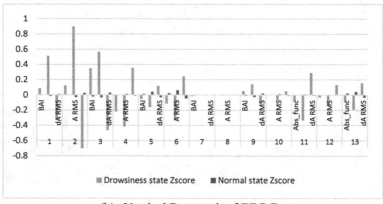

(b) Vertical Bar graph of EEG Features

Fig. 4. Graphs of mean values at the two states of each EEG feature

Table 2. ANOVA test result.

EEG feature	d.f.	F-value	P-value
BAI	1	11.0126	0.0031
A RMS	1	15.4335	0.0007
dA RMS	1	15.8506	0.0006

4 Discussion and Conclusion

The signs of the mean Z-score values of BAI and A RMS at the drowsy state were the same in all data. In four data BAI and A RMS had positive signs, but in the others BAI and A RMS had negative signs. By comparing the results with the previous studies [10, 11, 13], we confirmed that there is no problem even if BAI and A RMS have any sign. Therefore, the EEG features of this paper can be used to detect drowsiness for any drivers.

In the paper, only three of the EEG channels, i.e. Cz, Fz and POz were used, since the contaminations were severe in other channels. We performed a limited EEG analysis using a small number of EEG channels. Above all, the Z-score values of the EEG features were used in this paper, so it cannot be used for actual driving immediately. Therefore, it is a future work to develop a tool to measure EEG data without the driver feeling uncomfortable and collects EEG data which is not contaminated by movement artifacts.

Despite the limitation, the proposed EEG-based drowsiness detection model that has simple calculation process just using three EEG features and can be a real-time model because calculates the data in 0.1 s increments will be a promising approach in the near future.

Acknowledgements. This work was supported in part by a grant (code 18TLRP-B131486-02) from Transportation and Logistics R&D Program funded by Ministry of Land, Infrastructure and Transport of Korean government, and by DGIST R&D Program (18-BT-01) of the Ministry of Science and ICT of Korean government.

References

1. Advanced Brain Monitoring. http://www.advancedbrainmonitoring.com/xseries/x10/. Accessed 16 Mar 2018
2. Åkerstedt, T., Gillberg, M.: Subjective and objective sleepiness in the active individual. Int. J. Neurosci. **52**(1–2), 29–37 (1990)
3. Antoniol, G., Tonella, P.: EEG data compression techniques. IEEE Trans. Biomed. Eng. **44** (2), 105–114 (1997)
4. Bernstein, A.S., Riedel, J.A.: Psychophysiological response patterns in college students with high physical anhedonia: Scores appear to reflect schizotypy rather than depression. Biol. Psychiatry **22**(7), 829–847 (1987)
5. BIOPAC Systems, Inc. https://www.biopac.com/manual/acqknowledge-5-software-guide/. Accessed 16 Mar 2018
6. Borghini, G., Astolfi, L., Vecchiato, G., Mattia, D., Babiloni, F.: Measuring neurophysiological signals in aircraft pilots and car drivers for the assessment of mental workload, fatigue and drowsiness. Neurosci. Biobehav. Rev. **44**, 58–75 (2014)
7. Dingus, T.A., Hankey, J.M., Antin, J.F., Lee, S.E., Eichelberger, L., Stulce, K.E., McGraw, D., Perez, M., Stowe, L.: Naturalistic driving study: technical coordination and quality control (No. SHRP 2 Report S2-S06-RW-1) (2015)
8. Eoh, H.J., Chung, M.K., Kim, S.H.: Electroencephalographic study of drowsiness in simulated driving with sleep deprivation. Int. J. Ind. Ergonomics **35**(4), 307–320 (2005)

9. Jarrett, D.B., Greenhouse, J.B., Miewald, J.M., Fedorka, I.B., Kupfer, D.J.: A reexamination of the relationship between growth hormone secretion and slow wave sleep using delta wave analysis. Biol. Psychiatry **27**(5), 497–509 (1990)

10. Lal, S.K., Craig, A.: Driver fatigue: psychophysiological effects. In: 4th International Conference on Fatigue and Transportation, Fremantle, Western Australia (2000)

11. Lal, S.K., Craig, A.: A critical review of the psychophysiology of driver fatigue. Biol. Psychol. **55**(3), 173–194 (2001)

12. Mak, J.N., McFarland, D.J., Vaughan, T.M., McCane, L.M., Tsui, P.Z., Zeitlin, D.J., Sellers, E.W., Wolpaw, J.R.: EEG correlates of P300-based brain–computer interface (BCI) performance in people with amyotrophic lateral sclerosis. J. Neural Eng. **9**(2) (2012)

13. Santamaria, J., Chiappa, K.H.: The EEG of drowsiness in normal adults. J. Clinical Neurophysiol. **4**(4), 327–382 (1987)

14. Visu, P., Varunkumar, K.A., Srinivasan, R., Kumar, R.V.: Brainwave based accident avoidance system for drowsy drivers. Indian J. Sci. Technol. **9**(3) (2016)

15. Yeo, M.V., Li, X., Wilder-Smith, E.P.: Characteristic EEG differences between voluntary recumbent sleep onset in bed and involuntary sleep onset in a driving simulator. Clin. Neurophysiol. **118**(6), 1315–1323 (2007)

Head and Neck Supporting for Seating

Ghi-Hwei Kao[1,2(✉)] and T. K. Philip Hwang[1,3]

[1] National Taipei University of Technology, Taipei 110, Taiwan
ghi.box@gmail.com
[2] Oriental Institute of Technology, New Taipei City 22061, Taiwan
[3] Da-Yeh University, Changhua 51591, Taiwan
phwang@mail.dyu.edu.tw

Abstract. This study aimed to improve comfort of cabin seat. Traditional cabin seats provide the user with a pillow-like head support which might force the user bending the spine curvature. In this case, spinal vertebrae can not maintain a nature cervical curve to withstand gravity, resulting in neck and shoulder compressive stress. Moreover, maintaining a fixed sitting posture for long period of time might lead to static muscular efforts, which results in muscular aches or pain. In order to provide users with a proper support for head, a three V-shape headrest was proposed with carefully designed headrest height for optimal neck posture. The three V-shape headrests provide the user with changeable head position which helps maintain neck flexibility. Most importantly, the coordination of seat back and headrest would prevent forward head carriage which is often overlooked in terms of a cause for neck pain.

Keywords: Forward head posture (FHP) · Ergonomics · Seat design
Universal design

1 Introduction

Seating comfort is an important issue in long distance transportation vehicles.

The survey form Institute of Occupational Safety and Health (2003) pointed out that up to 86.3% of bus drivers have musculoskeletal discomfort, owing to that truck drivers have to maintain a fixed position for a long to in the limited space. Over time poor posture results in pain, muscle aches, tension and headache and can lead to long term complications such as osteoarthritis (2009).

1.1 Neck and Shoulder Stress

When travelling, passengers maintain a fixed posture for hours and often complain about neck and back pain. According to the observation, most of seat designs are using a pillow-like headrest on chair back which might force user's head forward. According to Cailliet (1993) M. D., former director of the department of physical medicine and rehabilitation at the University of Southern California, maintaining a forward head posture causes stress concentration in the neck and shoulder.

© Springer International Publishing AG, part of Springer Nature 2018
C. Stephanidis (Ed.): HCII Posters 2018, CCIS 852, pp. 375–380, 2018.
https://doi.org/10.1007/978-3-319-92285-0_50

In recent years, most of seat designs are more emphasis on innovative design, generous seat space; comfort features such as seat material, and rarely pay attentions to ergonomics like the neck and back pain caused by long time use.

1.2   Preventing a Forward Head Posture

According to the shortcomings of the traditional passenger seat which users familiar with, the most uncomfortable issue is difficult to sleep in the seat. One of reasons is hard to stably rest the head in the headrest which cause to neck and shoulder stress.

Traditional cabin seats provide a pillow-like head support for user as an ergonomics feature, which forces the user's head forward. Maintaining a forward head posture it will causes stress concentration in the neck and shoulder, resulting in neck and shoulder pain (Fig. 1).

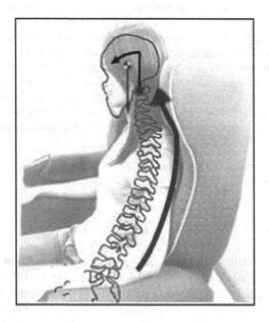

Fig. 1.   Static muscular efforts caused by an improper headrest that forces head forward.

2   Design Research

2.1   For Neck and Shoulder Stress Improvement

A tilted backward angle at about 22° on the seat from the shoulder height will keep the center of gravity of the head in a straight line on spine. Moreover, a proper neck support leads the head gravity, neck and spine in a naturally straight line, significantly reduce neck stress (Fig. 2).

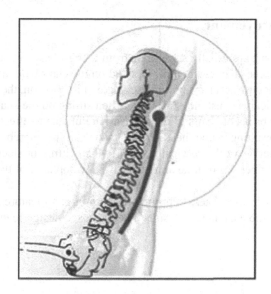

Fig. 2. To prevent a forward head posture (FHP), a backward angle from neck support of chair back was proposed.

2.2   For Head Fix

Moreover, maintaining a sitting posture for a long period of time might lead to static muscular efforts which cause discomfort. When shifting upper trunk, the passenger's head rest in different position on the headrest. A design of wide headrest with three V-shape notches would provide passengers with better head support following the upper trunk shifting (Fig. 3).

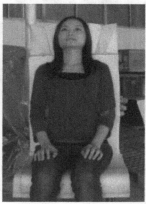

Fig. 3. A three V-shape notch was designed for passenger's head rest in different position when shifting upper trunk.

3   Design Improvement

Chairs of the prior art are usually structured from a chair base, a chair cushion and a chair back, wherein the chair cushion is disposed on the chair base, and the chair back is joined to the chair cushion at an appropriate angle of inclination, thereby enabling the back of the user to lean against the chair back when sitting on the chair cushion.

However, chair backs of chairs of the prior art are unable to effectively support the cervical vertebra, resulting in poor head postures when sitting, thereby causing pressure on the peripheral nerves of the cervical vertebra when sitting or sleeping on chairs of the prior art for long periods of time and affecting development of the central nervous system.

In addition to the head and neck support, other ergonomics feature will be integrated to achieve a comfortable cabin seat design. The proposed design features of cabin seat are as follows:

3.1   Headrest

A backward angle from neck support of chair back could shift the head gravity forward to keep head and trunk in a straight. It would decline the stress from the forward head posture (Fig. 4).

Fig. 4.

3.2   V-Shape Notches

The three V-shape headrest notches in various angles would enable the passenger to maintain a comfortable sitting posture when shifting upper trunk (Fig. 5).

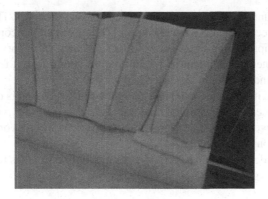

Fig. 5.

3.3 Neck Support

A proper convex cylindrical neck support would effectively relieve the neck stress (Fig. 6).

Fig. 6.

4 Conclusion

The present invention relates to an improved ergonomic chair for transportation cabin, and more particularly to an ergonomic chair which enables a chair back to appropriately support the cervical vertebra, and thereby avoid neck pains when sitting.

The design research is based on the question that the traditional passenger seat headrest is the main factor leading to neck and back pain. The severity of the neck issue may depend on the amount of tension on the cord or tension on the nerves. The design solution maintains a nature cervical curve which supports a relaxed spinal cord.

After design improvement, the seat headrests changed from forward to backward, users head and spine can maintain in a nature curve, these design features effectively improve the neck and back pain conditions.

In summary, the improvement of head and neck support design is new to the market, the user's experiences after functional model test are also positive. Although the user's experience is positive, professional ergonomic testing is required in order to achieve the optimal specifications.

The innovative design would benefit airlines and bus companies for better customer satisfaction in seating (Fig. 7).

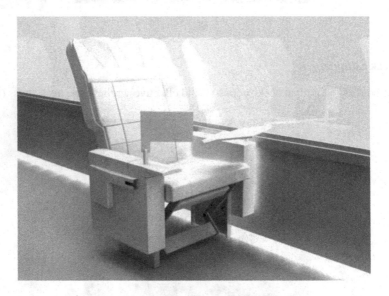

Fig. 7.   Seat design rendering

References

Albertsson, P., Falkmer, T.: Is there a pattern in European bus and coach incidents? A literature analysis with special focus on injury causation and injury mechanisms. Accid. Anal. Prev. **37**(2), 225233 (2005)

Cailliet, R., Gross, L.: Rejuvenation Strategy. Doubleday and Co., New York (1987)

Cailliet, R.: Pain. F.A. Davis, Philadelphia (1993)

Sanders, M.S., McCormic, E.J.: Human Factors in Engineer & Design, 7th edn. Mcgraw-Hill Inc., New York (1992)

Tanner, J.: Better Back. Dorling Kindersley Book, New York (2003)

Tilley, A.: The Measure of Man and Woman. Henry Dreyfess Associate, New York (1993)

Pheasant, S.: Bodyspace: Anthropometry, Ergonomics and the Design of Work, 2nd edn. Taylor & Francis, London (1998). ISBN 0748403264

Generating Training Images Using a 3D City Model for Road Sign Detection

Ryuto Kato[✉], Satoshi Nishiguchi, Wataru Hashimoto, and Yasuharu Mizutani

Faculty of Information Sciences and Technology, Osaka Institute of Technology,
1-79-1 Kitayama, Hirakata, Osaka 573-0196, Japan
sky-programmer@outlook.jp, {satoshi.nishiguchi,wataru.hashimoto,
yasuharu.mizutani}@oit.ac.jp

Abstract. In order to prevent traffic accidents due to mistakes in checking road signs, a method for detecting road signs from an image shot by an in-vehicle camera has been developed. On the other hand, Deep Learning which is frequently used in recent years requires preparing a large amount of training data, and it is difficult to photograph road signs from various directions at various places. In this research, we propose a method for generating training images for Deep Learning using 3D urban model simulation for detecting road signs. The appearance of road signs taken in the simulation depends on the distance and direction from the camera and the brightness of the scene. These changes were applied to Japanese road signs, and 303,750 types of sign images and their mask areas were automatically generated and used for training. As a result of training YOLO detectors using these training images, in detection for some road sign class groups, the F values of 66.7% to 88.9% could be obtained.

Keywords: Road sign · Object detection · Deep Learning
Generating training data · 3D simulation

1 Introduction

In 2012, Alex Net [1] which appeared in ILSVRC (ImageNet Large Scale Visual Recognition Competition) provided a great impact to the world. Currently six years have passed, the momentum of the development of this technology continues to be developed. Deep Learning has been contributing to excellent results in various fields such as image recognition, natural language processing, speech recognition and so on.

The growth of image recognition technology is particularly remarkable, and the technology enables to recognize more accurately than a human in object recognition. However, in order to identify objects in images by using Deep Learning, we need to prepare a large amount of training images with correct labels. Moreover, it is extremely time-consuming to prepare images obtained by photographing road signs in real space from various positions and directions.

Therefore, in this research, we propose a method to generate training images automatically for road sign detection using Deep Learning by simulation based on 3D city model.

© Springer International Publishing AG, part of Springer Nature 2018
C. Stephanidis (Ed.): HCII Posters 2018, CCIS 852, pp. 381–386, 2018.
https://doi.org/10.1007/978-3-319-92285-0_51

2 Classification of Road Signs Subject to This Study

Based on the classification [2] defined by the Japanese Ministry of Land, Infrastructure and Transport and Tourism, this study focuses on road signs which are applied to 225 kinds of road signs independently. The classification mentioned here is as of October 2017, but in the experiment of this paper, the data as of September 2016 was used. Therefore, we will not consider the changes including the crawl/guide sign [3] with English notation added in FY 2017.

Road signs in Japan are divided into principal sign and supplemental sign. Principal sign is further categorized into four types (guide signs, warning signs, regulatory signs and instruction signs). These five categories of 208 signs consist of 78 types of guide sings, 27 types of warning signs, 59 types of regulatory signs, 14 types of instruction signs and 30 types of supplemental signs in September 2016.

In this paper, we added 17 kinds of signs consist of both guide signs and auxiliary signs in order to classify the differences according to the layout, the presence of illustration, and the pattern of contents. A total of 225 signs were used as the detection targets in the experiment of this research and were based on image classification models.

3 Method for Generating Training Images of Road Signs

3.1 Outline of 3D City Model Simulation

In Deep Learning, a technique called "Data Augmentation" is generally used in object recognition using images in 2D space in order to increase the number of training images by geometrically transforming existing images. However, such transformed images are inadequate for efficient learning due to large difference from real images. Therefore, we propose a method for generating images of road signs in various directions, sizes, positions and lightness by using 3D road sign models located in 3D city model.

3.2 Preprocessing of Sign Images for Training Image Generation

To generate images used for training, 225 images were prepared by cutting out the area corresponding to each road sign from the image of road sign list provided at the website of the Ministry of Land, Infrastructure, Transport and Tourism of Japan in advance. These are the original images of 225 class images. Figure 1 shows examples of images obtained by cutting out only a sign region. The clipped image is pasted to the center of a transparent canvas of 640 * 480 pixels.

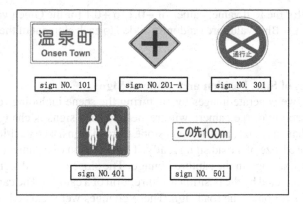

Fig. 1. Examples of images obtained by cutting out only the sign area

In order to apply to the 3D simulation environment to be used this time to each of the prepared 225 class sign images, a necessary area is cut out so that the width of the image becomes 300 pixels. The images of informatory sign s with a large difference in the size of them and the images of irregular signs of size were manually cut out. The images of remaining signs were automatically cut out after checking the size of necessary area.

Using the pre-processed images obtained by these method, training images are generated in the 3D simulation environment according to the procedures described in Sect. 3.3.

3.3   Method for Generating Training Images Using 3D Simulation

In generating various sign images, a simulation is carried out in a 3D model taking into consideration the changes in the brightness depending on the position of the sun regarded as a parallel light source, the color of the light source of the sun, the position, direction, distance of the camera towards signs. In this research, we used Unity that is game engine in order to handle a 3D simulation environment.

3.3.1   3D Model of an Urban City and Road Sign

We used Japanese Dosanko City model that is provided by Zenrin Co., Ltd. as a 3D urban model. We located 10 plane models for road signs in this city, and attached sign images to the surface of the plane model. The training images are generated by shooting plane models of signs from various positions.

3.3.2   Change of Light Source for 3D Road Signs

In order to reproduce the change of brightness and shadow of the light source in the real space, we change the position of the parallel light source variously. Furthermore, since the color change of the light source is also added, the RGB values of the original color are changed. Specifically, with respect to the RGB values normalized from 0 to 1, values of −0.4 to +0.4 for the Red value, values of −0.1 to +0.1 for the Green value, values of −0.2 to +0.2 for the Blue value are randomly added to each element of the original RGB values.

3.3.3   Changes of Size, Position and Slope of Signs

In this research, we generate images by capturing the scene including road signs. The position and direction of the camera with respect to road signs is changed in order to reproduce the change in size, position and slope of road signs. The position of a camera affects the captured size of a road sign greatly. The direction of a camera greatly affects the position of a road sign in the captured image. The slope of a road sign in a captured image is greatly affected by the position and direction of a camera. The camera is always oriented in the direction of the road sign. These changes were realized with a script in Unity.

3.3.4   Estimating a Road Sign Area in the Captured Image

It is possible to generate road sign images that reproduce actual changes by the above method. However, what is needed for giving these images as input images at the time of training detector is area information of road signs in the images. It takes a lot of labor to manually assign this area information for each image. In order to automatically generate this area information, we used a mask image of the road sign area.

First, an image as a base of the mask image is generated by using Unity. We used layer function and renderer function to generate an original image. Layer function is used by cameras to render only a part of the scene. In the layer function, the color image of a road sign and the mask image are saved as a pair by switching between the layer on which the color image is normally expressed and the layer for the mask image on which the background other than the road sign is expressed in white. In the renderer function, we switched the color of a road sign between black and color. An original image of the mask image is generated by combining these.

Next, a circumscribed rectangle of a road sign is estimated and the rectangle is used as the area information of road signs for training the detector. The outline for estimating a rectangle region including a road sign is shown in Fig. 2.

Fig. 2. Example of an estimated region of circumscribed rectangle of a road sign

4 Experiment and Results

4.1 Estimation of the Preparing Time of Training Images

The specifications of the computer used in the experiment are as follows. the CPU is Intel Core i7-7700K 4.2 GHz, the main memory is 32 GB, and the GPU is GeForce GTX 1080 Ti. In this study, 303,750 sets of the pair of the training images and the mask images, that is 607,500 images, were generated. Generating these images took about 9 h and 40 min. Also, the preprocessing time of the road sign image in Sect. 3.2, took about 13 h and 45 min. In addition to these, it took about 20 min to generate road sign area information from the original image of the mask image. Totally, it took 23 h and 45 min to generate 303,750 training images and area information. Therefore, training images and area information can be generated in about 0.28 s per road sign image.

On the other hand, when manually preparing images using a digital camera, it is assumed that it takes about 3 s for one image capturing and about 5 s for adding region information manually, and furthermore, considering the traveling time for it, the time and labor required per road sign image will increase. Based on the above, it can be said that the proposed image generation method is useful.

4.2 Estimation of Discrimination Performance by Generated Training Images

In order to estimate the validity of generated road sign images, we discriminated 87 images of road signs manually captured by a digital camera or cut off from the Google Street View screen. We used YOLO version 2 as a target detector for each of 87 images. Since the number of images for evaluation was small, the F value was calculated by replacing the output result of detection with the question of discrimination as to whether or not there are 225 target signs in the image.

As an experimental result, out of the 87 images for evaluation, the number of classes of labels included in the image was 52 out of 225 classes. The 13 classes of the 52 classes contained 4 or more training images. Table 1 shows the precision, recall, and F values of 7 classes out of 13 classes in which the F value was 20% or more. As can be seen from Table 1, F values of sign No. 206 were obtained in 88.9%, The sign No. 213 was 80%, and the sign No. 332 was 66.7%. The results of the F values of these classes are shown in Fig. 3. For all other 6 classes, the F values were 0%.

Table 1. Accuracy for each signs

Sign No.	Precision	Recall	f-measure
206	100.0%	80.0%	88.9%
213	100.0%	66.7%	80.0%
305	66.7%	40.0%	50.0%
312	100.0%	25.0%	40.0%
322	91.7%	35.5%	51.2%
328	100.0%	11.8%	21.1%
332	85.7%	54.5%	66.7%

As a result of this experiment, it was found that the signs No. 206, 213, 332 can be detected with relatively high accuracy from 66.7% to 88.9% by the method of this paper. The characteristics of the road sign in which the F value is relatively high is that discrimination by color is easily possible, that there is little information on letters, that there is little influence of left/right reversal, that there are few other signs around the sign, that the resolution of the area of the sign is high, that the difference of size between a test image and a training image of the detector model is small.

From these results, in order to obtain a detector with higher accuracy in the method of this research, it is considered that it is necessary to first design the system considering the size of the test image and the resolution of the region of signs. In addition to this, it is thought that not only the color information of the signs but also images for training in consideration of changes in the contents of letters and changes in left and right inversion are important. Furthermore, considering that not only one kind of signs of the real space but also a plurality of signs is installed, it is necessary to prepare an image reflecting the features of installation of the signs in the training image.

5   Conclusions

In this paper, we investigated the possibility to train the detection model which can detect the road sign using the training images automatically generated in 3D City model. In addition, it was understood that considering the resolution and size of the image as well as the actual change of the character of the sign and the setting environment etc., are important in order to train a highly accurate detection model by these methods.

In the future research, it is necessary to evaluate using more images and analyze the results, reflecting improvements of test images and training images found in this experiment. In addition, all of the images used in this study were taken in the scene of daytime. Therefore, it is necessary to investigate that our method is effect in the scene at night.

References

1. Krizhevsky, A., Sutskever, I., Hinton, G.E.: ImageNet classification with deep convolutional neural networks. In: Proceedings of Advances in Neural Information Processing Systems, (NIPS 2012), vol. 25, pp. 1097–1105 (2012)
2. Japanese Ministry of Land, Infrastructure and Transport and Tourism, Road: Road signs etc. Road signs overview etc. Road sign list. http://www.mlit.go.jp/road/sign/sign/douro/ichiran.pdf. Accessed 8 Oct 2017
3. Ministry of Land of Japan, Infrastructure and Transport, Press Release Presentation: About "Proposed Order to Revise Part of Order concerning Road Signs, Lines and Road Signs". http://www.mlit.go.jp/report/press/road01_hh_000829.html. Accessed 8 Oct 2017

Knowledge Based Health Monitoring
During Driving

Se Jin Park[1,2(✉)], Seunghee Hong[1], Damee Kim[1], Young Seo[1], and Iqram Hussain[1,2]

[1] Korea Research Institute of Standards and Science, Daejeon, South Korea
sjpark@kriss.re.kr
[2] University of Science & Technology, Daejeon, South Korea

Abstract. Knowledge based system is considered most innovative technology in smart healthcare monitoring system which is able to demonstrate real-time physiological parameters in computer and mobile platform and diagnosis health status. Driving has been an integrated part of our life and sometimes stress and health abnormality arises during driving, specially for elderly drivers. Among all kinds of health problems, stroke is most deadly diseases and real-time health monitoring is desired to detect stroke onset during regular activities. The aim of our study is to develop a knowledge base health monitoring system for elderly drivers using air cushion seat and IoT (Internet of things) devices in order to detect health abnormality such as stroke onset during driving. We have also developed a health monitoring system air cushion based body balance system and IoT devices. This system can monitor ECG, EEG, heart rate, seat pressure balance data, face/eye tracking etc. using IoT sensors, generate alert and send message to relatives and emergency services if any health abnormality happens during driving to provide emergency assistance. Knowledge based health monitoring system extract feature and pattern of physiological parameters; and compare extracted knowledge with real-time health data and deliver a significant status output as a service.

Keywords: Knowledge based system · Internet of things · Elderly healthcare
Real-time health monitoring · Brain stroke

1 Introduction

Knowledge Based Cloud Engine performs a significant role in the development of smart vehicles, which offers smart transportation, cloud connectivity, vehicle-to-vehicle interaction, smartphone integration, safety, security, and e-healthcare services. Recent development trends show that auto industries are already paying attention to develop IoT cars that could integrate driver's health status and driving safety. Both auto industry and key global original equipment manufacturers are integrating healthcare services into their next-generation products [1].

As health has become the major point of interest, many researches are focused on the development of smart health care system. Driving consumes a significant amount of time in our daily life. Sudden health issues like cardiac arrest, stroke etc., can happen during driving. In order to avoid those circumstances automotive manufacturers as well as users are interested to incorporate the real-time health monitoring system in the car [2, 3]. Driver's health abnormality may also effect safety of other vehicles. So, automotive manufacturers and users are interested to include real-time health monitoring in car system. World population is aging rapidly and aged population is getting much more concern nowadays. Aging originates from increasing longevity and results in deteriorating fertility [4]. Population aging is taking place in nearly all the countries of the world. As age increases, older drivers become more conservative on the road. Age-related decline in cognitive function hampers safety and quality of life for an elder. As the aged population in the developed world is increasing, so the number of older drivers is becoming higher [5]. Research on age-related driving has shown that an increased risk of being involved in a vehicle crash is more at around the driver's age of 65. Certain behavioral factors, in particular, may contribute to these statistics: drifts within the traffic lane, confusion in making left-hand turns, and decreased ability to adjust behavior in response to an unexpected or fast-changing situation [6].

Stroke is the second top reason of death above the age of 60 years, and its proportion is rising. Many health abnormality happens after stroke. Postural disorders is observed as one of the most common disabilities after stroke. [7]

Some developments in the wearables and embedded sensors to measure physiological and bio-signals during driving have been already done [8]. Faurecia developed an automotive seat which detects traveler's heart rate and breathing rhythm through unique types of embedded sensors [9]. IPPOCRTE designed a steering wheel could measure vital physiological parameters including ECG, eye gaze, body temperature, and pulse rate [10].

This paper focused on briefly explaining the design and framework of the elderly drivers' health monitoring services in connected car using IoT devices. The purpose of this study is to develop the knowledge based real-time health monitoring system for drivers during the sudden stroke onset using body balance air cushion and IoT devices.

2   Model and Methodology

2.1   Intelligent Car Seat Model

A model of automotive seat is designed for monitoring health status of driver. For monitoring body postural balance, an air cushion is designed that consists of four air chamber. Four chambers can indicate body inclination to four sides; front, rear, right and left side. Air chambers are pumped by a small air compressor to maintain inflation in order to detect symmetric body pressure. Air cushion is made of polyvinyl chloride, very common kind of synthetic plastic polymer.

For measuring body pressure over air cushion, each air chamber is equipped with air pressure sensor. This air cushion is inserted to inside of air seat and covered with seat cover. For better comfortability, air cushion top surface is placed in same level of car seat flat surface (Fig. 1). To add an air cushion in the seat cushion, small modifications have been done to make room for the air cushion. In order to get effective pressure response, air cushion has been placed in middle position of car seat. Identical air pressure in all chamber of air cushion indicate driver's body balance over car seat. Large variation of pressure in air cushion chambers represents tilting of driver's position in one side. Brain lesions may cause a difficulty of postural control, and postural disorder is found to be one of the most common disabilities after stroke onset [11].

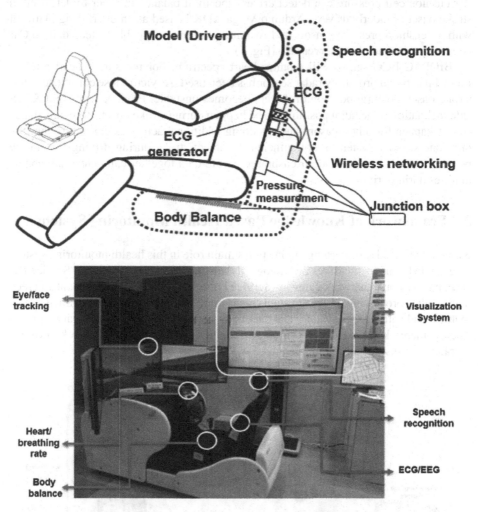

Fig. 1. Intelligent car seat model embedded with IoT sensors.

In back part of the seat, ECG sensor is attached and remains in contact with wearable clothes. Wearable clothes are made of woven conductive fabric. In front of seat, proximity heartbeat sensor is placed in order to measure driver's heart rate. Face tracking and eye tracking camera will monitor face pattern and eye movement from the front side of driver.

2.2 Components of Driver's Health Monitoring System

IoT sensors such as ECG/EEG sensor will monitor heart spectrum, pressure sensors will monitor body pressure balance, and heart rate will be measured using proximity sensors. Air cushion cell pressure can detect drivers' postural balance in order to detect brain stroke onset of elderly drivers. Arduino Mega ADK is used as an interfacing platform with air cushion pressure sensors and Arduino platform is capable to feed data to Car control system and cloud server also (Fig. 1).

BIOPAC ECG sensor will monitor heart spectrum. For measuring heart rate, TI Launchpad based proximity radar sensor has been used. As victim lose conscience after stroke onset, postural position of drivers becomes unstable. Front & rear, right & left side inclination of postural position can be happen during stroke onset. Body unbalance can be happen for other reasons such as doing additional activities during driving. So, only one sensory system is not sufficient to detect stroke during driving for elderly people. ECG, Heart rate and air cushion pressure data together can detect any abnormalities during driving.

3 Framework of Knowledge Based Health Monitoring System

Knowledge based self-learning engine plays main role in this health monitoring system (Fig. 2). IoT sensors measures physiological data and data is transmitted to Service DB (Database) through network gateway. Service DB takes care data management and feed data for data processing. In Health status measurement model, algorithm extracts useful features and patterns of physiological parameter corresponding to specific target group. Then gathered knowledge stored in Knowledge DB for future use. These knowledge extraction trains up self-learning engine.

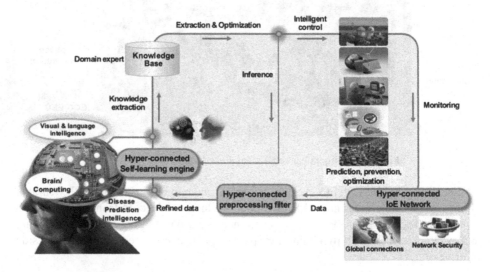

Fig. 2. Knowledge extraction process of physiological data.

Framework of knowledge based health monitoring is showed in Fig. 3. During real-time health service, real-time biodata is feed to self-learning engine and compared with reference data knowledge. Health status/Stroke Expert intelligence model predicts and detects health abnormality if any abnormal pattern found in real-time data. Health Status alert service receives health updates and always ready to respond if any health risk, more specifically stroke happens. System will also generate an alert and deliver messages to emergency services, family of the victim, people around the victim, and hospitals in order to ensure the immediate medical assistance. Each sensor prediction result contributes in large set of IoT sensor network. The more sensor in health monitoring system, the more reliability of monitoring system.

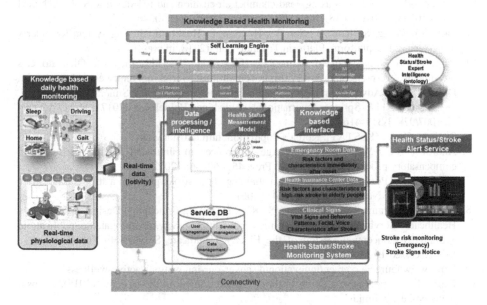

Fig. 3. Framework of knowledge based health monitoring system.

4 Conclusion

Knowledge based health monitoring system is expected to be promising service for real-time health monitoring. This study introduces an intelligent sensor based car seat model and also provides a basic framework Real-time knowledge based health monitoring; such as stroke detection system using body balance air cushion and IoT sensors for elderly drivers. Body balance system using air cushion, we can expect that the developed car seat is expected to identify stroke in tilted unbalanced postural position. In addition, ECG/EEG, heart rate sensor embedded in car seat can provide an intelligent in-car health monitoring platform and detect abnormality when health risk; such as brain stroke onset happens. Analysis of Stroke monitoring data has not been presented here. In future, health monitoring data analysis will be presented and study would consider a range of bio-sensors and technique in order to improve reliability of system for real-time health risk prediction during driving.

References

1. Park, S.J., Subramaniyam, M., Kim, S.E., Hong, S., Lee, J.H., Jo, C.M., Seo, Y.: Development of the elderly healthcare monitoring system with IoT. In: Duffy, V.G., Lightner, N. (eds.) Advances in Human Factors and Ergonomics in Healthcare. AISC, vol. 482, pp. 309–315. Springer, Cham (2017). https://doi.org/10.1007/978-3-319-41652-6_29
2. Park, S.J., Hong, S., Kim, D., Seo, Y., et al.: Development of a real-time stroke detection system for elderly drivers using quad-chamber air cushion and IoT devices. SAE Technical Paper 2018-01-0046 (2018). https://doi.org/10.4271/2018-01-0046
3. Park, S.J., Hong, S., Kim, D., Seo, Y., Hussain, I.: Health monitoring system for elderly drivers using IoT platform. Platform Technol. Lett. (2018, in press)
4. Park, S.J., Subramaniyam, M., Kim, S.E., Hong, S.H., Lee, J.H., Jo, C.M.: Older driver's physiological response under risky driving conditions–overtaking, unprotected left turn. In: Duffy, V. (ed.) Advances in Applied Digital Human Modeling and Simulation. AISC, vol. 481, pp. 107–114. Springer International Publishing, Heidelberg (2017). https://doi.org/10.1007/978-3-319-41627-4_11
5. Statistics Korea (KoSTAT): Korea's Population. http://kostat.go.kr
6. Andrews, E.C., Westerman, S.J.: Age differences in simulated driving performance: compensatory processes. Accid. Anal. Prev. **45**, 660–668 (2012)
7. Pérennou, D.: Postural disorders and spatial neglect in stroke patients: a strong association. Restor. Neurol. Neurosci. **24**, 319–334 (2006)
8. Park, S.J., Subramaniyam, M., Hong, S., Kim, D., Yu, J.: Conceptual Design of the Elderly Healthcare Services In-Vehicle using IoT. https://www.researchgate.net/publication/315858925_Conceptual_Design_of_the_Elderly_Healthcare_Services_In-Vehicle_using_IoT. Accessed 16 Mar 2018
9. http://www.faurecia.com/en/innovation/discover-our-innovations/active-wellness
10. Parti, D.: Ippocrate: a new steering wheel monitoring system (2015). https://www.politesi.polimi.it/
11. Pérennou, D.: Postural disorders and spatial neglect in stroke patients: a strong association. Restorative Neurol. Neurosci. **24**, 319–334 (2006)

"Voice Unlock" Function

Harim Seo and Younei Soe[(⊠)]

Indiana University, 107 S Indiana Ave, Bloomington, IN 47405, USA
seohari@iu.edu, ysoe@indiana.edu

Abstract. Most unlock methods for smartphones are unproblematic if users can use their phones freely but can be inconvenient and dangerous in some situations. For example, unlocking might take a user's attention away from another activity, such as a driver attempting to use a fingerprint-unlock feature. Since a driver should not have to look at or touch his or her phone while driving but may need to receive a call or text, a passenger should be able to unlock the driver's phone instead. However, a passenger asking the driver to unlock the phone (e.g., via fingerprint) can become uncomfortable and risky. By employing a case-study method through observations of and interviews with drivers and their passengers, this research presents the participants' unmet needs. The key findings are (a) drivers need a voice-activated unlocking method, (b) passengers need a way to find and play songs and control other functions comfortably without repeatedly having to ask the driver to unlock the phone with his or her fingerprint, and (c) drivers want to protect their privacy by allowing passengers to use only the apps and menus set in a pre-specified "use while driving" mode. Based on these findings, this study suggests a new smartphone unlock method called "Voice Unlock." The prototype and details of this feature are presented to explain why it provides a more convenient, comfortable, and safer unlocking method than fingerprint recognition for drivers who use a phone when driving with a passenger and passengers who want to use the driver's phone.

Keywords: Smartphone · Unlock method · Voice unlock · Driving
Safety · Case study

1 Introduction

1.1 Problem Description

The unlock function of smartphones has recently added a way to recognize the fingerprint of the user when unlocking a phone to protect the user's personal privacy, unlike past functions in which a pattern or password input was the main unlocking method. In fact, most people now use fingerprints to unlock their smartphones. This unlocking method is not a problem when people can freely use their smartphone, but it can be inconvenient in situations where the user's hands aren't free, such as needing to use a smartphone while driving. For example, a person may need to manipulate navigation while driving or change the music on their smartphone when it's connected `to their car. Because the driver can't see or touch the phone while driving, someone else should use it instead. However, the driver has to unlock the phone with one hand each time the passenger needs to use it, which can be very dangerous if the driver looks at the smartphone to unlock it while driving. Also, every time someone in the passenger seat wants to use the smartphone, they will ask the driver to unlock it, and this situation may feel uncomfortable for both the driver and other users.

1.2   The Purpose of Study

Using a smartphone while driving can cause very dangerous situations. Therefore, through a case study conducted by observation, this study suggests a more convenient, comfortable, and safer smartphone unlocking method than fingerprint recognition: the "Use While Driving" feature for users who use phones when driving with a passenger. This method ensures protection of privacy, a user-friendly system, and safety support service.

2   Related Work

Several researches have been conducted regarding smartphone applications or devices to help safe driving situations. [2] devises a mobile application that gauges driving habits based on in-vehicle acceleration measurements and gives corresponding feedback to drivers. Also, [3] created the "CafeSafe" app for Android phones which has sensors on the phone to find and notice dangerous driving conditions in and outside of the vehicle. "CafeSafe" monitors the driver's conditions or detects road situations using the car's front and back camera by utilizing computer vision and a machine learning algorithm. [4] also suggests "TEXIVE," a system leveraging internal sensors in regular smartphones by recognizing the micro-movements of smartphone users and detecting the driving and texting behaviors of users, which distinguishes drivers from passengers. In other words, they propose the critical task of detecting the user behavior of driving and texting at the same time. "TEXIVE" can identify dangerous operations with good sensitivity, specificity, and accuracy. According to these researches, many services and functions are continually developed to support people's driving situations and these functions will receive attention from various fields.

3   Methodology

3.1   Data Gathering

Driving a car and using a smartphone with a passenger in the car is a situation that happens in everyday life. Therefore, this study wanted to collect data directly from natural situations through the method of observation. For this study, the subjects of this observation are people who have their own smartphone or cars. However, a person who doesn't have a smartphone or a car can be the subject of this observation if they have experience using someone else's smartphone.

In the first participant case, MJ usually uses smartphone to connect the Bluetooth for playing music and making phone calls. Also, he often uses navigation when going places outside of Bloomington. However, he often changes the song while driving, and if he has a passenger, he makes the passenger choose the song they want to hear. However, soon after choosing a song, the screen of the smartphone turns off and the phone is locked again. MJ needs to unlock the smartphone each time but doesn't want to be disturbed when driving due to safety concerns. Therefore, he needs a way for his passengers to play other songs and operate other functions comfortably without unlocking the phone with his fingerprints.

Next, Elisa is the second participant. When she drives, her friends often use her smartphone. The friend can use her navigation app on her behalf or play a song they like listening to. Although they have a close relationship, she sometimes feels that she needs a way to have a certain amount of privacy from her friends. In other words, she wants others to be able to use only the apps and menus she pre-specified in a driving setting mode.

Lastly, the third participant, Elena often uses someone else's car because she doesn't have her own car. When she rides in someone else's car, the driver needs to concentrate on driving, but in cases when they need to use navigation, she has experience using the driver's smartphone. However, she feels uncomfortable asking the driver to unlock the smartphone every time she wants to search for or change a song because she feels sorry that she seems to be obstructing the driver's driving. She wants the smartphone to have a less rigorous smartphone unlock when driving so only limited functions can be used (Fig. 1).

Fig. 1. The figures of participants during observation (Driver and passenger)

3.2 Findings Based on Observations and Interviews

Observation and interviews revealed participants wanted some of the following features.

Drivers and passengers need a different unlocking method from fingerprint recognition. For example, they want an added voice-activated unlocking method. Drivers also need a way to protect private data such as photo albums, text records, and phone call history. Once the phone is unlocked, passengers need a way to find and play songs and control other functions comfortably without having to ask the driver again to unlock the phone with their fingerprint (Table 1).

Table 1. Recommended features based on user needs.

The driver	The passenger
Recognize the driving mode	Find and play songs comfortably without asking driver to unlock the smartphone
Unlock the smartphone using a voice unlock method instead of using the fingerprint recognition method	
A limited use function for the user's privacy which means others can use only the apps pre-specified by the owner	Freely use some applications set by the driver in advance

4 Conclusion

4.1 Prototype of "Use While Driving"

The "Use While Driving" mode works by separating functions for the driver and passenger. First, the new mode will allow the drivers to unlock the phone by clicking the Voice Unlock button without having to use the fingerprint recognition method. This could help drivers safely concentrate on their driving because they will not need to look at their smartphone to use some apps. Also, it protects the driver's privacy by only allowing others to use the apps and menus the owner pre-specified for the mode by using protected, limited use functions. The brief description of this mode is expressed as follows.

Fig. 2. Prototype of "Use While Driving" mode

- When a user needs to unlock the smartphone through voice, user clicks "voice unlock."
- When user wants to quit this mode, they click the "quit" button.
- Specific apps can be used without owner's authorization.
- When the user wants to change the easy-accessapps (in the Fig. 2 case, 'music, map, and internet'), he or she clicks the "Home" button, and the user can change the settings of these app options.

4.2 Limitations and Recommendations for Future Research

This project sets up a situation that is common in everyday life. Since the situation of driving a car with other people happens frequently, the process of selecting the subjects to observe and the observation of the problem situations were comparatively easy. However, there is something that I feel is lacking from this project. The participant selection process lacks objectivity because they were acquaintance of myself. Therefore, my perception could have affected the observation. In other words, it was not confirmed whether the users who felt the need to allow the passengers to access their smartphone when driving the car were in a general situation. This means the sample size in this study was small, so the findings cannot be applied to the smartphone user population as a whole. Therefore, when proposing these new ideas, it will be necessary to carry out observations on a wider range of users to verify the user needs. It is also helpful to support the new idea by considering examples that can be used in general as well as other perspectives, rather than assuming new ideas are limited to specific situations. In addition, a more in-depth study of smartphone use patterns in various driving situations would provide more insight.

References

1. Rogers, Y., et al.: Interaction Design: Beyond Human-Computer Interaction. Wiley, Chichester (2011)
2. Paefgen, J., Zhai, Y.: Driving behavior analysis with smartphone: insights from a controlled field study. In: Proceedings of the 11th International Conference on Mobile and Ubiquitous Multimedia, vol. 36 (2012)
3. You, C.-W., et al.: CarSafe: a Driver Safety App that detects dangerous driving behavior using dual-cameras on smartphones. In: Proceedings of the 2012 ACM Conference on Ubiquitous Computing, vol. 10, pp. 671–672 (2012)
4. Bo, C., et al.: You're Driving and Texting: detecting drivers using personal smartphones by leveraging inertial sensors. In: Proceedings of the 19th Annual International Conference on Mobile Computing & Networking (2013)
5. Fazeen, M., Gozick, B., Dantu, R., Bhukhiya, M., González, M.C.: Safe driving using mobile phones. IEEE Trans. Intell. Transp. Syst. **13**(3), 1462–1468 (2012)

A Simulator-Based Approach to Assess Take-over Performance in a Conditionally Automated Vehicle

Joonwoo Son[1,2(✉)], Sungryul Park[1], Myoungouk Park[1],
Jinwoo Park[1], Jihyuk Park[2], Jonghwa Kim[3], and Yongwon Yun[3]

[1] HumanLAB, DGIST (Daegu Gyoengbuk Institute of Science
and Technology), Daegu 42988, Republic of Korea
json@dgist.ac.kr
[2] Autonomous Driving R&D Team, Sonnet.AI,
Daegu 42988, Republic of Korea
[3] Automated Vehicle Center, Korea Automobile Testing & Research Institute
(KATRI), Hwaseong, Republic of Korea

Abstract. The interaction between the driver and the automated driving systems (ADS) will remain a key element of automated driving because drivers are expected to be available to take over control for the case of system failure or limitation in a conditionally automated vehicle, i.e. SAE level 3. A number of studies reported that various factors such as the time budget, the traffic complexity, and the driver's inattention may influence take-over time and quality. Therefore, the driver's take-over performance must be carefully analyzed to ensure a safe transition. This study aims to propose a take-over performance assessment method using a driving simulator. A systematic review was conducted to design a driving scenario for unintended take-over events. As a result, a take-over performance test protocol with four take-over situations such as missing lines on a straight and a curved road, road construction, and system failure was designed. Visual and cognitive non-driving related tasks, which influence a driver's situation awareness and take-over performance, were also considered. It will be proposed as Korean Traffic Safety Regulation to assess the safety of the take-over control in a conditionally automated vehicle from the perspective of the driver.

Keywords: Take-over performance · Conditionally automated vehicle
Simulator-based assessment

1 Introduction

Improvement of the automation level frees drivers from the primary driving tasks and allows to perform non-driving related tasks by shifting attentional resources to other tasks during driving [1]. However, the existing automated driving systems (ADS) are still considering a driver as a fallback-ready user who is receptive to the ADS-issued requests to take-over [1, 2]. Previous studies on automation and human factors found that a high level of automation can cause out-of-the-loop problems [3] and humans are not good at tasks that require vigilance for prolonged periods of time [4]. Thus, the driver's take-over performance must be carefully investigated to ensure a safe transition in a conditionally automated vehicle. This paper aims to propose a harmonized experimental protocol to assess drivers' take-over performance in a driving simulator and compare the results around the world.

2 Research Frameworks

In order to design an experimental protocol, we adopted a framework for human factors of transitions in automated driving [1, 5] and categorized the factors for the simulator-based take-over experiment design (Table 1). The factors are assigned to four simulation design elements such as participants, driving contexts, control contexts and ADS design. Among the simulation design elements, the participants and the ADS design were not considered because the recruitment of participants is dependent on the size and budget of the experiment and the ADS design are related to the individual design philosophy. The driving contexts was further investigated to propose a harmonized experimental scenario and summarized in Table 2. Except the system failure, most of the driving context factors were used in the previous studies. Although the system failure may affect the participant's perceived reliability and safety, it is worth considering as a safety-critical event.

Table 1. The factors of transitions in automated driving

Factors				Conditions	Simulation Design
Initiator of the transition (From)				Driver Car	Control Contexts (Apparatus Support)
Control after transition (To)				Driver Car	Control Contexts (Apparatus Support)
Situation Awareness	Situation Variables	Traffic Complexity	Roadway Type	Number of lanes Geometry (Straight/Curved)	Driving Contexts
			Events	System Failure / Limitation External Object	Driving Contexts
			Traffic Density	Number of vehicles per km	Driving Contexts
		HMI	Informing Interface	Visual Vocal Acoustic Tactile	ADS Design (Apparatus Support)
			Deactivation Interface	Button / Lever Steering wheel Pedals	ADS Design (Apparatus Support)
		Non-Driving Related Task		Visual Manual Cognitive	Control Contexts (Apparatus Support)
	Driver Variables	Age		Younger Older	Participants
		Gender		Male Female	Participants
		Driving skill		Experienced Novice	Participants
		Knowledge of ADS		Low High	Participants
		Take-over Readiness		Low High	Control Contexts (by NDRT)

Table 2. Summary of driving contexts in previous studies

Previous studies	Traffic complexity					
	Roadway	Take-over events			Traffic density	
	Geometry	Missing lane mark	External objects	System failure	Surrounding car	Defined density
Zeeb et al. [6]	S[a], C[a]	O	–	–	O	–
Zeeb et al. [7]	S, C	O	O	–	O	O
Zeeb et al. [8]	S	–	O	–	O	–
Chae et al. [9]	S, C	–	O	–	O	–
Melcher et al. [10]	S	–	O	–	–	–
Kuehn et al. [11]	S	O	–	–	–	O
Lorenz et al. [12]	S, C	–	O	–	O	–
Hergeth et al. [13]	S	–	O	–	–	–
Forster et al. [14]	S	–	–	–	O	–
Naujoks et al. [15]	S, C	O	–	–	O	–
Radlmayr et al. [16]	S	–	O	–	O	–
Happee et al. [17]	S	–	–	–	O	–
Gold et al. [18]	S	–	–	–	O	O
Clark and Feng [19]	S	–	O	–	O	–
Braunagel et al. [20]	S, C	–	–	–	O	O
Gibson et al. [21]	S, C	–	O	–	–	–
Korber et al. [22]	S, C	O	–	–	–	–

[a]S: straight, C: curved

3   Proposed Experimental Protocol

3.1   Experimental Design

In this study, the factors including 'take-over events', 'traffic density' and 'NDRT' were selected as independent variables. They are expected to affect situation awareness and drivers' readiness. As mentioned in the previous section, age, gender, and experience are considered as latent variables that can influence the take-over quality and take-over performance. Therefore, it is worth to note to recruit participants considering the proportion of sample size.

3.2   Take-over Situations in Driving Contexts

Based on the literature survey of the previous studies, this study proposes the driving contexts of four representative situations such as "Lane marking is missing on a straight road (S1)", "Lane marking is missing on a curved road (S2)", "Roadwork appears during driving a straight road (S3)", and "An automated system is deactivated due to system failure on a straight road (S4)". As shown in Table 3, S1 is the scenario with the lowest complexity and S4 is the highest.

Table 3. Take-over situations in the driving contexts

	S1	S2	S3	S4
Roadway	Straight	Curved	Straight	Straight
Lane marking	Missing	Missing	Visible	Visible
Roadwork	X	X	O	X
System failure	X	X	X	O
Surrounding cars	O	O	O	O
Traffic density (vehicles/km)	10	10	10, 30	10, 30

3.3 Take-over Performance Measures

Reaction time, take-over time and take-over quality measures are typical dependent variables in take-over related studies. The potential measures to assess take-over performance are summarized in Table 4.

Table 4. Summary of take-over performance measures

Measures	Description
Reaction times	
Time to eyes on (s)	First gaze at road (video labelling) [6]
Time to hand on (s)	First gaze at road (video labelling) [6]
Time to driver intervention (s)	Steering: steering wheel angle velocity $\geq$ 10/s [6]
	Braking: standardized brake pedal travel $\geq$ 10% [6]
Take-over time	
Time to disengage automation	[7, 8]
Steering response time (RT_{steer})	the point in time where the steering wheel angle exceeded 2° in the direction of the lane change [6]
Brake response time (RT_{brake})	the first point in time where the brake pedal was depressed more than 10% of the available stroke [6]
Take-over quality	
Maximum accelerations	[8, 13, 23]
Minimum time headway to an obstacle	[24–26]
Reaction type	Steering only, braking only, steering and braking [6]
Lateral maneuver	
Max. deviation from lane center (m)	Max. deviation of the ego-vehicle from the center of the ego-lane [6]
Min. Time to lane crossing (TLC)	Min. time to lane crossing (as measured by half of the ego-vehicle crossing the lane marking) [6]
Longitudinal maneuver	
Min. Distance (m)	Min. distance to leading vehicle [6]
Min. Time gap (s)	Min. time gap to leading vehicle [6]
Time to collision (TTC)	The time required for two vehicles to collide if they continue at their present speed and on the same path

4 Summary and Concluding Remarks

This paper proposed a simulator-based method to evaluate the take-over performance of the conditionally automated vehicle. In this study, we categorized a driving simulator experimental protocol into four components, i.e., driving contexts, control contexts, ADS design and participants. Then the driving context related parameters were selected based on the previous studies. Finally, four take-over events and performance measures were proposed. The result of this study may contribute to establish a guideline for take-over experiments. A pilot test will be conducted based on this experimental design.

Acknowledgements. This work was supported in part by a grant (code 18TLRP-B131486-02) from Transportation and Logistics R&D Program funded by Ministry of Land, Infrastructure and Transport of Korean government, and by DGIST R&D Program (18-BT-01) of the Ministry of Science and ICT of Korean government.

References

1. SAE, Taxonomy and definitions for terms related to driving automation systems for on-road motor vehicles. Standard No. J3016, SAE International (2016)
2. Son, J., Park, M.: Situation awareness and transitions in highly automated driving: a framework and mini review. J. Ergonomics **7**(5), 1–6 (2017)
3. Endsley, M.R., Kiris, E.O.: The out-of-the-loop performance problem and level of control in automation. J. Hum. Factors Ergonomics Soc. **37**(2), 381–394 (1995)
4. Casner, S.M., Hutchins, E.L., Norman, D.: The challenges of partially automated driving. Commun. ACM **59**(5), 70–77 (2016)
5. Lu, Z., Happee, R., Cabrall, C.D., Kyriakidis, M., de Winter, J.C.: Human factors of transitions in automated driving: a general framework and literature survey. Transp. Res. Part F Traffic Psychol. Behav. **43**, 183–198 (2016)
6. Zeeb, K., Härtel, M., Buchner, A., Schrauf, M.: Why is steering not the same as braking? The impact of non-driving related tasks on lateral and longitudinal driver interventions during conditionally automated driving. Transp. Res. Part F Traffic Psychol. Behav. **50**, 65–79 (2017)
7. Zeeb, K., Buchner, A., Schrauf, M.: Is take-over time all that matters? The impact of visual-cognitive load on driver take-over quality after conditionally automated driving. Accid. Anal. Prev. **92**, 230–239 (2016)
8. Zeeb, K., Buchner, A., Schrauf, M.: What determines the take-over time? An integrated model approach of driver take-over after automated driving. Accid. Anal. Prev. **78**, 212–221 (2015)
9. Chae, H., Jeong, Y., Yi, K., Choi, I., Min, K.: Safety performance evaluation scenarios for extraordinary service permission of autonomous vehicle. Trans. Korean Soc. Automot. Eng. **24**(5), 495–503 (2016)
10. Melcher, V., Rauh, S., Diederichs, F., Widlroither, H., Bauer, W.: Take-over requests for automated driving. Procedia Manuf. **3**, 2867–2873 (2015)
11. Kuehn, M., Vogelpohl, T., Vollrath, M.: Takeover times in highly automated driving (Level 3). In: 25th International Technical Conference on the Enhanced Safety of Vehicles (ESV) National Highway Traffic Safety Administration (2017)

12. Lorenz, L., Kerschbaum, P., Schumann, J.: Designing take over scenarios for automated driving. Proc. Hum. Factors Ergonomics Soc. Annu. Meet. **58**(1), 1681–1685 (2014)
13. Hergeth, S., Lorenz, L., Krems, J.F.: Prior familiarization with takeover requests affects drivers' takeover performance and automation trust. Hum. Factors **59**(3), 457–470 (2017)
14. Forster, Y., Naujoks, F., Neukum, A., Huestegge, L.: Driver compliance to take-over requests with different auditory outputs in conditional automation. Accid. Anal. Prev. **109**, 18–28 (2017)
15. Naujoks, F., Purucker, C., Wiedemann, K., Neukum, A., Wolter, S., Steiger, R.: Driving performance at lateral system limits during partially automated driving. Accid. Anal. Prev. **108**, 147–162 (2017)
16. Radlmayr, J., Gold, C., Lorenz, L., Farid, M., Bengler, K.: How traffic situations and non-driving related tasks affect the take-over quality in highly automated driving. Proc. Hum. Factors Ergonomics Soc. Annu. Meet. **58**(1), 2063–2067 (2014)
17. Happee, R., Gold, C., Radlmayr, J., Hergeth, S., Bengler, K.: Take-over performance in evasive manoeuvres. Accid. Anal. Prev. **106**, 211–222 (2017)
18. Gold, C., Korber, M., Lechner, D., Bengler, K.: Taking over control from highly automated vehicles in complex traffic situations: the role of traffic density. Hum. Factors **58**(4), 642–652 (2016)
19. Clark, H., Feng, J.: Age differences in the takeover of vehicle control and engagement in non-driving-related activities in simulated driving with conditional automation. Accid. Anal. Prev. **106**, 468–479 (2017)
20. Braunagel, C., Rosenstiel, W., Kasneci, E.: Ready for take-over? A new driver assistance system for an automated classification of driver take-over readiness. IEEE Intell. Transp. Syst. Mag. **9**(4), 10–22 (2017)
21. Gibson, M., Lee, J., Venkatraman, V., Price, M., Lewis, J., Montgomery, O., et al.: Situation awareness, scenarios, and secondary tasks: measuring driver performance and safety margins in highly automated vehicles. SAE Int. J. Passeng. Cars Electron. Electr. Syst. **9**(1), 237–242 (2016)
22. Korber, M., Prasch, L., Bengler, K.: Why do i have to drive now? Post Hoc explanations of takeover requests. Hum. Factors, 18720817747730 (2017)
23. Gold, C., Damböck, D., Lorenz, L., Bengler, K.: "Take over!" How long does it take to get the driver back into the loop? Proc. Hum. Factors Ergonomics Soc. Ann. Meeting **57**(1), 1938–1942 (2013)
24. Merat, N., Jamson, A.H., Lai, F.C.H., Daly, M., Carsten, O.M.J.: Transition to manual: driver behaviour when resuming control from a highly automated vehicle. Transp. Res. Part F Traffic Psychol. Behav. **27**, 274–282 (2014)
25. Louw, T., Merat, N., Jamson, H.: Engaging with highly automated driving: to be or not to be in the loop? In: Proceedings of the 8th International Driving Symposium on Human Factors in Driver Assessment, Training, and Vehicle Design: Driving Assessment, pp. 190–196 (2015)
26. Louw, T., Kountouriotis, G., Carsten, O., Merat, N.: Driver inattention during vehicle automation: how does driver engagement affect resumption of control? In: 4th International Conference on Driver Distraction and Inattention (2015)

Detection of Checking Action on Parking Significant for Cognitive Dysfunction Patients

Tomoji Toriyama[✉], Akira Urashima, and Kanada Taisei

Toyama Prefectural University, Toyama, Japan
{toriyama,a-urasim}@pu-toyama.ac.jp

Abstract. Cognitive dysfunction patient could have symptoms such as attention disorder, execute function disorder and so on. These symptoms may cause unsafe driving in daily life. The degree of these symptoms can be evaluated by neuropsychological examination, however, the correspondence relationship between these symptoms and unsafe driving is uncertain. Therefore, it is difficult to judge the patient's driving aptitude only by neuropsychological examination. To solve this problem, we are developing unsafe driving detection system. It requires some small wireless sensors measuring triaxial angular velocity and acceleration to be attached on user's head, toes and steering wheel, and GPS sensor on a car. Since many of the cognitive dysfunction patients have symptom of attention disorder, it assumed that safety checking actions tend to be careless. Based on this assumption, we have analyzed the driver's checking action on intersections and changing lane. Here discusses the result of analysis assumingly complex checking action on parking cars. When parking a car, driver must control the car and pay attention to rear, front and both side simultaneously. From the video analysis of the experiment with small wireless sensors and a real car, cognitive dysfunction patients tend to use rear view mirror to accomplish their safety checking. Especially, the right side mirror checking action was significantly high compare to the one without cognitive dysfunction. Safety checking action, accomplished only by rear view mirror is more dangerous than checking directly by turning around. On investigating of how much the attached sensors can acquire these driver's checking actions, it was clarified that these sensors can identify only the direction of head, however cannot identify if the drivers were looking at the target object directly or through rear view mirror. It should be studied further that how much can our unsafe driving detection system distinguish direct and indirect one.

Keywords: Cognitive dysfunction · Wearable sensor
Checking action on parking

1 Introduction

When a part of the brain is affected by apoplexy, brain tumor or injury to the head, cognitive dysfunction symptoms including attention disorder and execute function disorder may appear. Although these symptoms can be improved by medical treatment, it may be dangerous to drive a car in daily life, depending on the degree of the symptom. In Japan, under the road traffic law, driving license can be suspended or canceled in case

© Springer International Publishing AG, part of Springer Nature 2018
C. Stephanidis (Ed.): HCII Posters 2018, CCIS 852, pp. 404–409, 2018.
https://doi.org/10.1007/978-3-319-92285-0_55

of problems with recognition, judgment or operation, which are identified through apti-tude tests. However, there are no standard guidelines to judge the driving aptitude of the cognitive dysfunction patients. In some hospitals, neuropsychological examination is used to evaluate the degrees of symptoms and driving simulators are used to measure the reaction time to sudden dangers on the road and avoidance operation such as braking and steering. However, the correspondence relationship between these symptoms and unsafe driving is uncertain and such simulators do not give the sense of acceleration and deceleration to the user, and visual resolution or coverage angle of the display is limited, there is a certain gap between real and virtual driving. We have been developing the Driving Skill Evaluation System [1] for cognitive dysfunction drivers, which acquires the driver's behaviors with wearable and wire-less motion sensors and GPS sensor [2, 3]. In this paper, we focus on the difference of safety checking action between drivers with cognitive dysfunction and drivers without cognitive dysfunction. We report the result of analysis on patients' driving data acquired from the experiments by using our system on a designed "private course".

2 Experiment on Designed Parking Area

The experiments are conducted with subjects equipped with wearable wireless motion sensors using real cars on "private course" in Toyama Driving Education Center, Japan. Figure 1 shows the top view of designed "private course" for the experiment. The course includes several kinds of road conditions, such as signalized/nonsignalized, intersections with/without stop sign and parking area, and roads with several kinds of speed limitation that take 10–15 min to drive. Figure 1 also shows enlarged view of the parking area and expected car parking trajectory. On parking the car, drivers must go pass the front of parking space, stop once and move backward to the parking space. Drivers can retry this parking procedure as much as they need.

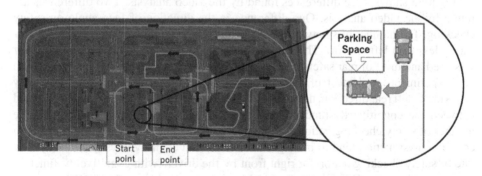

Fig. 1. Designed "private course" and enlarged view of parking area

The subjects are 14 cognitive dysfunction patients and 13 adults without cognitive dysfunction. Six video cameras are installed inside and outside of the car in order to record driving behavior in detail. These video cameras record the drivers from forward, side and backward. One video camera is also attached near the driver's foot in order to record pedal action.

3   Detected Differences from Video Analysis

As shown in Fig. 2, the direction of safety check on parking was classified subjectively to following five groups, front forward, right front, left front, right rear and left rear.

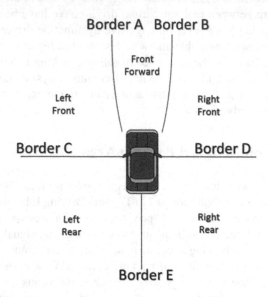

Fig. 2. Classification of safety checking directions

Figure 3 shows three differences found by the video analysis. Two differences are found by the video analysis. One difference is the direction of face angle on safety checking. The number of safety checking actions for the right rear direction is significantly less than left rear (a). The reason is assumed that right-side steering wheel car was used and most of rear safety checking were accomplished with turning lest-side in this experiment. And most of these checking actions were classified as the safety checking of left rear direction, not a right rear direction. Another difference can be found between the cognitive dysfunction drivers and without cognitive dysfunction. The number of safety checking actions for the left front and left rear by the drivers without cognitive dysfunction tend to be larger than ones with cognitive dysfunction (b). The rate of safety checking action for right front by the drivers with cognitive dysfunction drivers are significantly larger than ones without cognitive dysfunction (c). These result can indicate the difference of means to conduct rear safety check. The rear checking by the drivers with cognitive dysfunction is mainly accomplished through the right-side mirror, on the contrary, drivers without cognitive dysfunction mainly accomplished them directly by turning around. However, in the video analysis, checking rear, through the mirror or direct check to right front could not be separated precisely. With eye direction tracking system, these two actions can be distinguished.

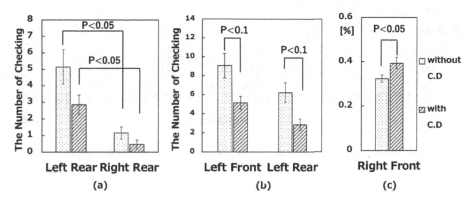

Fig. 3. Differences found by video analysis

4 Unsafe Driving Detection System

We have been developing the Driving Skill Evaluation System with small wireless sensors and evaluate driving aptitude of patients with cognitive dysfunction [4]. In this experiment, this system was used to capture driver's action. We put the sensors on the driver's head and toes, as well as the car's steering wheel and body, in order to measure their movements. The data from a car, once stopped after passing the front of the parking space until when the car is entirely stopped on the parking space, was captured as the safety checking action data on parking. Face direction angle was calculated and analyzed as safety checking action from these data.

We obtain yaw angle (relative angle around the vertical axis from the ground) of the head from sensor data of acceleration and angular velocity by Kalman filter, where constant offset of angular velocity is removed based on the data while the car stops before starting. In order to obtain relative yaw angle from the car body, we subtract yaw angle of a car body from that of the driver's head. However, there still remains irregular offset drift of angular velocity, which affects the estimated yaw angle. To remove the irregular offset, we calculate the reference value from the middle point between the minimal and maximal values of the yaw angle obtained above in a certain period. We obtain a corrected yaw angle (face direction) by subtracting the reference value from the yaw angle. Furthermore, we also obtain rotation angle of the steering wheel from sensor data of acceleration and angular velocity by Kalman filter.

5 Deference Detection by the Sensors

Figures 4 and 5 shows the accumulated safety checking time, for each head angle of the drivers with cognitive dysfunction and without cognitive dysfunction on parking respectively calculated from the attached sensor data.

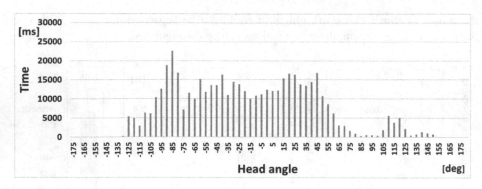

Fig. 4. Accumulated safety checking time (without cognitive dysfunction driver)

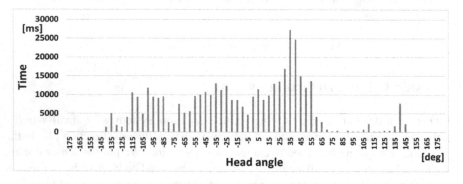

Fig. 5. Accumulated safety checking time (with cognitive dysfunction driver)

In Figs. 4 and 5, 0-degree angle indicates right in front forward, and negative value indicates left angle of front forward, positive value indicates right angle of front forward. To compare with the result of video analysis shown in chapter three, these safety checking actions must be classified into five groups which are used in video analysis. In Figs. 3 and 4 it is confirmed that the accumulated time of safety checking action around $-75°$ and $75°$ looks less than other close angles. Then, the border line C and the border line D was decided to $\pm75°$ respectively. And border A and B decided to $\pm10°$ respectively because the scope of both side check should include the front corner check of the car and measured angle of the right corner is $75°$. Using these decided value, captured safety checking actions were classified to five groups. It is confirmed that the result of comparing video analysis, the sensor data also indicates that the number of safety checking action for rear directly is significantly less than those for other directions. However, the rate of are not significant while both has same tendency on the video analysis.

It cannot be detected that the difference of the number of safety checking actions for the left front and left rear between the drivers with cognitive dysfunction and ones without cognitive dysfunction, which was detected on the video analysis. While the rate of safety checking action for right front by the drivers with cognitive dysfunction drivers tends to be larger than ones without cognitive dysfunction.

6   Conclusion

We conducted experiments equipped with wearable wireless motion sensors using real cars. The video analysis of the safety checking action found the typical safety check action to the rear direction by the cognitive dysfunction patients which can be the candidate of their feature. However, it is uncertain why the feature appears, but the following hypothesis are considered. The cognitive dysfunction patients tend to check rear through rear view mirror, while drivers without cognitive dysfunction tend to check directly by turning around. To verify this hypothesis, the experiment with eye tracking system should be conducted. And we investigated adaptability of our Driving Skill Evaluation System [1] to distinguish above typical checking actions of cognitive dysfunction drivers and clarified that our system can detect a part of those typical safety checking action.

It should be studied further that with eye tracking system, in order to analyze the reason why the typical safety checking action occurs. Accordingly, our Driving Skill Evaluation System [1] must be improved to judge more detailed information.

Acknowledgment. We would like to thank Toyama Driving Education Center and Toyama rehabilitation Hospital for the cooperation in the experiments. This work was supported by JSPS KAKENHI Grant Number 15K01472.

References

1. Toriyama, T., Urashima, A., Nakamura, M., Nomura, T., Ohshima, J., Yoshino, O.: A study of driving skill evaluation system using wearable sensors for cognitive dysfunction. IEICE Technical report, vol. 113, no. 272, WIT2013-48, pp. 29–34, October 2013. (in Japanese)
2. Objet. http://www.sensetech.jp/ATR-SensetechGV.html. (in Japanese)
3. Tada, M., Nayo, F., Ohmura, R., Okada, M., Noma, H., Toriyama, T., Kogure, K.: A method for measuring and analyzing driving behavior using wireless accelerometers. IEICE Trans. Inf. Syst. (Jpn. Edn.) **J91-D**(4), 1115–1129 (2008). (in Japanese)
4. Toriyama, T., Urashima, A., Yoshikuni, S.: Detection system of unsafe driving behavior significant for cognitive dysfunction patients. In: Stephanidis, C. (ed.) HCI 2017. CCIS, vol. 713, pp. 391–396. Springer, Cham (2017). https://doi.org/10.1007/978-3-319-58750-9_54

Study on UI of Charger in EV Charging Station

Wonseok Yang[1(✉)], Takanori Hirohashi[1], and Yeongchae Choi[2]

[1] Engineering and Design, Shibaura Institute of Technology,
3-9-14, Shibaura, Minato-ku, Tokyo, Japan
yang@shibaura-it.ac.jp
[2] Graduate School of Engineering and Science,
Shibaura Institute of Technology, 3-7-5, Toyo-su, Koto-ku, Tokyo, Japan

Abstract. Since the current Quick Charging system is different from the conventional gas station in terms of operation procedures and information display, it is highly likely that a person not accustomed to the Quick Charging system will be confused when charging. Problems related to operability are studied to occur due to mismatch of conceptual models owned by designers and users in smart phones, home appliances, and the like. However, research on charging infrastructure and battery problems has been made for current EV related research, but research on operation is few in the use of Quick Charging system. Therefore, from the viewpoint of UI/UX, we thought that it was necessary to study the design of the operation method in the Quick Charging station. In this research, we conducted a survey of the current Quick Charging system, and created a task and a UI model for usability test. As a research result, "redesign the configuration of UI at password acquisition time and simplify information" on smartphone "and" review information given to people not accustomed to charging EV and improve understanding of operation "are required It was confirmed that it was. Based on the results, we reconsidered the operation method of fast charging stand for charging.

Keywords: EV charging station · Quick Charging system · UX/UI
Usability

1 Introduction

Many automobile manufacturers are working on the development of EV (Electric vehicle) to solve environmental and energy issue. At the Beijing Motor Show in 2016, more than 50 types of vehicles that can be directly charged from the outside of car, such as EV and PHV, were announced, and it is thought that popularization will continue in near future. [1] Although EV charging stations with authentication systems are spreading, charging infrastructure for running long distances with peace of mind is not enough. However, research on charging infrastructure and battery problems has been made for current EV related research, but research on operation is few in the use of Quick Charging system. Therefore, from the viewpoint of UI/UX, we believe that it was necessary to study the design of the operation method in the Quick Charging station [2].

C. Stephanidis (Ed.): HCII Posters 2018, CCIS 852, pp. 410–417, 2018.
https://doi.org/10.1007/978-3-319-92285-0_56

When investigating user-centric information-communication devices from an operational perspective, it is observed that contemporary devices have been changing their operational methodology owing to the advent of smartphones and information. In addition, the information device itself is also directly connected to the Internet, and in the past where one complex operation was not possible without several terminals, it is now possible to perform several operations with one device [3, 4]. Also, in recent years, various things have been connected to the Internet, and IoT-converted devices that can be controlled and managed automatically are rapidly proliferating. In addition to the above information-communication devices, furniture such as tables and chairs, automobile-related products, and the like are also becoming possible to operate via a smartphone. For this reason, the user's lifestyle is becoming centered on information-communication devices such as smartphones. Therefore, we think that it is necessary to design a new user interface to keep pace with the changes in technology and users' lifestyles [5]. Our research shows that the configuration of the UI during password acquisition needs to be redesigned, the simplify information on the smartphone needs to be simplified, and the information given to people not accustomed to charging EV and improve understanding of operation must be reviewed (Fig. 1).

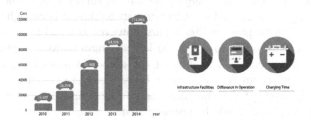

Fig. 1. Number of units owned by EV etc. Statistics and current problems

2   Research Method

In this research, in order to design a new operational method by obtaining the current status of a quick charging stand and the user's ability to operate it, we proceeded with the following steps:

(1) Get the current situation and conduct a survey at the quick charge station
(2) Test usability on the operation screen of the quick charge system.

3   Research Result

3.1   Observation Survey and Interview at Quick Charging Station

On May 30, 2016, an interview and current-situation survey were conducted at Nissan Prince Tokyo Sales Co. Ltd. at their Kamata shop. During the interview, there were several cards used in the quick charging station, so it became heavy, and the fee was not displayed. In the current-situation survey, the users were able to grasp that they misunderstood it as a touch panel, but they were perplexed by password entry and so on (Fig. 2).

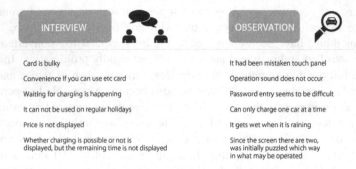

Fig. 2. Interview and observation results

3.2   Summary of Operational Configuration of Charging Station

Physical buttons are used in the charging station we surveyed this time. Therefore, it was relatively easy to understand the selection part because it is enough to press either "OK" or "Return." In the password-input part, however, one had to select the numbers 0 to 9 laid out in a horizontal row with the left and right buttons, so we received the impression that the operation was difficult for users. Also, as the charging station couples the charging controller to the main body, there are two displays. Therefore, when standing in front of the charging stand for the first time, it was difficult to understand which display should be operated first.

3.3   Usability Test on Operation Screen

A usability test using a test model with more than 2 years of smartphone experience, no experience of using a gas station (GS), and no driving history (26 people) in order to ascertain whether the user can operate smoothly from the start to the end of charging was carried out. We gave the subjects the following tasks to perform. After the test, we conducted a questionnaire and interview on a series of operations. In the survey, we asked a free questionnaire and 15 questions were to be answered using the SD method. Principal component analysis was carried out based on the data obtained via the questionnaire (Fig. 3).

Fig. 3. Task flow

(1) **Experimental setting**

We explained the service provided by the charging station, the assumptions, and the series of operations of the charging in advance using a picture of the actual charging device. We shot the actual viewpoint with a head camera and the whole scene with a video camera. The observer walked behind and arranged them side by side in anticipation of people lining up to the charging station (Fig. 4).

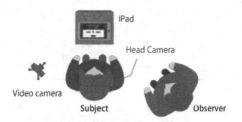

Fig. 4. Experimental setting

(2) **Results of principal component analysis**

From the principal component analysis to interpret the overall meaning based on the questionnaire survey, "composition" and "comprehension degree" were cited as the principal components, so it is necessary to review the charging configuration. We found that it is necessary to provide icons and easy-to-understand designs such as charging status, and provide information in an easy-to-understand manner.

- **Satisfaction rating of operating the charging station**

  As a result of the principal component analysis, six principal components with high explanatory sentences with eigenvalues exceeding 1 were detected (Table 1).
  - The first principal component contained "easy to understand operation", "easy to understand button operation", and "prompt response to operation." In other words, it can be inferred that it means "good operability."
  - The second principal component contained "it takes more time than expected", "cannot understand how to use immediately", and "the screen is unfamiliar." In other words, it can be judged that it means "the degree of understanding of the UI and the operational procedure is low."
  - The third principal component contains "the on-screen information cannot be trusted", "after the operation is completed, the next operation can be expected", and "there is a sense of unity in the sequence of operations". In other words, it can be judged that "reliability of operations is low."
  - The fourth principal component contains "the writing is difficult to understand", "feels like more information is asked than necessary". In other words, it can be judged that "the information displayed in the UI is insufficient."
  - The fifth principal component contains "there is a word which you do not under stand", "screen coloration is easy to understand", "there is unity in button

operation and screen display". In other words, it can be judged that "the text is bad but the design is good."

- The sixth principal component contains "it is hard to return to the previous screen." It can be simply judged to mean "hard to return to the previous screen".

Table 1. Satisfaction rating for charging station Principal component analysis

NO	1	2	3	4	5	6
Eigenvalue	3.4176	2.4931	1.6578	1.5577	1.2995	1.2140
Proportion	21.360	15.582	10.362	9.735	8.122	7.588
Cumulative	21.360	36.942	47.303	57.039	65.161	72.748

Variable	PCA1	PCA2	PCA3	PCA4	PCA5	PCA6
Text sentence is easy to understand	-0.081	0.357	0.137	-0.392	0.154	0.261
Trusted above the screen	0.205	0.316	-0.469	0.115	0.057	-0.115
Do not understand a word	-0.382	-0.085	0.041	-0.137	0.392	0.086
Feel that I need more information when charging	0.014	-0.043	0.173	0.590	-0.156	0.281
It takes longer than I expected	0.109	0.465	0.033	0.122	-0.229	-0.298
The operation procedure is easy to understand	0.330	-0.298	0.084	-0.060	-0.046	0.235
How to use can be understood immediately	0.205	-0.256	0.133	-0.154	0.076	0.098
After completing the operation, the next operation can be predicted	0.113	0.301	0.444	-0.261	-0.305	-0.104
There is unity in the flow of operations	0.363	0.040	0.358	0.127	-0.040	0.196
Screen color scheme is easy to understand	-0.069	0.083	0.192	0.425	0.429	0.182
The screen has familiarity	0.234	-0.419	0.165	-0.006	-0.142	-0.380
Easy to understand button operation	0.376	0.090	0.025	-0.241	0.275	0.292
Quick response to operation comes back	0.332	0.211	-0.177	0.259	0.125	0.051
There is unity in button operation and screen display	0.282	0.153	0.193	-0.053	0.423	-0.273
Easy to return to the previous screen	-0.133	-0.011	0.364	0.159	0.333	-0.493

- **Comparison with sex, license status, and gas station stand experience**
  Next, we made a comparison based on sex, license possession, and gasoline stand experience. The comparison result is as follows: when comparing by sex and license retention, the difference was in "amount of information when charging", "ease of button operation", etc. When compared with "license understanding", "easy to return to previous screen" was returned. On comparison with the gas station experience, we can find a difference in "understanding of usage" (Table 2).
- **Survey on usability of charging stand**
  Regarding the usability of the charging station, the results of "time taken", "total number of taps", and "number of erroneous taps" are as follows.

  1. **Time**
     Regardless of license or gas station experience, we can confirm that it takes three tries to start the charging operation and four tries to terminate the charging operation when taking the password (Fig. 5).

- **Number of taps and number of erroneous taps**
  The number of erroneous taps at the start of the charging operation is found to be 12 times as high as the time of completion, and the number of erroneous taps is large until the user gets used to the device. Moreover, it can be confirmed that a person

Table 2. Comparison with sex, license hold status and gas station stand experience

	SEX	Absence of license holders	Absence of GS experience
Text sentence is easy to understand	n.s.	n.s.	n.s.
Trusted above the screen	n.s.	n.s.	n.s.
Do not understand a word	n.s.	n.s.	n.s.
Feel that I need more information when charging	$p < 0.1$	n.s.	n.s.
It takes longer than I expected	n.s.	n.s.	n.s.
The operation procedure is easy to understand	n.s.	n.s.	n.s.
How to use can be understood immediately	n.s.	$p < 0.1$	$p < 0.05$
After completing the operation, the next operation can be predicted	n.s.	n.s.	n.s.
There is unity in the flow of operations	n.s.	n.s.	n.s.
Screen color scheme is easy to understand	n.s.	n.s.	n.s.
The screen has familiarity	n.s.	n.s.	n.s.
Easy to understand button operation	$p < 0.05$	n.s.	n.s.
Quick response to operation comes back	$p < 0.05$	n.s.	$p < 0.05$
There is unity in button operation and screen display	n.s.	n.s.	n.s.
Easy to return to the previous screen	n.s.	$p < 0.05$	n.s.

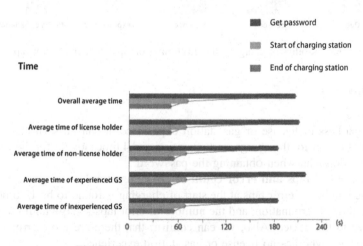

Fig. 5. Usability of charging Station (time)

who has no license or gas station experience has more erroneous taps than a person with a license. Regardless of license availability or gas station experience, there was a difference in the usability of the charging station at the beginning and the end of charging.

As a result, it is necessary to "improve the UI design at the time of password acquisition", "shorten operation time", "reduce the number of errors", and "redesign the UI for charging start and charging end", as interpreted from our analysis (Fig. 6).

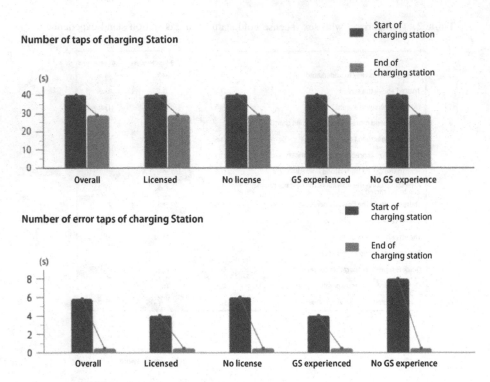

Fig. 6. Usability of charging stand (number of taps/number of error taps)

- **Usability**

  (1) **Time**

      Regardless of license or gas station experience, it can be seen that it takes 3 times longer for the charge start operation and 4 times longer for the charge end operation than when obtaining the password.

  (2) **Number of taps and error count of charging stand**

      The number of error taps at the start of charging is found to be 12 times that at the time of termination, and the number of error taps is large until the user gets used to the device. Also, we can confirm that there are more error taps from someone who has no license or gas station experience.

- **Opinion**

  Positive opinions are many, such as "few buttons makes it so simple", and "less annoying." There are many negative opinions, such as "password input is hard", "people around can see", and "the password acquisition page is difficult to understand". As for suggestions, we see that there are many opinions saying "QR code", "detailed information on charging situation", and "numeric keypad".

4   Conclusion

In this research, we conducted a survey on the current status of quick charging stations and examined a new charging method. As a result of the survey, in the principal component analysis result on the satisfaction level, we found "low understanding of operation procedures and UI" and "the information displayed on the UI is insufficient." As for the usability survey results, it took about 5 min from one charging operation to the next, so we felt it was necessary to shorten the operation time. Together with the above problems, "redesign the configuration of the UI when acquiring passwords on smartphones and simplify information" and "review the information given to people who are not accustomed to charging EVs and understanding operability" are improvements to be considered.

References

1. Next Generation Vehicle Promotion Center, Case Studies of Infrastructure for Charging EVS and PHVS (2009)
2. Akatsu, H., Miki, H., Komatsubara, A.: Principles guiding the design of IT equipment based on the cognitive behavioral characteristics of elderly users, use of experimentally designed ATM prototypes. J. Jpn. Ind. Manag. Assoc. 61(6), 337–346 (2010)
3. Urokohara, H., Tatsubuchi, M., Sato, D., Furuta, K.: A case study of "efficiency of an operation" evaluation and the following tool development by NEM (quantitative usability evaluation method). In: Human Interface Society Symposium (2001)
4. Yuasa, N., Ihara, M., Nakamura, M., Matsumoto, K.: Evaluating usability of integrated services in home network services. EICE Tech. Rep. 106(578), 399–404 (2007)
5. Katsuo, I.: Interface Design Textbook. Maruzen, Reston (2011)
6. Johnson, J.: Designing with the Mind in Mind: Simple Guide to Understanding User Interface Design Guidelines, 2nd edn. Morgan Kaufmann, San Francisco (2014)
7. Masaaki, K.: Human Centered Design Basics. Kindaikagakusa Publishing (2016)
8. Nielsen, J.: Usability Engineering (Interactive Technologies). Morgan Kaufmann, San Francisco (1994)
9. Masaaki, K.: Usability Testing - Towards User-Centered Manufacturing. Kyoritsu-Publishing, Tokyo (2003)
10. Fukaya, M.: Usability Engineering: usability engineering for home appliances. IPSJ Mag. 44(2), 145–150 (2003)
11. Wake, H., Wake, T., Mogi, K., Nonaka, E.: Evaluation of the automatic teller machine guided by pictorial representation in touch and voice information for the persons with visual impairments. J. Psychol. Educ. Kanagawa Univ. 22, 104–162 (2003)

Experimental Design for Multi-modal Take-over Request for Automated Driving

Hanna Yun[1], Ji Won Lee[1], Hee Dong Yang[1], and Ji Hyun Yang[2(✉)]

[1] Graduate School of Automotive Engineering, Kookmin University,
Seoul 02707, Korea
[2] Department of Automotive Engineering, Kookmin University,
Seoul 02707, Korea
yangjh@kookmin.ac.kr

Abstract. Despite recent advancement in autonomous vehicles, limitations of autonomous driving system still remain. When the autonomous driving system encounters failure, it hands over dynamic driving task to the driver. In the event of a failure of the autonomous driving system, effective take-over request should be issued according to driver's status to guarantee safety and comfort of a driver. To devise the optimal alert modalities for take-over request that can minimize the risk of failure in the autonomous driving system, the following factors were drawn out for the experimental design: 4 scenarios for take-over request through the case analysis of cause of autonomous driving disengagement; and verifiable vehicle alert modalities of visual, auditory, and tactile aspects for take-over request through the literature search and market research. Then, we have established a virtual reality simulator for experiment environment that can effectively identify driver's status based on human factors. This study will find out effective multi-modality for take-over request through an analysis of statistically significant differences according to driver's status based on human factors by drawing the quantitative/qualitative data based on scenarios for take-over request and combinations of vehicle alert modalities of visual, auditory, and tactile aspects obtained from the results of previous studies analyzed in this experiment environment.

Keywords: Autonomous driving system · Take-over request · Human factor
Alert · Modality · Vehicle interface

1 Introduction

Car manufacturers in the world recently release vehicles equipped with diverse cutting-edge functions, providing safety and convenience for drivers effectively. Such cutting-edge functions are defined as the Advanced Driver Assistance System (ADAS) and cars with ADAS are called autonomous vehicles. Car makers and engineering scientists over the world focus on developing the sensor technology of autonomous vehicles. When developing an autonomous vehicle, it is important to develop high-performance sensors but it is also essential to consider HMI (Human-Machine Interaction) [1]. Amid the rising issues over autonomous vehicles these days, research on the HMI aspect has begun to be stimulated.

© Springer International Publishing AG, part of Springer Nature 2018
C. Stephanidis (Ed.): HCII Posters 2018, CCIS 852, pp. 418–425, 2018.
https://doi.org/10.1007/978-3-319-92285-0_57

In autonomous vehicles, their automation levels are defined under diversified criteria; and, depending upon the levels, HMI research should be progressed differently. At the lowest level (e.g., no automation, or level 0 in [2]) of automation the human driver is in full control of the car. Cars at automation level 3 have lower human participation in driving task of driver. But, when the autonomous driving system reaches its limit, human drivers are required to involve in driving. Such an autonomous vehicle is defined as a conditional autonomous vehicle (e.g., level 3 in [2]). In full automation (e.g., level 5 in [2]), the human driver is not involved in any driving task anymore [3].

Compared to existing work [4, 8], in this present study, experimental design was implemented for the designing of a multi-modality alert capable of making request alerts in the most effective manner in the take-over situation that can happen in partial or conditional autonomous vehicles. This study seeks to design a multi-modal take-over request which can enhance the safety of autonomous vehicle by delivering take over requests to human drivers most effectively based on take-over cases analysis, take-over scenario design, and alert modalities of visual, auditory and tactile aspects.

2 Take-over Case Study and Scenario Design

2.1 Analysis of Cases of Autonomous Driving Disengagement

Various companies are developing autonomous driving system, and doing real road driving tests with the license on the temporary operation of such autonomous vehicles in CA, US. The manufacturers record and present in report events of autonomous driving disengagement during their real road tests. Such reports contain the frequency of autonomous driving disengagement events, cause of disengagement, reaction time in the event of take-over request, etc. Eleven manufacturers organized the 2015 and 2016 records of test and submitted them as the autonomous driving disengagement reports to the Department of Motor Vehicles in State of California by January 1, 2017 [5–7].

In this study, 3,271 disengagement cases were analyzed in reports by 7 organizations, which seemed to have been prepared in an analyzable manner. The circumstances and causes of take-over request recorded in the reports were expressed in key words and categorized under driver, vehicle, and environment factors. The driver factor means disengagement by drivers as they felt uncomfortable due to the delay of deceleration in autonomous vehicle, failure of lane keeping control, etc. The vehicle factor means disengagement by the system based on the failure of perception, decision, control and network of the autonomous system or vehicle failure. The environment factor means autonomous driving system disengagement because of traffic participants, road, weather, traffic flow, and obstruction. As a result of statistical analysis, the driver factor accounted for 21.7% of the disengagement causes; vehicle factor, 53.4%; and environment factor, 24.8%.

2.2 Design of Take-over Request Scenario

To design the optimal take-over multi-modal request alert method, take-over scenario design was implemented in this study. This study looks at only the system disengagement to explore an effective take-over request alert method.

First, the causes of take-over request can be divided into two groups at a higher level. Type A is defined as unplanned take-over circumstances and Type B, planned take-over circumstances. Type A is subdivided into autonomous system failure, vehicle failure, and unplanned ODD (Operational Design Domain) exit. Type B is classified under Planned ODD Exit, meaning that the autonomous system is ended as its planned driving task is finished. Examples of Type A and Type B take-over circumstances are shown in Table 1.

Table 1. Examples of take-over request according to disengagement causes.

Type	Cause of disengagement	Example of take-over request
A type	Autonomous System Failure	Faulty sensor perceptions such as RADAR/LiDAR to halt autonomous driving
		Localization failure to halt autonomous driving
	Vehicle Failure	ECU (engine control unit) failure to lose basic vehicle functionality
	Unplanned ODD Exit	Insufficient lane mark to halt autonomous driving
		Construction zone not registered with route information to halt autonomous driving
B type	Planned ODD Exit	Autonomous driving mode finished upon the completion of a planned route

For the implementation of take-over request scenario, scenario design elements were identified [9]. As in Table 2, the scenario design elements were classified based on vehicle type, driving agent, conditions of autonomous driving system and driving speed. Take-over request scenario can be established by adding the design elements to the examples of take-over request identified previously in Table 1. The examples of take-over request scenario are in Table 3.

Table 2. Take-over request scenario design elements.

Classification		Design elements
Vehicle type		Car, truck
Driving agent		Driver, system
Autonomous system	Automation Level	0, 1, 3, 4, 5 (e.g., level in [2])
	Task	Lateral control, longitudinal control, monitor driving environment, fallback performance
	Duration	Short time, continuous
Speed range		Low, mid, high

Table 3. Examples of take-over request according to disengagement causes.

Take-over request circumstance	Scenario design element	Resulted scenario
Perception sensor failure such as RADAR/LiDAR to halt autonomous driving	Vehicle type: Car	When the SAE L3 autonomous vehicle performs longitudinal/lateral control and monitors driving environment at 60 km/h, the system requests the driver to take over due to perception sensor failure
	Driving agent: System	
	Automation level: 3	
	Task: lateral control, longitudinal control, monitor driving environment	
	Duration: Continuous	
	Speed Range: High (more than 60 km)	

3 Previous Study on Alert Modality

3.1 Guidance on the Alert Modalities for Non-autonomous Vehicle

Since there is no guidance on alert modalities of visual, auditory, and tactile aspects for autonomous vehicles; those on alert modalities for non-autonomous were investigated first before producing such guidance for autonomous vehicles. As a result, design elements to consider according to visual, auditory and tactile modalities were organized and such design elements can be differently applied to alert interface depending upon circumstantial urgency and a driver's status.

First of all, the visual modality-based information delivery device is one of the means to communicate information with drivers effectively. Conditions can vary according to visual display type and locating, alert color, character height, legibility, temporal characteristics, and display glare to form an alert interface. Next, the auditory modality-based information delivery device can have an alert interface by varying the conditions according to perceived urgency, perceived annoyance, loudness, distinctiveness, localization cues, and using speech. Lastly, the tactile modality information delivery device is divided into vibrotactile interface and kinesthetic interface and can have an alert interface by setting different conditions according to haptic display type, frequency band that human can detect, and period.

3.2 Previous Study on Alert Modality of Autonomous Vehicle

As the roles of human drivers change in autonomous vehicles, research on new DVI (Driver-Vehicle Interaction) related to autonomous vehicles is going on actively. Although there are not enough studies on the alert methodology in take-over request circumstances, studies on take-over request time and autonomous vehicle alert interface were inspected before producing take-over request alert modality.

With respect to the visual modality-based studies, Walch et al. [10] showed it was effective to vary the alert times using visual modality and give a take-over request 6 s prior to an incident. Eriksson et al. [11] found in their study that an arrow form was the most effective for successful take-over to human drivers.

Among the auditory modality studies, the study by Naujoks et al. [12] showed that, in the event of take-over request in autonomous vehicles, speech was preferred over simple tone. Hester et al. [13] analyzed drivers' trust on warnings in mutually different types in the event of a vehicle failure in autonomous vehicles and found that more drivers successfully avoided collision when they had received speech warning describing emergency.

Among the tactile modality studies, the study by Petermeijuer et al. [14] looked into drivers' reaction time, availability, and pleasantness in relation to tactile modality in the event of a take-over request in autonomous vehicles. They found that, rather than alerting solely based on tactile modality, alerting via both tactile modality and auditory modality was more effective. Telpaz et al. [15] also studies whether a tactile modality alert through the seat improved driver's awareness to achieve effective take-over. They found that the tactile modality helped drivers react to take-over request more swiftly.

3.3   Alert Modality of Mass-Produced Autonomous Vehicle

Prior to establishing a take-over request alert methodology for conditional driving autonomous vehicle, the alert methods of partial autonomous vehicles (e.g., level 2 in [2]) produced by 8 manufacturers were investigated. As of now, there are only mass-produced vehicles at the SAE L2 and one manufacturer, Tesla Motors, provides a take-over request alert function.

In the event of failure to keep the distance between cars or lane departure, the visual modality-based alert devices in the presently mass-produced partial autonomous vehicles provide warnings through an icon or light on their instrument panel or HUD (Head-up Displayer). Next, the auditory modality-based alert interface sounded warning at a set frequency band in a set period if a driver does not operate the steering wheel for a long while or driving speed exceeds 37 miles per hour. A8, produced by Audi, alerts driver if it exceeds 37 miles per hour. Lastly, the tactile modality-based alert interface warned by sending vibration at certain intervals through the steering wheel or seat motor in the event of lane departure or potential collision. Leaf, produced by Nissan, gives an alert if it exceeds 37 miles per hour.

3.4   Establishment of Uni-modal Alert Design

A set of uni-modal alert design was established, which can be considered as the top priority in take-over request studies, based on the investigation on the guidelines on alert methods of existing non-autonomous vehicles, preceding studies on autonomous vehicles' alert methods and alert methods of autonomous vehicles mass-produced so far.

The visual-based alert method can provide a warning sign containing the phrase, "Take Over Immediately", on the head-up display in 3 Hz period until take-over is complete, as its first method described in Method 1 in Fig. 1. Subsequently, as shown in Method 2, it provides a warning sign containing the phrase, "Take Over Immediately" on the room mirror in 3 Hz period until the take-over is complete. Lastly, as in

Method 3, it can provide a warning icon to a bar-formed model with red-colored background and a warning sign including the phrase, "Take Over" on the instrument panel or head-up display in 3 Hz period until the take-over is completed.

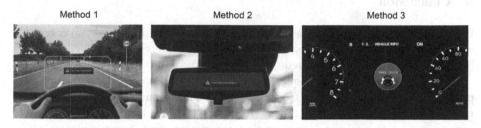

Fig. 1. Example of visual-based alert method.

The auditory-based alert method borrows the warning sound of presently mass-produced partial autonomous vehicles and repeats 0.2-second-long warning sound two times at 0.06-s intervals at 533 Hz in the event of any take-over request incident; or provides 0.09-second-long warning sound three times at 0.03 intervals at 1498 Hz. It also employs these two warning sounds and the signal from previous study to mix 880 Hz and 1760 Hz single tones and sound 0.05-second-long warning three times at 0.03-s intervals.

In the tactile-based method, motor is horizontally arranged in the widest possible range around the back and gluteus of human drivers' seat and vibration alerts can be gradually increased from the lowest level of 60 Hz up to 250 Hz. Until the take-over is completed, 0.2-second-long pulse can be provided through the back and gluteus of human drivers' seat at 0.05-s intervals. Also, 0.2-second-long pulse at the lowest level of 200 Hz up to 250 Hz can be given through the gluteus of human drivers' seat at 0.05-s intervals.

4   Experimental Environment Setup

A driving simulator was constructed, which can materialize the take-over request scenario in virtual reality, provide take-over request alert to drivers, and measure their reactions.

Huyndai's medium-sized sedan, LF SONATA, was utilized as a cabin. To implement the virtual driving environment and autonomous vehicle functions, the SCANeR 1.7 program was employed. To realize take-over request alert modality, visual, auditory and tactile alert interfaces were equipped. The visual modality alert interface was made with center fascia, instrument panel, rear-view mirror, and side mirrors LED monitor. The auditory modality alert interface was established by utilizing 5.1Ch speaker; and the tactile device, the vibration of seat, steering wheel, and accelerator pedal.

In order to measure drivers' status, NVR Camera was installed, which can provide video monitoring of driver behaviors. Drivers' sight patterns are identified through

Face Lab's eye tracker. In addition, BioPac's bio-signal interface was employed to gain drivers' bio-signals such as electrocardiogram, and GSR (Galvanic Skin Response).

5 Conclusion

In this study, a previous study was performed on alert modalities for take-over request, which can secure take-over safety in conditional autonomous vehicles (e.g., level 3 in [2]) expected to be commercialized.

The established take-over request scenario and multi-modality combination proposals will be materialized with the virtual environment simulator to build an experiment device capable of assessing drivers' reaction and gain vehicle and driver data. We plan to implement a take-over request alert experiment, draw quantitative/qualitative data, analyze statistically significant difference in driver and vehicle data according to take-over request multi-modal alert method, and establish a take-over request multi-modal alert method.

Acknowledgment. This research was supported by a grant (code 17TLRP-B131486-01) from Transportation and Logistics R&D Program funded by the Ministry of Land, Infrastructure and Transport of Korean government. The first author was partly supported by Basic Science Research Program through the National Research Foundation of Korea (NRF), funded by the Ministry of Science, ICT, and Future Planning (2017R1A2B4008615).

References

1. Kim, H., Yang, J.: Takeover requests in simulated partially autonomous vehicles considering human factors. IEEE Trans. Hum. Mach. Syst. **PP**(99), 1–6 (2017)
2. Taxonomy and definitions for terms related to on-road motor vehicle automated driving systems. SAE Standard J3016. SAE On-road Automated Vehicle Standards Committee. SAE International (2016)
3. Remo, M.A., Shamsi, T., Christian, P.: Priming drivers before handover in semi-autonomous cars. In: CHI 2017, USA (2017)
4. Gold, C., Dambock, D., Lorenz, L., Bengler, K.: "Take over!" How long does it take to get the driver back into the loop? Proc. Hum. Factors Ergonomics Soc. Ann. Meet. **57**(1), 1938–1942 (2013)
5. California Legislation Information, Division 16.6. Autonomous Vehicles. https://leginfo. legislature.ca.gov/faces/codes_displayText.xhtml?lawCode=VEH&division=16.6.&title= &part=&chapter=&article=. Accessed 20 Jan 2018
6. State of California Department of Motor Vehicles, Order to Adopt. https://www.dmv.ca.gov/ portal/wcm/connect/d48f347b-8815-458e-9df2-5ded9f208e9e/adopted_txt.pdf?MOD= AJPERES. Accessed 20 Jan 2018
7. Google self-driving car testing report on disengagements of autonomous mode, December 2015. https://www.dmv.ca.gov/portal/wcm/connect/dff67186-70dd-4042-bc8c-d7b2a9904665/ google_disengagement_report.pdf?MOD=AJPERES. Accessed 15 Dec 2017
8. Yun, Y.: Trend and issue of driver-vehicle interface for autonomous vehicle. J. Korean Soc. Automot. Eng. **38**(2), 34–40 (2016)

9. System Classification and Glossary. Deliverable D2.1. Automated Driving Applications and Technologies for Intelligent Vehicles. https://www.adaptive-ip.eu/index.php/deliverables_ papers.html. Accessed 02 Mar 2018
10. Walch, M., Muehl, K.: Autonomous driving: investigating the feasibility of car-driver handover assistance. In: Proceedings of the 7th International Conference on Automotive User Interfaces and Interactive Vehicular Applications (2015)
11. Eriksson, A., Petermeijer, S.M., Zimmerman, M., De Winter, J.C.F., Bengler, K.J., Stanton, N.A.: Rolling out the red (and green) carpet: supporting driver decision making in automation-to-manual transitions. IEEE Trans. Hum. Mach. Syst. Subj. Correct. **102C**, 227–234 (2017)
12. Naujoks, F., Forster, Y., Wiedemann, K., Neukum, A.: Speech improves human-automation cooperation in automated driving. In: Mensch und Computer 2016–Workshopband (2016)
13. Hester, M., Lee, K., Dyre, B.P.: "Driver Take Over": a preliminary exploration of driver trust and performance in autonomous vehicles. In: Proceedings of the International Annual Meeting of Human Factors and Ergonomics Society (2017)
14. Petermeijer, S.M., Cieler, S., De Winter, J.C.F.: Comparing spatially static and dynamic vibrotactile take-over requests in the driver seat. Accid. Anal. Prev. **99**, 218–227 (2017)
15. Telpaz, A., Rhindress, B., Zelman, I., Tsimhoni, O.: Haptic seat for automated driving: preparing the driver to take control effectively. In: Proceedings of the 7th International Conference on Automotive User Interfaces and Interactive Vehicular Applications. ACM (2015)

Designing Autonomous Driving HMI System: Interaction Need Insight and Design Tool Study

Yinshuai Zhang[1(✉)], Chun Yu[2], and Yuanchu Shi[2]

[1] Academy of Art and Design, Tsinghua University, Beijing 100084, China
516578981@qq.com
[2] Department of Computer Science and Technology, Tsinghua University,
Beijing 100084, China

Abstract. With the development of high precision sensing, automation, artificial intelligent and etc., human may experience a fully autonomous vehicle in commercial operation in 2021 [1], where passengers might engage in none-driving activities during journeys. There can be more possibilities to design car interior infrastructure and interaction without providing driving interface to drivers. Thus, we can re-design the whole HMI system to provide brand new user experience [2]. Based on an actual project, we summarize the design method and process, we obtained insights of user needs and design the HMI system accordingly. We explain why and how to use the process and tools in the context of our project. Finally, we evaluated our need insight and design tool by contrasting the HMI designed with our process with another HMI designed with a normal process (first think-aloud and then focus group). We also outline a design proposal to express our vision for the interaction design of future autonomous vehicle.

Keywords: Design thinking · Autonomous car · HMI · Need finding
Multi-sense · Intelligent agent

1 Introduction

Nowadays, the user experience study of autonomous car is getting more and more attention. As seen in auto shows, there are lots of HMI concepts describing the outlook of future autonomous car interaction systems. Nissan PIVO uses a physical robot as interaction system. Eleven years later, in their IDS concept car, we can see the same concept with a robot on a movable screen. Daimler uses holographic display in Vision Tokyo concept car. BMW uses HUD display, LED ambient light, at least 9 interactive devices and so on in their HMI system. Not only in concept cars, we can also find the big change of design in production car like Tesla model 3 which only has screen, steering wheel, screen, brake, and accelerator. The HMI concept and study of autonomous car are widely divergent. The interaction of autonomous car today is much like the "faster horse" which people want a century ago. There are enough technology and ideas about the future autonomous cars interaction. So we hold the opinion that the insight of user need and design process is more necessary now.

© Springer International Publishing AG, part of Springer Nature 2018
C. Stephanidis (Ed.): HCII Posters 2018, CCIS 852, pp. 426–433, 2018.
https://doi.org/10.1007/978-3-319-92285-0_58

Highly automated system like autonomous car has a concomitant rise in the breadth and complexity of interaction. Thus, we need a clear, consistent, logical, and holistic design method to design and analyze human-vehicle interaction environment [3]. As most of the product focus on human-centered design process, researchers always involve users in participatory design. But in our study, we found that it is hard for users to put forward ideas in a brand new product which they never experience before. So, we want to propose an innovative method about need insight and interaction design for highly automated human-vehicle interaction system, then design a HMI system using our method and compared our system with another one using normal design method to evaluate our method.

2   Related Works

The work of Sven Krome introduces a context-based design process and a method called "car storm" to provide unique experience for the autonomous car passengers [4]. Bo Zhou utilizes a four steps design process based on service system design method to define the Service-Defined Intelligent Vehicle [5]. Ingrid studies the design techniques for exploring automotive interaction and discuss unmet needs in interaction design for the future [6]. In another area of research, some low cost experimental methods to simulated unmanned vehicle environment are studied due to the difficulty of building an autonomous car. Raphael uses a scale model to do the user test [7]. Tom uses "The Wizard of Oz" [8]. We use a real autonomous test car provided by an enterprise to do the on-road experiment. Our main contribution is that we introduce a design process to insight interaction needs and design HMI system for the autonomous car.

3   The Interaction Model and Definition of Self-driving Car

3.1   The Context of Self-driving Car

The U.S. Department of Transportation's National Highway Traffic Safety Administration (NHTSA) has created the most common definition breaking down autonomous vehicles into 5 categories, which shows the deployment path from none-automation to fully self-driving automation. Since driving task still exists in level 0–3, all the interaction have to be designed as a secondary task [9]. We want to set a free environment that makes our passengers get rid of driving. So we choose level 4 full self-driving automation as the target we design for.

3.2   The Model of Self-driving Car Based on Intelligent Agent

As described in Patrick A.M. Ehlert's work, self-driving car can be defined as an intelligent agent. An intelligent agent is an autonomous, computerized entity capable of sensing environment and acting intelligently based on its perception [10]. Obviously, compared with normal interactive system, to interact with an intelligent agent can result in a more complex interface and task. To be specific, we are facing inaccessible, non-deterministic, non-episodic, dynamic and continuous environment [11].

Our autonomous car can be defined as an intelligent agent through comparison with the model described in Nilsson's "principles of artificial intelligence" [12]. Based the definition in Nilsson's book people should also be seen as an intelligent agent. So in our design process, we do not only think about the users' needs but also find the "car needs". For example, to recognize the user is one of the car needs.

3.3   The Interaction Model of Autonomous Car: Application Scenario

We need to define an interaction between people and vehicle. The human-vehicle inter-action is transforming from an interface for controlling a machine to an interface helping people to communicate with information, intelligent agent and other people [13]. To find a universal model in our system, we need to describe the relationship between people, vehicle, technologies, user needs and so on. With reference to the PACT model put forward by David Benyon, we propose an application scenario used to describe the interaction model between intelligent agents.

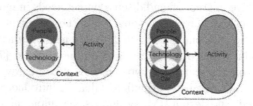

Fig. 1. PACT model (left) and PCACT model (right)

As shown in Fig. 1 we add an agent to the model to make up the new scenario. That is because, in the old model, the car should be part of the technologies. But some scenario doesn't contain people. For example, the Summon function updated in Tesla v7.1 can pick you up wherever you want by the car itself. Autonomous car should be the same as people in the system. Both people and car are agents. They use technologies to act in context. So it should be concluded as a PCACT model as the figure shows. In this model, interface exists between people and technology, people and car, people-car-technology system and activity. Furthermore, there are three different interfaces between people-car-technology system and activity. They are P-T-A, C-T-A, P-C-T-A. What we need to do next is to design interaction system for the 5 different kinds of interface.

4   Interaction Needs Insight and Design Method

4.1   Principle

First of all, we need to define interaction design for autonomous cars. In our opinion, it is to find application scenario, which can prove the technology is useful through the understanding of human need and activities. Finally, we can generate requirement of technology [14]. Thus, we will introduce a design process from need insight to design tool and find the technology needs finally. That will help us to translate users' needs to technical demands.

Design should focus on human needs. There are serval methods to insight the human needs such as user interview, brainstorm, and concepts from other products and so on. But, there will be difference of needs in terms of description and integrity. Therefore, in order to standardize the requirements, we find with different methods. We use the interactive model described in this paper as a script, by supplementing the necessary content in the script, to obtain a large number of application scenario list from different sources but have the same format. The format is the PVACT model we describe before.

In our study, we conducted user interview, brainstorming and network survey to collect application scenarios with details filled and similar ones merged. Finally, we obtained 153 scenarios. There are 21 techniques satisfying the requirements in the 153 scenarios. Obviously, if we put all of the 21 techniques in one product, it will result in a bad user experience because of high complexity and poor efficiency although it can meet all the user needs. Thus, we need a technology convergence to satisfy the needs selectively.

It should be noted that keeping an open mind when filling PCACT model helps to find more needs.

4.2   Need-Technology Matrix

We collected 16 classes of people, 9 classes of autonomous vehicles, 21 classes of technologies, 153 classes of activities and 9 classes of contexts. In order to assist decision making, it is better to show these elements in a visual way. We can fill them in the two-dimension matrix. In general, in the early phase, different classes of people and vehicles do not need to be seen as variables in the matrix (Fig. 2).

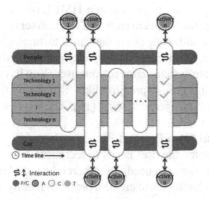

Fig. 2. PCACT matrix

So we can show all the PCACT we found in the two-dimension matrix as the picture show. But it is a concept model, the real matrix in our study should have more information.

The matrix shows us the relationship between the technologies and user needs clearly. Based on this matrix and the needs finding before, we change from design-driven to technology-driven in this phase. Then, we need to analysis the matrix to obtain technology requirements.

4.3   Design with the Matrix

The design process can be summarized in the following steps

Step 1: To Filter High Frequency Ratio Technologies.
It is easy to find that some technologies can be chosen for multiple times in one raw compared with others. Some technologies can only fit for 1, 2 requirements. To make a universal and cost-effective system, we should choose high demanded technology and just site the low demand technology aside.

Step 2: To Identify Special Requirements
After the first requirement screening, we choose the technology which can fit for user needs as much as possible. But the needs can't be satisfied due to technical reduction maybe are important for users. So we should double check the low demand technologies in case of missing some key application scenario. For example, the accelerometer in your smart phone is a high demand technology. You can use it in serval different application scenarios such as Game, human motion data acquisition, auto rotate screen and so on. Fingerprint identification looks like a low demand technology in the matrix which only have two scenarios. But fingerprint unlocks and pay are high frequency scenarios. So Finger print identification is also a high demand technology. In a word, there are two indicators needed to be considered to calculate the demand for technologies, one is the frequency at which the scenarios are triggered, the other one is the number of scenarios.

Step 3: To Optimize Technical Path
After the two focus step, we can get a rough HMI layout and technology list. Next step, we should optimize the technical path. We can find serval different paths to satisfy the application scenario although using the same technologies. What we need is to find the best path. Then, to optimize the best expressing method. For example, when you want to communicate system status to your user. You have at least two expressing methods. One is system centric expressing like "Reliability 64%". Another is human centric expressing like "Engagement 36%" [16]. The expressing method decides the ease and experience of use.

Step 4: To Define Your Own Product
We have already translated the user needs to technical demands. The final step is to define the product with your own needs, commercial needs, branding needs and so on. We can combine the technologies to create a product. Ideally, there is no limit to what product it is. In our study, we do not have to add all of the interactive devices on the car. We can also design a mobile device using the same technologies to make a better in-vehicle experience. In one sentences, the combination of technologies is product design.

5 Result

5.1 Result

Finally, we solicited 4 from the 21 technologies we collected to form the whole vehicle HMI system. We hope to use a minimum of technologies to achieve the greatest effects. To ensure the integrity of the system, there should be at least one input and one output device. For a better user experience and richer application scenarios, we need to combine soft and hard interaction together [15]. So we need to make sure that input and output system have both implicit and explicit interaction devices. Depending on the ranking of technologies demands, we choose the top one to fill in each quadrant. And we get the HMI technology matrix as the Fig. 3 shows.

Fig. 3. HMI technology matrix and result 1

Fig. 4. 1:1 concept car

Based on the matrix, we redesign the HMI layout, as shown in Fig. 5. This system has two inputs and two outputs. The eye-gaze can be used to monitor user status, identify users and so on. Speech control can input the users' command. And the status monitored by eye-gaze can help the system understand the users' voice command better. We cite an instance when user tells the car to stop there the system will park in the area where the user stares at. The output devices consist of 3D sound cue and ambient LED light. They can provide spatial light, 3D VUI, 3D earcon and so on as the output. The light and sound combine together via the space position. Cite an instance, we can set up the voice and LED move together from back to front to express speed up. Based on the HMI layout we designed with our process, we make a 1:1 concept car to test our HMI system (Fig. 4).

Fig. 5. Result 2

5.2   Result Designed with General Method

In order to evaluate how the design method impacts on output of design result in this paper more intuitively, we design another HMI system using the normal design method to compare with result 1. Method 2 is an on-road test. The user is told before test that the car would be driving itself and we have an official security to protect passengers. We encourage the user to think aloud. The users can express their dissatisfaction, creativity, improvement suggestions and so on. Then, all the ideas we collected from the users can be used in the focus group. Finally, we received 89 ideas about the interaction design. After evaluated by users, we designed a HMI layout as shown.

In consideration of the limit of in-vehicle time, users prefer to use their own devices to reduce learning cost. But they still need a larger screen as an extend screen to get a better visual effect. So we will allow user to connect their smart devices with our car system to adapt to our system quickly.

Acknowledgement. Feng zhou and Gansha Wu from UISEE gave many great comments and shared his thoughts generously. Thank you for UISEE to provide the autonomous test car for user test. Thanks you the concept car team for making the car become reality. This project is supported by National Social Science Fund of China under Grant 15CG147.

References

1. Autonomous (2021). https://corporate.ford.com/innovation/autonomous-2021.html
2. Large, D.R., Banks, V., Burnett, G., Margaritis, N.: Putting the joy in driving: investigating the use of a joystick as an alternative to traditional controls within future autonomous vehicles. In: Proceedings of the 9th International Conference on Automotive User Interfaces and Interactive Vehicular Applications, pp. 31–39. ACM, September 2017
3. Heymann, M., Degani, A.: Automated driving aids: modeling, analysis, and interface design considerations. In: Proceedings of the 5th International Conference on Automotive User Interfaces and Interactive Vehicular Applications, pp. 142–149. ACM, October 2013
4. Krome, S., Goddard, W., Greuter, S., Walz, S.P., Gerlicher, A.: A context-based design process for future use cases of autonomous driving: prototyping AutoGym. In: Proceedings of the 7th International Conference on Automotive User Interfaces and Interactive Vehicular Applications, pp. 265–272. ACM, September 2015
5. Zhou, B., Sun, X., Zhang, B.: SDIV: service-defined intelligent vehicle towards the 2020 urban mobility. In: Rau, P.-L.P. (ed.) CCD 2017. LNCS, vol. 10281, pp. 288–298. Springer, Cham (2017). https://doi.org/10.1007/978-3-319-57931-3_23

6. Pettersson, I., Ju, W.: Design techniques for exploring automotive interaction in the drive towards automation. In: Proceedings of the 2017 Conference on Designing Interactive Systems, pp. 147–160. ACM, June 2017
7. Zimmermann, R., Wettach, R.: First step into visceral interaction with autonomous vehicles. In: Proceedings of the 9th International Conference on Automotive User Interfaces and Interactive Vehicular Applications, pp. 58–64. ACM, September 2017
8. van Huysduynen, H.H., Terken, J., Meschtscherjakov, A., Eggen, B., Tscheligi, M.: Ambient light and its influence on driving experience. In: Proceedings of the 9th International Conference on Automotive User Interfaces and Interactive Vehicular Applications, pp. 293–301. ACM, September 2017
9. Summary of levels of driving automation for on-road vehicles. http://cyberlaw.stanford.edu/files/blogimages/LevelsofDrivingAutomation.pdf
10. Lungaro, P., Tollmar, K., Beelen, T.: Human-to-AI interfaces for enabling future onboard experiences. In: Proceedings of the 9th International Conference on Automotive User Interfaces and Interactive Vehicular Applications Adjunct, pp. 94–98. ACM, September 2017
11. Chakraborty, N., Patel, R.S.: Intelligent agents and autonomous cars: a case study. Int. J. Eng. Res. Technol. (IJERT) 2, 1–7 (2013)
12. Nilsson, N.J.: Principles of Artificial Intelligence, 1st edn. Springer, Heidelberg (1982)
13. Benyon, D., Turner, P., Turner, S.: Designing Interactive Systems: People, Activities, Contexts, Technologies. Pearson Education, Harlow (2005)
14. Benyon, D.: Designing Interactive Systems: A Comprehensive Guide to HCI and Interaction Design, 2nd edn. Pearson Education, Harlow (2010)
15. Are we there yet? Thoughts on in-car HMI. https://usweb-cdn.ustwo.com/ustwo-production/uploads/2016/07/AreWeThereYet_V1.2.pdf
16. Noah, B.E., Gable, T.M., Chen, S.Y., Singh, S., Walker, B.N.: Development and preliminary evaluation of reliability displays for automated lane keeping. In: Proceedings of the 9th International Conference on Automotive User Interfaces and Interactive Vehicular Applications, pp. 202–208. ACM, September 2017

Smart Cities and Smart Environments

Automation and Complacency: Insights from a Planning Task in the Transportation Domain

Eugénie Avril[1]([⌧]), Jordan Navarro[2], Liên Wioland[3], Benoit Valery[1],
Virginie Govaere[3], Didier Gourc[4], Koosha Khademi[1],
Christos Dimopoulos[5], Elisabeth Dargent[7], Nathalie Renaudeau[6],
and Julien Cegarra[1]

[1] Science de la Cognition, Technologie, Ergonomie (SCoTE),
University of Toulouse, INU Champollion, Albi, France
{eugenie.avril,benoit.valery,koosha.khademi,
julien.cegarra}@univ-jfc.fr
[2] Laboratoire d'Etude des Mécanismes Cognitifs,
University Lyon 2, Bron, France
jordan.navarro@univ-lyon2.fr
[3] INRS Working Life Department, Paris, France
{lien.wioland,virginie.govaere}@inrs.fr
[4] University of Toulouse, IMT Mines, Albi, France
didier.gourc@mines-albi.fr
[5] Department of Computer Science and Engineering,
European University Cyprus, Engomi, Cyprus
C.Dimopoulos@euc.ac.cy
[6] Deret, Saran, France
nrenaudeau@deret.com
[7] Main Forte, Lille, France
elisabeth.dargent@main-forte.fr

Abstract. Automated systems are becoming increasingly prevalent in our environment. This leads to a new tasks repartition between the human operator and automation. Understanding human-machine cooperation including potential failures has become a hot topic. In this study we focus on a possible negative consequence of automation: the complacency phenomenon. This phenomenon has been repeatedly observed in dynamic situations in which automation execute an action in order to relieve the human operator from his/her activity. In static task, automation often serves to simplify/pre-process the data and not to directly make a decision. The goal of automation in a static task (like planning) is to optimize an external representation and allow the human operator to make his choices more easily. The Eye Tracker is used to understand human behaviors and their strategies in these static situations. The purpose of this study is therefore to compare complacency to "action execution" from complacency to "data simplification". We confronted 96 participants to these two automation types on the Multi Attribute Task Battery. We also manipulated four levels of automation reliability (0%; 56.25%; 87.5%, 100%). In all these conditions we assessed complacency through the detection rate of automation failure. In addition, we used an eye tracker to assess a potential low level of suspicion regarding automation failure.

© Springer International Publishing AG, part of Springer Nature 2018
C. Stephanidis (Ed.): HCII Posters 2018, CCIS 852, pp. 437–442, 2018.
https://doi.org/10.1007/978-3-319-92285-0_59

Keywords: Automation · Reliability · Complacency · Detection failures Trust

1 Introduction

Automation might provide large differences in functioning when comparing dynamic situation such as aircraft piloting to static situation as the planning of delivery in the transportation domain. Since the 1970s, different decompositions of degrees of automation have been proposed in the literature [1, 2]. It also has been proposed to include human-human model of cooperation to human-machine activities [3]. According to Parasuraman [4], different failures in the cooperation between the human operator and the automated system can occur such as the complacency phenomenon. This phenomenon occurs when the human operator is not questioning the actions of the automated systems even if these were wrong. Automation is often considering in the ergonomic literature as an action execution intervening in a dynamic situation. The ecological interface design (EID) [5], allow extending this point of view by focusing on the importance of problem representation. Thus, the design of external representations has become central in this new type of automation [6, 7]. That is the case in the planning of delivery in the transportation domain where the human operator faces a large set of information. The automation is present through an interface where data is pre-processed, thus facilitating information seeking and finally decision making. The objective of the study is to demonstrate that the failures of the cooperation between the human operator and the automation can relate to "action execution" (automation of command) but also to "data simplification" (automation of signaling). We hypothesized an effect of the degree of reliability of the signaling automation and of the degree of reliability of the command automation on the error detection rate.

2 Related Work

Many studies showed the emergence of complacency between human and automation [8–10]. This is particularly present in studies where the reliability of automation is modulated. Unability to detect automation failures is used to demonstrate the evidence of this phenomenon [8–10]. The study of eye movements also supports the hypothesis of the complacency through the attention allocation of the participant [11]. Bagheri and Jamieson [8] did compare different levels of automation reliability. They showed that when the reliability was constant and high, the mean time between fixations in the automated task was higher compared than the other reliability levels. These authors explained the importance of eye movement analysis to better understand the participant's allocation strategies, in addition to the failure detection performance.

Trust of the human operator towards the system is also related to this phenomenon. Here the trust in the system is related to the automation performance [12]. All of these studies have in common to use the Multi Attribute Task Battery, a micro world of aircraft piloting that can present both "action execution" and "data simplification" automation [13].

In our study, we hypothesize that when automation reliability is high, the participant will tend to be "complacent" with the automated system and therefore will not necessarily detect and react correctly to automation failures. Contrary, with a highly unreliable automated system, the participant will regain control (ie. a lower confidence) and will more easily detect errors (ie. a lower complacency). Indeed, when automation fails in the task, the participant does the task instead of automation and thus regain control.

3   Research Methodology

3.1   Design

We confronted 96 participants to 4 conditions of reliability of automation (24 in each condition).

The 4 levels of reliability of the automation were 0%; 56.25%; 87.5% and 100%. Two types of automation were used: an automation of command and an automation of signaling. The reliability of the command automation was an intra-subject variable; the participants performed the 4 levels of reliability. Conversely, the reliability of signaling automation was inter-subject; each condition corresponding to a level of reliability (and therefore the 4 levels of reliability "execution").

As the experiment is currently underway, only two conditions could be performed by the participants at the moment (0% and 56.25% of signaling automation).

3.2   The Multi Attribute Task Battery

Each participant has to perform three tasks in parallel. The first task was a monitoring task (Fig. 1. Top left). This task consisted of four columns. In a normal situation, the cursor fluctuated around the center of the column. In case of failure, the cursor froze

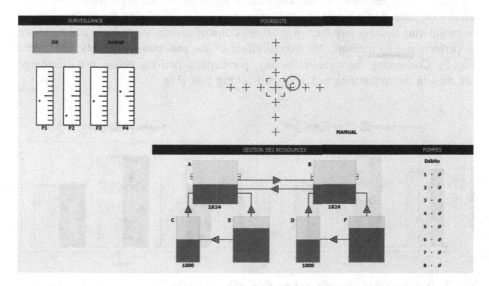

Fig. 1. The multi attribute task battery.

in the lower part or the upper part of the column (and not in the center) and the "failure" light changed to red. When there was a failure, the participant had to press F1 (if the cursor was blocked in column 1), F2 (column 2), F3 (column 3) and F4 (column 4).

In our study, this task was automated. The cursor was automatically unblocked after 10 s when there was a failure. However, the automated system might dysfunction: sometimes, the cursor could not be unblocked (command automation) and the light did not change to red (signaling automation) while there was a failure. In these cases, the participant had to regain control by pressing the corresponding key. The participant was warned of "possible automation failures, in the release of cursor to nominal state or in the color signalling."

The resource management task consisted of several tanks (Fig. 1 bottom). The goal is to maintain tanks A and B at 2500 units each (optimal value). However, the fuel emptied into these two tanks and the participant had to activate pumps to use the safety tanks and to keep the values in these tanks. The reserve tanks E and F were unlimited unlike other tanks whose liquid level was displayed under them. The different tanks did not have the same rate of fluctuation of the liquid. Thus, the pumps 1 and 2 had a flow rate of 800; pumps 3, 4, 5 and 6 had a flow rate of 600; pumps 7 and 8 had a flow rate of 400. When the participant activated a pump, the flow rate appeared on the right. To fill the main tanks, participants had to use the number located on their keyboard.

The last task is a compensatory tracking task and the subject's task is to keep the target in the center of the window with a Joystick (Fig. 1 top right).

We used an SMI Eye Tracker to measure eye movements (at a 120 Hz sampling rate).

4   Results

The results are not final because the experiment is still underway. Therefore only the first results on two conditions are described below (0% and 56.25% of signaling automation).

The effect of reliability of the automation signaling on the performance was analyzed. Condition 4 of reliability (100%) was excluded in calculating the performance of the monitoring task because there was no detection of automation failures and therefore no performance to measure. No overall effect of the command reliability was found (Fig. 2). Concerning the signal reliability, participants perform better in the resource task than in the monitoring task and the tracking task (Fig. 3).

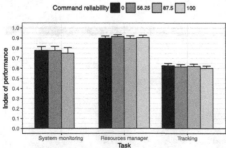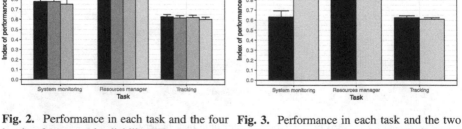

Fig. 2. Performance in each task and the four levels of command reliability. The higher the index the better is the performance.

Fig. 3. Performance in each task and the two levels of signal reliability. The higher the index the better is the performance.

The performance in the monitoring task is also better with a high reliability. More precisely, we can note an effect of the signal reliability on performance in the system monitoring task $F(1, 30) = 4.64$, $p < .05$.

The analysis of eye movements showed no effect for the command reliability (Fig. 4). However concerning the signal reliability (Fig. 5) the dwell time proportion is more important in the tracking task than in the resource management task and last in the tracking task $F(2, 60) = 32.84$, $p < .05$.

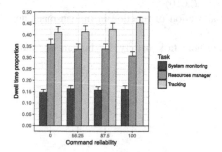

Fig. 4. Dwell time proportion for each task and the four levels of command reliability

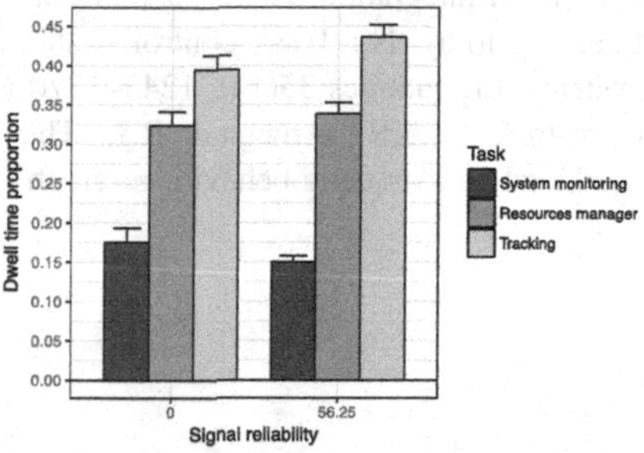

Fig. 5. Dwell time proportion for each task and the two levels of signal reliability.

Therefore, reliability of the automation signaling impacts the performance of the participants and their eye movements (task sampling). Full results (87.5% and 100%) are however necessary to confirm (or not) our hypothesis about a complacent behaviour. They will be discussed at the light of Bagheri and Jamieson's study on automation reliability [8, 10].

References

1. Sheridan, T.B., Verplank, W.L.: Human and computer control of undersea teleoperators (Technical report, Man-Machine Systems Laboratory, Department of Mechanical Engineering). MIT, Cambridge, MA (1978)
2. Endsley, M.R., Kaber, D.B.: Level of automation effects on performance, situation awareness and workload in a dynamic control task. Ergonomics **42**(3), 462–492 (1999)
3. Hoc, J.M.: From human-machine interaction to human-machine cooperation. Ergonomics **43**, 833–843 (2000)
4. Parasuraman, R., Riley, V.: Humans and automation: use, misuse, disuse, abuse. Hum. Factors **39**(2), 230–253 (1997)
5. Vicente, K.J., Rasmussen, J.: Ecological interface design: theoretical foundations. IEEE Trans. Syst. Man Cybern. **22**(4), 589–606 (1992)
6. Vicente, K.J.: Ecological interface design: progress and challenges. Hum. Factors **44**(1), 62–78 (2002)
7. Zhang, J., Norman, D.A.: Representations in distributed cognitive tasks. Cogn. Sci. **18**(1), 87–122 (1994)

8. Bagheri, N., Jamieson, G.A.: Considering subjective trust and monitoring behavior in assessing automation-induced "complacency". In: Human Performance, Situation Awareness, and Automation: Current Research and Trends, pp. 54–59 (2004)

9. Parasuraman, R., Molloy, R., Singh, I.L.: Performance consequences of automation-induced 'complacency'. Int. J. Aviat. Psychol. 3(1), 1–23 (1993)

10. Bagheri, N., Jamieson, G.A.: The impact of context-related reliability on automation failure detection and scanning behaviour. In: 2004 IEEE International Conference on Systems, Man and Cybernetics, vol. 1, pp. 212–217. IEEE, October 2004

11. Parasuraman, R., Manzey, D.H.: Complacency and bias in human use of automation: an attentional integration. Hum. Factors 52(3), 381–410 (2010)

12. Lee, J., Moray, N.: Trust, control strategies and allocation of function in human-machine systems. Ergonomics 35(10), 1243–1270 (1992)

13. Comstock Jr., J.R., Arnegard, R.J.: The multi-attribute task battery for human operator workload and strategic behavior research (1992)

A Human Recognition System for Pedestrian Crosswalk

Chyi-Ren Dow[✉], Liang-Hsuan Lee, Ngo Huu Huy, and Kuan-Chieh Wang

Department of Information Engineering and Computer Science,
Feng Chia University, Taichung, Taiwan
{crdow,M0403762,P0564319,P0630393}@fcu.edu.tw

Abstract. The concept of pedestrian priority has been taken gradually in recent years. However, there are still many vehicles and motorcycles caused traffic accidents due to ignoring the pedestrian right. In this work, we design and implement a human recognition system based on image processing techniques for pedestrians crosswalk. This system can be used to improve the safety level and reduce the probability of intersection accidents. We use the environment feature vectors obtained by the system to detect the zebra-crossing and find out the range of the zebra-crossing. We propose a dual-camera mechanism to maintain the detection accuracy and improve the fault tolerance of the proposed system. We design an Enhanced-Motion-HOG classification scheme to recognize pedestrians at the road intersection. To verify the feasibility and efficiency of our system, we implement a prototype system and compared the accuracy of the pedestrian detection scheme with the original HOG method and the motion detection method. Experimental results demonstrate that our scheme outperforms these schemes in terms of detection accuracy and processing time.

Keywords: Pedestrian recognition · Zebra-crossing · Motion-HOG

1 Introduction

Pedestrians are a powerful indicator of the social and economic health and safety of a community. The recent studies about the casualties of the accident presented that among the road users, pedestrians are the most vulnerable groups [8]. They quite need to be protected in dangerous road intersections.

In the last few years, researchers have focused on pedestrian detection technology, for enhancing pedestrian detection accuracy and simplifying pedestrian detection processing time. Many pedestrian detection algorithms have been developed [2, 10].

In this research study, we take a new approach with HOG in the past which apply suitable detect pedestrians at the intersection. We also show that analysis specifically, comprehensive about processing time and detection accuracy. The remainder of this paper is organized as follows. Section 2 describes the recent relevant research and technology. The design and architecture of the proposed system are explained in Sect. 3. Section 4 details the system prototype. Finally, Sect. 5 presents conclusions.

© Springer International Publishing AG, part of Springer Nature 2018
C. Stephanidis (Ed.): HCII Posters 2018, CCIS 852, pp. 443–447, 2018.
https://doi.org/10.1007/978-3-319-92285-0_60

2   Related Work

In this section, we will introduce some related work. First, we discussed some image processing schemes about how to recognize zebra pattern. Then, we present related studies which involve the pedestrian detection based on HOG.

Many researchers have already studied the zebra-crossing region detection. Se [9] proposed a method to detect zebra-crossing which can be considered as a group of consecutive edges. Khaliluzzaman and Deb [5] proposed a zebra-crossing detection framework based on unique geometrical features of zebra-crossing. Ahmetovic et al. [1] presented the ZebraRecognizer algorithm that rectifies the ground plane hence removing the projection distortion of the extracted features.

Beiping et al. [2] presented a real-time Human detection algorithm based on HOG features and SVM architecture. He et al. [4] improved the HOG + SVM pedestrian detector with the semantic regions of interest obtained from a fully-convolutional neural network. Kim et al. [6] proposed the HOG-UDP algorithm that included a dimension reduction functionality based on the manifold.

3   System Architecture

This section details the architecture of the pedestrian crosswalk recognition system. Figure 1 shows an overview of the system. In this system, Camera is used to collect the frame images from real-time video. After that, we have to detect the target region which includes the crossing region and the waiting region. To identify the crossing region, we need to recognize zebra-crossings and find the boundaries of them. The waiting region is detected following the crossing region. These regions will not the same depending on each intersection environment.

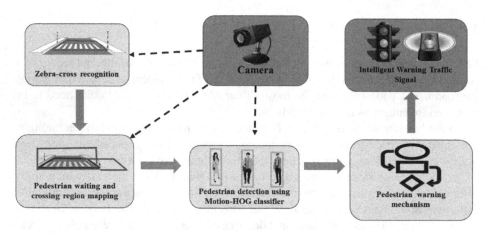

Fig. 1. System overview

After target region detection, we will perform to recognize pedestrian in there. We design a set of Motion-HOG classifier with mobility. The mobility rate and pedestrian's characteristics as the screening factor for pedestrian recognition.

The camera is vulnerable to wind, earthquake, rain and the impact of various environmental factors shaking, change the location, so the pedestrian waiting line and the area is not static. To obtain the crossing region and the waiting region accurately, we observed that all the intersections are recognizable features zebra-crossing so that we can see the zebra line as a picture calibration point to slightly correct the screen deviation. The location of the zebra-crossing is mapped to the waiting region. After obtaining the environmental parameters, we use these parameters as the control values of the zebra-detection algorithm. We set up a dual-lens camera on both sides of the zebra crossing. The system will combine the detection results from both sides, we can fix the detection errors caused by long distance.

The Motion-HOG classifier is shown in Fig. 2. First, when the nth frame in the webcam stream was inputted to the system, the background subtraction phase first establishes the background model through the mean-background method [4, 9] and then extracts the foreground object dataset.

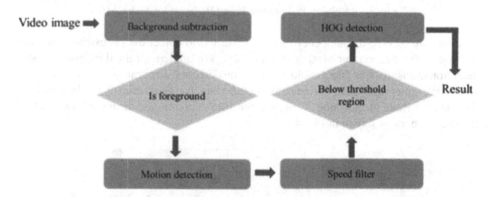

Fig. 2. The pedestrian detection progress using motion-HOG classifier

In the Motion detection phase, we use object tracking method to find out if there is any movement object belong to the dataset. And the velocity of $speed_{object}$ would be calculated. When the velocity $speed_{object}$ of the $object_j$ is lower than the speed threshold value $speed_{threshold}$, the $object_j$ will be delivered to the HOG detection phase and analyze whether it is Pedestrian objects and output the results. We use two threads in our method to handle HOG detection and Motion detection functions and detect all the motion objects at the same time, and then detect all HOG features simultaneously. It can reduce the detection time.

4   System Prototype

The prototype system is implemented to provide an adaptive zebra-crossing finding function and pedestrians detection function in the intersection.

We use Raspberry Pi 3 (RPi3) Module B [11] as our system device which is equipped with a ARM Cortex-A53 CPU 1.2 GHz, 64-Bit, Quad-Core and 1 GB RAM, as shown in Fig. 3. The Python language is used to implement the system interface and OpenCV library was chosen to implement our main function in OS system Raspbian.

Fig. 3. Raspberry Pi 3 module B and Webcam logitech C615

After we receive the area coordinate, we started to detect the pedestrians who are waiting in the area via our Motion-Hog method. We implement the dual camera view detection to ensure our system could decrease the detection error rate and there is a signal light in the upper right corner to indicate whether there has pedestrian or not. We selected the Kaixuan Road in Taichung, Taiwan as the study site for case design with setting up the dual camera as shown in Fig. 4.

Fig. 4. Experimental environment in Kaixuan Road, Taichung, Taiwan

5 Conclusions

In this paper, we design and implement a human recognition system which aimed to detect pedestrians crosswalk. The zebra-crossing recognizer adapts the variation of environmental illumination. We can obtain the crossing region and waiting region. After that, we can know whether pedestrians are passing or are going to pass the zebra-crossing by our proposed Motion-HOG classifier. In the future, we will develop the pedestrian crossing warning system based on the pedestrian detection results in this research. Furthermore, we will implement the detection of the vehicle to expand the ability of our system.

References

1. Ahmetovic, D., Bernareggi, C., Gerino, A., Mascetti, S.: ZebraRecognizer: efficient and precise localization of pedestrian crossings. In: 2014 22nd International Conference on Pattern Recognition, Stockholm, Sweden, pp. 2566–2571 (2014)
2. Beiping, H., Wen, Z.: Fast human detection using motion detection and histogram of oriented gradients. J. Comput. 6(8), 1597–1604 (2011)
3. Gradinescu, V., Gorgorin, C., Iftode, L., Diaconescu, R., Cristea, V.: Adaptive traffic lights using car-to-car communication. In: Vehicular Technology Conference (VTC 2007), Dublin, Ireland, pp. 21–25 (2007)
4. He, M., Luo, H., Chang, Z., Hui, B.: Pedestrian detection with semantic regions of interest. Sensors 17(11), 1–16 (2017)
5. Khaliluzzaman, M., Deb, K.: Zebra-crossing detection based on geometric feature and vertical vanishing point. In: 2016 3rd International Conference on Electrical Engineering and Information Communication Technology (ICEEICT), Dhaka, Bangladesh, pp. 1–6 (2016)
6. Kim, P.-K., Kim, H.-H., Kim, T.-W.: An improved pedestrian detection system that utilizes the HOG-UDP algorithm. In: Park, J., Chen, S.-C., Raymond Choo, K.-K. (eds.) MUE/ FutureTech -2017. LNEE, vol. 448, pp. 218–225. Springer, Singapore (2017). https://doi.org/10.1007/978-981-10-5041-1_37
7. Koonce, P., Rodegerdts, L., Lee, K., Quayle, S., Beaird, S., Braud, C., Urbanik, T.: Operational and safety analysis. In: Traffic Signal Timing Manual, pp. 56–87. Federal Highway Administration, Turner-Fairbank Highway Research Center, McLean, VA, USA (2008)
8. Najada, H.A., Mahgoub, I.: Big vehicular traffic data mining: towards accident and congestion prevention. In: International Wireless Communications and Mobile Computing Conference (IWCMC), Paphos, Cyprus, pp. 256–261 (2016)
9. Se, S.: Zebra-crossing detection for the partially sighted. In: IEEE Conference on Computer Vision and Pattern Recognition, CVPR 2000, Hilton Head Island, SC, USA, pp. 211–217 (2000)
10. Sladojević, S., Anderla, A., Ćulibrk, D., Stefanović, D., Lalić, B.: Integer arithmetic approximation of the HoG algorithm used for pedestrian detection. Comput. Sci. Inf. Syst. 14(2), 329–346 (2017)
11. Raspberry Pi. https://www.raspberrypi.org/

Modeling Design of Six-Freedom-Degree Collaboration Robot

Rongrong Fu[✉] and Ye Zhang

East China University of Science and Technology,
No. 130 Meilong Road, Shanghai 200237, China
Muxin789@126.com, Missccchina@yeah.net

Abstract. The development of manufacturing industry made the structure composition of productivity have changed a lot, as a new kind of production tools, the industrial robot has imponderable advantages compared with other tools, it can better meet the needs of mass production manufacturing, enhance productivity capacity and play a better role of decreasing labor costs. However, the existing industrial robots are far from meeting market demands, they are just only meeting the function and manufacturing needs, which ignores the user's psychological needs, makes uncoordinated human-computer interaction and poor competitiveness and backward development of industry. Based on the problem and manufacturing demand, combing existing products, using design theories and principles of psychology, ergonomics, chromatology and so on, highlight the emotional needs, from perspectives of safety and customers, to conduct the develop and research of industrial robot. Through the design of six-freedom-degree collaboration robot which is applied generally, and by scheme optimization to reach the final result as well, to improve the interactive experience between users and industrial robot, and develop a kind of six-freedom-degree collaboration robot which meets the demand currently, further improve manufacturing efficiency as well as we can. And hoping it can provide a design direction reference for the future development of industrial robot

Keywords: Manufacturing industry · Emotional · Interactive experience
Six-freedom-degree collaboration robot · Modeling design

1 Introduction

The collaboration robot is the result of the changes in components of productivity, and the category widely applied currently is six-freedom-degree one. As the representation of intelligent productivity, it can realize automated production, increase social production capacity and is an effective method for productivity growth. However, we found the blank area between handled and auto assembled production line in the investigation, which is especially obvious in application of light installations and automation. Here we introduce the collaboration robot to help

© Springer International Publishing AG, part of Springer Nature 2018
C. Stephanidis (Ed.): HCII Posters 2018, CCIS 852, pp. 448–454, 2018.
https://doi.org/10.1007/978-3-319-92285-0_61

production, but we also found that the existing industrial robot cannot meet requirements by industrial robot status analysis. From modeling perspective, the lack of affinity leads to fear feeling of the operators, absence of human-computer interactive mode and difficulty of MRK. Product modeling actually is the information communication media, and its nature is coding various visual signs. As the first element for information transmitting, modeling can turn the intrinsic factors of products to external appearance ones, such as organization, structure and connotation, its ultimate goal is to transmit product information and change human physiological and psychological status by vision as well [1, 2]. Good modeling accords with operator's psychology, which creates a good and safe working condition for efficiency improving [3]. Thus for helping operators overcome their fear to machine, we try to solve the problem by a modeling design scheme based on the human-computer interactive modes from the perspectives of emotion and design psychology (For the gradually matured existing internal technology, here only discuss the modeling application in the blank area).

The remainder of the article is organized as follows. In section two, we do modeling features comparison analysis of industrial robots both at home and abroad, grab key elements for design analysis, and conduct design positioning on the basis of related design theories and principles, which includes psychology, ergonomics and Kansei, and the interactive mode between operators and robots as well. Based on the design positioning, getting design scheme which meets the emotional needs of operators and collaborators from aspects of crowd, shape, color, function and materials. Section three concludes the paper.

2 Scheme Design

We choose several representative brands, and do comparative analysis from the aspects of color, shape, application and so on. Due to the interactive mode between human and machine is related to human mental state which is influenced by product modeling, we codified the data and get universals, shortages and trends in modeling, then analyze the design requirements from mentality and application, and get a solution finally.

2.1 Status at Home and Abroad

Domestic robot industry bias low-end market, here we conclude several examples for universals, the details are as follows.

From Table 1, we conclude that modeling features of the existing domestic six-freedom-degree collaboration robot are heavy, naked wires and unnatural transition. Over mechanized shape not only influences aesthetic but also the relationship among humans, environment and machine, especially the semi-automatic assemble application. Operators will be anxious and lack of security without trust in machine, which will lead to assembly line inefficiency.

Table 1. Modeling features of domestic collaborative robots.

Brand	Color	Appearance features
SIASUN	White	Thin, special-shaped base; no corner in head; exposed wires on the side
MITSUBISHI ELETRIC	Bias white	Round, strong but heavy; double-sided structure joints
JARI	White and black	Light and nimble; three-section joints in arm; semi-naked wires; round-in-square-shaded style
ESTUN	Medium yellow	Concise and easy; slender; exposed bottom electric machine; round-in-square-shaded style
EFFORT	Light yellow	Half naked wires; heavy and mechanized; protection device in joints; dynamic feeling for its shape from small to large overall

From Table 2, we conclude that modeling features of the existing abroad six-freedom-degree collaboration robot are high-end, more in six and over six degrees. Though some are similar to domestic ones, more are slender, emotional and compact. Bulky joints are disappearing, wires and other components are inside, and mechanized shapes are turning into colorful, dynamic, smarter and more reliable. Those trends increase confidence, and beautiful modeling even encourages operators' collaboration desire.

Table 2. Modeling features of abroad collaborative robots.

Brand	Color	Appearance features
YASKAWA	Blue	Slender appearance; thicker and low square base; corner in head; bare wires besides
EPSON	Almost white	No diversified shape; round; high and cylinder base; corner in head; thicker middle arm; no naked wires
FANUC	Lemon yellow	Slender; round chamfered base; no corner in head; bare wires besides
KUKA	Orange	Round base; diversified arm; no corner in head; bare wires besides
NACHI	Cream	Shaped base; low height base; no corner in head; bare wires besides; rough in vision
KAWASAK	White	Round and chamfered base; no corner in head; thin middle and thick joints arm
ABB	Ochre	Circular table base; thick shape; corner in head; thick joints; bare wires behind
COMAU	Red	Slender; circular table base; no corner in head; wires in round shell body; beautiful

Therefore, from the two tables, we get the overall modeling features of collaboration robots: From low-end to high-end market, more human, and more considerations about psychology, all of those shows in vision are more emotional instead of mechanized and indifferent, more colorful and bionic. And we will do design based on the modeling features analysis, application, function and human-computer interactive mode between operators and machine.

2.2 Application and Function Analysis

For design goal, we conduct analysis to application and function after modeling analysis.

Application. The environments of MRK between handled and auto assembled production line are not all with clean air, constant temperature and humidity. For components assembly production, it is full of harmful gas, noise, radiation and other problems. Pollution such as oil and dust adsorption can leads to mechanical wear, thus the problem should be taken into consideration. And due to long time production process and continuous operating time, the abrasion resistance of joints and the robot's stability are very important, otherwise, it will cause collision between robots and safety hazard. So the structure and material should be paid more attention and an emergency stop device is necessary as well.

Function Requirements. The scheme is mainly to fill the blank area between handled and auto assembled production line in, especially in application of light installations and automation. According to the function goal, the structure requirements are as follows.: Supporting part should be connected with the frame to support the machine; Pinion rack and motor which provides power in front arm; Upper arm equips with mechanical transmission device and motor as well; And the joint can be installed with different parts to achieve the operation target, for example the drill bit.

2.3 Design Positioning

In the early stage, we conducted research and analysis to the existing collaborative robots and got the current modeling development trend. Based on the existing technology, for MRK, this paper aims at a solution to meet the needs of industrial production from the perspective of human-computer interactive mode and users. Since the users mostly are assembler of MRK, to achieve better production target, the design should be with affinity and sense of security. Round modeling makes feel soft, which can reduce mistrust in the process of human-computer interaction and relieve stress. Thus try to avoid structures that may cause injuries, such as straight lines and sharp corners. Color should be soft and friendly, the operation process should be simple and clear, the materials should be non-toxic and high temperature as well. Combined with application and function requirements, the final modeling design requirements are as follows: More bionics, more compact and slender, more arc and curves to reduce user insecurity and interaction difficulties in the process. And integrated design of the body is better for longer service life, new material for weight reduce and the wall-mounted way for space saving is better.

2.4   Scheme Design

Based on Sect. 2.3, we conduct a modeling design scheme of six-freedom-degree collaboration robot to solve the problem of MRK. The details are as follows (see Fig. 1).

Fig. 1. Modeling scheme of six-freedom-degree collaboration robot. (Color figure online)

With the design method of anthropomorphic, like human arms and curves in the edge, it can avoid dangers in homework. And wall installed two arms can not only improve efficiency, but more secure and reliable, and save space as well. Small liftable and lowerable hydraulic equipment and capturing part make move more freely, and it also can be hided inside the external shell structure under stopped state, which prevents dangers to workers and protects the internal structure. The scheme makes people feel comfortable and safe, which leads to higher efficiency in production.

We make a special design on the structure for the problem proposed before. The cantilever structure is used to save space and set a movable frame for better factory area division. The movement direction is the upper and lower dimensions, which decrease the horizontal range, reduces the fixed XY axis moving, and avoids workers' hurts. Its body is relatively closed shell structure, which can withstand strong strength, better protect internal components, and prevent dust interference. Two arms are connected with parallel mechanism, synchronous motion, and the turbine worm structure realizes movement, which improve work efficiency. Considering safety and maintenance factors, we install several LED work lights, when the light is green shows working state while red means danger and stop working automatically.

For color, the affinity color is the representative of light industry. In addition, the stimulus of color has certain psychological implication to the operators, and the objects that they operate with can also increase vigilance and avoid mis-operation. Operators in factory are stressful, they must have more strong sense of responsibility and vigilance when in working. Moderate color can relief the pressure of workers and reduce the occurrence of accidents. So from the psychological perspective of workers, right color is crucial to them, and types, environment and requirements of different works also differ. We consider from aspects of raising attention, psychological coordination and security, based on color's influence to workers, and select white finally. The details are as follows.

(a) Pure white. White represents spirit, space and thinking in the east, and existing domestic manufacturing industry robot mostly are white, which makes operators feel calm with intense industrial working. It is the main application color of various light industries, shows clean and calm, gives the worker quiet and comfortable visual experience.

(b) Warm white. Getting rid of the traditional color obstacle, adding a bit of emotion into the boring, repetitive and monotonous industrial work, more humane concern.

(c) Cold white, symbolizing sagacity and rationality, but more about science and technology sense, giving people insight, inspiration, interplanetary power and intuition, which can inspire workers' creativity and working passion to some extent. And it makes people naturally keep safe distance.

Here we combine product positioning and application, choose warm white finally.

In the selection of materials, the basic requirements are high strength, large elastic modulus, light weight, large damping and low material price. According to the investigation, the existing industrial robots using materials mainly are cast iron and cast aluminum, which cannot maintain balance in strength and quality. After extensive research, we found that carbon fiber composite materials can be used to replace traditional ones as structure, support, and even the pedestal parts. It has light weight and strong strength, and many mechanical properties are better than steel, aluminum alloy and other metal materials. Here due to cost, performance and other considerations, most of the materials use carbon fiber composite materials.

3 Conclusion

For the existing monotonous modeling of collaboration robots and production problem caused by lack of trust to robots in interactive process, this paper tried to propose a modeling design strategy of six-freedom-degree collaboration robot and conduct scheme design based on user requirements, Kansei Engineering and other design principles from the perspective of emotion and bionics design. It is an exploration in the trend of manufacturing transformation, the ultimate goal is to develop the light industry. However, we still don't know enough about the other using areas and applications of the six-freedom-degree collaboration robot in the scheme.

References

1. Li, H.: Researches based on product appearance design. China New Technol. Prod. **10**, 112–112 (2009)
2. Gu, W.: On the modeling consciousness in packaging design. J. Jiamusi Educ. Inst. **127**, 116–117 (2013)
3. Wang, W.: The art design of machine tools. China Acad. J. **2**, 33–35 (1992)

Implementation and Evaluation of a Reminder Registration Interface for Daily Life Objects

Kenro Go[✉], Nagomu Horikoshi, Shion Tominaga,
Jinta Nakamura, and Akihiro Miyata

Nihon University, 3-25-40, Sakurajousui, Setagaya-Ku, Tokyo, Japan
ken.ken664@gmail.com

Abstract. There are many tasks regarding objects that are conducted according to specific date and time in daily life. To avoid forgetting to handle a task, reminder applications are useful. However, these tools require some effort on the part of the user to verbalize her or his task, e.g., "Read the book taken out from the library," and input it to the system. To address this issue, we devised a model in which the user physically registers "the existence information of the task" to the object. This enables the user to notice the existence of a task related to the object and recall the content of the task every time he or she sees it. To realize this model, we propose a method for registering an object reminder by attaching clips to it. This makes it possible for the user to set the reminder only by attaching *clips* that have the specified duration information. Each clip has a full-color LED and displays the existence of task and deadline information associated to it. The evaluation result demonstrates that the proposed method yields better operability and acceptability for registering reminders than those of the conventional method.

Keywords: Reminder · Real environment oriented interface · Clip

1 Introduction

In daily life, there are objects connected to many tasks planned for specific dates and times. To ensure tasks are not forgotten, reminder applications are useful. However, existing reminder applications have problems. To use a reminder application, the user has to verbalize their task (e.g., "Read the book borrowed from the library") and input it into the system. If this is a business task, such as "send quotation data to customers today," the cost of verbalization and system inputting seems to be worthwhile. However, the cost outweighs the benefits for everyday tasks such as reading books. In this research, we will study future tasks related to such objects in daily life. To make the research subject clearer, we will organize where these tasks will be positioned among future tasks. Future tasks can be divided into *time-based* tasks and *event-based* tasks [1–3]. When a *time-based* task is detailed, it can be divided into a *by-time task* (a future task to be executed by a certain time) and an *on-time* task (a future task to be performed at a specific time). In this research, we focus on *by-time* tasks. Also, when an *event-based* task is refined, future tasks concerning objects, people, places, and situations can be classified as *object-based* tasks, *person-based* tasks, *location-based* tasks, and *situation-based*

C. Stephanidis (Ed.): HCII Posters 2018, CCIS 852, pp. 455–462, 2018.
https://doi.org/10.1007/978-3-319-92285-0_62

tasks. We focus on *object-based* tasks. Based on the above, this research focuses on future tasks that are *by-time* and *object-based* in daily life.

2   Research Goal

Future tasks are generally considered to consist of Step (1) formation of intention, Step (2) memorization of intention, Step (3) recall of intention, Step (4) execution of intention [3, 4]. A reminder aiming to memorize and notify of future tasks needs to support Steps 2 and 3, but considering the application to future tasks that are *by-time* and *object-based* tasks in daily life, some existing technologies have some problems.

As a first problem, in Step 2, the user needs to verbalize their task. Although [5] demonstrated an automatic notification time setting, they have not yet automated task content verbalization.

As a second problem, in Step 3, with existing technologies, it is necessary to constantly carry the electronic device to confirm the contents set via the reminder [6–9]. In a *by-time* task, it is likely that Step 3 will be performed several times before the deadline of the task. Therefore, for reminders used in daily life, it is desirable to be able to confirm task contents/deadlines without carrying devices.

As a third problem, there is the issue that the objects to which information can be related are limited. In the field of real environment-oriented interfaces, many methods of associating information with real world objects have been proposed. However, since it is based on the use of dedicated tools, it cannot be general purposed to various objects entering and leaving a daily living space. When setting a reminder related to various daily life objects, it is a burden to prepare dedicated tools for each object.

From the above, the case in which the user sets a reminder for the object-related daily life task deadline, we outline three research subject categories:

1. Reminders can be set without task verbalization
2. Task contents and deadlines can be confirmed without using an electronic terminal
3. The system is generalized to any daily life object

3   Proposal Method

To address the problems mentioned in Sect. 2, we decomposed the entire reminder system model. In the conventional model, it is necessary for the user to register the task contents in the system after verbalizing their task, which is burdensome for the user (see upper half of Fig. 1). For this reason, we hypothesized that, even if the system does not memorize task contents, the user can recall the task contents from their own memory if they view the related object in combination with the presence of an additional item that contains task information. Based on this hypothesis, we have devised a model in which the user physically registers the existing task and deadline information to the object (see lower half of Fig. 1). Consequently, each time the user sees an object, they can recognize that there is a task related to it, and can thus recall the task from their own memory. To realize this model, we propose a method for registering a reminder to an object by attaching clips to it. This allows the user to set the reminder by merely attaching clips containing the specified deadline information (see the upper half of Fig. 2). Each clip has a full-color LED indicating the existence of a task and the deadline information. Furthermore, by adding multiple clips, time addition can be performed (see the lower half of Fig. 2). For example, by attaching a clip with respective holding times of 1 d and 12 h to an object, it is possible to set a reminder with a deadline of one and a half days later.

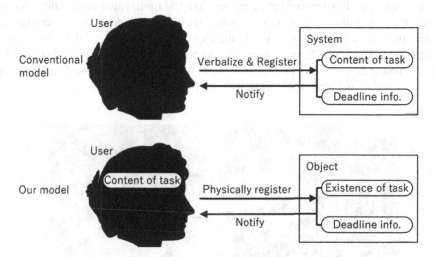

Fig. 1. The difference between the conventional model and our model.

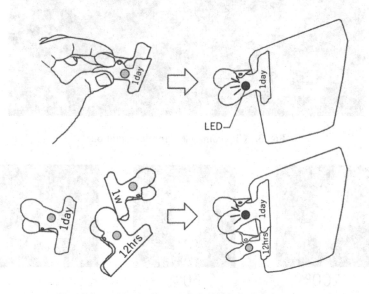

Fig. 2. Attached-clip reminder registration concept.

4 Implementation

The prototype system is comprised of multiple clip components and one clip control component. Each clip wirelessly communicates with the clip control component in real time using a WebSocket. Figure 3 shows the clip component in use; the LED and current sensor are attached. The LED color changes according to the time remaining until the deadline (Fig. 4). Gradation is implemented to incorporate a smooth-transitioning intermediate state for each color; the LED lights up before the deadline and flashes after the deadline. A color change of green, yellow, red refers to a traffic signal, which is familiar in everyday life. Figure 5 provides a sectional side view of the clip component showing the current sensor configuration. This mechanism enables the clip component to determine whether it has been attached to the object by detecting insulation. As previously mentioned, multiple clips can be attached to an object to add holding times (see lower part of Fig. 2).

Fig. 3. Clip component implementation.

100%
(Green)

50%
(Yellow)

0%
(Blinking red)

Fig. 4. LED color indicator of the remaining time. (Color figure online)

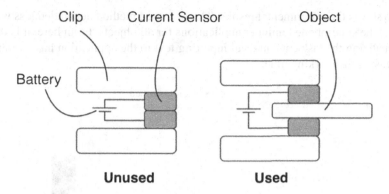

Fig. 5. Sectional side view of current sensor configuration for in-use detection.

5 Evaluation

5.1 The Evaluation Design

The intent of this research is to propose a new interface and model to provide reminders of tasks in daily life. To confirm the effectiveness of the proposed method, it is necessary to use the system and verify it in daily life. However, there are various external factors during everyday life, and the daily life of each subject is diverse. Therefore, to gradually and strictly proceed with the evaluation, we first verify the usability of the interface of the system itself (Sect. 5.2) and evaluate the practicality common to each subject during daily life (Sect. 5.3).

5.2 Evaluation 1

To verify the usability of the proposed method, we conducted an experiment comparing the smartphone reminder application with the time taken to set a reminder. The procedure of the experiment is as follows. The objects used in the experiment are books, a milk carton, and a potato chips packet.

Step 1: In the case of the proposed method, put an opaque box containing the clips in front of the subject. In case of the baseline method, have the reminder application launched on the subject's smartphone.

Step 2: The experimenter selects objects in random order and places them in front of the subjects and notifies the subjects of the deadline, for example, "the deadline is in xx weeks". In the case of the proposed method, the experimenter opens the box containing the clips immediately after notification.

Step 3: In the case of the proposed method, the subject selects the necessary clips from the box and attaches them to the object. In the case of the baseline method, subjects verbalize task themselves, and register the task names and deadlines in the reminder application.

Figure 6 shows the experimental results. The proposed method demanded less working time than the smartphone reminder applications for all objects. From here, it is thought that verbalizing the task contents and inputting text to the application has an influence on increasing the working time.

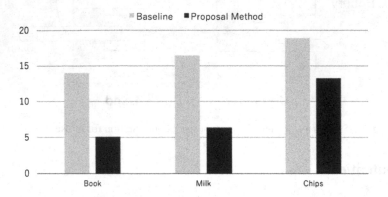

Fig. 6. The mean operation times in evaluation 1 (sec, N = 12).

5.3 Evaluation 2

To evaluate the practicality of our system, we have tested the hypothesis in Sect. 3 via a two-week experiment involving ten subjects. The procedure of the experiment is as follows. As the experimental site, we selected our laboratory which is a daily living space where all the subjects spend most of their school days. In addition, we prepared six types of objects, two books (a comic, a novel), two types of snacks (chips, jelly), and two documents (a report, a questionnaire). Steps 2 and 3 were carried out twice, about once a week, after Step 1.

Step 1: Set reminders on objects using the proposed method. At that time, the subject tells the experimenter the task.
Step 2: Give the subject a voice recorder and have the subjects clean the laboratory for 5 min.
Step 3: When a subject notices that another subject set a reminder, the subject records the recalled task and remaining deadline in the voice recorder.

In performing the steps above, the experimenter calculates the task content recall rate and the recall time of the remaining time limit. The task content recall rate is calculated by comparing the tasks set by the subject with the tasks recorded when the subject recalled, and by discussing how accurately they are recalled. The recall error of the remaining time limit compares the actual remaining time limit with the remaining time limit remembered by the subject and calculates the error.

The results of the experiment are shown below. Figure 7 shows the percentage of people noticing the object that set the reminder. The horizontal axis shows the elapsed time from Step 1, and the vertical axis represents the percentage (%) noticed.

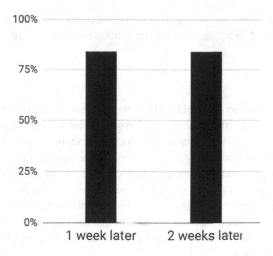

Fig. 7. The mean percentage of objects noticed in evaluation 2 (%, N = 10).

Figure 8 shows the rate of task content recall when the object that set the reminder is noticed. The horizontal axis shows the elapsed time from Step 1, and the vertical axis represents the percentage (%) correctly recalled. Both one week and two weeks later, the user could remember the tasks he himself performed with an accuracy of 100%. Therefore, if a user can notice the object that set the reminder, the hypothesis is that a task recalled from a user's memory is considered correct.

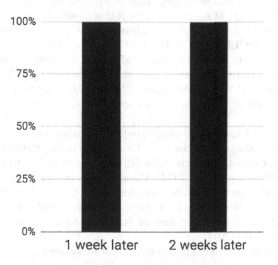

Fig. 8. The mean percentage of recalled task contents in evaluation 2 (%, N = 10).

In addition, regarding the recalling error of the remaining time limit, the error was 13.3% after 1 week and 5.5% after 2 weeks. The percentage of expirations noticed was 85.7% after 1 week and 87.7% after 2 weeks. As compared with the time after 1 week and after 2 weeks, the accuracy of both the recall of the remaining time limit and the recall of the expiration has improved. It is thought that this is because the subjects once recalled their tasks and deadlines, so that the deadline was established more in memory.

6   Conclusion

In this research, we devised a model in which the user physically registers "the existence information of a task" directly in the object. To realize this model, we proposed a method for registering the reminders associated to object by attaching clips to it, and constructed a prototype system combining clips and LEDs. In the experiments, we confirmed the effectiveness of the proposed system on interface usability and practicality in daily life. In the future, we plan to apply the objects to be applied. Given that the current system determines whether clips are attached to an object by the current sensor, if the object is a conductive object, it cannot be determined whether the clips are attached to the object. This problem can be solved by a method such as attaching a mechanical opening or closing sensor to the clips.

References

1. Einstein, G.O., McDaniel, M.A.: Retrieval processes in prospective memory: theoretical approaches and some new empirical findings. In: Prospective Memory: Theory and Applications, pp. 115–141 (1996).
2. McDaniel, M.A., Einstein, G.O.: Strategic and automatic processes in prospective memory retrieval: a multiprocess framework. Appl. Cognit. Psychol. **14**(7), S127–S144 (2000)
3. Wang, Y., Pérez-Quiñones, M.A.: Exploring the role of prospective memory in location-based reminders. In: Proceedings of the 2014 ACM International Joint Conference on Pervasive and Ubiquitous Computing (UbiComp 2014), pp. 1373–1380 (2014)
4. Ellis, J.: Prospective memory or the realization of delayed intentions: a conceptual framework for research. In: Prospective Memory: Theory and Applications, pp. 1–22 (1996)
5. Graus, D., Bennett, P.N., White, R.W., Horvitz, E.: Analyzing and predicting task reminders. In: Proceedings of the 2016 Conference on User Modeling Adaptation and Personalization, pp. 7–15 (2016).
6. Zhang, X., Pina, L.R., Fogarty, J.: Examining unlock journaling with diaries and reminders for in situ self-report in health and wellness. In: Proceedings of the International Conference on Human Factors in Computing Systems (CHI 2016), pp. 5658–5664 (2016)
7. Kortuem, G., Segall, Z., Thompson, T.G.C.: Close encounters: supporting mobile collaboration through interchange of user profiles. In: Gellersen, H.-W. (ed.) HUC 1999. LNCS, vol. 1707, pp. 171–185. Springer, Heidelberg (1999). https://doi.org/10.1007/3-540-48157-5_17
8. Lin, C., Hung, M.: A location-based personal task reminder for mobile users. Pers. Ubiquit. Comput. **18**(2), 303–314 (2014)
9. Dey, A.K., Abowd, G.D.: CybreMinder: a context-aware system for supporting reminders. In: Thomas, P., Gellersen, H.-W. (eds.) HUC 2000. LNCS, vol. 1927, pp. 172–186. Springer, Heidelberg (2000). https://doi.org/10.1007/3-540-39959-3_13

Reconfigurable Spaces and Places in Smart Built Environments: A Service Centric Approach

Denis Gračanin[1]([✉]), Mohamed Eltoweissy[2], Liang Cheng[3], and Reza Tasooji[1]

[1] Department of Computer Science, Virginia Tech, Blacksburg, VA 24060, USA
gracanin@vt.edu
[2] Department of Computer and Information Science,
Virginia Military Institute Lexington, Lexington, VA 24450, USA
[3] Department of Computer Science and Engineering, Lehigh University,
Bethlehem, PA 18015, USA

Abstract. A smart built environment (SBE) contains connected, interactive smart objects that have sensing and actuating capabilities. A network of such objects provides an Internet of Things infrastructure that changes the way how SBEs behave and how the inhabitants interact with them. If SBE components, such as walls and furniture pieces, are mobile and controllable, the geometry and interior design of SBE spaces can be changed in response to inhabitants actions and social activities. An added complexity is the mobility of smart objects and their ability to reconfigure. We describe a preliminary work on a service-based framework that includes SBE reconfiguration services. The layered architecture provides access to the reconfigurable smart objects that react to the user activities and behavior. Initial simulation and preliminary findings are included.

Keywords: Smart Built Environments · Internet of Things
Service-oriented middleware

1 Introduction

The "smart" house or Smart Built Environment (SBE) augments a traditional home by adapting new technology. The technology is adapted into the existing patterns of use with a rich computational and communicational infrastructure. This infrastructure incorporates smart objects, devices and sensors that observe the built environment and interact with the inhabitants in novel ways [1]. However, the physical and social structures within a home are subject to continuous changes that create the need for reconfigurable spaces and places in SBEs. Dourish emphasizes the difference between space and place, defining place as space with added socio-cultural understandings that frames behavior [2].

The concept of Internet of Things (IoT) describes the pervasive presence of things or objects that interact and cooperate with each other to reach common

© Springer International Publishing AG, part of Springer Nature 2018
C. Stephanidis (Ed.): HCII Posters 2018, CCIS 852, pp. 463–468, 2018.
https://doi.org/10.1007/978-3-319-92285-0_63

goals. IoT provides sensing, communication, computing, and actuation infrastructure for ubiquitous interactions and pervasive services. Sensors, actuators, and services distributed across the spaces and places need to collaborate with each other and render adaptive behaviors to changing environmental and functional contexts of the spaces and places for their reconfigurability.

These physical smart objects have a social existence that could be supported through the IoT (an Internet of social things) [3]. Designing and deploying IoT infrastructure into SBEs provides capabilities that can change how systems behave and how users interact with them. Such SBEs enhanced with technology can improve the lives of individuals, groups, and the broader community.

We describe a preliminary work on a service-based framework that identifies and supports reconfiguration capabilities in SBEs. The layered architecture provides access to the reconfigurable smart objects, integrates environmental and biometric data and identifies the patterns of user activities and behavior.

2   Reconfigurable Spaces and Places

Reconfigurable IoT-based SBEs [4] can provide significant benefits by enabling mobile, flexible and collaborative spaces. Such SBEs can include reconfigurable social spaces for dining, entertaining or other activities. Reconfigurable SBEs include reconfigurable,mobile furniture pieces that can adjust to the changing floor plan and room sizes. While that has been an ongoing trend for office spaces, it is now becoming more relevant for residential spaces, especially for smaller apartments and houses. This new opportunities and capabilities of architecture and built spaces brings new challenges in terms of user experience and interaction design [5].

As an example, robotic buildings robots can perform tasks of physical and sensorial reconfiguration to support behaviors ranging from responsive to interactive [5]. The challenge is how to incorporate adaptivity, spatial and functional reconfigurability within SBEs and provide it as services across the multiple time scales (e.g., seasonal, daily, ad-hoc).

In an adaptive architecture feedback loop, an SBE gathers data from inhabitants and uses them to inform actuations of architectural elements to change the SBE thus providing a feedback to inhabitants [6]. The enactive approach to architectural experience in underlined by sense-making, constitutive relatedness, and embodied action [7]. An inhabitant is embedded in a specific architectural context and extends the body in to the physical space through human senses [8]. Architectural thinking has to be combined with interactive technologies to design interactive SBEs from an architectural point of view [9].

Household members interactions are expressed through sequences of practical actions that identify domestic routines and communications [10]. Such communications must be considered for design and the deployment of new computing devices and applications in the home [11]. Usability of end-user composition interfaces for SBEs play an important role in safety consideration.

Some of the factors include predictability of composition model, readability of composition representation, overview and means for planning compositions, and attractiveness and desirability [12]. When dealing with smart things like smart appliances, usefulness is the strongest predictors for the intention to use. However, the emotional response is also an important explanatory variable that can be used to inform the safety features.

Mobile robotics can be applied to create automated, self-moving furniture components that can be controlled, coordinated and configured based on the actions taking place in SBEs [13]. An example of a self-reconfiguring modular robotic system are Roombots that can move in their environment and that change shape and functionality during the day [14]. Some of the features that characterize mobile robots are reconfiguration, docking, degrees of freedom, locomotion, control, communications, size, and powering [15].

3   Framework

We build on our work on the design of interaction independence middleware and context sensitive interaction interoperability frameworks, and a service infrastructure for human-centered IoT-based SBEs [16] to define a layered service architecture for the reconfigurable SBEs. The IoT layer provides connectivity and communication to embedded devices, sensors and actuators. The data layer provides data collection and fusion. The energy layer supports energy analysis and management for ad-hoc and periodic activities (daily, seasonal) (Fig. 1).

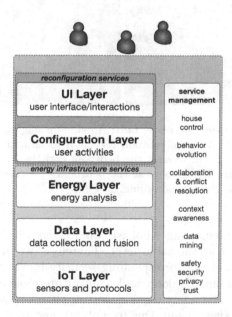

Fig. 1. Service framework: The lower three layers mange the data collection and overall energy consumption (sustainability). The upper two layers provide reconfiguration services that can be triggered automatically or by inhabitants' requests.

The configuration layer allows inhabitants to manage the space configuration and overall comfort settings. Finally, the UI layer supports multi-modal interactions across variety of interface and interaction devices in SBEs. The service management subsystem manages the service lifecycle and deals with reconfiguration and conflict resolution, context awareness, behavior detection and safety/security/privacy issues.

Figure 2 illustrates a simple simulation of a reconfiguration service in an SBE. The SBE recognizes a pattern of daily social activities (e.g., a family time) and changes the space configuration (i.e., room sizes) by moving (sliding) the wall. The corresponding interior reconfiguration takes place by rearranging the smart mobile furniture pieces. Providing the occupancy data and related services enables addressing the inhabitants's safety in a reconfigurable, dynamic physical space.

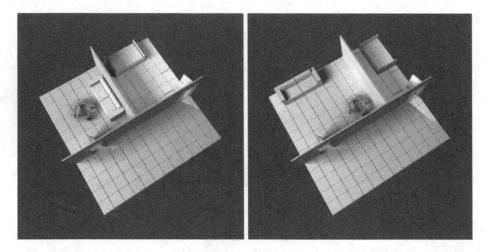

Fig. 2. Reconfigurable space and place. **Left:** A default configuration for a living room and a bedroom. **Right:** A reconfiguration for the a social activities that take place in the living room. The wall between the bedroom and the living room moves thus increasing the size of the living room at the bedroom's expense. The interior design (furniture arrangement) changes accordingly.

While there is an emerging emphasis on IoT security, the safety aspects are not yet addressed at the same level. Therefore, we are investigating the safety requirements and the corresponding security implications. For example, a movement of an automated door, wall or furniture piece can result in almost instantaneous injury. The safety requirements apply not only to the inhabitants but also to the SBE they live in. Due to mobility and reconfigurability of SBE components, it is possible to cause damage to the SBE.

Since reconfigurable SBEs are distributed, "multi-robotics" systems with autonomous mobile components, the framework must provide real-time obstacles (inhabitants, SBE damage) avoidance services in the SBE's physical space and state space.

Implementing an IoT-based SBE involves interconnecting a variety of devices, some of which with limited resources, through a communication network. We use the MQTT protocol as representative communication protocol for the IoT layer. The collected data is stored in the OSIsoft PI system data infrastructure (data layer) to support energy analysis and activity monitoring (energy layer). The configuration layer facilitates proactive decision making with real-time access and visualization of data (reconfiguration services).

We created an example that models SBE safety in a simulated small physical environment (Fig. 2). The example is based on an SBE prototype currently under construction. The SBE prototype includes several movable walls, actuated doors, drawers, etc. We are using it to test and iteratively develop the preliminary service-based framework to support reconfigurable SBE.

4 Conclusion

We presented some challenges faced by IoT-based SBEs related to the design and implementation of reconfigurable spaces and places. A preliminary service-based framework is described and illustrated using a simple example. The ongoing development of a reconfigurable SBE (a smart home) will provide ground truth and allow for iterative improvements of the service framework based on the real-world testing.

Acknowledgements. This work has been partially supported by a grant from the Virginia Tech Institute for Creativity, Art, and Technology.

References

1. Crabtree, A., Rodden, T.: Domestic routines and design for the home. Comput. Support. Coop. Work **13**(2), 191–220 (2004)
2. Dourish, P.: Re-space-ing place: "place" and "space" ten years on. In: Proceedings of the 2006 20th Anniversary Conference on Computer Supported Cooperative Work (CSCW 2006), pp. 299–308. ACM, New York, 4–8 November 2006
3. Nansen, B., van Ryn, L., Vetere, F., Robertson, T., Brereton, M., Douish, P.: An internet of social things. In: Proceedings of the 26th Australian Computer-Human Interaction Conference on Designing Futures: The Future of Design, pp. 87–96. ACM, New York (2014)
4. Konomi, S., Roussos, G. (eds.): Enriching Urban Spaces with Ambient Computing, the Internet of Things, and Smart City Design. IGI Global, Hershey (2017)
5. Dalton, N.S., Schnädelbach, H., Wiberg, M., Varoudis, T. (eds.): Architecture and Interaction: Human Computer Interaction in Space and Place. Springer, Cham (2016)
6. Schnädelbach, H.: Adaptive architecture. Interactions **23**(2), 62–65 (2016)

7. Jelić, A., Tieri, G., De Matteis, F., Babiloni, F., Vecchiato, G.: The enactive app-roach to architectural experience: a neurophysiological perspective on embodiment, motivation, and affordances. Front. Psychol. **7**(481), 1–20 (2016)
8. Jäger, N.: Interacting with adaptive architecture. Interactions **24**(6), 62–65 (2017)
9. Wiberg, M.: Interaction design meets architectural thinking. Interactions **22**(2), 60–63 (2015)
10. Suchman, L.A.: Human-Machine Reconfigurations: Plans and Situated Actions, 2nd edn. Cambridge University Press, Cambridge (2007)
11. Crabtree, A.: Design in the absence of practice: breaching experiments. In: Proceed-ings of the 5th Conference on Designing Interactive Systems: Processes, Practices, Methods, and Techniques, pp. 59–68. ACM, New York (2004)
12. Dahl, Y., Svendsen, R.-M.: End-user composition interfaces for smart environ-ments: a preliminary study of usability factors. In: Marcus, A. (ed.) DUXU 2011. LNCS, vol. 6770, pp. 118–127. Springer, Heidelberg (2011). https://doi.org/10.1007/978-3-642-21708-1_14
13. Yuliana, A., Felipe, O., Byron, S., Liliana, L., Andres, V.: Configuration of work environments with smart furniture. In: Proceedings of the III International Congress of Engineering Mechatronics and Automation (CIIMA), pp. 1–5, October 2014
14. Spröwitz, A., Moeckel, R., Vespignani, M., Bonardi, S., Ijspeert, A.J.: Roombots: a hardware perspective on 3D self-reconfiguration and locomotion with a homoge-neous modular robot. Rob. Auton. Syst. **62**(7), 1016–1033 (2014)
15. Brunete, A., Ranganath, A., Segovia, S., de Frutos, J.P., Hernando, M., Gambao, E.: Current trends in reconfigurable modular robots design. Int. J. Adv. Rob. Syst. **14**(3), 1–21 (2017)
16. Gračanin, D., Handosa, M., Elmongui, H.G.: A service infrastructure for human-centered IoT-based smart built environments. In: Streitz, N., Markopoulos, P. (eds.) DAPI 2017. LNCS, vol. 10291, pp. 262–274. Springer, Cham (2017). https://doi.org/10.1007/978-3-319-58697-7_19

Measurement of Motion Range to Improve of Body Balance and Its Training Contents

Dong-Yeon Kim, Sung-Wook Shin, Se-Jin Goo, and Sung-Taek Chung[(✉)]

Department of Computer Engineering, Korea Polytechnic University, Seoul, Korea
{kim2917,napalza,rntpwls7,unitaek}@kpu.ac.kr

Abstract. Wrong lifestyle habits can be a major factor for reduced balance ability that may cause difficulties in performing daily activities due to musculoskeletal disorders, gait abnormality, a fall, and other problems. This study assessed range of motion (ROM) using Inertial Measurement Unit (IMU) sensors placed at the waist or upper and lower limbs by measuring the maximum rotation angle of the body to the directions of the sagittal, coronal and transverse planes in real time. Directions with a low body balance are identified using ROM data and based on the analysis results, training content is recommended to improve reduced balance ability in corresponding directions. Furthermore, this content is designed to offer intensive balance training toward a specific direction by providing selection modes of balance training in the desired directions. Motivation for training can be enhanced by comparing changes in measurements assessed before and after balance training. The results of this study are expected to aid improving reduced physical activities in elderly individuals with reduced muscle strength, body balance and walking ability using the content tailored to measure changes in range of motion and improve balance ability.

Keywords: IMU · Balance training · Range of motion · Training contents

1 Introduction

Balance ability is divided into static balance ability to maintains a certain posture on a fixed surface and dynamic balance ability to maintain a posture while performing movement. This is fundamental for normal daily activities and maintained through diverse interactions between musculoskeletal system and nervous system [1, 2]. The elderly population is growing as Korea becomes an aging society recently. These elder people or people with wrong life or exercise habits increasingly experience problems in their balance ability. The aging-caused muscle strength reduction and muscular atrophy rapidly undermine balance ability, causing brain damage or fracture by fall [3, 4]. Moreover, since wrong life or exercise habits are repeated unconsciously, they could cause a problem in muscular function and balance ability leading to musculoskeletal diseases such as spinal deformity, left-right shoulder imbalance, and twisted pelvis [5]. Methods to prevent such diseases include core muscle reinforcement exercise that balances the body and holds the spine and pelvis not to be shaken [6]. This exercise is to help enhance the body joint motion range, flexibility, muscular strength, endurance, coordination, etc.

© Springer International Publishing AG, part of Springer Nature 2018
C. Stephanidis (Ed.): HCII Posters 2018, CCIS 852, pp. 469–474, 2018.
https://doi.org/10.1007/978-3-319-92285-0_64

Methods include that a therapist induces certain postures and their repetition or that a patient looks in a mirror to see his or her own moves to train [7, 8]. Such training methods are to repeat simple moves and do not tell patients about any quantitative change in their present status in real time. In addition, the boredom of such a training method undermines patients' voluntary engagement or training flow [9]. For this reason, motivational ways of exercise have been proposed for voluntary training engagement, which form scenarios for patients to enjoy their training with fun by giving contents in connection with devices measuring their body movements [10, 11].

In this study, wireless IMU sensor was employed to develop an analysis program that measures the joint motion range before and after the balance training of sagittal plane, coronal plane and transverse plane; and compares changes. This study sought to utilize this program to analyze users' physical measurement data and recommend efficient training contents according to the degree of their physical imbalance.

2 Methods and Results

2.1 Range of Motion (ROM) Measurement Program

Figure 1(a) shows the status of attaching to body the IMU sensor (LP-Research's LPMS-B2) for ROM measurement and contents implementation in this study. Here, the IMU sensor wirelessly transmits each value of acceleration, angular speed, Euler angle, and Quaternion angle using Bluetooth in real time; thus, it can measure ROM and physical movement without any spatial restriction. ROM is measured in order of, as in Fig. 1(b), a user's coronal, sagittal, and transverse planes. Their Euler angle values are measured in real time then, the max Euler angle values are extracted at each direction. The max angle values extracted from here are utilized as parameters necessary to determine the difficulty level of training contents. Training contents at an appropriate difficulty level for users' body balance status gives users the sense of achievement for their body balance improvement and

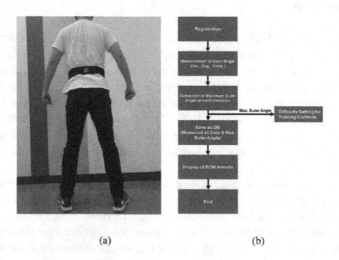

(a)   (b)

Fig. 1. (a) Location of IMU attached to the body (b) Flow chart of ROM measurement

is also an efficient way. Moreover, users' ROM results are measured at every direction in real time and the saved data are visually presented for everyone to check their present body balance status easily and compare pre/post-training change in ROM.

ROM measurement in the coronal, sagittal, and transverse planes are shown in Fig. 2. shows the left/right motion range measurement in the coronal plane. First, when the Test button is pressed, Euler angle is measured for the 2 s when a posture is maintained and their mean value is set as the reference value for the corresponding user's ROM measurement. This value is utilized to represent a user's max ROM measured via coronal left/right turn. In Fig. 2(a), the pie graph in the screen center visualizes ROM in real time. The red-colored area represents the presently-measured max motion range. With respect to the coronal left/right-side ROM, the red-colored bar represents the presently-measured ROM; and green bar, previously-measured motion range mean. Figure 2(b) and (c) show the ROM measurement in the sagittal and transverse planes just as the measurement method in the coronal plane.

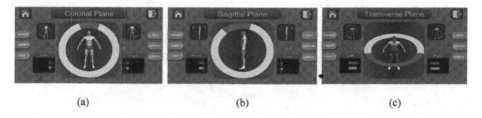

(a)   (b)   (c)

Fig. 2. Motion range measurement (a) coronal (b) sagittal (c) transverse (Color figure online)

After the measurement of coronal, sagittal, transverse Euler Angle values is generally completed, the results are presented in Fig. 3. The result page shows up/down or three-directional left/right ROM in bar graph. The presently-measured values are red colored and previous mean values, green colored. Users can check their motion range in each direction in real time. The measured Euler Angle values are saved in the internal DB and utilized to compare pre/post-interventional ROM changes. Max Euler Angle value is employed as a parameter to determine content difficulty levels.

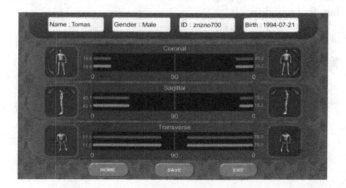

Fig. 3. Result page of ROM measurement

2.2 Body Balance Ability Training Contents

Balance ability training contents were made for users to select necessary training programs or receive recommendations based on the motion range measurement results. In the system, a character was utilized to follow the move of users to help improve their interest and flow while implementing the contents for proactive training engagement. During the content move to maintain balance on unstable platform, users do the trunk exercise reinforcing their core muscles. Physical movements are measured with IMU sensor and the moves are mapped to the moving route of the character. Figure 4(a) is the main contents execution page. After clicking Start, users can select a training direction they wish as in Fig. 4(b) then follow the corresponding training. The materialized contents support 5 modes (Auto, Front, Rear, Left, Right). The Auto mode allows a user to train his or her weak direction based on the ROM values. As presented in Fig. 4(c), training difficulty was differentiated into Easy, Normal and Hard. As the difficulty level moves up, users have smaller-sized mission objects and character requiring more detailed moves to keep a posture.

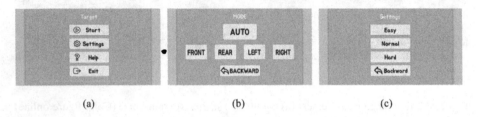

      (a)   (b)   (c)

Fig. 4. Basic Screen Construction (a) Start (b) Training Mode Selection (c) Difficulty Setting

Figure 5 shows a content screen where an Indian character eats cheese. In Fig. 5(a), the Indian character follows the move of a user and the user has to move the character to the cheese and keep a posture for 2 s to win the cheese. Then, while moving to the house in the center of the page as in Fig. 5(b), the user has to repeat the content 5 times for posture arrangement. The figures on the upper right part of the page informs the number of present round of ongoing work. The Pause button allows users to suspend the game if they feel any difficult.

      (a)   (b)

Fig. 5. Content page following users' move

3   Conclusions

In this study, a program was developed based on wireless IMU sensor, which measures the ROM of pre/post-training of sagittal, coronal, and transverse planes; and compares any changes in there. The developed program allows users to measure their max turn range in each area and check their status; and sets up the necessary training mode for each user automatically in connection with training contents. In this manner, users can follow training contents at an appropriate difficulty level for their own status and, by receiving the necessary training intensively, training process efficiency can elevate. Moreover, pre/post-training change in motion range can help increase users' sense of achievement and motivation to encourage proactive training engagement. The training contents aim at reinforcing the core muscles for enhanced balance ability. In the training, IMU sensor is attached to the body and Euler angle is measured to move the content character to a target. In order for users to fully enjoy the contents, diverse kinds of modes are provided at different difficulty levels so that users can select an appropriate training program for themselves or receive recommendation to enjoy training with high efficiency. Together with the motion range measurement developed in the present study, pressure sensor will be employed to measure plantar pressure and understand balance ability in diversified aspects in further research. By doing so, users' present status will be more precisely analyzed and enhancement in personalized training recommendation will be additionally studied.

Acknowledgement. This research was supported by Basic Science Research Program through the National Research Foundation of Korea (NRF) funded by the Ministry of Education (NRF-2017R1D1A1B03036406).

References

1. O'Sullivan, S.B., Schmitz, T.J., Fulk, G.: Physical Rehabilitation. FA Davis, Duxbury (2013)
2. Tinetti, M.E., Baker, D.I., McAvay, G., Claus, E.B., Garrett, P., Gottschalk, M., Koch, M.L., Trainor, T., Horwitz, R.I.: A multifactorial intervention to reduce the risk of falling among elderly people living in the community. N. Engl. J. Med. **331**(13), 821–827 (1994). https://doi.org/10.1056/NEJM199409293311301
3. Nicholson, V.P., McKean, M.R., Burkett, B.J.: Low-load high-repetition resistance training improves strength and gait speed in middle-aged and older adults. J. Sci. Med. Sport **18**(5), 596–600 (2015). https://doi.org/10.1016/j.jsams.2014.07.018
4. Hatch, J., Gill-Body, K.M., Portney, L.G.: Determinants of balance confidence in community-dwelling elderly people. Phys. Ther. **83**(12), 1072–1079 (2003). https://doi.org/10.1093/ptj/83.12.1072
5. Kang, S.R., Kim, U.R., Jung, H.C., Kwon, T.K.: Effect of correction to muscle imbalance in lower limbs according to reduction of weight bearing methods of four point of horizontal shaft. J. Rehabil. Welf. Eng. Assistive Technol. **7**(2), 101–107 (2013)
6. Mori, A.: Electromyographic activity of selected trunk muscles during stabilization exercises using a gym ball. Electromyogr. Clin. Neurophysiol. **44**(1), 57–64 (2004)

7. Knapik, J.J., Wright, J.E., Mawdsley, R.H., Braun, J.: Isometric, isotonic, and isokinetic torque variations in four muscle groups through a range of joint motion. Phys. Ther. **63**(6), 938–947 (1983). https://doi.org/10.1093/ptj/63.6.938
8. Bromley, I.: Tetraplegia and paraplegia: a guide for physiotherapists, 6th edn. Churchill Livingstone, Edinburgh (2006)
9. Sluijs, E.M., Kok, G.J., Van der Zee, J.: Correlates of exercise compliance in physical therapy. Phys. Ther. **73**(11), 771–782 (1993). https://doi.org/10.1093/ptj/73.11.771
10. Fitzgerald, D., Trakarnratanakul, N., Smyth, B., Caulfield, B.: Effects of a wobble board-based therapeutic exergaming system for balance training on dynamic postural stability and intrinsic motivation levels. J. Orthop. Sports Phys. Ther. **40**(1), 11–19 (2010). https://doi.org/10.2519/jospt.2010.3121
11. Burke, J.W., McNeill, M., Charles, D., Morrow, P., Crosbie, J., McDonough, S.: Serious games for upper limb rehabilitation following stroke. In: Games and Virtual Worlds for Serious Applications. VS-GAMES 2009 Conference, pp. 103–110, March 2009. https://doi.org/10.1109/vs-games.2009.17

Developing a Human Behavior Simulation System Based on Geometry Affordance

Yun Gil Lee[(✉)]

Department of Architecture, Hoseo University, Asan, Korea
yglee@hoseo.edu

Abstract. This research develops a human behavior simulation system that can be used in the architectural design process. Specifically, the proposed system, called PlayGA, is intended for use in the non-Euclidian architectural design process. PlayGA is a type of export system that can simulate human behaviors while taking into account design geometry. After geometrical shapes are designed using a geometrical design tool, PlayGA can deploy non-player characters (NPCs) in the design alternatives. These NPCs play freely and behave in a variety of different ways in the simulation. The autonomous behavior of NPCs is based on the intelligence of recognizing geometric affordance. In this paper, we introduce how to develop a technology that simulates geometric affordance.

Keywords: Building information modeling · Architectural design
Human behavior simulation

1 Introduction

To design a building is to create a number of environmental settings for its users' activities. For this reason, architectural designers should always consider how situations change when crafting environmental settings that support users' behaviors. The human factor is one of the most important standards for judging the quality of design alternatives [1].

Recently, many architectural features with non-Euclidian shapes have appeared in the urban environment, in response to social demands for innovative building shapes. In the educational field of architectural design, non-Euclidian design has become an important part of the curriculum, because generating these shapes is not an easy task for students who have been trained in conventional design education. In this challenging pedagogical situation, one significant problem involves the difficulty that students may simply be attracted to the notion of creating unusual forms while ignoring important factors like human behaviors during the non-Euclidian architectural design process, because many instructors focus primarily or even entirely on the technical methods needed to create non-Euclidian shapes [2].

To resolve this issue, we suggest a technical solution. This research develops a human behavior simulation system, called PlayGA, which can be used in the non-Euclidian architectural design process. PlayGA is a type of export system that can simulate human behaviors while taking into account design geometry. After geometrical shapes

© Springer International Publishing AG, part of Springer Nature 2018
C. Stephanidis (Ed.): HCII Posters 2018, CCIS 852, pp. 475–479, 2018.
https://doi.org/10.1007/978-3-319-92285-0_65

are designed using a geometrical design tool, PlayGA can deploy non-player characters (NPCs) in the design alternatives. These NPCs play freely and behave in a variety of different ways in the simulation. The autonomous behavior of NPCs is based on the intelligence of recognizing geometric affordance. In this paper, we introduce how to develop a technology that simulates geometric affordance.

2　3D Object Recognition Techniques

3D object recognition is a basic requirement for comprehending the NPCs' reactions to geometrical shapes. There are two commonly known methods for 3D object recognition: the pattern recognition approach and the feature-based approach. Pattern recognition approaches use pre-captured (or pre-computed) images of an object to recognize that object. However, they cannot consider an object's 3D context and do not handle occlusion [3, 4]. On the other hand, feature-based approaches work well in recognizing distinctive featured objects that contain vivid edge features, blob features, etc. However, it is not appropriate for recognizing the smooth surfaces objects without texture [5].

Several architectural objects like doors, windows, and furniture contain typical patterns, and previous approaches might well be able to recognize them successfully. However, those methods are not appropriate for this research, the goal of which is to extract geometrical affordances from non-Euclidian shapes, which are not easily specified as patterns. In order to extract NPC behaviors according to objects of various shapes, we developed a method using those objects' basic attributes: vertices, edges, and surfaces. All architectural shapes have those attributes, and humans generally display certain behaviors in the context of a given shape. Thus, we have introduced a strategy to match possible behavioral information related to the properties of basic objects and reproduce it according to the characters' traits. Figure 1 shows NPC behavior allocation strategy in PlayGa.

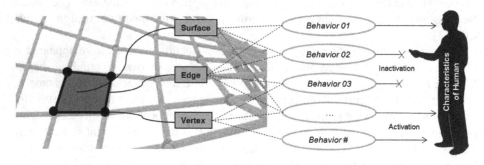

Fig. 1. NPC behavior allocation strategy in PlayGA

3   PlayGA: A Human Behavior Simulation System Based on Geometry Affordances

In order to perform human behavioral simulation in the design process of non-Euclidian shaped buildings, a human behavioral simulation module (PlayGA) has been developed, based on the commercial modeling tools SketchUp Make 2017. Figure 2 shows the process of using PlayGA as a plug-in with SketchUp. PlayGA is developed on Unity3D, a game-based platform. After architects design non-Euclidian shapes, PlayGA can be executed in a real-time manner. It generates a virtual place based on the designed geometries and automatically deploys NPCs in that space. NPCs behave freely according to the geometric shapes, which are associated with pre-assigned behaviors. NPC behavior is also constrained by the characteristics of the human NPC figure and the object's configuration status. Figure 3 shows NPCs' reactions according to the direction and height of the contextual geometry.

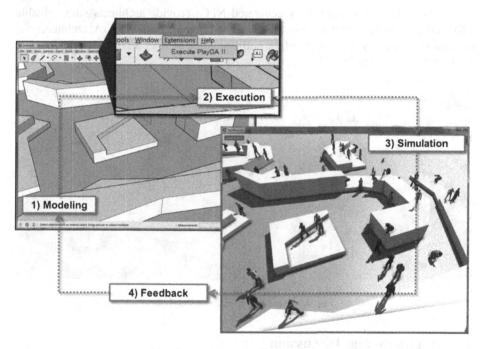

Fig. 2. The process of using PlayGA

Fig. 3. NPCs' reactions according to the direction (left) and height (right) of geometry

The behaviors of automatically generated NPCs provide architects with valuable information regarding the usability of the designed shapes. With PlayGA, architects can evaluate functionality in the midst of the non-Euclidian architectural design process and produce the optimal alternative (Fig. 4).

Fig. 4. Execution images in PlayGA

4   Conclusion and Discussion

This research presents PlayGA, a human behavior simulation system that can be used in the non-Euclidian architectural design process. In PlayGA, the autonomous behavior of NPCs is based on the intelligence of recognizing geometric affordances. In this paper, we have introduced how to develop a technology that simulates geometric affordances. PlayGA appears to be helpful in evaluating the functionality of design alternatives in a non-Euclidian architectural design process. However, in further research, the effect of PlayGA should be evaluated through rigorous field tests, and further development is required to stabilize its functions.

Acknowledgment. This research was supported by Basic Science Research Program through the National Research Foundation of Korea (NRF) funded by the Ministry of Education (NRF-2015R1D1A1A01057525).

References

1. Lee, Y.G., Park, C.H., Lim, D.H.: A study on the development of the user behavior simulation technology using a perceived action possibilities. J. Korea Multimedia Soc. **17**(11), 1335–1344 (2014)
2. Dourish, P.: Where the Footprints Lead: Tracking Down Other Roles for Social Navigation, pp. 273–291. Springer, London (2003)
3. Murase, H., Nayar, S.K.: Visual learning and recognition of 3-D objects from appearance. Int. J. Comput. Vis. **14**(1), 5–24 (1995)
4. Selinger, A., Nelson, R.: A perceptual grouping hierarchy for appearance-based 3D object recognition. Comput. Vis. Image Understand. **76**(1), 83–92 (1999)
5. Tomasi, C., Kanade, T.: Shape and motion from image streams: a factorization method. Int. J. Comput. Vis. **9**(2), 137–154 (1992)

ParkCDMX: A Customized Parking App

Leticia Luna Tlatelpa[✉] and Rocío Abascal-Mena

Master in Design, Information and Communication (MADIC),
Universidad Autónoma Metropolitana, Cuajimalpa, Mexico
letyludigital@gmail.com, mabascal@correo.cua.uam.mx

Abstract. Parking in Mexico City is a real challenge. Although this city is North America's worst city for parking [2], there is not a real parking system. There are people in charge of parking cars on the public street for a fee together with public or private parking garages. Meanwhile, there are also parking meters in some of the neighborhoods and also some apps for finding paid parking. This paper presents ParkCDMX, a new app to help people to find a place in a public garage in Mexico City. It provides a map of all registered public parking lots in the city. The actual geographic position of the user can be the starting point to search either by street or neighborhood. The approach is based on User Centered Design methodology, including interviews of potential users in order to know their needs and offer a pertinent app according to the city.

Keywords: Parking app · Usability · User experience
User-centered design methodology · Evaluation

1 Introduction

The problem of finding a good parking place in a big city, like Mexico City, really matters. In a study conducted by IBM in 2011 [1], it was found that 73% of the drivers in this city have been frustrated enough that they gave up looking and drive away. This survey also reports that 30 percent of the traffic in a city is caused by drivers searching for a parking lot, which in turn produces subsequent air pollution.

In the Valley of Mexico metropolitan area[1], almost 6.8 millions of vehicles circulate every day [3]. The total of parking spots constructed in the city is about 6.5 million, according to IMCO[2] [4]. Most of them are private. They belong to offices, malls, restaurants, supermarkets, shops, apartment buildings and housing complexes [5]. There are 2128 public parking garage, that means, there is no place enough for each vehicle to park [6]. To make matters worse only around 50% of the parking complies with security norms and accident coverage; the others are irregular [6]. Added to this, the information about public parking contains the data of only 698 of them [7] and corresponds only to

---

[1] Zona Metropolitana del Valle de México. This area corresponds to Mexico City and the suburbs, which are part of the neighbor state Estado de Mexico.
[2] Mexican Institute for Competitiveness. A think tank dedicated to generate public policy proposals to boost competitiveness.

© Springer International Publishing AG, part of Springer Nature 2018
C. Stephanidis (Ed.): HCII Posters 2018, CCIS 852, pp. 480–486, 2018.
https://doi.org/10.1007/978-3-319-92285-0_66

the city and not to the Valley of Mexico metropolitan area. There is also no information about the quality of parking[3] [7].

2 Exploratory Research

In many countries, there has been a great effort to help the drivers to find a parking spot. The schemes applied are very different. Some of the apps need to be used within a functional system of parking system, like EasyPark [8], developed in Denmark and active in many European countries. This is not the case for Mexico City, as mentioned in the introduction of this paper.

There are other apps that were developed considering the scenario of this city. One of them, called Leopark [9], which shows the parking garages of an area on the map and the user can drive there by using Waze [11] or Google Maps [12] and in some places it is also possible to pay with a credit card. Arriv.io [10] is other app similar to Leopark, but it works only with associated parking lots and has a staff of valet parking that help you to park your car.

Even though these apps have many advantages and useful features, none of them allows the driver to rate the user experience of the parking garage, which is essential to bring confidence for future users. The confidence and security provided by a parking lot are key characteristics to consider when designing an app to find a parking space in Mexico City. The prototype ParkCDMX intents to build a database with information related with the driver's experiences and the evaluations of the parking places that he has already visited. In the next section, the design process of ParkCDMX is presented.

3 Design Process of ParkCDMX

The conducted design process was based on the User Centered Design approach, which is a design method whose process is directed by information about the people who are going to make use of the product [13]. A main concept in this approach is usability, which is defined by the standard ISO 9241-11 as *"the extent to which a product can be used by specified users to achieve specified goals with effectiveness, efficiency and satisfaction in a specified context of use"* [14]. In this project, the usability principle was the guide that allowed to determine the needs of the users, through knowing them and understanding their activities, in order to design a product that would satisfy these needs, in an iterative process of design and evaluation.

The first stage of the process is the acquisition of the user needs in form of *Personas*. Then a storyboard and a paper prototype were designed. This prototype was given to different users to get usability feedback. Their evaluations were translated to heuristics metrics. After that, the prototype was redesigned and implemented as a digital prototype or mockup, which in turn was tested by five different users and evaluated using

---

[3] The data base with information with the public parking garages in the city is open data and it is provided by Laboratorio de Datos de la Ciudad de México.

the heuristics metrics again. The mockup was redesign again to obtain a final version of the app.

3.1 Research Design

During the research process, some of the common users of parking lots[4] were observed. Then, several in-depth interviews were conducted with different parking users to learn about their context. With some users, the interview was done in a parking lot chosen by the user to observe in detail the problems of the place. Afterward, a brainstorm was conducted with some of the interviewees to find their needs. The data collected during the interviews and the brainstorm sessions was analyzed to create the Personas and the scenarios. The information was very helpful to develop a more complete representation and concrete understanding of the user. The latter describe the use that the potential user can give to the final product. Otherwise, designing without knowing the user can result in a bad product [15].

Some of the needs detected were the following:

- To know where there are parking places.
- To search a parking lot without stress.
- To be sure that the parking place is secure.
- To have an idea of the time to reach the parking place.
- To know if the parking lot has damage insurance.
- To pay with credit card.
- To know where the cheapest parking lots are.
- To know the ranking of a parking lot given from other drivers.
- To know if there are free places in a parking lot.
- To make a reservation.
- To know if the parking lot has places with enough space for a large car.
- The need of a photo of the establishment.

3.2 Personas and Scenarios

Personas and scenarios are very useful to design because they are based on the specific needs of a user or group of users [15]. For this project, three Personas and three scenarios were created; one of them is shown in Figs. 1 and 2. The first Persona, Mr. Cano, represents a successful doctor, father of two children, who doesn't have much free time and avoids visiting museums, theaters or going to concerts because he doesn't know if he will find a place to park. Also, he has a large car. The second Persona is a young girl, Ms. Ana García, who lives far from her job. She doesn't like to take public transport and she prefers to use a car, although she has trouble finding where to park safely and not very expensive. The third Persona is a 53-year-old woman, Ms. Lupita, who does

---

[4] The users of the parking meters were not considered because the parking meters belong to private companies that do not publish their data.

social work and usually parks her car in the street, but many times the places are occupied, so she loses a lot of time looking for cheap but safe parking.

Two principles of design were chosen: (1) time and (2) visualization.

Persona

FOTO & NOMBRE	DETALLES	NECESIDADES
 Esta es Lupita, esposa de Ricardo y mamá de Andrés, Juan y Paty.	Lupita tiene 54 años y vive en el poniente de la CDMX. Dos veces a la semana colabora en una ONG y trabaja como freelance para una agencia de mercadeo y para una inmobiliaria, por lo que debe moverse entre Santa Fé y la Condesa. No tiene salario fijo y debe cuidar sus gastos. Dos de sus hijos trabajan y uno estudia. Le gusta salir con sus amigas y su familia. No usa el transporte público por temor a la inseguridad. Tiene un coche Sentra 2009. Si puede, evita los estacioamientos públicos porque son caros, prefiere estacionar en la calle. Usa tarjeta de crédito.	Lupita quiere llegar a tiempo a sus citas. Quisiera saber si tiene alguna posibilidad de estacionarse en la calle antes de salir de casa. Eso le ayudaría a estimar su tiempo de llegada y si debe optar por un estacionamiento público seguro y no muy caro.

Fig. 1. One of the Personas, Ms. Lupita, who is married with kids and needs to arrive in time to her meetings.

ESCENARIO

UN DÍA TÍPICO

Lupita se levanta temprano para dar de desayunar. Después hace algo de ejercicio. Se arregla para salir. Mira su teléfono y verifica que necesita 45 min para llegar a su cita. Afortunadamente, en la zona donde quiere estacionar hay muchos cafés con WiFi así que podrá revisar algunos detalles de su entrevista.
El estacionamiento "Ramírez" es el que más le conviene pero no tiene lugares disponibles, según le indica la aplicación. El sistema le ofrece una alternativa. Revisa y el lugar está bien calificado. Además, no es muy caro el lugar ya que a esa hora no hay mucha demanda aunque, tiene que caminar un poco más. Indica al sistema que se dirige al estacionamiento "Parking Seguro". Esta vez, ella prefiere hacer la reservación cuando ya se encuentre cerca de donde quiere estacionar. Puede que haya más posibilidades de que se libere un lugar en el estacionamiento "Ramírez".
Durante el trayecto escucha las notificaciones que le da el sistema. Se liberó un lugar en el estacionamiento "Ramírez" pero dada la demanda cuesta más de lo usual. Rechaza la sugerencia y hace la reservación para el estacionamiento "Parking Seguro". Continúa su ruta hacia allí.
Lo que le indicó la aplicación acerca del lugar es cierto y así lo verifica.
Todavía tiene tiempo para revisar sus notas antes de su cita.

Fig. 2. One of the Scenarios for Ms. Lupita: her typical day consists in arriving early to her meeting and having time before it starts.

3.3 Storyboard

For the design of ParkCDMX the following point of view was important: *"It is very useful at the moment of choosing a parking place to have an accurate approximation of the time needed to reach it"*. With this in mind two storyboards were drawn. The storyboard is a Lo-fi prototype that focuses in the different tasks to be resolved and to communicate ideas. The user is always the central part. Figure 3 shows one of these storyboards.

Fig. 3. Example of Storyboard that shows a woman that is using a computer or laptop device to find the parking lot that has available places.

The inspiration for the storyboards were some apps, like Airbnb[5] and Uber[6], that use the recommendations given by the community and establish a direct connection between the user and the service provider. Another source of inspiration were colors and design concepts like minimalism design and simplicity.

Afterwards, a paper prototype was made and its usability was evaluated applying different heuristics. For Nielsen [16], a usability problem was any aspect of the user interface that could be a complication. It can be a severe, moderate or a minor problem. The author proposed ten heuristics to evaluate usability [17]. In this project, this approach was chosen because it is cheap and intuitive.

Some important findings were reported by the evaluators at this first stage of the design: (1) time was not the principal issue for the app, because it should use Waze [11] or Google Maps [12] to indicate the route to reach the parking place and (2) truthful information about a parking lot was very important in order to choose one. The last one modified the concept completely so that the new point of view to follow was: *"it is very useful at the moment of choosing a parking place to have an instrument which can give truthful information about it"*. Some of the proposed screen changed to bring more detailed information in the digital version of the prototype.

The evaluators had different background, young people used to do everything with a smartphone and older people with little experience use some apps like Waze or Uber.

For the digital version of the prototype only one function was implemented: the possibility to search for a parking place. This prototype was evaluated again using the

---

[5] https://www.airbnb.mx/.
[6] https://www.uber.com/.

heuristics approach. This time the changes were more about small modifications in some of the screens and about simplifying the design by eliminating unnecessary screens.

4   Conclusions and Future Work

In this article, we have presented the process that was followed to determine the needs of the people in terms of mobility in the City of Mexico. Until now there is no application that allows to locate available parking spaces. So, based on the findings, although that the time of arriving to a parking place is important, the principal issue for a potential user of a parking place is the price and the quality of the service. Last one can be estimated on the basis of the qualification given by other drivers. In this way, ParkCDMX can help to construct a confident database of parking places of Mexico City. This could be helpful also for visitors, tourists or simply for people who have to go from one extreme of the city to the other. Using Waze or Google Maps as the routing tools can make the calculation of the time needed to reach the destination more easily. It is important to note that it would be interesting to apply other types of heuristic evaluation, such as one that considers the cultural context [18] and one that can be applied in specific domains [19].

References

1. Armonk, N.Y.: Drivers share worldwide parking woes, IBM global parking survey. https://www-03.ibm.com/press/us/en/pressrelease/35515.wss. Accessed 2 Mar 2018
2. México como la peor ciudad del mundo para estacionarse. http://www.msn.com/en-ca/news/other/the-20-worst-cities-for-parking-in-the-world/ss-AA2o757#image=10. Accessed 2 Mar 2018
3. INEGI, Statistics about registered automobiles in Mexico. http://www.inegi.org.mx/est/contenidos/proyectos/registros/economicas/vehiculos/descripciones.aspx#. Accessed 2 Mar 2018
4. IMCO, El peso de los estacionamientos (2016). http://imco.org.mx/competitividad/el-peso-de-los-estacionamientos/. Accessed 2 Mar 2018
5. Nota periodística, La Silla Rota. http://lasillarota.com/cdmx-donde-no-hay-lugar-para-estacionarse#.WEHcN6J97_8. Accessed 2 Mar 2018
6. Estadísticas sobre estacionamientos piratas en CDMX. https://www.maspormas.com/2016/04/06/la-mitad-de-los-estacionamientos-en-la-cdmx-son-piratas/. Accessed 2 Mar 2018
7. Laboratorio de Datos, Base de datos de los estacionamientos públicos de la CDMX. http://datos.labplc.mx/datasets/view/estacionamientos_publicos. Accessed 2 Mar 2018
8. EasyPark. https://easyparkgroup.com/. Accessed 2 Mar 2018
9. LeoPark. https://www.leopark.mx/. Accessed 2 Mar 2018
10. Arriv.io. http://arriv.io/. Accessed 2 Mar 2018
11. Waze. https://www.waze.com/es/. Accessed 2 Mar 2018
12. Google Maps. https://maps.google.com.mx. Accessed 2 Mar 2018
13. Pribeanu, C.: A revised set of usability heuristics for the evaluation of interactive systems. Informatica Economica 21(3), 31 (2017)

14. ISO 9241-11, Ergonomics Requirements for Office Work with Visual Display Terminals (VDT's) - Part 11: Guidance on Usability, International Organization for Standardization, Geneva, (1998)
15. Cooper, A., Reimann, R., Cronin, D.: About Face 3: The Essentials of Interaction Design. Wiley, Hoboken (2007)
16. Nielsen, J.: Usability Engineering. Academic Press, New York (1993)
17. Nielsen, J.: Usability Inspection Methods. Wiley, Hoboken (1994)
18. Díaz, J., Rusu, C., Collazos, C.A.: Experimental validation o a set of cultural-oriented usability heuristics: e-Commerce websites evaluation. Comput. Stand. Interfaces **50**, 160–178 (2017)
19. Hermawati, S., Lawson, G.: Establishing usability heuristics for heuristics evaluation in a specific domain: is there consensus? Appl. Ergon. **56**, 34–51 (2016)

Overcoming Space Inequalities in City Building Games Through Negotiation

Paola Monachesi[✉]

Utrecht University, Trans 10, 3512JK Utrecht, The Netherlands
P.Monachesi@uu.nl

Abstract. Serious games for urban planning can support the process of consensus building among various stakeholders. They make possible to negotiate among different scenarios about the use of space. We present You Place It!, a prototype for a multiplayer geo-game dealing with negotiations related to the development of the road infrastructure of Dharavi, a complex low-income area in Mumbai (India). We discuss the implementation choices being carried out and the relevance of introducing a language component in the game to deal with negotiations.

Keywords: Serious games · Urban planning · Dharavi · Negotiations
Language

1 Introduction

Serious games for urban planning can provide an effective platform for decision-making and conflict resolution in urban development. They can support the process of consensus building among different stakeholders and allow to test different scenarios about the use of space and its resources.

We present You Place It!, a prototype version of a geo-game for urban planning. It takes as case study Dharavi, one of the largest low-income areas in Mumbai (India). The game is a multiplayer one and focuses on negotiations related to planning and building road infrastructure in Dharavi and the obstacles (i.e. spatial and financial) that are encountered in the process. It can play an important role in the process of consensus building among different stakeholders: government, developers and citizens. The main aim is to achieve common ground by taking into account individual needs and those of the community. Reaching consensus about the use of resources is crucial in spatial planning, especially for urban poor communities. Local governments often cannot provide solutions, it is thus worth assessing an alternative path in which communities can get involved spelling out their needs and their knowledge by proposing their own solutions [1].

Communication plays a crucial role in negotiation processes even though its role is often neglected in (urban planning) digital games. The proposed game, through the introduction of a chat-box, allows for negotiations among the players to be carried out through communication. It creates an innovative conceptual framework to investigate

© Springer International Publishing AG, part of Springer Nature 2018
C. Stephanidis (Ed.): HCII Posters 2018, CCIS 852, pp. 487–493, 2018.
https://doi.org/10.1007/978-3-319-92285-0_67

whether certain spatial configurations (physical/F2F vs. digital/online) can support consensus finding (in urban planning) better than others.

2   You Place It!

Serious games for urban planning can provide an effective platform for decision-making and conflict resolution in urban development since they focus on spatial and real- world problems. For example, [2] carried out a pilot project set in Boston to develop a park and used Second Life but also meetings in physical space. NextCampus, a game to evaluate the implications related to moving the campus of the University of Hamburg to a new location was developed by [3].

You Place It! Is a serious game for urban planning with the goal to support the process of consensus building among different stakeholders that can play and test different scenarios about the use of space and its resources, as well as possible responses to these scenarios. The game focuses on one of the largest low-income areas in India, Dharavi. Its population is estimated to more than 1 million inhabitants. It is located in Mumbai and was founded in 1880s during the British colonial area. It is a very diverse and multi-religious settlement. It currently covers an area of about 230 hectares. The value of the land occupied by Dharavi has increased substantially due to its central location, the vicinity of the airport and the business area BKC. Dharavi is the basis of many local industries dealing with pottery, leather goods, embroidery and garments, food, among others. It has a turnover between $650 million and 1 billion annually. Figure 1 shows a bird's eye perspective of this area. Figure 2 demonstrates the study area on the satellite image.

Fig. 1. View of Dharavi

Fig. 2. Satellite image of area

Dharavi represents a very complex urban area: several plans have been proposed during the years which didn't succeed in their realization. There is the need to involve diverse stakeholders in order to design an acceptable urban plan and a game such as You Place It! might represent an opportunity to interact and to facilitate participation.

The game was originally conceived as a single player one [4]. It focuses on negotiations related to planning and building road infrastructure in Dharavi and the obstacles (i.e. spatial and financial) that are encountered in the process. The player plays against the system that takes the role of the road developer. The implementation was based on the level-k negotiation model ([5, 6]). The player negotiates on the basis of the space occupied and the costs related to removing obstacles.

We have extended the initial implementation that is described in [4], into a multi-player game with the goal of achieving consensus in building a road infrastructure by relying on negotiations supported by communication. The main aim is to achieve common ground and build the roads by taking into account individual needs and those of the community. The space represented in the game is the actual geographical area of Dharavi and the application is built on top of Google Maps, as can be seen in Fig. 3 which shows the start of the game: players can log into the application and are assigned a role to play and a budget.

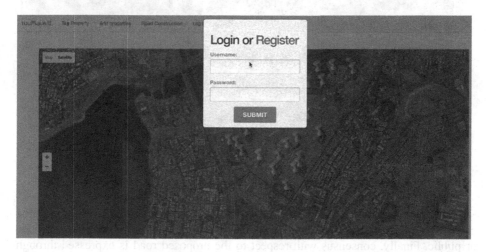

Fig. 3. Login You PlaceIt!

Different roles are envisaged: residents, representatives of the government, real-estate developers, commercial representatives that have business in the area and NGOs. Residents own properties in Dharavi and they need roads to connect to other properties, they do not have a budget to build the roads but they can vote for various proposals. They can influence the decisions of the others by raising or lowering the price of their own property. The representatives of the government are in charge of planning the roads, but they do not have a big budget for their development so they need the cooperation of the residents to accomplish their plans: they own properties and they have the most influential vote. The real-estate developers aim to redevelop the area for business purposes, they do not own properties but have a significant budget: their vote is the least important. The commercial representatives own properties and need a better infrastructure to connect to clients, suppliers and the rest of the city: they have a vote and a budget. NGOs own properties having public utility, they have a small budget and a vote.

Several objects are accessible to the players (they are represented by the colored pins distinguishing them) and are tagged beforehand with their properties associated to them (prices and negotiation margins), they include commercial buildings, houses, school buildings, hospital, market places, civic facilities such as religious buildings, water plants, parks.

Players can propose a road to be constructed as can be seen in Fig. 4. A requirement is that it should connect properties. Negotiations take place if the road development occurs into obstacles such as properties that need to be demolished or take a path that is not beneficial for the community.

Fig. 4. Proposed road in black

Negotiation includes a financial transaction but also communication through the chat-box. Players can try to influence each other by using messages that are either private or public. Finally, consensus with respect to the proposed road is expressed through voting so that it is decided whether the road can be maintained or removed.

3 Language and Negotiations

The multiplayer implementation has been enhanced with a chat-box in order to add the possibility to use language in negotiations. Negotiation is a process of communication and language offers insights in this process (i.e. conditions of bargaining, introduction and closure) as well as in the social aspects. Furthermore, an analysis of the information of messages exchanged by negotiators based on linguistic signals (i.e. presence or absence of degree, comparative word categories) shows correlations with negotiation success or failure [7]. Therefore, adding a chat box in the game provides complementary information to the actions related to the negotiation process, as can be seen in Fig. 5. The use of text-based forms of communications in online games has not received much attention in the literature: they have been addressed mainly in the educational context, especially with respect to language learning [8]. However, language plays an important role in online games especially in the case of a multiplayer game since it gives insights in the discourse strategies. Language is virtually the only means in online games to enact authority in order to become group leader as well as to create group identity [9]. In the context of YouPlaceIt!, it can be employed not only in building consensus but also in the creation of social interaction, roles and identities [10].

Fig. 5. Negotiations through the chat box

The analysis of communicative interactions in digital games has not received much attention. The inclusion of a language component in the game is an innovative extension that allows for corpus creation of the language data that can be extracted. More specifically, the data is collected in the database for retrieval and it includes the sender and receiver ids, the message id, the message text and the time the message has been sent. It allows for a quantitative analysis of the role of language in digital space that can offer new insights in online interactions. It creates the conditions for a comparison with F2F interactions in similar settings that make possible to assess the role of language and eventually that of spatial configurations (physical/F2F vs. digital/online) in negotiations within a (web-based urban planning) game.

Urban planning games can be of relevance in analyzing whether certain spatial configurations (physical/F2F vs. digital/online) can support negotiation and consensus finding better than others so that communication and knowledge exchange is facilitated. While physical space plays an important role in triggering socialization, in online games this function is taken over by language. The style of communication or the vocabulary adopted can be a relevant indicator of a community and identify cultural and social differences [11].

4   Implementation

An SQL database is used for storing both the information related to the user and the game objects. It includes tables related to the user identification, those related to the connection among players and game rounds (including the id of all players involved and their roles), tables concerning the properties (including location, type of owner, costs, margins for negotiation) and tables concerning the roads (including its coordinates and the id of the player that proposed it).

There are individual actions possible within the game such as login, add new tagged properties, propose roads, visualize proposed roads and delete proposed roads while multiplayer actions include the possibility of private chat or with the whole community of players to carry out negotiations at different levels.

The implementation carried out is available in a Github dedicated page at https://github.com/YouPlaceIt/Dharavi.

5   Evaluation

The prototype has been evaluated by Computer Science students of Utrecht University in the context of a game development course. They pointed out several bugs and gave suggestions with respect to the user interface that was supposed to be more intuitive, it should include more explanations concerning the game actions and have self-explanatory labels for the buttons. In addition, it was suggested to give the possibility to delete roads proposed if there was not enough consensus. Furthermore, it was mentioned to start the game with objects already tagged regarding their type and owners. This feedback has been worked out in the current implementation. It was also suggested to move away from Google Earth and have a schematic representation of the area. This suggestion was not taken into account since the current implementation has the advantage that it can be easily adapted to new environments.

The game was also evaluated by students of the summer school on Arts, Fashion and Culture at the University of Macerata (Italy) that suggested to relate the road development to the cultural and religious buildings present in the area in order to support the cultural heritage.

At the Workshop on Urban Futures and Urban Utopia in South-Asian Megacities organized at the Institute of Development Studies in Kolkota (India), the game was perceived as a useful instrument for community empowerment in order to learn how to negotiate with the government.

6   Conclusions

The You Place It! game is conceived as a tool to reach consensus in the negotiation of space in a complex urban planning context such as that of Dharavi. It can constitute an alternative, bottom up way to achieve consensus in urban development by focusing on the needs of the citizens and the requirements of the stakeholders involved. It is a multiplayer game enhanced with a language component to carry out the negotiations.

There is a shortcoming in the development of current City Building Games since their game mechanics and interface don't allow for development of utopic visions [12]: spatial inequalities are often ignored and there are no possibilities to explore different models. You Place it! has the potential to fill this gap since it confronts the players with the challenges and the problems of mega-cities while creating the possibility to imagining alternative solutions for their development.

Acknowledgements. We would like to thank Fabiano Dalpiaz and Joske Houtkamp for their suggestions during the development of the prototype and Ioana Cocu for its implementation. Thanks to Kavita Vemuri for making the original single player implementation available. The pilot was made possible thanks to the seed funding granted by the Utrecht Center for Game Research at Utrecht University.

References

1. Papeleras, R., Bagotlo, O., Boonyabancha, S.: A conversation about change-making by communities: some experiences from ACCA. Environ. Urbanization **24**(2), 463–480 (2012)
2. Gordon, E., Manosevitch, E.: Augmented deliberation: merging physical and virtual interaction to engage communities in urban planning. New Media Soc. **13**(1), 75–95 (2010)
3. Poplin, A.: Playful public participation in urban planning: a case study for online serious games. Comput. Environ. Urban Syst. **36**, 195–206 (2012)
4. Vemuri, A., Poplin, A., Monachesi, P.: YouPlaceIt!: a serious digital game for achieving consensus in urban planning. In: AGILE 2014 Workshop (2014)
5. Costa-Gomes, M., Crawford, V.P., Broseta, B.: Cognition and behavior in normal-form games: an experimental study. Econometrica **69**(5), 1193–1235 (2001)
6. Nagel, R.: Unraveling in guessing games: an experimental study. Am. Econ. Rev. **85**(5), 313–1326 (1995)
7. Sokolova, M., Lapalme, G.: How much do we say? Using informativeness of negotiation text records for early prediction of negotiation outcomes. Group Decis. Negot. **21**, 363–379 (2012)
8. Kardan, K.: Computer role-playing games as a vehicle for teaching history, culture and language. In: Sandbox Symposium Proceedings, Boston, MA, July 2006
9. Rusaw, E.: Language and social interaction in the virtual space of World of Warcraft. Studies in the Linguistic Sciences: Illinois Working Papers 2011, pp. 66–88 (2011)
10. Newon, L.: Online multiplayers games. In: Georgakopoulou, A., Spilioti, T. (eds.) The Routledge Handbook of Language and Digital Communication. Routledge, London (2016)
11. Monachesi, P., Markus, T.: Using social media for ontology enrichment. In: Aroyo, L., Antoniou, G., Hyvönen, E., ten Teije, A., Stuckenschmidt, H., Cabral, L., Tudorache, T. (eds.) ESWC 2010. LNCS, vol. 6089, pp. 166–180. Springer, Heidelberg (2010). https://doi.org/10.1007/978-3-642-13489-0_12
12. Bereitschaft, B.: Gods of the City? Reflecting on City Building Games as an Early Introduction to Urban Systems. Geography and Geology Faculty Publications. Paper 8 (2015)

Instruvis: Play Music Virtually
and Visualize the Data

Ismail Ayaz and Elumalai Monisha(✉)

University of Texas at Dallas, Richardson, TX, USA
{aai103020,mxe160530}@utdallas.edu

Abstract. The use of micro-inertial and magnetic sensors in day-to-day life is becoming more and more common with the introduction of IoT devices. Using the concept of these sensors we have designed Instruvis - a virtual platform for musicians to produce music using wearable devices that use machine learning algorithms to train gestures representing notes using MIDI in Digital Audio Workstation. Instruvis has been developed using Intel-Curie chips that is designed with motion sensors and modules involving pattern matching engine. Wearing the devices makes it possible for musicians to produce and enjoy quality music on-the-go in place of confining them to a setup. We evaluated our prototype on music enthusiasts and are further improving Instruvis based on our findings.

Keywords: Virtual music · Gesture recognition · Pattern recognition
Music visualization

1 Introduction

Sensors and data have been essential to today's technology. The concept of capturing data with wearable devices helps a user understand the proximity level of pulses and reacts to the command. Micro inertial sensors are gradually becoming popular, and magnetic sensors are commonly used within inertial sensors for accurate and drift-free orientation estimation. Both of these sensors have been proven to estimate the orientation of body segments without the use of external cameras [1].

Using the data of the orientation returned by these sensors and appropriate machine learning algorithms one can help in pushing the boundaries on how an individual uses musical instruments. The notion of playing instruments virtually and visualizing data in electronic music can be fundamental as musicians can make music on the go. Our goal in Instruvis, is to develop a virtual platform for musicians to produce music using wearable devices that use machine learning algorithms to train gestures representing notes using MIDI in Digital Audio Workstation. To achieve this, we have decided to use Intel Curie Chip as our wearable which is a tiny system that can provide compute power for wearable devices. However, before implementing the Intel Curie chip, we experimented with Leapmotion and MYO that already exist in the market to make gesture based virtual instruments, but these devices produced lots of constraints with static gestures. A key element in music is to visualize the sound generated to help the audience understand the mood of the composition, hence we incorporate this with Instruvis using colors to

© Springer International Publishing AG, part of Springer Nature 2018
C. Stephanidis (Ed.): HCII Posters 2018, CCIS 852, pp. 494–500, 2018.
https://doi.org/10.1007/978-3-319-92285-0_68

represent the amplitude, frequency and the pitch of the sound. Henceforth, we are making our own wearable device with neural network processor as the core for sensing and recognizing gestures to produce music.

1.1 Gestures for Music

We often observe musicians from the classics to the modern using gestures of a particular form to understand music. Some gestures are based out of culture and some more help other musicians talk the same language as the one performing. Keeping this in mind, the control system developed as a part of the project concentrates on pattern recognition using neural networks that has an ability to learn from the training data fed to it. The data fed to the neural network represents gesture of a form along the x-axis, y-axis and z-axis. Since gestures often have variations it is important for a system built for music or sound to have an ability to learn and adapt to the user, hence enabling the user to enjoy and produce music very naturally like with the physical instruments that respond to one's own style of gestures which is constrained in the Theremin/Doumbak/Violin/E-Guitar.

Using the Intel curie compute module to develop these devices will help us assign a pattern to a particular MIDI sound and at the same time provides us with an in-built machine learning algorithm that helps train a gesture or a pattern and can be used going further to learn different gestures made by the user. This is a required feature as often the gestures made by different people are different by certain values along the horizontal and vertical axes. This algorithm will help learn these gestures and if a pattern is not found in an existing pattern set, it can be added and assigned to a particular class that fits close to the existing patterns on the device. Hence giving the user the flexibility required to customize the device. The learned patterns are assigned to notes corresponding to the keys of various instruments and further tested while running the application. The notes for the various keys are played using MIDI. This enables us to connect with any device that consists of a MIDI controller. As a result the user would be able to use the controller with any such device giving them the freedom to pick a device of their choice. The system is Bluetooth enabled, hence providing easy access to connect and work with mobile devices. For example, as a part of the testing procedure, we used the Garage Band application available in most iOS devices. We connected the control system to the iPad device using Bluetooth to play various musical devices available on the application.

1.2 Gesture Tracking and Electronic Sound Design

The control system from hands-on technology is gradually changing to hand gesture tracking. It's dynamic ability to control an application without touching a device identifies gesture within the human system. The structure of hand gesture relies on identified control signals. These control signals capture data of your hand movements to function the desired objective. The Lucas-Kanade algorithm is the basis for the hand gesture system. The most important step for the algorithm is identifying and computing the Region of Interest (ROI) in the most efficient manner. The algorithm uses a velocity equation and tracks the each feature from one point to the other in every frame presented using an iterative approximation with a Newton-Raphson type method [2]. The Newton-Raphson allows the algorithm to find successively better hence providing the most optimal region of interest.

The innovation of new instruments has helped musicians develop new electronic sounds which creates an ambience among the audience. The creativity aspect of producing new age sound helps the acoustic part of the world. Acoustic and Electronic sound has certainly bought a new kind of vibe to todays music. Digital audio workstations (DAW) like Logic Pro X and Pro Tools has made it easy for users to make music. Hence, these DAWs are even used in live concerts today. Musicians program electronic beats and sound in these DAWs and use them at their live concerts with acoustics instrument. The interesting part of this whole acoustic and electronic sound is the vibe and appearance. The appearance part of this is the design of the instrument. The currently popular ROLI keyboard [3], which allows for simultaneous keyboard-like, string-like, drum-like, and touch-pad-like action, well beyond previous incarnations of multidimensional musician-keyboard-interaction, as seen in advanced organ-type instruments of the 20th century, such as the 1920s "Ondes Martenot" [4].

Electronic music is not cautious departure from certain traditional paths, but rather, in the radical character of its techniques, gives access to sound phenomena hitherto unknown in the field of music. In traditional music, the repertoire of instruments is generally limited to a fixed set [5]. It's interesting how electronic music provides the depth of color in region of performance and music-making. Roads, the author of the seminal "computer music tutorial" and a more recent textbook on "composing electronic music", points out, the instruments are visible onstage, and we witness the correlation between the performer's gestures and the sounds they produce. The identity of the sound sources is unambiguous. Music played back from a table computer are often ambiguous. The open approach to sounds in electronic music creates structures of notes which can rearranged in terms of modulation and pitch. The culture of electronic music production is now supported by industrial base development, marketing, and sales of music technology. Composing music in this medium changes the environment of certainty and curiosity [6]. Can we imagine someone playing drums sitting on the couch without having the physical kit in front of him? The answer to the question lies within certainty and curiosity. The sound palette of electronic music can closely approximate traditional instruments through techniques such as camping, additive synthesis, and synthesis by physical models. As in traditional music, electronic music benefits from visual representation. Visuals in electronic music is implemented by instrumental music. These scores may serve as a guide for an instrumental performer, as a document construction, or any illustration of an analysis by a music scholar. Illustration can be interesting in terms of graphic representation. If you are playing a drum kit, you can replicate the elements of the kit in graphical representation. It opens the domain of composition from a closed homogeneous set of notes to an unlimited universe of heterogeneous sound objects. The notes in traditional music are homogeneous and in electronic music its heterogeneous. Traditional music can be described by the same four properties: pitch, dynamic marking, duration, and instrument timbre. In electronic music diverse musical materials may not sure common properties. The sound objects can be unique and it can be cast into a strange new acousmatic land without conventional language [5].

1.3 Visualization

Color and Music is an illustration of notes in which its integrated into sound and it is an expression of mood. Graphical representation helps user understand the notion of sound that is being generated in terms of visual elements. The most common way to learn music is to study musical scores and technical essays. Visualization in musical scores creates a strong visual cognition ability for a person to understand the core element of the notes that are being played. The interaction between visualization and musical notes is like macro-micro relationship. In the macro-micro relationship themes and layers can be compared. Themes can be visualization and layers can be musical compositions. Music Composition comprises various layers, which are known as instrumentations and voices. Compositions are inspired by themes, story, or script [7]. In a romantic theme we can think of instruments like Piano, Flute, Saxophone, Violins, etc. While these instruments are being played, an expression of musical notes can be visualizing semantically to the layers that are created. Interestingly, Arc Diagrams are the first attempt to visualize repetitions in music using information visualization [7]. Digital music and visual feedback enhances the environment in terms of modernity feel and artist's performance. In traditional setting, one conducts a classical symphony orchestra via gesture, but the visual feedback is programmed ahead of time. As where in digital music, one can run multiple devices such as Arduino to program visuals to music in a real time manner. In digital music, the observance of real time responsive visuals is embedded within amplitude, frequency, and pitch. The responsive visuals depend on the parameters derived from the music hence helping the audience understand the mood of the music and help a musician observe the parameters of his music. In Instruvis, we are currently using Arduino based program that takes music from an external mic to translate the MIDI data into colors showing harmonic function (Fig. 1).

Fig. 1. Visualization used with Instruvis translating MIDI data to colors

2 System Design

The Intel curie compute module used to design the gesture controller is a low-power hardware module designed for wearables with a software platform that supports the design of IoT devices. It consolidates various highlights that make it perfect for the for playing music on the go. The module consists of motion sensors, Bluetooth Low Energy (Bluetooth® LE) for communication, and a scope of interfaces for Pattern Matching Engine(PME) with a battery charge controller [8]. The motion sensor is a combo sensor that includes a six-axis and a three-axis accelerometer and a three-axis gyroscope, thus helping the user measure the rotation along all the three axes providing approximately precise values. Along with the sensors, it consists of a digital signal processor (DSP) sensor hub which allows us to easily and accurately identify minor motions on the device using the data from the motion sensors. Figure 2 shows the design of a simple intel curie Module used for this project.

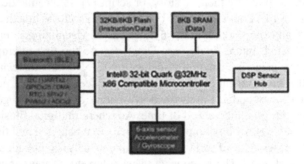

Fig. 2. Simple block diagram of the Intel Curie Module

Once the data from the curie axes are available the next step involves data cleaning. The data obtained from the pattern-matching accelerator contains values of the axes from when code is uploaded into the controller and the respective data obtained from performed gestures. To get the perfect learning rate in the machine learning algorithm used by curie to match patterns and gestures, its trivial that the data to be fed into the algorithm has data that has highest significance. To obtain this we clean the data and place data corresponding to every gesture in a separate file. The multiple files are then fed into the algorithm which generates a combined file of patterns with its corresponding learning rate. Every individual pattern is assumed to be a class by the algorithm.

The machine learning algorithm uses the pattern set file generated for comparison while testing the controller. Now the controller takes the user gesture as an input and derives its similarity with the already available patterns. If the similarity value for the comparison is above the set threshold value, then the pattern is assigned to the respective class identified class with the closest similarity. Every class of pattern is assigned to a particular note of an instrument, which is played one the class of the testing input pattern is identified.

2.1 Proposed Interface Design

Instruvis currently makes use of GarageBand's User Interface in correspondence with the usage of Intel Curie kit which represents the hardware part of the project. One of the major hindrances of using this already existing app UI is that it does not have the option of visualization which can be produced from the music being created, and thus to overcome the mentioned obstacle we have proposed a custom system where we can have sound visualization to be shown to the end user in real-time as he/she is playing a specific instrument or while loading an already saved track from the device. Thus, having our proposed system will meet our particular needs unlike the existing apps in the market which do not fulfill our goals in the exact way we are striving to achieve (Fig. 3).

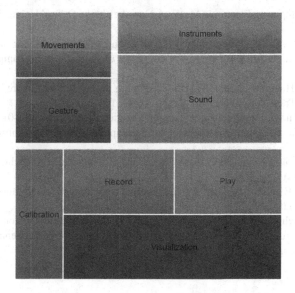

Fig. 3. Outlined system design of the system

3 Conclusion

In conclusion, after testing out Leap Motion and MYO, Intel Curie Chip provides the required flexibility for our design of Instruvis. However, there are bugs and errors in pattern recognition, which can be resolved with the proposed system with and internal design. In the proposed system, visualization will be a key element which will allow users to express music to its audience effectively in terms of composition and genre.

References

1. Fang, B., Sun, F., Liu, H., Guo, D.: Development of a wearable device for motion capturing based on magnetic and inertial measurement units. Sci. Program. **2017** (2017)
2. Pinoli, J.-C.: Mathematical Foundations of Image Processing and Analysis, vol. 1. Wiley-ISTE, Hoboken (2014). Print
3. ROLI Tutorials: Seaboard Playing Techniques and Sounds - Classic Pad. YouTube, 24 August 2015 (2015). https://www.youtube.com/watch?v=WUV79eVugTk. Accessed 04 Dec 2017
4. Electronic music in the 1920s – the ondes Martenot. Audio and sound. http://www.noiseaddicts.com/2009/01/ondes-martenot-electronic-music-theremin/. Accessed 04 Dec 2017
5. Roads, C.: Composing Electronic Music: A New Aesthetic. Oxford University Press, Oxford (2015)
6. Premaratne, P., Ajaz, S., Premaratne, M.: Hand gesture tracking and recognition system using Lucas-Kanade algorithms for control of consumer electronics. Neurocomputing **116**, 242–249 (2013)
7. Chan, W.-Y., Huamin, Q., Mak, W.-H.: Visualizing the semantic structure in classical music works. IEEE Trans. Visual Comput. Graph. **16**(1), 161–173 (2010)
8. ZDNet: Design with the Intel Curie Compute Module. Digit, 14 June 2017 (2017). https://www.digit.in/apps/design-with-the-intel-curie-compute-module-35608.html. Accessed 03 Dec 2017
9. Collopy, F.: Color, form, and motion: dimensions of a musical art of light. Leonardo **33**(5), 355–360 (2000)
10. ® Quark™ SE microcontroller, by Intel. http://www.mouser.com/pdfdocs/IntelQuarkSE ProductBrief.pdf
11. NeuroMem technology Guide, rev 4.0.1, revised 5/6/2016. General Vision
12. General Vision Homepage. http://www.general-vision.com/documentation/TM_Neuro Mem_Technology_Reference_Guide.pdf

Identity Verification for Attendees of Large-Scale Events Using Face Recognition of Selfies Taken with Smartphone Cameras

Akitoshi Okumura[✉], Takamichi Hoshino, Susumu Handa,
Eiko Yamada, and Masahiro Tabuchi

NEC Solution Innovators, Ltd., Kawasaki, Japan
a-okumura@bx.jp.nec.com

Abstract. This paper proposes an identity-verification system for attendees of large-scale events using face recognition from selfies taken with smartphone cameras. Such a system has been required to prevent illegal resale such as ticket scalping. The problem in verifying ticket holders is how to simultaneously verify identities efficiently and prevent individuals from impersonating others at a large-scale event at which tens of thousands of people participate. We previously developed two ticket ID systems for identifying the purchaser and holder of a ticket that uses two types of face-recognition systems, i.e., tablet-based and non-stop face-recognition, that require ID equipment such as a tablet terminal with a camera, card reader, and ticket-issuing printer. These systems were proven effective for preventing illegal resale by verifying attendees at large concerts of popular music groups. Simplifying the ID equipment is necessary from an operational view-point. It is also necessary to secure clear facial photos from a technical view-point of face-recognition accuracy because face recognition fails when unclear face photos are obtained, that is to say, when individuals have their eyes closed, not looking directly forward, or have hair covering their face. Our proposed system uses attendees' selfies as input photos for face recognition, which simplifies ID equipment by only requiring smartphone cameras, enabling clear face photos to be obtained the allowing attendees to take their own photos. The system achieved 97.5% face-recognition accuracy in preliminary tests of 240 photos taken under various brightness and background conditions.

Keywords: Face recognition · Biometrics · Identity verification
Illegal ticket resale prevention · Selfie · Smartphone app

1 Introduction

The problem in verifying ticket holders is how to simultaneously verify identities efficiently and prevent individuals from impersonating others at a large-scale event at which tens of thousands of people participate. To solve this problem, we previously developed two ticket ID systems that identify the purchaser and holder of a ticket by using face-recognition software, which require ID equipment such as a tablet terminal with a camera, card reader, and ticket-issue printer [1–3]. Since the two systems were proven

© Springer International Publishing AG, part of Springer Nature 2018
C. Stephanidis (Ed.): HCII Posters 2018, CCIS 852, pp. 501–509, 2018.
https://doi.org/10.1007/978-3-319-92285-0_69

effective for preventing illegal resale by verifying attendees at large concerts of popular music groups, they have been used at more than 100 concerts. However, simplifying the ID equipment is necessary from an operational view-point. It is also necessary to secure the cooperation of individuals in obtaining facial photos from a technical view-point of face-recognition accuracy because face recognition fails when unclear facial photos of individuals are obtained, i.e., when the individuals have their eyes closed, are not looking directly forward, or have hair covering their face. This paper proposes an identity-verification system that uses attendees' selfies as input photos for face recognition, which simplifies ID equipment by using the attendees' smartphone cameras and secures clear facial photos from attendees by allowing them to take their own photos.

2   Methods

2.1   Identity-Verification System Using Face Recognition from Selfies

The proposed system solves the following problems with conventional systems:

(1) Simplifying ID equipment

Attendees open an identity-verification app with their smartphone cameras to show a venue attendant the verification result, as shown in Fig. 1.

Fig. 1. Admission by using identity-verification app

The app recognizes attendees' selfies and makes it possible for them to check-in. It is not necessary for an event organizer to prepare card readers for check-in, cameras for taking facial photos of attendees, tablet-terminals for face recognition, and ticket-issuing printers.

(2) Securing clear facial photos

Selfies are helpful for securing clear facial photos because it is possible for attendees to take their own photos with the identity-verification app. The app helps attendees take acceptable photos by showing their registered facial photos as good examples together with an instruction message, as shown in Fig. 2 (left). The message suggests that they should directly face the camera without having their eyes closed or having their face covered by their hair. They are able to re-try if they were not successful.

Fig. 2. Self-photographing screen (left) and soft-flash screen (right)

2.2 Requirements for Using Selfies

(1) Pre-screening of Attendee's Operational Skills

All attendees do not possess smartphones and do not always have sufficient skills to operate a smartphone camera for selfies. Therefore, attendees who would like to enter an event venue with the app have to be verified as to whether they succeeded in identity verification with the app in advance of the event. Successful attendees are allowed to verify themselves by using their selfies with the app on the day of the event. Unsuccessful attendees as well as those who do not want to use the app at an event site are arranged to be verified with conventional systems. The pre-screening makes it possible for an event organizer to estimate the necessary equipment and number of venue attendants by figuring out the number of attendees verified with the proposed and conventional systems.

(2) Preventing impersonation

Selfies should be checked when and where they were taken because it is possible for attendees to use ticket winners' smartphones with which identity verification succeeded by using the winners' selfies in advance. Therefore, the app is designed to verify the time and location of selfies, i.e., whether the selfies were appropriately taken at the right place and time of the event, by using the built-in clock and GPS of smartphones.

(3) Self-photographing under dark conditions

Face recognition from selfies at an event site is impossible when it is too dark to detect facial areas. Though flash photography is useful for face recognition under dark conditions, the front-facing built-in cameras used for selfies are not currently equipped with a flash. Therefore, the app provides a soft-flash screen for selfies under dark conditions, which has a wide white area except for a small viewfinder with the highest brightness, as shown in Fig. 2 (right). The soft-flash screen makes it possible for attendees to execute face recognition by illuminating their faces.

2.3 Identity-Verification Procedure

The proposed system meets the above-mentioned requirements according to the following operational procedure from the first step of ticket application to the last step of admission supported by the app:

Step 1
Individuals applying for tickets register their membership information as well as their facial photos in the same way as with conventional systems [1–3]. The photos are stored in the membership database.

Step 2
After an event organizer notifies ticket winners, i.e., successful applicants that have been selected, the winners can download the identity-verification app. The organizer gives permission to attendees who succeeded in the identity verification by using their selfies with the app in advance of the event. The permitted attendees can enter the event venue with the app.

Step 3
The permitted attendees open the app to execute face recognition by taking their selfies at a specified date and place. They show a venue attendant a message displayed on their smartphone when the verification was successful, as shown in Fig. 1. Checking the execution date and place prevents attendees from borrowing or obtaining ticket winners' smartphones with which identity verification succeeded in advance.

Step 4
A venue attendant carries out the admission procedure in accordance with a message on the smartphone display. When the attendant invalidates a ticket on the attendees' smartphone, the same way as an electronic tearing ticket [4], it is reported to the event organizer.

2.4 Configuration of Identity-Verification App

The identity-verification app consists of four modules, i.e., face recognition, time-location verification, identity-verification control, and check-in, as shown in Fig. 3. In the face-recognition module, the face-photographing function makes it possible for attendees to take selfies even under dark conditions by means of a soft-flash screen. The face-recognition module stores the encoded facial image of the attendee that is registered at the time of ticket application. The module collates the selfie with the registered facial photo then transmits the recognition result to the identity-verification control module together with the selfie and registered photo. When the face-recognition module transmits a signal of face-photographing to the time-location verification module, the module extracts the time and location data. The module checks whether the extracted data are consistent with the pre-stored time and location data of the event at which an attendee can participate as a ticket winner. After the check, the module transmits the verification result to the identity-verification control module. The identity-verification control module determines that the verification result is successful if both results of face-recognition and time-location verification are successful. Otherwise, the control module determines that the verification result is a failure. The control module transmits the result to the check-in module together with the selfie and registered facial photo. The check-in module stores the attendee's data, such as name and seat, in advance. This module generates a success message from the attendee's data, the transmitted selfie and registered photo, and a sentence telling the attendee to enter the venue if the verification was successful. Otherwise, it generates an unsuccessful message from the attendee's data, the transmitted selfie and registered photo, and a sentence prompting the attendee to retry identity verification. When a venue attendant carries out the admission procedure on the attendee's smartphones, the app transmits the attendee's check-in information to the event organizer as well as expressing an appreciation message on the display.

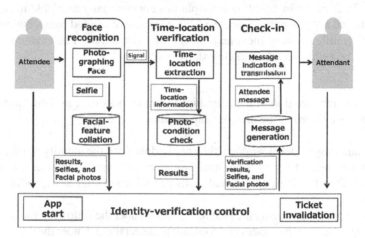

Fig. 3. Configuration of identity-verification app

3   Preliminary Tests and Results

3.1   Face-Recognition Parameters

The proposed system should be evaluated before the identity-verification app is used for actual events from the view-point of face-recognition accuracy. Though time-location verification is reliable because commercial smartphones have practically proven results, face-recognition accuracy has to be scrutinized regarding the feasibility under actual event conditions because attendees take photos of themselves using their smartphones in various environments. Face recognition is controlled using intrinsic, extrinsic, and operational parameters [2]. The intrinsic parameters are due purely to the physical nature of the face and are independent of the observer. They include age, expression, and facial paraphernalia such as facial hair, glasses, and cosmetics. Extrinsic parameters are related to the appearance of the face. They include lighting, pose, background, and imaging such as resolution and focus. Operational parameters are related to the interaction between attendants and attendees. They include how many times the face-recognition process should be repeated per attendee until his/her identity is verified, whether an attendee should stop for the face-recognition process, and whether an attendee should face the camera. The proposed system makes it possible for attendees to control the intrinsic and operational parameters using selfies they have taken. However, attendees are not able to control several extrinsic parameters such as resolution, lighting, and background. Though resolution is not a problem for a commercial smartphone from the view-point of face recognition, it is necessary to evaluate face-recognition accuracy under actual venue conditions with regard to brightness and background conditions.

3.2   Test Methods

The identity-verification app was developed based on the tablet-based face-recognition system [1, 2]. It can be installed on smartphones commercially available in Japan with Android OS and iOS. As preliminary tests, 30 examinees executed face recognition with the app under different brightness and background conditions. The examinees carried out the tests according to the following steps:

Step 1

Examinees registered their membership information as well as their facial photos. The photos were stored in the membership database.

Step 2

In the same way as ticket winners, they could download the identity-verification app on their smartphones. They were permitted to operate the app at any time and any place for the tests. They had their operational skills pre-screened after downloading the app.

Step 3

They started the app to execute face recognition under the following two conditions: bright enough to detect their faces and too dark to detect them. Under the dark condition, they used the soft-flash screen for face recognition. Both conditions contained four backgrounds, i.e., indoor, outdoor, crowds, and under-umbrella. This means that all the examinees tested eight selfie patterns, i.e., taken under the two conditions multiplied by four backgrounds. The total number of selfies were 240, i.e., 8 patterns multiplied by 30 examinees.

3.3   Results

The identity-verification app was downloaded and operated normally without any problems by all examinees. The face-recognition accuracy was 97.5%, (the false reject rate was 2.5%); 6 photos failed in face recognition among the 240 photos. Table 1 lists the results in the form of the number of failure photos/total number of photos with regard to the two brightness and four background conditions. One failure under the bright outdoor condition was due to the examinees closing their eyes during photographing. There were no failure photos due to the fact that examinees were not looking directly forward or that they had hair covering their faces. Five failures in crowds were due to face-detection errors. Since the five photos contained several people behind the examinees, faces of the different people were detected for face recognition. There was no failure photo among those taken with soft-flash or under-umbrella.

Table 1. Face-recognition results under various brightness and background conditions

	Indoor	Outdoor	Crowds	Under-umbrella
Bright	0/30	1/30	5/30	0/30
Soft-flash	0/30	0/30	0/30	0/30

4 Discussion

4.1 Problems with Conventional Systems

The identity-verification app was downloaded and operated normally for the preliminary tests with the commercial smartphones of all examinees. It was not difficult for the examinees to operate the app. The face-recognition accuracy was 97.5%, which is higher than that of the conventional systems [1–3]. This could be helpful for simplifying ID equipment in comparison with conventional systems. Though one facial photo happened to be unclear, the others were all clear for face recognition. Therefore, selfies are regarded as helpful for securing clear facial photos.

4.2 Background Conditions

Face detection exhibited a problem in that faces of incorrect people were detected when selfies contained other people behind the examinees. It could be practically solved by choosing the face with the largest face area among all the detected faces. The detected face areas could be equal when two people are photographed abreast intentionally. The app will be improved with the re-try function with a message telling attendees to take a photo of one person again when it detects same-sized faces.

4.3 Brightness Conditions

The soft-flash screen made it possible for attendees to execute face recognition even under conditions in which it was too dark to detect their faces. In general, brightness is more than 1000 lx in bright offices such as department stores, 750 lx under shopping arcades at night or just after sunset, 200 lx under street lights or in bedrooms, and 30 lx in moonlight or candlelight [5]. The soft-flash screen provided a brightness of more than 80 lx for face recognition. Since the soft-flash illuminated the face of only the person close to the smartphone screen, it prevented the detection of those of other people in crowds.

4.4 Future Issues

The preliminary tests could ensure the feasibility for simplifying ID equipment by using selfies with attendees' smartphones. They also clarified that selfies are helpful for securing clearer photos than with conventional systems. After improving face detection, we will address the following issues before applying the proposed system for actual large-scale events:

(1) Time of identity verification by a venue attendant

The proposed system is expected to decrease identity-verification time because venue attendants do not have to execute face recognition and ticket issuing. We are currently measuring how long attendants should spend for admission procedure per person in step 4 mentioned in Subsect. 2.3 to estimate the number and allocation of necessary venue attendants according to the event scale.

(2) Rehearsal at actual event sites

Larger-scale tests are planned at actual event sites where the proposed system is expected to be used. All the modules of the identity-verification app will be checked as a rehearsal for actual events. At the rehearsal, we will install the proposed system as well as conventional systems in case of any problems that will make it impossible for attendees to use the identity-verification app. We are also developing operational guidelines for dealing with disruptive individuals.

5   Conclusion

We developed an identity-verification system for attendees of large-scale events using face recognition from selfies. The proposed system simplifies ID equipment by using attendees' smartphone cameras and ensures clear facial photos from attendees by allowing them to take their own photos. The system achieved 97.5% face-recognition accuracy in preliminary tests of 240 photos taken by 30 examinees under various brightness and background conditions. The soft-flash screen made it possible for attendees to execute face recognition under conditions in which it would be too dark to detect faces. However, it is necessary to improve the face-detection method for choosing the foremost face when several faces are detected. We are developing clear guidelines for system introduction by estimating the number and allocation of necessary venue attendants through larger-scale tests at actual sites.

Acknowledgements. Thanks are expressed to all the personnel related to our systems, especially to Mr. Hiroshi Sakuma, Executive Vice President and Director of NEC Solution Innovators, Ltd. for his constant encouragement and support.

References

1. Okumura, A., Handa, S., Hoshino, T., Nishiyama, Y.: Identity confirmation to issue tickets using face recognition. In: Stephanidis, C. (ed.) HCI 2016. CCIS, vol. 617, pp. 488–493. Springer, Cham (2016). https://doi.org/10.1007/978-3-319-40548-3_81
2. Okumura, A., Hoshino, T., Handa, S., Nishiyama, Y., Tabuchi, M.: Identity verification of ticket holders at large-scale events using face recognition. J. Inf. Process. **25**, 448–458 (2017)
3. Okumura, A., Hoshino, T., Handa, S., Nishiyama, Y., Tabuchi, M.: Improving identity verification for ticket holders of large-scale events using non-stop face recognition system. IPSJ Trans. Consum. Devices Syst. **8**(1), 27–38 (2018). (in Japanese)

4. fringe watch: "tixee" ticketless management system realized "Denshi Mogiri" service for smart phones without barcode or QR code. http://watch.fringe.jp/2013/0613200357.html. (in Japanese)
5. National Institute of Advanced Industrial Science and Technology: Let's make the brightness standards of Japan. http://www.aist.go.jp/science_town/standard/standard_03/standard_03_04.html. (in Japanese)

Developing an Internet of Things (IoT) Service System Based on Spatial Context

Hyo Jun Sim and Yun Gil Lee(✉)

Department of Architecture, Hoseo University, Asan, Korea
shimhyojun@naver.com, yglee@hoseo.edu

Abstract. The Internet of Things (IoT) is considered to be one of the most significant fields in modern research. The IoT offers innovative services via the networking of various objects; such connectivity had heretofore been impossible, as each object had traditionally been disconnected from its possible companions. According to the IoT concept, all existing objects can be connected both to the Internet and to other objects in the built environment. However, existing studies have ignored the importance of spatial information, which serves to limit not only users' behaviors but also the services offered to them. All IoT devices are deployed within the built environment and can be executed in architectural spaces consisted by building components. In order to develop advanced IoT services, it is essential to understand the spatial context. This research aims to develop an IoT service system that is based on spatial information. The majority of existing IoT services consist of one-to-one services offered to users via their devices; this study aims to improve the quality of these services by utilizing spatial information. This study also intends to establish that IoT service systems can determine a user's situation by analyzing the user's location, thereby providing the user with more appropriate services than ever before. This is a form of LBS (Location Based Service) that utilizes spatial information as a semantic location map.

Keywords: IoT (Internet of Things) · Spatial context · Location Based Service
Building information modeling · Architectural design

1 Introduction

The Internet of Things (IoT) is considered to be one of the most significant fields in modern research. The IoT offers innovative services via the networking of various objects; such connectivity had heretofore been impossible, as each object had traditionally been disconnected from its possible companions. According to the IoT concept, all existing objects can be connected both to the Internet and to other objects in the built environment. However, existing studies have ignored the importance of spatial information, which serves to limit not only users' behaviors but also the services offered to them. All IoT devices are deployed within the built environment and can be executed in architectural spaces consisted by building components. In order to develop advanced IoT services, it is essential to understand the spatial context [1, 2].

© Springer International Publishing AG, part of Springer Nature 2018
C. Stephanidis (Ed.): HCII Posters 2018, CCIS 852, pp. 510–514, 2018.
https://doi.org/10.1007/978-3-319-92285-0_70

This research aims to develop an IoT service system that is based on spatial information. The majority of existing IoT services consist of one-to-one services offered to users via their devices; this study aims to improve the quality of these services by utilizing spatial information. This study also intends to establish that IoT service systems can determine a user's situation by analyzing the user's location, thereby providing the user with more appropriate services than ever before. This is a form of LBS (Location Based Service) that utilizes spatial information as a semantic location map.

2   IoT Service System Based on Spatial Context

Figure 1 illustrates the concept of a proposed IoT service system that is based on spatial information. This diagram demonstrates the systemic framework that is used to provide IoT services during a quarrel between a wife and a husband. Through wearable devices, a user's emotional data and position data are recorded and delivered to the IoT service server. Numerical 'Position Data' is translated into semantic 'Locational Situation' markers via the utilization of 'Spatial Information' and then delivered to the 'Situation Manager.' The 'Situation Manager' determines which service should be offered to the user in this locational situation and asks the 'User Service Manager' to provide the IoT service in the proper position. This process is similar to existing IoT services, though it differs in that it can provide users with more appropriate IoT services by understanding situations based on spatial information and by providing suitable services [3].

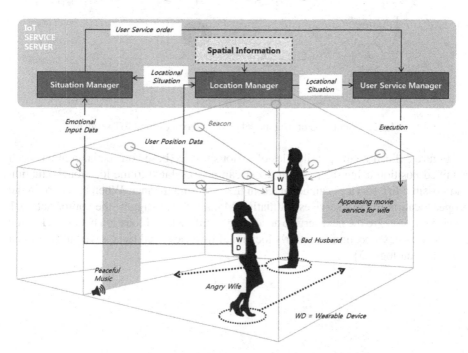

Fig. 1. An IoT service system based on spatial context

3   How to Use Spatial Context for IoT Service?

Figure 2 shows the concept of interaction of data model of spatial context and IoT service. The data model of spatial context is developed based on the traditional building data modeling method which is a kind of object oriented data modeling regarding all building components as an object. Static building components play a role of locational standard like a map and 'Node' which is position tracer like Beacon delivery the current numerical position of 'Human'. According to this data model, 'Situation Manager' can calculate the proper service and the proper location of providing it based on the user's current locational situation.

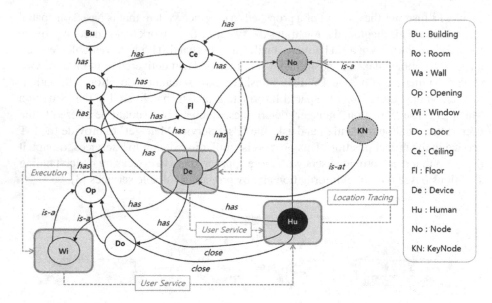

Fig. 2.   Interaction of data model of spatial context and IoT service

Figure 3 illustrate the possibilities of various service based on spatial context. Each obtained position using the position tracer can be translated to the locational situation and possible IoT services can be linked in the real-time manner. When users are in the proper location for IoT services, 'Situation Manager' can suggest the appropriate IoT service and prepare the next service according to inference of location histories. For the inference of next location, the user's locational histories need to be saved as relational data like ontology [5].

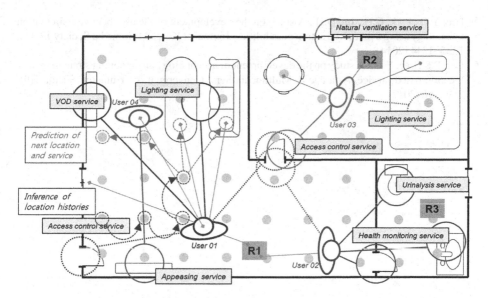

Fig. 3. The possibilities of various services using spatial context

4 Conclusion and Discussion

This research aims to develop an IoT service system that is based on spatial information. In this paper, we suggested overall structure of the proposed system and methods to use spatial context for IoT Service. The proposed idea could be expect to overcome the limitation of the existing IoT service system which consists of one-to-one services offered to users via their devices. In the further research, we need to apply this idea to real world and evaluate the effeteness of using spatial context for IoT service.

Acknowledgment. This research was supported by Basic Science Research Program through the National Research Foundation of Korea (NRF) funded by the Ministry of Education (NRF-2015R1D1A1A01057525).

References

1. Gubbia, J., Buyyab, R., Marusica, S., Palaniswamia, M.: Internet of Things (IoT): a vision, architectural elements, and future directions. Future Gener. Comput. Syst. **29**(7), 1645–1660 (2013)
2. Feki, M.A., Kawsar, F., Boussard, M., Trappeniers, L.: The Internet of Things: the next technological revolution. Computer (2013)
3. Wang, X., Shang, J., Yu, F., Yan, J.: Indoor semantic location models for location-based services. Int. J. Smart Home **7**(4), 127–136 (2013)
4. Lee, Y.G., Choi, J.W., Lee, I.J.: Location modeling for ubiquitous computing based on the spatial information management technology. J. Asian Architect. Build. Eng. **5**(1), 105–111 (2006)

5. Lee, Y.G., Park, C.H., Im, D.H.: A study on the development of the user behavior simulation technology using a perceived action possibilities. Journal of Korea Multimedia Society **17**(11), 1335–1344 (2014)
6. Lee, P.S., Lee, Y.G.: A study on the development of a technology anger coping strategies using location-based service. Asia Pac. J. Multimedia Serv. Convergent Art Humanit. Sociol. **7**(9), 289–296 (2017)

A CDF-Based Symbolic Time-Series Data Mining Approach for Electricity Consumption Analysis

I-Chin Wu[1]([⊠]), Yi-An Chen[2], and Zan-Xian Wang[2]

[1] Graduate Institute of Library and Information Studies, National Taiwan Normal University, Taipei, Taiwan
icwu@ntnu.edu.tw
[2] Department of Information Management, Fu-Jen Catholic University, New Taipei City, Taiwan

Abstract. Electricity is critical for industrial and economic advancement, as well as a driving force for sustainable development. This study collects the energy consumption data of annealing processes from an annealing furnace of a co-operating steel forging plant. We propose a CDF-based symbolic time-series data mining and analytic framework for electricity consumption analysis and prediction of machine operating states by machine-learning techniques. We computed the breakpoint value relying on a density-based notion – namely, the cumulative distribution function (CDF) – to improve the original breakpoint table in the SAX algorithm for symbolizing the time-series data. The main contribution of this work is that the modified SAX algorithm can achieve better prediction the operating state of the machine in comparison to the original SAX algorithm.

Keywords: Cumulative distribution function
Electricity consumption analysis · Symbolic aggregate approximation
Time-series data mining

1 Introduction

Given the problems of gradual oil depletion and global warming, energy consumption has become a critical factor for energy-intensive sectors, especially the semiconductor, manufacturing, iron and steel, and aluminum industries. Without a doubt, energy is a vital resource for modern civilization and economic growth, especially for long-term competitive sustainability. To reduce unnecessary energy consumption and improve energy efficiency, it is critical to make informed decisions in real time. To that end, we collected data regarding energy consumption as well as information from the corresponding production and manufacturing domains from the co-operating steel-forging plant. Based on load profiles determined from data stream mining, we propose a refined symbolic time-series data mining approach for electricity consumption analysis and typical patterns extraction based on the load profiles. The objectives of our research is we have tried to improve the breakpoint table of the SAX algorithm. Breakpoint is the key factor for the SAX algorithm to symbolize values, and SAX converts different

© Springer International Publishing AG, part of Springer Nature 2018
C. Stephanidis (Ed.): HCII Posters 2018, CCIS 852, pp. 515–521, 2018.
https://doi.org/10.1007/978-3-319-92285-0_71

numerical data to different symbols through the breakpoint table. Compared to the SAX breakpoint table proposed by Lin et al. [1], this study computes the breakpoint value by using cumulative distribution function (CDF) that relies on a density-based notion to improve the accuracy of the symbolization [2]. We adopt the tightness of lower bound (TLB) measure to evaluate the performance of our refined distance measure.

2   Framework

To confirm the advantage of adopting the symbolic time-series data mining framework for electricity consumption analysis proposed in this study, we collected electricity consumption data and corresponding product information from an annealing furnace during April 1–December 31, 2014 to carry out our research. The following content describes the three-phase operational process of the framework in this research, as shown in Fig. 1.

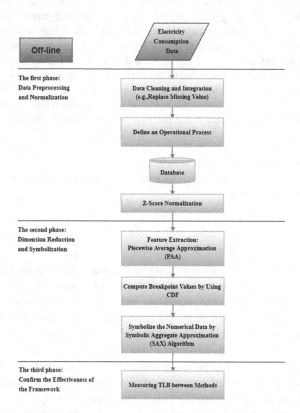

Fig. 1. The process of CDF-based symbolic time-series data mining for electricity consumption analysis

- **Phase 1: Data preprocessing and normalization.** In this phase we carried out the data-cleaning integration, for example, replacing the missing values and defining a complete machining procedure. After data preprocessing, we took these data to execute z-score normalization.
- **Phase 2: Dimensionality reduction and symbolization.** In this phase we reduced the dimensionality of data and then symbolized the numerical time-series data. The SAX algorithm follows a two-step process: (1) Piecewise Aggregate Approximation (PAA) and (2) conversion of a PAA sequence into a series of letters. PAA divides the data set of length n into w equally spaced segments or bins, and computes the average of each segment. This essentially means that we reduce the number of dimensions from n to w ($n > w$). The SAX algorithm is a symbolic representation of a time series and uses a synthetic set of symbols to reduce the dimensionality of the numerical series. In this work, we refined the breakpoint value by using the cumulative distribution function (CDF) and took the results to build the breakpoint table. Breakpoint is the key factor for the SAX algorithm to transform numerical data into symbolic data. The methods and the adjusted algorithm of SAX will be explained in Sect. 3.
- **Phase 3: Identification of machine operational states.** In this phase we identified the operational states of the machine and measured the tightness of lower bound (TLB) between methods to measure the effectiveness of the modified SAX algorithm in our application domain. In addition, we improved the lower-bounding distance measure that calculates the similarity among symbolized energy-load profiles by considering the variance of time-series data to get the new distance of two continuous strings. The methods and experimental results will be explained in Sects. 4 and 5.

3 Modified Breakpoint Table of SAX Algorithm

When dealing with time-series data efficiently, it is important to develop data representation techniques that can reduce the dimensionality of time-series while still preserving the fundamental characteristics of the data [3, 4]. Data- size reduction techniques may be helpful in the process of categorizing the electrical load consumption patterns on the basis of their shape. The SAX, a symbolic representation of a time series, uses a synthetic set of symbols to reduce the dimensionality of the numerical series. As we introduced it in the basic concepts, the SAX algorithm follows a two-step process: (1) Piecewise Aggregate Approximation (PAA) and (2) conversion of a PAA sequence into a series of letters. PAA divides the data set of length n into w equally spaced segments or bins, and computes the average of each segment. This essentially means that we reduce the number of dimensions from n to w.

Having transformed a time-series database into the PAA we can apply a further transformation to obtain a discrete representation. It is desirable to have a discretization technique that will produce symbols with equal probability. The amplitude intervals may be regular or determined according to the quantiles of the statistical distribution that represents the probability density of the amplitudes in the entire data set, Lin et al. [1]

used the former case and this study used the latter case. In the latter case, the entire data set has to be processed to determine the probability distribution of the amplitudes, this study represented through its CDF. The CDF of a random variable is a method to describe the distribution of random variables. The advantage of the CDF is that it can be defined for any kind of random variable, including discrete, continuous, and mixed random variables. Starting from the CDF, the amplitude breakpoints can be identified by the quantiles of the probability curve to partition the amplitude axis into intervals and obtain partitioning of the amplitude intervals with equal probability. The SAX converts different numerical data into different symbols through the breakpoint table. Compared to the SAX's breakpoint table proposed by Lin et al. [1] (shown as Table 2), this study computed the breakpoint value by using CDF, that is, by relying on a density-based notion, in which the number of symbolized data points is the same in every amplitude interval.

The cumulative distribution function (CDF) of random variable X is defined as

$$F_X(\mathcal{X}) = P(X \leq \mathcal{X}), \; for \; all \; \mathcal{X} \in \mathbb{R} \tag{1}$$

$F_X(\mathcal{X})$ accumulates all of the probability less than or equal to $\mathcal{X}$. The CDF for continuous random variables is a straightforward extension of that of the discrete case. The CDF calculates the cumulative probability for a given X-value. For continuous distributions, the CDF gives the area under the probability density function, up to the given x-value. And for discrete distributions, the CDF gives the cumulative probability for the given X-value.

4 The Distance Measure of the SAX Algorithm

The most common distance measure for time series data is the Euclidean distance. The weakness of the Euclidean distance is its sensitivity to distortion in the time axis [5], that is, when there are two time series sequences that have an overall similar shape but are not aligned in the time axis. Given two time series $T1$ and $T2$, with the same length, n, we then conducted dimension reduction using the PAA approach to transform the original $T1$ and $T2$ into $T1'$ and $T2'$, respectively. Based on Chakrabarti et al. [6], we obtained a lower bounding Euclidean distance approximation between the original time-series data by Eq. (2). The lower bounding Euclidean distance measure can be applied using the reduced-dimension time series representation method, which ensures the reduced dimension can be less than or equal to the true distance on the raw time-series data (Ding et al. 2008).

$$D_{LB}(T_1', T_2') = \sqrt{\frac{n}{w}} \sqrt{\sum_{i=1}^{w} (t_{1i}' - t_{2i}')^2} \tag{2}$$

We further transformed the data into the symbolic representation, that is, SAX, with a lower-bounding distance measure. In the SAX algorithm Lin et al. (2007) define a D_{min_dist} function to calculate the minimum distance between two sequences of symbols as shown in Eq. (3).

$$D_{\min\_dist}(T_1'', T_2'') = \sqrt{\frac{n}{w}} \sqrt{\sum_{i=1}^{w} dist((t_{1i}'' * i - t_{2i}'' * i))^2} \qquad (3)$$

The distance between two symbols can be read off by checking the corresponding row and column by checking the look up table [7]. The equation is shown in Eq. (4) below:

$$Dist(R, C) = \begin{cases} 0, & if |R - C| \le 1 \\ \beta_{\max(R,C)-1} - \beta_{\min(R,C)}, & otherwise \end{cases} \qquad (4)$$

Where βi is the element of the breakpoint list B = (β1, β2,...β_{W-1}) and $\beta i - 1 < \beta i$. R denotes row and C denotes column in the look up table which can be referenced in Wu et al. [7].

5 Experimental Design and Results

5.1 Distance Evaluation Metrics: Measuring the Tightness of Lower Bound

Lin et al. [1, 8] have proposed empirically determining the best values by simply measuring the TLB, defined as the ratio in the range [0,1] of the lower bound distance to the actual true Euclidean distance. The higher the ratio, the tighter is the bound. Based on previous researches [3, 8], we adopted the TLB measure to evaluate the performance of our adjusted distance measure using SAX algorithm. Since we aimed to achieve the tightest possible lower bounds, we can simply estimate the lower bounds over all possible parameters and select the best settings. To identify the TLB, we used Eq. (5):

$$\text{TLB} = \frac{lower \ bounds \ distance}{true \ euclidean \ distance} \qquad (5)$$

The lower bound distance represents the distance after symbolization, whereas the true Euclidean distance represents the true distance of two time-series data. The value range of the TLB is always between 0 and 1; the higher the TLB value, the closer it is to the true Euclidean distance, which indicates better results.

5.2 Effectiveness of the Modified Breakpoint Table of the SAX Algorithm

Firstly, we examined the degree of distortion of two time-series data with the SAX algorithm and modified the breakpoint table of the SAX algorithm by the CDF. Lin et al. [1] used the former case and this study used the latter case. In the latter case, the entire data set has to be processed in order to determine the probability distribution of the amplitudes. This study represented through its CDF. We set α to be 10 (i.e., 10 amplitude intervals) in our electricity consumption data to have alphabetical labels. As such, we can get the best symbolized results. Herein, we focused on the electricity consumption data from one of the annealing furnaces to conduct the experiment to evaluate the effectiveness of the proposed CFD-refined breakpoint table approach (SAX_CDF) compared to the original SAX algorithm (SAX_Orginal).

Observation1: Table 1 show a comparison of TLB between Lin's breakpoint table and the CDF breakpoint table for the machine. Apparently, the results show that the CDF-based SAX approach can achieve 10.38% improvements, compared to the original SAX approach. The results confirm the effectiveness of our refined CDF-based SAX algorithm.

Table 1. Comparison of TLB with Lin's and CDF's breakpoint table

Windows number (n)	SAX_Original	SAX_CDF
300	0.430	0.454
400	0.478	0.516
500	0.516	0.531
600	0.505	0.562
700	0.539	0.579
800	0.559	0.611
900	0.565	0.618
950	**0.583**	**0.634**
1000	0.474	0.492
1100	0.562	0.566
1200	0.574	0.595
1300	0.589	0.658
1400	0.595	0.674
1450	**0.595**	**0.678**
Average	0.443	**0.489 (+10.38%)**

Observation 2: There are two optimum solutions, one is n (time window) is 1450, the other is n is 950. Setting n to 1450 can get the highest TLB value, while setting n to 950 is the most efficient parameter setting for the machine. The breakpoints when n is 1450 are $\{-0.6024, -0.5987, -0.5945, -0.5933, -0.45, -0.2688, 0.1377, 1.6334, 1.6965\}$, and the breakpoints when n is 950 are $\{-0.7455, -0.7355, -0.7267, -0.7202, -0.7177, -0.5321, -0.2688, 1.9060, 2.0317\}$. It provides reference values for our future research.

6   Conclusion

Here is a summary of the preliminary findings of this research. First, our experimental results show that the modified CDF-based SAX algorithm can achieve better results in terms of higher TLB values compared to the one without any modification, representing a 10.38% improvement. In the future, we will adopt the results for further normal and abnormal electricity-pattern retrieving tasks. We also aim to deploy a visualized electricity consumption system for conducting real-time decisions in a real context.

References

1. Lin, J., Keogh, E.J., Wei, L., Lonardi, S.: Experiencing SAX: a novel symbolic representation of time series. Data Min. Knowl. Disc. **15**(2), 107–144 (2007)
2. Notaristefano, A., Chicco, G., Piglione, F.: Data size reduction with symbolic aggregate approximation for electrical load pattern grouping. IET Gener. Transm. Distrib. **7**(2), 108–117 (2013)
3. Ding, H., Trajcevski, G., Scheuermann, P., Wang, X., Keogh, E.: Querying and mining of time series data: experimental comparison of representations and distance measures. Proc. VLDB Endowment **1**(2), 1542–1552 (2008). https://doi.org/10.14778/1454159.1454226
4. Han, J., Kamber, M., Pei, J.: Data Mining: Concepts and Techniques, 3rd edn. Morgan Kaufmann, Waltham (2011)
5. Keogh, E., Ratanamahatana, C.A.: Exact indexing of dynamic time warping. Knowl. Inf. Syst. **7**(3), 358–386 (2005). https://doi.org/10.1007/s10115-004-0154-9
6. Chakrabarti, K., Keogh, E., Mehrotra, S., Pazzani, M.: Locally adaptive dimensionality reduction for indexing large time series databases. ACM Trans. Database Syst. **27**(2), 188–228 (2002). https://doi.org/10.1145/568518.568520
7. Wu, I.-C., Chen, T.-L., Hong, G.-Q., Chen, Y.-M., Liu, T.-C.: A symbolic time-series data mining framework for analyzing load profiles of electricity consumption. J. Libr. Inf. Stud. **15**(2), 21–44 (2017)
8. Lin, J., Keogh, E., Lonardi, S., Chiu, B.: A symbolic representation of time series, with implications for streaming algorithms. In: Proceedings of the 8th ACM SIGMOD Workshop on Research Issues in Data Mining and Knowledge Discovery, San Diego, CA, USA, pp. 2–11 (2003)

Author Index

Printed in the United States
By Bookmasters